Praise for *Feminist Literary Theory*

"*Feminist Literary Theory: A Reader* is an indispensable guide, companion and handbook for students and teachers of women's literature. No other anthology offers so many bite-sized tasters of work on gendered authorship, literary production, critical reception, sexuality and genre – from romantic fiction to travel writing. Mary Eagleton's clear and informative introductions contextualize the debates represented by each extract, suggest connections between them and point to further reading. This third edition maintains and develops the irreplaceable breadth of the previous editions with several new pieces on such areas as autobiography, science fiction and border talk. The extra section, 'Writing "Glocal"', investigates dynamically evolving dialogues between feminism and postcolonialism, diaspora narratives and transculturalism. Whether you read from start to finish or choose to sample selectively, this rich collection will expand your knowledge and understanding of feminist thought, both as an historical discipline and as an excitingly relevant and progressive set of ideas."

Jane Dowson,
De Montfort University

FEMINIST LITERARY THEORY

A Reader

Third Edition

Edited by
Mary Eagleton

WILEY-BLACKWELL

A John Wiley & Sons, Ltd., Publication

This edition first published 2011
© 2011 Blackwell Publishing Ltd except for editorial material and organization
© 2011 Mary Eagleton

Edition history: Blackwell Publishing Ltd (1e, 1986); Blackwell Publishers Ltd (2e, 1996);

Blackwell Publishing was acquired by John Wiley & Sons in February 2007. Blackwell's publishing program has been merged with Wiley's global Scientific, Technical, and Medical business to form Wiley-Blackwell.

Registered Office
John Wiley & Sons Ltd, The Atrium, Southern Gate, Chichester, West Sussex, PO19 8SQ, United Kingdom

Editorial Offices
350 Main Street, Malden, MA 02148-5020, USA
9600 Garsington Road, Oxford, OX4 2DQ, UK

The Atrium, Southern Gate, Chichester, West Sussex, PO19 8SQ, UK

For details of our global editorial offices, for customer services, and for information about how to apply for permission to reuse the copyright material in this book please see our website at www.wiley.com/wiley-blackwell.

The right of Mary Eagleton to be identified as the author of the editorial material in this work has been asserted in accordance with the UK Copyright, Designs and Patents Act 1988.

Library of Congress Cataloging-in-Publication Data

Feminist literary theory: a reader / Mary Eagleton. – 3rd ed.
    p.   cm.
  Includes bibliographical references and index.
  ISBN 978-1-4051-8313-0 (pbk. : alk. paper)
1. Feminist literary criticism.   I. Eagleton, Mary.   II. Title.
  PN98.W64F44 2011
  801′.95082–dc22
                                                      2010016557

A catalogue record for this book is available from the British Library.

Set in 10/12pt Sabon by SPi Publisher Services, Pondicherry, India
Printed in Malaysia by Ho Printing (M) Sdn Bhd

1   2011

Contents

Preface to the Third Edition

The first edition of *Feminist Literary Theory: A Reader* was published in 1986. It was an attempt to give an introduction – chiefly for students – to the outpouring of material following the rise in feminist activism and critiques in the late 1960s and the early 1970s. This work profoundly impacted on education, on what was seen as legitimate knowledge and, for our purposes here, on the field of imaginative and critical writing: who wrote, in what ways, for whom, about what, and in what locations became highly significant questions. Many of the names included in the 1986 edition continued through the second edition in 1996 and into this third edition. Critics such as Elaine Showalter, Gayatri Chakravorty Spivak, Hélène Cixous, Sandra Gilbert and Susan Gubar, and many more, have achieved a status as key figures in their fields, both defining a particular moment or position and opening up debates to ongoing scrutiny. Now in its third edition, the *Reader* has inevitably become, to some extent, a history of feminist literary studies. In addition to earlier extracts from Virginia Woolf, it spans the period from 1965 to the present and one of my strongest pieces of advice to those using this volume would be always to check the date of the extracts you are reading. In so doing, you will get a sense of the ideas current at any particular period, the differences amongst those ideas and how responses have developed, changed and endured over time. In fact, a whole other way of reading this volume would be to ignore the chapter divisions and read the material historically.

You will notice my use of plurals in that sentence above – 'ideas', 'differences', 'responses'. Readers of this book have sometimes expressed the view that they would like rather *fewer* ideas, differences and responses; they felt overwhelmed by the amount and range of material and thought that having fewer, longer extracts or full essays would be more manageable and allow them to follow through an argument to a conclusion. I understand that point of view and there are many excellent collections that do precisely that, but this volume is trying to do something different. In the Preface to the second edition I wrote: 'I have kept to passages which succinctly summarize one or two important points. The aim is to provide readers with a taster – if you want a different metaphor, a snap-shot – and my hope is that they will then pursue further the ideas that interest them.' This is still the aim. With 122 extracts, 57 of them new, all chapters updated and a new chapter, 'Writing "Glocal"', with the Introduction to each chapter fully revised and the footnotes providing extensive guidance on further study, I believe that every reader will find material of relevance and provocation which can then be the basis for more research. There is no demand to start at the beginning and work through. Just as an historical perspective offers a different approach, so too following a single idea across several chapters and in the extended reading suggested in the footnotes can be highly illuminating. Most especially, the plethora of material guards against over-simplifications. For example, one cannot say that 'seventies feminism' or 'postmodern feminism' is synonymous with this or that position, or that 'French feminism' signifies 'x', or that stylistically women's writing has 'y' as a common characteristic because, repeatedly, within and between the extracts one finds such simplicities becoming more complicated and nuanced. There is no single, direct road through feminist literary theory, but there are many fascinating parallel routes, interchanges, detours and crossroads. Thus, to study feminist literary theory is both a diachronic and synchronic activity. It is concerned with a history, development, continuity and change over time, but it is also preoccupied with the diversity of the moment, the richness of and dialogue between different positions.

My other piece of advice would be to focus on these dialogues and debates, and although at various points in the Introductions I alert readers to possible links, I would encourage them to seek out their own connections. I have employed three strategies. Firstly, within each chapter, I deliberately introduce a variety of material and positions with respect to the chapter topic. I am keen to counter any sense of feminism having a party line within its politics or definitive theoretical conclusions. On occasions, extracts are responding directly to earlier material; for example, in Chapter 4, Madhu Dubey comments on bell hooks' extract concerning the meaning of the marginal, while Robyn Wiegman responds to Nancy Fraser and Linda J. Nicholson on postmodern feminism. But the aim of the second extract is not to counter the first but to question and supplement; it is to dispute rather than refute, to add to the ebbs and flows of a critical discourse. Secondly, the millennium greatly encouraged retrospective and prospective assessments, and many extracts from around that period engage in reviews of the field and mappings of future lines of enquiry. Most notably, individual critics – Toril Moi or Judith Butler, for example – are able to return to their early, formative work to reassess it. Thirdly, I have enhanced discussion of pre-nineteenth-century literature. To read Margaret J. M. Ezell or Betty A. Schellenberg on feminist historiography (Chapter 1), or Paula McDowell on earlier forms of women's literary production (Chapter 2), or Clare Brant on the multiple genres employed in eighteenth-century women's writing (Chapter 3) once again leads us into questioning presumptions and making necessary comparisons.

The chapter divisions with which, from the start, I structured this *Reader* remain valid. One cannot imagine *not* raising questions of authorship, literary tradition, production, readership, genre, difference, interactions with other literary theories; such topics are the bedrock of any discussion. In the second edition, I added a new chapter in response to the impact of postmodernism in the early 1990s and the wide interest, through both postmodernism and psychoanalysis, in subjectivity. In this edition, I include a chapter which explores literary feminism's concern with place, space and location. This springs in part from feminism's conversation with postcolonial theory and, more widely, with feminism's understanding of how writing may be precisely situated culturally and geographically, but also the product of imperial, diasporic and transnational forces. Thus, our critical perspective in the twenty-first century is both local and global and, in a globalized world, those questions with which we started – who wrote, in what ways, for whom, about what – take on another inflection.

This new chapter also encourages the cross-readings I am advising. For example, the problem of defining terms and the often tricky relation between terms, discussed in Chapter 4, is revisited; how do 'first world' and 'third world' speak and read each other would be one instance. Dialogues are again established. So Sara Suleri and Rey Chow respond to Chandra Talpade Mohanty and Trinh T. Minh-ha, while Caren Kaplan questions Adrienne Rich. As elsewhere, issues of production and genre are important. Hence, the interest in marketing, touched on in Chapter 2, is discussed here in the work of Amal Amireh and Lisa Suhair Majaj, and the generic forms considered in Chapter 3 are extended, in the final chapter, to include travel writing. Finally, that focus on 'the literary', so central to the whole collection, is further explored in this chapter in, for instance, Mary Louise Pratt's and Elleke Boehmer's comments on narrative strategies or in Laura E. Franey's discussion of 'verbal violence'.

There is then, I trust, an openness in this collection to the diversity of feminist literary theory, to its changing narrative across the decades and within different locations, and to the multiple ways it has related to other critical discourses. But, for good or ill, one has to set parameters on one's topic; one can never be all things to all people. Hence, whenever I have been unsure about the relevance of a particular extract, I have always returned to the title of the collection, *Feminist Literary Theory: A Reader*, and asked myself a series of questions: does this extract spring from or speak to a feminist politics; though the term is problematic, does this extract engage with 'the literary' as a formal, stylistically conscious, communicative activity; does the extract raise issues about the production, reception, reading or interpretation of women's writing; will the extract inform and stimulate the reader? If, in my own mind, I can answer 'yes' to those four questions then there is a possibility the extract will be included, but even then, there are still a whole number of invidious choices to make and difficulties to confront with respect to volume, range, accessibility and gaining permission to reprint. One treads a wobbly line between recognizing the porous borders and conceptual vitality of feminist literary theory and, at the same time, the intellectual and practical need to put some shape and limits on that heterogeneity.

I am very grateful to colleagues at Wiley-Blackwell who have been so helpful, patient and professional throughout the production of this third edition and to my colleagues at Leeds Metropolitan University, past and present, who have supported me in so many ways, not least by their intellectual liveliness and warm collegiality. I am especially thankful to my friends in the Contemporary Women Writers' Network and on the journal, *Contemporary Women's Writing*, who give daily proof of the continued importance of feminist literary theory and of feminist practice as both possible and productive. Finally, I give my loving thanks to David and Matt for always being there.

Acknowledgments

Linda Alcoff: extract from 'Cultural Feminism versus Post-structuralism: The Identity Crisis in Feminist Theory', *Signs: Journal of Women in Culture and Society*, vol. 13, no. 3 (1988). Published by University of Chicago. © 1988 The University of Chicago. All rights reserved.

Amal Amireh and Lisa Suhair Majaj: extract from *Going Global: The Transnational Reception of Third World Women Writers* (New York and London: Garland., 2000).

Gloria Anzaldúa: extract from *Borderlands/La Frontera: The New Mestiza* (San Francisco: Aunt Lute Books, 1987).

Isobel Armstrong: extract from Isobel Armstrong, 'Christina Rossetti: Diary of a Feminist Reading', in Sue Roe (ed.), *Women Reading Women's Writing* (Brighton: Harvester Press, 1987). Reprinted with permission. Extract from *The Radical Aesthetic* (Oxford: Blackwell, 2000).

Nancy Armstrong: extract from *Desire and Domestic Fiction: A Political History of the Novel* (Oxford: Oxford University Press, 1987). Reprinted with permission.

Michèle Barrett: extract from 'Feminism and the Definition of Cultural Politics' in Rosalind Brunt and Caroline Rowan (eds.) *Feminism, Culture and Politics*. London: Lawrence and Wishart, © 1982.

Catherine Belsey: extract from *Critical Practice* © 1980 by permission of Taylor & Francis Books UK.

Seyla Benhabib: extract from 'Sexual Difference and Collective Identities: The New Global Constellation', *Signs: Journal of Women in Culture and Society*, vol. 24, no. 2 (1999), © 1999 by The University of Chicago. All rights reserved.

Shari Benstock: extract from 'Afterword: The New Woman's Fiction', in Suzanne Ferriss and Mallory Young (eds.), *Chick Lit: The New Woman's Fiction*. New York: Routledge, 2006. Reprinted with permission.

Black Woman Talk Collective: extract from 'Black Woman Talk', *Feminist Review* 17 (Autumn 1984). Reprinted by permission from Macmillan Publishers Ltd: Feminist Review – Black Woman Talk Collective 'Black Woman Talk', copyright 1984, published by Palgrave Macmillan.

Elleke Boehmer: extract from *Stories of Women: Gender and Narrative in the Postcolonial Nation*. (Manchester: Manchester University Press, 2005). Reprinted with permission.

Rachel Bowlby: extract from 'Flight Reservations: The Anglo-American/ French Divide in Feminist Criticism' in *Still Crazy After All These Years: Women, Writing and Psychoanalysis* © 1992. Reproduced by permission of Taylor & Francis Books UK.

Carole Boyce Davies: extract from *Black Women, Writing, and Identity: Migrations of the Subject*. Copyright © 1994 by permission of Taylor & Francis Books UK.

Avtar Brah: extract from *Cartographies of Diaspora: Contesting Identities*. Copyright © 1996 by permission of Taylor & Francis Books UK.

Rosi Braidotti: extract from *Nomadic Subjects: Embodiment and Sexual Difference in Contemporary Feminist Theory* (New York: Columbia University Press, 1994). Reprinted with permission.

Clare Brant: extract from 'Varieties of Women's Writing' in Vivien Jones (ed.) *Women and Literature in Britain 1700–1800*, 2000. © Cambridge University Press 2000, reproduced with permission.

Judith Butler: extract from *Undoing Gender* (New York and London: Routledge, 2004). Reprinted with permission.

Rey Chow: extract from *Writing Diaspora: Tactics of Intervention in Contemporary Cultural Studies*. Bloomington and Indianapolis: Indiana University Press, © 1993. Reprinted with permission of Indiana University Press.

Barbara Christian: extract from 'The Race for Theory' in Linda Kauffman (ed.), *Gender and Theory: Dialogues on Feminist Criticism* (Oxford: Basil Blackwell, 1989). Reprinted with permission.

Hélène Cixous: extract from Hélène Cixous et al., 'Conversations', in Susan Sellers (ed.), *Writing Differences: Readings from the Seminar of Hélène Cixous* (Milton Keynes: Open University Press, 1988). Reprinted with permission. Extract from 'The Laugh of the Medusa', in Elaine Marks and Isabelle de Courtrivron (eds.), *New French Feminism: An Anthology* (Brighton: Harvester, 1980). Trans. Keith Cohen and Paula Cohen. First published in English in *Signs: Journal of Women in Culture and Society*, vol. 1, no. 4 (1976). Revised from 'Le Rire de la Méduse', *L'Arc* (1975). Reprinted with permission. Extract from 'Castration or Decapitation?' in *Signs: Journal of Women in Culture and Society*, vol. 7, no. 1 (Autumn, 1981). Trans. Annette Kuhn.

Hélène Cixous and Mireille Calle-Gruber: extract from *Hélène Cixous Rootprints: Memory and Life Writing*. Trans. Eric Prenowitz. (London: Routledge, 1997).

Rosalind Coward: extract from *Female Desire: Women's Sexuality Today* (London: Paladin, Granada Publishing, 1984). HarperCollins Publishers Ltd © 1984 Rosalind Coward. Extract from ' "This Novel Changes Lives": A Response to Rebecca O'Rourke's Article "Summer Reading" ', *Feminist Review* 5 (1980).

Jonathan Culler: extract from 'Reading as a Woman', *On Deconstruction: Theory and Criticism after Structuralism* © 1983. Reproduced by permission of Taylor & Francis Books UK.

Marysa Demoor and Jürgen Pieters: extract from 'Discursive Desire: Catherine Belsey's Feminism', *Feminist Review*, no. 66 (Autumn 2000). Reprinted with permission.

Madhu Dubey: extract from *Signs and Cities: Black Literary Postmodernism* © University of Chicago Press, 2003.

Anne duCille: extract from 'On Canons: Anxious History and the Rise of Black Feminist Literary Studies' in Ellen Rooney (ed.) *The Cambridge Companion to Feminist Literary Theory*, 2006, © Cambridge University Press 2006, reproduced with permission.

Mary Eagleton: extract from 'Mapping Contemporary Women's Fiction after Bourdieu', *Women: A Cultural Review*, vol. 19, no. 1 (Spring 2008). Reprinted with permission.

Mary Ellmann: excerpts from *Thinking about Women* copyright © 1968 by Mary Ellmann, reproduced by permission of Houghton Mifflin Harcourt Publishing Company.

Margaret J. M. Ezell: Ezell, Margaret J. M. *Writing Women's Literary History*. © 1993 The Johns Hopkins University Press. Reprinted with permission of The Johns Hopkins University Press.

Lillian Faderman: extract from 'What Is Lesbian Literature? Forming a Historical Canon', in George E. Haggerty and Bonnie Zimmerman (eds.), *Professions of Desire: Lesbian and Gay Studies in Literature* (New York: The Modern Language Association of America, 1995). Reprinted by permission of the Modern Language Association of America.

Marilyn R. Farwell: extract from *Heterosexual Plots and Lesbian Narratives* (New York and London: New York University Press, 1996).

Shoshana Felman: extract from 'Women and Madness: The Critical Phallacy', *Diacritics*, vol. 5, no. 4 © 1975 The Johns Hopkins University Press. Reprinted with permission of The Johns Hopkins University Press. Extract from *What Does a Woman Want? Reading and Sexual Difference* (Baltimore: Johns Hopkins University Press, 1993). Reproduced by permission of Shoshana Felman.

Rita Felski: extract from *Doing Time: Feminist Theory and Postmodernist Culture* (New York: New York University Press, 2000).

Jan Fergus: extract from *Provincial Readers in Eighteenth-Century England* (Oxford: Oxford University Press, 2006). By permission of Oxford University Press.

Judith Fetterley: extract from *The Resisting Reader: A Feminist Approach to American Fiction*, Indiana University Press, 1978. Reprinted with permission of Indiana University Press.

Kate Flint: extract from *The Woman Reader, 1837–1914* (Oxford: Oxford University Press, 1993). By permission of Oxford University Press.

Viviane Forrester: extract from 'What Women's Eyes See', in Elaine Marks and Isabelle de Courtivron (eds.), *New French Feminisms: An Anthology*. Trans. Isabelle de Courtivron (Brighton, Sussex: Harvester Press, 1981).

Laura Franey: extract from *Victorian Travel Writing and Imperial Violence*, published 2003, Palgrave. Reproduced with permission of Palgrave Macmillan.

Nancy Fraser and Linda J. Nicholson: extract from 'Social Criticism without Philosophy: An Encounter between Feminism and Postmodernism', in Linda J. Nicholson (ed.), *Feminism/Postmodernism* (New York and London: Routledge, 1990). Reprinted with permission.

Susan Stanford Friedman: *Mappings*. © 1998 Princeton University Press. Reprinted by permission of Princeton University Press.

Diana Fuss: extract from *Essentially Speaking: Feminism, Nature and Difference*. New York and London: Routledge, 1989. Reprinted with permission.

Sandra M. Gilbert and Susan Gubar: extract from *The Madwoman in the Attic: The Woman Writer and the Nineteenth-Century Literary Imagination* (New Haven and London: Yale University Press, 1979). Copyright © 1979 Yale University Press.

Donna J. Haraway: extract from 'A Cyborg Manifesto: Science. Technology, and Socialist-Feminism in the Late Twentieth Century', in *Simians, Cyborgs and Women: The Reinvention of Nature* (London: Free Association Books, 1991). Reprinted with permission.

Jenny Hartley: extract from *Reading Groups*, A Survey Conducted in Association with Sarah Turvey (Oxford: Oxford University Press, 2001). By permission of Oxford University Press.

Clare Hemmings: extract from 'Telling Feminist Stories', *Feminist Theory*, vol. 6, no. 2 (2005). Reprinted with permission.

bell hooks: extract from 'Choosing the Margin as a Space of Radical Openness', *Yearning: Race, Gender, and Cultural Politics* (London: Turnaround, 1991). Reprinted with permission.

Graham Huggan: extract from *The Postcolonial Exotic: Marketing the Margins*, London: Routledge. Copyright © 2001 by permission of Taylor & Francis Books UK.

Nicola Humble: extract from *The Feminine Middlebrow Novel, 1920s to 1950s: Class, Domesticity and Bohemianism* (Oxford: Oxford University Press, 2001). By permission of Oxford University Press.

Luce Irigaray: extract from 'The Powers of Discourse and the Subordination of the Feminine', in *This Sex Which Is Not One* (Ithaca, New York: Cornell University Press, 1985). Trans. Catherine Porter with Carolyn Burke. First published 1977. Reprinted with permission.

Rosemary Jackson: extract from *Fantasy: The Literature of Subversion* © 1981 by permission of Taylor & Francis Books UK.

Mary Jacobus: extract from *Reading Women: Essays in Feminist Criticism* (London: Methuen, 1986).

Alice A. Jardine: extract from *Gynesis: Configurations of Woman and Modernity* (Ithaca, New York and London: Cornell University Press, 1985). Reprinted with permission.

Peggy Kamuf: extract from 'Writing Like a Woman' in Sally McConnell-Ginet, Ruth Borker and Nelly Furman (eds.) *Women and Language in Literature and Society*. New York. Copyright © 1980 by Praeger Publishers. Reproduced by permission of ABC-CLIO, LLC.

Caren Kaplan: extract from 'This Question of Moving and Postmodern Geographies', in *Questions of Travel*. Copyright, 1996, Duke University Press. All rights reserved. Used by permission of the publisher.

Cora Kaplan: extract from 'Editor's Introduction' to Elizabeth Barrett Browning, *Aurora Leigh and Other Poems* (London: Women's Press, 1978). Reprinted with permission.

Annette Kolodny: extract from 'Dancing through the Minefield: Some Observations on the Theory, Practice, and Politics of Feminist Literary Criticism', *Feminist Studies*, vol. 6, no. 1 (Spring 1980). Reprinted with permission.

Julia Kristeva: extract from 'Woman Can Never Be Defined', in Elaine Marks and Isabelle de Courtrivron (eds.), *New French Feminism: An Anthology* (Brighton: Harvester, 1980). Trans. Marilyn A. August. First published as 'La femme, ce n'est jamais ça' an interview by 'psychoanalysis and politics' in *Tel Quel* (Autumn 1974). Reprinted with permission. Extract from 'Talking about Polylogue' in Toril Moi (ed.), *French Feminist Thought: A Reader* (Oxford: Blackwell 1987). Trans. Sean Hand. First published as 'A partir de *Polylogue*', interview with Francoise van Rossum-Guyon in *Revue des Sciences Humaines*, vol. XLIV, no. 168 (Oct.–Dec. 1977). Extract from Julia Kristeva, 'A Question of Subjectivity: An Interview', in Philip Rice and Patricia Waugh (eds.), *Modern Literary Theory: A Reader* (London: Edward Arnold, 1989).

Susan S. Lanser: extract from 'Towards a Feminist Narratology', *Style*, vol. 20, no. 3 (Fall 1986). Reprinted with permission.

Teresa de Lauretis: extract from 'Upping the Anti (Sic) in Feminist Theory', in Marianne Hirsch and Evelyn Fox Keller (eds.), *Conflicts in Feminism* (New York and London: Routledge, 1990). Reprinted with permission.

Paul Lauter: extract from 'Race and Gender in the Shaping of the American Literary Canon: A Case Study from the Twenties' in Judith Newton and Deborah Rosenfelt (eds.) *Feminist Criticism and Social Change: Sex, Class and Race in Literature and Culture* (New York and London: Methuen, 1985). Essay first published in *Feminist Studies* 9 (1983) © Paul Lauter.

Reina Lewis: extract from *Rethinking Orientalism: Women, Travel and the Ottoman Harem* © 2004. I. B. Tauris.

Alison Light: extract from *Forever England: Femininity, Literature and Conservatism between the Wars* (London and New York: Routledge, 1991). Reprinted with permission.

Terry Lovell: extract from 'Writing Like a Woman: A Question of Politics' in Francis Barker et al. (eds.) *The Politics of Theory* (Essex: The University of Essex).

Anne McClintock: extract from *Imperial Leather: Race, Gender, and Sexuality in the Colonial Context.* (New York and London: Routledge, 1995). Reprinted with permission.

Paula McDowell: extract from *The Women of Grub Street: Press, Politics, and Gender in the Literary Marketplace 1678–1730* (Oxford: Clarendon Press, 1998). By permission of Oxford University Press.

Kathryn McGrath: extract from 'Pushed to the Margins: The Slow Death and Possible Rebirth of the Feminist Bookstore', *Feminist Collections*, vol. 25, no. 3 (Spring 2004).

Nancy K. Miller: extract from 'Parables and Politics: Feminist Criticism in 1986', *Paragraph* 8 (October 1986). Extract from *Subject to Change: Reading Feminist Writing* (New York: Columbia University Press, 1988). Reprinted with permission.

Juliet Mitchell: extract from 'Femininity, Narrative and Psychoanalysis', *Women: the Longest Revolution: Essays in Feminism, Literature and Psychoanalysis* (London: Virago, 1984). Copyright © Juliet Mitchell. Reproduced by permission of the author c/o Rogers, Coleridge & White Ltd., 20 Powis Mews, London W11 1JN.

Ellen Moers: extract from *Literary Women* (London: Women's Press, 1978; first published in the UK by W. H. Allen and Co., 1977). Extract from *Literary Women* (London: Women's Press 1978; first published in the UK by W. H. Allen and Co., 1977).

Chandra Talpade Mohanty: extract from 'Under Western Eyes: Feminist Scholarship and Colonial Discourses' in Chandra Talpade Mohanty, Ann Russo and Lourdes Torres, *Third World Women and the Politics of Feminism*: Indiana University Press, © 1991. Reprinted with permission of Indiana University Press.

Toril Moi: extract from *Sexual/Textual Politics: Feminist Literary Theory* © 1985 Reproduced by permission of Taylor & Francis Books UK. Extract from *What is a Woman? And Other Essays*, Oxford: Oxford University Press 1999. By permission of Oxford University Press.

Claire Goldberg Moses: extract from 'Made in America: "French Feminism" in Academia' originally published in *Feminist Studies*, vol. 24, issue 2 (Summer 1998) 241–75 by permission of the publisher *Feminist Studies, Inc.*

Simone Murray: extract from *Mixed Media: Feminist Presses and Publishing Politics* (London: Pluto Press, 2004). Reprinted with permission.

Lauretta Ngcobo: extract from 'Editor's Introduction', in *Let It be Told: Black Women Writers in Britain* (London: Virago, 1988). First published Pluto Press, 1987. Reprinted with permission.

Carol Ohmann: extract from 'Emily Brontë in the Hands of the Male Critics', *College English*, Vol. 32, No. 8 (May, 1971). Published by NCTE.

Tillie Olsen: extract from *Silences* (1965, 1972, 1978) (London: Virago, 1980). Reprinted with permission.

Benita Parry: extract from *Postcolonial Studies: A Materialist Critique*. Copyright © 2004 by permission of Taylor & Francis Books UK.

Meenakshi Ponnuswami: extract from 'Small Island People: Black British Women Playwrights' in Elaine Aston and Janelle Reinelt (eds.) *The Cambridge Companion to Modern British Women Playwrights*, 2000 © Cambridge University Press 2000, reproduced with permission.

Mary Louise Pratt: extract from *Imperial Eyes: Travel Writing and Transculturation*. Copyright © 2008 by permission of Taylor & Francis Books UK.

Janice A. Radway: extract from *A Feeling for Books: The Book-of-the-Month Club, Literary Taste, and Middle-Class Desire*. Copyright © 1997 by the University of North Carolina Press.

Sangeeta Ray: extract from 'New Woman, New Nations: Writing the Partition in Desai's Clear Light of Day and Sidhwa's Cracking India', in *En-Gendering India*. Copyright, 2000, Duke University Press. All rights reserved. Used by permission of the publisher.

Cherie Register: extract from 'American Feminist Literary Criticism: A Bibliographical Introduction', in Josephine Donovan (ed.), *Feminist Literary Criticism: Explorations in Theory* (Kentucky: Kentucky University Press, 1975). Reprinted with permission.

Adrienne Rich: excerpts from 'Compulsory Heterosexuality and Lesbian Existence', Excerpts from 'Notes toward a Politics of Location', from Blood, Bread, and Poetry: Selected Prose 1979–1985 by Adrienne Rich. Copyright © 1986 by Adrienne Rich. Used by permission of the author and W. W. Norton and Company, Inc.

Jacqueline Rose: extract from 'Femininity and its Discontents', *Feminist Review*, no. 14 (Summer 1983).

Betty A. Schellenberg: extract from *The Professionalization of Women Writers in Eighteenth-Century Britain*, 2005 © Betty A. Schellenberg 2005, published by Cambridge University Press, reproduced by permission.

Robert Scholes: extract from 'Reading Like a Man' in Alice Jardine and Paul Smith (eds.), *Men in Feminism* (New York and London: Methuen, 1987).

Eve Kosofsky Sedgwick: extract from *Epistomology of the Closet*. © 1991 University of California Press.

Susan Sellers: extract from *Myth and Fairy Tale in Contemporary Women's Fiction*, published 2001, reproduced with permission of Palgrave Macmillan.

Elaine Showalter: extract from *A Literature of Their Own: British Women Novelists from Brontë to Lessing*, London: Virago Ltd., 1978. (First published by Princeton University Press, 1977). © 1977 Princeton University Press, 2005 renewed PUP, 1999 exp. Paperback edition. Reprinted by permission of Princeton University Press. Extract from 'Towards a Feminist Poetics' in Mary Jacobus (ed.) *Women Writing and Writing about Women* © 1979 by permission of Taylor & Francis Books UK.

Barbara Smith: extract from 'Toward a Black Feminist Criticism', in Elaine Showalter (ed.), *The New Feminist Criticism: Essays on Women, Literature and Theory* (London: Virago, 1986). First published in *Conditions: Two*, vol. 1, no. 2 (Oct. 1977).

Kate Soper: extract from 'Of OncoMice and Female Men: Donna Haraway on Cyborg Ontology', *Women: A Cultural Review*, vol. 10, no. 2 (1999). Reprinted with permission.

Jane Spencer: extract from *Literary Relations: Kinship and the Canon 1660–1830* (Oxford: Oxford University Press, 2005). By permission of Oxford University Press. Extract from *The Rise of the Woman Novelist: From Aphra Behn to Jane Austen* (Oxford: Blackwell, 1986). Reprinted with permission.

Gayatri Chakravorty Spivak: extract from 'How to Read a "Culturally Different" Book', in Francis Barker, Peter Hulme and Margaret Iverson (eds.), *Colonial Discourse/Postcolonial Theory* (Manchester: Manchester University Press, 1994). Extract from 'French Feminism from an International Frame', *Yale French Studies*, no. 62 (1981). Reprinted with permission.

Claire Squires: extract from *Marketing Literature: The Making of Contemporary Writing in Britain* (Basingstoke: Palgrave Macmillan, 2007). Reprinted with permission.

Domna C. Stanton: extract from 'Language and Revolution: The Franco-American Dis-Connection', in Hester Eisenstein and Alice Jardine (eds.), *The Future of Difference* (New Brunswick, NJ: Rutgers University Press, 1994). First published Barnard Women's Center, 1980.

Susan Strehle: extract from *Transnational Women's Fiction: Unsettling Home and Homeland*, published 2008, Palgrave. Reproduced with permission of Palgrave Macmillan.

Sara Suleri: extract from 'Woman Skin Deep: Feminism and the Postcolonial Condition', from *Cultural Critique*, no. 18 (1992), University of Minnesota Press.

Trinh T. Minh-ha: extract from Woman, *Native, Other: Writing, Postcoloniality and Feminism*. Bloomington and Indianapolis: Indiana University Press, 1989. Reprinted with permission of Indiana University Press.

Robyn R. Warhol: extract from *Having a Good Cry: Effeminate Feelings and Pop-Culture Forms* (Columbus, Ohio: Ohio State University Press, 2003). Reproduced by permission of the Ohio State University Press.

Elizabeth Weed: extract from Elizabeth Weed, 'Introduction' in Weed and Naomi Schor (eds.) *Feminism Meets Queer Theory* © 1997. Reprinted with permission of Indiana University Press.

Chris Weedon: extract from *Feminist Practise and Poststructuralist Theory* (Oxford: Basil Blackwell, 1987). Reprinted with permission.

Robyn Wiegman: extract from 'Introduction: Mapping the Lesbian Postmodern', in Laura Doan (ed.), *The Lesbian Postmodern* (New York: Columbia University Press, 1994). Reprinted with permission.

Linda R. Williams: extract from Linda R. Williams 'Happy Families? Feminist Reproduction and Matrilineal Thought' in Isobel Armstrong (ed.) *New Feminist Discourses: Critical Essays on Theories and Texts* © 1992. Reproduced by permission of Taylor & Francis Books UK.

Monique Wittig: extract from *The Straight Mind*. Copyright © 1992 by Monique Wittig. Reprinted by permission of Beacon Press, Boston.

Virginia Woolf: extracts from *A Room of One's Own and Three Guineas* (Harmondsworth, Middlesex: Penguin, 1993). Introduction and notes by Michèle Barrett. The Society of Authors as the literary representative of the Estate of Virginia Woolf (UK/EEA Rights). Extract from 'Professions for Women', *The Death of the Moth and Other Essays* (London: Hogarth Press, 1942), reproduced in Virginia Woolf, *Women and Writing*. Edited and with an Introduction by Michèle Barrett. (New York and London: Harcourt Brace Jovanovich, 1979). Reprinted with permission.

Despite every effort to trace and contact copyright holders prior to publication this has not always been possible. We apologise for any apparent infringement of copyright and if notified, we will be pleased to rectify and errors or omissions at the earliest opportunity.

1

Finding a Female Tradition

INTRODUCTION

Breaking the Silence

> It is the women's movement, part of the other movements of our time for a fully human life, that has brought this forum into being; kindling a renewed, in most instances a first-time, interest in the writings and writers of our sex.
>
> Linked with the old, resurrected classics on women, this movement in three years has accumulated a vast new mass of testimony, of new comprehensions as to what it is to be female. Inequities, restrictions, penalties, denials, leechings have been painstakingly and painfully documented; damaging differences in circumstances and treatment from that of males attested to; and limitations, harms, a sense of wrong, voiced.[1]

Tillie Olsen's essay, from which this quotation comes, was first published in 1972 and, later, became part of a volume entitled *Silences*. Both the date and the title are significant. British and American feminist critics in the 1970s were preoccupied with the idea that women writers had been silenced by, and largely excluded from, literary history. The Olsen quotation exemplifies the key interests of many feminist critics at that time – the desire to rediscover the lost work of women writers, while providing a context that would be supportive of contemporary women writers, and the wish to manifest 'what it is to be female', to declare the experience and perceptions that have been unheard. Aware that critical attention concentrated mostly on male writers, these critics demanded a status and recognition for women authors. But the aim was not simply to fit women into the male-dominated tradition; that was dismissed as an 'add women and stir' model. Rather, they wanted to produce the history of a tradition *among* women themselves. The writing of this period,

Feminist Literary Theory: A Reader, Third Edition By Mary Eagleton © 2011 Mary Eagleton

building on the earlier work of Virginia Woolf, reveals the affinity which women writers have felt for each other, the interest – sometimes encouraging, sometimes anxiously competitive – that they have taken in each other's work, the way the writing of one might prepare the ground for another, the problems women writers faced, and still face, in handling the institutions of literary production.[2] The expansion of feminist literary criticism and of courses about women's writing, and the establishment of feminist publishing houses or feminist lists within existing houses, introduced to readers an extensive new area of research. It became increasingly difficult for a teacher to use the 'lack of material' argument to explain the absence of women writers from a course.

Elaine Showalter offers two cautionary notes. Firstly, she questions Ellen Moers's use of the term 'movement', which suggests a steady and continuous development in women's writing, and mentions the 'holes and hiatuses', the absences, gaps and disruptions, which have broken that history. Though no writer ever enjoys continuous critical acclaim, Showalter believes that women writers have disappeared more easily from literary history, leaving their sisters bereft and struggling to reconstruct the fractured tradition. Secondly, Showalter feels that Patricia Meyer Spacks's concept of a 'female imagination' can confirm the belief in 'a deep, basic, and inevitable difference between male and female ways of perceiving the world'. Such essentialist or biologistic viewpoints imply that there is something both intrinsic in the experience of being female and common to all women. The danger is that gender is privileged at the expense of other differences and that the approach can too easily become ahistorical and apolitical in the assumption of an unproblematic unity among women, across culture, class and history.[3]

At the same time, Showalter would be among the first to stress that the search for women writers has constituted an important political challenge. To ask the questions – Where are the women writers? What has aided or inhibited their writing? How has criticism responded to their work? – introduces into literary criticism the determinant of gender and reveals literary tradition as a construct. The commonplace idea that 'talent will out', that 'great' writers will spontaneously and inevitably reveal their quality, is shown to be false. To the questioning from Marxist criticism about the class bias of the literary tradition are added feminist queries about its androcentricity. What have been proposed by conservative criticism as impartial and objective academic judgements begin to look value-laden and ideologically suspect.

Who Belongs to the Female Tradition?
The quotation from Olsen hints at two contradictions that have dogged feminist criticism for many years. On the one hand, how can feminism speak of the relentless silencing of women while at the same time maintaining that there is a formidable tradition to uncover? On the other hand, how can

feminism claim a rich plurality of female voices and then produce a rather narrow and homogeneous literary heritage – chiefly that of white, middle-class, heterosexual (or presented as heterosexual) women, living in England and the USA during the nineteenth and twentieth centuries? This description would apply to many of the critical works produced in the USA in the late 1960s and throughout the 1970s, books which are, rightly, considered founding texts in feminist literary criticism: Mary Ellmann's *Thinking about Women* (1968), Patricia Meyer Spacks's *The Female Imagination* (1975), Ellen Moers's *Literary Women* (1977, although parts of the book go back to 1963), Elaine Showalter's *A Literature of Their Own: British Women Novelists from Brontë to Lessing* (1977). Not surprisingly, then, by the end of the 1970s, a strong counter-voice from lesbians and 'women of color' began to question feminism's own processes of inclusion and exclusion. Sexism might be challenged in the white, heterosexual work, but heterosexism or homophobia or racism or ethnocentricity may not be. For example, Afra-American feminist critics pointed out that the female stereotypes which so preoccupy white feminists – the Southern belle, or the Angel in the House, or the submissive wife – simply do not apply to them, though they are offered in the criticism as the dominant stereotypes and as widely relevant.[4] Where writing from a different position does exist, its place is frequently marginal – the odd paragraph, the single essay.

We see in Adrienne Rich's work an eagerness to seek out new traditions, looking for names, for a history, for foremothers.[5] This activity inevitably disputes the dominant literary values, confronts feminism's own failings and, yet, illustrates how feminist literary criticism has always been in critical dialogue with itself. Rich's emphasis on the *political* importance of lesbianism and on heterosexuality as an institution challengingly moves the debate beyond the level of liberal pluralism. Lesbianism exists not as a 'sexual preference' or an 'alternative lifestyle' but as a fundamental critique of the dominant order and as an organizing principle for women. It is worthwhile comparing Rich's views with the even more challenging thesis of Monique Wittig (Chapter 6). Yet the problem of conceptualizing a literary tradition remains as intractable for 'women of color' and lesbians as it does for white women and heterosexuals. Chris Weedon, reflecting on the work of Rich and, particularly, Bonnie Zimmerman, examines the key question of defini-tion. The meaning of lesbianism, she maintains, is not fixed or dependent solely on the lifestyle of the author or the subject matter of the text; rather, the meaning 'changes with historical shifts in the discursive construction of female sexuality'. How, then, can one define what a lesbian tradition is?[6] Similarly, Ann duCille, looking back at the rise of black feminist literary studies in the 1970s from the perspective of 2006, sees another history of selection and exclusion and that 'missing in action' is, particularly, the work of nineteenth-century black women writers.

Omission might be caused by all manner of factors – antipathy or blind-spots, personal self-interest, poor scholarship, restrictions of the format – but it would be wrong to explain this phenomenon solely at the level of the individual and individual inadequacies. duCille suggests a more subtle ideological process, how the black feminist critics of the 1970s had difficulty in incorporating the nineteenth-century material into the vision they were creating of a black women's literary heritage; it did not 'fit' with the tenor, politics or aspirations of the moment.[7] Paul Lauter's and Clare Hemmings's extracts point to other factors, namely the social determinants operating within institutions and discourse. In Lauter's case study, the focus is the creation, in American higher education of the 1920s, of a middle-class, male, white, professoriate, which was in a position to determine the content of the American literary canon and, in Lauter's view, 'virtually eliminated black, white female and all working-class writers'.[8] Hemmings's extract is concerned with the production, through citation, of a particular narrative of poststructuralist feminist thought which certainly does disservice to 1970s feminism but, equally, simplifies the diversity of feminist positions in play at any moment and the range of interest held by the theorists themselves.[9] Both Lauter and Hemmings show the importance of a micro analysis and the significance of detail.

New Wine in Old Bottles?
A further problem in creating a female literary tradition is that feminists may unwittingly continue to employ aesthetic concepts that are compromised and intrinsically linked with the very social order they wish to undermine. Understanding this is complicated by the fact that debates sometimes range rather uncertainly across three aspects: searching for a literary tradition; critiques of canonical ranking while, at the same time, constructing one's own canon; and questions of aesthetic value. Thus, to talk of a female tradition of writing can reinforce the canonical view which looks upon liter-ary history as a continuum of significant names. Rather than disrupting the individualistic values by which the mainstream has been created, feminist critics may merely replace a male First Eleven with a female one: so you can study Aphra Behn instead of Dryden, Edith Wharton instead of Henry James, Dorothy Wordsworth instead of William.[10] The very approach which has always seemed to find the majority of women writers lacking is trans-posed, uncritically, to a separate female tradition, and the humanist ethic which supports that approach is accepted as basically valid, only in need of extending its franchise.[11] Yet, even if we reject the canonical in favour of a more dispersed sense of literary history, the problem of aesthetic value remains. Why do we find certain works more pleasurable, relevant, impor-tant than others; how do gender and other determinants impact on those responses; and are we, then, inevitably making a claim for these works as

having a privileged place in a female literary tradition?[12] Rita Felski's response in a chapter notably entitled 'Why Feminism Doesn't Need an Aesthetic (and Why It Can't Ignore Aesthetics)' – the contradiction says it all – turns to David Carroll's concept of 'paraesthetics' and its uncertain, unsettling, resistant view of aesthetics.[13]

Equally, concern has focused on the generational thinking involved in creating a literary tradition.[14] Though Woolf advises us to 'think back through our mothers' and Alice Walker to go 'in search of our mothers' gardens', other commentators have been less sure about embracing a familial and, specifically, matrilineal history. For Linda Williams, the matrilineal heritage again reinforces the notion of a commonality among women and dangerously substitutes a female paradigm of mother and daughter for the male Oedipal model of father and son. However, Jane Spencer, while certainly not endorsing any sense of 'happy families', productively analyses the biological, social and metaphorical meanings of kinship. Her detailed literary history from 1660 to 1830 reveals a dense, shifting field where the woman author can feature as Muse and as the biological or metaphorical mother, daughter or sister to both male and female authors. Like Williams, Nancy K. Miller notes the haunting presence in feminist criticism of Oedipal relations, that 'biological and murderous simplicity' recycled through Harold Bloom. Using the analogy of letter writing and the example of Germaine de Staël's *Corinne or Italy* (1809), Miller hopes to 'return to sender' all the accepted assumptions and values of literary criticism and to produce a more nuanced sense of generational legacy.

The View from Elsewhere
Despite all the problems and qualifications, Anglo-American criticism rests on the presumption that there definitely is a female tradition, buried like hidden treasure in literary history, and that the task of the feminist critic is to dig it out, brush it down and exhibit it; Showalter uses a different simile and compares feminist literary tradition to the lost continent of Atlantis rising from the sea. As we have already seen from Weedon's and Miller's pieces, critics approaching the problem from a different theoretical position, chiefly influenced by French deconstructive and psychoanalytical thought, are not quite so sure that such an entity exists. Viviane Forrester contends that we cannot know what women are. The feminine is that which has been repressed and women's vision – in Forrester's case with regard to film – is only evident in 'what you don't see'. It is not that women are hidden or silent; rather they are lacking. While Anglo-American critics are looking for women in history, French women writers, Elaine Marks tells us, are: 'looking for women in the unconscious, which is to say in their own language. "Cherchez la femme" might be one of their implied mottos; where repression is, she is'.[15] Thus, although we may uncover a whole list of forgotten novels by women or

films with female directors, feminists of this school are unwilling to see that as necessarily a female tradition. They want to put the questions that Shoshana Felman asks. Are these novelists and directors speaking 'as women' or are they 'speaking the language of men'? Can they be said to be speaking 'as women' simply because they are born female? Who is speaking 'for women' and how?

A second 'view from elsewhere' comes from feminist interest in historiography. We have already seen in the extracts from duCille and Hemmings the importance of self-reflexive assessments of how feminism is constructing its own history – as Hemmings indicates, the *stories* we tell ourselves and others. This work has been greatly enabled by research into women's pre-nineteenth-century writing. Literary feminism has constructed a history, claims Margaret J. M. Ezell, which reads backwards, with the result that women's earlier writing has been, to use Jerome McGann's term, 'gerrymandered'. Moreover, this linear approach is based on a nineteenth-century model of narrative historiography which has built into it a presumption of progress. Like Ezell, Betty A. Schellenberg sees the problem in diachronic readings but also in the 'binary synchronic structure' of the dominant feminist model which produces oppositional relationships. She shows how effectively subsequent work has challenged the simple binary view but, interestingly, has, on occasions, confirmed the diachronic.[16] What this work points to is a more subtle study of the woman author, situated in history and discourse, and viewed through a range of interpretative categories, including gender.

Notes

1   Tillie Olsen, *Silences* (London: Virago, 1980), p. 23. Note that parts of this volume go back to 1965.
2   An example of the continuing problems would be the production of *The Field Day Anthology of Irish Writing*, the first three volumes of which were published in 1991 with a notable absence of women writers. The furore that greeted the publication led in 2002 to the publication of two subsequent volumes on Irish women's writing: Angela Bourke (ed.), *The Field Day Anthology of Irish Writing: Irish Women's Writing and Traditions* Vols. IV and V (Cork: Cork University Press). For discussion of this issue and the politics of canon making, see: John Greene et al., 'Wealth, Gender, Politics: Three Views of the *Field Day Anthology of Irish Writing*', *Eire-Ireland: A Journal of Irish Studies*, vol. 27, no. 2, pp. 111–31 (1992); Anne Fogarty, 'Challenging Boundaries', *Irish Literary Supplement*, 22 Mar. 2003; Elvira Johnston, '*The Field Day Anthology of Irish Writing* Vols. 4 and 5 and the Invention of the Medieval Woman', *Irish University Review*, vol. 33, no. 2 (2003), pp. 392–9; Helen Thompson, *The Current Debate about the Irish Literary Canon* (Lewiston, New York: Edward Mellen, 2006).

3   Spacks's work is again used as an example of possible biologism in Peggy Kamuf's extract in Ch. 5.

4   See Deborah E. McDowell, 'New Directions for Black Feminist Criticism', *Black American Literature Forum*, vol. 14, no. 4 (Winter 1980); Andrea B. Rushing, 'Images of Black Women in Modern African Poetry: An Overview' in *Sturdy Black Bridges: Visions of Black Women in Literature*, eds. Roseann P. Bell, Bettye J. Parker, Beverly Guy-Sheftall (New York: Anchor/Doubleday, 1979); Alice Walker, 'A Letter of the Times, or Should this Sado-Masochism Be Saved?' in *You Can't Keep a Good Woman Down* (New York: Harcourt Brace Jovanovich, 1982).

5   Further examples here would be the essays of Alice Walker in *In Search of Our Mothers' Gardens* (New York: Harcourt Brace Jovanovich, 1983) and Bonnie Zimmerman, 'What Has Never Been: An Overview of Lesbian Feminist Literary Criticism', *Feminist Studies*, vol. 7, no. 3 (Autumn 1981).

6   An extract from the Barbara Smith article to which Weedon refers can be found in Chapter 2. The issue of definition is considered again in Chapter 4.

7   The response can operate in a contrary way. As Rita Felski has remarked on Sandra Gilbert and Susan Gubar's *The Madwoman in the Attic*: 'By depicting Victorian writers as seething rebels rather than moral guardians, as maimed victims of patriarchy rather than prim and censorious foremothers, they created precursors very much after their own heart' (*Literature After Feminism*, Chicago: University of Chicago Press, 2003), pp. 66–7.

8   Lauter's essay was subsequently included in his *Canons and Contexts* (Oxford: Oxford University Press, 1991), a collection which extensively discusses the professional, academic and publishing production of a canon. For a more recent examination of literary feminism as an institutional and critical production, see Sharon Marcus, 'Feminist Criticism: A Tale of Two Bodies', *PMLA*, vol. 121, no. 5 (Oct. 2006), pp. 1722–8.

9   The discussion of the possibility/ impossibility of constructing an adequate feminist history continued in a later volume of *Feminist Theory*. See Rachel Torr, 'What's Wrong with Aspiring to Find Out What Has Really Happened in Academic Feminism's Recent Past? Response to Clare Hemmings' "Telling Feminist Stories"', *Feminist Theory*, vol. 8, no. 1 (2007), pp. 59–67, and, in the same volume, Hemmings's reply, 'What Is a Feminist Theorist Responsible For? Response to Rachel Torr', pp. 69–76. See also Mary Eagleton, 'Who's Who and Where's Where: Constructing Feminist Literary Studies', *Feminist Review*, no. 53 (Summer 1996), pp. 1–23 on the historiography of feminist criticism; the chapter 'Perverse Presentism' in Judith Halbestam, *Female Masculinity* (Durham, NC, and London: Duke University Press, 1998); Katherine Binhammer and Jeanne Wood (eds.), *Women and Literary History: 'For There She Was'* (Newark: University of Delaware Press, 2003); and Alison Donnell, *Twentieth-Century Caribbean Literature: Critical Moments in Anglophone Literary History* (London: Routledge, 2006).

10 Note how the focus on the individual woman author can serve a different purpose in tracing the long-term reception of women writers and the intricate patterning of readerships, affects, literary evaluations, reputations and influences. See, for example, Jane Spencer, *Aphra Behn's Afterlife* (Oxford: Oxford

University Press, 2000) and Robert McClure Smith and Ellen Weinauer (eds.), *American Culture, Canons, and the Case of Elizabeth Stoddard* (Tuscaloosa and London, University of Alabama Press, 2003).

11   A more recent strategy has been to think of literary history in a gendered but non-separatist way. See Karen K. Kilcup (ed.), *Soft Canons: American Women Writers and Masculine Tradition* (Iowa City: University of Iowa Press, 1999) and Cathy N. Davidson and Jessamyn Hatcher (eds.), *No More Separate Spheres! A Next Wave American Studies Reader* (Durham, NC, and London: Duke University Press, 2002).

12   In addition to Felski, other work on feminist aesthetic value would include: Gayatri Chakravorty Spivak, 'Scattered Speculations on the Question of Value', in *In Other Worlds: Essays in Cultural Politics* (New York and London: Methuen, 1987); Steven Connor, *Theory and Cultural Value* (Oxford: Blackwell, 1992); Isobel Armstrong, *The Radical Aesthetic* (Oxford: Blackwell, 2000); Janet Wolff, *The Aesthetics of Uncertainty* (New York: Columbia University Press, 2008).

13   Other strategies would include Griselda Pollock's suggestion that we should concentrate not on inclusion or on exclusion from the canon but on 'differencing' the canon: see *Differencing the Canon: Feminist Desire and the Writing of Art's Histories* (London and New York: Routledge, 1999). See also John Guillory's suggestion in *Cultural Capital: The Problem of Literary Canon Formation* (Chicago: University of Chicago Press, 1993) that we focus on cultural capital rather than representation when thinking about literary canons.

14   See also on generational thinking Devoney Looser and E. Ann Kaplan (eds.), *Generations: Academic Feminists in Dialogue* (Minneapolis: University of Minnesota Press, 1997) and Stacy Gillis and Rebecca Munford, 'Genealogies and Generations: The Politics and Praxis of Third Wave Feminism', *Women's History Review*, vol. 13, no. 2, pp. 165–82. Hemmings's essay is also strongly informed by a sense of genealogies and generations.

15   Elaine Marks, 'Women and Literature in France', *Signs: Journal of Women in Culture and Society*, vol. 3, no. 4 (1978), p. 836.

16   In addition to the titles noted by Schellenberg, see also Anne E. Boyd, *Writing for Immortality: Women Writers and the Emergence of High Literary Culture in America* (Baltimore and London: Johns Hopkins University Press, 2004) and Catherine Gallagher, 'A History of the Precedent: Rhetorics of Legitimation in Women's Writing', *Critical Inquiry*, vol. 26 (2000), pp. 309–27 for explorations of women's strategic positioning of themselves in literary culture, again questioning the accepted binary relationship.

VIRGINIA WOOLF

A Room of One's Own

And with Mrs Behn we turn a very important corner on the road. We leave behind, shut up in their parks among their folios, those solitary great ladies who wrote without audience or criticism, for their own delight alone. We come to town and rub shoulders with ordinary people in the streets. Mrs Behn was a middle-class woman with all the plebeian virtues of humour, vitality and courage; a woman forced by the death of her husband and some unfortunate adventures of her own to make her living by her wits. She had to work on equal terms with men. She made, by working very hard, enough to live on. The importance of that fact outweighs anything that she actually wrote, even the splendid 'A Thousand Martyrs I have made', or 'Love in Fantastic Triumph sat', for here begins the freedom of the mind, or rather the possibility that in the course of time the mind will be free to write what it likes. For now that Aphra Behn had done it, girls could go to their parents and say, You need not give me an allowance; I can make money by my pen. Of course the answer for many years to come was, Yes, by living the life of Aphra Behn! Death would be better! and the door was slammed faster than ever. That profoundly interesting subject, the value that men set upon women's chastity and its effect upon their education, here suggests itself for discussion, and might provide an interesting book if any student at Girton or Newnham cared to go into the matter. Lady Dudley, sitting in diamonds among the midges of a Scottish moor, might serve for frontispiece. Lord Dudley, *The Times* said when Lady Dudley died the other day, 'a man of cultivated taste and many accomplishments, was benevolent and bountiful, but whimsically despotic. He insisted upon his wife's wearing full dress, even at the remotest shooting-lodge in the Highlands; he loaded her with gorgeous jewels', and so on, 'he gave her everything – always excepting any measure of responsibility'. Then Lord Dudley had a stroke and she nursed him and ruled his estates with supreme competence for ever after. That whimsical despotism was in the nineteenth century too.

But to return. Aphra Behn proved that money could be made by writing at the sacrifice, perhaps, of certain agreeable qualities; and so by degrees writing became not merely a sign of folly and a distracted mind, but was of practical importance. A husband might die, or some disaster overtake the family. Hundreds of women began as the eighteenth century drew on to add to their pin money, or to come to the rescue of their families by making translations or writing the innumerable bad novels which have ceased to be recorded even in text-books, but are to be picked up in the fourpenny boxes in the Charing Cross Road.[7] The extreme activity of mind which showed itself in the later eighteenth century among women – the talking, and the meeting, the writing of essays on Shakespeare, the translating of the classics – was founded on the solid fact that women could make money by writing. Money dignifies what is frivolous if unpaid for. It might still be well to sneer at 'blue stockings with an itch for scribbling', but it could not be denied that they could put money in their purses. Thus, towards the end of the eighteenth century a change came about which, if I were rewriting history, I should describe more fully and think of greater importance than the Crusades or the Wars of the Roses. The middle-class woman began to write. For if *Pride and Prejudice* matters, and *Middlemarch* and *Villette* and *Wuthering Heights* matter, then it matters far more than I can prove in an hour's discourse that women generally, and not merely the lonely aristocrat shut up in her country house among her folios and her flatterers, took to writing. Without those forerunners, Jane Austen and the Brontës and George Eliot could no more have written than Shakespeare could have written without Marlowe, or Marlowe without Chaucer, or Chaucer without those forgotten poets who paved the ways and tamed the natural savagery of the tongue. For masterpieces are not single and solitary births; they are the outcome of many years of thinking in common, of thinking by the body of the people, so that the experience of the mass is behind the single voice. Jane Austen should have laid a wreath upon the grave of Fanny Burney, and George Eliot done homage to the robust shade of Eliza Carter[8] – the valiant old woman who tied a bell to her bedstead in order that she might wake early and learn Greek. All women together ought to let flowers fall upon the tomb of Aphra Behn which is, most scandalously but rather appropriately, in Westminster Abbey, for it was she who earned them the right to speak their minds. It is she – shady and amorous as she was – who makes it not quite fantastic for me to say to you tonight: Earn five hundred a year by your wits.

(1929)

Notes

7   *Charing Cross Road*: in London, a centre for second-hand bookshops.
8   *Eliza Carter*: Elizabeth Carter (1717–1806), translator of Epictetus, letter-writer, friend of Dr Johnson and an original 'blue stocking'. The 'blue stockings' were a group of women who hosted evening parties in the 1750s. Eschewing card games and evening dress in favour of literary conversation, they invited eminent men of letters to take part in their discussions. One member of the group, Benjamin Stillingfleet, regulary attended wearing blue worsted stockings instead of black evening clothes, giving rise to the nickname 'blue stocking' for a woman with literary tastes.

Elaine Showalter

A Literature of Their Own: British Women Novelists from Brontë to Lessing

As the works of dozens of women writers have been rescued from what E. P. Thompson calls 'the enormous condescension of posterity,'[16] and considered in relation to each other, the lost continent of the female tradition has risen like Atlantis from the sea of English literature. It is now becoming clear that, contrary to Mill's theory, women have had a literature of their own all along. The woman novelist, according to Vineta Colby, was 'really neither single nor anomalous,' but she was also more than a 'register and a spokesman for her age.'[17] She was part of a tradition that had its origins before her age, and has carried on through our own.

Many literary historians have begun to reinterpret and revise the study of women writers. Ellen Moers sees women's literature as an international movement, 'apart from, but hardly subordinate to the mainstream: an undercurrent, rapid and powerful. This "movement" began in the late eighteenth century, was multinational, and produced some of the greatest literary works of two centuries, as well as most of the lucrative pot-boilers.'[18] Patricia Meyer Spacks, in *The Female Imagination*, finds that 'for readily discernible historical reasons women have characteristically concerned themselves with matters more or less peripheral to male concerns, or at least slightly skewed from them. The differences between traditional female preoccupations and roles and male ones make a difference in female writing.'[19] Many other critics are beginning to agree that when we look at women writers collectively we can see an imaginative continuum, the recurrence of certain patterns, themes, problems, and images from generation to generation.

This book is an effort to describe the female literary tradition in the English novel from the generation of the Brontës to the present day, and to show how the development of this tradition is similar to the development of any literary subculture. Women have generally been regarded as 'sociological chameleons,' taking on the class, lifestyle, and culture of their male relatives. It can, however, be argued that women themselves have constituted a subculture within the framework of a larger society, and have been unified by values, conventions, experiences, and behaviors impinging on each individual. It is important to see the female literary tradition in these broad terms, in relation to the wider evolution of women's self-awareness and to the ways in which any minority group finds its direction of self-expression relative to a dominant society, because we cannot show a pattern of deliberate progress and accumulation. It is true, as Ellen Moers writes, that 'women studied with a special closeness the works written by their own sex';[20] in terms of influences, borrowings, and affinities, the tradition is strongly marked. But it is also full of holes and hiatuses, because of what Germaine Greer calls the 'phenomenon of the transience of female literary fame'; 'almost uninterruptedly since the Interregnum, a small group of women have enjoyed dazzling literary prestige during their own lifetimes, only to vanish without trace from the records of posterity.'[21] Thus each generation of women writers has found itself, in a sense, without a history, forced to rediscover the past anew, forging again and again the consciousness of their sex. Given this perpetual disruption, and also the self-hatred that has alienated women writers from a sense of collective identity, it does not seem possible to speak of a 'movement.'

I am also uncomfortable with the notion of a 'female imagination.' The theory of a female sensibility revealing itself in an imagery and form specific to women always runs dangerously close to reiterating the familiar stereotypes. It also suggests permanence, a deep, basic, and inevitable difference between male and female ways of perceiving the world. I think that, instead, the female literary tradition comes from the still-evolving relationships between women writers and their society. Moreover, the 'female imagination' cannot be treated by literary historians as a romantic or Freudian abstraction. It is the product of a delicate network of influences operating in time, and it must be analyzed as it expresses itself, in language and in a fixed arrangement of words on a page, a form that itself is subject to a network of influences and conventions, including the operations of the marketplace. In this investigation of the English novel, I am intentionally looking, not at an innate sexual attitude, but at the ways in which the self-awareness of the woman writer has translated itself into a literary form in a specific place and time-span, how this self-awareness has changed and developed, and where it might lead.

I am therefore concerned with the professional writer who wants pay and publication, not with the diarist or letter-writer. This emphasis has required careful consideration of the novelists, as well as the novels, chosen for discussion. When we turn from the overview of the literary tradition to look at the individuals who composed it, a different but interrelated set of motives, drives, and sources becomes prominent. I have needed to ask why women began to write for money and how they negotiated the activity of writing within their families. What was their professional self-image? How was their work received, and what effects did criticism have upon them? What were their experiences as women, and how were these reflected in books? What was their understanding of womanhood? What were their relationships to other women, to men, and to their readers? How did changes in women's status affect their lives and careers? And how did the vocation of writing itself change the women who committed themselves to it? In looking at literary subcultures, such as black, Jewish, Canadian, Anglo-Indian, or even American, we can see that they all go through three major phases. First, there is a prolonged phase of *imitation* of the prevailing modes of the dominant tradition, and *internalization* of its standards of art and its views on social roles. Second, there is a phase of *protest* against these standards and values, and *advocacy* of minority rights and values, including a demand for autonomy. Finally, there is a phase of *self-discovery*, a turning inward freed from some of the dependency of opposition, a search for identity.[22] An appropriate terminology for women writers is to call these stages, *Feminine, Feminist,* and *Female.* These are obviously not rigid categories, distinctly separable in time, to which individual writers can be assigned with perfect assurance. The phases overlap; there are feminist elements in feminine writing, and vice versa. One might also find all three phases in the career of a single novelist. Nonetheless, it seems useful to point to periods of crisis when a shift of literary values occurred. In this book I identify the Feminine phase as the period from the appearance of the male pseudonym in the 1840s to the death of George Eliot in 1880; the Feminist phase as 1880 to 1920, or the winning of the vote; and the Female phase as 1920 to the present, but entering a new stage of self-awareness about 1960.

It is important to understand the female subculture not only as what Cynthia Ozick calls 'custodial'[23] – a set of opinions, prejudices, tastes, and values prescribed for a subordinate group to perpetuate its subordination – but also as a thriving and positive entity. Most discussions of women as a subculture have come from historians describing Jacksonian America, but they apply equally well to the situation of early Victorian England. According to Nancy Cott, 'we can view women's group consciousness as a subculture uniquely divided against itself by ties to the dominant culture. While the ties to the dominant culture are the informing and restricting ones, they provoke within the subculture certain strengths as well as weaknesses, enduring values as well as accommodations.'[24] The middle-class ideology of the proper sphere of womanhood, which developed in post-industrial England and America, prescribed a woman who would be a Perfect Lady, an Angel in the House, contentedly submissive to men, but strong in her inner purity and religiosity, queen in her own realm of the Home.[25] Many observers have pointed out that the first professional activities of Victorian women, as social reformers, nurses, governesses, and novelists, either were based in the home or were extensions of the feminine role as teacher, helper, and mother of mankind. In describing the American situation, two historians have seen a subculture emerging from the doctrine of sexual spheres:

> By "subculture" we mean simply "a habit of living" ... of a minority group which is self-consciously distinct from the dominant activities, expectations, and values of a society. Historians have seen female church groups, reform associations, and philanthropic activity as expressions of this subculture in actual behavior, while a large and rich body of writing by and for women

articulated the subculture impulses on the ideational level. Both behavior and thought point to child-rearing, religious activity, education, home life, associationism, and female communality as components of women's subculture. Female friendships, strikingly intimate and deep in this period, formed the actual bonds.[26]

For women in England, the female subculture came first through a shared and increasingly secretive and ritualized physical experience. Puberty, menstruation, sexual initiation, pregnancy, childbirth, and menopause – the entire female sexual life cycle – constituted a habit of living that had to be concealed. Although these episodes could not be openly discussed or acknowledged, they were accompanied by elaborate rituals and lore, by external codes of fashion and etiquette, and by intense feelings of female solidarity.[27] Women writers were united by their roles as daughters, wives, and mothers; by the internalized doctrines of evangelicalism, with its suspicion of the imagination and its emphasis on duty; and by legal and economic constraints on their mobility. Sometimes they were united in a more immediate way, around a political cause. On the whole these are the implied unities of culture, rather than the active unities of consciousness.

From the beginning, however, women novelists' awareness of each other and of their female audience showed a kind of covert solidarity that sometimes amounted to a genteel conspiracy. Advocating sisterhood, Sarah Ellis, one of the most conservative writers of the first Victorian generation, asked: 'What should we think of a community of slaves, who betrayed each other's interests? of a little band of shipwrecked mariners upon a friendless shore who were false to each other? of the inhabitants of a defenceless nation, who would not unite together in earnestness and good faith against a common enemy?'[28] Mrs. Ellis felt the binding force of the minority experience for women strongly enough to hint, in the prefaces to her widely read treatises on English womanhood, that her female audience would both read the messages between her lines and refrain from betraying what they deciphered. As another conservative novelist, Dinah Mulock Craik, wrote, 'The intricacies of female nature are incomprehensible except to a woman; and any biographer of real womanly feeling, if ever she discovered, would never dream of publishing them.'[29] Few English women writers openly advocated the use of fiction as revenge against a patriarchal society (as did the American novelist Fanny Fern, for example), but many confessed to sentiments of 'maternal feeling, sisterly affection, *esprit de corps*'[30] for their readers. Thus the clergyman's daughter, going to Mudie's for her three-decker novel by another clergyman's daughter, participated in a cultural exchange that had a special personal significance.

(1977)

Notes

16 *The Making of the English Working Class*, New York, 1973, p. 12.
17 Vineta Colby, *The Singular Anomaly: Women Novelists of the Nineteenth Century*, New York, 1970, p. 11.
18 'Women's Lit: Profession and Tradition,' *Columbia Forum 1* (Fall 1972): 27.
19 Spacks, p. 7.
20 Moers, 'Women's Lit.' 28.
21 'Flying Pigs and Double Standards,' *Times Literary Supplement*, (July 26, 1974): 784.
22 For helpful studies of literary subcultures, see Robert A. Bone, *The Negro Novel in America*, New York, 1958; and Northrop Frye, 'Conclusion to *A Literary History of Canada*,' in *The Stubborn Structure: Essays on Criticism and Society*, Ithaca, 1970, pp. 278–312.
23 'Women and Creativity,' p. 442.
24 Nancy F. Cott, introduction to *Root of Bitterness*, New York, 1972, pp. 3–4.
25 For the best discussions of the Victorian feminine ideal, see Françoise Basch, 'Contemporary Ideologies,' in *Relative Creatures*, pp. 3–15; Walter E. Houghton, *The Victorian Frame of Mind*, New Haven, 1957, pp. 341–3; and Alexander Welsh's theory of the Angel in the House in *The City of Dickens*, London, 1971, pp. 164–95.
26 Christine Stansell and Johnny Faragher, 'Women and Their Families on the Overland Trail, 1842–1867,' *Feminist Studies* 11 (1975): 152–3. For an overview of recent historical scholarship on the 'two cultures,' see Barbara Sicherman, 'Review: American History.' *Signs: Journal of Women in Culture and Society* 1 (Winter 1975): 470–84.
27 For a sociological account of patterns of behavior for Victorian women, see Leonore Davidoff, *The Best Circles: Society, Etiquette and the Season*, London, 1973, esp. pp. 48–58, 85–100.
28 Sarah Ellis, *The Daughters of England*, New York, 1844, ch. ix, p. 90.
29 Dinah M. Craik, 'Literary Ghouls,' *Studies from Life*, New York, n.d., p. 13.
30 Letter of October 6, 1851, in *Letters of E. Jewsbury to Jane Welsh Carlyle*, ed. Mrs. Alex Ireland, London, 1892, p. 426. For Fanny Fern, see Ann Douglas Wood, 'The "Scribbling Women" and Fanny Fern: Why Women Wrote,' *American Quarterly* XXIII (Spring 1971): 1–24.

ADRIENNE RICH

'Compulsory Heterosexuality and Lesbian Existence'

III

I have chosen to use the term *lesbian existence* and *lesbian continuum* because the word *lesbianism* has a clinical and limiting ring. *Lesbian existence* suggests both the fact of the historical presence of lesbians and our continuing creation of the meaning of that existence. I mean the term *lesbian continuum* to include a range – through each woman's life and throughout history – of woman-identified experience, not simply the fact that a woman has had or consciously desired genital sexual experience with another woman. If we expand it to embrace many more forms of primary intensity between and among women, including the sharing of a rich inner life, the bonding against male tyranny, the giving and receiving of practical and political support, if we can also hear in it such associations as *marriage resistance* and the 'haggard' behavior identified by Mary Daly (obsolete meanings: 'intractable,' 'willful,' 'wanton,' and 'unchaste' ... 'a woman reluctant to yield to wooing')[45] – we begin to grasp breadths of female history and psychology which have lain out of reach as a consequence of limited, mostly clinical, definitions of 'lesbianism.'

Lesbian existence comprises both the breaking of a taboo and the rejection of a compulsory way of life. It is also a direct or indirect attack on male right of access to women. But it is more than these, although we may first begin to perceive it as a form of nay-saying to patriarchy, an act of resistance. It has of course included isolation, self-hatred, breakdown, alcoholism, suicide, and intrawoman violence; we romanticize at our peril what it means to love and act against the grain, and under heavy penalties; and lesbian existence has been lived (unlike, say, Jewish or Catholic existence) without access to any knowledge of a tradition, a continuity, a social underpinning. The destruction of records and memorabilia and letters documenting the realities of lesbian existence must be taken very seriously as a means of keeping heterosexuality compulsory for women, since what has been kept from our knowledge is joy, sensuality, courage, and community, as well as guilt, self-betrayal, and pain.[46]

Lesbians have historically been deprived of a political existence through 'inclusion' as female versions of male homosexuality. To equate lesbian existence with male homosexuality because each is stigmatized is to erase female reality once again. Part of the history of lesbian existence is, obviously, to be found where lesbians, lacking a coherent female community, have shared a kind of social life and common cause with homosexual men. But there are differences: women's lack of economic and cultural privilege relative to men; qualitative differences in female and male relationships, for example, the patterns of anonymous sex among male homosexuals, and the pronounced ageism in male homosexual standards of sexual attractiveness. I perceive the lesbian experience as being, like motherhood, a profoundly *female* experience, with particular oppressions, meanings, and potentialities we cannot comprehend as long as we simply bracket it with other sexually stigmatized existences. Just as the term 'parenting' serves to conceal the particular and significant reality of being a parent who is actually a mother, the term 'gay' may serve the purpose of blurring the very outlines we need to discern, which are of crucial value for feminism and for the freedom of women as a group.[47]

As the term 'lesbian' has been held to limiting, clinical associations in its patriarchal definition, female friendship and comradeship have been set apart from the erotic, thus limiting the erotic itself. But as we deepen and broaden the range of what we define as lesbian existence, as we delineate a lesbian continuum, we begin to discover the erotic in female terms: as that which is unconfined to any single part of the body or solely to the body itself; as an energy not only diffuse but, as Audre Lorde has described it, omnipresent in 'the sharing of joy, whether physical, emotional, psychic,' and in the sharing of work; as the empowering joy which 'makes us less willing to accept powerlessness, or those other supplied states of being which are not native to me, such as resignation, despair, self-effacement, depression, self-denial.'[48] In another context, writing of women and work, I quoted the autobiographical passage in which the poet H. D. described how her friend Bryher supported her in persisting with the visionary experience which was to shape her mature work:

> ... I knew that this experience, this writing-on-the-wall before me, could not be shared with anyone except the girl who stood so bravely there beside me. This girl had said without hesitation, "Go on." It was she really who had the detachment and integrity of the Pythoness of Delphi. But it was I, battered and dissociated ... who was seeing the pictures, and who was reading the writing or granted the inner vision. Or perhaps, in some sense, we were "seeing" it together, for without her, admittedly, I could not have gone on....[49]

If we consider the possibility that all women – from the infant suckling her mother's breast, to the grown woman experiencing orgasmic sensations while suckling her own child, perhaps recalling her mother's milk-smell in her own; to two women, like Virginia Woolf's Chloe and Olivia, who share a laboratory;[50] to the woman dying at ninety, touched and handled by women – exist on a lesbian continuum, we can see ourselves as moving in and out of this continuum, whether we identify ourselves as lesbian or not.

We can then connect aspects of woman identification as diverse as the impudent, intimate girl-friendships of eight-or nine-year olds and the banding together of those women of the twelfth and fifteenth centuries known as Beguines who 'shared houses, rented to one another, bequeathed houses to their room-mates ... in cheap subdivided houses in the artisans' area of town,' who 'practiced Christian virtue on their own, dressing and living simply and not associating with men,' who earned their livings as spinners, bakers, nurses, or ran schools for young girls, and who managed – until the Church forced them to disperse – to live independent both of marriage and of conventual restrictions.[51] It allows us to connect these women with the more celebrated 'Lesbians' of the women's school around Sappho of the seventh century BC; with the secret sororities and economic networks reported among African women; and with the Chinese marriage resistance sisterhoods – communities of women who refused marriage, or who if married often refused to consummate their marriages and soon left their husbands – the only women in China who were not footbound and who, Agnes Smedley tells us, welcomed the births of daughters and organized successful women's strikes in the silk mills.[52] It allows us to connect and compare disparate individual instances of marriage resistance: for example, the type of autonomy claimed by Emily Dickinson, a nineteenth-century white woman genius, with the strategies available to Zora Neale Hurston, a twentieth-century black woman genius. Dickinson never married, had tenuous intellectual friendships with men, lived self-convented in her genteel father's house in Amherst, and wrote a lifetime of passionate letters to her sister-in-law Sue Gilbert and a smaller group of such letters to her friend Kate Scott Anthon. Hurston married twice but soon left each husband, scrambled her way from Florida to Harlem to Columbia University to Haiti and finally back to Florida, moved in and out of white patronage and poverty, professional success, and failure; her survival relationships were all with women, beginning with her mother. Both of these women in their vastly different circumstances were marriage resisters, committed to their own work and selfhood, and were later characterized as 'apolitical.' Both were drawn to men of intellectual quality; for both of them women provided the on-going fascination and sustenance of life.

(1980)

Notes

45   Daly, *Gyn/Ecology*, p. 15.
46   'In a hostile world in which women are not supposed to survive except in relation with and in service to men, entire communities of women were simply erased. History tends to bury what it seeks to reject' (Blanche W. Cook, ' "Women Alone Stir My Imagination": Lesbianism and the Cultural Tradition,' *Signs: Journal of Women in Culture and Society* 4, no. 4 [Summer 1979]: 719–20). The Lesbian Herstory Archives in New York City is one attempt to preserve contemporary documents on lesbian existence – a project of enormous value and meaning, working against the continuing censorship and obliteration of relationships, networks, communities, in other archives and elsewhere in the culture.
47   [A. R., 1986: The shared historical and spiritual 'crossover' functions of lesbians and gay men in cultures past and present are traced by Judy Grahn in *Another Mother Tongue: Gay Words, Gay Worlds* (Boston: Beacon, 1984). I now think we have much to learn both from the uniquely female aspects of lesbian existence and from the complex 'gay' identity we share with gay men.]

48 Audre Lorde, *Uses of the Erotic: The Erotic as Power* in *Sister Outsider* (Trumansburg, NY: Crossing Press, 1984).

49 Adrienne Rich, 'Conditions for Work: The Common World of Women,' in *On Lies, Secrets, and Silence* (p. 209); H. D., *Tribute to Freud* (Oxford: Carcanet Press, 1971), pp. 50–4.

50 Woolf, *A Room of One's Own*, p. 126.

51 Gracia Clark, 'The Beguines: A Mediaeval Women's Community,' *Quest: A Feminist Quarterly* 1, no. 4 (1975): 73–80.

52 See Denise Paulme, ed., *Women of Tropical Africa* (Berkeley: University of California Press, 1963), pp. 7, 266–7. Some of these sororities are described as 'a kind of defensive syndicate against the male element' – their aims being 'to offer concerted resistance to an oppressive patriarchate,' 'independence in relation to one's husband and with regard to motherhood, mutual aid, satisfaction of personal revenge.' See also Audre Lorde, 'Scratching the Surface: Some Notes on Barriers to Women and Loving,' in *Sister Outsider* pp. 45–52; Marjorie Topley, 'Marriage Resistance in Rural Kwangtung,' in *Women in Chinese Society*, ed. M. Wolf and R. Witke (Stanford, Calif.: Stanford University Press, 1978), pp. 67–89; Agnes Smedley, *Portraits of Chinese Women in Revolution*, ed. J. MacKinnon and S. MacKinnon (Old Westbury, NY: Feminist Press, 1976), pp. 103–10.

Chris Weedon

Feminist Practice and Poststructuralist Theory

Similar questions need to be asked of feminist criticism which is concerned with discovering particular women's experience in women's writing. At the present time attempts are being made to describe black and lesbian female experience as expressed in women's writing and to construct traditions of black and lesbian women's writing. As with all traditions, readers assume that texts are connected, that earlier writers influence later ones and that the analysis of such influences comes before the detailed historical location of women's writing within the specific social relations of cultural production, structured by class, gender and race, which produce texts.

The problems facing this approach are at their most extreme in the case of lesbian writing and the construction of a lesbian aesthetic and tradition expressing a lesbian experience. Not only does this project share the problems of approaches which assume that texts express women's experience, it is also faced with the primary problem of defining lesbian texts. In her overview of lesbian-feminist literary criticism, written in 1981, Bonnie Zimmerman addresses the complexities of these issues. She points out that contemporary discourses of lesbianism are wide-ranging. They include the exclusive definition of lesbianism as a sexual practice, the extension of the term lesbian to all 'woman-identified experience' as in the work of

Adrienne Rich, or some point between the two. Zimmerman herself endorses Lillian Faderman's definition in *Surpassing the Love of Men* (Faderman, 1981):

> 'Lesbian' describes a relationship in which two women's strongest emotions and affections are directed toward each other. Sexual contact may be part of the relationship to a greater or lesser degree, or it may be entirely absent. By preference the two women spend most of their time together and share most aspects of their lives ... with each other. (Faderman in Showalter, [*The New Feminist Criticism*] 1985, p. 206)

This definition may indeed serve the interests of current lesbian research and attempts to construct a lesbian tradition. It is important to remember, however, that it is a contemporary definition and that the meaning of lesbianism changes with historical shifts in the discursive construction of female sexuality. The different meanings of lesbianism in the past gave rise to different forms of oppression and resistance, knowledge of which helps to denaturalize the present and sharpen our awareness of the contemporary modes through which gender and sexual power are exercised.

As a group who are socially defined by others in terms of a sexual preference which is not heterosexual and therefore not 'normal', lesbians write from different subject positions than most heterosexual feminists. It is not impossible for heterosexual women to occupy fundamentally anti-heterosexist discourses but this takes a political commitment beyond their own immediate day-to-day interests. While all feminists would agree 'that a woman's identity is not defined only by her relation to a male world and a male literary tradition ... that powerful bonds between women are a crucial factor in women's lives' (Showalter, 1985, p. 201), this is not enough to counter a heterosexism which is a fundamental structuring principle of discourses of gender and the social practices which they imply.

If it is difficult to decide on the meaning of lesbianism in women, a decision which can only ultimately be political, determined by present and future objectives, the question of what constitutes a lesbian text is equally open to a range of answers: 'This critic will need to consider whether a lesbian text is one written by a lesbian (and if so, how do we determine who is a lesbian?), one written about lesbians (which might be by a heterosexual woman or man), or one that expresses a lesbian 'vision' (which has to be satisfactorily outlined) (Zimmerman in Showalter, 1985, p. 208).

The questions asked by self-defined lesbian critics tend to focus on the relationship between author and text. Zimmerman, for example, assumes that 'the sexual and emotional orientation of a woman profoundly affects her consciousness and thus her creativity' (Showalter, 1985, p. 201). While this is very likely to be the case, we cannot know the intimate details of an author's consciousness; at best we have access to the competing range of subject positions open to her at a particular historical moment. Moreover we cannot look to authorial consciousness for the meaning of a text, since this is always open to plural readings which are themselves the product of specific discursive contexts.

Alternatively lesbianism in fiction can be seen in terms of textual strategies as, for example, in Barbara Smith's exposition of Toni Morrison's *Sula* in the same volume of essays (Showalter, 1985, pp. 168–84). There is a danger, however, of masking important and productive differences by assuming that fiction which contests particular forms of heterosexual practice and family life is necessarily lesbian in its implications.

How we define lesbianism and how we read lesbian texts will depend on how we define our objectives. Bonnie Zimmerman opts for a 'lesbian "essence" that may be located in all these specific historical existences, just as we may speak of a widespread perhaps universal structure of marriage or the family' (Showalter, 1985, pp. 215–16). She stresses, however, that 'differences are as significant as similarities'. If we are searching for positive lesbian role models or for a recognizable lesbian aesthetic, then a fixed concept of lesbianism is important. From a post-structuralist perspective, however, this fixing is always historically specific and temporary and will determine in advance the type of answers we get to our questions. If we want to understand and challenge past and present heterosexism we need to start from the discourses which constitute it and the forms of sexuality, sexual regulation and gendered subjectivity which they construct. We need to look for the possibilities of challenge and resistance to specific modes of heterosexuality. Fictional texts play their part in this process.

ANN DUCILLE

'The Rise of Black Feminist Literary Studies'
The Cambridge Companion to Feminist Literary Theory

But there was something else about the critical practice that began to call itself "feminist" in the 1970s. While it took back, blackened, and politicized the term, it did not historicize it by connecting it to the pioneering black feminists of the nineteenth century, with the possible exception of Sojourner Truth. Still in the revolutionary mode of the 1960s, black feminist literary studies shot from the hip-huggers in the beginning. When it did become anxious enough about its origins to go back in search of its mothers' gardens – to use Alice Walker's metaphor – it too often stopped at the front porch of Zora Neale Hurston, the self-proclaimed queen of the Harlem Renaissance, who had died in 1960 out of print and out of favor. Replicating the great author/great book model of mainstream canon construction, the new black feminist criticism resurrected Hurston as its literary fore-mother and her 1937 novel *Their Eyes Were Watching God* as its classic text in much the same way that white feminist criticism had reclaimed Kate Chopin and *The Awakening* and Charlotte Perkins Gilman and *The Yellow Wallpaper*. And like its white counterpart, it often reconstructed its picked-to-click precursor in a cultural and intellectual vacuum that treated her as if she gave birth to herself, Alice Walker, Toni Morrison, and the entire identifiable tradition of black women writers.

What was often lost or at least overshadowed in the translation was the work of Hurston's precursors and contemporaries such as Alice Dunbar-Nelson, Nella Larsen, Dorothy West, Marita Bonner, and Jessie Fauset, and of other black women writers whose settings are urban or whose characters are middle class. (There are striking similarities between Dunbar-Nelson's unpublished novella, "A Modern Undine," and Hurston's fourth novel, *Seraph on the Suwanee* [1948], suggesting an anxiety of influence that, to my knowledge, no one has yet explored.) Also largely missing in action in this emerging discourse in the early 1970s was the fiction of a number of nineteenth-century black women writers. There is considerable irony in this last elision in particular because these early writers had already fought some of the same battles over sexism and racism, over failed sisterhood and the double jeopardy of race and gender difference, and over the exclusionary practices of the black male and white female communities that should have been allies. Not only had their black feminist ancestors traversed similar ground, they had also come to similar conclusions about the need for self-expression, self-representation, and, in a manner of speaking, self-publication. And they, too, had undertaken their own efforts to combat stereotypical representations of black womanhood by publishing their own counter-narratives.

In particular, the 1890s (what Harper dubbed the "Woman's Era") was the site of furious literary activity on the part of African American women similar to the productivity of the 1970s, but, if anything, written against an even stiffer grain and published against even greater odds. In the 1970s and 1980s black women were a commodity on the cusp of becoming in vogue, though by no means in power, in the academy and the publishing industry. In the 1890s black women were not in favor with anyone anywhere, except perhaps within the separate women's clubs, political organizations, and educational networks they built to continue the fight for both racial and gender justice. Their crusades intensified and solidified at the turn of the century in the wake of the failures of Reconstruction, the rise of the Ku Klux Klan, the proliferation of lynch law and Jim Crow, and the increasingly patriarchal character of their own black communities.

Challenging the white male authority and racist characterizations of plantation tradition writers like Joel Chandler Harris and Thomas Nelson

Page, Pauline Hopkins, writer, political activist, and literary editor of the *Colored American Magazine*, urged black women and men to use literature as an instrument of liberation. "*No one will do this for us*," she wrote in the introduction to her first novel, *Contending Forces: A Romance Illustrative of Negro Life North and South* (1900); "*we must ourselves develop the men and women who will faithfully portray the inmost thoughts and feelings of the Negro with all the fire and romance which lie dormant in our history*, and, as yet unrecognized by writers of the Anglo-Saxon race."[29]

In attempting to help "raise the stigma of degradation" from the race, Hopkins's "little romance" tackles all the major political and social crises of the day: the systematic rape and sexual exploitation of black women, lynching and other mob violence, women's rights, job discrimination, and black disenfranchisement. Much the same is true for the fiction, prose, and poetry of Frances Harper, whose body of work consistently addresses the interplay of racial and sexual ideology. Published in 1892, the same year as Ida B. Wells's antilynching manifesto *Southern Horrors: Lynch Law and All Its Phases* and Anna Julia Cooper's feminist manifesto *A Voice from the South*, Harper's political novel *Iola Leroy; or, Shadows Uplifted* was long believed to be the first novel published by an African American woman. But even before it was dislodged from its premier position by the recovery of *Our Nig* and other earlier novels (Amelia Johnson's *Clarence and Corinne* [1890] and Emma Dunham Kelley's *Megda* [1891]), and eventually three other earlier novels by Harper herself, *Iola Leroy* garnered little cultural capital from the designation "first."[30]

There are, of course, exceptions to the tendency to ignore the black feminist past – the work of Frances Smith Foster, for one, and later Claudia Tate and Carby. More often, however, early black feminist criticism either ignores nineteenth-century writers like Harper and Hopkins or dismisses them for writing sentimental fiction in the Anglo-American mode – "courtesy book[s] intended for white reading and black instruction," Houston Baker calls them, even though the stated audience for many of these works is the black community.[31] Unlike Hurston's colorful prose (whose misogyny was overlooked or explained away), their fiction was condemned for not being authentically black or feminist enough, despite its consistently critical stance toward the heterosexual institutions of racism, rape, sexual blackmail, lynching, and, in some instances, marriage itself.

In 1988 the Schomburg Library, in conjunction with Oxford University Press, reissued dozens of previously lost and out-of-print texts by nineteenth-century African American women. Gates, the general editor of the collection, noted in his foreword that black women published more fiction between 1890 and 1910 than black men had published in the preceding half-century. He questioned why this "great achievement" had been ignored.

"For reasons unclear to me even today," he wrote, "few of these marvelous renderings of the Afro-American woman's consciousness were reprinted in the late 1960s and early 1970s, when so many other texts of the Afro-American literary tradition were resurrected from the dark and silent graveyards of the out-of-print and were reissued in facsimile editions aimed at the hungry readership for canonical texts in the nascent field of black studies."[32]

Gates may not know why so few of these renderings were taken up in the late 1960s and early 1970s, but there are some obvious possible answers. It is not just that many of these texts were accessible only in rare book rooms, as Gates acknowledges. It is also – perhaps even more so – that these books were known only through their *mis*readings and through the bad rap that the "women's fiction" of the period had received historically, mostly at the hands of male critics – white and black. But an even fuller answer to Gates's conundrum may lie in that nagging word "tradition." None of this nineteenth-century fiction easily fits within the 1970s model of an identifiable black feminist literary tradition, a tradition that, by definition, privileges the "authentic" voices and experiences of black women of the rural South such as Hurston's heroine Janie Crawford in *Their Eyes Were Watching God*. Articulating the sentiments of many black feminist critics, Sherley Anne Williams invokes this privilege in her preface to the 1978 reprint of *Their Eyes*, where she describes her discovery of the novel in graduate school as a close textual encounter that made her Hurston's for life. "In the speech of her characters I heard my own country voice and saw in the heroine something of my own country self. And this last was most wonderful because it was most rare."[33]

Self-expression as a cultural imperative is one thing, but however wonderful, however rare, self-recognition as a critical prescription is inherently limiting and exclusionary. Written in an intellectual rather than a vernacular tradition – in the master's tongue rather than the folk's – nineteenth-century narratives contain neither the specifically black female language nor the valorized black female activities that Barbara Smith identified as emblems of authentic black womanhood. In other words, within the 1970s black feminist dream of a common language, this early writing was judged grammatically incorrect, out of step with the established tempo of the literary tradition. Ironically, however, this canon construction of the close encounter kind also excluded some of the work by the very same writer it had claimed as its founding mother, Zora Neale Hurston. While Hurston's second novel, *Their Eyes Were Watching God*, was heralded as the quintessential black feminist text, her fourth novel, *Seraph on the Suwanee*, was panned along with nineteenth-century narratives like *Iola Leroy* and *Contending Forces* because of its move away from folklore and its focus on white characters instead of black.[34] Inexplicably, by the logic of 1970s and 1980s canon construction, Hurston was a card-carrying black feminist writer when she published *Their Eyes* in 1937 but not when she published *Seraph* in 1948.

(2006)

Notes

29 Pauline Hopkins, *Contending Forces: A Romance Illustrative of Negro Life North and South* (Boston: Colored Co-operative Publishing House, 1900), pp. 13–14; reprinted with an introduction by Richard Yarborough (New York: Oxford University Press in conjunction with the Schomburg Library, 1988). Emphasis in the original.

30 In the early 1990s, more than a hundred years after *Iola Leroy* first appeared, Frances Smith Foster recovered and brought back into print three long-lost novels by Frances Harper, all of which were originally serialized in the *Christian Recorder*, the journal of the African Methodist Episcopal Church. Through years of painstaking research and detective work, Foster managed to piece together most of the texts of each of the lost novels: *Minnie's Sacrifice*, which was serialized in twenty installments between March 20 and September 25, 1869; *Sowing and Reaping*, which ran from August 1876 to February 1877; and *Trial and Triumph*, which appeared between October of 1888 and February of 1889. See Frances Smith Foster, ed., *Minnie's Sacrifice, Sowing and Reaping, Trial and Triumph: Three Rediscovered Novels by Frances E. W. Harper* (Boston: Beacon Press, 1994. Recent evidence suggests that Kelley may not have been black.

31 Houston A. Baker, Jr, *Workings of the Spirit: The Poetics of Afro-American Women's Writing* (Chicago: University of Chicago Press, 1991), p. 32.

32 Henry Louis Gates, Jr, foreword to *The Schomburg Library of Nineteenth-Century Black Women Writers* (New York: Oxford University Press, 1988), p. xix.

33 Sherley Anne Williams, foreword to *Their Eyes Were Watching God* (Bloomington: University of Illinois Press, 1978), p. vii.

34 For example, Alice Walker, who was so instrumental in reclaiming *Their Eyes Were Watching God* from obscurity, condemned Hurston's later work as "reactionary, static, shockingly misguided and timid." This is particularly true of *Seraph on the Suwanee*, Walker maintains, "which is not even about black people, which is no crime, but *is* about white people for whom it is impossible to care, which is." In his definitive literary history, *The Afro-American Novel and Its Tradition*, Bernard Bell asserts that Hurston's focus on white characters places *Seraph* outside the scope of his study, suggesting that black writers can focus only on black characters. See Alice Walker, "Zora Neale Hurston: A Cautionary Tale and a Partisan View," in Walker, *In Search of Our Mothers' Gardens* (New York: Harcourt Brace Jovanovich, 1984); and Bernard Bell, *The Afro-American Novel and Its Tradition* (Amherst, MA: University of Massachusetts Press, 1987).

PAUL LAUTER

'Race and Gender in the Shaping of the American
Literary Canon: A Case Study from the Twenties'
Feminist Criticism and Social Change

Demographic factors were also at work, as historian Laurence Veysey has pointed out. The proportion 'of the mature working-age population in America' who were college and university professors and librarians was rising 'spectacularly' in the decades leading to 1920 – especially in relation to older, static learned professionals, like doctors, lawyers and the clergy. Although they constituted only a tiny portion of people at work, professors had enormously larger impact 'as the universities increasingly took over training for a wide variety of prestigious occupations'. In fact, Veysey writes that

> the social effect of intellectual specialization [occurring in universities among other areas of American life] was to transfer authority, most critically over the printed word and what was taught in colleges to sons and daughters of the elite, away from the cultivated professions considered as an entirety and toward a far smaller, specially trained segment within them, those who now earned Ph.D. degrees.... Concretely, this meant vesting such authority in a group that, as of 1900, numbered only a few hundred persons spread across the humanistic fields. The immediate effect was thus the intensification of elitism as it was transferred onto a new academic basis. A double requirement was now imposed – intellectual merit, at least of a certain kind, defined far more rigorously, as well as a continuing expectation of social acceptability.[19]

In short, the professoriat exercised increasing control of the definition of a 'literate' reader, including those who were to become the next generation's writers.[20]

The social base of that professoriat was small. The professors, educators, critics, the arbiters of taste of the 1920s, were, for the most part, college-educated white men of Anglo-Saxon or northern European origins. They came, that is, from that tiny, élite portion of the population of the United States which, around the turn of the century, could go to college. Through the first two decades of the new century, this dominant élite had faced a quickening demand for some power and control over their lives from Slavic, Jewish, Mediterranean and Catholic immigrants from Europe, as well as from black immigrants from the rural South. Even women had renewed their demand for the vote, jobs, control over their bodies. The old élite and their allies moved on a variety of fronts, especially during and just after World War I, to set the terms on which these demands would be accommodated. They repressed, in actions like the Prohibition Amendment and the Palmer raids, the political and social, as well as the cultural, institutions of immigrants and of radicals. They reorganized schools and professionalized elementary and secondary school curriculum development, in significant measure as a way to impose middle-class American 'likemindedness' on a heterogeneous, urban, working-class population.[21] Similarly, calling it 'professionalization', they reorganized literary scholarship and teaching in ways that not only asserted a male-centered culture and values for the college-educated leadership, but also enhanced their own authority and status as well.[22]

The Modern Language Association, for example, underwent a major reorganization just after World War I, the effect of which was to concentrate professional influence in the hands of groups of specialists, most of whom met at the annual convention. The convention thus took on much greater significance, practically and symbolically in terms of defining professional leadership. As professionalism replaced gentility, the old all-male 'smoker' at the convention was discontinued. With it also disappeared a female and, on occasion, modestly feminist institution: the ladies' dinner. We do not fully know how, or even in this instance whether, such institutions provided significant support for women scholars, nor do we know what was lost with their disappearance in the 1920s.[23] Clearly, women were left without any significant organizational base within the newly important convention. For when, in 1921, specialized groups were established for MLA conventions, women's roles in them were disproportionately small, minor and largely confined.[24] If the men gave up the social institution that had helped sustain their control, they replaced it with professional authority in the new groups. Not only were women virtually excluded from leadership positions in them and given few opportunities to read papers, but they also appear to have been pushed toward – as men were certainly pushed away from – subject areas considered 'peripheral' to the profession. For example, folk materials and works *by* women became particularly the province *of* women – as papers, dissertation topics and published articles illustrate.[25]

As white women were excluded from the emerging scholarly power structures, and blacks – female or male – were kept almost entirely ghettoized in black colleges, 'their subjects', women and blacks, remained undeveloped in a rapidly developing profession. For example, in the first ten years of its existence, *American Literature* published twenty-four full articles (as distinct from Notes and Queries or Reviews) by women scholars out of a total of 208. Nine of these appeared in the first two volumes, and a number of women published more than once. An article on Dickinson appeared in volume 1, and others in volumes 4 and 6. These apart, the *only* article on a woman writer until volume 10 was one on American comments, mostly by men, on George Sand. In volume 10 one finds a piece, by a male scholar, on Cather, as well as another trying to show that Ann Cotton derived her material from husband John. It is not, I should add, that the journal confined itself to 'major' writers or to authors from the early or mid-nineteenth century. Quite the contrary, it ran pieces on stalwarts like John Pendleton Kennedy, not to speak of *Godey's Ladies' Book*, as well as articles dealing with a number of twentieth-century male authors.

While professionalization was thus erecting institutional barriers against women, their status was being attacked in other ways. Joan Doran Hedrick has shown how the ideology of domesticity and the bogey of 'race suicide', which re-emerged around the turn of the century, was used during the next thirty years to attack women teachers, both the proverbial spinster school-marm and the female college professor.[26] The extent to which such attacks arose from the pressure of job competition, general political conservatism, antisuffrage backlash or other factors is not yet clear. It was true, however, that women had not only been competing more and more effectively for positions in the humanities, but also that the predominance of women students in undergraduate literature courses had long worried the male professoriat. In 1909, for example, the chairman of the MLA's Central Division had devoted his address to the problem of 'Coeducation and literature'. He wondered whether the predominance of women taking literary courses 'may not contribute to shape the opinion that literature is preeminently a study for girls, and tend to discourage some men.... This is not yet saying,' he continued, 'that the preference of women turns away that of men. There are many factors to the problem. But it looks that way.' How, he asked, can we deal with the problem that the 'masculine ideal of culture' has largely rejected what the modern languages, and we as its professors, have to offer? 'What may we teachers do more or better than we have done to gain for the humanities as represented by literature a larger place in the notion of masculine culture?'[27]

Something of an answer is provided in an unusually frank way in the *Annual Reports* of Oberlin College for 1919–20. In the section on the faculty, Professor Jelliffe, on behalf of Bibliography, Language, Literature and Art, urged the hiring of an additional teacher of composition. He writes:

> In my opinion the new instructor, when appointed, should be a man. Of sixteen sections in Composition only three are at present being taught by men instructors. This is to discredit, in the opinion of our students, the importance of the subject, for despite the excellent teaching being done by the women of the English faculty, the students are quick to infer that the work is considered by the faculty itself of less importance than that to which the men devote their time.[28]

Such ideas, the institutional processes I have described, and other historical forces outside the scope of the paper, gradually eroded the gains women had made in higher education in the decades immediately following the turn of the century. By the early 1920s, women were earning 16 per cent of all doctorates; that proportion gradually declined (except for the war years) to under 10 per cent in the 1950s. Similarly, the proportion of women in the occupational category of college presidents, professors and instructors rose from 6.4 per cent in 1900 to 32.5 per cent around 1930, but subsequently declined to below 22 per cent by 1960.[29] The proportion of women earning advanced degrees in the modern languages and teaching these subjects in colleges was, of course, always somewhat higher, but the decline affected those fields in a similar way. Because more women were educated in these fields, they were particularly vulnerable in the 1930s to cutbacks ostensibly instituted to preserve jobs for male 'breadwinners' or to nepotism regulations newly coined to spread available positions among the men. Not surprisingly, by the 1950s only 19 per cent of the doctorates being earned in the modern languages were awarded to women,[30] a proportion higher than in fields like sociology, history or biology, but significantly lower than it had been thirty years earlier. As a result, the likelihood of one's encountering a female professor even in literature – and especially at élite male or coeducational institutions – was perhaps even slighter than the chances of encountering a female writer.

Blacks, female or male, faced a color line that professionalization did nothing to dispel. Black professors of literature were, for the most part, separated into their own professional organization, the College Language Association, and into positions at segregated black colleges. The color line persisted in *American Literature* so far as articles on black writers were concerned, until 1971, when the magazine printed its first piece, on James Weldon Johnson. The outlook apparently shared by *American Literature*'s editors comes clearest in a brief review (vol. 10 (1938), pp. 112–13) by Vernon Loggins, then at Columbia, of Benjamin Brawley's collection of *Early Negro American Writers*.

> The volume … gives a hint of American Negro literature before Dunbar, but scarcely more than a hint. Yet it should be of practical value in American literature courses in *Negro colleges*. Professor Brawley obviously had such an aim in mind in making the compilation. [Italics mine]

Over the years a few articles appeared on images of blacks in the writings of white authors, but in general, as such reviews and notes on scholarly articles make clear, those interested in black writers were effectively referred to the *Journal of Negro History* or to the *College Language Association Journal*.[31]

Although the existence of such black professional organizations and periodicals reflected the pervasiveness of institutional racism in American life, such black-defined groups and magazines like the *Crisis* had at least the advantage of providing black writers and scholars with outlets for and encouragement of their work. Women, especially white professional writers, faced rather a different problem in this period: one can observe a significant shift in cultural authority from female-defined to male-defined institutions – in symbolic terms, one might say, from women's literary societies to *Esquire* magazine. The analogy may, at first, seem far-fetched, but it is probably more accurate than the cartoon view of women's clubs with which we have lived since the 1920s. In fact, the taste of the older generation of genteel professors and magazine editors largely accorded with that of the female literary clubs; the outlook of the new professoriat and *Esquire*, the *Playboy* of its day, largely coincided, at least with respect to the subjects and writers of fiction, as well as to certain conceptions of male camaraderie and culture.[32] To understand why, we must now turn to the aesthetic theories which helped to shape the canon.

(1983)

Notes

19   Laurence Veysey, 'The humanities, 1860–1920', typescript of paper for volume on the professions, c. 1974, pp. 21, 24.

20   Pattee remarks that 'American literature today is in the hands of college-educated men and women. The professor has molded the producers of it'. See Pattee, *Tradition and Jazz*, p. 237.

21   Barry M. Franklin, 'American curriculum theory and the problem of social control, 1918–1938' (paper presented at the Annual Meeting of the American Educational Research Association, Chicago, 15–19 April 1974), ERIC, ED 092 419. Franklin quotes Edward A. Ross, *Principles of Sociology* (New York: Century, 1920): 'Thoroughly to nationalize a multitudinous people calls for institutions to disseminate certain ideas and ideals. The Tsars relied on the blue-domed Orthodox church in every peasant village to Russify their heterogeneous subjects, while we Americans rely for unity on the "little red school house".'

22   Whatever its ostensible objectives, in practice, professionalization almost invariably worked to the detriment of female practitioners – and often female 'clients' as well. The details of this argument have been most fully worked out for medicine; see, for example, Barbara Ehrenreich and Deirdre English, *Complaints and Disorders: The sexual politics of sickness* (Old Westbury, NY: Feminist Press, 1973), and *For Her Own Good: One hundred and fifty years of the experts' advice to women* (New York: Pantheon, 1979). See also Janice Law Trecker, 'Sex, science and education', *American Quarterly* 26 (October 1974): pp. 352–66; and Margaret W. Rossiter, *Women Scientists in America: Struggles and strategies to 1940* (Baltimore: Johns Hopkins University Press, 1982), especially the chapters titled 'A manly profession', pp. 73–99, which includes a wonderful discussion of the professionally exclusionary function of the male 'smoker', and 'Academic employment: protest and prestige', pp. 160–217.

23   The ladies' dinner had disappeared by 1925. A good deal of work on female cultures of support has recently been published, beginning with Carroll Smith-Rosenberg, 'The female world of love and ritual: relations between women in nineteenth-century America', *Signs* 1 (Autumn 1975), pp. 1–27. In another professional field, history, women apparently felt so excluded from the mainstream and in need of mutual support that in 1929 they formed the Berkshire Conference of Women Historians, an institution extended in the 1970s to include sponsorship of a large conference on women's history. In most academic fields, however, while the proportion of *individual* women obtaining doctorates might have increased or been stable during the 1920s, female-defined *organizations* seem virtually to have disappeared – and with them, I suspect, centers for women's influence.

24   From 1923 on, the MLA gathered in what was called a 'union' meeting, rather than in separate conventions of the Eastern, Central and Pacific divisions – another indication of the new importance of the convention. That year 467 registered as attending the session. Fifty-nine women attended the ladies' dinner; some of the women were probably wives and other women members probably did not attend. About 24 per cent of the MLA members were female; very likely a smaller proportion attended the convention. Among the divisions and sections there were 37 male chairpersons, and 1 female, Louise Pound, who chaired the Popular Culture section. There were 29 male secretaires, and 1 woman, Helen Sandison, served as secretary for two sections. Of the 108 papers, 6 were delivered by women.

In 1924, 978 persons registered, and 121 women went to the ladies' dinner. There continued to be 1 female chairperson, Louise Pound, and now 43 men. The female secretarial corps had increased to 5, Helen Sandison still serving twice, and 'Mrs Carleton Brown' now serving as secretary for the Phonetics section. Of the 128 papers, 7 were by women.

In *PMLA*, the proportion of women remained, relatively, much higher. In 1924, women were 7 of 47 authors; in 1925, 9 of 47; and in 1926, 11 of 55.

25   For example, of those seven papers delivered by women in the 1924 MLA meeting, two were in Popular Literature, two on Phonetics – where, perhaps not incidentally, women were officers – one in American Literature. Similarly, the entry for American Literature prepared by Norman Foerster for the 1922 American Bibliography (*PMLA*, 1923) contains one paragraph devoted to works about Indian verse, black writers and popular ballads. Four of the scholars cited in this paragraph are women, 5 are men. Otherwise, 58 men and 9 women scholars are cited in the article. Of the 9 women, 2 wrote on women authors, 2 are cobibliographers and 1 wrote on Whittier's love affair.

26   Joan Doran Hedrick, 'Sex, class, and ideology: the declining birthrate in America, 1870–1917', unpublished MS, c. 1974. Hedrick demonstrates that many of the sociologists and educators who developed the idea of utilizing curriculum for social control were involved with the supposed problem of 'race suicide' and active in efforts to restrict immigration as well as to return women to the home.

27   A. G. Canfield, 'Coeducation and literature', *PMLA* 25 (1910), pp. lxxix–lxxx, lxxxiii.

28   *Annual Reports of the President and the Treasurer of Oberlin College for 1919–20* (Oberlin, Ohio: Oberlin College, 10 December 1920), pp. 231–2.

29   Rudolph C. Blitz, 'Women in the professions, 1870–1970', *Monthly Labor Review* 97 (5 May 1974): pp. 37–8. See also Pamela Roby, 'Institutional barriers to women students in higher education', in *Academic Women on the Move*, ed. Alice S Rossi and Ann Calderwood (New York: Russell Sage Foundation, 1973), pp. 37–40; and Michael J. Carter and Susan Boslego Carter, 'Women's recent progress in the professions, or, Women get a ticket to ride after the gravy train has left the station', *Feminist Studies* 7 (Fall 1981), pp. 477–504.

30   Laura Morlock, 'Discipline variation in the status of academic women', in *Academic Women on the Move*, pp. 255–309.

31   In 1951, the Committee on Trends in Research of the American Literature Group circulated a report on research and publications about American authors during 1940–50, together with some notes on publications during the previous decade. For the 1885–1950 period, the report (basing itself on categories established by the *Literary History of the United States*) provided information on ninety-five 'major authors'. Of these, four were black: Charles Chesnutt, Paul Laurence Dunbar, Langston Hughes, Richard Wright – in context a surprisingly 'large' number. Chesnutt is one of the few of the ninety-five about whom no articles are listed for either period; for Dunbar, one three-page article is listed and a 'popular' book; for Hughes, there are four articles, two by Hughes himself. Only Wright had been the subject of a significant number of essays. Among 'minor authors', as defined by *LHUS*, Countee Cullen had two articles, totaling five pages, written about him; W. E. B. DuBois nothing; and James Weldon Johnson, Claude McKay and Jean Toomer, among others, were not even listed. Available in Modern Language Association, American Literature Group Files, University of Wisconsin Memorial Library Archives, Madison, Wisconsin.

32   One suggestive illustration.

I was pleased to get your letter and hear about the hunting. I don't know whether you realize how fortunate you people are to live where the game is still more plentiful than the hunters. It is no fun up here where hunting frequently resembles a shooting duel.

   I am vastly amused by the report of the situation of the good and important woman who thought we should have more women on our committees in the American Literature Group.... Beyond ... [Louise Pound and Constance Rourke] I cannot think of another woman in the country who has contributed sufficiently to be placed on a par with the men on our Board and committees. If you can think of anyone, for heaven's sake jog up my memory. We must by all means keep in the good graces of the unfair sex.

   Sculley Bradley to Henry A. Pochmann, 12 January 1938, Modern Language Association, American Literature Group Files, University of Wisconsin Memorial Library Archives, Madison, Wisconsin.

CLARE HEMMINGS

'Telling Feminist Stories'
Feminist Theory

Citation is a central technique in consolidating the trajectory that I am tracing here, and the move is consistently from a relative lack of citation, through to a precise and limited choice of authors. Judith Butler, Donna Haraway and Gayatri Spivak, in particular, are invoked as threshold figures, heralding the dawn of a new feminist era of difference, and representing in themselves the increased sophistication understood to attend that era. Butler, the most cited of all, carries the heaviest teleological burden, frequently single-handedly inaugurating a move away from 'woman' as the invariant ground and subject of oppression, knowledge and resistance. This extract puts the case succinctly: 'Perhaps more than any other feminist theorist, she [Butler] has systematically elaborated a way of understanding gender identity as deeply entrenched but not immutable and has thereby pushed feminist theory beyond the polarities of the essentialist debate' (*Theory, Culture & Society*, 1999). Citation of Haraway tends to occur in accounts charting the move away from essentialist conceptions of the body, and specifically away from a sexually differentiated understanding of the body within feminism. And citation of Spivak seems by turns to mark a black feminist critique of feminism's white presumption, and an account of that difference as postcolonial rather than biological.[18] Their citation thus seems to signal 'the death' of one way of thinking and the inception of a newer, more flexible way of thinking; it never evidences ongoing contests within feminism over precisely these issues. And as the quotation above suggests, this transition is understood to be one that feminism pre-difference is forced or pushed into rather than one that it is already engaged in.

Of particular interest to me here is how attributing such a shift to difference to a few named authors detaches those authors from their own feminist trajectories. If Butler, Haraway and Spivak are 'responsible' for feminism's reluctant acknowledgment of the epistemological problematics of 'woman'; they are grammatically as well as temporally posed as distinct from that history which they have now allowed us to surpass. Citation is once again a key way that a narrative separating poststructuralism from feminism is under-written. The influences on Butler, Spivak and Haraway are consistently cited as male theorists, affirming the sense of a break in feminist inquiry. For example, in the paper the following extract is taken from, Derrida is the *only* referenced source of inspiration for Haraway's (1985) cyborg figure: 'Haraway must acknowledge a siblingship with Derrida over those central questions of humanism concerning origin, authenticity and universality. The project for both is to dissolve categorical distinctions, which Haraway pursues most particularly by challenging the concept of the natural' (*Body & Society*, 1996).[19]

And despite her engagement with a range of Third World and postcolonial feminist writers, one could be forgiven for thinking that Spivak had only ever read Marx and Derrida from the persistence of such casual introductory phrases such as 'To certify the Derridean assumptions upon which thinkers like Spivak draw ...' (*Critical Inquiry*, 1998).[20] Similarly, Foucault, Lacan and Derrida are more consistently seen as Butler's primary influences than Irigaray and Wittig, despite *Gender Trouble's* substantial engagement with these feminist authors. Repeated statements such as 'Judith Butler transformed the study of gender by using Foucault to apply poststructuralist conceptions of the subject to it' (*Australian Feminist Studies*, 2003),[21] and 'because of the influence of Foucault and Derrida, recondite abstractions characterize postmodernist feminist theory in general and Butler's books in particular' (*Critical Inquiry*, 1998), allow Butler to be critically reviewed as marking a break with rather than as having an ongoing engagement with feminist theory.

To recap then: the familiar story is thus. The feminist seventies is ignorant or innocent of racial and sexual diversity at best, or indeed actively exclusionary through its whiteness and heterosexism. The poststructuralist nineties emerges on the other side of the eighties as champion of multiplicity and difference, although significantly an indeterminate rather than located difference – *difference in general*. The teleology could not be more firmly solidified than in the following: 'By the eighties, changes were taking place that laid the groundwork for the third phase of feminist criticism, which I will call the engendering of differences' (*Critical Inquiry*, 1998). The seventies and the nineties loom large in such a statement, despite frequently not being directly mentioned. In order for this teleology to be maintained a number of other binaries are overlaid onto this linear trajectory as I have shown (sexual difference–gender theory, singularity–multiplicity, empiricism–deconstruction, and feminism–poststructuralism), and different perspectives within the feminist seventies' literature squashed, erased, or deemed exceptions to the rule.

Let me be as clear as possible. In order for poststructuralism to emerge both as beyond particularized difference and as inclusive of those differences, this narrative actively requires the misrepresentation of interventions within feminism as decade-specific. A universalized essentialist feminism is directly or indirectly associated with the seventies, and racial and sexual critiques contained in the eighties in order for poststructuralism to have finally both surpassed the essentialisms and incorporated the identities associated with sexual difference, sexuality and race.

[...]

Conclusion
Thus far, I have been mapping some of the ways in which narratives of the recent feminist past, whether seen as successes or failures, fix its teleological

markers in very similar ways. One might simply argue that it is in the nature of all story-telling to generalize, but to return to the genealogical inquiry I began this article with, my concern is with which markers stick over others, and with where our narratives position us as subjects of feminist history and theory. This particular selective story detaches feminism from its own past by generalizing the seventies to the point of absurdity, fixing identity politics as a phase, evacuating poststructuralism of any political purchase, and insisting we bear the burden of these fantasized failings. In the process we disappear class, race and sexuality only to rediscover them 'anew' as embodiment and agency. Small wonder it is not clear what the future of feminist theory holds. In closing, let me ask the following. How might feminist theory generate a proliferation of stories about its recent past that more accurately reflect the diversity of perspectives within (or outside) its orbit? How might we reform the relationship between feminism's constituent parts to allow what are currently phantom presences to take shape? Can we do feminist theory differently?

My starting point, in what will inevitably be a longer set of reflections, concerns the role of the citation of key feminist theorists. As I have argued, in the doubled story of Western feminist theory, Butler, Haraway and Spivak are imaginatively positioned at the threshold of the 'death of feminism' in several ways. They are celebrated for pointing to the failures of an 'early' feminist emphasis on sisterhood, and heralded as marking the long-awaited theoretical sophistication of feminist theory. Yet in this narrative, and in the counter narratives that dispute this celebration, these authors are split from their own legacies within feminism, symbolically, textually and politically situated as 'other' to and 'after' that imagined past. In the counter narratives that position poststructuralism as apolitical and self-referential, these same theorists are understood both as marking the death of politically accountable feminism, and as embodying that death through their own self-referential academic style, frequently denoted in classroom and conference contexts as aggressive inaccessibility. In both versions of the story, it is the specificity of feminist accounts of difference, power and knowledge at all points in the recent past that is elided.

Instead, I would advocate an approach stressing the links rather than the discontinuities between different theoretical frameworks, as a way of challenging the linear 'displacement' of one approach by another. Firstly, schools of thought conventionally pitted against one another, for example sexual difference and gender theories, might productively be read for their rather different approaches to the common problem of power in the production of sexual and gendered meaning. Might there be a methodological rigour to be extrapolated from my perhaps naïve equal enjoyment of Rosi Braidotti and Judith Butler, despite their own insistence on their irreducible difference from one another (Braidotti, 2002; Butler, 2004)? Might it be productive to think through the still harder task of reconnecting Gayatri Spivak with Luce Irigaray, so that the latter's consistent citation predominantly as object of postcolonial critique becomes more difficult to justify (Spivak, 1987; Irigaray, 1985)?

A closely related second genealogical approach would start from the citational absences in the secondary readings of those feminist theorists overburdened with marking a shift away from feminism. If we insist that, from a feminist perspective, Butler takes her deconstructive cue from Monique Wittig, as she clearly does, the former's role as 'the first' to challenge (1981) 'woman' as the ground of feminist inquiry becomes impossible to sustain. If we rewrite one of the statements introduced earlier – 'Judith Butler transformed the study of gender by using Foucault to apply poststructuralist conceptions of the subject to it' (*Australian Feminist Studies*, 2003) – to 'Judith Butler transformed the study of gender by using Wittig to apply Marxist/lesbian concepts of the subject to it' we see that the shift is more than citational. A valuing of the citational absences used to cement the doubled story I am contesting here repositions both Wittig and Butler, and tells the story of *Gender Trouble* as continuous with its feminist points of reference.[28] What I am suggesting as a feminist alternative to changing the historical record here is a process of revaluing currently sidelined traces of already key rather than marginal feminist figures. In doing so I hope this work might have two primary effects: firstly to highlight the restricted nature of what we already think we know about those figures and their histories; and secondly, to suggest a way of imagining the feminist past somewhat differently – as a series of ongoing contests and relationships rather than a process of imagined linear displacement.

(2005)

Notes

18   As Susan Gubar notes, as 'the most often cited authority on the matter of white feminists' racism ... [Spivak] combines an attention toward racial identity politics with ... poststructuralist methodologies' (1998: 892). In this sense, Spivak is more of a transitional figure than the other two.

19   *Body & Society* was launched in 1995 to cater for the upsurge of interest in the social and cultural analysis of the human body that has taken place in recent years ... *Body & Society* centrally concerns itself with debates in feminism, technology, ecology, postmodernism, medicine, ethics and consumerism which take the body as the central analytic issue in the questioning of established paradigms. (Extract from http://tcs.ntu.ac.uk/body/. Journal published by SAGE)

20   The first thirty years of *Critical Inquiry* witnessed the emergence of structuralism and poststructuralism, cultural studies, feminist theory and identity politics, media and film studies, speech act theory, new historicism, new pragmatism, visual studies and the new art history, new cognitive and psychoanalytic systems, gender studies, new forms of materialist critique,

postcolonial theory, and discourse analysis, queer theory and (more recently) 'returns' to formalism and aesthetics, and to new forms of public and politically committed intellectual work. (Extract from http://www. uchicago.edu/research/jnl-crit-inq/features/specialsymposium.html. Journal published by University of Chicago Press)

21   As an international, peer reviewed journal, *Australian Feminist Studies* publishes academic articles from throughout the world which contribute to current developments in the new and burgeoning fields of Women's Studies and feminist research ... We also aim to encourage discussion of interactions between feminist theory and practice; consideration of government and trade union policies that concern women; comment on changes in educational curricula relevant to Women's Studies; sharing of innovative course outlines, reading lists and teaching/learning strategies; reports on local, national and international conferences; reviews, critiques, enthusiasm and correspondence. (Extract from http://www.tandf.co.uk/journals/titles/08164649.asp. Journal published by Carfax Publishing)

28   But surely *Gender Trouble* favours Foucault over Wittig? In fact, in direct discussion of their work, Butler devotes 18 pages to Foucault and 17 to Wittig, and the author's critical knife is applied rather equally in both quantitative and qualitative terms. Foucault's 'sentimental indulgence' (Butler, 1990: 96) mirrors Wittig's 'thoroughgoing appropriation' (1990: 128).

Rita Felski

Doing Time: Feminist Theory and Postmodernist Culture

Paraesthetics

How, then, can feminism come to grips with the aesthetic instead of either hoping it will go away or resorting to traditional ideas about the canon? David Carroll has opened up another way of thinking about aesthetics. His term "paraesthetics" is an attempt to explain the importance of literature and art in the work of contemporary philosophers such as Derrida, Lyotard, and Foucault. For these thinkers, Carroll suggests, the value of art lies in resisting abstraction, dogmatism, and claims to truth. A line of poetry or a painting demands our attention in a specific way, inviting us to dwell on the particular and the nonidentical, on that which resists systematic thinking and confounds conceptual mastery. Yet poststructuralist thinkers are also at odds with traditional aesthetic theory. They reject any notion of the artwork as an organic, unified whole or of art as an autonomous, self-contained, transcendental sphere.

Here Carroll coins the term paraesthetics, meaning "an aesthetics turned against itself, pushed beyond or beside itself, a faulty, irregular, disordered improper aesthetic."[10] Poststructuralist theory draws on the heritage of aesthetics because it directs our attention to the metaphoric, self-reflexive, and polysemic aspects of literature and art rather than trying to extract a political message or evaluating a work in terms of its practical value. It is interested in art as a form of resistance to meaning and use. However, while classical aesthetics speaks of the harmony, totality, and integrity of the artwork, paraesthetics prefers the language of contradiction and undecidability. Art is important because it crystallizes and comments self-consciously on a general cultural condition: the end of metaphysics, the lack of foundations, and the slippery and indeterminate nature of language and communication.

Feminist critics influenced by poststructuralism draw on similar ideas to tackle the relations between art and gender. They begin by stressing the importance of language and representation in defining who we are as men or women. Language and culture go all the way down, shaping our most intimate sense of self. It is not that female experience comes to self-knowledge and then strives to express itself in language. Rather, our experiential reality at the most primal and instinctual level is always already soaked in culture. Our sense of what it means to be a woman, of how women look, talk, think, and feel, comes from the books we read, the films we watch, and the invisible ether of everyday assumptions and cultural beliefs in which we are suspended. Rather than subjects producing texts, in other words, texts produce subjects. Thus language and culture play a crucial part in reproducing the unequal relations between women and men. Patriarchal power pervades verbal and visual systems of meaning. Within such systems, woman is always connected to and inseparable from man. Men's ability to symbolize the universal, the absolute, and the transcendental depends on the continuing association of femaleness with difference, otherness, and inferiority.

These arguments lead us to a very different feminist aesthetic, or perhaps more accurately "textual politics." Clearly, we can no longer appeal to female experience as a ground for female creativity. The very idea of a single, common femaleness is a metaphysical illusion produced by a phallocentric culture. The goal of feminist criticism is not to affirm universal woman as counterpart to universal man. This is not only because of the many empirical differences of race, class, sexuality, and age that render notions of shared female experience untenable. It is also because all such visions of woman are contaminated by male-defined notions of the truth of femininity. This is true not only of the negative cultural images of women (prostitute, demon, medusa, bluestocking, vagina dentata) but also of positive ones (woman as nature, woman as nurturing mother, or innocent virgin, or heroic amazon ...). Woman is always a metaphor, dense with sedimented meanings.

Rather than expressing the truth of female identity, then, art becomes a means of questioning identity. Art has the power to be uncanny and unsettling, to estrange us from the everyday and challenge our routine assumptions. For example, Jacqueline Rose questions the view of women's writing as a reflection of women's experience and suggests that "writing undermines, even as it rehearses at its most glaring, the very model of sexual difference itself."[11] Instead of subordinating aesthetic experience to feminist goals, we should recognize the power of literature and art to subvert taken-for-granted truths, including the truths of gender.

This strangeness and uncanniness, according to some critics, can be found in all significant art. Shoshana Felman, for example, suggests that works of literature are great to the extent that "they are self-transgressive with respect to the conscious ideologies that inform them."[12] Here, it is not the gender of the author that dictates how feminist scholars should value art. Rather, it is the formal elements of the work itself, the extent to which these elements come together to question our everyday assumptions about the reality, coherence, and separateness of male and female identity. This feminist approach has obvious parallels to Marxist aesthetics, which has also argued that great art can cast a critical light on the work of ideology.

Marxist critics were often divided on which forms and styles of writing were most radical. Was realism or modernism the most appropriate form for capturing the complex social and psychological realities of modern life? Similar debates have afflicted feminist criticism. Some feminist critics sympathetic to poststructuralist ideas have concluded that an experimental poetics is the best way of unsettling norms of femininity. The appeal of *écriture féminine* and Julia Kristeva's theories of poetic language to many feminist critics in the 1980s stemmed from the belief that subverting syntax, eschewing narrative, and using avant-garde strategies to question reality would help to shatter conventional ideas about gender.

Feminist visual artists also turned to a negative aesthetics of rupture, fragmentation, and disidentification. In her abovementioned *Post-Partum Document*, for example, Mary Kelly explored the experience of motherhood by juxtaposing her child's dirty diapers with psychoanalytic accounts of maternal fantasy and women's fetishistic desire for children in patriarchal culture. Kelly's work flatly refuses to offer the viewer an iconic representation of motherhood and to gratify feminist desires for positive images of women. How, after all, could any image of the maternal ever transcend the suffocating weight of the endless madonnas and pietàs that have over the centuries rendered women such easily consumable objects of the male gaze?[13]

The "paraesthetic" turn within feminist theory thus leads to a more serious and substantial engagement with the aesthetic as both a negative and a positive phenomenon. Negative because male-defined images, metaphors, and narratives are powerful and all-pervasive. We cannot simply cast off these false representations to uncover an unblemished and authentic female reality. Any attempt by women to depict women's perspective is enmeshed within rhetoric, narrative, and figure, shaped by the symbols and conventions of a phallocentric culture. Feminism cannot, in this sense, exist outside the male-defined heritage of aesthetic representation.

But the aesthetic also acquires a positive value. Given the importance of language and culture in shaping reality, questioning representation can become a powerful means of questioning the social world. In the twentieth century, art has often been another name for this questioning. Much modern art has sought to estrange us from everyday reality, to shatter the fiction of a unified, stable ego and to explore the opaque, enigmatic qualities of language. Art is not just a means to truth, but also a way of questioning the desire for truth. There are thus obvious affinities between avant-garde art and a feminist poststructuralism that seeks to undermine phallocentric norms. Ingrid Richardson writes, "feminism has embraced the aesthetic as that one final realm which has not been and cannot be subsumed into reason, as that place which sidesteps-undercuts preoccupations with identity, boundaries and norms, as the space where female desire can finally be written into discourse and spill out new matrices of subjectivity and experience."[14]

Aesthetics, in other words, can be a space of resistance as well as conformism. Feminist attacks on art as a bastion of male authority and linchpin of the status quo are too simple and reductive. Within modernity, at least, the role of the artist has often been that of dissident and outsider. Aesthetic experience has a complicated and often conflict-ridden relationship to a social order whose primary values are those of efficiency, rationality, and profit. This is not to suggest that male artists have always been friends and allies of feminism. If anything, the opposite has been true. But modern art does contain a rich and complex history of experimenting with differing styles and techniques of representation, with questioning everyday realities and imagining alternative worlds. As feminist critics and artists struggle to rethink the meaning of gender, they have found aspects of that history inspiring.

From the standpoint of paraesthetics, then, gender and the aesthetic are intertwined in a manner quite unlike conventional feminist aesthetics. Art is not subordinated to a feminist demand for a fixed and coherent female identity. Rather, art is the place where identity fails, where the fictions of separate, unitary and complementary male and female selves are revealed as fictions. This art is "feminine" in a metaphorical sense, in embracing everything that is elided and repressed by the binary logic of a patriarchal culture. Femininity is thus the space of non-identity rather than identity, heterogeneity and otherness rather than the will to truth. In this sense, there would appear to be no necessary relationship between the (female) gender of the author and the (feminine) gender of art. Some feminist critics, however, have insisted that the two are linked, and that the fragmented, chaotic, polysemic forms of experimental art have a close affinity with women's bodies and women's psyches. Feminine sexuality engenders feminine textuality.

This perspective in turn raises new questions about social meanings and effects of art. How revolutionary, after all, is poetic language? Does the shattering of form reach out beyond the aesthetic sphere? Art may offer new ways of seeing, but do these new ways translate into social change? Should they? Who are the audiences of experimental and avant-garde art and how does this fact affect claims about the subversive nature of feminine writing or antirepresentational art? Feminist critics sometime use the language of transgression too glibly, without thinking about the specific contexts in which literature and art are interpreted. Art may no longer offer positive truth, but it can easily slide into a form of negative truth or negative theology, whose subversive effects are assumed rather than demonstrated.

(2000)

Notes

10 David Carroll, *Paraesthetics: Foucault, Lyotard, Derrida* (New York: Methuen, 1987), xiv.
11 Jacqueline Rose, *Sexuality in the Field of Vision* (London: Verso, 1986), 121.
12 Shoshana Felman, *Reading and Sexual Difference* (Baltimore: Johns Hopkins University Press, 1993), 6.
13 For an overview of *écriture féminine* and the work of Julia Kristeva, see Toril Moi, *Sexual/Textual Politics* (London: Methuen, 1985). Griselda Pollock discusses an aesthetics of disidentification in "Screening the Seventies: Sexuality and Representation in Feminist Practice – A Brechtian Perspective," in *Vision and Difference: Femininity, Feminism, and Histories of Art* (London: Routledge, 1988).
14 Ingrid Richardson, "Feminism and Critical Theory," unpublished manuscript.

Linda R. Williams

'Happy Families? Feminist Reproduction and Matrilineal Thought' *New Feminist Discourses*

Feminist Family Romances

Mother/daughterhood is then one of the most persistent ways that feminism has articulated women's alternative networks of communication. As metaphor it has profoundly affected our reading of women's literary history, and I want to explore more closely what is at stake in this. It is, I think, not so simple. However strongly this 'pure' bond is asserted, however much it is seen to be a democratic exchange of feeling and information, its intervention as a controlling metaphor in feminist studies, and particularly in feminist criticism, needs to be challenged. From the premiss that women have access to purity of sublime or semiotic communication comes the notion that authentic female communication takes place through matriarchal and matrilineal networks, networks which are purified from the distortions of the symbolic. Hegel's women conceive immaculately because for them no defiling or politicized process of transmission takes place in thought. They 'gather' knowledge in an apparently unmediated way – it is 'exchanged' or absorbed, and therefore not subject to the problems of transmission.

Against this, and with Alice Jardine, I would

> like to avoid the mother/daughter paradigm here (so as not to succumb simply to miming the traditional father/son, master/disciple model), but it is difficult to avoid at this point being positioned by the institution as mothers and daughters. Structures of debt/gift (mothers and increasingly daughters control a lot of money and prestige in the university), structures of our new institutional power over each other, desires and demands for recognition and love – all of these are falling into place in rather familiar ways.[18]

Her 'Notes for an Analysis' is written in anticipation of a 'new kind of feminist intellectual' who 'fully inscribes herself within the ethics of impossibility, concluding by calling for the wiping away of 'the concept of "generation" altogether' when feminist women place themselves 'across the generations'. She suggests an embrace of intra-generational solidarity which would erase the power of differentials bound up in the relationship of debt between mothers and daughters, towards a totality of unified radical feminist intellectuals. It is a pity that such a complex analysis of the contemporaneity of feminism and psychoanalysis ends before suggesting how this embrace of generational forgetting is to take place, and at what point it would resist undifferentiated unity with a dynamic of different, *afamilial* powers.

How, then, can feminism interpret the transmission of ideas, knowledge; systems of thought outside of an Oedipal dynamic? With what language do we currently discuss the channels through which information is passed on? When Hegel writes the offhand 'Women are educated – who knows how?' he invites us to presume that the way in which men are educated is no problem at all. That's obvious – it's women who are the mystery. I want to ask a series of questions about how we pass on information to each other and what we want it to do. What is feminist transmission? Why do we so often employ familial metaphors to interpret our conceptual and scholarly relationships with each other? What are the power relations at stake in setting up feminist networks of thinking which rely on mother-daughter or sisterly ties? Why are we so reluctant to rid ourselves of the family? These questions focus not only on the problem of mother–daughter relations in history or psychoanalysis, but crucially on the way we have interpreted women's *literary* history as a *family* history, glued together by those 'unknowable' feminine relations discussed above: 'the unique bonds that link women in what we might call the secret sisterhood of their literary subculture'.[19] Thus it seems, ironically, that the very force which some writers have drawn upon to signal the breakdown of patriarchal family relations – a feminine communication which disrupts normal epistemologies – has then been used to make coherent an alternative Great (female) Tradition.

Virginia Woolf's famous statement, 'we think back through our mothers if we are women'[20] has engendered a whole family of feminisms dedicated to the recovery of an intellectual matriarchy. As Rachel Bowlby writes, 'Woolf has herself become foremother to a generation of feminists who "think back through our mothers".'[21] What Bowlby is indicating, then, isn't just that Woolf thought that there is a literary history which works matrilineally, but that this has in turn engendered a feminist critical family line. Matriarchal thinking has become a primary feminist characteristic, and its language acts as the freemason's handshake of Gilbert and Gubar's 'secret sisterhood'. I want briefly to outline here the arguments of a few kinswomen who display the family resemblances most strongly. Is it a happy family? I think not. Its members squabble constantly over who mother is. Is she Dale Spender's mother, stable source of a comfortable literary tradition, legitimized and authentic? Is she the sublime, pre-Oedipal mother, with whom closeness opens up revolutionary possibilities of disruption?

Dale Spender's *Mothers of the Novel* – dedicated to the author's mother, presumably the grandmother of this text – is an unashamedly evangelical eulogy to 'our' literary matriarchs. Her project is to reclaim the 'treasure chest'[22] of 'women's traditions' which 'we have been missing'.[23] Indeed, her fervent championing of a tradition mothered and reproduced by women – 'it is my contention that women were the mothers of the novel and that any other version of its origin is but a myth of male creation' – is uncannily like that of F. R. Leavis who, in his early work, also occupied an inspired dissident position, championing the canonically repressed. And, like Leavis, what Spender wants to do is to produce an 'authentic' or 'legitimated female tradition',[24] thus exemplifying a feminist critical position which turns to the fecund mother figure as guarantor of a sense of stability and genealogical truth.

Gilbert and Gubar's *The Madwoman in the Attic* is perhaps a more interesting example of matriarchal reading. They take the problem of how creativity is engendered head-on, and partly inherit Harold Bloom's interpretation of literary movement as energized by the anxiety of influence. 'Criticism', for Bloom, 'is the art of knowing the hidden roads that go from poem to poem'[25] – it is the detection of the literary violation of fathers by sons. Writing that 'Poetry (Romance) is Family Romance',[26] Bloom rewrites literary history as the history of Oedipal conflict.

> True poetic history is the story of how poets as poets have suffered other poets, just as any true biography is the story of how anyone suffered his own family – or his own displacement of family into lovers and friends.

Summary – Every poem is a misinterpretation of a parent poem.[27]

For Bloom, imagination is *mis*interpretation; creativity is the deliberate violation of what's come before. A feminism which would assemble all the fragments of women's literary history into 'the career of a single woman artist, a "mother of us all"',[28] which would conform in part to the notion that female imagination is osmotically communicated through that 'unique bond', would undoubtedly have enormous problems with such a violating tradition. What Gilbert and Gubar want to do is take Bloom's model and strip it of its anxiety as far as literary daughters and mothers are concerned, neatly retaining father as the bad relation. Patriarchal tradition takes on the image of the wicked stepfather in a romance of positive feminine relations: the father remains the one to be killed, and although today's women writers are 'the daughters of too few mothers', nevertheless a dedicated enough act of feminist critical genealogy can trace a whole matriarchal history, putting together the history of 'a woman whom patriarchal poetics dismembered and whom we have tried to remember'. Re-membering thus becomes a process dedicated to unity; fragments of written selves are made to undergo a rite of matrilineal coherence. Remembering phallically assembles fragments into a unity of 'membership'. If patriarchal history was the process of splitting women exogamically from each other, disseminating their powers and dismembering their tradition, certain feminist histories would bring the parts back into the organic whole again. Coherence, progress, growth, community, all combine to produce a stable tradition of women's literary history. The female artist can then begin the struggle which Gilbert and Gubar call 'the anxiety of authorship', 'only by actively seeking a female precursor who, far from representing a threatening force to be denied or killed, proves by example that a revolt against partriarchal literary authority is possible'.[29]

Furthermore, not only has the reintroduction of a sense of tradition restabilized our understanding of women's writing but ironically enough the very fact that women have been able to draw upon matrilineal metaphors has given that tradition the weight of genetic verification. To assert that paternity is undecidable whilst maternity is undeniable is a fairly commonplace idea; as Freud writes in *Moses and Monotheism*,

> this turning from the mother to the father points in addition to a victory of intellectuality over sensuality – that is, an advance in civilization, since maternity is proved by the evidence of the senses while paternity is a hypothesis, based on an inference and a premiss.[30]

Hélène Cixous, champion of fiction if ever there was one, is, however, quite prepared to denigrate it in contrast with this primary 'fact' of maternity: 'Paternity, which is a fiction, is fiction passing itself off as truth.'[31] To extend this into the metaphorics of writing generations, feminist literary history has reversed and rewritten Cixous' statement as: 'literary maternity, which is a fact, is fact which has historically been passed off as untruth'. Some feminist criticisms have challenged this 'historical passing off' in order to establish a framework within which feminist scholarship is meaningful. Thus in pursuit of matrilineal stability, feminism has been able to deploy the metaphor of the most concrete human given of all: the fact that one is the issue of one's mother. So, patriarchal literary tradition has acted only to render women writers temporary orphans; the happy ending of the family romance is that given sufficiently skilful sleuthing, the truth will out and our true mother will be found.

(1992)

Notes

18   Alice Jardine, 'Notes for an Analysis', in Teresa Brennan (ed.), *Between Feminism and Psychoanalysis* (London, 1989), p. 77.
19   Sandra Gilbert and Susan Gubar, *The Madwoman in the Attic* (New Haven and London, 1979), p. 51.
20   Virginia Woolf, *A Room of One's Own* (1929) (St Albans, 1977), pp. 72–3.
21   Rachel Bowlby, *Virginia Woolf: Feminist Destinations* (Oxford, 1988), p. 25.
22   Dale Spender, *Mothers of the Novel: 100 Good Women Writers Before Jane Austen* (London, 1986), p. 2.
23   ibid., p. 6.
24   ibid., pp. 262–3.
25   Harold Bloom, *The Anxiety of Influence* (Oxford, 1973), p. 96.
26   ibid., p. 95.
27   Bloom, op. cit.
28   Gilbert and Gubar, op. cit., p. 101.
29   ibid., p. 49.
30   Freud, *Moses and Monotheism* (1939 [1934–8]), in Pelican Freud Library vol. 13, *The Origins of Religion*, p. 361.
31   Hélène Cixous and Catherine Clément, *The Newly Born Woman* (1975), trans. Betsy Wing (Manchester, 1986), p. 101.

JANE SPENCER

Literary Relations: Kinship and the Canon 1660–1830

Nevertheless, I find kinship relations and kinship metaphors crucial both to the literary lives of writers from the Restoration to the Romantics, and to the creation of the canon. First, while the long-term account of the separation of kinship and economy is justified, the extent to which kinship was in decline in the period under discussion can easily be exaggerated. Capitalist organization did not necessarily mean that the family group lost its economic role. Leonore Davidoff and Catherine Hall, in a classic study, showed how important family businesses were to the expanding economy of the late eighteenth and early nineteenth centuries, and Richard Grassby's large empirical study of London business families in an earlier period concludes that the business world, organized around kinship relations, can be described as a world of 'familial capitalism'.[9] These historians offer helpful ways of thinking about writers working together in the eighteenth century. People did not only compete in the literary market as isolated individuals. For the married couple Richard and Elizabeth Griffith, who published their premarital correspondence as *Letters of Henry and Frances*, or sisters Harriet and Sophia Lee, who ran a school together and collaborated on a volume of fictional tales, or the several generations of Sheridans who worked in various literary genres, writing was a kind of family enterprise. How a family setting for literary life nurtured and constrained writers, and how it affected their sense of themselves as authors and the ways they were received (or not) into the developing canon, will be a part of my focus in the following chapters.

Secondly, even when there are significant changes in economic and social organization, older ways of cultural understanding retain a great deal of their power, and show themselves in commonly used metaphors. Kinship metaphors are a particularly strong example of this, for while kinship has lost ground as a structuring principle for trade and industry, and individuals today are less likely than those of 300 years ago to centre their lives in their families of origin, the psychological importance of primary kinship relations remains. The importance of the idea of paternal generation and authority is evident in the common habit of referring to inventors as fathers of their inventions, artists and writers as fathers of movements and traditions, or scientists as fathers of different specialisms.[10] Kinship metaphors can even be understood as a fundamental kind of metaphor, because we understand all kinds of resemblance 'in terms of kin relation and family resemblance', ideas which therefore underlie our patterns of language and cognition.[11] This is not to say, though, that the ideas that necessity is the mother of invention and J. Robert Oppenheimer was the father of the atomic bomb express universal truths. Current anthropological thought is moving away from the view that kinship is transhistorically, cross-culturally central to all societies. Rather, it is the huge importance of kinship within Western views of the world that has led Western anthropologists to impose it as a pattern for understanding societies which understand themselves in quite different terms.[12] The centrality of the concepts of generative literary fatherhood, mythical literary motherhood, and competitive and co-operative literary brotherhood and sisterhood, to the creation of the British literary tradition should be seen as part of a culturally and historically specific (though widespread and long lasting) complex of ideas about kinship relations.

(2005)

Notes

9   Leonore Davidoff and Catherine Hall, *Family Fortunes: Men and Women of the English Middle Class 1780–1850* (London: Hutchinson, 1987); Richard Grassby, *Kinship and Capitalism: Marriage, Family, and Business in the English-Speaking World, 1580–1740* (Cambridge: Woodrow Wilson Center Press and CUP, 2001).

10   Robert K. Merton lists the fathers of pathology, palaeontology, electrotechnics, mathematical physics, histology, protozoology and bacteriology, preventive medicine, modern acoustics, scientific pedagogy, experimental psychology, biometry, 'and, of course, Comte, the Father of Sociology': his names, he points out, are selected from a much longer list of generally acknowledged fathers. See 'Priorities in Scientific Discovery: A Chapter in the Sociology of Science', in Bernard Barber and Walter Hirsch (eds.), *The Sociology of Science* (New York: Free Press of Glencoe, 1962), 447–85. For a discussion of the sinister implications of the modern competition for scientific paternity see Brian Easlea, *Fathering the Unthinkable: Masculinity, Scientists and the Nuclear Arms Race* (London: Pluto Press, 1983).

11   Mark Turner, *Death is the Mother of Beauty: Mind, Metaphor, Criticism* (Chicago: University of Chicago Press, 1987), 11. Turner classifies a number of 'basic' metaphors dependent on parenthood and siblinghood, and notes the gender prejudices implicit in them, e.g. in metaphors in which 'a female state generates a male activity' (ibid. 56). For the cognitive linguistic view of metaphor, which sees metaphors not as arbitrary rhetorical devices but as rooted in sensorimotor experiences, see Mark Johnson, *The Body in the Mind: The Bodily Basis of Meaning, Reason and Imagination* (Chicago: University of Chicago Press, 1987), and Zoltán Kövecses, *Metaphor: A Practical Introduction* (Oxford: OUP, 2002).

12   The challenge to the anthropological consensus on kinship is found in David Schneider, *A Critique of the Study of Kinship* (Ann Arbor: University of Michigan Press, 1984). For a discussion of current trends in kinship studies see Ladislav Hóly, *Anthropological Perspectives on Kinship* (London: Pluto Press, 1996).

Nancy K. Miller

'Parables and Politics: Feminist Criticism in 1986'
Paragraph

Throughout his overview of feminist literary studies, Ruthven complains about and protests against what he calls 'separatist feminism' (13); what he understands to be an exclusive/exclusionist attention to women's writing: 'It would be a pity', he worries, by way of a conclusion:

> if the feminist critique, which has been so successful in identifying androcentric bias against women writers and in making possible a critical discourse free of such

prejudices, should be betrayed by a gynocritics developed along separatist lines. For that would simply reproduce the polarity between women's writing and men's which feminist criticism set out to combat in the first place. And it would also make it that much harder next time to persuade men and women that they have far too much to learn from one another to risk going their separate ways. (128)

Since I myself have been dubbed a 'partisan of separatist criticism',[7] I would like in closing to suggest a more accurate and useful way to think about women's writing. I would argue that it is precisely through the processes of recovery, revision and 'revisionary rereading' (Kolodny) which constitute the characteristic gestures of the work on women's writing, that we can learn how to challenge the false continuities ('origins' and influences) of the canon: a collection of texts that might more truthfully be designated as 'men's writing'.[8]

In many ways the reconstruction of feminism, like deconstruction which involves two principles or steps, is a doubled dealing: 'a *reversal* of the classical opposition *and* a general *displacement* of the system'.[9] But the reconstruction sought by feminist literary theory necessarily operates a specific inflection (and displacement) of that set of gestures: the establishment of a female tradition – a move that by its own claims to representation seeks to unsettle the claims of literary history – *and* a steady, Medusa-like gaze from its own genealogies at a tradition that has never thought to think back through its mothers. Put another way, my argument here is that a feminist look at the canon (the system) will reveal the petrification of the gender hierarchies that regulate the institutionalization of literature; and displace the asymmetries those hierarchies install. Contrary to what Ruthven imagines, then, I would argue that by its attention to the questions of feminist literary theory – who reads, who writes, whose interests are served by this reading and writing? – the study of women's writing *returns* separatism from the margins to the nervous 'I' of the dominant beholders. And in my view, meaningful change within the institution will come only from this return to sender that dislocates the universal subject from his place at the centre of the dominant discourse.

The third parable. In the literature of female signature there is a text, a long novel, though that term domesticates the work's explosion of generic restraints (or rather a kind of Bakhtinian heteroglossia reigns instead), that takes up the question of the pantheon, the canon and the place in it for the woman writer. This work is Germaine de Stael's *Corinne or Italy* (1807). Corinne, the heroine, begins the tour of Rome she has designed to capture the imagination of Oswald, the melancholy Englishman who has come to Italy to recover his health, and recover from the grief brought on by the death of his Father.

Corinne, a poet and improviser whose crowning on the steps of the Capitol dramatically introduces the lovers to each other, takes Oswald first to the Pantheon where one can see 'the busts of the most famous artists: they decorate the niches where the gods of the ancients had been placed' (96). Corinne explains that her deepest desire is to have her place there as well: 'I've already chosen mine, she said, showing him an empty niche' (97).

If we ask again, 'how does the inclusion of women's writing alter our view of the tradition', *Corinne* offers an exemplary set of answers: it rereads the Greek myth through Roman architecture; it incarnates cultural relativism; it articulates the history of Classicism and Romanticism; it politicizes, by making it a question of public display, the notion of genius (Moers); it stages the problem of subjectivity; and dramatizes the question of the artist's relation to the social. The novel had enormous impact on (women) writers in France, England and America. Need I say that it belongs neither to the canon of French literature – though because of Staël's status as an intellectual the novel gets honourable mention – nor to the pantheon of world literature. In other words, the niche still remains empty.

When Corinne realizes she is about to die (young), and is too ill to perform, she has her verses read, in a final theatrical, by a young girl. She also arranges before her death to have her tiny niece, Juliette (the daughter of Oswald and Corinne's English half-sister), learn to speak Italian and play the harp: just like Corinne, but of course with the difference a generation makes. Thus the artist in her lifetime arranges for and underwrites her legacy: what I will call a feminist 'aftertext' (Berg, 219).

Barthes, we know, has argued that the Death of the Author is co-terminous with, if not brought about by, the Birth of the Reader. Although he records the former event with a jubilation feminist critics will not all necessarily share, there is, perhaps, good reason to appropriate and revise the paradigm. For this is our only hope. Confronted with the persistence of the empty niche, it becomes our task to stage the possibility of a different sort of continuity. Not the biological and murderous simplicity that appeals so much to the father and son teams of our cultural paradigms (à la Harold Bloom after Sigmund Freud), but a more complex legacy that like Corinne's passes on its values in life to another generation through reading and its performatives (Berg, 214); and like Lucy Snowe's authorizes its passions from another and finally ambiguous scene of writing.

(1986)

Notes

7   Adrienne Munich, 'Notorious signs, feminist criticism and literary tradition', in *Making a Difference*. In *Reading Woman* Mary Jacobus performs an astute analysis of Ruthven's obsession with separatism: Ruthven's 'own discourse on feminist criticism retains its imaginary mastery of the discourse of feminism. The measure is separation (feminist criticism as castration) or a reassuring image of wholeness (feminist criticism as the imaginary, narcissistic completion of critical

lack): the phallic woman, in short, has something to offer the institution of criticism after all.'

8   There is a proposal on the floor at Dartmouth College, put forward by a man, that the catalogue should accurately designate what is taught. What flows from this is that 'Modern British and American Poetry', for example, would read, 'White European Male Modern British and American Poetry'; and the great works would read: men's writing. In the recorded discussion about the establishment at Barnard College of a Women's Studies Programme and major in 1977, the Professor of Music 'stated that he found it difficult to envision a men's studies programme and therefore found it equally difficult to conceive of a women's studies programme'.

9   The argument continues: 'It is on that condition alone that deconstruction will provide the means of *intervening* in the field of oppositions it criticizes and which is also a field of non-discursive forces' (*Marges*, 392; in Culler, 86). Whether the operations of displacement actually effect an intervention in the scene of non-discursive structures, in the hierarchies of university life, for example, is to my mind the great question of deconstructive criticism as a politics.

VIVIANE FORRESTER

'What Women's Eyes See'
New French Feminisms

We don't know what women's vision is. What do women's eyes see? How do they carve, invent, decipher the world? I don't know. I know my own vision, the vision of one woman, but the world seen through the eyes of others? I only know what men's eyes see.

So what do men's eyes see? A crippled world, mutilated, deprived of women's vision. In fact men share our malaise, suffer from the same tragedy: the absence of women particularly in the field of cinema.

If we were responsible for this absence, couldn't they complain about it? 'After all,' they would say, 'we have communicated our images, our vision to you; you are withholding yours. That is why we present a castrated universe, a life whose essential answers are unknown to us. We make films, we attempt to say, to translate, to destroy, to know, to invent, and you condemn us to a monologue that confines us to stale repetition, an isolation such that we are becoming petrified in endless narcissism. We have only fathers. We see only through our own fantasms, our malaise, the tricks we play on you, our renunciations (this network of conventions which replaces you and propagates itself dangerously at every level of our work) and the vacuum created by your absence and the dolls who fill it and whom we have fabricated. And we do not know how you see us. You do not look at us, etc.'

We don't hear such complaints and for obvious reasons. Because this blindness to women's vision, which in fact prohibits any global vision of the world, any vision of the human species, has been fashioned by men for our mutual impoverishment.

How can male directors today not beg women to pick up the camera, to open up unknown areas to them, to liberate them from their redundant vision which is deeply deformed by this lack? Women's vision is what is lacking and this lack not only creates a vacuum but it perverts, alters, annuls every statement. Women's vision is what you don't see; it is withdrawn, concealed. The images, the pictures, the frames, the movements, the rhythms, the abrupt new shots of which we have been deprived, these are the prisoners of women's vision, of a confined vision.

The quality of this vision is not the point – in the hierarchical sense – it is not better (how absurd to speak of a 'better' vision), it is not more efficient, more immediate (certain women will assert that it is, but that's *not* the point); but it is lacking. And this deficiency is suicidal.

Women are going to seize (they are beginning to do so) what they should have acquired naturally at the same time as men did, what men after this bad start should have eventually begged women to undertake: the practice of film making. Women will have to defend themselves against an accumulation of clichés, of sacred routines which men delight in or reject and which will frequently trap women as well. They will need a great deal of concentration and above all of precision. They will have to see, to look, to look at themselves unaffectedly, with a natural gaze that is so difficult to maintain; they will have to dare to see not only their own fantasms, but also, instead of an old catalogue, fresh, new images of a weary world. Why will they be more apt to rid themselves of whatever obstructs men's vision? Because women are the secret to be discovered, they are the fissures. They are the source where no one has been.

(1976)
Translated by Isabelle de Courtivron

SHOSHANA FELMAN

'Women and Madness: The Critical Phallacy'
Diacritics

A question could be raised: if 'the woman' is precisely the Other of any conceivable Western theoretical locus of speech, how can the woman as such be speaking in this book? Who is speaking here, and who is asserting the otherness of the woman? If, as Luce Irigaray suggests, the woman's silence, or the repression of her capacity to speak, are constitutive of philosophy and of theoretical discourse as such, from what theoretical locus is Luce Irigaray herself speaking in order to develop her own theoretical discourse about the woman's exclusion? Is she speaking the language of men, or the silence of women? Is she speaking *as* a woman, or *in place of* the (silent) woman, *for* the woman, *in the name of* the woman? Is it enough to *be* a woman in order to *speak* as a woman? Is 'speaking as a woman' a fact determined by some biological *condition* or by a strategic, theoretical *position*, by anatomy[1] or by culture? What if 'speaking as a woman' were not a simple 'natural' fact, could not be taken for granted? With the increasing number of women and men alike who are currently choosing to share in the rising fortune of female misfortune, it has become all too easy to be a speaker *'for* women.' But what does 'speaking *for* women' imply? What is 'to speak *in the name of* the woman'? What, in a general manner, does 'speech in the name of mean? Is it not a precise repetition of the oppressive gesture of *representation*, by means of which, throughout the history of logos, man has reduced the woman to the status of a silent and subordinate object, to something inherently *spoken for*? To 'speak in the name of,' to 'speak *for*,' could thus mean, once again, to appropriate and to silence. This important theoretical question about the status of its own discourse and its own 'representation' of women, with which any feminist thought has to cope, is not thought out by Luce Irigaray, and thus remains the blind spot of her critical undertaking.

(1975)

Note

1   Freud has thus pronounced his famous verdict on women: 'Anatomy is destiny,' But this is precisely the focus of the feminist contestation.

MARGARET J. M. EZELL

Writing Women's Literary History

Those who have ventured where Greer warns us not to tread, writing women's literary history, do encounter the problem of scarcity of texts and critical studies which Greer cites. To solve this problem and to establish common ground over a historical line, diachronically, the solution has been to investigate using a linear cause and effect analysis, either to start in the past and work forward in time, looking for development and searching for patterns of influence, or to read backward, starting with the present and looking for predecessors, a sort of literary genealogy. Because, until recent years, it was extremely difficult to obtain materials by and about women writers before 1800 (the causes of which are analyzed in chapters 3 and 4), the tendency has been to read backward. The starting point for establishing commonality and for generalizing about women's writing and women's lives as authors has been either from the present or from the nineteenth century, defined by Moers as the "epic age" of women writers. Because of this choice, as we shall see, recent critical assumptions about earlier women's writings and about patterns of female authorship have tended to be based on nineteenth- and twentieth-century examples.

In its search for a commonality through which to create a female literary tradition, women's literary history has scanned the biographies of early women writers. We seek to relate to the past through shared life experiences or shared responses. As Alice Walker phrased it, we search for our mothers' gardens: in describing the composition of "The Revenge of Hannah Kemhuff," Walker observed:

> In that story I gathered up the historical and psychological threads of the life my ancestors lived, and in the writing of it I felt joy and strength and my own continuity. I had that wonderful feeling writers get sometimes, not very often, of being *with* a great many people, ancient spirits, all very happy to see me consulting and acknowledging them, and eager to let me know, through the joy of their presence, that, indeed, I am not alone.[7]

This metaphor of the female literary family is frequently found in studies of women's literary history. Moers's landmark study of nineteenth-century women writers makes use of this image of the literary community as a family of women to emphasize its stabilizing effect on the female author, the confidence given by the possession of predecessors. While modern women writers have more educational opportunities than their restricted Victorian ancestors, Moers argues, they, too, "appear to benefit still from their membership in the wide-spreading family of women writers."[8]

Ultimately, one can see the attempt to write women's literary history as having the same goal as the original one of genealogy. One very great need expressed in this search for the tradition is to provide literary ancestors; ancestors document the legitimacy of current women's literary activities. The re-creation of a female family of authorship also suggests that it will provide the emotional security and support lacking in society at large.

The danger in searching out one's relatives, however, is whom one might find. For ideological reasons this search is an important step in reclaiming significance for women's history, which then helps to enable future study. But are we actually seeing all that there is to see in the past, meeting all our relatives, in our genealogical sweeps? Or are we so concerned with establishing continuity that our vision of the life of a woman writer, before 1700 in particular, is exclusive and selective? Have we, to use Jerome McGann's terms, gerrymandered the past in order to support a particular present concept of the woman writer?

[...]

A feminist/new historicist approach to this particular construction of the past raises several issues. Given the heavy dependence on nineteenth-century women's literature in the construction of a theory of female authorship, one must question the extent to which the image of the woman writer in earlier periods has been made to conform to a Romantic or Victorian concept of the artist. One must also wonder about the extent to which the analysis of pre-1700 literature in critical studies is based on a nineteenth-century model of literature as a commercial activity.

Thus, I find myself agreeing with Todd, whose own work focuses on the eighteenth century, that one of the central problems in existing women's literary history is the critics' lack of familiarity with early texts, that "we avoid listening to a past that might be annoying through its resolute refusal to anticipate us" (p. 46). However, I do not believe her assertion that this lack of familiarity is a characteristic of "the early phase of feminist criticism in general," a phase now supposedly superseded. I believe it arises in part from the insistence on women's literary history following a nineteenth-century model of narrative historiography. Narrative history is a linear mode of organization, which, in its ordering of events, concentrates on locating events on a time line to discover cause and effect solutions, on defining separate periods to serve as the bases for comparison and ranking, on finding "origins" and significant turning points in an evolutionary pattern that leads up to and explains the contemporary situation.

For example, the assumptions about the evolutionary nature of the technology of authorship permeate the very questions we bring to texts written before 1700. As we shall see, even studies on seventeenth-century women writers, such as Jacqueline Pearson's analysis of women dramatists in the Restoration and Goreau's reading of Aphra Behn and Lady Falkland, tend to adopt a nineteenth-century construction of the practice of authorship and the nature of literature as being the norm against which earlier practices are ranked. As I suggested in the Introduction, while the last decade has seen a rise in the number of studies of women writing before 1700, it has not yet seen a systematic challenge to the original conceptualization of an evolutionary pattern of female authorship proposed by Virginia Woolf in *A Room of One's Own,* which has been elaborated by Showalter, Moers, Gilbert, and Gubar into a theory of female creativity.

Instead, accounts of early women's writing have tended to push back the dates on the time line without questioning the system behind it. This adherence to a linear narrative of women's literary history has directed the type of questions we ask about early women writers. Thus we now debate whether Mary Astell or Jane Anger was the "first" English feminist, a debate that can only be decided by ranking the earlier woman's "feminism" against the latter's; likewise, Mary Sidney now contests with Aphra Behn for the title of "the first woman in the period who sought a clear literary vocation" without a question being raised concerning the point of this competition. Being "first," of course, establishes the model against which others are measured, but it also indicates a more rudimentary accomplishment – being the first is not usually equated with being the best.

And the current theoretical model of women's literary history is very much concerned with who wins, who is better than another. Not only does Showalter's model of the evolution of women's texts from the feminine, to the feminist, to the female rank the different periods in ascending order through chronological history, but studies devoted to Renaissance and Restoration periods adopt the same narrative strategy as well. When we study women writing in the Renaissance as a group, the ultimate question posed is, "is there evidence of evolution, both for the individual and for the group? Unsurprisingly, they write better the more they write; surprisingly in so small a group, each poet surpasses her predecessor"; we are offered an immediate cause and effect explanation in the scheme of the linear progress of women writing in the Renaissance: "Time would allow women to evolve poetically because once there was one published woman poet, other women would not only start practicing, they would realize that women could be poets without sacrificing their character."[10]

The problem with this type of linear historiography that focuses on unique events – whether it is involved in identifying the first feminist, or the first woman with a "true" literary vocation, or a more general event such as middle-class women beginning to write commercially, which Woolf cites as the turning point in women's history – is that it has an unstated notion of evolutionary progress built into it. Events are interpreted as they lead up to or follow a major event. As a result, this history can easily negate those events preceding the chosen significant one on the time line; for example, women who do not fit the pattern of development signposted by the special events get labeled "anomalies" or are defined as doing something different and less important (writing "closet" literature), or, as we shall see in the case of the late seventeenth-century Quaker women writers, they are simply left out.

(1993)

Notes

7   Alice Walker, *In Search of Our Mothers' Gardens: Womanist Prose* (New York: Harcourt Brace Jovanovich, 1983), 13.

8   Ellen Moers, *Literary Women: The Great Writers* (Garden City, NY: Doubleday, 1976), 44.

10   Elaine V. Beilin, *Redeeming Eve: Women Writers of the English Renaissance* (Princeton: Princeton Univ. Press, 1987), 116–17.

BETTY A. SCHELLENBERG

The Professionalization of Women Writers
in Eighteenth-Century Britain

My inquiry took root in graduate student days in the late 1980s, when my discovery of eighteenth-century studies coincided with a reinvigoration of the field through exciting new historicist, materialist, print culture, and above all, feminist approaches. The novelty of the attention paid to noncanonical women writers in such overviews of the period as Jane Spencer's *The Rise of the Woman Novelist: From Aphra Behn to Jane Austen* (1986), Kathryn Shevelow's *Women and Print Culture: The Construction of Femininity in the Early Periodical* (1989), and Janet Todd's *The Sign of Angellica* (1989) was captured by Patricia Meyer Spacks, who in 1990 reviewed *The Sign of Angellica* as responding to "a great recent shift in literary assumptions" with what "only a few years [before], would have seemed inconceivable to write, or to read, a literary history of the Restoration and eighteenth century focused entirely on women."[4]

The influence of these studies was equally felt in the form of an interpretive frame they had adopted – the model of a separate-spheres gender economy, established with the rise of a bourgeois class in the eighteenth century, which relegated women to the private (domestic) sphere, and to rigid codes of sexual chastity, propriety, and silence.[5] From this starting point, women writers' interventions in the public realm of print were by definition transgressive. As Shevelow put it, women writers were permitted to enter the public sphere of letters only to reinforce the figure of "the domestic woman, constructed in a relation of difference to men, a difference of kind rather than degree." Forays into print had therefore to present a legitimizing face to the public, whether that of an authorizing male literary figure or that of the author herself in an apologetic preamble about "domestic distress, financial necessity, and the urge to instruct other women."[6] The actual matter of such publications, it followed, would either be genuinely orthodox, and in that case produced by the appropriated voice of a submissive woman, or itself in masquerade, its subversion peeping slyly out from beneath a surface orthodoxy, in the case of a writer of genuine feminist convictions. Thus this account of eighteenth-century women writers, using gender as fundamental binary cause, produced layers of oppositional and inevitably value-laden categories of masculine and feminine, cultural gatekeeper and supplicant, surface and depth, orthodox and subversive, appropriated and feminist.

I must emphasize that in Spencer, Shevelow, and Todd the model I have just described is more nuanced than its influence on subsequent literary criticism would suggest.[7] Nevertheless, the interpretive frame had a tendency to become increasingly schematic with each application, especially in the area that concerns me here, the height of the eighteenth century. For the binary synchronic structure of this model was given narrative momentum by a diachronic explanation of the long eighteenth century which might be called, if somewhat disrespectfully, the "sandwich model." Restoration and early eighteenth-century writers such as Aphra Behn and Delarivier Manley engaged in a brief flowering of feminism characterized by what Todd described as "sophisticated insights and techniques," displayed in productions which were "erotic and worldly." A century later, fiction "seem[ed] to gain a new strength from an assumption of the moralist's authority" with Frances Burney, Ann Radcliffe, and Mary Wollstonecraft. Between these endpoints, writers such as Frances Brooke, along with Sarah Fielding, Frances Sheridan, and Sarah Scott, on the other hand, represented an eclipse of feminism by the so-called "modest muse," constrained and appropriated by patriarchal figures like Samuel Richardson, and characterized by "a moralistic ... colluding with the growing ideology of femininity, preaching and greatly rewarding self-sacrifice and restraint."[8] Spencer argued, similarly, that eighteenth-century women writers increasingly succeeded in the public sphere through skillful reinforcement of the ideology locating women's lives in the domestic realm. In other words, they learned to meet "the Terms of Acceptance" for their writing in order to gain acknowledgment of their talents.[9]

As Spacks noted in her review, "Todd's sympathy appears fully engaged" with Restoration and early eighteenth-century writers, but she "has more difficulty" with mid-century writers of sentiment, making their works "sound unappealing indeed," only to have "her interest intensif[y] as she considers the century's final decade."[10] Not surprisingly, such treatments led to much further work on those early and later writers where evidence of feminist convictions, or at least subversion, was relatively easy to find, especially when it took the form of representations of female sexual desire. The Restoration and early eighteenth-century writers Behn, Manley, and Eliza Haywood, for example, have been reexamined in their significantly different political and professional contexts, not only by Todd and Spencer, but also by Ros Ballaster, Catherine Ingrassia, and others.[11] Ultimately, one effect of such work has been to put pressure on a rigid separate-sphere thesis, resulting in a more nuanced approach to all women writers of this time. Recent work has increasingly represented the relation between gender ideology and the individual writer's experience and works as contested and variable. Exploiting the potential for a much-broadened perspective of eighteenth-century publication enabled by the ongoing *English Short Title Catalogue (ESTC)* project, Paula McDowell, in her exemplary 1998 study *The Women of Grub Street: Press, Politics and Gender in the London Literary Marketplace 1678–1730*, employs the methods of book history to challenge the public–private gender dichotomy in the sphere of

print publication. One effect of McDowell's discovery of women's extensive engagement in a wide range of publishing activities is to challenge
notions of their lack of agency in the political public sphere.[12] With respect
to an individual writer, the late Restoration royalist Jane Barker, Kathryn
King has in turn pointed out that reading Barker "*within* a narrative of
the emerging bourgeois femininity and *against* the more flamboyant literary practices of the sex-and-scandal school of female popular fiction" is at
best unhelpful for this writer marginalized in multiple senses as a Catholic,
a Jacobite, an intellectual woman, and a spinster. King's study demonstrates that "gender-driven, oppositional accounts of early modern women
writers, so hugely productive over the last couple of decades, have reached
a point of diminishing returns and will need to be supplemented by more
inclusive pictures of women's involvement in early modern culture if feminist literary history is to move forward."[13]

Indeed, feminist historians of the pre-twentieth century have for some
time been raising concerns about the value of this broad-brush model as
an analytical tool, in part because of its seeming applicability to any
number of historical moments and because of its reliance on suspect com-
binations of prescriptive and descriptive sources. In her 1993 article
"Golden Age to Separate Spheres? A Review of the Categories and
Chronology of English Women's History," Amanda Vickery helpfully
reviewed theoretical and methodological critiques from the late 1980s,
while noting the continued reliance of historians of British women's experience on the assumption that a gendered public–private dichotomy developed in England from the late seventeenth to the early nineteenth centuries.
Vickery concluded that

> the notion of separate spheres ... has done modern women's history a great
> service. With this conceptual framework women's history moved beyond a
> Whiggish celebration of the rise of feminism, or a virtuous rediscovery of
> those previously hidden from history. In asserting the instrumental role of the
> ideology of separate spheres in modern class formation, historians asserted the
> wider historical significance of gender. Thereby the interpretation offered
> powerful justification for the study of women when the field was embattled.
> Yet strategic concerns do not in themselves justify the deployment of an artifi-
> cial and unwieldy conceptual vocabulary. In the attempt to map the breadth
> and boundaries of female experience, new categories and concepts must be
> generated, and this must be done with more sensitivity to women's own
> manuscripts.[14]

In a similar vein, but dealing more directly with historiography of the
eighteenth century, Lawrence E. Klein, in a 1995 article on "Gender and
the Public/Private Distinction in the Eighteenth Century," has questioned
the "domestic thesis" for superimposing the two binary oppositions of male/

female and public/private to argue for "the persistent exclusion of women from public roles, power and citizenship." Klein notes that this model fails to take into account evidence that "even when theory was against them, women in the eighteenth century had [conscious] public dimensions to their lives."[15] Such work revisits Jürgen Habermas's influential discussion of the rise of the bourgeois public sphere in eighteenth-century England, in order to pry open the fissure between Habermas's scheme of a public sphere of letters which is broadly inclusive and a public political sphere which grows out of the former, but is made up of private individuals who are male, middle-class heads of households.[16]

(2005)

Notes

4   Patricia Meyer Spacks, review in *Eighteenth-Century Fiction* 2 (1990), p. 364.
5   For a full outline of the model, see Jane Spencer, *The Rise of the Woman Novelist: From Aphra Behn to Jane Austen* (Oxford: Blackwell, 1986), especially chapter 1's section on "The New Ideology of Femininity" and chapter 3, "The Terms of Acceptance," and Todd, *Sign of Angellica*, Part Two, especially chapters 6 to 8.
6   Kathryn Shevelow, *Women and Print Culture: The Construction of Femininity in the Early Periodical* (London: Routledge, 1989), p. 5; Todd, *Sign of Angellica*, p. 4.
7   Spencer, for example, in identifying three strands of "response" to the ideological climate for women writers – the novel of protest, the novel of conformity, and the novel of escape – acknowledges overlap between her categories, and traces manifestations of each throughout the long eighteenth century (*Rise of the Woman Novelist*, pp. ix–x, chapters 4–6).
8   Todd, *Sign of Angellica*, p. 2.
9   Spencer, *Rise of the Woman Novelist*, p. 95.
10 Spacks review, p. 365.
11 See especially the essay collection *Aphra Behn Studies*, edited by Todd (Cambridge: Cambridge University Press, 1996); Spencer's *Aphra Behn's Afterlife* (Oxford: Oxford University Press, 2000); Ros Ballaster, *Seductive Forms: Women's Amatory Fiction from 1684 to 1740* (Oxford: Clarendon, 1992); Catherine Ingrassia, *Authorship, Commerce, and Gender in Early Eighteenth-Century England: A Culture of Paper Credit* (Cambridge: Cambridge University Press, 1998); Kirsten T. Saxton and Rebecca P. Bocchicchio (eds.), *The Passionate Fictions of Eliza Haywood: Essays on Her Life and Work* (Lexington: University Press of Kentucky, 2000).
12 Paula McDowell, *The Women of Grub Street: Press, Politics and Gender in the London Literary Marketplace 1678–1730* (Oxford: Clarendon, 1998).
13 Kathryn R. King, *Jane Barker, Exile: A Literary Career, 1675–1725* (Oxford: Clarendon, 2000), pp. 7–20.

14   Amanda Vickery, "Golden Age to Separate Spheres? A Review of the Categories and Chronology of English Women's History," *The Historical Journal* 36 (1993), p. 413. See also Vickery's own "attempt to map the breadth and boundaries of female experience," in *The Gentleman's Daughter: Women's Lives in Georgian England* (New Haven: Yale University Press, 1998).

15   Lawrence E. Klein, "Gender and the Public/Private Distinction in the Eighteenth Century: Some Questions about Evidence and Analytic Procedure," *Eighteenth-Century Studies* 29 (1995), p. 97, 102; see also Kathleen Wilson, "Citizenship, Empire, and Modernity in the English Provinces, c. 1720–1790," pp. 69–96 in the same journal issue.

16   Jürgen Habermas, *The Structural Transformation of the Public Sphere: An Inquiry into a Category of Bourgeois Society*, trans. Thomas Burger with the assistance of Frederick Lawrence (Cambridge, MA: MIT Press, 1989), pp. 51–6.

2

Women and Literary Production

INTRODUCTION

Problems for the Woman Writer

Why have women traditionally been under-represented as published writers? The extracts by Virginia Woolf and Tillie Olsen point not to a maliciously planned conspiracy by top male publishers to keep women out of print, but to a tricky combination of material and ideological factors that inhibit the potential woman writer. The catalogue of material problems is long – inequalities in the educational system, lack of privacy, responsibilities for child-bearing and rearing, domestic obligations – but equally decisive are the restrictions of family and social expectations. Even if women writers solve the material problems that prevent their writing, an anxiety about their chosen role and how they are perceived continues to surface. Woolf, for instance, writes about women's awareness of an oppressive male presence constraining their work; Olsen comments on the 'leeching of belief, of will'. Woolf illustrates how deeply entrenched is the problem, beyond conscious decision making. Despite her strong belief that 'it is fatal for anyone who writes to think of their sex', despite her privileged position of economic independence and a room of her own, despite her high level of understanding of the issues, she still has to admit, in 'Professions for Women', that she has 'many ghosts to fight, many prejudices to overcome'.

Repeatedly, the woman writer finds herself at a point of tension, aware that her writing both challenges the conventional view of what is appropriate for women and encroaches on what some see as a male preserve. If the woman writer writes about women, she risks the labels of 'partiality', 'narrowness', 'a woman's book'; if she tries to write about her own deepest responses,

Feminist Literary Theory: A Reader, Third Edition By Mary Eagleton   © 2011 Mary Eagleton

particularly sexual, she feels anxious at revealing 'the truth about my own experiences as a body' (Woolf); if she writes at all, she risks being seen as usurping a position which is not hers. Sandra Gilbert and Susan Gubar explore this predicament. With what must be among the most memorable opening sentences in literary criticism – 'Is a pen a metaphorical penis?' – they trace that literary history which sees writing as a kind of extension of the male generative act and which confers on the male writer authority, the right to create and control.[1] In trying to negotiate this situation, Gilbert and Gubar believe the woman writer is involved in a difficult balancing act between apparent conformity to certain patriarchal literary norms and a trenchant critique, expressing the unacceptable, the authorial rage and desire and antagonism.[2]

Possibilities for the Woman Writer

Both Terry Lovell and Jane Spencer take issue with the claims of Gilbert and Gubar. The emphatic assertions of the male writers whom Gilbert and Gubar quote, speaking so conclusively of the masculine nature of literary production, reveal to Lovell not a confident and consolidated tradition, but a deep insecurity about femininity and how it might relate to writing. Lovell maintains that in Western culture imaginative writing is not 'male' but 'gender ambiguous', and she supports her argument by setting alongside the male-dominated canon the popular, 'feminine' image of creative writing, the involvement of female students in the study of languages and literature, and the centrality of women in the development of the novel.

Lovell's suggestions are important. Most of the work on gender and literary production has looked at the *problems* of female literary production. The marked difference in the number of male and female writers and the prevalence, since the early 1970s, of the debate about gaining access have prompted such an approach. Yet, it is equally necessary to turn the question on its head and ask not what has inhibited women's writing, but what has made it possible: historically, there have been more women writers than, say, women sculptors or concert pianists. Lovell's method is to look chiefly at the relationship between social attitudes to writing and the practicalities of production. But other variables, such as literary form, also need to be taken into account.[3] Spencer's comments prompt the question: why is it the novel, *par excellence*, which has been colonized by the woman author? The production of poetry is a domestic activity and yet there are far fewer female poets than male. The theatre is not associated in the popular imagination with 'manliness' and, as students of drama, women are well represented; yet the public production of theatre seems to determine that women should be under-represented as both playwrights and directors. As Woolf makes clear, the reason why 'Judith Shakespeare' could not become 'Shakespeare' had nothing to do with lack of talent or determination. Even within the novel, as Lovell and Spencer indicate, the situation is double-edged. The woman novelist gains status as a writer during a period when women are losing political power; she creates, and yet is confined by, a certain construction of femininity; she finds a public voice and uses it to praise private virtue. All this indicates that the justifiable complaint about women's exclusion from literary production is but the first line in a multi-layered argument. One cannot presume a consistent relation of female exclusion and male inclusion, across history, across cultures, across all literary genres or that this relation produces uniform effects.

Critical Reception
Writing is only the first stage in the production process. The work has to be published, marketed, distributed and, hopefully, reviewed. What Gilbert and Gubar call women's 'anxiety of authorship' has been created and maintained in part through the practices of reviewing and literary criticism. The quotes in their extract from eminent men reveal a striking combination of prohibition, marginalization and casual dismissiveness. In *Thinking about Women*, Mary Ellmann referred to this practice as 'phallic criticism' and produced a devastating catalogue of examples.[4] As we see in Carol Ohmann's work, such criticism can have its funnier moments. Bound by a rigid sex stereotyping, *Wuthering Heights* produced for its reviewers one set of characteristics when they thought the author male, quite a different set when they knew her to be female.[5] Ohmann's analysis acutely exposes any claims to critical objectivity.

Perhaps phallic criticism is all that can be expected of one's enemies, but what if the response of one's friends is equally unsatisfactory? Lack of attention, attention, and the nature of that attention can all be problematic. Writing in 1977, Barbara Smith recognizes how black literature, generally, exists only as a 'discrete subcategory of American literature', while black feminist criticism, specifically, does not exist in *any* concerted sense. Smith sees literary criticism not simply as a subordinate interpreter of the primary imaginative text, but as an important contributor to the possibility of creative writing: it establishes a context in which that writing can be produced and understood. She makes the case for a 'non-hostile' (which, of course, need not mean non-critical), 'perceptive', knowledgeable criticism, one which links to the political movement of black women and provides a method of analysis for black feminist writing.[6] It is salutary to compare Smith's model with Woolf's 'Judith Shakespeare' story (Chapter 1). Towards the end of the Judith Shakespeare extract, Woolf makes one of her characteristic rapid developments of an idea, moving within a few lines from the silence of women, to the desire of men to mark, name and possess, to the imperialist claim for the control of land and other people. Not only is Woolf's contention that a white *woman* would not wish to dominate and refashion a black woman somewhat dubious, her positioning of the black woman as a victim of imperialism rather than as a potential writer also raises issues. For the contemporary critic, it is vital that the history is not forgotten but, equally, that the black woman becomes the subject of her own discourse, creating a new imagery and symbolism, and constructing, as Smith hopes, a critical framework for the writing of black women.[7]

Other commentators have complained that feminism has produced its own set of limitations – not only the kind of incipient racism that Smith mentions, but an unhelpful deference to critical theory, or a kind of prescriptive orthodoxy of its own, or, at best, a list of well-meaning expectations which, nevertheless, no writer could fulfil.[8] In 1987, Isobel Armstrong produced a perceptive reading of Christina Rossetti in the midst of questions, qualifications, hesitancies, worries about what might be 'allowed' or 'permitted' within criticism and feminism. With wit and some exasperation, she tries to position both her poet and herself but, for some, Armstrong's writing is clearly not feminist enough. 'But *I* want to write poetry which men will read' is the confession extracted from Armstrong. Yet, who is to say what *is* a feminist text/reading and how that text/reading is to be produced? Pierre Salesne, who takes part in the Hélène Cixous seminar, would probably equate any prescriptive demands, even feminist prescriptive demands, with 'a certain fantasy of mastery'. The participants in 'Conversations' employ a very different vocabulary. Their aim is not to determine a text but to 'espouse a text', to 'listen to a text', to 'work on a text'; reading is 'a work of love', 'a flowing process of exchange between the reader and the text'. The emphasis is not on control or definition or political correctness, but rather on responsiveness, interaction and a bodily apprehension.[9]

Marketing the Woman Author

Looking along the shelves of any high-street or academic bookshop today, it seems that the question of women writers' presence or absence, once again, needs reframing. Women writers feature as a notably marketable commodity. There are lots of them; they figure in front-of-shop and best-seller displays; they appear at readings and festivals. Feminist criticism, however, features hardly at all. While one market has expanded in the last twenty-five years, the other has declined. The three extracts considered here illustrate how, in getting writing into the public domain and actually bought, everything counts, from significant policy decisions by major publishers to the paratextual detail of an individual novel, and, equally, everything contributes to the construction of particular ways of reading and particular appreciations of value.[10] My own extract takes as its starting point a number of literary critical texts published between 1999 and 2006 to see how they construct the category 'contemporary women's writing'. The evidence is that this category – like many others – inhabits an uneasy ground where critical responses and academic feminism meet with marketing strategies. Literary criticism, reviewing, a place in school or university curricula, prize winning, television programmes and promotional labels all play their part in determining who is read and how. Claire Squires gives us a particularly illuminating example of marketing at work in her analysis of the impact of Arundhati Roy's *The God of Small Things* (1997). We see here the cultural production of an author at a specific moment, in a specific context, the myriad range of contributing forces, the shifting relationships. Previews, reviews, Roy's appearance, book-prize nominations, book-buying habits in India, the comparative reception of the book in India and the UK, the placing of Roy in a lineage from Salman Rushdie at once sell Roy, interpret her and construct her readership. She is created as 'India's next big thing'.[11]

Squires mentions at one point Graham Huggan's concept of the 'postcolonial exotic'; as Huggan's sub-title indicates, the West is in the business of 'marketing the margins' and exoticizing them is an important strategy. Exoticism, he tells us, is 'a kind of semiotic circuit that oscillates between the opposite poles of strangeness and familiarity. Within the circuit, the strange and the familiar, as well as the relation between them, may be recoded to serve different, even contradictory, political needs and ends.'[12] In this section of the book he considers Aboriginal women's life narratives and the function of the paratextual in Alice Nannup's *When the Pelican Laughed* (1992) and Sally Morgan's *My Place* (1987).[13] The paratexts strive to establish authenticity, legitimacy and value, the transnational and 'interethnic endorsement'. But, as Huggan shows, they are at once carefully selective – no mention of race – and yet excessive. The plethora of material – cover image, blurbs, writer endorsements, editors' introduction, postscript, biography, photo, tributes – can be strangely at odds with the texts, attempting to authenticate them through identification and refusing the texts' difference. The paratexts both market and constrain the texts.

Publishing and Distribution

At the start of this chapter, we were thinking of the individual author sitting at her desk and of what is necessary in the conditions of her life and in her own sense of subjectivity to make writing possible. We broadened the debate to issues of reception in reviewing and literary criticism and to the contemporary marketing of the woman author. In what ways are these practices affected by gender? What I should like to focus on, finally, is a further element in the production process, namely the often fraught attempts by women to control the printing, publishing and distribution of their writing and to establish a supportive infrastructure. As early as 1938, Virginia Woolf was voicing this demand for women's control of the means of literary production as a way of avoiding what she refers to as 'adultery of the brain':

> Still, Madam, the private printing press is an actual fact, and not beyond the reach of a moderate income. Typewriters and duplicators are actual facts and even cheaper. By using these cheap and so far unforbidden instruments you

can at once rid yourself of the pressure of boards, policies and editors. They will speak your own mind, in your own words, at your own time, at your own length, at your own bidding.[14]

Woolf did have access to a press, the Hogarth Press; if only she had had desk-top publishing at her disposal. But Paula McDowell shows that women's involvement in printing and publishing has a much longer history. 'In the late seventeenth and early eighteenth centuries in England, for the first time in history, a significant body of politically literate women who were neither aristocratic nor genteel obtained access to the closest thing their culture had to a "mass medium": the press.'[15] Here we see the importance of literary production as a domestic economy, how women could maintain their roles as wife and mother, the varied ways in which skills were acquired, the commercial power that women could attain.

Making sense of the potential of any moment is not easy, and maintaining that potential is even more difficult. The Black Woman Talk Collective, writing in 1984, indicates the lack of interest on the part of the British publishing industry in black British women writers; the only available space is for Afra-American writers. They advocate taking control of the means of production by forming a workers' publishing co-operative. Three years later, Lauretta Ngcobo is more optimistic, believing that the UK market has been stimulated by the US imports and that the publishing industry has begun to open up. She is still shrewdly aware of the problems of dissemination and how a devaluing of black women's writing might be countered by getting into educational curricula. Twenty years on, as I note in my extract, Afra-American writing has largely lost its place in the UK market and, like Ngcobo, I too saw the significance of educational curricula in maintaining a profile. At the same time, The Women's Press, mentioned by the Black Woman Talk Collective, Ncgobo and myself as central in this field, has endured, like most sections of the publishing industry, a roller-coaster existence – but survived. Many of the other companies listed by the Black Woman Talk Collective and Ncgobo have gone.[16] The cultural paradox within which all this operates is that of an expanding, though narrowly targeted, market for certain kinds of women's writing alongside an uncertain progress for feminism.

The ups and downs of the feminist publishing industry relate, in no small measure, to the difficulty in producing a politics while, and through, producing marketable writing. Simone Murray suggests that one way forward might lie in an astute combination of the digital and the bibliocentric, but, ultimately, feminist publishing will have to find a way of situating itself with respect to the 'globalised media conglomerates'.[17] It will need to assess the commercial possibilities of, respectively, new writers, established living writers and 'classics', and to assess the possibilities of different media. Books might not always be best. But, if they are, will there be any feminist bookshops to stock them? Kathryn McGrath is cautiously hopeful – the 'possible rebirth of the feminist bookstore' is part of her article's title, after 'slow death'. This rebirth will have to come from a fundamental rethinking about what a feminist bookstore is and does, but from the examples she quotes, there seems no shortage of willingness to adapt.

Notes

1   For studies on the relation between gender, 'genius' and aesthetic status, see: Christine Battersby, *Gender and Genius: Towards a Feminist Aesthetics* (London: The Women's Press, 1989); Peggy Zeglin Brand and Carolyn Korsmeyer (eds.), *Feminism and Tradition in Aesthetics* (Pennsylvania: Pennsylvania State University Press, 1995); Carolyn Korsmeyer, *Gender and Aesthetics: An Introduction* (London and New York, Routledge, 2004).

2   For a return to this problem of how to be both 'a woman' and 'a writer', see: Toril Moi, ' "I am not a woman writer": About Women, Literature and Feminist Theory Today', *Feminist Theory*, vol. 9, no. 3 (2008), pp. 259–71.

3   Chapter 3 considers more extensively the relation between gender, genre and literary form.

4   See Mary Ellmann, *Thinking About Women* (New York: Harcourt Brace Jovanovich, 1968), Chapter 2.

5   The construction of gender stereotypes in Victorian periodical reviews is discussed also by Elaine Showalter in *A Literature of Their Own: British Women Novelists from Brontë to Lessing* (London: Virago, 1978; 2nd edition 2009) and Nicola Diane Thompson, *Reviewing Sex: Gender and the Reception of Victorian Novels* (London: Macmillan, 1996).

6   With respect to Afra-American writing, this challenge has been met since then in the work of, among others: Gloria Bowles, Hazel Carby, Barbara Christian, Carole Boyce Davies, Ann duCille, bell hooks, Deborah McDowell, Mary Evans, Barbara Smith, Valerie Smith, Hortense Spillers, Claudia Tate, Alice Walker and Mary Helen Washington.

7   It is interesting to see how Alice Walker rewrites the Judith Shakespeare story in the title essay of *In Search of Our Mothers' Gardens* (New York: Harcourt Brace Jovanovich, 1983) so as to rescue the black woman from the position of sympathetic object.

8   Some of the issues concerning prescriptive criticism and an extract from Barbara Christian on the problems of applying critical theory to black feminist criticism are considered further in Chapter 4. For recent reflections on the position of feminism after twenty-plus years of dialogue with contemporary critical theory, see Toril Moi, 'Feminist Theory after Theory', in Michael Payne and John Schad (eds.), *Life. After. Theory* (London and New York: Continuum, 2003).

9   A comparative description of the process of reading can be found in Jane Marcus, 'Still Practice, A/Wrested Alphabet', *Feminist Issues in Literary Scholarship*, ed. Shari Benstock, (Bloomington: Indiana University Press, 1987) and Susan Sellers, 'Learning to Read the Feminine', in Helen Wilcox et al. (eds.), *The Body and the Text: Hélène Cixous, Reading and Teaching* (London: Harvester Wheatsheaf, 1990).

10   For further examples of work on the marketing of the woman writer, see: Simon Brown, *Consuming Books: The Marketing and Consumption of Literature* (London: Routledge, 2006); Catherine Gallagher, *Nobody's Story: The Vanishing Acts of Women Writers in the Marketplace 1670–1820* (Oxford: Clarendon Press, 1994); Judy Simons and Kate Fullbrook (eds.), *Writing: A Woman's Business* (Manchester: Manchester University Press, 1998).

11   In studies of the marketing of the postcolonial writer, Roy has been a particularly interesting example. In addition to Squires' work, see Graham Huggan, *The Postcolonial Exotic: Marketing the Margins* (London: Routledge, 2001) and Elleke Boehmer, *Stories of Women: Gender and Narrative in the Postcolonial Nation* (Manchester: Manchester University Press, 2005). Other studies of literary celebrity include: Joe Moran, *Star Authors: Literary Celebrity in America* (London: Pluto Press, 2000) with a chapter on Kathy Acker; and Lorraine York, *Literary Celebrity in Canada* (Toronto: University of Toronto Press, 2007) with chapters on Margaret Atwood and Carol Shields. Further comment on the marketing of the postcolonial writer can be found in Chapter 7.

12   Huggan, *The Postcolonial Exotic*, p. 13. For a critique of Huggan's concept, see Sarah Brouillette, *Postcolonial Writers in the Global Literary Marketplace* (London: Palgrave, 2009). It is unfortunate for our purposes that Brouillette does not actually consider the postcolonial woman writer in this study.

13   For further work on women authors and the paratextual, see: Stephanie Harzewski, 'New Voice, Old Body: The Case of Penelope Fitzgerald', *Contemporary Women's Writing*, vol. 1, no. 1/2 (Dec. 2007), pp. 24–33; Peta Mayer, 'The Paratextual Construction of Anita Brookner: Chronotopic Conflict in the Book Review and the Author Review', *Women: A Cultural Review*, vol. 19, no. 1 (Spring 2008), pp. 49–68; Amanda Nettlebeck, 'Presenting Aboriginal Women's Life Narratives', *New Literatures Review*, 34 (1997), pp. 43–56; Richard Watts, *Packaging Post/Coloniality* (Lanham, MD: Lexington Books, 2005).

14   Virginia Woolf, *Three Guineas* in the combined volume of *A Room of One's Own* and *Three Guineas*, ed. Michèle Barrett (London: Penguin, 1993), p. 223.

15   Paula McDowell, *The Women of Grub Street: Press, Politics and Gender in the Literary Marketplace 1678–1730* (Oxford: Clarendon Press, 1998), p. 11. McDowell continues this work in her chapter, 'Women and the Business of Print', in Vivien Jones (ed.), *Women and Literature in Britain 1700–1800* (Cambridge: Cambridge University Press, 2000), pp. 135–54.

16   In the 1996 edition of this reader, I commented on the lack of work on women's publishing: 'One hopes, though, that someone, somewhere *is* writing a thesis on this aspect of feminist literary production since much knowledge and experience will otherwise be lost.' I am glad to say that work has been very ably done in Simone Murray, *Mixed Media: Feminist Presses and Publishing Politics* (London: Pluto Press, 2004). For earlier work in this area, see: Eileen Cadman et al., *Rolling Our Own* (London: Minority Press Group, 1981); Gail Chester and Julienne Dickey (eds.), *Feminism and Censorship* (Bridport, Dorset: Prism Press, 1988); Nicci Gerrard, *Into the Mainstream* (London: Pandora, 1989).

17 For work on the impact of the digital and new technologies on women's writing, see: N. Katherine Hayles, *My Mother Was a Computer: Digital Subjects and Literary Texts* (Chicago and London: University of Chicago Press, 2005); Hayles, 'Intermediation: The Pursuit of a Vision', *What Is Literature Now? Special issue of New Literary History*, vol. 38, no. 1 (2007), pp. 99–125; Liedeke Plate, 'Is Contemporary Women's Writing Computational? Unraveling Twenty-First Century Creativity with Penelope at her Loom', *Contemporary Women's Writing*, vol. 1, no. 1/2 (2007), pp. 45–53.

Virginia Woolf

A Room of One's Own

Let me imagine, since facts are so hard to come by, what would have happened had Shakespeare had a wonderfully gifted sister, called Judith, let us say. Shakespeare himself went, very probably – his mother was an heiress[3] – to the grammar school, where he may have learnt Latin – Ovid, Virgil and Horace – and the elements of grammar and logic. He was, it is well known, a wild boy who poached rabbits, perhaps shot a deer, and had, rather sooner than he should have done, to marry a woman in the neighbourhood, who bore him a child rather quicker than was right. That escapade sent him to seek his fortune in London. He had, it seemed, a taste for the theatre; he began by holding horses at the stage door. Very soon he got work in the theatre, became a successful actor, and lived at the hub of the universe, meeting everybody, knowing everybody, practising his art on the boards, exercising his wits in the streets, and even getting access to the palace of the queen. Meanwhile his extraordinarily gifted sister, let us suppose, remained at home. She was as adventurous, as imaginative, as agog to see the world as he was. But she was not sent to school. She had no chance of learning grammar and logic, let alone of reading Horace and Virgil. She picked up a book now and then, one of her brother's perhaps, and read a few pages. But then her parents came in and told her to mend the stockings or mind the stew and not moon about with books and papers. They would have spoken sharply but kindly, for they were substantial people who knew the conditions of life for a woman and loved their daughter – indeed, more likely than not she was the apple of her father's eye. Perhaps she scribbled some pages up in an apple loft on the sly, but was careful to hide them or set fire to them. Soon, however, before she was out of her teens, she was to be betrothed to the son of a neighbouring wool-stapler. She cried out that marriage was hateful to her, and for that she was severely beaten by her father. Then he ceased to scold her. He begged her instead not to hurt him, not to shame him in this matter of her marriage. He would give her a chain of beads or a fine petticoat, he said; and there were tears in his eyes. How could she disobey him? How could she break his heart? The force of her own gift alone drove her to it. She made up a small parcel of her belongings, let herself down by a rope one summer's night and took the road to London. She was not seventeen. The birds that sang in the hedge were not more musical than she was. She had the quickest fancy, a gift like her brother's, for the tune of words. Like him, she had a taste for the theatre. She stood at the stage door; she wanted to act, she said. Men laughed in her face. The manager – a fat, loose- lipped man – guffawed. He bellowed something about poodles dancing and women acting[4] – no woman, he said, could possibly be an actress. He hinted – you can imagine what. She could get no training in her craft. Could she even seek her dinner in a tavern or roam the streets at midnight? Yet her genius was for fiction and lusted to feed abundantly upon the lives of men and women and the study of their ways. At last – for she was very young, oddly like Shakespeare the poet in her face, with the same grey eyes and rounded brows – at last Nick Greene[5] the actor-manager took pity on her; she found herself with child by that gentleman and so – who shall measure the heat and violence of the poet's heart when caught and tangled in a woman's body? – killed herself one winter's night and lies buried at some cross-roads where the omnibuses now stop outside the Elephant and Castle.

That, more or less, is how the story would run, I think, if a woman in Shakespeare's day had had Shakespeare's genius. But for my part, I agree with the deceased bishop, if such he was – it is unthinkable that any woman in Shakespeare's day should have had Shakespeare's genius. For genius like Shakespeare's is not born among labouring, uneducated, servile people. It was not born in England among the Saxons and the Britons. It is not born today among the working classes. How, then, could it have been born among women whose work began, according to Professor Trevelyan, almost before they were out of the nursery, who were forced to it by their parents and held to it by all the power of law and custom? Yet genius of a sort must have existed among women as it must have existed among the working classes. Now and again an Emily Brontë or a Robert Burns blazes out and proves its presence. But certainly it never got itself on to paper. When, however, one reads of a witch being ducked, of a woman possessed by devils, of a wise woman selling herbs, or even of a very remarkable man who had a mother, then I think we are on the track of a lost novelist, a suppressed poet, of some mute and inglorious[6] Jane Austen, some Emily Brontë who dashed her brains out on the moor or mopped and mowed about the highways crazed with the torture that her gift had put her to. Indeed, I would venture to guess that Anon, who wrote so many poems without signing them, was often a woman. It was a woman Edward Fitzgerald,[7] I think, suggested who made the ballads and the folk-songs, crooning them to her children, beguiling her spinning with them, or the length of the winter's night.

This may be true or it may be false – who can say? – but what is true in it, so it seemed to me, reviewing the story of Shakespeare's sister as I had made it, is that any woman born with a great gift in the sixteenth century would certainly have gone crazed, shot herself, or ended her days in some lonely cottage outside the village, half witch, half wizard, feared and mocked at. For it needs little skill in psychology to be sure that a highly gifted girl who had tried to use her gift for poetry would have been so thwarted and hindered by other people, so tortured and pulled asunder by her own contrary instincts, that she must have lost her health and sanity to a certainty. No girl could have walked to London and stood at a stage door and forced her way into the presence of actor-managers without doing herself a violence and suffering an anguish which may have been irrational – for chastity may be a fetish invented by certain societies for unknown reasons – but were none the less inevitable. Chastity had then, it has even now, a religious importance in a woman's life, and has so wrapped itself round with nerves and instincts that to cut it free and bring it to the light of day demands courage of the rarest. To have lived a free life in London in the sixteenth century would have meant for a woman who was poet and playwright a nervous stress and dilemma which might well have killed her. Had she survived, whatever she had written would have been twisted and deformed, issuing from a strained and morbid imagination. And undoubtedly, I thought, looking at the shelf where there are no plays by women, her work would have gone unsigned. That refuge she would have sought certainly. It was the relic of the sense of chastity that dictated anonymity to women even so late as the nineteenth century. Currer Bell, George Eliot, George Sand,[8] all the victims of inner strife as their writings prove, sought ineffectively to veil themselves by using the name of a man. Thus they did homage to the convention, which if not implanted by the other sex was liberally encouraged by them (the chief glory of a woman is not to be talked of, said Pericles, himself a much-talked-of man), that publicity in women is detestable. Anonymity runs in their blood. The desire to be veiled still possesses them. They are not even now as concerned about the health of their fame as men are, and, speaking generally, will pass a tombstone or a signpost without feeling an irresistible desire to cut their names on it, as Alf, Bert or Chas, must do in obedience to their instinct, which murmurs if it sees a fine woman go by, or even a dog. Ce chien est à moi. And, of course, it may not be a dog, I thought, remembering Parliament Square, the Sieges Allee[9] and other avenues; it may be a piece of land or a man with curly black hair. It is one of the great advantages of being a woman that one can pass even a very fine negress without wishing to make an Englishwoman of her.

[...]

But for women, I thought, looking at the empty shelves, these difficulties were infinitely more formidable. In the first place, to have a room of her own, let alone a quiet room or a sound-proof room, was out of the question, unless her parents were exceptionally rich or very noble, even up to the beginning of the nineteenth century. Since her pin money, which depended on the good will of her father, was only enough to keep her clothed, she was debarred from such alleviations as came even to Keats or Tennyson or Carlyle, all poor men, from a walking tour, a little journey to France, from the separate lodging which, even if it were miserable enough, sheltered them from the claims and tyrannies of their families. Such material difficulties were formidable; but much worse were the immaterial. The indifference of the world which Keats and Flaubert and other men of genius have found so hard to bear was in her case not indifference but hostility. The world did not say to her as it said to them, Write if you choose; it makes no difference to me. The world said with a guffaw, Write? What's the good of your writing? Here the psychologists of Newnham and Girton might come to our help, I thought, looking again at the blank spaces on the shelves. For surely it is time that the effect of discouragement upon the mind of the artist should be measured, as I have seen a dairy company measure the effect of ordinary milk and Grade A milk upon the body of the rat. They set two rats in cages side by side, and of the two one was furtive, timid and small, and the other was glossy, bold and big. Now what food do we feed women as artists upon? I asked, remembering, I suppose, that dinner of prunes and custard. To answer that question I had only to open the evening paper and to read that Lord Birkenhead is of opinion – but really I am not going to trouble to copy out Lord Birkenhead's opinion upon the writing of women. What Dean Inge says I will leave in peace. The Harley Street specialist may be allowed to rouse the echoes of Harley Street with his vociferations without raising a hair on my head. I will quote, however, Mr Oscar Browning, because Mr Oscar Browning was a great figure in Cambridge at one time, and used to examine the students at Girton and Newnham. Mr Oscar Browning was wont to declare 'that the impression left on his mind, after looking over any set of examination papers, was that, irrespective of the marks he might give, the best woman was intellectually the inferior of the worst man.' After saying that Mr Browning went back to his rooms – and it is this sequel that endears him and makes him a human figure of some bulk and majesty – he went back to his rooms and found a stable-boy lying on the sofa – 'a mere skeleton, his cheeks were cavernous and sallow, his teeth were black, and he did not appear to have the full use of his limbs.... "That's Arthur" [said Mr Browning]. "He's a dear boy really and most high-minded." '[15] The two pictures always seem to me to complete each other. And happily in this age of biography the two pictures often do complete each other, so that we are able to interpret the opinions of great men not only by what they say, but by what they do.

But though this is possible now, such opinions coming from the lips of important people must have been formidable enough even fifty years ago. Let us suppose that a father from the highest motives did not wish his daughter to leave home and become writer, painter or scholar. 'See what Mr Oscar Browning says,' he would say; and there was not only Mr Oscar Browning; there was the *Saturday Review*; there was Mr Greg – the 'essentials of a woman's being', said Mr Greg emphatically, 'are that *they are supported by,* *and they minister to, men'*[16] – there was an enormous body of masculine opinion to the effect that nothing could be expected of women intellectually. Even if her father did not read out loud these opinions, any girl could read them for herself; and the reading, even in the nineteenth century, must have lowered her vitality, and told profoundly upon her work. There would always have been that assertion – you cannot do this, you are incapable of doing that – to protest against, to overcome. Probably for a novelist this germ is no longer of much effect; for there have been women novelists of merit. But for painters it must still have some sting in it; and for musicians, I imagine, is even now active and poisonous in the extreme. The woman composer stands where the actress stood in the time of Shakespeare. Nick Greene, I thought, remembering the story I had made about Shakespeare's sister, said that a woman acting put him in mind of a dog dancing. Johnson repeated the phrase two hundred years later of women preaching. And here, I said, opening a book about music, we have the very words used again in this year of grace, 1928, of women who try to write music. 'Of Mlle Germaine Tailleferre one can only repeat Dr Johnson's dictum concerning a woman preacher, transposed into terms of music. "Sir, a woman's composing is like a dog's walking on his hind legs. It is not done well, but you are surprised to find it done at all." '* So accurately does history repeat itself.

* *A Survey of Contemporary Music*, Cecil Gray, p. 246.

(1929)

Notes

3 *his mother was an heiress*: in the manuscript version Woolf originally named Shakespeare's sister after his mother: 'Let us call her Mary Arden', she wrote. She was an extraordinary child, born around 1564. 'Her father was a small tradesman, perhaps a butcher or a dealer in wool.' See *Women and Fiction*, p. 73.

4 *poodles dancing and women acting*: the reference here is to Samuel Johnson's much-quoted view that a woman preaching was like a dog walking on its hind legs: 'It is not done well; but you are surprised to find it done at all' (from Boswell's *Life of Samuel Johnson*, 31 July 1763).

5 *Nick Greene*: the character of Nicholas Greene, an imaginary poet and critic, had been elaborated in Orlando (1928; Penguin Books, 1993, p. 59ff).

6 *some mute and inglorious*: Woolf refers to Thomas Gray's 'Elegy Written in a Country Church-Yard' (1751) ('Some mute inglorious Milton here may rest'). There are both direct and oblique references to John Milton (1608–74) throughout *AROO*, who can be understood as representing, for Woolf, the masculine appropriation of writing.

7 *Edward Fitzgerald*: (1809–83) translator of *The Rubáiyát of Omar Khayyám* and Victorian man of letters.

8   *Currer Bell ... George Sand*: Currer Bell was Charlotte Bronte's (1816–55) pseudonym, under which her early work was published; George Eliot and George Sand were the names under which Mary Ann Evans (1819–80) and Amandine Dupin (1804–76) published.

9   *Ce chien ... the Sieges Allee*: 'This dog is mine', from Blaise Pascal's (1623–62) *Pensées*. The Siegesallee (Victory Avenue) is in Berlin.

10 *a very fine negress*: Woolf's remark is rather disturbing now. It demonstrates the rare, exoticized status of black women in England at that time, and many years were to pass before an identity of 'black British' people would be accepted. More positively, Woolf's belief that 'as a woman I have no country' (elaborated in *TG*) enables her here to recognize cultural and 'racial' differences without harnessing them to nationalistic dogmas.

[...]

15 *He's a dear boy really and most high-minded*: Oscar Browning was a Fellow of King's College, Cambridge; the reference to 'high-minded' Arthur implies a link between misogyny and homosexuality and might thus be seen as somewhat homophobic on Woolf's part. Jane Marcus has interpreted this in terms of a history in which Sir Leslie Stephen had acted to protect Browning and his nephew, J. K. Stephen, from scandal. Browning had been sacked from Eton, with an implication of sexual scandal, and J. K. Stephen was a favoured pupil there who followed him to Cambridge. Marcus reads Woolf's scorching remarks on Browning as, to some extent at least, a displacement of her anger at the patriarchalism of her father and male relatives. See Jane Marcus, *Virginia Woolf and the Languages of Patriarchy* (Indiana University Press, 1987, pp. 181ff.). Browning recorded his own *Memories of Sixty Years* (1910) and his nephew H. E. Wortham published a biography of him in 1927 (the source of Woolf's anecdote).

16 *they are supported by, and they minister to, men*: Woolf encountered this remark in Barbara Stephen's *Emily Davies and Girton College*, published in 1927. *Two Women*, her review of the book, is reprinted in *WE*, pp. 115–20.

Virginia Woolf

'Professions for Women'
The Death of the Moth

What could be easier than to write articles and to buy Persian cats with the profits? But wait a moment. Articles have to be about something. Mine, I seem to remember, was about a novel by a famous man. And while I was writing this review, I discovered that if I were going to review books I should need to do battle with a certain phantom. And the phantom was a woman, and when I came to know her better I called her after the heroine of a famous poem, The Angel in the House. It was she who used to come between me and my paper when I was writing reviews. It was she who bothered me and wasted my time and so tormented me that at last I killed her. You who come of a younger and happier generation may not have heard of her – you may not know what I mean by the Angel in the House. I will describe her as shortly as I can. She was intensely sympathetic. She was immensely charming. She was utterly unselfish. She excelled in the difficult arts of family life. She sacrificed herself daily. If there was chicken, she took the leg; if there was a draught she sat in it – in short she was so constituted that she never had a mind or a wish of her own, but preferred to sympathize always with the minds and wishes of others. Above all – I need not say it – she was pure. Her purity was supposed to be her chief beauty – her blushes, her great grace. In those days – the last of Queen Victoria – every house had its Angel. And when I came to write I encountered her with the very first words. The shadow of her wings fell on my page; I heard the rustling of her skirts in the room. Directly, that is to say, I took my pen in my hand to review that novel by a famous man, she slipped behind me and whispered: 'My dear, you are a young woman. You are writing about a book that has been written by a man. Be sympathetic; be tender; flatter; deceive; use all the arts and wiles of our sex. Never let anybody guess that you have a mind of your own. Above all, be pure.' And she made as if to guide my pen. I now record the one act for which I take some credit to myself, though the credit rightly belongs to some excellent ancestors of mine who left me a certain sum of money – shall we say five hundred pounds a year? – so that it was not necessary for me to depend solely on charm for my living. I turned upon her and caught her by the throat. I did my best to kill her. My excuse, if I were to be had up in a court of law, would be that I acted in self-defence. Had I not killed her she would have killed me. She would have plucked the heart out of my writing. For, as I found, directly I put pen to paper, you cannot review even a novel without having a mind of your own, without expressing what you think to be the truth about human relations, morality, sex. And all these questions, according to the Angel of the House, cannot be dealt with freely and openly by women; they must charm, they must conciliate, they must – to put it bluntly – tell lies if they are to succeed. Thus, whenever I felt the shadow of her wing or the radiance of her halo upon my page, I took up the inkpot and flung it at her. She died hard. Her fictitious nature was of great assistance to her. It is far harder to kill a phantom than a reality. She was always creeping back when I thought I had despatched her. Though I flatter myself that I killed her in the end, the struggle was severe; it took much time that had better have been spent upon learning Greek grammar; or in roaming the world in search of adventures. But it was a real experience; it was an experience that was found to befall all women writers at that time. Killing the Angel in the House was part of the occupation of a woman writer.

[...]

I want you to figure to yourselves a girl sitting with a pen in her hand, which for minutes, and indeed for hours, she never dips into the inkpot. The image that comes to my mind when I think of this girl is the image of a fisherman lying sunk in dreams on the verge of a deep lake with a rod held out over the water. She was letting her imagination sweep unchecked round every rock and cranny of the world that lies submerged in the depths of our unconscious being. Now came the experience, the experience that I believe to be far commoner with women writers than with men. The line raced through the girl's fingers. Her imagination had rushed away. It had sought the pools, the depths, the dark places where the largest fish slumber. And then there was a smash. There was an explosion. There was foam and confusion. The imagination had dashed itself against something hard. The girl was roused from her dream. She was indeed in a state of the most acute and difficult distress. To speak without figure she had thought of something, something about the body, about the passions which it was unfitting for her as a woman to say. Men, her reason told her, would be shocked. The consciousness of what men will say of a woman who speaks the truth about her passions had roused her from her artist's state of unconsciousness. She could write no more. The trance was over. Her imagination could work no longer. This I believe to be a very common experience with women writers – they are impeded by the extreme conventionality of the other sex. For though men sensibly allow themselves great freedom in these respects, I doubt that they realize or can control the extreme severity with which they condemn such freedom in women.

These then were two very genuine experiences of my own. These were two of the adventures of my professional life. The first – killing the Angel in the House – I think I solved. She died. But the second, telling the truth about my own experiences as a body, I do not think I solved. I doubt that any woman has solved it yet. The obstacles against her are still immensely powerful – and yet they are very difficult to define. Outwardly, what is simpler than to write books? Outwardly, what obstacles are there for a woman rather than for a man? Inwardly, I think, the case is very different; she has still many ghosts to fight, many prejudices to overcome. Indeed it will be a long time still, I think, before a woman can sit down to write a book without finding a phantom to be slain, a rock to be dashed against. And if this is so in literature, the freest of all professions for women, how is it in the new professions which you are now for the first time entering?

(1942)

Tillie Olsen

Silences

Work first:

> Within our bodies we bore the race. Through us it was shaped, fed and clothed... Labour more toilsome and unending than that of man was ours.... No work was too hard, no labour too strenuous to exclude us.[1]

True for most women in most of the world still.

Unclean; taboo. The Devil's Gateway. The three steps behind; the girl babies drowned in the river; the baby strapped to the back. Buried alive with the lord, burned alive on the funeral pyre, burned as witch at the stake. Stoned to death for adultery. Beaten, raped. Bartered. Bought and sold. Concubinage, prostitution, white slavery. The hunt, the sexual prey, 'I am a lost creature, O the poor Clarissa.' Purdah, the veil of Islam, domestic confinement. Illiterate. Denied vision. Excluded, excluded, excluded from council, ritual, activity, learning, language, when there was neither biological nor economic reason to be excluded.

Religion, when all believed. In sorrow shalt thou bring forth children. May thy wife's womb never cease from bearing. Neither was the man created for the woman but the woman for the man. Let the woman learn in silence and in all subjection. Contrary to biological birth fact: Adam's rib. The Jewish male morning prayer: thank God I was not born a woman. Silence in holy places, seated apart, or not permitted entrance at all; castration of boys because women too profane to sing in church.

And for the comparative handful of women born into the privileged class; being, not doing; man does, woman is; to you the world says work, to us it says seem. God is thy law, thou mine. Isolated. Cabin'd, cribb'd, confin'd; the private sphere. Bound feet: corseted, cosseted, bedecked; denied one's body. Powerlessness. Fear of rape, male strength. Fear of aging. Subject to. Fear of expressing capacities. Soft attractive graces; the mirror to magnify man. Marriage as property arrangement. The vices of slaves:[2] dissembling, flattering, manipulating, appeasing.

Bolstering. Vicarious living, infantilization, trivialization. Parasitism, individualism, madness. Shut up, you're only a girl. O Elizabeth, why couldn't you have been born a boy? For twentieth-century woman: roles, discontinuities, part-self, part-time; conflict; imposed 'guilt'; 'a man can give full energy to his profession, a woman cannot.'

> How is it that women have not made a fraction of the intellectual, scientific,
> or artistic-cultural contributions that men have made?

Only in the context of this punitive difference in circumstance, in history, between the sexes; this past, hidden or evident, that (though objectively obsolete – yes, even the toil and the compulsory childbearing obsolete) *continues so terribly, so determingly to live on, only in this context can the question be answered or my subject here today – the women writer in our century: one out of twelve – be understood.*

How much it takes to become a writer. Bent (far more common than we assume), circumstances, time, development of craft – but beyond that: how much conviction as to the importance of what one has to say, one's right to say it. And the will, the measureless store of belief in oneself to be able to come to, cleave to, find the form for one's own life comprehensions. Difficult for any male not born into a class that breeds such confidence. Almost impossible for a girl, a woman.

The leeching of belief, of will, the damaging of capacity begin so early. Sparse indeed is the literature on the way of denial to small girl children of the development of their endowment as born human: active, vigorous bodies; exercise of the power to do, to make, to investigate, to invent, to conquer obstacles, to resist violations of the self; to think, create, choose; to attain community, confidence in self. Little has been written on the harms of instilling constant concern with appearance; the need to please, to support; the training in acceptance, deferring. Little has been added in our century to George Eliot's *The Mill on the Floss* on the effect of the differing treatment – 'climate of expectation' – for boys and for girls.

But it is there if one knows how to read for it, and indelibly there in the resulting damage. One – out of twelve.

In the vulnerable girl years, unlike their sisters in the previous century, women writers go to college.[3] The kind of experience it may be for them is stunningly documented in Elaine Showalter's pioneering "Women and the Literary Curriculum."[4] Freshman texts in which women have little place, if at all; language itself, all achievement, anything to do with the human in male terms – *Man in Crises, The Individual and His World*. Three hundred thirteen male writers taught; seventeen women writers: That classic of adolescent rebellion, *A Portrait of the Artist as a Young Man*; and sagas (male) of the quest for identity (but then Erikson, the father of the concept, propounds that identity concerns girls only insofar as making themselves into attractive beings for the right kind of man).[5] Most, *not all*, of the predominantly male literature studied, written by men whose understandings are not universal, but restrictively male (as Mary Ellmann, Kate Millett, and Dolores Schmidt have pointed out); in our time more and more surface, hostile, one-dimensional in portraying women.

In a writer's young years, susceptibility to the vision and style of the great is extreme. Add the aspiration-denying implication, consciously felt or not (although reinforced daily by one's professors and reading) that (as Virginia Woolf noted years ago) women writers, women's experience, and literature written by women are by definition minor. (Mailer will not grant even the minor: 'the one thing a writer has to have is balls.') No wonder that Showalter observes:

> Women [students] are estranged from their own experience and unable to perceive its shape and authenticity, in part because they do not see it mirrored and given resonance in literature.... They are expected to identify with masculine experience, which is presented as the human one, and have no faith in the

validity of their own perceptions and experiences, rarely seeing them confirmed in literature, or accepted in criticism ... [They] notoriously lack the happy confidence, the exuberant sense of the value of their individual observations which enables young men to risk making fools of themselves for the sake of an idea.

Harms difficult to work through. Nevertheless, some young women (others are already lost) maintain their ardent intention to write – fed indeed by the very glories of some of this literature that puts them down.

But other invisible worms are finding out the bed of crimson joy.[6] Self-doubt; seriousness, also questioned by the hours agonizing over appearance; concentration shredded into attracting, being attractive; the absorbing real need and love for working with words felt as hypocritical self-delusion ('I'm not truly dedicated'), for what seems (and is) esteemed is being attractive to men. High aim, and accomplishment toward it, discounted by the prevalent attitude that, as girls will probably marry (attitudes not applied to boys who will probably marry), writing is no more than an attainment of a dowry to be spent later according the needs and circumstances within the true vocation: husband and family. The growing acceptance that going on will threaten other needs, to love and be loved; ('a woman has to sacrifice all claims to femininity and family to be a writer').[7]

And the agony – peculiarly mid-century, escaped by their sisters of pre-Freudian, pre-Jungian times – that 'creation and femininity are incompatible.'[8] Anaïs Nin's words.

> The aggressive act of creation; the guilt for creating. I did not want to rival man; to steal man's creation, his thunder. I must protect them, not outshine them.[9]

The acceptance – against one's experienced reality – of the sexist notion that the act of creation is not as inherently natural to a woman as to a man, but rooted instead in unnatural aggression, rivalry, envy, or thwarted sexuality.

And in all the usual college teaching – the English, history, psychology, sociology courses – little to help that young woman understand the source or nature of this inexplicable draining self-doubt, loss of aspiration, of confidence.

It is all there in the extreme in Plath's *Bell Jar* – that (inadequate)[10] portrait of the artist as young woman (significantly, one of the few that we have) – from the precarious sense of vocation to the paralyzing conviction that (in a sense different from what she wrote years later)

> Perfection is terrible. It cannot have children.
> It tamps the womb.

And indeed, in our century as in the last, until very recently almost all distinguished achievement has come from childless women: Willa Cather, Ellen Glasgow, Gertrude Stein, Edith Wharton, Virginia Woolf, Elizabeth

Bowen, Katherine Mansfield, Isak Dinesen, Katherine Anne Porter, Dorothy Richardson, Henry Handel Richardson, Susan Glaspell, Dorothy Parker, Lillian Hellman, Eudora Welty, Djuna Barnes, Anaïs Nin, Ivy Compton-Burnett, Zora Neale Hurston, Elizabeth Madox Roberts, Christina Stead, Carson McCullers, Flannery O'Connor, Jean Stafford, May Sarton, Josephine Herbst, Jessamyn West, Janet Frame, Lillian Smith, Iris Murdoch, Joyce Carol Oates, Hannah Green, Lorraine Hansberry.

Most never questioned, or at least accepted (a few sanctified) this different condition for achievement, not imposed on men writers. Few asked the fundamental human equality question regarding it that Elizabeth Mann Borghese, Thomas Mann's daughter, asked when she was eighteen and sent to a psychiatrist for help in getting over an unhappy love affair (revealing also a working ambition to become a great musician although 'women cannot be great musicians'). 'You must choose between your art and fulfillment as a woman,' the analyst told her, 'between music and family life.' 'Why?' she asked. 'Why must I choose? No one said to Toscanini or to Bach or my father that they must choose between their art and personal, family life; fulfillment as a man.... Injustice everywhere.' Not where it is free choice. But where it is forced because of the circumstances for the sex into which one is born – a choice men of the same class do not have to make in order to do their work – that is not choice, that is a coercive working of sexist oppression.[11]

(1978)

Notes

1   Olive Schreiner, *Women and Labour.*
2   Elizabeth Barrett Browning's phrase; other phrases throughout from the Bible, John Milton, Richardson's *Clarissa*, Matthew Arnold, Elizabeth Cady Stanton, Virginia Woolf, Viola Klein, Mountain Wolf Woman.
3   True almost without exception among the writers who are women in *Twentieth Century Authors* and *Contemporary Authors.*
4   *College English*, May 1971. A year later (October 1972), *College English* published an extensive report, "Freshman Textbooks," by Jean Mullens. In the 112 most used texts, she found 92.47 percent (5,795) of the selections were by men; 7.53 percent (472) by women (One Out of Twelve). Mullens deepened Showalter's insights as to the subtly undermining effect on freshman students of the texts' contents and language, as well as the minuscule proportion of women writers.
5   In keeping with his 1950s–60s thesis of a distinctly female 'biological, evolutionary need to fulfil self through serving others.'
6   O Rose thou art sick./The invisible worm,
        That flies in the night/In the howling storm:
        Has found out thy bed/Of crimson joy:
        And his dark secret love/Does thy life destroy.
                      William Blake

7   Plath. A letter when a graduate student.
8   *The Diary of Anais Nin*, Vol. III, 1939–44.
9   A statement that would have baffled Austen, the Brontës, Mrs Gaskell, Eliot, Stowe, Alcott, etc. The strictures were felt by them in other ways.
10   Inadequate, for the writer being ('muteness is sickness for me') is not portrayed. By contrast, how present she is in Plath's own *Letters Home*.
11   'Them lady poets must not marry, pal,' is how John Berryman, poet (himself oft married) expressed it. The old patriarchal injunction: 'Woman, this is man's realm. If you insist on invading it, unsex yourself – and expect the road to be made difficult.' Furthermore, this very unmarriedness and childlessness has been used to discredit women as unfulfilled, inadequate, somehow abnormal.

SANDRA M. GILBERT AND SUSAN GUBAR

The Madwoman in the Attic: The Woman Writer and the Nineteenth-Century Literary Imagination

And the lady of the house was seen only as she appeared in each room, according to the nature of the lord of the room. None saw the whole of her, none but herself. For the light which she was both her mirror and her body. None could tell the whole of her, none but herself.

Laura Riding

Alas! A woman that attempts the pen
Such an intruder on the rights of men,
Such a presumptuous Creature is esteem'd
The fault can by no virtue be redeem'd.

Anne Finch, Countess of Winchilsea

As to all that nonsense Henry and Larry talked about, the necessity of 'I am God' in order to create (I suppose they mean 'I am God. I am not a woman') ... this 'I am God,' which makes creation an act of solitude and pride, this image of God alone making sky, earth, sea, it is this image which has confused woman.

Anaïs Nin

Is a pen a metaphorical penis? Gerard Manley Hopkins seems to have thought so. In a letter to his friend R. W. Dixon in 1886 he confided a crucial feature of his theory of poetry. The artist's 'most essential quality,' he declared, is 'masterly execution, which is a kind of male gift, and especially marks off men from women, the begetting of one's thought on paper, on verse, or whatever the matter is.' In addition, he noted that 'on better consideration it strikes me that the mastery I speak of is not so much in the mind as a puberty in the life of that quality. The male quality is the creative gift.'[1] Male sexuality, in other words, is not just analogically but actually the essence of literary power. The poet's pen is in some sense (even more than figuratively) a penis.

Eccentric and obscure though he was, Hopkins was articulating a concept central to that Victorian culture of which he was in this case a representative male citizen. But of course the patriarchal notion that the writer 'fathers' his text just as God fathered the world is and has been all-pervasive in Western literary civilization, so much so that, as Edward Said has shown, the metaphor is built into the very word, *author*, with which writer, deity, and *pater familias* are identified. Said's miniature meditation on the word *authority* is worth quoting in full because it summarizes so much that is relevant here;

> *Authority* suggests to me a constellation of linked meanings: not only, as the OED tells us, 'a power to enforce obedience,' or 'a derived or delegated power,' or 'a power to influence action,' or 'a power to inspire belief,' or 'a person whose opinion is accepted': not only those, but a connection as well with *author* – that is, a person who originates or gives existence to something, a begetter, beginner, father, or ancestor, a person also who sets forth written statements. There is still another cluster of meanings: *author* is tied to the past participle *auctus* of the verb *augere*; therefore *auctor*, according to Eric Partridge, is literally an increaser and thus a founder. *Auctoritas* is production, invention, cause, in addition to meaning a right of possession. Finally, it means continuance, or a causing to continue. Taken together these meanings are all grounded in the following notions: (1) that of the power of an individual to initiate, institute, establish – in short, to begin; (2) that this power and its product are an increase over what had been there previously; (3) that the individual wielding this power controls its issue and what is derived therefrom; (4) that authority maintains the continuity of its course.[2]

In conclusion, Said, who is discussing 'The Novel as Beginning Intention,' remarks that 'All four of these [last] abstractions can be used to describe the way in which narrative fiction asserts itself psychologically and aesthetically through the technical efforts of the novelist.' But they can also, of course, be used to describe both the author and the authority of any literary text, a point Hopkins's sexual/aesthetic theory seems to have been designed to elaborate. Indeed, Said himself later observes that a convention of most literary texts is 'that the unity or integrity of the text is maintained by a series of genealogical connections: author – text, beginning-middle-end, text – meaning, reader – interpretation, and so on. *Underneath all these is the imagery of succession, of paternity, or hierarchy*' (italics ours).[3]

There is a sense in which the very notion of paternity is itself, as Stephen Dedalus puts it in *Ulysses*, a 'legal fiction,'[4] a story requiring imagination if not faith. A man cannot verify his fatherhood by either sense or reason, after all; that his child is *his* is in a sense a tale he tells himself to explain the infant's existence. Obviously, the anxiety implicit in such storytelling urgently needs not only the reassurances of male superiority that patriarchal misogyny implies, but also such compensatory fictions of the Word as those embodied in the genealogical imagery Said describes. Thus it is possible to trace the history of this compensatory, sometimes frankly stated and sometimes submerged imagery that elaborates upon what Stephen Dedalus calls the 'mystical estate' of paternity[5] through the works of many literary theoreticians besides Hopkins and Said. Defining poetry as a mirror held up to nature, the mimetic aesthetic that begins with Aristotle and descends through Sidney, Shakespeare, and Johnson implies that the poet, like a lesser God, has made or engendered an alternative, mirror-universe in which he actually seems to enclose or trap shadows of reality. Similarly, Coleridge's Romantic concept of the human 'imagination or esemplastic power' is of a virile, generative force which echoes 'the eternal act of creation in the infinite I AM,' while Ruskin's phallic-sounding 'Penetrative Imagination' is a 'possession-taking faculty' and a 'piercing ... mind's tongue' that seizes, cuts down, and gets at the root of experience in order 'to throw up what new shoots it will.'[6] In all these aesthetics the poet, like God the Father, is a paternalistic ruler of the fictive world he has created. Shelley called him a 'legislator.' Keats noted, speaking of writers, that 'the antients [*sic*] were Emperors of vast Provinces' though 'each of the moderns' is merely an 'Elector of Hanover.'[7]

In medieval philosophy, the network of connections among sexual, literary, and theological metaphors is equally complex: God the Father both engenders the cosmos and, as Ernst Robert Curtius notes, writes the Book of Nature: both tropes describe a single act of creation.[8] In addition, the Heavenly Author's ultimate eschatological power is made manifest when, as the *Liber Scriptus* of the traditional requiem mass indicates. He writes the Book of Judgment. More recently, male artists like the Earl of Rochester in the seventeenth century and Auguste Renoir in the nineteenth, have frankly defined aesthetics based on male sexual delight. 'I ... never Rhym'd, but for my Pintle's [penis's] sake,' declares Rochester's witty Timon,[9] and (according to the painter Bridget Riley) Renoir 'is supposed to have said that he painted his paintings with his prick.'[10] Clearly, both these artists believe, with Norman O. Brown, that 'the penis is the head of the body,' and they might both agree too, with John Irwin's suggestion that the relationship 'of the masculine self with the feminine-masculine work is also an autoerotic act ... a kind of creative onanism in which through the use of the phallic pen on the "pure space" of the virgin page ... the self is continually spent and wasted....'[11] No doubt it is for all these reasons, moreover, that poets have traditionally used a vocabulary derived from the patriarchal 'family romance' to describe their relations with each other. As Harold Bloom has pointed out, 'from the sons of Homer to the sons of Ben Jonson, poetic influence [has] been described as a filial relationship,' a relationship of '*sonship*.' The fierce struggle at the heart of literary history, says Bloom, is a 'battle between strong equals, father and son as mighty opposites, Laius and Oedipus at the crossroads.'[12]

Though many of these writers use the metaphor of literary paternity in different ways and for different purposes, all seem overwhelmingly to agree that a literary text is not only speech quite literally embodied, but also power mysteriously made manifest, made flesh. In patriarchal Western culture, therefore, the text's author is a father, a progenitor, a procreator, an aesthetic patriarch whose pen is an instrument of generative power like his penis. More, his pen's power, like his penis's power, is not just the ability to generate life but the power to create a posterity to which he lays claim, as, in Said's paraphrase of Partridge, 'an increaser and thus a founder.' In this respect, the pen is truly mightier than its phallic counterpart the sword, and in patriarchy more resonantly sexual. Not only does the writer respond to his muse's quasi-sexual excitation with an outpouring of the aesthetic energy Hopkins called 'the fine delight that fathers thought' – a delight poured seminally from pen to page – but as the author of an enduring text the writer engages the attention of the future in exactly the same way that a king (or father) 'owns' the homage of the present. No sword-wielding general could rule so long or possess so vast a kingdom.

Finally, that such a notion of 'ownership' or possession is embedded in the metaphor of paternity leads to yet another implication of this complex metaphor. For if the author/father is owner of his text and his reader's attention, he is also, of course, owner/possessor of the subjects of his text, that is to say of those figures, scenes, and events – those brain children – he has both incarnated in black and white and 'bound' in cloth or leather. Thus, because he is an *author*, a 'man of letters' is simultaneously, like his divine counterpart, a father, a master or ruler, and an owner: the spiritual type of a patriarch, as we understand that term in Western society.

Where does such an implicitly or explicitly patriarchal theory of literature leave literary women? If the pen is a metaphorical penis, with what organ can females generate texts? The question may seem frivolous, but as our epigraph from Anaïs Nin indicates, both the patriarchal etiology that defines a solitary Father God as the only creator of all things, and the male metaphors of literary creation that depend upon such an etiology, have long 'confused' literary women, readers and writers alike. For what if such a profoundly masculine cosmic Author is the sole legitimate model for all earthly authors? Or worse, what if the male generative power is not just the only legitimate power but the only power there is? That literary theoreticians from Aristotle to Hopkins seemed to believe that this was so no doubt prevented many women from ever 'attempting the pen' – to use Anne Finch's phrase – and caused enormous anxiety in generations of those women who were 'presumptuous' enough to dare such an attempt. Jane Austen's Anne Elliot understates the case when she decorously observes, toward the end of *Persuasion*, that 'men have had every advantage of us in telling their story. Education has been theirs in so much higher a degree; the pen has been in their hands' (II, chap. 11).[13] For, as Anne Finch's complaint suggests, the pen has been defined as not just accidentally but essentially a male 'tool,' and therefore not only inappropriate but actually alien to women. Lacking Austen's demure irony. Finch's passionate protest goes almost as far toward the center of the metaphor of literary paternity as Hopkins's letter to Canon Dixon. Not only is 'a woman that attempts the pen' an intrusive and 'presumptuous Creature,' she is absolutely unredeemable: no virtue can outweigh the 'fault' of her presumption because she has grotesquely crossed boundaries dictated by Nature:

> They tell us, we mistake our sex and way;
> Good breeding, fassion, dancing, dressing, play
> Are the accomplishments we shou'd desire;
> To write, or read, or think, or to enquire
> Wou'd cloud our beauty, and exaust our time,
> And interrupt the conquests of our prime;
> Whilst the dull mannage, of a servile house
> Is held by some, our outmost art and use.[14]

Because they are by definition male activities, this passage implies, writing, reading, and thinking are not only alien but also inimical to 'female' characteristics. One hundred years later, in a famous letter to Charlotte Brontë, Robert Southey rephrased the same notion: 'Literature is not the business of a woman's life, and it cannot be.'[15] It cannot be, the metaphor of literary paternity implies, because it is physiologically as well as sociologically impossible. If male sexuality is integrally associated with the assertive presence of literary power, female sexuality is associated with the absence of such power, with the idea – expressed by the nineteenth-century thinker Otto Weininger – that 'woman has no share in ontological reality.' As we shall see, a further implication of the paternity/creativity metaphor is the notion (implicit both in Weininger and in Southey's letter) that women exist only to be acted on by men, both as literary and as sensual objects. Again one of Anne Finch's poems explores the assumptions submerged in so many literary theories. Addressing three male poets, she exclaims.

> Happy you three! happy the Race of Men!
> Born to inform or to correct the Pen
> To proffitts pleasures freedom and command
> Whilst we beside you but as Cyphers stand
> T increase your Numbers and to swell th' account
> Of your delights which from our charms amount
> And sadly are by this distinction taught
> That since the Fall (by our seducement wrought)
> Our is the greater losse as ours the greater fault.[16]

Since Eve's daughters have fallen so much lower than Adam's sons, this passage says, *all* females are 'Cyphers' – nullities, vacancies – existing merely and punningly to increase male 'Numbers' (either poems or persons) by pleasuring either men's bodies or their minds, their penises or their pens.

In that case, however, devoid of what Richard Chase once called 'the masculine *élan*,' and implicitly rejecting even the slavish consolations of her 'femininity,' a literary woman is doubly a 'Cypher,' for she is really a 'eunuch,' to use the striking figure Germaine Greer applied to all women in patriarchal society. Thus Anthony Burgess recently declared that Jane Austen's novels fail because her writing 'lacks a strong male thrust,' and William Gass lamented that literary women 'lack that blood congested genital drive which energizes every great style.'[17] The assumptions that underlie their statements were articulated more than a century ago by the nineteenth-century editor-critic Rufus Griswold. Introducing an anthology entitled *The Female Poets of America*, Griswold outlined a theory of literary sex roles which builds upon, and clarifies, these grim implications of the metaphor of literary paternity.

> It is less easy to be assured of the genuineness of literary ability in women than in men. The moral nature of women, in its finest and richest development, partakes of some of the qualities of genius; it assumes, at least, the similitude of that which in men is the characteristic or accompaniment of the highest grade of mental inspiration. We are in danger, therefore, of mistaking for the efflorescent energy of creative intelligence, that which is only the exuberance of personal 'feelings unemployed.' ... The most exquisite susceptibility of the spirit, and the capacity to mirror in dazzling variety the effects which circumstances or surrounding minds work upon it, may be accompanied by *no power to originate, nor even, in any proper sense, to reproduce.* [Italics ours][18]

Since Griswold has actually compiled a collection of poems by women, he plainly does not believe that all women lack reproductive or generative literary power all the time. His gender-definitions imply, however, that when such creative energy appears in a woman it may be anomalous, freakish, because as a 'male' characteristic it is essentially 'unfeminine.'

The converse of these explicit and implicit definitions of 'femininity' may also be true for those who develop literary theories based upon the 'mystical estate' of fatherhood: if a woman lacks generative literary power, then a man who loses or abuses such power becomes like a eunuch – or like a woman. When the imprisoned Marquis de Sade was denied 'any use of pencil, ink, pen, and paper,' declares Roland Barthes, he was figuratively emasculated, for 'the scriptural sperm' could flow no longer, and 'without exercise, without a pen, Sade [became] *bloated*, [became] a eunuch.' Similarly, when Hopkins wanted to explain to R. W. Dixon the aesthetic consequences of a *lack* of male mastery, he seized upon an explanation which developed the implicit parallel between women and eunuchs, declaring that 'if the life' is not 'conveyed into the work and ... displayed there ... the product is one of those *hens' eggs* that are good to eat and look just like live ones but never hatch' (italics ours).[19] And when, late in his life, he tried to define his own sense of sterility, his thickening writer's block, he described himself (in the sonnet 'The Fine Delight That Fathers Thought') both as a eunuch and *as a woman*, specifically a woman deserted by male power: 'the widow of an insight lost,' surviving in a diminished 'winter world' that entirely lacks 'the roll, the rise, the carol, the creation' of male generative power, whose 'strong/Spur' is phallically 'live and lancing like the blow pipe flame.' And once again some lines from one of Anne Finch's plaintive protests against male literary hegemony seem to support Hopkins's image of the powerless and sterile woman artist. Remarking in the conclusion of her 'Introduction' to her *Poems* that women are 'to be dull/Expected and designed' she does not repudiate such expectations, but on the contrary admonishes herself, with bitter irony, to *be* dull:

> Be caution'd then my Muse, and still retir'd;
> Nor be dispis'd, aiming to be admir'd:
> Conscious of wants, still with contracted wing.
> To some few friends, and to thy sorrows sing:
> For groves of Lawrell, thou wert never meant;
> Be dark enough thy shades, and be thou there content.[20]

Cut off from generative energy, in a dark and wintry world, Finch seems to be defining herself here not only as a 'Cypher' but as 'the widow of an insight lost.'

(1979)

Notes

Epigraphs: 'In the End,' in *Chelsea* 35:96; 'The Introduction,' in *The Poems of Anne Countess of Winchilsea*, ed. Myra Reynolds (Chicago: University of Chicago Press, 1903), pp. 4–5; *The Diary of Anaïs Nin. Vol. Two. 1934–1939*, ed. Gunther Stuhlmann (New York: The Swallow Press and Harcourt, Brace, 1967), p. 233.

1 *The Correspondence of Gerard Manley Hopkins and Richard Watson Dixon*, ed. C. C. Abbott (London: Oxford University Press, 1935), p. 133.

2 Edward W. Said, *Beginnings: Intention and Method* (New York: Basic Books, 1975), p. 83.

3 Ibid., p. 162. For an analogous use of such imagery of paternity, see Gayatri Chakravorty Spivak's 'Translator's Preface' to Jacques Derrida, *Of Grammatology* (Baltimore: Johns Hopkins University Press, 1976), p. xi: 'to use one of Derrida's structural metaphors, I a preface is I the son or seed ... caused or engendered by the father (text or meaning).' Also see her discussion of Nietzsche where

she considers the 'masculine style of possession' in terms of 'the stylus, the stiletto, the spurs,' p. xxxvi.

4   James Joyce, *Ulysses* (New York: Modern Library, 1934), p. 205.

5   Ibid. The whole of this extraordinarily relevant passage develops this notion further: 'Fatherhood, in the sense of conscious begetting, is unknown to man,' Stephen notes. 'It is a mystical estate, an apostolic succession, from only begetter to only begotten. On that mystery and not on the madonna which the cunning Italian intellect flung to the mob of Europe the church is founded and founded irremovably because founded, like the world, macro- and microcosm, upon the void. Upon incertitude, upon unlikelihood. *Amor matris*, subjective and objective genitive, may be the only true thing in life. Paternity may be a legal fiction' (pp. 204–5).

6   Coleridge, *Biographia Literaria*, chapter 13. John Ruskin, *Modern Painters*, vol. 2. *The Works of John Ruskin*, ed. E. T. Cook and Alexander Wedderburn (London: George Allen, 1903), pp. 250–51. Although Virginia Woolf noted in *A Room of One's Own* that Coleridge thought 'a great mind is androgynous' she added dryly that 'Coleridge certainly did not mean ... that it is a mind that has any special sympathy with women' (*A Room of One's Own* [New York: Harcourt Brace, 1929], p. 102). Certainly the imaginative power Coleridge describes does not sound 'man-womanly' in Woolf's sense.

7   Shelley, 'A Defense of Poetry.' Keats to John Hamilton Reynolds, 3 February 1818: *The Selected Letters of John Keats*, ed. Lionel Trilling (New York: Doubleday, 1956), p. 121.

8   See E. R. Curtius, *European Literature and the Latin Middle Ages* (New York: Harper Torchbooks, 1963), pp. 305, 306. For further commentary on both Curtius's 'The Symbolism of the Book' and the 'Book of Nature' metaphor itself, see Derrida. *Of Grammatology*, pp. 15–17.

9   'Timon, A Satyr,' in *Poems by John Wilmot Earl of Rochester*, ed. Vivian de Sola Pinto (London: Routledge and Kegan Paul, 1953), p. 99.

10   Bridget Riley, 'The Hermaphrodite,' *Art and Sexual Politics*, ed. Thomas B. Hass and Elizabeth C. Baker (London: Collier Books, 1973), p. 82. Riley comments that she herself would 'interpret this remark as expressing his attitude to his work as a celebration of life.'

11   Norman O. Brown, *Love's Body* (New York: Vintage Books, 1968), p. 134.; John T. Irwin, *Doubling and Incest. Repetition and Revenge* (Baltimore: Johns Hopkins University Press, 1975), p. 163. Irwin also speaks of 'the phallic generative power of the creative imagination' (p. 159).

12   Harold Bloom, *The Anxiety of Influence* (New York: Oxford University Press, 1973), pp. 11, 26.

13   All references to *Persuasion* are to volume and chapter of the text edited by R. W. Chapman, reprinted with an introduction by David Daiches (New York: Norton, 1958).

14   Anne Finch, *Poems of Anne Countess of Winchilsea*, pp. 4–5.

15   Southey to Charlotte Brontë, March 1837. Quoted in Winifred Gérin, *Charlotte Bronte: The Evolution of Genius* (Oxford: Oxford University Press, 1967), p. 110.

16   Finch, *Poems of Anne Countess of Winchilsea*, p. 100. Otto Weininger, *Sex and Character* (London: Heinemann, 1906), p. 286. This sentence is part of an extraordinary passage in which Weininger asserts that 'women have no existence and no essence: they are not, they are nothing,' this because 'woman has no relation to the idea ... she is neither moral nor anti-moral,' but 'all existence is moral and logical existence.'

17   Richard Chase speaks of the 'masculine *élan*' throughout 'The Brontës, or Myth Domesticated,' in *Forms of Modern Fiction*, ed. William V. O'Connor (Minneapolis: University of Minnesota Press, 1948), pp. 102–13. For a discussion of the 'female eunuch' see Germaine Greer, *The Female Eunuch* (New York: McGraw Hill, 1970). See also Anthony Burgess, 'The Book Is Not For Reading,' *New York Times Book Review*, 4 December 1966, pp. 1, 74, and William Gass, on Norman Mailer's *Genius and Lust*, *New York Times Book Review*, 24 October 1976, p. 2. In this connection, finally, it is interesting (and depressing) to consider that Virginia Woolf evidently defined *herself* as 'a eunuch.' (See Noel Annan, 'Virginia Woolf Fever,' *New York Review*, 20 April 1978, p. 22.)

18   Rufus Griswold, Preface to *The Female Poets of America* (Philadelphia: Carey & Hart, 1849), p. 8.

19   Roland Barthes, *Sade/Fourier/Loyola*, trans. Richard Miller (New York: Hill & Wang, 1976), p. 182; Hopkins, *Correspondence*, p. 133.

20   Finch, *Poems of Anne Countess of Winchilsea*, p. 5.

TERRY LOVELL

'Writing Like a Woman: A Question of Politics' *The Politics of Theory*

Literary Production and Gender

The penetration of capital, and the transformation of literature into a commodity, has been limited to the stages of printing and publishing, and distribution. The first stage of literary production has been untouched either by technological transformation or by the division of labour. Unlike other forms of intellectual work, novel writing has not become institutionalised within the University. In terms of masculine/feminine poles of ideology, novel-writing is deeply ambivalent, like all categories of so-called 'creative writing'. It is paid work, work for breadwinners; and despite recurrent male complaints of female competition, it is dominated by men. Richard Altick estimates that the proportion of female to male novelists remained at about 20%, from 1800–1935.[1] Yet novel-writing is frequently seen as 'feminine' rather than 'masculine'. Even male writers can be found who make this association. John Fowles links all kinds of creativity with femininity. However, this does not mean that he considers it fit work for women. 'There are', he tells us, 'Adam-women and Eve-men; singularly few of the world's great progressive artists and thinkers, have not belonged to the latter category'.[2]

John Fowles' views are of course his own. But I believe he articulates the gender ambiguity of literary production in our culture. However, a recent massive contribution to feminist literary theory has argued the opposite case. Sandra Gilbert and Susan Gubar claim that

> In patriarchal Western culture ... the text's author is a father, a progenitor, an aesthetic patriarch whose pen is an instrument of generative power like his penis.

They back up their claim with quotations from literary men and women:

> The artist's most essential quality is masterly execution, which is a kind of male gift, and especially marks off men from women ... (Gerard Manley Hopkins, 1886)

> Literature is not the business of a woman's life, and it cannot be ... (Robert Southey, 1837)

> Jane Austen's novels fail because her writing lacks a strong male thrust, (Anthony Burgess)

> Literary women lack that blood congested genital drive which energises every great style. (William Gass)[3]

These quotations fail to establish Gilbert and Gubar's claim – in fact they cast doubt upon it. Where femininity and masculinity are strongly marked in culture and ideology, they do not have to be stridently claimed. The writers she quotes protest too much. Their over-insistence paradoxically confirms the gender-ambiguity of 'creative writing' in Western culture, rather than establishing its masculine credentials.

Perhaps this is a further reason for the greater interest which feminism as opposed to socialism has displayed for literature. Literary production has been a contested area vis-à-vis gender in a way in which it has not been for class. I want to argue that this gender ambiguity has made it easier for women and for feminists to breach literary production, but that this has created particular problems for feminist literary theory.

First, though, it is necessary to substantiate my claim that literary production *is* gender ambiguous.

i. I would hazard a guess that there is no strong association among the population at large, of creative writing with 'manliness' – quite the opposite in fact.

ii. The study of literature and languages, through the school system and at university, is heavily dominated by female students.

iii. Women gained access to novel-writing and to other forms of literary work at a time when they were excluded from virtually all other (middle-class) professions except governessing. It was, moreover, the only paid occupation in which they could hope to achieve independence and financial parity with men.[4]

iv. Novel writing is a form of domestic production. Here, home and work-place have never been separated. It is an individual and personalised form of production.

v. Fictional worlds have been largely restricted to the sphere which is conventionally and ideologically assigned to women, or for which women are assumed to have a special responsibility – that of personal relations. ... the development of the novel has been closely bound up with the social and political position of women ... there is a fundamental continuity which firmly places them in a private domestic world where emotions and personal relationships are at once the focus of moral value and the core of women's experience. In the novel women are 'prisoners' of feeling and of private life.[5]

Naturally, male writers have struggled against this taint of feminine identification. Hence the sentiments quoted above. They have often done so by denigrating their female colleagues. Women, urged to write, if they must, like ladies, were despised as inferior when they did, attacked as 'unfeminine' when, like Charlotte Brontë, they did not.[6] Certain genres have been marked off as 'lesser' forms, and ceded to women (e.g. romantic fiction). Others have been developed and colonised as vehicles of strident masculinity (the Hemingway-Miller-Mailer school attacked by Kate Millett[7]). More recently, structuralist theory applied to literature has offered a new offensive in the field of literary criticism. Showalter argues that 'The new sciences of the text ... have offered literary critics the opportunity to demonstrate that the work they do is as manly and aggressive as nuclear physics – not intuitive, expressive, feminine'.[8] Where structuralism is allied to Lacanian psychoanalytic theory, the bid to masculinise is strongest. Variants of this approach have consigned the feminine *per se* to absence, silence, incoherence, even madness. Several feminists have attempted to construct theories of feminine identity and a feminist aesthetic upon this marginal territory ceded by a phallocentric theory of language. I believe this to be a mistaken strategy, for it abandons territory which can and ought to be defended against masculine imperialism; coherence, rationality, articulateness.

(1983)

Notes

1   Richard Altick, *The English Common Reader* (Chicago, University of Chicago Press, 1957).

2   John Fowles, *The Aristos* (London, Triad Granada, 1981), p. 157.

3   Sandra M. Gilbert and Susan Gubar, *The Madwoman in the Attic: The Woman Writer and the Nineteenth-Century Literary Imagination* (New Haven, Yale University Press, 1979).

4   Elaine Showalter, *A Literature of Their Own: British Women Novelists From Brontë to Lessing* (London, Virago, 1979).

5 Patricia Stubbs, *Women and Fiction: Feminism and the Novel, 1880–1920* (London, Methuen, 1979), p. x.
6 Showalter, *A Literature of Their Own.*
7 Kate Millett, *Sexual Politics* (London, Virago, 1977).
8 Elaine Showalter, 'Towards a Feminist Poetics', *Women Writing and Writing about Women*, edited by Mary Jacobus (London, Croom Helm, 1979).

JANE SPENCER

The Rise of the Woman Novelist: From Aphra Behn to Jane Austen

Nancy Armstrong has pointed out that feminist analyses of the obstacles to female creativity in patriarchal society may leave women's actual achievements unexplained.[3] To explain why women were sometimes successful and highly acclaimed writers not only in the nineteenth-century but for over 100 years before that, we could postulate that the oppressive ideology excluding women from writing has been neither consistent nor entirely successful. In the eighteenth century we can detect the presence of a view of writing that links it to the feminine role rather than opposing the two. This, as I will show, encouraged the expansion of women's professional writing. But at the same time as encouraging women to write, this feminization of literature defined literature as a special category supposedly outside the political arena, with an influence on the world as indirect as women's was supposed to be. Women's new status as authors did not necessarily mean new powers for women in general. *The Rise of the Woman Novelist*, then, is centrally concerned with the paradox that women writers may well be rising at a time when women's condition in general is deteriorating. My view of women's novels in the eighteenth century is in one sense positive: I am claiming that they occupy a much more important place in the development of the novel than is usually believed, and that they contributed a great deal to women's entry into public discourse. But I am wary of viewing that success as a simple gain: the terms on which women writers were accepted worked in some ways to suppress feminist opposition. Women's writing is not the same thing as women's rights.

[...]

By the beginning of the eighteenth century, then, a path was open for the woman writer, but it was full of pitfalls. There were common expectations about women's writing: their main subject would be love, their main interest in their female characters. The idea that women were naturally inclined to virtue, and could exert a salutary moral influence on men, was spreading; and so was the idea that it was through women's tender feelings and their ability to stimulate tender feelings in men, that this influence operated.

Hence women writers who wished to claim a special place in literature because of their sex were constrained by the twin requirements of love and morality. The two could be mutually antagonistic. The theme of love could lead to warm, and therefore immoral writing; and on the other hand didacticism could kill romance, a danger that was to be apparent later, in some of the eighteenth-century novels. Women writers had the delicate task of balancing a 'feminine' sensitivity to love with an equally 'feminine' morality.

The women novelists of the eighteenth century inherited a role from the women dramatists of the seventeenth century, but their relationship with those professional predecessors was not always easy. The novel, even more than the pathetic tragedy, allowed for concentration on women's sensibility and women's dilemmas; but the novelists, even more than the earlier dramatists, were affected by the double requirement to delight with romantic love yet instruct according to the strictest of contemporary moral standards. As they tried to fulfil this requirement, they defined their female characters in accordance with the developing ideology of femininity, and though the terms they used changed in line with the century's increasing delicacy, their concerns were similar throughout. Women were defined by their sexuality: and so were women writers. A woman's writing and her life tended to be judged together on the same terms. The woman novelist's sexual behaviour was as much a subject for concern as her heroine's. Her main subject – female sexuality, as controlled by female chastity – was established by the early 1700s. Not only this subject matter but her attitude to it had to be carefully controlled by the ever more onerous demands of proper femininity. Male writers too, of course, were affected by the simultaneous demand for passion and morality so typical of the century: but women writers left it as a demand on their entire selves, not just on their writings.

With these drawbacks, women's empire of wit was founded. It was an empire internally divided by the contradictory demands made by bourgeois society's ideals of femininity, and its attitude to the women who had first won it was deeply ambivalent. But its achievements are worth remembering in themselves and for the legacy they left to us. For as we watch the women novelists of the eighteenth century weighing passion against prudence, sexual attachment against female independence, desire against duty, and morality against romance, we will find them building, out of the contradictions of 'femininity', an identity for themselves as writers and a female tradition in literature.

(1987)

Note

3   See Nancy Armstrong, 'The Rise of Feminine Authority in the Novel', *Novel* 15, no. 2 (Winter, 1982), pp. 127–45.

CAROL OHMANN

'Emily Brontë in the Hands of Male Critics'
College English

The pseudonyms all the Brontës chose for their joint volumes of poems and for their novels were, Charlotte reported, deliberately selected to admit of ambiguous interpretation. They did not wish to choose names avowedly masculine; they would not call themselves, for example, Charles, Edward, and Alfred. On the other hand, as Charlotte wrote afterwards, 'We did not like to declare ourselves women, because – without at that time suspecting that our mode of writing and thinking was not what is called "feminine" – we had a vague impression that authoresses are liable to be looked on with prejudice; we had noticed how critics sometimes use for their chastisement the weapon of personality, and for their reward, a flattery, which is not true praise.'[2]

Contemporary reviews of *Wuthering Heights*, all five found in Emily Brontë's writing desk and others as well, referred to Ellis Bell as 'he.' 'He' had written a book which, give or take certain differences of emphasis, was declared to be powerful and original. Although an occasional review acknowledged that it was a story of love, its essential subject was taken to be a representation of cruelty, brutality, violence, of human depravity or wickedness in its most extreme forms. Its lack of moral statement or purpose was taken to be either puzzling or censurable. It was awkwardly constructed. But, even so, in spite of the degree to which the reviewers were, variously, displeased, inclined to melancholy, shocked, pained, anguished, disgusted, and sickened, a number of them allowed the novel to be the work of a promising, possibly a great, new writer.

Most of the reviewers simply assumed without comment that the writer's sex was masculine. Two American reviewers did more: they made much of the novelist's sex and found plain evidence of it in the novel itself. Percy Edwin Whipple, in *The North American Review*, found in *Jane Eyre* the signatures of both a male and a female mind.[3] He supposed that two persons had written it, a brother and a sister. To the sister, he attributed certain 'feminine peculiarities': 'elaborate descriptions of dress'; 'the minutiae of the sickchamber'; and 'various superficial refinements of feeling in regard to the external relations of the sex.' He went on to assert, 'It is true that the noblest and best representations of female character have been produced by men; but there are niceties of thought and emotion in a woman's mind which no man can delineate, but which often escape unawares from a female writer' (356).

From the brother, Whipple derived the novel's clarity and firmness of style, all its charm, and its scenes of profanity, violence, and passion. These scenes, he was virtually certain, were written by the same hand that wrote *Wuthering Heights*. Turning to *Wuthering Heights*, Whipple concentrated on the novel's presentation of Heathcliff, whom he found quintessentially bestial, brutal, indeed monstrous. He did allot a few lines to Heathcliff in love, but without mentioning Catherine. He scored the author of *Wuthering Heights* for 'coarseness' and for being a 'spendthrift of malice and profanity' (358).

George Washington Peck, in *The American Review*, did not overtly theorize on the sex of the author of *Wuthering Heights*. He assumed it to be masculine, then elaborated on the assumption in a rush of comparisons. The novel's language might be that of a Yorkshire farmer or a boatman or of frequenters of 'bar-rooms and steamboat saloons.'[4] He cautioned young ladies against imitating it, lest American social assemblies come to resemble certain scenes in Tammany Hall. The novel's author Peck likened to a 'rough sailor [with] a powerful imagination' (573). He is like a friend of whom one is fond and yet by whom one is continually embarrassed. He is not a gentleman. He would embarrass you with his *gaucheries* whether you were walking down Broadway with him or across the fields of Staten Island or dropping into a shop or store anywhere. Among his eccentricities or faults is a disposition to believe that he understands women. But he does *not* understand them. *He* cannot see *them* as *they* are. He can only see them as he is, and then, just slightly, refine them.

There are not so many reviews of the second edition of *Wuthering Heights*. But there are enough, I think, to show that once the work of Ellis Bell was identified as the work of a woman, critical responses to it changed. Where the novel had been called again and again 'original' in 1847 and 1848, the review in the *Athenaeum* in 1850 began by firmly placing it in a familiar class, and that class was not in the central line of literature. The review in the *Athenaeum* began by categorizing *Wuthering Heights* as a work of 'female genius and female authorship.'[5] The reviewer was really not surprised to learn that *Jane Eyre* and its 'sister-novels' were all written by women. The nature of the novels themselves, together with 'instinct or divination,' had already led the reviewer to that conclusion, which was now simply confirmed by Charlotte Brontë's 'Biographical Notice.' The review quotes a great deal from the 'Notice': Charlotte's description of the isolation of Haworth, her discovery of Emily's poems, the silence that greeted their publication in *Poems by Currer, Ellis, and Acton Bell*, and the deaths of both Emily and Anne. It is on Emily Brontë's *life* that the review spends most of its 2,000 words. References to *Wuthering Heights* are late and few, and then it is grouped not only with *Jane Eyre* but also with *Agnes Grey*. All three are 'characteristic tales' – characteristic of the Bell, that is to say the Brontë, sisters and, more generally, of tales women write. A single sentence is given to *Wuthering Heights* alone: 'To those whose experience of men and manners is neither extensive nor various, the construction of a self-consistent monster is easier than the delineation of an imperfect or inconsistent reality....' The review ends there, repeating still another time its classification of the novel. *Wuthering Heights*, with its 'Biographical Notice,' is a 'more than usually interesting contribution to the history of female authorship in England.'

I don't mean to suggest that this is the first time a reviewer for the *Athenaeum* was ever condescending; the particular terms of the condescension are my point. Emily Brontë the novelist is reduced to Emily Brontë the person, whose fiction in turn is seen to be limited by the experiential limitation of the life. *Wuthering Heights* is an addition to the 'history of female authorship in England.'

There are other consequences that attend the knowledge or the presumption that Ellis Bell is not a man but a woman. Sydney Dobell published a long essay titled 'Currer Bell' in the *Palladium* three months before he could have known on Charlotte's authority that her sister had written *Wuthering Heights*. But he already 'knew' from the intrinsic nature of *Jane Eyre, Wuthering Heights, Agnes Grey*, and *The Tenant of Wildfell Hall* that they were written by women; indeed, he thought them written by the same woman.[6] Approaching *Wuthering Heights* with that conviction, he stressed the youthfulness of its author. And he likened her to a little bird fluttering its wings against the bars of its cage, only to sink at the last exhausted. Later, when it had more practice writing novels, it would fly freely into the heavens. Dobell stressed also the 'involuntary art' of the novel. (Whipple, you may remember, had said that female authors sometimes wrote well 'unawares.') Finally, Dobell saw the novel primarily as a love story, and for the first time made the heroine Catherine the major focus of interest, but only insofar as she was in love. With Heathcliff, Dobell contended, the 'authoress' was less successful.

It is clear, I hope, in these instances (and the same can be argued of other contemporary responses) that there is a considerable correlation between what readers assume or know the sex of the writer to be and what they actually see, or neglect to see, in 'his' or her work. *Wuthering Heights* is one book to Percy Edwin Whipple and George Washington Peck, who quarrel strenuously with its 'morals' and its taste, but another to the reviewer for the *Athenaeum*, who puts it calmly in its place and discourses on the life of the clergyman's daughter who wrote it. And Peck's rough sailor is born anew as Dobell's piteous birds with wings too young to fly.

(1971)

Notes

2 'Biographical Notice of Ellis and Acton Bell,' *Wuthering Heights: An Authoritative Text with Essays in Criticism*, ed. William M. Sale, Jr (New York: W. W. Norton, 1963), p. 4. All quotations from *Wuthering Heights* are taken also from this edition.
3 'Novels of the Season,' *The North American Review*, LXVII (1848), 353. K. J. Fielding identifies the reviewer in 'The Brontës and "The North

American Review": A Critic's Strange Guesses,' *Brontë Society Transactions*, XIII (1957), 14–18.

4   'Wuthering Heights,' *The American Review*, NS I (1848), 573. Additional reviews of the first edition consulted are the following: *The Athenaeum*, Dec. 25, 1847, 1324–5; *The Atlas*, XXIII (1848), 59; *Britannia*, Jan. 15, 1848; *Douglas Jerrold's Weekly Newspaper*, Jan. 15, 1848; *The Examiner*, Jan. 8, 1848, 21–2; *Godey's Magazine and Lady's Book*, XXXVII (1848), 57, *Graham's Magazine*, XXXIII (1848), 60; *Literary World*, III (1848), 243; *The New Monthly Magazine and Humourist*, LXXXII (1848), 140; *The Quarterly Review*, LXXXIV (1848), 153–85; *The Spectator*, XX (1847), 1217; *Tail's Edinburgh Magazine*, XV (1848), 138–40; *The Union Magazine*, June, 1848, 287; and an unidentified review quoted in full by Charles Simpson in *Emily Brontë* (London: Country Life, 1929). I am indebted for references to reviews of *Wuthering Heights* both to Melvin R. Watson, '*Wuthering Heights* and the Critics,' *Trollopian*, III (1949). 243–63 and to Jane Gray Nelson. 'First American Reviews of the Works of Charlotte, Emily, and Anne Brontë,' *BST*, XIV (1964), 39–44. Nelson lists one review that I have not so far seen: *Peterson's Magazine*, June, 1848.

5   *The Athenaeum*, Dec. 28, 1850. All quotations are from pp. 1368–9.

6   'Currer Bell,' *Palladium*, I (1850). Reprinted in *Life and Letters of Sydney Dobell*, ed. E. Jolly (London, 1878), I. 163–86 and in *BST*, V (1918), 210–236. Additional reviews of the second edition consulted are the following: *The Eclectic Review*, XCIII (1851), 222–7: *The Examiner*, Dec. 21, 1850, 815: *The Leader*, Dec. 28, 1850, 953: *The North American Review*, LXXXV (1857), 293–329. The last review, later than the others, appeared in response to Mrs Gaskell's *Life of Charlotte Brontë*. It implies an apology for the first *North American* review of *Wuthering Heights*. Knowing the lives of the Brontës, the 1857 reviewer finds *Wuthering Heights* peculiar, but he also finds the novel easy to dismiss – its peculiarity or strangeness mirrors the 'distorted fancy' of the writer's life, lived in isolation and deprivation. The novel lies outside normal human experience; it would be inappropriate to bring moral judgment to bear on it. Virtually the same attitude is taken by the reviewer in *The Eclectic Review*. The review in *The Leader*, by G. H. Lewes, is probably the best of the contemporary ones. Still, it would not be difficult to trace in it the operation of sexual prejudice, although the argument would, I think, take more space than I have allotted to any single review here. Charlotte Brontë was quite alert to Lewes's bias, as she revealed in a letter to him dated Nov. 1, 1849. Allan R. Brick gives excerpts from the *Leader* review and comments revealingly on Charlotte Brontë's attitude toward it and toward other early reviews in 'Lewes's Review of *Wuthering Heights*,' *NCF*, XIV (1960), 355–9.

Barbara Smith

'Toward a Black Feminist Criticism'
Conditions: Two

The role that criticism plays in making a body of literature recognizable and real hardly needs to be explained here. The necessity for non-hostile and perceptive analysis of works written by persons outside the 'mainstream' of white/male cultural rule has been proven by the Black cultural resurgence of the 1960s and '70s and by the even more recent growth of feminist literary scholarship. For books to be real and remembered they have to be talked about. For books to be understood they must be examined in such a way that the basic intentions of the writers are at least considered. Because of racism Black literature has usually been viewed as a discrete subcategory of American literature and there have been Black critics of Black literature who did much to keep it alive long before it caught the attention of whites. Before the advent of specifically feminist criticism in this decade, books by white women, on the other hand, were not clearly perceived as the cultural manifestation of an oppressed people. It took the surfacing of the second wave of the North American feminist movement to expose the fact that these works contain a stunningly accurate record of the impact of patriarchal values and practice upon the lives of women and more significantly that literature by women provides essential insights into female experience.

In speaking about the current situation of Black women writers, it is important to remember that the existence of a feminist movement was an essential pre-condition to the growth of feminist literature, criticism and women's studies, which focused at the beginning almost entirely upon investigations of literature. The fact that a parallel Black feminist movement has been much slower in evolving cannot help but have impact upon the situation of Black women writers and artists and explains in part why during this very same period we have been so ignored.

There is no political movement to give power or support to those who want to examine Black women's experience through studying our history, literature and culture. There is no political presence that demands a minimal level of consciousness and respect from those who write or talk about our lives. Finally, there is not a developed body of Black feminist political theory whose assumptions could be used in the study of Black women's art. When Black women's books are dealt with at all, it is usually in the context of Black literature which largely ignores the implications of sexual politics. When white women look at Black women's works they are of course ill-equipped to deal with the subtleties of racial politics. A Black feminist approach to literature that embodies the realization that the politics of sex as well as the politics of race and class are crucially interlocking factors in the works of Black women writers is an absolute necessity. Until a Black feminist criticism exists we will not even know what these writers mean. The citations from a variety of critics which follow prove that without a Black feminist critical perspective not only are books by Black women misunderstood, they are destroyed in the process.

Jerry H. Bryant, the *Nation's* white male reviewer of Alice Walker's *In Love & Trouble: Stories of Black Women*, wrote in 1973.

The subtitle of the collection. 'Stories of Black Women,' is probably an attempt by the publisher to exploit not only black subjects but feminine ones. There is nothing feminist about these stories, however[2]

Blackness and feminism are to his mind mutually exclusive and peripheral to the act of writing fiction. Bryant of course does not consider that Walker might have titled the work herself, nor did he apparently read the book which unequivocally reveals the author's feminist consciousness.

In *The Negro Novel in America*, a book that Black critics recognize as one of the worst examples of white racist pseudo-scholarship, Robert Bone cavalierly dismisses Ann Petry's classic, *The Street*. He perceives it to be '... a superficial social analysis' of how slums victimize their Black inhabitants.[3] He further objects that:

> It is an attempt to interpret slum life in terms of *Negro* experience, when a larger frame of reference is required. As Alain Locke has observed, '*Knock on Any Door* is superior to *The Street* because it designates class and environment, rather than mere race and environment, as its antagonist.'[4]

Neither Robert Bone nor Alain Locke, the Black male critic he cites, can recognize that *The Street* is one of the best delineations in literature of how sex, race, *and* class interact to oppress Black women.

In her review of Toni Morrison's *Sula* for the *New York Times Book Review* in 1973, putative feminist Sara Blackburn makes similarly racist comments. She writes:

> ... Toni Morrison is far too talented to remain only a marvelous recorder of the black side of provincial American life. If she is to maintain the large and serious audience she deserves, she is going to have to address a riskier contemporary reality than this beautiful but nevertheless distanced novel. *And if she does this, it seems to me that she might easily transcend that early and unintentionally limiting classification 'black woman writer' and take her place among the most serious, important and talented American novelists now working.*[5] [Italics mine.]

Recognizing Morrison's exquisite gift, Blackburn unashamedly asserts that Morrison is 'too talented' to deal with mere Black folk, particularly those double nonentities, Black women. In order to be accepted as 'serious,' 'important,' 'talented,' and 'American,' she must obviously focus her efforts upon chronicling the doings of white men.

The mishandling of Black women writers by whites is paralleled more often by their not being handled at all, particularly in feminist criticism. Although Elaine Showalter in her review essay on literary criticism for *Signs* states that: 'The best work being produced today [in feminist criticism] is exacting and cosmopolitan,' her essay is neither.[6] If it were, she would not have failed to mention a single Black or Third-World woman writer, whether 'major' or 'minor' to cite her questionable categories. That she also does not even hint that lesbian writers of any color exist renders her purported overview virtually meaningless. Showalter obviously thinks that the identities of being Black and female are mutually exclusive as this statement illustrates.

> Furthermore, there are other literary subcultures (black American novelists, for example) whose history offers a precedent for feminist scholarship to use.[7]

The idea of critics like Showalter *using* Black literature is chilling, a case of barely disguised cultural imperialism. The final insult is that she footnotes the preceding remark by pointing readers to works on Black literature by white males Robert Bone and Roger Rosenblatt!

Two recent works by white women, Ellen Moers' *Literary Women: The Great Writers* and Patricia Meyer Spacks' *The Female Imagination* evidence the same racist flaw.[8] Moers includes the names of four Black and one Puertorriqueña writer in her seventy pages of bibliographical notes and does not deal at all with Third-World women in the body of her book. Spacks refers to a comparison between Negroes (sic) and women in Mary Ellmann's *Thinking About Women* under the index entry, 'blacks, women and,' '*Black Boy* (Wright)' is the preceding entry. Nothing follows. Again there is absolutely no recognition that Black and female identity ever co-exist, specifically in a group of Black women writers. Perhaps one can assume that these women do not know who Black women writers are, that they have had little opportunity like most Americans to learn about them. Perhaps. Their ignorance seems suspiciously selective, however, particularly in the light of the dozens of truly obscure white women writers they are able to unearth. Spacks was herself employed at Wellesley College at the same time that Alice Walker was there teaching one of the first courses on Black women writers in the country.

I am not trying to encourage racist criticism of Black women writers like that of Sara Blackburn, to cite only one example. As a beginning I would at least like to see in print white women's acknowledgement of the contradictions of who and what are being left out of their research and writing.[9]

Black male critics can also *act* as if they do not know that Black women writers exist and are, of course, hampered by an inability to comprehend Black women's experience in sexual as well as racial terms. Unfortunately there are also those who are as virulently sexist in their treatment of Black women writers as their white male counterparts. Darwin Turner's discussion of Zora Neale Hurston in his *In a Minor Chord: Three Afro-American Writers and Their Search for Identity* is a frightening example of the near assassination of a great Black woman writer.[10] His descriptions of her and her work as 'artful,' 'coy,' 'irrational,' 'superficial,' and 'shallow' bear no relationship to the actual quality of her achievements. Turner is completely insensitive to the sexual political dynamics of Hurston's life and writing.

In a recent interview the notoriously misogynist writer, Ishmael Reed, comments in this way upon the low sales of his newest novel:

> ... but the book only sold 8000 copies. I don't mind giving out the figure: 8000. Maybe if I was one of those young *female* Afro-American writers that are so hot now, I'd sell more. You know, fill my books with ghetto women who can *do no wrong*.... But come on, I think I could have sold 8000 copies by myself.[11]

The politics of the situation of Black women are glaringly illuminated by this statement. Neither Reed nor his white male interviewer has the slightest compunction about attacking Black women in print. They need not fear widespread public denunciation since Reed's statement is in perfect agreement with the values of a society that hates Black people, women and Black women. Finally the two of them feel free to base their actions on the premise that Black women are powerless to alter either their political or cultural oppression.

In her introduction to 'A Bibliography of Works Written by American Black Women' Ora Williams quotes some of the reactions of her colleagues toward her efforts to do research on Black women. She writes:

> Others have reacted negatively with such statements as, 'I really don't think you are going to find very much written.' 'Have "they" written anything that is any good?' and, 'I wouldn't go overboard with this woman's lib thing.' When discussions touched on the possibility of teaching a course in which emphasis would be on the literature by Black women, one response was, 'Ha, ha. That will certainly be the most nothing course ever offered!'[12]

A remark by Alice Walker capsulizes what all the preceding examples indicate about the position of Black women writers and the reasons for the damaging criticism about them. She responds to her interviewer's question, 'Why do you think that the black woman writer has been so ignored in America? Does she have even more difficulty than the black male writer, who perhaps has just begun to gain recognition?' Walker replies:

> There are two reasons why the black woman writer is not taken as seriously as the black male writer. One is that she's a woman. Critics seem unusually ill-equipped to intelligently discuss and analyze the works of black women. Generally, they do not even make the attempt; they prefer, rather, to talk about the lives of black women writers, not about what they write. And, since black women writers are not – it would seem – very likeable – until recently they were the least willing worshippers of male supremacy – comments about them tend to be cruel.[13]

(1977)

Notes

2   Jerry H. Bryant, 'The Outskirts of a New City,' in the *Nation*, 12 November 1973, p. 502.
3   Robert Bone, *The Negro Novel in America* (Yale University Press, New Haven: orig. c. 1958), p. 180.
4   *Ibid. (Knock on Any Door* is a novel by Black writer, Willard Motley.)
5   Sara Blackburn, 'You Still Can't Go Home Again,' in the *New York Times Book Review*, 30 December 1973, p. 3.
6   Elaine Showalter, 'Review Essay: Literary Criticism,' *Signs*, Vol. 1. no. 2 (Winter, 1975), p. 460.
7   Ibid., p. 445.
8   Ellen Moers, *Literary Women: The Great Writers* (Anchor Books, Garden City. New York: 1977, orig. c. 1976).
    Patricia Meyer Spacks, *The Female Imagination* (Avon Books, New York: 1976).
9   An article by Nancy Hoffman, 'White Women, Black Women: Inventing an Adequate Pedagogy,' in *Women's Studies Newsletter*, Vol. 5, nos. 1 & 2 (Spring, 1977), pp. 21–4, gives valuable insights into how white women can approach the writing of Black women.
10 Darwin T. Turner, *in a Minor Chord: Three Afro-American Writers and Their Search for Identity* (Southern Illinois University Press, Carbondale and Edwardsville: c. 1971).
11 John Domini, 'Roots and Racism: An Interview With Ishmael Reed,' in *The Boston Phoenix*, 5 April 1977, p. 20.
12 Ora Williams, 'A Bibliography of Works Written by American Black Women' in *College Language Association Journal*, March 1972, p. 355. There is an expanded book-length version of this bibliography: *American Black Women in the Arts and Social Sciences: A Bibliographic Survey* (The Scarecrow Press, Inc., Metuchen, NJ: 1973).
13 John O'Brien, ed., *Interviews With Black Writers* (Liveright, New York: c. 1973), p. 201.

ISOBEL ARMSTRONG

'Christina Rossetti: Diary of a Feminist Reading'
Women Reading Women's Writing

To begin with, the poem does not have an overtly 'female' content. I was dissatisfied with restricting myself to poems which could be literalised as accounts of women's experience because this circumscribes and isolates women as special cases, culturally and psychologically. What was I permitted to say? It is significant that an oppressive sense of what was 'allowed' hung over me. The sort of individualist feminist criticism I knew then (Kate Millett) pointed to the ideological repression of women expressed in female texts. Barbara Hardy had shaken me by the scruff of the neck with Millett a few years before but I did not want to resolve the poem into a sexual politics of this kind. It seemed to lead me to rage and anger (though I reflect that a little of this would have been useful in confronting my earlier education). It seemed to be a 'vulgar' feminism, like vulgar Marxism. People were beginning to describe women's writing in terms of its claims to an independent tradition. Though I liked the work of Cora Kaplan and Dolores Rosenblatt I was tentative – too much so – about making these claims. Like the cruder feminist individualism it seemed to make women special cases of oppression. But if you do not take this route, how do you prevent yourself from falling into a stodgy impartiality which is not impartiality at all?

I read biography avidly, trying to find out what Christina Rossetti read. If she belonged to a network of texts one could find one's way back to a set of cultural relationships, relationships with some 'central' discourse, which did not trap her into isolation. But in trying to do this I discovered the extraordinary passionate and traumatic story of her love for William Bell Scott and his casually brutal treatment of her, which is proposed in Lorna Morse Packham's biography. I noticed that Geoffrey Grigson's review of the first volume of R. W. Crump's edition (1979) of Rossetti's work in the *Times Literary Supplement* simply ignores Packham's hypotheses. Did he know of them? He prefers a more credible account of her life which is actually more tortuously ingenious. Was I 'allowed' to deal with this agony, and if so, how? My feeling that the biography was important did not seem to match with any form I could write in.

It is interesting that the sense that I was able or 'permitted' to say some things and not others remained as some undefined coercion even in a feminist reading. I believed, and still believe, that one must talk about a politics and simultaneously about language, but how? The politics must be in the form and in the language, I decided, because that frees one to think of structures which must belong to cultural patterns. And since poetry does not simply reproduce, but creates and becomes the materials of cultural forms themselves, this reciprocity seemed promising for the way out of the impasse which makes women the passive object of a special or marginalised experience. It makes the woman poet an agent.

'Winter Rain' is conjured out of rigorous repetition and the iteration of negations. '*Every valley* drinks,/*Every dell* and *hollow*:/ Where the kind rain *sinks* and *sinks* ...'. It is one of those pastoral lyrics so familiar in English writing that the form is virtually sourceless, speaking out of an idiom so generalised that it comes from everywhere and nowhere. The voice speaks from conventions which are both hidden and obvious. One meets this simultaneous sharing and not sharing in Christina Rossetti's poetry constantly. It is a scrupulous way of marking community with and dissociation from the pastoral tradition which is after all a male preserve. The action of 'fattening' rain appears to follow a conventional course, as it irrigates the concavities of dell and hollow, bursting buds, creating a natural environment for fertility, though the pregnant solidity of 'fattening' works oddly with the diffusing nature of rain. But then comes a systematic deviation into the denial of negatives – 'But for ... But for ... no ... never ... never ... no ... no ... no ... never ... not.' Without rain the natural processes of birth and propagation would cease, the poem says in its 'simplicity'. The frightful matching sterility of land and water, which would not be water but desert, is the final negation. The simple statement of lack goes much further however, questioning expectations about the teleological necessity of recurrence and regularity. What is 'natural' when this is denied?

It seemed that much could be understood when I got to this point. If the teleological order and the 'natural' is being questioned, so implicitly is the cultural. If the 'natural' order which exists in interdependence with the teleological order turns out to be neither natural nor ordered, then a great deal has been said about the coercive force of accepted assumptions. The constant action of doubling, repetition, iteration and duplication seemed to me to create an intransigently restricting order which the poem disrupts by using the processes of order themselves. It was tempting to think in terms of Kristeva's antithesis between the semiotic and the symbolic. The subversive, semiotic freedom of 'fattening' rain, which keels over from the sheer physicality of organic growth to the idea of fattening for slaughter, is in opposition, perhaps, to the repressive abstract patterns of symbolic 'masculine' syntax and repetition. But I was not happy with this. The 'repressive' pattern, if it was that, was overwhelmingly dominant and seemed to be tested in its capacity to sustain itself by showing that it collapsed of itself. There seemed to be a play in and with pattern which made order both restricting *and enabling*. Thus the antithesis between semiotic and symbolic maintained by Kristeva was not sustained, in this poem at least.

The idea that an order could be restricting *and* enabling took me some way for I saw that one could regard the dominant Victorian poetics of expression in a parallel way that seemed both psychoanalytically and politically important. Victorian poetics (Keble is an obvious example) assumes that expression occurs when the barrier of the customary restraints of consciousness is broken. Emotion breaks out of the self into representation. But by the same token, though this is never consciously theorised, the barrier constitutes repression. Each needs, and is predicated on, the other. Though there are significant differences, this does not seem far away from Freud's account of repression as effecting a continual displacement and indeed, creation of energy. I did not wish to use Freud at that time because the two sets of theories don't converge in very important ways, but I am bolder now. We can bring the two theories together. After all, without Freud one would not conceptualise any form of repression. Victorian poetics could be seen as a paradigm for both sexual and political life. I saw that in playing so daringly with the barrier of the symbolic and in recognising the interdependence of expression and repression, Christina Rossetti was both confirming and questioning the limits of both.

Goblin Market, where the 'good' Laura smears the goblins' forbidden fruit on the face of the 'bad' Lizzie, who had been denied the fruit she once bought with a piece of herself, her own hair, took on a new meaning. That there is a market price for the glory of Lizzie's experience which is paid for with one's identity is one gross fact. But we are not asked to 'choose' between a bad and a good girl because there is in reality no *moral* opposition here. The play of desire and restriction, Lizzie and Laura, create one another and the play of opposition is enabling. But Christina Rossetti chooses to distort and intensify the opposition between Laura and Lizzie in this poem because she sees that the play of desire and repression is subjected to a fierce economic and ethical code in their world. The dripping fruit crushed against the faces of both girls, one resisting, one rejoicing, becomes both outrage and orgy, a deliberate demonstration that what is literally 'expressed' here can only be so in the context of violation, abuse, scatological fury and aggression. For a structural condition has been turned into a moral order. The morbid aspect of Victorian culture is in this poem, but, it seems to say, can these facts ever be 'neutral'?

This is something I felt I 'could' say. I took a lecture to America on the problems of full-frontal feminism and its preoccupation with content at the expense of language and form. Elaine Showalter rose in majestic disagreement. She argued that I was colluding with a central academic discourse which always assimilated women to men's concerns. I was too ready to show that Christina Rossetti was part of a dominant Victorian aesthetics of expression. I was not making claims for a feminine tradition. After along argument I said, 'But *I* want to write poetry which men will read.' 'Ah', said Elaine. She was right to feel that I had not used the sanctions of feminist criticism powerfully. But there is a problem. What can be said about Christina Rossetti ought to be relevant to Tennyson, Browning and Hopkins.

(1987)

Hélène Cixous et al.

'Conversations', *Writing Differences: Readings from the Seminar of Hélène Cixous*

Pierre Salesne: In the early days of the seminar, we worked more closely with theoretical texts. They allowed us to overcome certain obstacles, especially in relation to Freud's work. I think that at that time, it was necessary for us to work on theory to undo in ourselves a certain fantasy of mastery, deconstructing what could otherwise become law and prevent us from getting close to the text. I also think it was in relation to what was happening around us. The seminar has never been outside history. We needed to go back over certain texts in order to reply to the weight of theoretical discourse which threatened the work we were trying to do.

Mara Négron Marreo: In Puerto Rico, literature students are trained in American and European theories of textual analysis. The desire to approach the text as an object characterizes most of these theories. One does a job of dissection on the text. Once all the parts are separated, no one knows how to re-assemble them. We forget that at the beginning there was beginning, a living source. The beating heart of the text is cut open on the operating table. The pulse is silenced.

Sarah Cornell: As far as theory is concerned, we do make use of theoretical tools from the fields of literary criticism, psychoanalysis, linguistics and philosophy, but we don't attempt to reduce the texts in order to make them fit into a so-called academic method or into the fixed framework of any given ideological system. In other words, we wouldn't want to attack the text with theoretical swords and daggers. Instead of keeping the text at a distance or burying it under a discourse of mastery, I'd say we try to approach it, not only with our minds, but also with our hearts and souls, trying to hear, and then say, what the text says to us.

Hélène Cixous: The space we work in qualifies itself by the grouping together of many strangenesses. The texts we work on are strange either because of their language or because of what they say. What binds us together is our belief in the need to ensure that the essence of each strangeness is preserved.

The image this meeting of strangenesses evokes for me is one of movement. When I first encountered the texts of Clarice Lispector I remembered Celan's image of the bottle and the sea: the poem's journey to the reader. Reading Clarice, I witnessed this journey. I saw the map of the world crossed by a voice, a message.

Sometimes in the seminar I feel as if we were replying to the curse of Babel. The biblical curse was finding oneself prey to a multiplicity of languages but I see it as a blessing to be in the midst of so many languages. For languages say different things. And our multiple collectivity makes these differences – this infinite enrichment – apparent to us.

There is a passage in Blanchot where the narrator says 'I espoused him in his language'. What we try to do is to espouse a text in its language. When we translate a text, for example, we don't try to *reduce* it to French. We work to preserve the essence of each different language as it passes from one language to the other.

The work we do is a work of love, comparable to the work of love that can take place between two human beings. To understand the other, it is necessary to go in their language, to make the journey through the other's imaginary. For you are strange to me. In the effort to understand, I bring you back to me, compare you to me. I translate you in me. And what I note is your difference, your strangeness. At that moment, perhaps, through recognition of my own differences, I might perceive something of you.

This movement is like a voyage. Sometimes I have worked on countries poetically. Cambodia is an example. In my mind, I had an imaginary Cambodia composed of everything I had read. But, of course, nothing could render the actual experience of going to Cambodia which is something that passes through the body, through the senses, something which happens between Cambodia and me – my encounter with its smell, its space, the colours of its sky.

I have always thought how much I should like to be able to keep all the various stages of this journey. The pre-journey; the imaginary journey. All the preparations for the journey. The first encounter. The moment of discovery. Then everything we bring back from the encounter.

All these different stages are, in reality, the history of a text. And our reading must be a movement capable of following all the stages of this vast journey from one to the other, to me, to you.

I believe that in order to read – to translate – well, we have to undertake this journey ourselves. We have to go to the country of the text and bring back the earth of which the language is made. And every aspect is important, including the things we don't know, the things we discover.

Sarah Cornell: The etymology of 'to translate' tells us a great deal about what translation actually does. 'Translate' comes from the Latin word *translatus* which is the past participle of *transferre* meaning 'to transfer' or 'to translate'. *Ferre* also gives the idea of 'to carry'. Translation is in fact this process of transferring or carrying across. It creates a bridge from one language to another and thus opens a passageway towards the encounter of the other where he or she dwells, speaks, cries or sings in a different tongue.

Violette Santellani: As a result of participating in the seminar, reading has become a new act. Now when I read, I have the impression of slowing down, of changing down to a lower gear. I am still looking at the text as a place of potential self-discovery, but now I am able to reject earlier positions of evasion and identification to enter the body of the text. The image that comes to mind is that of a mouse exploring all the various threads of a text, examining the different colours and knots of meaning, the patterns and designs, all the dark, shadowy creases and folds.

Sarah Cornell: For me, reading is a flowing process of exchange between the reader and the text. On the one hand, reading means working with the text where the text itself is working consciously or unconsciously. On the other hand, as Hélène wrote in 'Approach to Clarice Lispector',[1] reading is 'letting oneself be read' by the text.

Reading in this way calls for the acceptance of a certain position of non-mastery in order to let oneself go towards the mystery or the unknown in the text. However, I think it's important to point out that 'non-mastery' doesn't mean a total lack of orientation nor a failure to recognize the value of modern theory.

Hélène Cixous: Everything begins with love. If we work on a text we don't love, we are automatically at the wrong distance. This happens in many institutions where, in general, one works on a text as if it were an object, using theoretical instruments. It's perfectly possible to make a machine out of the text, to treat it like a machine and be treated by it like a machine. The contemporary tendency has been to find theoretical instruments, a reading technique which has bridled the text, mastered it like a wild horse with saddle and bridle, enslaving it. I am wary of formalist approaches, those which cut up structure, which impose their systematic grid.

If I set loving the text as a condition, I also set up the possibility that there will be people who will not love some of the text we work on. Some of us won't 'bite' into certain texts, certain texts won't mean anything to us. It doesn't matter. Others amongst us will be called by them and moved to reply.

There are thirty ways into a text. Reading together in this way we bring the text into play. We take a page and everyone comes individually towards it. The text begins to radiate from these approaches. Slowly, we penetrate together to its heart.

I choose to work on the texts that 'touch' me. I use the word deliberately because I believe there is a bodily relationship between reader and text. We work very close to the text, as close to the body of the text as possible; we work phonically, listening to the text, as well as graphically and typographically.

Sometimes I look at the design, the geography of the text, as if it were a map, embodying the world. I look at its legs, its thighs, its belly, as well as its trees and rivers: an immense human and earthly cosmos. I like to work like an ant, crawling the entire length of a text and examining all its details, as well as like a bird that flies over it, or like one of Tsvetaeva's immense ears, listening to its music.

We listen to a text with numerous ears. We hear each other talking with foreign accents and we listen to the foreign accents in the text. Every text has its foreign accents, its strangenesses, and these act like signals, attracting our attention. These strangenesses are our cue. We aren't looking for the author as much as what made the author take the particular path they took, write what they wrote. We're looking for the secret of creation, the same process of creation each one of us is constantly involved with in the process of our lives. Texts are the witnesses of our proceeding. The text opens up a path which is already ours and yet not altogether ours.

(1988)

Note

1 'Approche de Clarice Lispector', *Poetique*, No. 40, Paris, Editions du Seuil, November 1979, p. 407.

MARY EAGLETON

'Mapping Contemporary Women's Fiction after Bourdieu'
Women: A Cultural Review

Between the Academy and the Marketplace
In 1992 Tim Cook surveyed the literature syllabus in thirty-six higher education institutions in the UK. In the top ten of twentieth-century novelists there was a happy, male/female equity, the five women novelists being Virginia Woolf, Angela Carter, Toni Morrison, Margaret Atwood and Alice Walker. The current situation, however, is unknown. We *do* know that contemporary women's writing is popular and widely covered. A report by the English Subject Centre, UK, in 2003 had modules in women's writing on a par with Shakespeare in terms of popularity and second only to modules on contemporary literature which, of course, include many women writers. But we have no systematic sense of *which* contemporary women writers are being taught or where they might feature within various modules. Anecdotal evidence and the uneven data from university websites or publishers' marketing departments provide some insight; this listing can provide more.

James Acheson and Sarah C. E. Ross, *The Contemporary British Novel* (Edinburgh University Press, 2005).	Angela Carter, Zadie Smith, Marina Warner, Pat Barker, A. L. Kennedy, Janice Galloway, Rose Tremain, A. S. Byatt, Jeanette Winterson
Nick Bentley (ed.), *British Fiction of the 1990s* (London: Routledge, 2005).	Beryl Bainbridge, Pat Barker, A. L. Kennedy, Jane Rogers, Zadie Smith, Jeanette Winterson

Peter Childs (ed.), *Contemporary Novelists*: British Fiction Since 1970 (London: Palgrave, 2005).	Pat Barker, Angela Carter, Zadie Smith, Jeanette Winterson
James F. English (ed.), *A Concise Companion to Contemporary British Fiction* (Oxford: Blackwell, 2006).	In the chapter, 'The Woman Writer' by Patricia Waugh – Doris Lessing, Iris Murdoch, Muriel Spark, A. S. Byatt, Angela Carter, Margaret Drabble, Anita Brookner, Fay Weldon, Jeanette Winterson (*passim*)
Dominic Head, *The Cambridge Introduction to Modern British Fiction, 1950–2000* (Cambridge University Press, 2002).	The longer references are: Angela Carter, Margaret Drabble, Nell Dunn, Iris Murdoch, Fay Weldon, Jeanette Winterson
Richard Lane, Rod Mengham, Philip Tew (eds), *Contemporary British Fiction* (Cambridge: Polity Press, 2003).	Pat Barker, Angela Carter, A. L. Kennedy, Zadie Smith, Jeanette Winterson
Rod Mengham (ed.), *An Introduction to Contemporary Fiction* (Cambridge: Polity, 1999).	Muriel Spark, Jeanette Winterson, Afro-American Women's Fiction
Jago Morrison, *Contemporary Fiction* (London: Routledge, 2003).	Maxine Hong Kingston, Toni Morrison, Angela Carter, Buchi Emecheta, Alice Walker, Jeanette Winterson

The form of the text makes its own demands. These are introductions, surveys, collections of essays, companions, guides, and the attention given to the woman writer varies. For example, in Lane et al., there is a chapter on each name; in Bentley, most of the chapters focus on an individual text; in Head, the names I have listed are the most mentioned amongst a larger sample; in English, there is a focus on women authors and feminism in one chapter but other women writers feature elsewhere. Although authors and the marketing departments of publishers often give a spin to the material by suggesting it is 'comprehensive' or 'representative', this is difficult to substantiate, both because of the somewhat serendipitous way in which, particularly, edited collections can be put together and because the authors that feature in these books are, necessarily, highly selective. Thus, the name list cannot be 'comprehensive' and, on the basis of the small sample, it is impossible to judge whether it is 'representative' or, indeed, of what it might be representative.[8] One presumes that these selections are based on what is being taught in academic modules and I suspect also that there would be a relation to the demography of the critics who write or edit these texts: when did they come into higher education; what was the state of the field at that time; how determining are their particular interests and dispositions? If we had the data – but, once more, we have not – there would be a way of tracking the relation between a writer's publications, her entrée into academic teaching and publishing, the role of the critic (as Bourdieu says) as the 'creator of the creators', a wider non-academic market of literary reading, explored in recent years through the phenomenon of the book club, and the changing currency of individual writers and forms.[9] What is certain, however, is that to be named carries value. It may increase the economic capital of the author if the academic reader decides to put a title on a module. It certainly increases symbolic capital as the status of the work as 'serious' literature is confirmed.

As with any listing, these names are suggestive. Although the titles of the volumes tend towards 'Britishness', it is the Edinburgh University Press volume that features the strongest 'Scottishness' with Janice Galloway and A. L. Kennedy but, curiously, not Muriel Spark. Where the volume title does not mention 'British', this is because of the inclusion of, primarily, American authors. 'Afro-American Women's Fiction' exists as a category in the Mengham volume in a chapter written by Maud Ellmann; Maxine Hong Kingston, Toni Morrison and Alice Walker are discussed in the Morrison volume. The trajectory of Afro-American women's writing within the UK merits study. Walker and Morrison were the key names – Maya Angelou to a somewhat lesser extent – when it began making an impact in the UK in the early 1980s. The cross-over appeal of these authors to various markets was considerable: the educated 'common reader'; the activist reader involved in feminist and/or black politics; a much wider popular market, particularly for Walker after the filming of *The Color Purple*; and, as Tim Cook's survey indicated, an academic market. Bourdieu's opposition between the autonomous and the heteronymous fails to show how, in contemporary fiction, writers may be simultaneously positioned in various sectors of the field, accumulating different capitals. Now, neither Walker nor the category 'Afro-American women's writing' has the distinction it used to have. To understand that change, one would need to look at the history of The Women's Press in the UK, which played a central role in popularising Afro-American women's writing, but also at what happened in the late 1980s and into the 1990s as new critical theories were introduced into the academy at hectic speed and feminism lost some of its currency, while interest in the postcolonial and the introduction of the category 'Black British' eclipsed African-American writing.[10] 'Black British' was a product not only of the academy, as expressed in theoretical writing, but of the changing ethnic and social relations in the UK, evidenced in official reports and government policy, and across the media.

The literary histories of Toni Morrison and Zadie Smith, the most recent inclusion on the listing, are illustrative. In terms of the UK market, Morrison has been almost the sole survivor of that Afro-American female grouping and that because she has achieved a level of distinction which, to a certain extent, inures her to the ebbs and flows of both marketing strategies and academic interests.[11] With, amongst many other awards, her endowed Chair in the Humanities at Princeton, the Pulitzer Prize in 1988, the National Humanities Medal in 2000 and, above all, the Nobel Prize for Literature in 1993, Morrison has 'shot into the stratosphere, where you circulate in radiant mists, far beyond the ken of juries' (Atwood 2005: 343).[12] It is at this level that the 'interest in disinterestedness' can produce its strongest effects. Morrison is particularly notable in occupying both the most consecrated position (Nobel Prize winner) and the most heteronymous position (three times chosen for Oprah Winfrey's book club).[13] Smith, on the other hand, is the leading female light in the category 'Black British'. She operates under the marks of 'newness', woman, ethnicity, postcolonial, multicultural and marketability. As the headline of an article in the *Observer* in January 2000 reads: 'She's young, black, British – and the first publishing sensation of the millennium.' Smith is already gathering symbolic capital with the Whitbread Prize for her first novel, *White Teeth*, her shortlisting for the Man Booker Prize and the winning of the Orange Prize in 2006 for *On Beauty*. One could interestingly compare Smith's developing profile in the US with the established profile of Morrison in the UK market but such transnational positionings are never equivalent. In Bourdieu's terms, Smith could never become the British Morrison since there is no position in the UK literary field with the equivalent cultural resonance to that held by Morrison in the US. I am thinking particularly of the effects of the cultural hegemony of the US and the exceptional historical significance of slavery. Even if such a position were available, Smith would have to have the necessary dispositions to fit that position and she would have to be not simply productive but acquiring symbolic capital over a long period.

In the listing above, Smith is the only post-millennium woman writer to receive any consecration. Sarah Waters, another likely candidate, merits only a passing mention in Bentley, Childs and English.[14] Her first two novels, *Tipping the Velvet* (1998) and *Affinity* (1999) slightly predate Smith's *White Teeth* (2000). Both published books in 2002 (Waters's *Fingersmith* and Smith's *The Autobiography Man*) and Waters's *The Night Watch* (2006) followed Smith's *On Beauty* (2005). Waters has been just as enthusiastically reviewed as Smith and has enhanced her profile with the television adaptations of *Tipping the Velvet* and *Fingersmith*. Both were listed in 2003 in *Granta*'s Best of Young British Novelists and, like Smith, Waters has won a number of literary prizes, including being shortlisted for the Man Booker and the Orange Prize in both 2002 and 2006. But, looking more closely at Smith and Waters's prize-winning begins to tell another story. Smith is also winner of the Commonwealth Writers' Prize for *White Teeth* and two EMMAs (BT Ethnic and Multicultural Media Award). She has profited from her marketing within, what Graham Huggan calls, the 'postcolonial exotic'. For a metropolitan audience, says Huggan, 'postcolonial' functions as 'a sales tag for the international commodity culture of late (twentieth-century) capitalism, while the '[e]xoticist myths and stereotypes, apparently dismantled by the writers, reappear with a vengeance in the commercial packaging of their books' (Huggan 1994: 24; 26). In Smith's case, 'multiculturalism' is the exoticist tag that has been most energetically employed. Waters, on the other hand, has been shortlisted (for *Tipping the Velvet*) and once won (for *Affinity*) the Ferro-Grumley Award for Lesbian and Gay Fiction; she has been shortlisted once and twice won the Lambda Literary Award (Lesbian, Gay, Bisexual, Transexual); she has won the Stonewall Book Award and the Somerset Maughan Award for Lesbian and Gay Fiction. We could say Waters is profiting from a 'lesbian exotic'.

In a fuller analysis, one would need to assess the cultural meanings and values that surround 'lesbian' and their difference to those surrounding 'multicultural' – for instance, in how 'multiculturalism' has political and public policy agendas attached to it which is not, to the same extent, the case with 'lesbian'. For Bourdieu, Smith's 'multicultural' designation and Waters's 'lesbian' designation would be examples of how the field is structured by the positions available in it and the dispositions of authors to take up those positions. This latter point is notable. For every writer who is happy to accept the market designation, others will resist the position but they cannot resist too far or be too resistant too early in their career – that is, before garnering significant symbolic capital – without losing their place in the field. Writers often express an uneasy negotiation between position and disposition and this links, on a wider level, to the uneasy relationship between, on the one hand, the field of cultural production and an aesthetic disposition which likes to see itself as disinterested and, on the other, the interested moves of the economic field or the field of power. One can pursue these differences endlessly: is it really significant that Smith had a full entry in Wikipedia before Waters, or that the Continuum Contemporaries *Zadie Smith's White Teeth: A Reader's Guide*, written by Claire Squires, came out within two years of the novel's publication and nothing has yet appeared on Waters; how does one understand Smith's inclusion in the OCR A-level syllabus against the absence of Waters?

(2008)

Notes

8   See Eagleton (1996) and Hemmings (2005) for further comment on the politics of inclusion and exclusion.

9   On the 'creator of the creators', see Bourdieu (1993a), pp. 76–7; (1993b), pp. 139–48; (1996), pp. 166–73. On book clubs, see Radway (1997), Hartley and Turvey (2002) and Long (2003). Radway and Long make use of the work of Bourdieu in their studies.

10 On the role The Women's Press played in the promotion of Afro-American women's writing, see Murray (2004).

11 Maya Angelou, though now largely absent from university curricula, has continued as a writer on the English GCSE syllabus though, as government ministers once again re-vamp the syllabus, this is now in doubt. Alice Walker's presence in university curricula is, again, much reduced.

12 Atwood is actually speaking here, defensively, with respect to Alice Munro and Carol Shields.

13 Jonathan Franzen was chosen for Oprah's Book Club for *The Corrections* (2001), expressed reservations and was then dropped. The ensuing media coverage and his defence of his comments is another example of the intensity of struggles over cultural and symbolic capital.

14 Though not included in my listing, it is Waters, rather than Smith, who is entered in Renison (2005). This bio/bibliographical reference book covers fifty contemporary writers. In his Preface, Smith and Waters are mentioned together, Waters included because she has published three novels by the time of Renison's cut-off date, Smith mentioned as likely to be included in any future edition.

CLAIRE SQUIRES

Marketing Literature: The Making of Contemporary Writing in Britain

Primed as 'India's Next Big Thing' (as the *Independent* put it), Roy and her novel were also mentioned in several previews in the press at the turn of 1996 and 1997.[76] The opening of the novel was extracted in Granta's *India!* issue of Spring 1997, alongside writings by R. K. Narayan, Amit Chaudhuri and Vikram Seth.[77] Major review attention followed, which in terms of allotted space was not hindered by Roy's 'heart-breaking [...] beaut[y]' (*Sunday Times*) – her photograph made numerous appearances in the newspapers.[78] Although the praise was not unanimous, it was substantial, as the profusion of acclaim reprinted on the paperback edition of the novel makes evident.

With the short-listing and eventual award of the Booker in the autumn of 1997, *The God of Small Things*' miraculous few months reached their climax. Roy had accomplished in just over a year what most writers can only dream of achieving in a career: hundreds of thousands of pounds in advances from global rights sales; worldwide publicity; and the award of the Commonwealth's most prestigious and high-profile prize. In Roy's home country of India, *The God of Small Things* was not only successful in itself but also a stimulus to opening the market, as described by Peter Popham in the *Independent on Sunday* in 1999:

Picador, whose parent company Macmillan has been in India for nearly 150 years, woke up to the fact that suddenly a large number of Indians were buying books [...] When Seth's *A Suitable Boy* was published in India, it sold only

7000 copies in hardback. 'If it was published now,' says [Peter] Straus, 'it would sell a lot more than that. Arundhati Roy's book has given a new confidence to Indian publishers about the size of their market.' [...]

    The God of Small Things has altered the landscape, coaxed many more people into shelling out for a literary novel, and opened up new selling channels; Arundhati Roy herself tells of being approached in her car at a traffic light by a hawker offering paper tissues, women's monthly magazines, and a bootleg copy of *The God of Small Things*. (She bought it.) But the problem in India is always the same: infrastructure.[79]

An unmitigated, worldwide success, give or take the perils of piracy and the problem of infrastructure? Every fairytale has its dark side, though, and *The God of Small Things* is no exception. The award of the Booker Prize is habitually greeted with derision from some quarters – scandal being integral to the Prize, as English argues in his work on literary prizes.[80] In 1998 Ian McEwan should have been Beryl Bainbridge. In 1996 Pat Barker should have been Salman Rushdie. In 1995 Graham Swift should have thought up his own plot, rather than borrowing William Faulkner's, just as Yann Martel in 2002 wrote a book a little too similar to one by the Brazilian author Moacyr Scliar. In 1994 James Kelman should have written in polite English rather than obscene Scots. (To refer to only a few of the Booker scandals of the 1990s.) And so the litany of complaint extends to Roy. In the televised post-award coverage the publisher Carmen Callil, who had chaired the previous year's panel, said that, ' "I disliked the book so much. It has got a vulgarity about it that embarrasses me. The writing is execrable." '[81] Even before the final decision, one anonymous 'observer' reported in *The Times* dismissed Roy's selection as ' "compensation for them not putting Vikram Seth on the list last time" '.[82] This commentary heightened the 'subcontinental' references, as did several of the other positive and negative remarks and reviews. In a largely generous and thoughtful piece in the *London Review of Books*, Michael Gorra stated that Roy's style had been 'pawed by Rushdie's', like 'other Indian authors'.[83] Peter Kemp in the *Sunday Times* saw it as 'considerably derivative from Salman Rushdie [...] this is magic realism as recycled candyfloss'.[84] Adverse comparisons, overlaid with a whiff of plagiarism, were drawn between *Midnight's Children's* depictions of a pickle factory and *The God of Small Things'* scenes set in 'Paradise Pickles & Preserves'. Valentine Cunningham's *Prospect* article, 'Manufacturing a Masterpiece', whose title more than hints at its cynical take on the novel, was an example of such negative comparison.[85]

    Even before the award of the Booker, Roy commented to the *Sunday Times* that ' "People's response to my book is refracted through adulation or hostility" '.[86] Her remark was a telling one. Much criticism of the text grew from comparative analyses: to the size of her advance; to her origins; to her beauty; to other Indian writers. Some reviews were favourable in their comparisons, some detracted, but the majority conformed to this pattern. The reception in

India, however, had a different frame of reference. For, as Peter Popham wrote in an earlier *Independent on Sunday* article, Roy 'discovered that success in the West is an ambiguous commodity at home'.[87] The particular cause of offence was Roy's portrayal of a sexual relationship between an Untouchable man and a Syrian Christian woman. According to Simon Barnes in *The Times*, 'Roy's book, adored over here and part of the continuing love affair with the Indian novel, is inevitably the subject of an obscenity suit in India. The fact that this concerns a passage about caste taboo will only inflame the passions higher; Indian hostility, English fascination.'[88] Barnes's delineation of the reaction as 'Indian hostility, English fascination', for all its simplification of complex cultural issues, uses a similar terminology to that employed by Roy: the reading refracted either through adulation or hostility. Blake Morrison's review of the novel in the *Independent on Sunday* exemplifies the adulatory reading in his depiction of the peculiarly British fascination with Indian literature:

> The British traditionally look to Indian novels to provide something exotic yet familiar, and *The God of Small Things*, which features a family of larger-than-life Anglophiles 'trapped outside their own history', doesn't disappoint. The landscape is so lush, so teeming with insect and reptile life [...] so palpably there, that it's likely the novel will do for Kerala's already burgeoning tourist industry what John Berendts's *Midnight in the Garden of Good and Evil* has done for Savannah's.[89]

Morrison suggests that British readings give a holiday-maker's view of a country and its culture, rendering it 'exotic'. This is appreciation as literary tourism – or cultural voyeurism. Jackie Wullschlager, previewing forthcoming novels in the *Financial Times* in January 1998, notes the trend for 'the new genre of sexy eastern novels, written by young Indian and Chinese women with a talent for lush prose, whom every publisher in England has been chasing since the success last year of Arundhati Roy's *The God of Small Things*'.[90] The conjunction of desire and orientalism that Wullschlager comments on is an extreme example, but it is not untypical of the ideology behind more subtle representations.

This conjunction is bound up with the issue of mimesis. As Amit Chaudhuri argued in his 1999 *Times Literary Supplement* article, 'The Lure of the Hybrid', the prevalent Western mode of reception of Indian writing, although frequently celebrating postmodern traits of the polyvocal and the fantastic, or magic realist, paradoxically becomes 'a surprisingly old-fashioned and mimetic ['interpretive aesthetic']: Indian life is plural, garrulous, rambling, lacking a fixed centre, and the Indian novel must be the same'.[91] The tendency is thus, according to Chaudhuri, 'To celebrate Indian writing simply as overblown, fantastic, lush and non-linear'.[92] This is a critical act that 'risk[s] making it a figure for the subconscious, and to imply that what is ordinarily called thinking is alien to the Indian tradition – surely an old colonial prejudice.'[93] It is no doubt this school of criticism that some of

Roy's reviewers fall prey to, and subsuming her work into what Chaudhuri sees as an 'old-fashioned' and prejudiced 'interpretive aesthetic'. This is the 'postcolonial exotic' that Graham Huggan identifies as the representational process that 'market[s] the margins'.[94] This instance of marketing by ethnicity is thus not only symptomatic of the publicity machine of contemporary UK publishing, but also the interpretive parameters that it both nourishes and feeds upon.

The example of *The God of Small Things*, then, offers some salutary lessons in the understanding of marketing's construction of literature. In his essay arguing against Anglo-centric constructions of literature, '"Commonwealth Literature" Does Not Exist' (1983), Rushdie writes:

> One of the rules, one of the ideas on which the edifice rests, is that literature is an expression of nationality. What Commonwealth literature finds interesting in Patrick White is his Australianness; in Doris Lessing, her Africanness; in V. S. Naipaul, his West Indianness [...][95]

Literature as the expression of nationality, nationality as the emphasis of marketing: the relationship of author, ethnicity and text thus takes on a curious form. It works by metonymy, each entity eliding the others. The acquisition of the novel is a 'subcontinental gamble', Roy a 'female Vikram Seth', even a 'Goddess of Small Things'.[96] Beautiful, exotic author. Sultry Keralan landscape. Lush, descriptive prose. This jumble of constructions is indicative of marketing's parasitic processes. To be sure, it does Roy's career no disservice, providing plenty of hooks to hang media interest on and so to reel in consumers. The impact on the author, though, 'bewilder[ed] at the frenzied reception' as MacDonald put it in the *Independent*, with her book and herself manipulated into exotic icons, is a side-effect that could cause more distress, though it could also be argued that Roy is complicit in the processes of marketing.

(2007)

Notes

76 Boyd Tonkin, 'Preface to 1997', *Independent*, 28 December 1996, 4 (The Long Weekend section). Jackie Wullschlager's 'Hedonism – and Feminism', *Financial Times*, 28 December 1996, xiv (Weekend section) was another preview mentioning Roy's book.

77 Arundhati Roy, 'Things Can Change in a Day', *Granta 57: India*, Spring 1997, 257–88.

78 Harvey Porlock, 'Critical List', *Sunday Times*, 29 June 1997, 2 (Books section).

79 Peter Popham, 'Rushdie Started It. And It Won't Stop', *Independent on Sunday*, 7 February 1999, 4 (Culture section). Later in the same year Tarun J. Tejpal's

article 'New Gold-Rush in the East' in the *Guardian*, 14 August 1999, 3 (Saturday Review section), similarly suggests *The God of Small Things*' place in the altering landscape from the point of view of the Indian publisher of the novel.

80   English writes that 'The Booker's chief administrator, Martin [sic] Goff, who should be regarded as a major figure in the history of prizes, was fully and actively complicit in exploiting the association of the Booker with scandal, wagering that the prize stood to reap the greatest symbolic profit precisely from its status as a kind of cultural embarrassment' ('Winning the Culture Game', 115).

81   Damian Whitworth and Erica Wagner, 'Booker Prize Goes to Debut Novelist', *The Times*, 15 October 1997, 1 (main section).

82   Dalya Alberge, 'Literary Recluse Faces Booker Shortlist Limelight', *The Times*, 16 September 1997, 1 (main section).

83   Michael Gorra, 'Living in the Aftermath', *London Review of Books*, 19 June 1997, 22.

84   Peter Kemp, 'Losing the Plot', *Sunday Times*, 21 September 1997, 3 (Books section).

85   Valentine Cunningham, 'Manufacturing a Masterpiece', *Prospect*, December 1998, 56–8.

86   Jan McGirk, 'Indian Literary Star Faces Caste Sex Trial', *Sunday Times*, 29 June 1997, 19 (main section).

87   Peter Popham, 'Under Fire, but India is in my Blood', *Independent on Sunday*, 21 September 1997, 17 (main section).

88   Simon Barnes, 'Passage to the India in All of Us', *The Times*, 18 October 1997, 22 (main section).

89   Blake Morrison, 'The Country Where Worst Things Happen', *Independent on Sunday*, 1 June 1997, 33 (The Sunday Review section).

90   Jackie Wullschlager, 'Prose Full of Promise', *Financial Times*, 3 January 1998, v (Weekend section).

91   Amit Chaudhuri, 'Lure of the Hybrid', *Times Literary Supplement*, 3 September 1999, 5–6, 5.

92   Chaudhuri, 'Lure of the Hybrid', 5.

93   Chaudhuri, 'Lure of the Hybrid', 6.

94   Graham Huggan, *The Postcolonial Exotic*.

95   Salman Rushdie, ' "Commonwealth Literature" Does Not Exist', in *Imaginary Homelands: Essays and Criticism 1981–1991* (London: Granta, 1991), 61–70, 66.

96   Cowley, 'Goddess of Small Things', 16.

GRAHAM HUGGAN

The Postcolonial Exotic: Marketing the Margins

Nettlebeck's focus on the reception of Aboriginal literature by white Australians leads her to overlook the international market appeal of Aboriginal works such as, most notably, Sally Morgan's *My Place* (1987).

My Place, by any accounts a massively successful international bestseller with close to half a million copies sold in the decade since its publication, has taken on the status of a foundation text with a 'touchstone effect' for Aboriginal literature not dissimilar from that exercised for Indian writing in English by Rushdie's *Midnight's Children* (see Chapter 2). Thus, it comes as no surprise to find an authorising comment from Morgan on the back cover of *When the Pelican Laughed*, which helps situate Nannup's narrative within a tradition of embattled Aboriginal women's life-stories: 'Alice Nannup courageously tells us exactly what it was like to grow up as a black woman in Australia, and through her book she has passed on a precious heritage. There are many unsung heroines in Black Australia and Alice is one of them.' The blurb is interesting for its insistence on the unimpeachable authenticity of oral testimony ('Alice Nannup ... tells us *exactly* what it was like to grow up as a black woman in Australia'), offering an unambiguous reading cue that appears at odds with other paratextual indicators – and with the main body of the text itself. As in *Don't Take Your Love to Town*, the most striking aspect of the paratextual material is its superabundance: Morgan's eulogy is also reproduced on the inside leaf, along with an endorsement by another 'foundational' Aboriginal writer, the playwright Jack Davis; the narrative is framed by an explanatory introduction, which provides the editors' rationale for transcribing Nannup's story, and a brief postscript, which rationalises it further by inserting it into a memorial testimony of 'collective loss' (Nannup 1992: 225); and Nannup's biography is repeated twice, both on the inside cover outline and on the next page, where it stands alongside brief biographical blurbs for her two editors, Lauren Marsh and Stephen Kinnane (himself Aboriginal). (These latter also flank her in a group, 'happy-family' photograph at the top of the page, for which the blurbs serve as complementary captions.) The effect of paratextual excess is not just, as Waring claims, to reconfirm the heterogeneity of the book's reception by sending out a series of cues for interpretation by readers of different cultural backgrounds and competencies; it also works to relativise the truth-claims made on behalf of the main narrative, which emerges nonetheless as the central, though by no means overriding or unequivocal, authorising source.

If Morgan's endorsement is a significant feature in the multiple authorisation of Nannup's narrative, her own life-story is legitimised in its turn by a front-cover tribute from the African American writer Alice Walker. The choice of Walker, a writer best known for her marketable combination of ethereal mysticism and political activism, indicates an attempt both to reach out to politically conscious 'mid-Atlantic' readers (Waring 1995) and to assimilate Morgan's narrative to a transnational New Age parable of personal healing and spiritual awakening. The half-amazed tone and dreamy diction of Walker's blurb certainly suggest this, as she praises a book that is 'sad and wise, and funny'; a book that is 'unbelievably and unexpectedly [*sic*] moving'; a book, above all, 'with heart'. (It is interesting to reflect here on a phenomenon we might uncharitably call 'interethnic endorsement' – African Americans being called upon to legitimise works written by Australian Aboriginals, a minority group with an entirely different culture located on the other side of the world. Interethnic endorsement emerges as the paratextual by-product of a market-model of authenticity, one of whose effects – as already mentioned – is to posit the interchangeability of 'exotic' cultures and cultural goods.)[17] Not that other contributors are to be out-done; for a whole range of hyperbolic tributes are accumulated on the book's inside pages, drawing on as many American as Australian sources, and including such luminary publications as the *Staten Island Advance* and the *Rocky Mountain News*. This bestseller format, clearly designed to appeal to 'ordinary', mass-market readers ('a book for everyone', *New York Times Book Review*) as well as more sophisticated, academically minded ones ('[Morgan] writes well, with the art which conceals art, so that a series of narratives becomes a complex exploration of the meaning of the past', *Westerly*), complements a text which persists in being read in comfortable, unchallenging terms (Muecke 1988: 409). Yet even here, where the ideological mismatch between text and paratext seems so con-spicuous, the possibility remains to read the paratextual material in differ-ent, potentially conflicting, ways. Thus, adjoined to a text whose simple title belies its often painful charting of successive displacements is a body of explanatory/descriptive citation that is itself highly mobile, fractured, assembled in a series of disparate fragments. This paratextual machinery operates according to what we might call, loosely following Derrida, the logic of the supplement.[18] On the inner-leaf page, for example, we find the following sequence of non-identical declarative statements: 'What started out as a tentative search for information about her family turned into an overwhelming emotional and spiritual pilgrimage'/'[A] fascinating story unfolds – a mystery of identity, complete with clues and suggested solutions'/'Sally Morgan's *My Place* is a deeply moving account of a search for the truth, into which a whole family is gradually drawn'/'*My Place* is a powerful autobiography of three generations, by a writer with the gift for language of a born story-teller.' Once again, as with Langford's narrative, a sense of interpretive indeterminacy prevails over the attempt to pin down a text that refuses to respect generic rules. And once again, the various para-textual cues and clues offered up to Morgan's prospective readers carefully elide issues of race and racism – as if the universal language of affect ('over-whelming emotion', 'deeply moving account', etc.) were sufficient to con-firm a *shared* narrative of human(ist) concern. The illusion of identification with the embattled cultural other confirms the authenticity of the reading experience for the liberally minded 'market reader'; and yet this same

gesture paradoxically robs the text of the authenticating markers of inerad-
icable difference on which its validity, and potential commercial success, as
an 'Aboriginal text' would otherwise be most likely to depend. In this context, ironically enough, *My Place* raises the unanswered, possibly unan-
swerable question of where authenticity is *located*. Is authenticity situated
in the specificities of individual experience, or is it rather to be found in the
potential for shared humanity and collective knowledge? Is authenticity
located in a deep-seated understanding of the material conditions of cultural existence, or is it limited instead to a superficial appreciation for cultural phenomena purposefully dislodged from their everyday material
context? Does authenticity convey the illusion of unmediated access to
other people's life-experiences, or is it better seen as the symbolic representation of what is felt to be missing from one's own – the simulacrum of loss,
the manufactured nostalgic moment?

These alternatives suggest that the discourse of (cultural) authenticity is
deeply riven, and that the identitary concerns and anxieties it displays are
inextricably linked to differential relations of power. Hence the use of
authenticity as an empowering political strategy for disadvantaged minority
communities, even as its use by dominating cultures acts as a constraint on
those communities' political power. Hence the fear, as well, on the part of
several Aboriginal writers that the expansionist imperatives of multinational
publishing, allied to the no less powerfully appropriative impulses of national
projects of revisionist self-reckoning, might have the effect of assimilating
their work into some vast collective enterprise – one in which the appearance of co-operation masks continuing tensions and imbalances in the social
structure, and the fluid myth of Native authenticity continues to be deployed
as a resource for other people's needs and ends (Nettlebeck 1997; see also
Goldie 1989).

(2001)

Notes

17   Interethnic endorsement is consolidated in the 1990 First Arcade edition of *My
     Place*, obviously packaged for an American audience, by a cover reference to
     the text as 'The Australian *Roots*'. The cover photograph, meanwhile, features
     the touristic icon of Aboriginal spirituality – Uluru/Ayers Rock – thereby facili-
     tating the insertion of the text into a New Age context reaffirmed by Walker's
     sententious blurb.
18   For Derrida (if I may simplify), the text's lack of an overarching meaning – a
     'transcendental signified' – is compensated for by a surplus of signifiers; it is
     this surplus, whereby the final meaning of the text is forever deferred, that
     conveys the logic of the supplement. See Spivak's introduction to her transla-
     tion of Derrida's *Of Grammatology* (1974) for a lucid explanation of the
     supplement.

Paula McDowell

The Women of Grub Street: Press, Politics, and Gender in the London Literary Marketplace 1678–1730

In early modern England, the nature and extent of a woman's involvement in a given trade depended less on the trade's physical demands than on whether or not it could be carried on within the home. Home workshops made it possible for women to move back and forth between different kinds of 'domestic' labour, and allowed even women aspiring to genteel social status to do economically important labour still within domestic space. John Dunton praised Mrs Green, a printer's wife in Boston, for her versatility in moving from one type of labour to another – first and most visibly from her job as dutiful wife and mother, and second and more quietly to her duties as unofficial partner in the family business:

> Mrs. Green was not only a loving, faithful, and an obedient Wife, but an industrious Wife too; managing that part of his [Mr Green's] business which he had deputed to her, with so much application and dexterity as if she had never come into the House; and yet so managed her House as if she had never gone into the Warehouse.[2]

Home workshops gave women like Mrs Green crucial access to training, account books, and customers. While only a small proportion of women in the London book trade were ever formally apprenticed, any woman whose family allowed it could acquire skills, training, customers, and credit by watching, assisting, and sometimes taking over for relatives. While most women printers, booksellers, and binders in this period were in fact related to male or sometimes female members of the Stationers' Company, any woman could theoretically be admitted to the freedom of the Company in her own right by apprenticeship, patrimony, or redemption (purchase). The first woman to be formally apprenticed to the Company was Joanna Nye, daughter of an Essex parson, to Thomas Minshall, engraver, in 1666, and between 1666 and 1800 108 women were formally apprenticed to members of the stationery trades.[3]

It was fairly common for daughters to be trained in their parents' trade to carry on in the business after their death. The most important example of a woman admitted to the Stationers' Company by patrimony in this period was the Quaker printer Tace Sowle. The daughter of Andrew and Jane Sowle, Tace was made free of the Stationers' Company shortly after her father's death in 1695. Assisted by her mother and later her husband and then a foreman, she continued to manage the Sowle press for another fifty-four years. In a career spanning over half a century, she would become arguably the most important nonconformist printer of her generation.[4]

In 1705, John Dunton described Tace Sowle as

> both a Printer as well as a Bookseller, and the Daughter of one; and under-
> stands her Trade very well, being a good Compositor herself. Her love and
> piety to her aged Mother is eminently remarkable; even to that degree, that she
> keeps herself unmarried for this reason (as I have been informed) that it may
> not be out of her power to let her Mother have always the chief command of
> her house. (*Life and Errors*, i. 222–3)

Tace Sowle did in fact marry the following year, but she nevertheless ensured
that it would still 'not be out of her power to let her Mother have always the
chief command of her house'. Seventy-five-year-old Jane Sowle became the
nominal head of the Sowle press the same year that her daughter was married. Imprints after this date read 'J. Sowle', and for the next thirty years
Tace Sowle's own name disappears.

Perhaps because she sensed the commercial value of an established name,
Tace Sowle never gave up her name for that of her husband Thomas Raylton,
but instead used the unusual compound 'Tace Sowle Raylton'. (Family pride
may have played a role here also.) Thomas Raylton was not a member of the
Stationers' Company, and there is no evidence that he ever had anything to do
with the actual production of printed works in his wife's printing house. Unlike
his new wife and mother-in-law, Raylton had no training or experience as a
printer. His apprenticeship was as a blacksmith, and at the time of his marriage into the Sowle business he was working as a hosier. Records do show
that Raylton helped with warehousing and accounting, and with dealing with
distributors (customarily the wife's job in male-headed printing households).
But records also show that Tace Sowle Raylton continued to oversee the
production of publications as she had done for sixteen years before she was
married, and as she would continue to do for another twenty-six years after
she was widowed. When Tace's mother died in 1711 at the age of 80, imprints
began showing 'assigns of J. Sowle' – that is, Tace Sowle Raylton. Thomas
Raylton died in 1723 after a long illness, but Tace Sowle Raylton did not take
on a foreman for another thirteen years. In 1736, she finally began employing
Luke Hinde, a relative, as a foreman, and thirty years after her name disappeared from her own imprints it suddenly begins to reappear. Imprints begin
showing 'T. Sowle Raylton and Luke Hinde' until Tace's own death another
thirteen years later at 83 years of age.

While women running businesses are commonly assumed by modern historians to have been widows, the example of Tace and Jane Sowle will suggest
that it was not impossible for women to be the legal and/or practical heads of
family businesses even while a male relative was alive. As we will see in Chapter
2, women whose male relatives came into conflict with the law routinely managed family businesses while their husbands or brothers were in prison or in

hiding. One exceptional woman printer, Jane Bradford, was accused of keeping her husband a prisoner in his own home. A government press spy described
Bradford as 'the chief Orderer and Director in everything she undertakes,
keeping her Husband, as a Prisoner, to protect her in ill Practices'.[5]

Bookseller-author John Dunton says a great deal about women in the
book trade in his *Life and Errors*, and reveals the centrality of his own wife
to his bookselling business. Although Dunton repeatedly stressed his wife's
'obedience', it is clear that Elizabeth Annesley Dunton had far more power
in the family business than one or both of them cared to let on. 'Dear Iris',
Dunton confessed, 'gave an early specimen of her prudence and diligence', and
'commenced Bookseller, Cash-keeper, managed all my Affairs for me, and
left me entirely to my rambling and scribbling humours' (i. 79). Never fond
of 'haggling behind a shop-board', Dunton left such drudgery to his wife,
and set off for several journeys which took him out of London and even to
North America for lengthy periods. Coming home after one extended
absence, Dunton discovered that Iris had, as he put it, accomplished more in
his warehouse in a month than he could have done in a year. This only made
him feel comfortable departing once again – this time for more than a year.
'Plainly Mrs. Dunton had a finer head for business than her husband,'
Dunton's biographer concludes.[6] Dunton would have been the first to agree,
though he would also insist that it was he who 'always kept an eye over the
main chance' (i. 79). Dunton's successes were Elizabeth Annesley's. After
her death in 1697, his business never quite recuperated from the loss of her
pragmatism and ability to inspire self-discipline in her husband.

(1998)

Notes

2 *The Life and Errors of John Dunton Citizen of London* (1705), 2 vols. (rpt. New
   York: Burt Franklin, 1969), i. 105.
3 This number is from Hunt, 'The London Trade', 518. While substantial, it represents less than 2% of the total number of apprentices during this period.
   Furthermore, until exhaustive studies of primary, as well as secondary, sources
   for the study of women in the book trade are completed such statistics must be
   viewed as provisional.
      There is no record of Joanna Nye ever having been made free of the Company.
   To be admitted by redemption was to pay a fee for immediate membership, as when
   Sarah Andrews and Dorothy Sheldenslow were allowed to buy their way into the
   Company for £5 each in the 1680s booksellers' drive against stall-holders. In 1668,
   Elizabeth Latham, daughter of bookseller George Latham, became the first woman
   to be admitted by patrimony (Blagden, *The Stationers' Company*, 162).
4 In actuality Tace succeeded her father in 1691 and had probably assumed manage-
   ment of the printing house some time earlier. By 1690 Andrew Sowle was described

as 'an old man' and nearly blind, and after this date his name no longer appears in imprints. For further information on the Sowle press and Quaker publishing see my article in James K. Bracken and Joel Silver, eds., *The British Literary Book Trade, 1475–1700* (Columbia, SC: Bruccoli Clark Layman, 1996), 249–57.

5   Robert Clare, qtd. in Henry L. Snyder, 'The Reports of a Press Spy for Robert Harley: New Bibliographical Data for the Reign of Queen Anne', *Library*, 5th ser. 22 (1967), 326–45; 341. Mary Darly, the manager of an important London print shop and an etcher of political prints, appears to have had a similarly dominant role in the family business (Herbert M. Atherton, *Political Prints in the Age of Hogarth: A Study of the Ideographic Representation of Politics* (Oxford: Clarendon Press, 1974), 18–21 and *passim*). Among those wives whose diligence John Dunton praised were Mrs Bilingsley, who took over the family business when bookseller Mr Bilingsley suffered from bouts of madness, and Abigail Baldwin, wife of Richard, who 'eased him of all his publishing work; and since she has been a Widow, might vie with all the women in Europe for accuracy and justice in keeping accompts: and the same I hear of her beautiful Daughter, Mrs. Mary Baldwin' (i. 230, 260).

6   Stephen Parks, *John Dunton and the English Book Trade: A Study of his Career with a Checklist of his Publications* (New York: Garland, 1976), 20–37.

BLACK WOMAN TALK COLLECTIVE

'Black Woman Talk'
Feminist Review

Black Woman Talk is a collective of women of Asian and African descent living in Britain. As Black women we feel that the publishing industry has ignored and silenced the views and ideas of Black women living in Britain. It is important for us therefore to restore the lines of communication which have been historically destroyed and to re-establish the links between our scattered and isolated communities.

As Black women we experience oppression due to our sex, race, class and sexual orientation. This is reflected in every area of our lives and the publishing industry is no exception. It is a very powerful medium for communication and it reflects the racism and sexism of this society. The amount of work published for, by and about Black women is totally negligible and Black women's voices have gone unheard. Instead racist and sexist stereotypes have been perpetuated and until now been unchallenged.

More recently, it appears that there is a growing awareness amongst some of the established mainstream and feminist publishers of the need to make Black voices heard. Unfortunately, their enthusiasm to publish works by Black women, particularly from America, seems to stem from their recognition that such books have a lucrative market, rather than any genuine commitment to making publishing accessible to Black women writers in Britain. Afro-American women seem to be the vogue for feminist publishers such as the Women's Press. Such publishers are not only reluctant to hear the voices of Black women in Britain but there is little concern about including Black women in the publishing industry in a way which gives them any decision-making powers at all levels.

Black Woman Talk began as a small group of unemployed women who came together to form a workers' publishing co-operative. We feel there is an urgent need to see more publications available by Black women living in Britain to express our experiences and history. Our own varied experiences in working in Black organizations as well as our varied involvement in creative work such as writing, visual arts, theatre and music places us in contact with Black women who are writing and/or doing visual work. We are all writers and artists who want to see more Black women get access to publishing and the various skills involved in this field.

Black Woman Talk aims to provide a means by which women of Asian and African descent can publish their work, and through the publication of short stories, poetry, political writings, photo-essays, calendars reflect the wide variety of written and visual works produced by us. We would like to encourage more Black women to write and record their life experiences and to provide a greater knowledge and understanding of the lives and history of Black women in the wider community. We would also like to make alternative materials available for use in schools, libraries and other public information centres.

We will shortly be asking for manuscripts by Black women and as we grow we shall provide employment in a co-operative situation where Black women work with and for other Black women, thus sharing the skills and knowledge we gain, and providing encouragement and advice to other Black women. We would like to extend to cover typesetting and printing in the long term, which would give us greater self-determination and more skills to share.

The existence of *Black Woman Talk* is testimony to the strength of Black Women organizing to create our own means of communication. The international movement of Black women organizing in this way is illustrated by the existence of our sister press in America, Kitchen Table; Women of Color Press, and Kali Press; Third World Women Press in Delhi.

(1984)

LAURETTA NGCOBO

'Introduction'
Let It be Told: Essays by Black Women in Britain

Notwithstanding the general attitudes of mainstream commercial publishers, the picture would be incomplete if no mention were made of certain exceptional developments taking place within the publishing world. Much of it has little to do specifically with Blackwomen writers, but its effects, like ripples in a pool, touch us indirectly. During the past decade and a half there have been changes in the outlook of white, male-dominated publishers which would have rocked the industry were it not so well secured through power, finance and tradition. First the feminist lobby has pressured them into promoting women who, in the main, worked on sufferance within these companies. This, being a case of too little too late for some enterprising women, led to the founding of feminist publishing houses. Initially these too seemed to have no thought for the beleaguered Blackwoman writer, their paramount consideration being to serve the neglected needs of their marginalized fellow white sisters. It has taken the literary cloudburst of Blackwomen's writing from North American to force Britain's feminist presses to look nearer home for Black talent.

Until recently, few publishing houses concerned themselves with Third World writing: the handful who did include Longman, Heinemann and Macmillan, and even they produced almost entirely for the export market. The doors have widened somewhat to admit Blackwomen to the lists of prestigious houses such as Virago, The Women's Press, Zed Press and others. In addition, there is a growing number of small Black companies producing books by our women. One of the oldest is Bogle-L'Ouverture Publications, begun by Jessica Huntley. Another woman who has started her own company, publishing her own work, is Buchi Emecheta. And in 1987 we have seen yet another women's publishing house, Zora Press established by Iyamidè Hazeley and Adeola Solanke. Joining the swelling ranks of committed Black publishers, headed by the now long-established New Beacon Books, are Karnak House, Akira and Karia. We owe a debt to these fledgling Black concerns, as well as to the radical white presses who first provided an outlet for some of our now better known writers.

The books that Blackwomen do write are invariably considered a separate class of writing that is somehow discredited, less authentic, not part of the main body of literature. More often than not, they will be stocked mainly by alternative booksellers. This discrimination means that our books do not easily find their way into schools and universities, for their validity is in doubt. Organizations such as the Association for the Teaching of Caribbean and African and Asian Literature (ATCAL) have been formed by teachers and others with a particular interest in trying to change these prevailing attitudes. Having been in existence for several years, ATCAL has made slow progress in achieving its main aim – to convince the examining bodies to accord examination status to this literature, for it is essential for the young of whatever race to understand the Black experience.

(1987)

SIMONE MURRAY

Mixed Media: Feminist Presses and Publishing Politics

Book-Inds: Co-opting Digital Technology for the Book
How then should feminist publishers remain open to the opportunities presented by digital technologies without becoming so enslaved by the technical capabilities of specific digital formats that they squander their corporate knowledge and operating capital? Successful contemporary feminist publishing initiatives suggest that engaging in the digital sphere while retaining a bibliocentric outlook yields optimal results. Where the Internet has been utilised to expand publicity and sales opportunities for traditional format books, feminist publishers have been able to strike a happy medium. Virtually all women's publishers now boast homepages highlighting their company profile and frontlist titles, but several have pioneered more innovative applications: brand-name feminist presses Virago and The Feminist Press have designed their websites as community centres and guides to the presses' history; numerous houses – among them The Women's Press, Spinifex and Naiad – offer online purchasing through third-party distributors; and, in a sign that e.book boosterism may be terminally on the wane, Virago has pioneered online print-on-demand ordering for 15 out-of-print Virago Modern Classics titles in traditional book format.

Such recalibration of digital technology for bibliocentric ends represents a cannily circumspect approach to a rapidly changing and still evolving medium. Yet it can at best pose only an interim solution to the question of feminist publishing's future. The longer-term sustainability of feminist publishing can only be assured if the sector comes to terms with the nature of the modern media industries as content-warehousing operations. The globalised media conglomerates that dominate the contemporary mediascape aim to own a broad array of intellectual property brands, which can be reformatted and repurposed in a wide variety of media forms, be they textual, visual, audio or any combination of these. Reconceptualising books not as stand-alone entities, but as component products in the life of a larger content property, may offer feminist publishing its best chance of survival in a greatly expanded and increasingly converged media landscape. Specific presses must respond to such shifts in industry structures by crafting individually tailored strategies. For feminist lists within larger corporations, maximum benefit may lie in promoting book properties to affiliate film, television or magazine divisions, and in reaping the cross-promotional benefits of tie-in editions, much as Virago engineered with screen-adapted bestsellers such as Vera Brittain's *Testament of Youth* (1933, republished 1978), Virginia Woolf's *Orlando* (1928, republished 1993) or, more recently, Sarah Waters' *Tipping the Velvet* (1998). In the case of independent feminist houses lacking such a conglomerate niche, press interests may best be served by contracting with authors to acquire the maximum range of rights, and actively brokering these rights for sale to outside parties, again benefiting from resultant cross-promotion. To embrace such cross-media traffic in content is not to admit the obsolescence of the book, but rather to acknowledge public enthusiasm for re-engaging with content already encountered in other media, and to harness this enthusiasm for the book sector.

Transforming publishing's key product from 'books' to 'rights' in such manner does, however, present feminist publishing with an especially destabilising challenge. The women's classics with which many feminist presses cut their teeth become vulnerable in a twenty-first-century media landscape for precisely the reasons they formerly represented a solid business proposition. 'Classic' titles, generally being already typeset, out of copyright and without living authors requiring royalty payments, formerly represented a low-cost, high-profit publishing opportunity. But in a publishing environment characterised by rights brokerage, such titles' out of copyright status renders them commercially disadvantageous, in that their content is already in the public domain. Contemporary feminist publishers may therefore be best advised to redirect their frontlists towards newly acquired titles by living authors, and to retain 'classics' backlists as commercial ballast, albeit continually depreciating ballast. The snag lies, of course, in the industry reality that notable living authors are almost certain to engage literary agents who will scrutinise overly generous rights clauses in publishers' contracts with the vigilant eye of self-interest. The trend would thus seem to lead back to feminist publishers' traditional ground: emerging writers who stand to benefit by association with a strong imprint identity, but who are not yet sufficiently successful to market themselves as their own authorial brand. Once again, feminist publishing finds its identity in pushing cultural margins, adroitly trafficking ideas between the periphery and the mainstream.

Reframing the 'Feminist Publishing' Debate
Throughout the preceding three decades of second-wave feminist publishing, debate has continuously swirled around the properly 'feminist' nature of such an activity, resulting in often arid debates over political 'purity' as opposed to commercial 'co-optation'. Yet, as the foregoing two chapters demonstrate, traffic between the margins and the mainstream of cultural production is now so plentiful and complex that any such attempts at watertight classifications obscure more than they illuminate. The as yet underexamined second term in the 'feminist publishing' tag – the nature of book publishing itself – now emerges as the front on which feminist publishing must regroup. The sector faces the challenge of keeping feminist issues prominent in a media environment in which the book represents only one of a plethora of competing communications platforms, and not the most pervasive

or profitable platform at that. The skill lies in tactically engaging with ancillary media to promote book properties. To retain maximum manoeuvrability, and to be able to ride out battles between developing delivery mechanisms, book publishers need to prioritise control of rights in book properties. This involves the possibly chastening experience for publishers of accepting that the most profitable application of a book property may not necessarily be in book form, but that interest in content generated by a screen medium may be captured and redirected by publishers towards a textual form.

Such a strategic approach holds particular benefits for feminists interested in the interface of gender and communication. For if feminist ideas have historically been suppressed through denying women access to the most socially powerful media forms, there is always the possibility that feminists investing heavily in one specific communications platform will miscalculate the odds, and be relegated to a less pervasive or obsolescing medium. Directing movement energies into retaining ownership of feminist intellectual property by contrast insulates feminism from the unpredictable fates and rivalries of communications media, and ensures that premium women's content can be formatted in whichever media seem most appropriate at any given time. The strategy constitutes a quintessentially twenty-first-century reformulation of Virginia Woolf's assertion in *Three Guineas* (1938) that owning a printing press is *the* non-negotiable prerequisite for guaranteeing 'intellectual liberty'. Thirty years of feminist publishing activism have amply manifested the overriding importance of women controlling the medium. Yet in the emerging media environment, control of the medium is proving secondary to control of the message itself.

(2004)

KATHRYN MCGRATH

'Pushed to the Margins: The Slow Death and Possible Rebirth
of the Feminist Bookstore'
Feminist Collections

To keep themselves and their missions alive, the remaining women's bookstores are getting creative and adopting new strategies. Some are purely practical: With the exception of Women & Children First, every one of the bookstores mentioned above relies on fund-raising and contributions to keep afloat and pay rising rents. Others, including the nonprofit In Other Words Women's Books and Resources in Portland, Oregon, and the newly reopened Bluestockings, also rely on volunteer workers. (Susan Post of Book Woman is so committed to keeping Texas's last feminist bookstore alive that she forgoes her own salary.)

Sarah Cohen has filled Change Makers with jewelry, gifts, music, t-shirts, candles, oils, and incense. Although the majority of the store is devoted to new and used titles, Cohen isn't counting on them to be profitable, and hopes that the gift items will subsidize the books. The store closes at 7 p.m. to allow for evening events like full-moon gatherings, drumming, and the Talking Ovaries club. Women & Children First has successfully competed with Barnes & Noble over star speakers, getting authors like Margaret Atwood, Isabelle Allende, and Al and Tipper Gore to do readings. "I like competing with the big guys. I get a kick out of it," says co-owner Linda Bubon with a laugh.

Other bookstores also see the need for long-term survival and transition planning. As the oldest independent feminist bookstore in North America, Minneapolis's Amazon Bookstore Co-operative wants to ensure that its legacy continues. In 1999, the bookstore settled a lawsuit with Amazon.com over the startup's use of the name the cooperative has had since 1970, and although the terms of the settlement are not public, it benefited the store. During the last thirty-three years, Amazon has grown from a table of books on a front porch to a large sunny store on Chicago Avenue South in a building shared with the women's-services organization Chrysalis. Last summer, when Amazon was faced with an unexpected $10,000 property-tax bill, they raised $35,000 despite the fact that donations were not tax-deductible because the store is for-profit. According to Wieser, the money largely came in small donations. "That really showed us how much people want the store to be around."

Part of a younger generation of bookstores, In Other Words opened ten years ago as a nonprofit organization. Manager Sue Burns, the store's only full-time employee, cut her teeth working at Book Woman. In addition to selling books, the store rents videos and hosts meetings, performances, open-mic nights, and support groups, and it has a resource center with bulletin boards for everything from housing to networking. The store's status as a nonprofit makes it eligible for grants and tax-deductible donations. Local businesses frequently donate goods and services to silent auctions and raffles benefiting the store. Recently, more fund-raising efforts have been necessary, but Burns says that by hosting events tailored to specific groups like women's studies professors, tranny bois, and punk-rock girls, the store is surviving. In Other Words also champions local grassroots women's organizations with their Organization of the Month program. The group puts together a window display for the store, which in turn offers a reading list. Says Burns, "It keeps windows dynamic – people see that we have something to offer, come in, and maybe happen upon something else." A group of fat women called Queen Size Revolution is up next for the window treatment. "Primarily, we are an organization of social change," Burns says. "We're fighting to keep the voices of women not only visible but accessible."

Other stores are making even bigger changes in programming, such as broadening their focus beyond women's books or recommitting to their original missions in new guises. In Cincinnati, Ohio, the twenty-two-year-old Crazy Ladies Bookstore was reborn last November as the Greater Cincinnati Women's Resource Center, while Cambridge, Massachusetts's revered New Words Bookstore closed its doors after twenty-eight years to focus on a capital campaign to fund a non-profit Center for New Words, dedicated to supporting women's writing, voices, and ideas. Gilda Bruckman, one of the four founders of New Words, describes the thought process that led them to close the store: "A couple years ago we realized that something dramatic had to happen. It seemed like a terrible waste to have that history and expertise vanish – we didn't want to lose that. We wanted to pass on those assets that we had acquired, the intangible ones, so they could continue within the community."

Center for New Words will be dedicated to creating both "space and place" for women's words. The Center continues to host a series of readings, workshops, and events. After a successful weekend workshop with poet Ellen Bass, the Center debuted a full series of intensive workshops ranging from a two-day memoir-writing workshop with Michelle Tea to a two-month journal-writing course for women of color with Gabriel Atchison, in addition to fiction, poetry, and performance workshops. The Center hopes to have a board of directors in place by next year, and the funds to begin anew. "We're looking for pilot projects and organizations to partner with and trying to think innovatively about programs," Bruckman says. The possibilities include starting a bookmobile, working with immigrant women and women in transitional housing, hosting a web-based writing group, and offering literacy resources, a writer-in-residence program, and additional writing workshops. For the moment, however, the Center is subsisting on a lot of people's good work and dedication.

"We all miss the store," says Jaclyn Friedman, Center for New Words' programming director, of plans to resurrect the bookselling operation. "Spontaneous communication is harder to come by when it's not a drop-in space anymore. When September 11 happened, people came to the bookstore to be together somewhere. When the war started, no one came because there was no longer a bookstore. That's one of the reasons we're committed to having a bookstore in the new space."

Center for New Words is following in the footsteps of Charis Books & More, which was one of the first feminist bookstores to spin off its programming efforts as a nonprofit organization, effectively forging a new business model to ensure the store's survival. In 1996, the nonprofit Charis Circle assumed responsibility for the many educational, cultural, and community outreach programs already offered by the bookstore. "We'd been doing educational programming in addition to book readings for eighteen years," explains Linda Bryant. "But this was a financially brilliant idea to synergistically keep those things alive." The Circle's board of directors has increased the programming for young women, sponsoring a number of programs including Feminism 101, a monthly discussion of issues; the Gaia Collective, an intergenerational mutual mentoring group; the Thursday Community Program, a monthly topical discussion; a children's reading hour; and increasingly popular writing workshops. Meanwhile, Charis remains a successful feminist bookstore.

Other stores are coping with changing times by expanding both their missions and the range of books they sell in response to market demand. While materials by and for lesbians and gay men have become easier to find and ask for, feminist bookstores have recently discovered a growing need for books and events about transgender issues. Similarly, other progressive concerns like globalization and social justice have gained greater attention from leftist and mainstream media alike, prompting a whole new shelving category.

My Sisters' Words' stock was originally made up almost entirely of books from feminist and lesbian presses. Owner Kavanaugh has since expanded the inventory to include more mainstream and university presses, and over the years most sections of the store have been changed to include new topics and concerns like AIDS, bisexuality, gender studies, and, more recently, globalization. Last year, My Sisters' Words celebrated its fifteenth anniversary with a grand reopening as My Sisters' Words/The Next Wave: A Bookstore for All Progressive Minds. "There were ways in which I was feeling I had come to the end of what I could do within the parameters of how I was defining the store," Kavanaugh says. The expansion of the children's, social change, globalization, and peace sections has given the store a much-needed boost in sales. "[These] are areas of life that have been influenced by the feminism of the past 40 years – so, while the store isn't what people have come to expect of a feminist bookstore, it still is [one]. Maybe what needs to change is the concept of what a feminist bookstore is."

(2004)

3

Gender and Genre

Women and the Novel

Any discussion of gender and genre is dominated by the need to explain women's special relationship with the novel. When Ian Watt published his influential work, *The Rise of the Novel*, in 1957, his subtitle gave no indication that women had any part to play: *Studies in Defoe, Richardson and Fielding*.[1] Where women do feature in Watt's study, it is as an eager readership rather than as authors. But Virginia Woolf, writing in 1929, *was* struck by the number of women writers on her book shelves who were novelists and looked for reasons to explain this. Woolf thinks about class, domestic space, the demands of the form – her rather debatable contention that novel writing takes less concentration – and, elsewhere in *A Room of One's Own*, the fact that 'the novel alone was young enough to be soft in [their] hands'.[2] Here was a mode that was malleable and without a long history of male authorities. At its most disparaging, novels could be viewed dismissively as the best that women could accomplish: men study classics; women amuse themselves with novels. Yet, equally, the novel's lack of status and tradition and the belief that it demanded less intellectual rigour than other forms of writing opened up possibilities for women. Moreover, because the novel's genesis lay partly in forms of writing familiar to women – the diary, the journal, letters – the form could seem more accessible and approachable than a poetry dependent on Greek and Latin allusions. Like Woolf, Ellen Moers discusses the vital role that the novel played in the development of 'professions for women'.[3] Some women novelists earned significant sums of money and an independence they had not previously known. Moers's calculation of

Fanny Burney's earnings of £2,000 as equivalent to $50,000 in 1977 would now have to be recalculated as equivalent to almost $178,000.

Woolf's comments reinforce those discussed in Chapter 2 about the importance for women of the domestic production of some forms of writing, but more than that, they illustrate how central the geography of women's lives was, and is, to the novel; the traditional subject-matter of the novel – its plot, characters, sensibility – could all be encountered in the drawing room or the village. Tolstoy may have written novels that range over half of Europe, but it was equally possible, as Jane Austen proves, to write novels that go no further than Bath. For Woolf, the marking of the nuances of interpersonal relations constitutes women's distinct contribution and the 'training in the observation of character, in the analysis of emotion' becomes an education for novel writing. Furthermore, critics have situated the emergence of the woman novelist within a general 'feminization' of culture in the latter part of the eighteenth century. Both Juliet Mitchell and Nancy Armstrong see links between the development of the novel, the consolidation of bourgeois capitalism, and the creation of a new understanding of the term 'woman'. As Mitchell writes, 'the novel is the prime example of the way women start to create themselves as social subjects under bourgeois capitalism – create themselves as a category: women'. Armstrong puts the same point: 'I will insist that one cannot distinguish the production of the new female ideal either from the rise of the novel or from the rise of the new middle classes in England.' The new, ideal social subject is both female and domestic. Armstrong's emphasis is on 'female forms of power' and she makes considerable claims for the power of rhetoric and culture over economics and politics.[4] Mitchell is more concerned with the ambiguity and vulnerability of the position of the woman writer. Using the psychoanalytical approaches of Jacques Lacan and Julia Kristeva, Mitchell suggests that the woman writer will 'speak the discourse of the hysteric'. She will at once 'be feminine and ... refuse femininity'; she creates a woman's world within her novels while, at the same time, rejecting that world through the authoritative act of writing. Mitchell sees no alternative for the woman writer. She has to work within the dominant order, what is termed the 'symbolic', for to be outside the dominant order is to be mad or dead. But equally, she must disrupt that symbolic order with a new symbolism.

If the novel has featured prominently as the genre most identified with women and, historically, most involved in the production of certain kinds of femininity, it has also, since the late 1980s, had an important place in feminist interventions into narratology. Susan S. Lanser is writing at a juncture when the reassessment of literary history to take account of gender has begun but the rewriting of narratology has not.[5] Lanser wants to forge a relationship between feminism and narratology, and to query how each might benefit from the other. To do this, she suggests, would not simply include women's writing and critiques within narratology, but significantly change the terms of the debate. The argument here is similar to that we saw in Chapter 1 concerning women's relation to literary tradition. In a sense, Lanser is trying to move narratology away from any pretensions to being wholly systematic and scientific; it must remember the referential, the social and political contexts of production and be conscious of its own ideological investments.[6] Robyn R. Warhol skilfully makes such links in her 'narratology of good-cry techniques'. She lists seven patterns – from which I include two – which can be found in the narrative discourse of sentimental novels and films. While in one respect a typology, her listing equally attests to the pleasure of 'a good cry', not as masochistic identification with a tragic character, but as a sympathy encouraged by the narrative strategies and which affirms feelings of community, value and affective relationship. While Lanser, writing in 1986, felt that 'virtually no work in the field of narratology has taken gender into account', Marilyn R. Farwell, ten years later, finds narratological studies about heterosexuality and male homosexuality but little consciousness of 'a lesbian narrative function'. Farwell surveys the work of those critics who have made a rich contribution to this field, some offering thematic alternatives, some structural. Her own argument enters the debate with respect to 'a reading of the lesbian subject as a metaphor'. The figure of the lesbian subject – whether an individual, a couple or a community – is an uncertain, excessive figure with the potential to redraw the narrative space and interrogate narrative categories. Thus, narrative parameters are, suggests Farwell, 'stretched to accommodate different power relations'.[7]

Constraints and Consequences

In the history of gender and genre studies, we can see how, at different moments, genres and forms become more or less possible for the woman author, more or less accepted by the reading public. Cora Kaplan enters the debate about women and poetry, arguing, with reference to Elizabeth Barrett Browning, that it is her choice of the epic form in *Aurora Leigh* which is the real 'venture into a male stronghold'. For the conservative reader of the period, Barrett Browning's narrative poetry is unsettlingly bisexual, 'didactic and philosophical as well as passionate and female'. Its challenge extends beyond the literary to the political and the developing public voice of the nineteenth-century, middle-class woman. No wonder critics tried to confine Barrett Browning to the lyric.[8] Meenakshi Ponnuswami is also concerned with that charged configuration of femininity and public voice, this time in the theatre. She looks to a specific location and moment, British theatre in the mid-1980s, and shows the restrictions of the theatrical field, with few spaces for the woman playwright, and the political, economic and institutional pressures operating within it.[9] Ponnuswami's comments on state funding for black theatre are particularly interesting. The funding is productive while also determining particular agendas, and those agendas – for example, encouraging work on ethnic identities – may, in different contexts, be viewed as either controlling or enabling. Thus, exploring genre becomes also a way of understanding a whole range of literary, cultural and political consequences, and, for this reason, Clare Brant advocates its widest application. She points out how the contemporary emphasis on fiction and poetry is not always helpful to the writer of earlier periods – indeed, can unhelpfully narrow the debate. As Brant illustrates, to put the widest sense of genre at the centre of the debate when discussing the woman writer of the eighteenth century can raise relevant issues about canonicity, authorship, originality, authenticity, literary status and the distinctions between literary forms.

Female/Feminine Forms
Over the last forty years, feminist criticism has turned its attention to a proliferating number of literary genres, sub-genres and forms, both canonical and popular.[10] As we saw in Mitchell's piece, this analysis may be presented in socioeconomic terms but, equally, in psychosexual terms; Mitchell herself looks to a Lacanian reading of the Oedipal crisis. The extracts in this section consider forms of writing frequently associated with female authors and readers, and with femininity – the Gothic, romantic fiction, the middlebrow novel and chick lit – and reveal genre studies' range of interest across the political and ideological, the psychic, the formal adaptations. For example, Rosemary Jackson's comments on, as Moers coined, the 'female Gothic' relate the politically and psychically disordered to the form of the writing. She speaks of Mary Shelley's writing as fantasizing 'a violent attack on the symbolic order' and as part of a tradition of women Gothic writers whose writings 'subvert patriarchal society'. The 'structural indeterminacy' of Shelley's fiction, questioning linear narrative, is thought by Jackson to be an important aspect of that attack on the symbolic order. She sees in Shelley's work no strong narrative line but fragmentary and circular forms which, by leaving the work open, reject an authoritative and definitive resolution.[11] Rather than fantasies of disruption, Rosalind Coward finds in romantic fiction a much more conservative politics in the infantile fantasies for the adored, powerful father. The heroine's power is always in relation to the hero's. Her moments of dominance are but a prelude to the restoration of his power, and structurally the narrative conventions are formulaic – desire, accompanied by obstacles to be overcome, followed by resolution.[12]

Alison Light's and Nicola Humble's studies see a different emphasis as they move carefully between the historical moment, ideological shifts, generic possibilities and questions of aesthetic value. Both are especially interested in the borders between categories. As a recognizable genre of 'romance' is created in the inter-war period, so, Light claims, it moves downmarket: sensationalism, thrills, irrationality become marked as both female and working class. Desire is dangerous. It is better for the aspiring, socially conscious woman author and reader to look to crime fiction with its 'apparently masculine qualities of reason and logic' and its proximity to literariness. Light's consciousness of class difference and her mention of the 'middlebrow' and the 'highbrow' are echoed in Humble's extract. What she calls the 'feminine middlebrow novel' is flexible; it can both confirm and contest gender and class identities, and can be both domestic and innovative. Humble's focus is on 'the heavily patrolled border between intellectual, experimental fiction and the commercial middlebrow', a border which in crossing calls into question the categories of middlebrow and highbrow. For instance, a disdain of the middlebrow in this period produces a particular version of modernism, one which positions Woolf as the solitary, female voice. Placing Woolf among her female contemporaries might, Humble suggests, connect her to the middlebrow.[13]

The elasticity of these categories – 'romance', 'the woman's novel', 'the middlebrow' – permits their frequent reformulation. One recent example of this is chick lit. Much of the work in this area has been concerned with recuperating chick lit for feminism; the aspirations, anxieties, contradictions and compromises of the chick-lit heroine are all familiar to her mother's generation.[14] But equally striking is chick-lit's interest in literary form, not only in the many intertextual references to nineteenth-century heroines – most often from the work of Austen, the Brontës and Wharton – but in its play on genre. Shari Benstock notices historical links to epistolary fiction, the novel of psychological development, memoir and autobiography. Her extract is from the 'Afterword' to a collection of essays that often pursue chick-lit's generic connections: for example, Elizabeth Hale on the *Bildungsroman*, Stephanie Harzewski on the novel of manners, Juliette Wells on the romantic quest.

Generic Challenges

Throughout many of the extracts in this chapter, we can trace an ongoing debate in feminism about the political effectiveness of challenging generic and formal norms. Susan Sellers ably draws together the different arguments in asking how, or whether, a feminist rewriting of myth is possible in any significant way. She surveys a number of post-structuralist positions that respond to Derrida's sense of the revolutionary potential of writing, the 'supplement' in writing that can break logocentric control. To what extent are we confined by the dominant and the known; to what extent can we change and question; what tools would be best employed; are these strategies merely tinkering around the edges? Sellers advocates a double-pronged approach: 'This would involve keeping and benefiting from those elements which are still potent for us, while discarding or revitalising those which are dead, deadly, or simply no longer appropriate.' She indicates how 'the known forms operate as compass points around which we can weave new and different stories'. Like Jackson, Sellers is optimistic about the transformative potential of rewritings and, like Woolf, she recognises the malleability of forms. Marina Warner, whom Sellers mentions, makes this point in a similar way to Woolf: 'Myths convey values and expectations that are always evolving, in the process of being formed, but – and this is fortunate – never set so hard they cannot be changed again, and newly told stories can be more helpful than repeating old ones.'[15] Sellers likens this approach to the psychoanalytic concept of holding and to Kristeva's understanding of dissident writing; the safety and knowability of the existing socioeconomic world enables change, movement, critique.

Notes

1 Feminist critics have subsequently uncovered what one might call the 'maternal' origins of the novel. See: Jane Spencer, *The Rise of the Woman Novelist: From Aphra Behn to Jane Austen* (Oxford: Basil Blackwell, 1986); Dale Spender, *Mothers of the Novel: 100 Good Women Writers before Jane Austen* (London: Pandora Press, 1986); Ros Ballaster, *Seductive Forms: Women's Amatory Fiction from 1684 to 1740* (Oxford: Clarendon Pres, 1992); Margaret Anne Doody, *The True Story of the Novel* (New Brunswick, NJ: Rutgers University Press, 1996).

2 Virginia Woolf, *A Room of One's Own* in the combined volume of *A Room of One's Own* and *Three Guineas*, ed. Michèle Barrett (London: Penguin, 1993), p. 70.

3 See relevant essays in Michèle Barrett (ed.), *Virginia Woolf: Women and Writing* (London: The Women's Press, 1979); Virginia Woolf, *A Woman's* Essays, ed. Rachel Bowlby (London: Penguin, 1992).

4 Armstrong returns to her argument in 'What Feminism Did to Novel Studies', in Ellen Rooney (ed.), *The Cambridge Companion to Feminist Literary Theory* (Cambridge: Cambridge University Press, 2006) and situates her own work within feminist studies of the novel.

5 See also Robyn Warhol, *Gendered Interventions: Narrative Discourse in the Victorian Novel* (New Brunswick, NJ: Rutgers University Press, 1989) and her question, 'Why Don't Feminists "Do" Narratology?' and Madhu Dubey's comments on the tendency to discuss the work of black women novelists thematically rather than structurally or formally: *Black Women Novelists and the Nationalist Aesthetic* (Indiana: Indiana University Press, 1994). Kathy Mezei (ed.), *Ambiguous Discourse: Feminist Narratology and British Women Writers* (Chapel Hill: University of North Carolina Press, 1996) and Ruth E. Page, *Literary and Linguistic Approaches to Feminist Narratology* (London: Palgrave 2006) both provide helpful surveys of the debates within feminism and narratology since the late 1980s.

6 An early – and sharp – refutation of Lanser's 1986 claims came in Nilli Diengott, 'Narratology and Feminism', *Style*, vol. 22, no. 1 (1988), pp. 42–60. See also Lanser's later study, *Fictions of Authority: Women Writers and Narrative Voice* (Ithaca, NY, and London: Cornell University Press, 1992), in which her analysis

of the relation between authority, gender and narrative voice (authorial, personal and communal) leads her to a questioning of issues that traditional narratology has ignored.

7 For further work on lesbian narratology, see: Judith Roof, *A Lure of Knowledge: Lesbian Sexualities and Theory* (New York: Columbia University Press, 1991); Elizabeth A. Meese, *[Sem]erotics: Theorizing Lesbian Writing* (New York: New York University Press, 1992); Marilyn Farwell, 'The Lesbian Narrative', in George E. Haggerty and Bonnie Zimmerman (eds.), *Professions of Desire: Lesbian and Gay Studies in Literature* (New York: Modern Language Association of America, 1995); Patricia Juliana Smith, *Lesbian Panic: Homoeroticism in Modern British Women's Fiction* (New York: Columbia University Press, 1997). Material in Chapter 6 on the lesbian subject is also relevant.

8 One can see how this battle within gender, lyric and epic poetry becomes material for A. S. Byatt in *Possession: A Romance* (London: Chatto & Windus, 1990).

9 See also on British theatre of this period, Michelene Wandor, 'The Impact of Feminism on the Theatre', *Feminist Review*, no. 18 (1984). Lizbeth Goodman (ed.) (with Jane de Gay), *The Routledge Reader in Gender and Performance* (London: Routledge, 1998) and Gabriele Griffin, *Contemporary Black and Asian Women Playwrights in Britain* (Cambridge: Cambridge University Press, 2003) bring this scenario more up to date.

10 As indicative titles, see: Lucie Armitt, *Contemporary Women's Fiction and the Fantastic* (Houndmills, Basingstoke: Palgrave Macmillan, 2000); Diana Wallace, *The Woman's Historical Novel: British Women Writers 1900–2000* (Houndmills, Basingstoke: Palgrave Macmillan, 2004); Gill Plain, *Twentieth-Century Crime Fiction: Gender, Sexuality and the Body* (Edinburgh: Edinburgh University Press, 2001); Lyn Pykett, *The 'Improper' Feminine: The Women's Sensation Novel and the New Woman Writing* (London: Routledge, 1992); Jenny Wolmark, *Aliens and Others: Science Fiction, Feminism, and Postmodernism* (Iowa City: University of Iowa Press, 1994). For consideration of women's autobiography, see Chapter 6 and for women's travel writing, Chapter 7.

11 For further studies on the female Gothic, see: Paulina Palmer, *Lesbian Gothic: Transformative Fictions* (New York: Cassell, 1999); Susanne Becker, *Gothic Forms of Feminine Fictions* (Manchester: Manchester University Press, 1999).

12 For a study of the reader response to romantic fiction, see: Janice A. Radway, *Reading the Romance: Women, Patriarchy and Popular Literature* (Chapel Hill: University of North Carolina Press, 1984). For a discussion of the place of desire in romantic fiction, see: Catherine Belsey, *Desire: Love Stories in Western Culture* (Oxford: Blackwell, 1994).

13 For further studies on women's writing and the middlebrow, see: Nicola Beauman, *A Very Great Profession: The Woman's Novel 1914–1939* (London: Virago, 1983; 2nd edition 1995); Clare Hanson, *Hysterical Fictions: The 'Woman's Novel' in the Twentieth Century* (Houndmills, Basingstoke: Palgrave Macmillan, 2000); Hilary Radner, *Shopping Around: Feminine Culture and the Pursuit of Pleasure* (London: Routledge, 1995).

14   See, for example, Imelda Whelehan, *The Feminist Bestseller: From Sex and the Single Girl to Sex and the City* (Houndmills, Basingstoke: Palgrave Macmillan, 2005); Whelehan puts chick lit in a tradition from 1970s consciousness-raising novels. Also the second edition of Tania Modleski, *Loving with a Vengeance: Mass-Produced Fantasies for Women* (New York: Routledge, 2008).

15   *Managing Monsters: Six Myths of Our Time* (London: Vintage, 1994), p. 14. See also Warner, *From the Beast to the Blonde: On Fairy Tales and their Tellers* (London: Vintage, 1995).

Virginia Woolf

A Room of One's Own

Here, then, one had reached the early nineteenth century. And here, for the first time, I found several shelves given up entirely to the works of women. But why, I could not help asking, as I ran my eyes over them, were they, with very few exceptions, all novels? The original impulse was to poetry. The 'supreme head of song'[9] was a poetess. Both in France and in England the women poets precede the women novelists. Moreover, I thought, looking at the four famous names, what had George Eliot in common with Emily Brontë? Did not Charlotte Brontë fail entirely to understand Jane Austen? Save for the possibly relevant fact that not one of them had a child, four more incongruous characters could not have met together in a room – so much so that it is tempting to invent a meeting and a dialogue between them. Yet by some strange force they were all compelled, when they wrote, to write novels. Had it something to do with being born of the middle class, I asked; and with the fact, which Miss Emily Davies a little later was so strikingly to demonstrate, that the middle-class family in the early nineteenth century was possessed only of a single sitting-room between them? If a woman wrote, she would have to write in the common sitting-room. And, as Miss Nightingale was so vehemently to complain, – 'women never have an half hour ... that they can call their own' – she was always interrupted. Still it would be easier to write prose and fiction there than to write poetry or a play. Less concentration is required. Jane Austen wrote like that to the end of her days. 'How she was able to effect all this', her nephew writes in his Memoir, 'is surprising, for she had no separate study to repair to, and most of the work must have been done in the general sitting-room, subject to all kinds of casual interruptions. She was careful that her occupation should not be suspected by servants or visitors or any persons beyond her own family party.'* Jane Austen hid her manuscripts or covered them with a piece of blotting-paper. Then, again, all the literary training that a woman had in the early nineteenth century was training in the observation of character, in the analysis of emotion. Her sensibility had been educated for centuries by the influences of the common sitting-room. People's feelings were impressed on her; personal relations were always before her eyes. Therefore, when the middle-class woman took to writing, she naturally wrote novels, even though, as seems evident enough, two of the four famous women here named were not by nature novelists. Emily Brontë should have written

* *Memoir of Jane Austen*, by her nephew, James Edward Austen-Leigh.

poetic plays; the overflow of George Eliot's capacious mind should have spread itself when the creative impulse was spent upon history or biography. They wrote novels, however; one may even go further, I said, taking *Pride and Prejudice* from the shelf, and say that they wrote good novels. Without boasting or giving pain to the opposite sex, one may say that *Pride and Prejudice* is a good book. At any rate, one would not have been ashamed to have been caught in the act of writing *Pride and Prejudice*. Yet Jane Austen was glad that a hinge creaked, so that she might hide her manuscript before any one came in. To Jane Austen there was something discreditable in writing *Pride and Prejudice*. And, I wondered, would *Pride and Prejudice* have been a better novel if Jane Austen had not thought it necessary to hide her manuscript from visitors? I read a page or two to see; but I could not find any signs that her circumstances had harmed her work in the slightest. That, perhaps, was the chief miracle about it. Here was a woman about the year 1800 writing without hate, without bitterness, without fear, without protest, without preaching. That was how Shakespeare wrote, I thought, looking at *Antony and Cleopatra*; and when people compare Shakespeare and Jane Austen, they may mean that the minds of both had consumed all impediments; and for that reason we do not know Jane Austen and we do not know Shakespeare, and for that reason Jane Austen pervades every word that she wrote, and so does Shakespeare. If Jane Austen suffered in any way from her circumstances it was in the narrowness of life that was imposed upon her. It was impossible for a woman to go about alone. She never travelled; she never drove through London in an omnibus or had luncheon in a shop by herself. But perhaps it was the nature of Jane Austen not to want what she had not. Her gift and her circumstances matched each other completely. But I doubt whether that was true of Charlotte Brontë, I said, opening *Jane Eyre* and laying it beside *Pride and Prejudice*.

[...]

One could not but play for a moment with the thought of what might have happened if Charlotte Brontë had possessed say three hundred a year – but the foolish woman sold the copyright of her novels outright for fifteen hundred pounds; had somehow possessed more knowledge of the busy world, and towns and regions full of life; more practical experience, and intercourse with her kind and acquaintance with a variety of character. In those words she puts her finger exactly not only upon her own defects as a novelist but upon those of her sex at that time. She knew, no one better, how enormously her genius would have profited if it had not spent itself in solitary visions over distant fields; if experience and intercourse and travel had been granted her. But they were not granted; they were withheld; and we must accept the fact that all those good novels, *Villette, Emma, Wuthering*

Heights, Middlemarch, were written by women without more experience of life than could enter the house of a respectable clergyman; written too in the common sitting-room of that respectable house and by women so poor that they could not afford to buy more than a few quires of paper at a time upon which to write *Wuthering Heights* or *Jane Eyre*.

Note

9 *supreme head of song*: Woolf quotes Swinburne's *Ave Atque Vale*, for the early Greek woman poet Sappho (b. 612 BC). She wrote hymns and love poems, some of which Swinburne translated.

ELLEN MOERS

Literary Women

Fanny Burney, now Mme d'Arblay, became pregnant at forty-one and ground out a novel – *Camilla* is her most lifeless production – to support her family. For once in her life, she made the economics of publishing work for her (they were just beginning to be organized to favor the independent author) in the one way that mattered: the acquisition of enough money, all at once, to pay for a house on a little piece of land in the country, which she called Camilla Cottage.

The episode once again is instructive, and shows why novel-writing became the profession of choice for literary women, and even for not particularly literary women whose intelligence and talent might have led them to different kinds of work. Only the novel offered the reward of capital endowment, that lump of money without which middle-class women, whatever their charms, would for long be virtually unmarriageable. Fanny Burney's court post had paid her 200 pounds a year, a wretched sum as Macaulay complained, but probably the highest salary a woman had ever received for respectable work, or would receive for generations to come. *Camilla* made her more than 2,000 pounds, or at least $50,000 in today's money.

The career of journalism, while never so important to English literary women as to French or American, began to open up to a few rare women in England fairly early in the eighteenth century, perhaps because it was so ill paid (almost as poorly paid as translating, which women of George Eliot's caliber would do for a pittance for generations to come). In the nineteenth century Harriet Martineau, for example, held an editorial post for which she received 15 pounds a year; but her first fiction, the *Political Economy* tales which took Martineau not much over two years to write, earned her more than 2,000 pounds.

Charlotte Brontë was dazzled by the first payment from her publishers for *Jane Eyre*: it was 100 pounds, the largest sum of money she had ever seen. There would be five such payments for the novel (probably an unfairly small slice of her publisher's profits) as opposed to the 20 pounds a year Brontë had been earning as a governess. ('My salary is not really more than £16 p.a.,' she wrote a friend in 1841, 'though it is nominally £20, but the expense of washing will be deducted therefrom.' Thus, to arrive at a sense of the real value of a governess' salary, we know that it was five times as much as the cost of laundering a governess' not very extensive wardrobe; we also know that it was about eleven times as much as the price of *Jane Eyre*. Governesses could not afford to buy three-volume novels, or almost anything else.)

The same 20 pounds, on the other hand, was the munificent sum Mrs Gaskell was paid for a mere short story in 1850. 'I stared,' she wrote, 'and wondered if I was swindling them but I suppose I am not; and Wm has composedly buttoned it up in his pocket.' Through Mrs Gaskell's letters can be traced the subtle and subtly changing attitudes of a successful literary woman to her husband's absolute control, in principle, over her earnings. Married life, however, as we all know, is a matter of practice as well as principle. By the late 1850s Mrs Gaskell was paying for her own trips abroad out of the proceeds of her fiction, and in 1865 'I did a terribly grand thing! and a secret thing too!' she wrote Charles Eliot Norton. 'Only you are in America and can't tell. I bought a house ... for Mr Gaskell to retire and for a home for my unmarried daughters.' Including furnishings, the house would cost her 3,000 pounds or so, all to be paid for in the style of Camilla Cottage, by a literary woman's fiction.

The economic system that made novel-writing look particularly attractive to Fanny Burney was subscription publishing: that is, soliciting payment in advance of a guinea and a half direct from readers, whose names were printed at the head of the first edition. Among the three hundred subscribers to *Camilla* were some of the greatest names of the day. And there were three names on the list even better known to posterity than to Fanny Burney, for they were those of the leading women novelists, which is to say the leading novelists, of the next generation: Mrs Radcliffe, Miss Edgeworth, and Miss Austen of Steventon.

Jane Austen was only twenty when she subscribed to *Camilla*, but then, she was also only twenty when she began 'First Impressions,' the first version of *Pride and Prejudice*, and she had already, in her teens, done a good deal of brilliant apprentice writing in imitation of or satirical reaction to the work of her female predecessors. When *Pride and Prejudice* finally appeared in 1813, women's literature came of age and with it the English novel, for in pure artistry no work in the form has ever surpassed it. It was a remarkable accomplishment of female professionalism, in the mere seventy years or so since *Pamela*, and the mere thirty years or so since *Evelina*.[1] Nor can the two phenomena be separated: the rise of the novel and the rise of women to professional literary status. And ever afterward the makeshift novel, last-born of literary genres, has dominated the literature of the world.

(1977)

Note

1   Whose author was still alive, still writing fiction. Fanny Burney lived to almost ninety, and the posthumous publication of her diaries almost spanned the Victorian age; in the case of her longevity, her life was not characteristic of literary women after her. But her last exemplary act as a woman writer produced yet another manuscript treasure for the Berg Collection: a dozen densely written pages about the operation she underwent for breast cancer in 1811, before the invention of anesthetic.

JULIET MITCHELL

'Femininity, Narrative and Psychoanalysis'
Women: The Longest Revolution

I want to look very briefly at one kind of history: that pre-eminent form of literary narrative, the novel. Roughly speaking, the novel starts with autobiographies written by women in the seventeenth century. There are several famous men novelists, but the vast majority of early novels were written by large numbers of women. These writers were trying to establish what critics today call the 'subject in process'. What they were trying to do was to create a history from a state of flux, a flux in which they were feeling themselves in the process of becoming women within a new bourgeois society. They wrote novels to describe that process – novels which said: 'Here we are: women. What are our lives to be about? Who are we? Domesticity, personal relations, personal intimacies, stories ...' In the dominant social group, the bourgeoisie, that is essentially what a woman's life was to become under capitalism. The novel is that creation by the woman of the woman, or by the subject who is in the process of becoming woman, of woman under capitalism. Of course it's not a neat homogeneous construction: of course there are points of disruption within it; of course there are points of autocriticism within it. *Wuthering Heights*, for example, is a high point of autocriticism of the novel from within the novel. I shall discuss it soon in that light.

As any society changes its social structure, changes its economic base, artefacts are re-created within it. Literary forms arise as one of the ways in which changing subjects create themselves as subjects within a new social context. The novel is the prime example of the way women start to create themselves as social subjects under bourgeois capitalism – create themselves as a category: women. The novel remains a bourgeois form. Certainly there are also working-class novels, but the dominant form is that represented by the woman within the bourgeoisie. This means that when contemporary Anglo-Saxon feminist critics turn to women writers, resurrect the forgotten texts of these women novelists, they are, in one sense, being completely conformist to a bourgeois tradition. There is nothing wrong with that. It is an important and impressive tradition. We have to know where women are, why women have to write the novel, the story of their own domesticity, the story of their own seclusion within the home and the possibilities and impossibilities provided by that.

This tradition has been attacked by critics such as Julia Kristeva as 'the discourse of the hysteric'. I believe that it has to be the discourse of the hysteric. The woman novelist must be an hysteric. Hysteria is the woman's simultaneous acceptance and refusal of the organisation of sexuality under patriarchal capitalism. It is simultaneously what a woman can do both to be feminine and to refuse femininity, within patriarchal discourse. And I think that is exactly what the novel is; I do not believe there is such a thing as female writing, a 'woman's voice'. There is the hysteric's voice which is *the woman's masculine language* (one has to speak 'masculinely' in a phallocentric world) talking about feminine experience. It's both simultaneously the woman novelist's refusal of the woman's world – she is, after all, a novelist – and her construction from within a masculine world of that woman's world. It touches on both. It touches, therefore, on the importance of bisexuality.

I will say something very briefly about the psychoanalytical theories behind this position of the woman writer who must speak the discourse of the hysteric, who both refuses and is totally trapped within femininity. Then I'll lead on to some of the things that were said earlier about how to disrupt this.

There is much current interest in re-reading Freud in terms of the moment at which sexual division is produced within society: the moment of the castration complex, the moment when the heterogeneously sexual, polymorphously perverse, carnivalesque child has imposed on it the divisions of 'the law'; the one law, the law of patriarchy, the mark of the phallus. At that moment two sexes are psychologically created as the masculine and the not-masculine. At the point in which the phallus is found to be missing in the mother, masculinity is set up as the norm, and femininity is set up as what masculinity is not. What is not there in the mother is what is relevant here; that is what provides the context for language. The expression which fills the gap is, perforce, phallocentric.

In Lacanian thinking this is called the moment of the symbolic. The symbolic is the point of organisation, the point where sexuality is constructed as meaning, where what was heterogeneous, what was not symbolised, becomes organised, becomes created round these two poles, masculine and not-masculine: feminine.

What has gone before can be called the pre-Oedipal, the semiotic, the carnivalesque, the disruptive. Now one can take two positions in relation to that. Either the pre-divided child, the heterogeneous child, the pre-Oedipal child, exists with its own organisation, an organisation of polyvalence, of polyphony. Or alternatively that very notion of heterogeneity, of bisexuality, of pre-Oedipality, of union in a dyadic possibility of child with mother, that image of oneness and heterogeneity as two sides of the same coin, is, in fact, provided by the law, by the symbolic law itself. The question to me has a political dimension to it. If you think that the heterogeneous pre-Oedipal polyvalent world is a separate structure in its own right, then the law is disruptable, the carnival can be held on the church steps. But if this is not the case, if the carnival and the church do not exist independently of each other, the pre-Oedipal and the Oedipal are not separate, discrete states – if, instead, the Oedipal with the castration complex is what defines the pre-Oedipal, then the only way you can challenge the church, challenge both the Oedipal and its pre-Oedipal, is from within an *alternative symbolic universe*. You cannot choose the imaginary, the semiotic, the carnival as an alternative to the symbolic, as an alternative to the law. It is set up by the law precisely as its own ludic space, its own area of imaginary alternative, but not as a symbolic alternative. So that politically speaking, it is only the symbolic, a new symbolism, a new law, that can challenge the dominant law.

Now this does have relevance for the two alternative types of feminist literary criticism which exist today. It was suggested in another paper at this conference that this area of the carnival can also be the area of the feminine. I don't think so. It is just what the patriarchal universe defines as the feminine, the intuitive, the religious, the mystical, the playful, all those things that have been assigned to women – the heterogeneous, the notion that women's sexuality is much more one of a whole body, not so genital, not so phallic. It is not that the carnival cannot be disruptive of the law; but it disrupts only within the terms of that law.

This suggests a criticism of the French school associated with Kristeva, and to me it explains why that school is essentially apolitical. One needs to ask why Kristeva and her colleagues, while producing very interesting ideas, choose exclusively masculine texts and quite often proto-fascist writings as well. Disruption itself can be radical from the right as easily as from the left. This type of disruption is contained within the patriarchal symbolic. To me this is the problem.

I shall just mention some things about *Wuthering Heights* here so that we can use it if we like as a text on which to hang some ideas. I do not want to offer a psychoanalytic reading of this novel; I want to use *Wuthering Heights* simply to illustrate some of the points that I have tried to make here.

Emily Brontë is not writing a carnivalesque query to the patriarchal order; she is clearly working within the terms of a language which has been defined as phallocentric. Yet she is, through a kind of irony, posing questions about patriarchal organisation, and I'll sketch in some of the questions that I think are asked by the novel. First, who tells the story? Emily Brontë's manuscript was stolen from her and presented to a publisher by her sister, Charlotte. It was eventually published under a male pseudonym: Ellis Bell. The author is a woman, writing a private novel; she is published as a man, and acquires some fame and notoriety. She uses two narrators – a man, Lockwood, and a woman, the nurse, Nelly Dean. The whole novel is structured through those two narrators. Lockwood is a parody of the romantic male lover. He is set up as a foppish gentleman from the town who thinks he loves all the things the romantic gentleman is supposed to love, such as solitude, or a heart of gold beneath a fierce exterior. These things are criticised from within the novel, particularly through the character of Isabella, who thinks that Heathcliff is a dark, romantic Gothic hero who will prove to be the true gentleman beneath all his cruelty.

The story of Catherine and Heathcliff is a story of bisexuality, the story of the hysteric. Catherine's father had promised he would bring her back a whip from his visit to Liverpool. Instead he picks up a gypsy child who is fatherless, who never has had and never will have a father's name, who is given just one name: Heathcliff, the name of a brother of Catherine's who had died in infancy. Catherine looks in her father's pocket, finds the whip broken; instead of this whip she gets a brother/ lover: Heathcliff.

Heathcliff is what Cathy wants all the rest of her life. She, in fact, makes the conventional feminine choice and marries somebody with whom she cannot be fully united – Edgar Linton. Edgar provides only an illusion of complementarity. I do not mean that they do not have a sexual relation; they have a child whose birth in one sense – the most unimportant – causes Catherine's death. The person that Catherine wants to be 'one' with is Heathcliff. Breaking the incest taboo, she says, 'I *am* Heathcliff, he's more myself than I am.' And Heathcliff says the same of Catherine. Each is the bisexual possibility of the other one, evoking a notion of oneness which is the reverse side of the coin of diverse heterogeneity. This type of 'oneness' can only come with death. Catherine dies; she haunts Heathcliff for twenty years, which is the date when the novel opens: it opens with Lockwood, who is given Heathcliff's dream, thinking (because he is the parodic romantic figure) that he can also get oneness. Heathcliff himself waits the whole stretch of the novel to have his own dream, which is to get back to Catherine. He dies getting back to her. 'Oneness' is the symbolic notion of what happens before the symbolic; it is death and has to be death. The choices for the woman within the novel, within fiction, are either to survive by making the hysteric's ambiguous choice into a femininity which doesn't work (marrying

Edgar) or to go for oneness and unity, by suffering death (walking the moors as a ghost with Heathcliff).

I want to end with my beginning, and with a question. I think the novel arose as the form in which women had to construct themselves as women within new social structures; the woman novelist is necessarily the hysteric wanting to repudiate the symbolic definition of sexual difference under patriarchal law, unable to do so because without madness we are all unable to do so. Writing from within that position can be conformist (Mills and Boon romantic novels) or it can be critical (*Wuthering Heights*). I think the novel starts at a point where society is in a state of flux, when the subject is in the process of becoming a woman (or man) as today we understand that identity. If we are today again talking about a type of literary criticism, about a type of text where the subject is not formed under a symbolic law, but within what is seen as a heterogeneous area of the subject-in-process, I would like to end with asking a question: *in the process of becoming what*? I do not think that we can live as human subjects without in some sense taking on a history; for us, it is mainly the history of being men or women under bourgeois capitalism. In deconstructing that history, we can only construct other histories. What are we in the process of becoming?

(1984)

NANCY ARMSTRONG

Desire and Domestic Fiction: A Political History of the Novel

To describe the history of domestic fiction, then, I will argue several points at once: first, that sexuality is a cultural construct and as such has a history: second, that written representations of the self allowed the modern individual to become an economic and psychological reality; and third, that the modern individual was first and foremost a woman. My argument traces the development of a specific female ideal in eighteenth and nineteenth century conduct books and educational treatises for women, as well as in domestic fiction, all of which often were written by women. I will insist that one cannot distinguish the production of the new female ideal either from the rise of the novel or from the rise of the new middle classes in England. At first, I will demonstrate, writing about the domestic woman afforded a means of contesting the dominant notion of sexuality that understood desirability in terms of the woman's claims to fortune and family name. But then, by the early decades of the nineteenth century, middle-class writers and intellectuals can be seen to take the virtues embodied by the domestic woman and to pit them against working-class culture. It took nothing less than the destruction of a much older concept of the household for industrialization to overcome working-class resistance. In time, following the example of fiction, new kinds of writing – sociological studies of factory and city, as well as new theories of natural history and political economy – established modern domesticity as the only haven from the trials of a heartless economic world. By the 1840s, norms inscribed in the domestic woman had already cut across the categories of status that maintained an earlier, patriarchal model of social relations.[4] The entire surface of social experience had come to mirror those kinds of writing – the novel prominent among them – which represented the existing field of social information as contrasting masculine and feminine spheres.[5]

This book, which links the history of British fiction to the empowering of the middle classes in England through the dissemination of a new female ideal, necessarily challenges existing histories of the novel. For one thing, it insists that the history of the novel cannot be understood apart from the history of sexuality. In dissolving the boundary between those texts that today are considered literature and those that, like the conduct books, are not, my study shows that the distinction between literary and nonliterary was imposed retrospectively by the modern literary institution upon anomalous works of fiction. It shows as well that the domestic novel antedated – was indeed necessarily antecedent to – the way of life it represented. Rather than refer to individuals who already existed as such and who carried on relationships according to novelistic conventions, domestic fiction took great care to distinguish itself from the kinds of fiction that predominated in the eighteenth and nineteenth centuries. Most fiction, which represented identity in terms of region, sect, or faction, could not very well affirm the universality of any particular form of desire. In contrast, domestic fiction unfolded the operations of human desire as if they were independent of political history. And this helped to create the illusion that desire was entirely subjective and therefore essentially different from the politically encodable forms of behavior to which desire gave rise.

At the same time and on the same theoretical grounds, my study of the novel challenges traditional histories of nineteenth century England by questioning the practice of writing separate histories for political and cultural events. Rather than see the rise of the new middle class in terms of the economic changes that solidified its hold over the culture, my reading of materials for and about women shows that the formation of the modern political state – in England at least – was accomplished largely through cultural hegemony. New strategies of representation not only revised the way in which an individual's identity could be understood, but in presuming to discover what was only natural in the self, they also removed subjective experience and sexual practices from their place in history. Our education does much the same thing when it allows us to assume that modern consciousness is a constant of human experience and teaches us to understand modern history in economic terms, even though history itself was not understood in those terms until the beginning of the nineteenth century. We are taught to divide the political world in two and to detach the practices that belong to a female domain from those that govern the marketplace. In this way, we compulsively replicate the symbolic behavior that constituted a private domain of the individual outside and apart from social history.

In actuality, however, the changes that allowed diverse groups of people to make sense of social experience as these mutually exclusive worlds of information constitute a major event in the history of the modern individual. It follows, then, that only those histories that account for the formation of separate spheres – masculine and feminine, political and domestic, social and cultural – can allow us to see what this semiotic behavior had to do with the economic triumph of the new middle classes. In effect, I am arguing, political events cannot be understood apart from women's history, from the history of women's literature, or from changing representations of the household. Nor can a history of the novel be historical if it fails to take into account the history of sexuality. For such a history remains, by definition, locked into categories replicating the semiotic behavior that empowered the middle class in the first place.

(1987)

Notes

4 By "the patriarchal model," I mean specifically the historical phenomenon that linked the political authority of the father over the household to that of the king in a mutually authorizing relationship. On this point, for example, see Gordon J. Schochet, *Patriarchalism in Political Thought* (New York: Basic Books, 1975) and Lawrence Stone, *The Family, Sex, and Marriage in England 1500–1800* (New York: Harper and Row, 1977), pp. 239–40.

5 I draw here on David Musselwhite's argument which implicitly challenges such notions of the politics of the novel as Bahktin articulates in *The Dialogic Imagination: Four Essays* trans. Michael Holquist (Austin, University of Texas Press, 1981). Rather than view the novel as a form that – like carnival – resisted hegemony, Musselwhite argues that the novel appropriates symbolic practices that would otherwise behave as forms of resistance. I intend to suggest that the politics of the novel are determined, on the one hand, by the genre's tendency to suppress alternative forms of literacy and to produce the homogenized discourse we know as polite standard English. I will push this argument further and suggest that, on the other hand, the novel's politics depend on how we use the genre today. In writing this book, I am assuming that one may expose the operations of the hegemony by reading the novel as the history of those operations. If there is any truth in this claim, then in adopting the novel's psychologizing strategies, one only perpetuates the great nineteenth century project that suppressed political consciousness. David Musselwhite, "The Novel as Narcotic," *1848: The Sociology of Literature* (Colchester, England: University of Essex, 1978), pp. 208–9.

Susan S. Lanser

'Towards a Feminist Narratology'
Style

There are compelling reasons why feminism (or any explicitly political criticism) and narratology (or any largely formal poetics) might seem incompatible. The technical, often neologistic, vocabulary of narratology has alienated critics of many persuasions and may seem particularly counterproductive to critics with political concerns. Feminists also tend to be distrustful of categories and oppositions, of "a conceptual universe organized into the neat paradigms of binary logic" (Schor ix)[8] – a distrust which explains part of the attraction of feminist theory to Derridean deconstruction. But there are (at least) three more crucial issues about which feminism and narratology might differ: the role of gender in the construction of narrative theory, the status of narrative as mimesis or semiosis, and the importance of context for determining meaning in narrative.

The most obvious question feminism would ask of narratology is simply this: upon what body of texts, upon what understandings of the narrative and referential universe, have the insights of narratology been based? It is readily apparent that virtually no work in the field of narratology has taken gender into account, either in designating a canon or in formulating questions and hypotheses. This means, first of all, that the narratives which have provided the foundation for narratology have been either men's texts or texts treated as men's texts. Genette's formulation of a "Discours du récit" on the basis of Proust's *A la recherche du temps perdu*, Propp's androcentric morphology of a certain kind of folktale, Greimas on Maupassant, Iser on male novelists from Bunyan to Beckett, Barthes on Balzac, Todorov on the *Decameron* – these are but evident examples of the ways in which the masculine text stands for the universal text. In the structuralist quest for "invariant elements among superficial differences" (Lévi-Strauss 8), for (so-called) universals rather than particulars, narratology has avoided questions of gender almost entirely. This is particularly problematic for those feminist critics – in this country, the majority – whose main interest is the "difference or specificity of women's writing" (Showalter, "Women's Time" 38). The recognition of this specificity has led not only to the rereading of individual texts but to the rewriting of literary history; I am suggesting that it also lead to a rewriting of narratology that takes into account the contributions of women as both producers and interpreters of texts.[9]

This challenge does not deny the enormous value of a body of brilliant narrative theory for the study of women's works; indeed, it has been applied fruitfully to such writers as Colette (Bal, "The Narrating and the Focalizing") and Eliot (Costello) and is crucial to my own studies of narrative voice in women's texts. It does mean that until women's writings, questions of gender, and feminist points of view are considered, it will be impossible even to know the deficiencies of narratology. It seems to me likely that the most abstract and grammatical concepts (say, theories of time) will prove to be adequate. On the other hand, as I will argue later in this essay, theories of plot and story may need to change substantially. And I would predict that the major impact of feminism on narratology will be to raise new questions, to add to the narratological distinctions that already exist, as I will be suggesting below in my discussions of narrative level, context, and voice.

A narratology for feminist criticism would also have to reconcile the primarily semiotic approach of narratology with the primarily mimetic orientation of most (Anglo-American) feminist thinking about narrative. This difference reminds us that "literature is at the juncture of two systems"; one can speak about it as

> a representation of life
> an account of reality
> a mimetic document

and as

> a non-referential linguistic system
> an enunciation supposing a narrator and a listener
> primarily a linguistic construct.
>
> (Furman 64–65)

Traditionally, structuralist narratology has suppressed the representational aspects of fiction and emphasized the semiotic, while feminist criticism has done the opposite. Feminist critics tend to be more concerned with characters than with any other aspect of narrative and to speak of characters largely as if they were persons. Most narratologists, in contrast, treat characters, if at all, as "patterns of recurrence, motifs which are continually recontextualized in other motifs"; as such, they "lose their privilege, their central status, and their definition" (Weinsheimer 195). This conception could seem to threaten one of feminist criticism's deepest premises: that narrative texts, and particularly texts in the novelistic tradition, are profoundly (if never simply) referential – and influential – in their representations of gender relations. The challenge to both feminism and narratology is to recognize the dual nature of narrative, to find categories and terms that are abstract and semiotic enough to be useful, but concrete and mimetic enough to seem relevant for critics whose theories root literature in "the real conditions of our lives" (Newton 125).

The tendency to pure semiosis is both cause and effect of a more general tendency in narratology to isolate texts from the contexts of their production and reception and hence from what "political" critics think of as literature's ground of being – the "real world." This is partly a result of narratology's desire for a precise, scientific description of discourse, for many of the questions concerning the relationship of literature to the "real world" – questions of why, so what, to what effect – are admittedly speculative. Thus "when narratology does attempt to account for the contextual, it does so in terms of narrative conventions and codes. Yet their capacity to account for social, historical or contextual differences always remains limited by the original formalist closure within which such codes and conventions are defined" (Brewer 1143). This is why early in the history of formalism, critics like Medvedev and Bakhtin called for a "sociological poetics" that would be dialectically theoretical and historical: "Poetics provides literary history with direction in the specification of the research material and the basic definitions of its forms and types. Literary history amends the definitions of poetics, making them more flexible, dynamic, and adequate to the diversity of the historical material" (30). My insistence on writing women's texts into the historical canon of narratology has precisely this aim of making it more adequate to the diversity of narrative.

Finally, feminist criticism would argue that narratology itself is ideological, indeed in an important sense fictional. One need not agree wholeheartedly with Stanley Fish that "formal units are always a function of the interpretive model one brings to bear (they are not 'in the text')" (13), to recognize that no interpretive system is definitive or inevitable. But as Fish also reminds us, every theory must believe itself the best theory possible (361). Formalist-structuralist narratology may "know" that its categories are not immanent, but it proceeds as if there were "a stable and immediately knowable text, directly available to classificatory operations that are themselves neutral and innocent of interpretive bias" (Chambers 18–19). Feminist criticism has simply not had this luxury: in its critique of masculine bias, it has of necessity taken the view that theory sometimes says more about the reader than about the text.

A narratology for feminist criticism would begin, then, with the recognition that revision of a theory's premises and practices is legitimate and desirable. It would probably be cautious in its construction of systems and favor flexible categories over fixed sets. It would scrutinize its norms to be sure of what they are normative. It would be willing to look afresh at the question of gender and to re-form its theories on the basis of women's texts, as Robyn Warhol's essay on the "engaging narrator," just published in *PMLA*, begins to do. In both its concepts and its terminology, it would reflect the mimetic as well as the semiotic experience that is the reading of literature, and it would study narrative in relation to a referential context that is simultaneously linguistic, literary, historical, biographical, social, and political. Granted, narratology might have to be willing to cede some precision and simplicity for the sake of relevance and accessibility, to develop terminology less confusing, say, than a series like analepsis, prolepsis, paralepsis, and metalepsis. The valuable and impressive work that has been done in the field would be opened to a critique and supplement in which feminist questions were understood to contribute to a richer, more useful, and more complete narratology. For as I have been trying to suggest, a narratology that cannot adequately account for women's narratives is an inadequate narratology for men's texts as well.

A re-formed narratology should be of particular interest to feminist critics because fiction is the dominant genre in the study of women and literature. The necessarily semiotic nature of even a revised narratology will help to balance feminist criticism's necessarily mimetic commitments. The comprehensiveness and care with which narratology makes distinctions can provide invaluable methods for textual analysis. As Mieke Bal argues, "The use of formally adequate and precise tools is not interesting in itself, but it can clarify other, very relevant issues and provide insights which otherwise remain vague" ("Sexuality" 121). Narratology and feminist criticism might profitably join forces, for example, to explore the teleological aspects of narrative, which have concerned narratologists like Ann Jefferson and Marianna Torgovnick and feminist critics like Rachel Blau DuPlessis. I can imagine a rich dialogue between Armine Mortimer Kotin's and Nancy K. Miller's analyses of the plot of *La Princesse de Clèves*. And a major benefit of narratology is that it offers a relatively independent (pre-textual) framework for studying groups of texts. It could, for example, provide a particularly valuable foundation for exploring one of the most complex and troubling questions for feminist criticism: whether there is indeed a "woman's writing" and/or a female tradition, whether men and women do write differently. For given the volatile nature of the question, the precision and abstraction of narratological systems offers the safety for investigation that more impressionistic theories of difference do not. This kind of research would demonstrate the particular responsiveness of narratology to certain problems for which other theories have not been adequate and hence illustrate its unique value for feminist scholarship.

(1986)

Notes

8   Oppositional thinking has, of course, been sharply disadvantageous to women, as to other dominated groups. Binary pairs of the variety P/not-P are precisely the structures that create hierarchy (as in nonwhite, illiterate, un-American).

Categories and classifications, while sometimes also used by feminists, are ripe for Procrustean distortions, for premature closures, for stifling rigidities.

9   In *The Narrative Act* I have in fact worked with women's texts as well as with men's, and I have also included the narrative theories of neglected women like Vernon Lee and Käte Friedemann. But I did not really undertake the radical reevaluation I am now calling for, one which would mean *beginning* with women's writings (both narrative and theoretical) in order not to remarginalize the marginal, in compensation for a training that has been so strongly biased in favor of male discourse.

MARILYN R. FARWELL

Heterosexual Plots and Lesbian Narratives

How, then, can we think about a lesbian narrative when systematic descriptions of narrative patterns, especially those aware of the gender implications, suggest the hegemony of not only male heterosexual but also of male homosexual/homosocial desire and offer as alternatives plots which rely on heterosexual women's experience and a narrative position related to men? How would a lesbian narrative function as an alternative narrative model? Literary critics of the last twenty-five years have more often provided thematic rather than structural alternatives. Catharine R. Stimpson proposed what has become the classic division of lesbian narratives into "the dying fall, a narrative of damnation ... and the enabling escape, a narrative of the reversal of such descending trajectories" ("Zero" 244). To these distinctions Terry Castle adds the division between the " 'dysphoric' " story – "female homosexual desire as a finite phenomenon – a temporary phase in a larger pattern of heterosexual *Bildung*" – or the " 'euphoric' " story in which a "new world is imagined in which male bonding has no place" (85–6). On that last description hangs lesbian theory's clearest alternative structural paradigm. Castle proposes that we think of lesbian narratives as "counterplotting" (82). Using Sedgwick's triangle of male-female-male relationships as the master plot, Castle suggests that lesbian novels plot against the normal paradigm by first subverting that triangle with a female-male-female triangle and then by eliminating the male middle. The result is fiction that always has "a profoundly attenuated relationship with what we think of, stereotypically, as narrative verisimilitude, plausibility, or 'truth to life' " (88). While Castle's theory unveils sameness as one structural element in lesbian narratives, Toni A. H. McNaron isolates it as the central dynamic of lesbian literature. In an essay entitled "Mirrors and Likeness: A Lesbian Aesthetic in the Making," McNaron claims that "sexual likeness or mirroring" provides an "alternative aesthetic to the thrust and parry, sticks and bowls school" traditionally favored (305). The subject-other dynamic of language and literature can then be reread in Penelope J. Engelbrecht's terms as "the inter/action of a lesbian Subject and a lesbian Other/self," a relationship in which the two terms "are more than interchangeable; they are synonymous" (86). But McNaron refuses to accept the reduction of sameness to blandness, sexual or aesthetic; in fact, she claims that when "liking is based on likeness ..., the connection often becomes electric" (294). The resulting literature is not without an aesthetic or narrative tension, but its movement mitigates the oppositional polemics of gender division and, as Mieke Bal illustrates, highlights the narrative's potential to distribute power more evenly. Thus both critics point to structural relationships among characters as central to the narrative's rules and the revisioning of these structural relationships as central to a lesbian narrative.

While my definition of the lesbian narrative depends on both of these astute suggestions, it also attempts to combine and extend the parameters of each. Sameness is differently structured in gay male writing than in lesbian writing, and is not to be equated with identity or with a unitary subject. Sameness is determined by positioning, by a direction rather than by identical somatic or psychic characteristics, and this similar positioning also assumes a doubled positionality of desired/desiring and active/passive wherein each character occupies either both positions at the same time or at different times. Terry Castle's reworking of Sedgwick is seductive, but lesbian counterplotting is not only the elimination of the male figure but also a complex readjustment of male characters. However important the elimination of male bonding or male figures may be to primarily white, lesbian narratives, for women of color the elimination of the male often threatens racial unity, even in their construction of the lesbian subject. More important, because Sedgwick's paradigm exists in conjunction with the heterosexually mandated mechanics of narrative, those gendered positionalities that reside in the interaction of a character and its abstract narrative space, excising a male character from the text does not necessarily change the gendered structure of narrative or, what might be called in a less formalist manner, the reader's expectations about active and passive narrative functions. In fact, as Jeanette Winterson proves in *Sexing the Cherry*, it should be possible to position a male character in a lesbian text that revolutionizes narrative mechanics. Finally, while both Castle and McNaron make possible a reading of the lesbian subject as a metaphor, McNaron creating more potential than Castle, neither emphasizes that as the centerpiece of her theory. It is at this point that my theory of the lesbian narrative begins.

In any definition of a lesbian narrative, the first problem is to explain the various meanings attached to the term "lesbian" and then to construe the resulting possibilities for the lesbian subject in narrative. The narrativized lesbian is not simply a given – a character whose sexuality is obvious or hinted at or even a coded image of two intensely involved women friends – rather, it is a trope, developed in the twentieth century and especially in the last twenty-five years, that functions in a variety of literal and nonliteral ways. This figure, which can function as a single character, as a couple, or as a community, is gendered female, but an excessive or grotesque female because by refusing to position itself in opposition to the male, it exceeds cultural and narrative boundaries. The lesbian subject's gendered excess implies that it is perceived as an ambiguously gendered figure – one that occupies both active and passive positions at the same time or crosses these boundaries. But the narrative consistently attempts to force this figure into recognizable gender categories. If, for instance, a male remains in a traditional story, the narrative – or the reader – will attempt to force the female figure into the narrative space of subordination. Thus the film *Aliens* refuses to allow Ripley to fall in love because she would lose her agency under those circumstances. Like Queen Elizabeth I, who knew that she would lose her power if she were to heed Parliament's directives for her to marry, the writers of this film know instinctively that a love relationship for Ripley will make her less than the actor and protagonist of the story. The lesbian subject, however, is a text image that refuses to align itself with the gendered mechanics and instead challenges those mechanics for its own narrative space, a lesbian narrative space. Because narrative space is, in effect, the structural function of narrative elements, lesbian narrative space is the combination and interchangeability of the conventional active and passive functions that have been strictly divided into male and female and, most often, male and female characters. As a result, the lesbian subject realigns some of the accepted narrative categories, particularly those of protagonist and object, narrator, and closure. In other words, the lesbian subject redraws the gender boundaries in the narrative categories in which subjectivity is posited. The narrative system, then, is unavoidable, but also can be stretched to accommodate different power relations. This approach, I believe, will make easier the identification as lesbian texts that do not contain specific lesbian characters, themes, or lesbian authors and yet not exclude more traditionally defined lesbian narratives.

As an interloper in narrative, the lesbian subject must take on the existing structure, function within some of its parameters, yet question its movement and arrangement of subject positions. This interrogation happens first, when female bonding breaks up male bonding, realigning any remaining male characters; second, when the asymmetrical structural patterns of active agent and passive object are revised by the structural interjection of sameness; and finally, when these changes on a structural level affect the movement and thematics of the traditional narrative. One technique, for instance, that affects these shifts is multiple plots or voices. As Susan S. Lanser notes, "polyphony is more pronounced and more consequential in women's narratives and in the narratives of other dominated peoples" (350). Multiple plots or voices heighten our awareness of the arbitrariness of the traditional plot by either imitating it, or parodying it, or referring obliquely to it, or recalling it through images. It is as if the story is instead a series of stories, telling and retelling itself. These counterplots often occur in the multiple voices of the narrators who direct the story's internal strategy. It is not, then, linearity that is poison to a lesbian subject and therefore to the lesbian narrative, but the lack of structural realignments that in turn affect the narrative thematics. Only when a lesbian character does not effect structural change and is consequently absorbed into a single, linear trajectory does the traditional narrative triumph. The lesbian figure who does realign structural categories is the lesbian subject who represents more than transparent literalness.

(1996)

ROBYN R. WARHOL

Having a Good Cry: Effeminate Feelings and Pop-Culture Forms

3. Sentimental narrative discourse requires a particular handling of "internal focalization," Genette's (1979) term for the technique of limiting narrative perspective to a single character's consciousness, despite the fact that the character does not speak the narration. Scenes in sentimental novels and films tend to be focalized either through victims (such as the many slaves separated from their families in *Uncle Tom*, the overworked and underappreciated George Bailey in *It's a Wonderful Life*, and the long-suffering Emma in *Terms*) or triumphant figures who have formerly been represented as oppressed (such as each of the March daughters in her little moment of glory, as when Meg receives praise from her husband, Jo gets a piece of writing accepted for publication, Beth receives the gift of a piano, and Amy accepts Laurie's marriage proposal). This focalization invites the reader to participate emotionally from the subject-position of the oppressed, in the diegetic good times and the bad. Sentimental novels can use embedded first-person narratives to achieve this effect, as when Cassie narrates to Uncle Tom the miserable story of her life as a "quadroon" slave sexually abused by her "master" (*Uncle Tom's Cabin*, 514–22). More often, the "omniscient" narrative focus simply shifts to the perspective of the sufferer, rendering the scene as he or she sees it, for instance, in the chapter of *Little Women* called "Amy's Valley of Humiliation," in which the youngest of the heroines is physically punished at school. As Fisher has pointed out, the focalization in sentimental narrative sometimes comes through sympathetic intermediary

figures who are not, themselves, directly oppressed – such as Eva in *Uncle Tom* – but it is seldom if ever granted to those who oppress the protagonists in the fictional world. This careful limiting of the narrative point of view to those who suffer and triumph after tribulation can effect a powerful pull on the sensations of a susceptible reader. In sentimental novels, moreover, the "good cry" is much more often evoked by scenes of triumph than by scenes of sadness: it is not Eva's death that inspires the cry, but her conviction that she is going to a "better place"; Beth March's death scene is notorious for making readers cry, but so is the earlier scene in which Beth does not die while her mother is out of town, but survives for a mother–daughter reunion.

Attention to the role narrative focalization plays in the affective dynamic of reading fiction and film is important, as it presents a challenge to the idea that readers sympathize with suffering characters when they can "identify" with them.[8] As a concept within psychoanalytic interpretation of texts, identification puts the crying reader in a position of enjoying pleasures that are specifically masochistic. If we think about the reader's consciously feeling that the miserable or triumphant sufferer is "just like me," however, audiences' participation in sentimentalism becomes more positively performative, less revealing of some presumed hidden truth about the readers' "real feelings."

4. The narrators of sentimental novels frequently use earnest, direct address to a narratee, calling upon him or her to recognize parallels between lived experience and the situations represented in the fiction. This, of course, is the notorious "preachy" tendency of sentimental novels that so many twentieth-century readers could not abide. Direct address to the reader is, however, central to the sentimental novelists' project, in that it does *not* rely on the actual audience's "identification" with characters to be the grounds for readers' taking the fiction seriously. The sentimental narrator (usually an example of what I have called elsewhere the feminine "engaging narrator") enforces comparisons between a flesh-and-blood reader's experience and characters' experiences which readers might not "naturally" have made on their own.

Rowson does it often: "My dear young readers, I would have you read this scene with attention, and reflect that you may yourselves one day be mothers.... Then once more read over the sorrows of poor Mrs. Temple, and remember, the mother whom you so dearly love and venerate will feel the same" (*Charlotte Temple*, 54). Stowe does it even more often: "In such a case, you write to your wife, and send messages to your children; but Tom could not write" (*Uncle Tom's Cabin*, 228); "And if you should ever be under the necessity, sir, of selecting out of two hundred men, one who was to become your absolute owner and disposer, you would, perhaps, realize, just as Tom did, how few there were that you would feel at all comfortable in being made over to" (476). Any given reader's ability to answer such an appeal would depend on that reader's willingness to step into the role constructed by the narrator's utterance (does Rowson's reader have to be female, to feel the agony of a mother's potential loss? Does Stowe's have to be male, to answer to the threat of freedom curtailed?). But those readers who could respond, whether on a literal or an imaginative level, might be effectively invited to participate in the represented emotions.

(2003)

Note

8 Michael Steig's remarkable reader-response study, *Stories of Reading* (1989), for example, attributes Steig's own crying over Charles Dickens's *Bleak House* to identification with the characters. Steig reports, "I still find my eyes filling with tears at the same old points. I have felt in the past that I must have some residue of sentimentality in my soul, and have been annoyed that Dickens manipulates me into that reaction, but that is probably unfair" (70). Steig finds the "coy" narrator, Esther Summerson, consistently irritating, "and yet at the same time I must be identifying with her strongly, on the evidence of the way my tears so easily flow." Emphasizing the intrinsically personal psychology of such identification, Steig remarks, "To get at the reasons for this will require some digging into my past" (70).

CORA KAPLAN

'Introduction'
Aurora Leigh and Other Poems

In the opening of Book V of *Aurora Leigh* there is a long discursive section on the poet's vocation where the author dismisses the lyric mode – ballad, pastoral and Barrett Browning's own favourite, the sonnet – as static forms: the poet 'can stand/Like Atlas in the sonnet and support/His own heavens pregnant with dynastic stars;/But then he must stand still, nor take a step.' The move into epic poetry chipped at her reputation in establishment circles, but enhanced her popularity. It was a venture into a male stronghold; epic and dramatic verse are associated with the Classicists and with Shakespeare, Milton, Shelley and Tennyson, and later, Browning. In 1893 the influential critic Edmund Gosse wrote that women have achieved nothing 'in the great solid branches of poetry in epic, in tragedy, in didactic and philosophical verse.... The reason is apparently that the artistic nature is not strongly developed in her.' This typical retrospective judgment may be a clue to *Aurora Leigh*'s modern oblivion, and one reason why such an important and diverse poet as Barrett Browning is now known almost exclusively as the author of *Sonnets from the Portuguese* (1850), her brilliant series of love lyrics to her husband. Twentieth-century male poet-critics echo Gosse's belief that women's voice in poetry, as in life, should be confined to the lyric. How can one account then for a sustained narrative poem that is both didactic and philosophical as well as passionate and female, an unmannerly intervention in the 'high' patriarchal discourse of bourgeois culture? *Aurora Leigh* makes few apologies for this rude eruption into the after-dinner subjects that go with the port and cigars. Barrett Browning knew less about 'this live throbbing age,/That brawls, cheats, maddens, calculates, aspires,' than Mrs Gaskell. But it is the latter, in *Mary Barton*, who intervenes with the authorial voice to offer a timid sop to male expertise: 'I am not sure if I can express myself in the technical terms of either masters or workmen...'

The taboo, it is stronger than prejudice, against women's entry into public discourse as speakers or writers, was in grave danger of being definitively broken in the mid-nineteenth century as more and more educated, literate women entered the arena as imaginative writers, social critics and reformers. The oppression of women within the dominant class was in no way as materially brutal as the oppression of women of the working class, but it had its own rationale and articulation. The mid-century saw the development of a liberal 'separate but equal' argument which sometimes tangled with, sometimes included the definition of women's sphere and the development of the cult of true womanhood. The publicity given on the woman question hardly dented the continued elaboration of mores and manners which ensured that daughters were marriageable, i.e. virgins. Patriarchal dominance involved the suppression of women's speech outside the home and a rigorous censorship of what she could read or write. All the major women writers were both vulnerable to and sensitive about charges of 'coarseness'. The Brontë sisters, Sand and Barrett Browning were labelled coarse by their critics, and, occasionally, by other women. Sexual impurity, even in thought, was *the* unforgivable sin, the social lever through which Victorian culture controlled its females, and kept them from an alliance with their looser lived working-class sisters.

The debates on the woman question which took up so many pages of leading British periodicals between 1830 and 1860 should not be seen as marginal to a male-dominated ruling class, increasingly threatened from below by an organising proletariat. Caught between this and the need to accommodate a limited demand for equity from informed women of their own class, they were equally committed to the absolute necessity of maintaining social control over females, and its corollary, the sexual division of labour. To get a sense of the space and importance given to the issue, one only has to leaf through the major quarterlies for a given year. The winter 1857 issue of the *North British Review* had both a substantial review of *Aurora Leigh* and a long review article dealing with eight books, titled 'The Employment of Women', which ranges from an abrupt dismissal of Margaret Fuller's *Woman in the Nineteenth Century* for its romantic obscurity, to a serious discussion of Anna Jameson's *The Communion of Labour*, a work which argued that middle-class women should be 'employed' in ameliorating the condition of the female poor. In support of Mrs Jameson the article quotes both Tennyson's *The Princess* and *Aurora Leigh*.

The right to write was closely connected with every wider choice that women might wish to make. In an age characterised by the importance of the popular press as the place of ideological production and the spread of female literacy, it was of prime importance to warn women off questioning traditional sexual morality. Public writing and public speech, closely allied, were both real and symbolic acts of self-determination for women. Barrett Browning uses the phrase 'I write' four times in the first two stanzas of Book I, emphasising the connection between the first person narrative and the 'act' of women's speech; between the expression of woman's feelings and thoughts and the legitimate professional exercise of that expression. Barrett Browning makes the link between women's intervention into political debate and her role as imaginative writer quite clear in her defence of Harriet Beecher Stowe's *Uncle Tom's Cabin*. She rejoices in Stowe's success as 'a woman and a human being' and pushes the message home to her timid female correspondent:

> Oh, and is it possible that you think a woman has no business with questions like the question of slavery? Then she had better use a pen no more. She had better subside into slavery and concubinage herself I think as in the times of old, shut herself up with the Penelopes in the "women's apartment", and take no rank among thinkers and speakers.

Writing is a skilled task learnt at the expense of 'Long green days/Worn bare of grass and sunshine, – long calm nights/From which the silken sleeps were fretted out ... with no amateur's/Irreverent haste and busy idleness/I set myself to art!' *Aurora Leigh* enters, however tentatively, into debates on *all* the forbidden subjects. In the first person epic voice of a major poet, it breaks a very specific silence, almost a gentlemen's agreement between women authors and the arbiters of high culture in Victorian England, that allowed women to write if only they would shut up about it.

(1978)

MEENAKSHI PONNUSWAMI

'Small Island People: Black British Women Playwrights'
The Cambridge Companion to Modern British Women Playwrights

It has been argued that increased activity in black arts in the mid-to-late 1980s was related to increased state funding for 'ethnic' social programmes which followed the urban uprisings of 1980 and 1981 and the subsequent recommendations of the 1982–3 Scarman Report on Brixton. The relationship between the theatre, political activism, and the state is a particularly important issue for any analysis of post-war British theatre, black or white; indeed, the rapid expansion of *all* theatrical activity during the 1960s and 1970s can be directly linked to state funding, which in turn may be seen as one part of the state's more-or-less planned efforts in the post-war era to contain the radicalism threatened by the social restructuring experienced during the war. A central debate for many of the fringe groups of the period, especially those on the Left, was whether to accept subsidies and perform to larger audiences (thereby risking the possibility of complicity with the state and the arts elite) or to refuse subsidy and perform only among the true folk (risking permanent ghettoisation and the possibility of never finding an audience).

The state's cultivation of black arts in the aftermath of Brixton did pose some problems. Juliet Jarrett, for example, has argued that the effect of such programmes was to create a handful of poorly funded and marginalised spaces for black artists; she cites the example of Lubaina Himid, curator of 'The Thin Black Line', the ICA's mid-1980s exhibition of works by black women, who wrote: 'The Greater London Council threatened to withdraw its considerable funding to the ICA if something black did not appear that financial year.'[17] As early as 1987, Pratibha Parmar despaired that the 'assumption of shared subjectivities' which had fired black feminisms a few years earlier had somehow 'led to a political practice which employs a language of "authentic subjective experience"': 'many women have retreated into ghettoised lifestyle "politics" and find themselves unable to move beyond personal and individual experience'.[18] Sociologist Amina Mama suggested further that the 'state-funded projects' (which, as she puts it, 'gained ascendance under the contradictory conditions of Thatcherism and municipal socialism') dispersed the radical energies of the earlier grass-roots black British feminisms precisely because such projects were 'constituted along ... ethnically specific lines': 'a growing focus on identity and a new competitive cultural politics', argues Mama, 'replaced the 1970s/early 1980s notions of black unity and wider anti-imperialist and black liberation struggles'.[19] In other words, subsidy was able to divide and rule by encouraging the development of inward-looking groups whose interests were obliged to centre on questions of selfhood and identity rather than political coalition.

Of course, dilemmas about whether to accept state funding can only vex those who have access to subsidy in the first place, and this was, as we have seen, rarely the case for black British theatres. In any case, although some groups do seem to have coalesced along specific ethnic axes, it is not at all clear that subsidy entailed political compromise or ethnocentric wrangling. Moreover, as May Joseph argues, the declaration of 'positionality' can be a means for black British women to contest the state's colonising of immigrant women's bodies, given the need for an 'emergent' and repressed citizenry – 'bodies "outside the state"' – to demand political participation within a state which at once controls and denies such participation. In such a context, writes Joseph, the announcement of one's location 'implies locating oneself as a subject already overdetermined by various contingent narratives' (p. 205). Implicit in this analysis is the suggestion that identity politics do not repudiate the anti-imperialist and global political imperatives of the mid-1980s; rather, the theatre produced by that political moment performs 'new kinds of multicultural citizenship' ('Borders', p. 199). The ideological legacy of the community activism of the mid-1980s, which drew attention to the need for new articulations of race, gender, and citizenship, is clearly discernible in this performance.

(2000)

Notes

17 Juliet Jarrett, 'Creative Space?: The Experience of British Women in British Art Schools', in Delia Jarrett-Macauley (ed.) *Reconstructing Womanhood, Reconstructing Feminism: Writings on Black Women* (London and New York: Routledge, 1996), pp. 121–3.

18 Pratibha Parmar, 'Other Kinds of Dreams', *Feminist Review*, 31, Spring 1989, pp. 55–65. Reprinted in Mirza, *Black British Feminism*, pp. 67–9.

19 Amina Mama, 'Black Women and the British State: Race, Class and Gender Analysis for the 1990s', in Peter Braham, Ali Rattansi, and Richard Skellington (eds.) *Racism and Anti-Racism: Inequalities, Opportunities and Policies* (London: Sage Publications, 1992), p. 97.

CLARE BRANT

'Varieties of Women's Writing'
Women and Literature in Britain 1700–1800

Feminist recuperation of eighteenth-century women's writing acquired two landmarks in the 1980s: Jane Spencer's book on women novelists, and Roger Lonsdale's anthology of women poets.[1] These rehabilitations challenged the canon, but at the price of a conservative attitude to genre. Many women writers in eighteenth-century Britain were not novelists, poets, or dramatists. They were writers of letters, diaries, memoirs, essays – genres of sometimes uncertain status then and certainly liminal status now. Indeed, one of the most popular titles for women (as well as for men) in this period was *Miscellanies*; another was *Poems on Several Occasions*, in which 'several' points to diversity as well as multiplicity, to several sorts of occasions. To modern minds, writers who present themselves as miscellaneous or occasional are only half in the picture; if those writers are women, as feminist critics are well aware, they run the risk of being pushed out of the picture altogether. Miscellaneity is critically awkward, it's true: a volume which includes letters, essays, and poems is harder to discuss than a volume of poems, even though those poems can be separated into epistles, pastorals, and so on; and the generic variety within 'prose' has had less critical attention or been understood predominantly in relation to fiction. But genres supposedly marginal to print culture had some advantages – indeterminacy, informality – and should not be read simply as the consequence of patriarchal disempowerment. This is not to overlook the fact that many women were prevented from becoming published authors, but so-called 'private' genres like letters are often highly social, and engage with public-sphere subjects like travel and politics in ways which go beyond the formation of a gendered subject.

I want to show the rewards of using genre to uncover some of the diversity of eighteenth-century women's writing, whilst recognising its limits. Genre has three drawbacks. Firstly, genres are not always distinct. For example, Sylviana Sola's 1752 volume entitled *Various Essays* consists of themed letters, dialogues, an allegory, verses, and a series of reflections headed 'Various Thoughts'. The templates of several genres can fit the same text. Secondly, genre has an ambivalent relationship with biography. If writings are generically diverse, the figure of the author can stabilise them. Thus Lady Mary Wortley Montagu's letters, essays, poems, and romance writings, or Hannah More's poems, tracts, dialogues, letters, and educational and political writings, are brought together. Biography remembers the sex of a writer, and a female author can be connected to other sorts of women. The figure of an author also supplies a literary cohesion which can then be 'discovered' in other works. Thus once Samuel Johnson is understood to be an author, any work by him can be read as Johnsonian. But there is a slippage between 'writing' and 'author' which makes it harder for women to attain the status of being authors. The third problem is that author figures can erase the significance of genre even when critics are particular about it: so a letter, a satire, or a poem by Swift have virtually equal potential to disclose that Swiftian irony beloved by an older generation of male eighteenth-century scholars. It is harder to find paradigms which relate, say, the poems of

Laetitia Pilkington to the memoirs in which she published them in 1748–54. It is tempting for feminist critics to make gender itself such a paradigm: hence displays of wit or expressions of desire can be read in terms of orthodoxies and transgressions within norms of femininity. This makes women writers inescapably *women* writers, even with attention to class or race as equally powerful constituents of identity.[2] Without advocating androgyny, genre-based criticism can relate women's writing to a variety of literary discourses.

A stress on the diversity of women's writing raises questions of canonicity particular to the study of eighteenth-century literature. Though new canons usually begin with single works – Behn's *Oroonoko*, or Wollstonecraft's *Vindication of the Rights of Woman*, for example – canonicity can serve diversity, as 'complete works' appear and show an author to be various in herself. Conversely, it can mean more of a writer's works reductively marketed as classics: hence Jane Austen stays commercially evergreen. The debate about what to claim in the absence of canonicity should also consider impersonation, ventriloquism and transvestism as varieties of women's writing, since male authors of fiction in particular invented heroines who became patterns, and rivals, for writing women. As Kathryn Shevelow has shown, many letters which purported to come from women were probably male-authored.[3] The tragic Portuguese Nun, supposed author of the popular *Lettres Portugaises* (first translated 1678), and Rousseau's Julie, heroine of *La Nouvelle Héloïse* (1761), became patterns of feminine desire, and Richardson's *Pamela* was a landmark for working-class texts. So the editor of Hannah Snell's life-story declared that Snell's determination to preserve her chastity was greater than Pamela's, and her story more sensational.[4] This competition between working-class woman and fictional heroine has been explained by Dianne Dugaw as the intrusion of middle-class discourses into the world of rumbustious ballads about cross-dressing; the polite colonises the popular.[5] A reverse disjunction of high life and middle-class fictions can be seen in the claims of some memoirists that they did not read novels. However unlikely this seems, it was as strategic for them to claim ignorance of fictional models of seduction as it was for Snell's editor to assume his readers' familiarity with them. The complex relations between fiction, male-authored or otherwise, and non-fictional women's writing, add to the difficulties of classification.

Anyone trying to comprehend the variety of women's writing has to reconsider anonymity, pseudonymity, and (un)originality. The commonplace book, for instance, used by many readers to make copies of favourite texts or extracts, could involve more than functional transcription. In 1705, Frances Lady Norton published two devotional works composed mostly of other people's words, but, unusually, signed by herself. Her daughter also took up the genre, if one can call it that, as something more authored than

we usually understand.[6] To cite an authority made writing culturally defer-
ential to men, but more authorised for women. As Lady Mary Walker put
it, 'you must not call me a plagiarist, for sometimes having recourse to my
common place-book'.[7] Again, Hester Thrale's marginalia, usually paragraph-
length reflections containing criticism, witticisms, or anecdotes, blur the
dividing line between primary and secondary texts, making annotation
almost a form of dialogue.

There were three kinds of eighteenth-century misconceptions about wom-
en's writing. The first was, predictably, that what women wrote was not in
fact written by women. So Sarah Chapone reported that on a visit to Oxford,
her brother ' "heard a whole room full of [men] deny that a thing was or
could be written by a woman" '.[8] Conversely, the second misconception
assumed female authorship on the basis of stereotypical feminine discourse.
So the Bishop of Rochester wrote to Pope that he thought the Arabian Tales
were wild and absurd: worse, 'observing how full they are in the descriptions of Dress, Furniture &c. I cannot help thinking them the product of
some Woman's imagination'.[9] That attention to daily life which made travel-
writing by women such as Lady Mary Wortley Montagu authentic and
authoritative was grossly material to a hostile male reader. If good books
could not be written by women, and bad books must be written by women,
a third and most peculiar view of women's writing reduced its variety to a
single corrupting effect. The following comment is by Oliver Goldsmith,
and I quote it at length because Goldsmith is himself a writer whose variety
has not hampered his canonical status, and because his paranoid fusion of
different genres into a single negative category shows how the concept of
'women's writing' expels literary particularity.

> The female miss, it must be owned, has of late been tolerably fruitful. Novels
> written by ladies, poems, morality, essays and letters, all written by ladies,
> show that this beautiful sex are resolved to be, one way or another, the joyful
> mothers of children. Happy it is that the same conveyance which brings an
> heir to the family shall at the same time produce a book to mend his manners,
> or teach him to make love, when ripe for the occasion. Yet, let not the ladies
> carry off all the glories of the late production ascribed to them; it is plain by
> the style, and a nameless somewhat in the manner, that pretty fellows, coffee-
> critics, and dirty shirted dunces have sometimes a share in the achievement.
> We have detected so many of these imposters already, that in future we shall
> look on every publication that shall be ascribed to a lady as the work of one
> of this amphibious fraternity.[10]

Collapsing procreation into literary creativity, Goldsmith is resentful that
women should correct men or instruct them even as he concedes the part
women's writing plays in upholding conservative family values. Women, no
more than bodies, are simultaneously denounced and erased. The feminine

is a semiotic blank, 'a nameless something in the manner' which turns male authors into pseudo-men, adulterous 'imposters'. Just as their role mushrooms from 'sometimes' to 'every' literary occasion, so the diversity of women's writing is read as uniformly corrupting and doubly false, neither genuinely by a woman, nor by a genuine man. It's true that literary competition between men generated abuse of Grub Street rivals as effeminate, ephemeral, and abject. But so long as men denounced men's writing through a discourse abusive of femininity, women's writing was likely to be seen as a bodily mass.

If this chapter was about varieties of men's writing, it would look slightly different. It would cover more historiography, political and doctrinal literature, more protest writing, more things we classify under the umbrella of the pamphlet. It would address, as this will, letters, essays, life-writings, and dialogues, but it would cover more of the sorts of texts entitled An Enquiry into, An Account of, Remarks on, A Defence of – genres in which authorship is anchored by a seemingly confident place in discourse. It is these genres in which women writers are fewer. But they may be found discussing the same subjects in an unexpected place. So political economy turns up not just in tracts but in novels and poems.[11]

(2000)

Notes

1 Jane Spencer, *The Rise of the Woman Novelist: From Aphra Behn to Jane Austen* (Oxford: Basil Blackwell, 1986); Roger Lonsdale (ed.), *Eighteenth-Century Women Poets: an Oxford Anthology* (Oxford and New York: Oxford University Press, 1990).

2 See Donna Landry, *The Muses of Resistance: Laboring-Class Women's Poetry in Britain, 1739–1796* (Cambridge University Press, 1990) and Paula R. Feldman and Theresa M. Kelley (eds.), *Romantic Women Writers: Voices and Countervoices* (Hanover and London: University Press of New England, 1995).

3 Kathryn Shevelow, *Women and Print Culture: the Construction of Femininity in the Early Periodical* (London and New York: Routledge, 1989).

4 *The Female Soldier; Or, The Surprising Life and Adventures of Hannah Snell* (1750), Augustan Reprint Society, no. 257 (Los Angeles: William Andrews Clark Memorial Library, 1989).

5 *The Female Soldier*, pp. vii–ix, and for further discussion by Dugaw of versions of the Hannah Snell story, see ch. 12 of this volume, pp. 276–9.

6 Lady Grace Gethin, *Misery's Virtues Whet-stone. Reliquae Gethinianae* (London: D. Edwards for the author, 1699).

7 Lady Mary Walker, *Letters from the Duchess de Crui and Others*, 2nd edn, 5 vols. (London: Robson; Walter; and Robinson, 1777), 1, 3.

8 Margaret J. Ezell, *Writing Women's Literary History* (Baltimore: Johns Hopkins University Press, 1993), p. 82.

9   Alexander Pope, *Mr Pope's Literary Correspondence*, 5 vols. (London: E. Curll, 1735), v, 89.
10   *Critical Review,* August 1759; quoted by Alison Adburgham, *Women in Print: Writing Women and Women's Magazines From the Restoration to the Accession of Victoria* (London: George Allen & Unwin, 1972), pp. 114–15.
11   See Isobel Armstrong's brilliant reading of a poem by Barbauld in relation to Burke, Malthus, Adam Smith, and Hume, 'The Gush of the Feminine: How Can We Read Women's Poetry of the Romantic Period?' in Feldman and Kelley, *Romantic Women Writers*, pp. 13–32.

ROSEMARY JACKSON

Fantasy: The Literature of Subversion

Mary Shelley's other prolonged fantasy, *The Last Man*, is even more extreme as a text unable to imagine a resolution of social contradictions except through complete holocaust. Whereas *Frankenstein* depends upon *Political Justice*, *Caleb Williams*, various utopian fantasies, and Coleridge's *Ancient Mariner*, *The Last Man* depends upon a revolutionary political text, Volney's *Ruins of Empires*. This was an anti-despotic publication, brought over from France to be circulated amongst London's Jacobin circles during the 1790s. It celebrates the destruction of patriarchal empire through death's levelling, and many of its powerful, graphic images provide Mary Shelley with dramatic material: 'And now a mournful skeleton is all that subsists of this opulent city, and nothing remains of its powerful government but a vain and obscure remembrance.'[8]

From this revolutionary material, Mary Shelley constructs a remarkable fantasy of cultural annihilation. It is a long, slow-moving narrative, as it tells of a global plague which spreads gradually across the world. Its panorama of decay presents a complete erasure of the human species. Only Verney, the last man (like Frankenstein's creation of a parodic 'first' man, another inversion of Adam), remains to tell the tale of order lapsing into undifferentiation and decay: it is a vast fantasy of entropy. 'One by one we should dwindle into nothingness.' All civilized forms collapse with the plague's levelling: society becomes amorphous. 'I felt as if, from the order of the systematic world, I had plunged into chaos, obscure, contrary, unintelligible.' Through the plague, ordinary life is uncovered and metamorphosed into its opposite.[9]

Verney, as the last man, mourns for the death of culture, weeping over 'the ruins of the boundless continents of the east, and the desolation of the western world.' It is important to distinguish between his voice, as narrator, and Mary Shelley's position, as author. His human (male) lamentation is not hers. In 'dialogue' with his voice of distress is a huge silence: the plague itself, Mary Shelley's fantasy of annihilation of the human. Her writings open an alternative 'tradition', of 'female Gothic'.[10] They fantasize a violent attack upon the symbolic order and it is no accident that so many writers of a Gothic tradition are women: Charlotte and Emily Brontë, Elizabeth Gaskell, Christina Rossetti, Isak Dinesen, Carson McCullers, Sylvia Plath, Angela Carter, all of whom have all employed the fantastic to subvert *patriarchal* society – the symbolic order of modern culture.

A remarkable narrative feature of Mary Shelley's texts is their structural indeterminacy. *The Last Man* is a series of 'fragments', the end being left open. *Frankenstein* is similarly indefinite. Structured like a line of receding mirror images, it moves from the outer tale of Walton, to the inner tale of Frankenstein, to the tale-within-the-tale of the monster's confessions. The reader is progressively seduced from a straightforward epistolary 'realism' into the vortex at the centre where the monster is strangely present (i.e. absent), surrounded by the text's webs of language, 'embedded in the innermost circle ... like the middle ring of a vast inferno'.[11] The three circles of narrative are not neatly re-situated within each other by the end, but collapse together, as Walton records the progressive vanishing of the monster, its end unknown. This open structure introduces a space within the initial 'closed' realistic form: through the monster, a 'place' has been given to non-human desires.

(1981)

Notes

8   Volney, *Ruins of Empires* (London, undated), p. 4.
9   This anticipates Artaud's metaphorical use of the plague in *The Theatre and its Double*: 'Society's barriers became fluid with the effects of the scourge. Order disappeared. He witnessed the subversion of all morality, the breakdown of all psychology.' (p. 7).
10 Ellen Moers, *Literary Women*, pp. 90–110, identifies a tradition of 'female Gothic'. It is surely no coincidence that so many writers and theorists of fantasy as a countercultural form are women – Julia Kristeva, Irène Bessière, Hélène Cixous, Angela Carter. Non-realist narrative forms are increasingly important in feminist writing: no breakthrough of cultural structure seems possible until linear narrative (realism, illusionism, transparent representation) is broken or dissolved.
11 M. A. Goldberg, 'Moral and Myth in Mrs Shelley's *Frankenstein*', *Keats-Shelley Journal*, 8 (1959), pp. 27–38.

ROSALIND COWARD

Female Desire: Women's Sexuality Today

In the adoration of the powerful male, we have the adoration of the father by the small child. This adoration is based on the father as all-powerful, before disillusionment and the struggle for autonomy set in. Sometimes the patriarchal nature of the fantasy becomes explicit:

His words hit her physically, so forcibly did they remind her of her father: he had been the only person who had ever used that word to describe the colour of her hair. And now to hear Stephen do so – the man she loved, who could only see her as a machine – was more than she could bear. Eyes blinded by tears, she ran out.

Roberta Leigh

The way in which these men are portrayed certainly involves a journey back to a world before any struggle for autonomy has occurred. It isn't even an adolescent fantasy; it's pre-adolescent, very nearly pre-conscious. As a fantasy, it represents the adoration of a person on whom your welfare depends, the exaggerated evaluation which children experience before the process of becoming a separate person begins. As the child becomes more independent there's invariably a re-estimation of the parent, perhaps even a disillusionment. The parent who is no longer omnipotent in the child's welfare is no longer seen as omnipotent in the world. The child begins the difficult process of recognizing social valuation as well as personal valuation of the parents. The struggle for autonomy also brings its problems. By adolescence, there's usually a full-scale struggle for independence. Power which might previously have been adored – after all, it ensured the welfare of a dependent child – becomes controlling and suffocating for a child struggling to become independent. The power of one person is seen as depriving another of autonomy. Especially for women, the relationship to patriarchal authority is bound to be hazardous. Men have power and authority only if women's equality is denied.

But in the fantasies represented by these novels, the power of men is adored. The qualities desired are age, power, detachment, the control of other people's welfare. And the novels never really admit any criticism of this power. Occasionally the heroines 'protest' their right to gainful employment, or rebel against the tyranny of the loved men. But in the end they succumb to that form of power. And what attracted them in the first place were precisely all the attributes of the unreconstructed patriarch. The qualities which make these men so desirable are, actually, the qualities which feminists have chosen to ridicule: power (the desire to dominate others); privilege (the exploitation of others); emotional distance (the inability to communicate); and singular love for the heroine (the inability to relate to anyone other than the sexual partner).

It is interesting to realize that obstacles do exist in the way of the heroine's adoration of her man. But the obstacles are never the criticisms or ambiguity which a woman might really feel towards that kind of man. The obstacles come from the outside, from material circumstances or misunderstandings. The work of the narrative is to remove these misunderstandings and obstacles, one by one. Instead of contradictory feelings towards such men, or feelings of suffocation, we have a number of frustrating circumstances which are finally cleared away to allow for the heroine safely to feel her respect and love for the man. In other words, these fantasies admit a belief that everything would be all right between the sexes were it not for a series of foolish misperceptions and misunderstandings.

There are a number of other factors which indicate a powerful infantile fantasy at work. For instance, there's the jealousy to which the heroine is invariably exposed. A rival for the hero's affections is almost obligatory, and the rival is usually better suited by class or by temperament. The crunch point in the narrative often comes when the heroine sees the hero and the other woman embracing, or meets the other two together. When the narrative is resolved, we discover that the hero was thinking about our heroine all along. He was either seeking consolation in another's arms, or was taken in by some scheming type. A satisfactory resolution of this obstacle is the discovery that the hero was after all loyal to the heroine, at least with the emotions if not the body.

The obliteration of a rival is another standard component of an infantile fantasy. The sight of the hero in another's arms is reminiscent of Freud's accounts of one of the forms taken by infantile jealousy provoked by the sight of the parents embracing. The child sees this and is jealous, seeking in fantasy to obliterate the intruding parent. Common childhood fantasies are of obliterating that parent and taking her/his place, becoming the rightful and only recipient of the other parent's love. In pulp romance, the disappointments based on discovering that others have claims on the loved one's attention are obliterated. There aren't really obstacles to total monomaniacal love, only temporary frustrations which the narrative then removes.

There is another significant way in which these narrative fantasies are regressive. It is the way in which sexual desire is portrayed. The hero's power is not only reminiscent of the father's perfection before the fall, so to speak; the power also works to absolve the women from any responsibility for the sexual engagement. Heroes are usually established as either sexually active (lots of girlfriends) or as almost untouchable. In the first case, the heroes are the objects of intense sexual interest, and have active sexual lives but refuse to settle down. In the end it is the overwhelming nature of their special desire for the heroine which is eventually secured. She alone has kindled the overwhelming desire that is going to end in marriage. The 'untouchable' syndrome is really very similar. In these cases, the hero is remote, too good for sexual intrigue, better still a priest – someone, in short, who ought not to feel sexual passion. The heroine alone awakens his desire. The desire he feels for her is so great that he has to come off his pedestal, gather her in his arms and crush her to his chest.

All the frustrations and delays integral to a good romance only heighten this outcome, where the hero's desire is made suddenly explicit. The hero's desire is so great that it borders on the uncontrollable. One journalist called it the 'bruised lips' syndrome, and it is certainly the case that the uncontrollable desire has close resemblances with descriptions of rape. The heroine keeps her blouse buttoned up only with the greatest difficulty until they can breathlessly mutter the marriage vows at each other and bring the novel to a satisfactory close: ' "Please put your dress on," he murmured huskily, "so we can go talk to your parents about our wedding" ' (Janet Dailey).

This fantasy is the ultimate expression of passive sexuality. The heroine may well be 'in love' with the hero. She may well adore him and admire him. But her *desire* is only ever triggered as a response, crushed out of her, as it were, as a series of low moans. Again psychoanalytic writing is illuminating about this kind of fantasy. It represents the projection of active desires by yourself on to another person, who then becomes responsible for that desire.

[...]

One thing about these fantasies, though, is that however passive the female, she is not actually powerless. The conclusion of marriage isn't necessary so much for reasons of morality, but because these fantasies are very obviously about a certain transfer of power, from the man to the woman. The woman is not annihilated by her subordination to the patriarch; she also assumes some power over him since his great power is finally harnessed to one woman – the heroine. Indeed, there are often other elements in romantic novels where the men are rendered helpless and dependent, like children. There's often a scene where the hero falls ill, suffers from hallucinations in the desert, or is even injured:

> The human frailty of Stephen Brandon's sickness – even though momentary – robbed Julia of her awesome fear with which she had regarded him. One could not see a man prostrate and not feel sorry for him; and sympathy – however fleeting – left change in its wake.
>
> Roberta Leigh

Rendering the hero ill, dependent, or injured is a narrative device which crops up all over the place. There's a common theme in fiction and films of women being attracted to cripples, or having fantasies about nursing men through illness during which the man suddenly realizes that 'what he's been feeling is love'. Dick Francis's racing thrillers, which are extremely popular with women, have this theme of male mutilation down to a fine art. We can be sure that if the hero isn't brutalized within the first few pages, he'll certainly get shot, beaten up or fall off his horse pretty soon. Now, all this is extremely interesting; it points to a push for power in female fantasy.

In romantic fiction, the hero is made dependent only 'fleetingly', as Roberta Leigh would undoubtedly have it. But this momentary impotence allows the woman to acquire power, the power of a mother caring for a child. And the concluding marriage is the symbol of the woman achieving power. The men are castrated and then restored. The power which the heroine achieves is the power of the mother; the daughter has taken the mother's place.

(1984)

ALISON LIGHT

Forever England: Femininity, Literature and Conservatism Between the Wars

The question of 'genre' is a useful one to raise, however. In the first place it reminds us of the modernity of many of these critical adjudications; in the second, of the modernity of many of the forms themselves, and finally, that the shaping of bestselling forms of fiction into a recognisable typology, which took significantly new commercial impetus in the period between the wars, altered the conditions for all writers. Once it became possible for readers to ask for a 'detective story' or a 'romance', 'an Edgar Wallace' or 'a Georgette Heyer', and to know what to expect, any writer, and especially those aiming at a broad readership, was up against the question of genre and could expect to be measured in some way against those categories. Moreover, they were categories which frequently confirmed the expectation that particular forms of writing spoke especially to women or to men.

The meanings of romance and of 'romantic' as terms of literary description became more narrowly specialised between the wars, coming to signify only those love-stories, aimed ostensibly at a wholly female readership, which deal primarily with the trials and tribulations of heterosexual desire, and end happily in marriage. At the same time, there is a sense in which, as part of the creation of this 'genre', romance went downmarket as it was boosted by the growth in forms of 'mass entertainment' in the period and its commercialisation made it a bestselling form for a much larger group of readers. Cheaper paperback editions and a plethora of new fiction weeklies for working women and girls (or 'books' as they called them), including *Peg's Paper* (1919), *Red Star* (1929), *Secrets* (1932) and *Oracle* (1933), offered them a staple of 'really grand stories', especially romances, 'that will make you eager to draw up your chair to the fire and have a real good read'.[8] Whereas before the war 'leisure' might be seen as primarily the property of the 'leisured', that is, wealthy, classes, a new market of 'leisure consumers' amongst the working classes was in the process of being created.

Those women's magazines wishing to dissociate themselves from this cheap entertainment, laid their stress not on fiction (which was a mere sideline) but on 'services' to readers (the range of 'experts' to deal with readers' problems which the new *Good Housekeeping* introduced, for example), on household management and 'constructive' uses of free time.[9]

Film, and especially Hollywood cinema, together with the spate of film magazines which became a craze in the late 1920s and '30s, made romance even more visible as the major form for a more heterogeneous class of audience.[10] And for many critics of the new forms of mass entertainment, it was romance which provided the model of all that was meretricious about the popular cultural forms of modernity: the creation of a reader or viewer whose individuality is effaced as they abandon themselves to the screen or to the 'tide of cheap, easy fiction', 'waiting passively to be stimulated'.[11] What might strike the reader now examining these criticisms is how much the descriptions echo traditional views of feminine sexuality as a whole, and can be readily collapsed into a vocabulary of distaste for the lower-class woman in particular. It is as though these new audiences and readerships can only be forgiven if they are seen as experiencing a kind of moral and intellectual violation against their will; if they enjoy it, they must be, like the fictions, 'cheap and easy'. The language in which F. R. Leavis condemns the experience of cinema in his attack on mass culture conjures up again a debased, because feminine, position:

> [Films] provide now the main form of recreation in the civilised world; and they involve surrender, under conditions of hypnotic receptivity, to the cheapest of emotional appeals.[12]

Progressive bourgeois women writers, and university women, were in the van of the attack on this lower class of fiction, of which Q. D. Leavis's pioneering study of 1932, *Fiction and the Reading Public*, is only the best-known example. Rebecca West deplored 'Marie Corelli's incurably commonplace mind' (whilst generously admitting that if 'she had a mind like a milliner's apprentice', she was nevertheless 'something more than a milliner's apprentice').[13] In her review of Ethel M. Dell's *Charles Rex*, West advised the critic who was trying to understand the appeal of best sellers to remember that

> whistles can be made sounding certain notes which are clearly audible to dogs and other of the lower animals, though man is incapable of hearing them.[14]

Storm Jameson (an admirer of the Leavises and an English graduate herself) lamented a fiction 'infected with film technique' and feeding 'herd prejudice', in which

Deep calls to deep, and the writer's thought is sucked into the immense vacuum created in women's minds by a civilisation in which they have either
nothing much to do or too much (too much machine-minding).[15]

The inclusion of that last sympathetic parenthesis suggests how far 'empty'
leisure was no longer the sign of the aristocratic or idle, wealthy woman but
of the worker; increasingly a new pressure is felt to differentiate the cultural
pleasures of women who might count themselves in the middle classes, not
just from the excesses of the class above, but from the reading and viewing
of those below.

When Virginia Woolf in 1929 looked forward to the day when women's
writing 'would no longer be the dumping ground for the personal emotions',[16] her version of feminism was in keeping with a horror of 'gush' or
'tosh', of the emotionality with which the pre-war bourgeois woman had
been burdened, and whose rejection was now *de rigueur*. Many writers of
fiction adopted a tone of irony toward the emotions which would have
caused consternation to their mothers. E. M. Delafield, for example, was
typical of her flippant generation in wryly asking the rhetorical question of
her readers which presupposed their own disavowal of such things:

Imagination, emotionalism, sensationalism, what woman is not the victim of
these insidious and fatally unpractical emotions?'
(*The Way Things Are*, p. 336)

The revelation of inner desires and emotional depths was traumatic not just
for 'severely political' or public women,[17] however, but for all those aiming
at a modern female respectability, different both from the image of bourgeois femininity in the past and from a contemporary sexuality displayed
across more proletarian forms. We might speculate that the modern bourgeois woman between the wars retreats from the visibly erotic or from displays of femininity, as the working classes become more publicly sexualised.
Certainly, with intensity of feeling and expressivity such thorough bad taste,
many writers left romance well alone or found ways of writing from a less
'feminine' position in the culture.[18]

Crime fiction, for example, was one place within the more popular literatures that 'middlebrow' and 'highbrow' could meet, and where both men
and women of the middle classes could be united in despising romantic literature. No 'shopgirl, factory girl, skivvy or housewife'[19] was likely to read
Christie, but if she did, it was surely with a sense of its superiority to Bertha
Ruck, *Peg's Paper* or Mills & Boon, if only because it did not advertise its
femininity. Regardless of how many women wrote detective fiction between
the wars, it was still considered to be a masculine form, mainly read by
men.[20] Neither gushy nor confessional, the crime story laid a stress on those

apparently masculine qualities of reason and logic; its modernist emphasis was upon surface, form and contemplation – the antithesis of romance's depth, substance and emotional involvement. It is an opposition maintained with a superb lack of self-consciousness by some critics today:

> the sort of mind that likes well-made plots is not likely to go in for formless romance and affection as well – murder (in fiction, at least) conforms to disciplines that love does not.[21]

Given the inferiority afforded to 'formless romance', writing detective fiction was, and is, for many women writers not only a way of claiming the 'unfeminine' qualities of orderliness and control, but also of attempting to avoid the 'stigma' of gender altogether. As crime fiction included university dons and 'highbrows' amongst its authors, there was always a meagre portion of cultural *cachet* which writers like Dorothy L. Sayers were only too happy to seize upon. Detective stories (so the argument runs), because of their emphasis upon cerebration, if nothing else, take more 'work' than other popular forms of novel, are closer to 'real novels', and thereby occupy a more elevated position amongst the 'pulp' fictions.[22] Dorothy L. Sayers was the first of many crime writers who sought to 'improve' the detective story, turn it from a mere crossword puzzle into a 'proper' novel: romance writers, on the other hand, were usually content to 'entertain'.

(1991)

Notes

8   From *Miracle*, 1938, cited by Cynthia White, *Women's Magazines 1693–1968* (Michael Joseph, 1970), p. 98.

9   White, *Women's Magazines*, discusses some of these shifts. Kirsten Drotner, *More Next Week! English Children and Their Magazines 1751–1945* (Aarhus University, Aarhus, 1985) offers a thoughtful analysis of the growth of new markets for women's fiction; Asa Briggs, *Mass Entertainment* (Griffin, London, 1960) and W. H. Fraser, *The Coming of the Mass Market 1850–1914* (Macmillan, London, 1981) provide an overview and some statistics. There is as yet no critical history of the development of forms of romance fiction in the late nineteenth and early twentieth century, or indeed a study of the reading of working women on a par with Louis James's *Fiction for the Working Man 1830–1850* (Oxford University Press, Oxford, 1963); Rachel Anderson, *The Purple Heart Throbs: The Sub-literature of Love* (Hodder & Stoughton, London, 1974) is a mainly descriptive account of popular writers like Marie Corelli and Elinor Glyn; Mirabel Cecil, *Heroines in Love 1750–1974* (Michael Joseph, London, 1974) and Nicola Beauman, *A Very Great Profession: The Woman's Novel 1914–39* (Virago, London, 1983) are also helpful; Helen

Taylor also provides a helpful retrospective on contemporary feminist debates about popular romance in 'Romantic readers', in H. Carr (ed.), *From My Guy to Sci-Fi: Genre and Women's Writing in the Postmodern World* (Pandora, London, 1989).

10 See Billie Melman, *Women and the Popular Imagination: Flappers and Nymphs* (Macmillan, London, 1988); A. Huyssen, 'Mass culture as woman: modernism's Other', in T. Modleski (ed.), *Studies in Entertainment – Critical Approaches to Mass Culture* (Indiana University, Bloomington, 1986). Film-going does not seem to have been seen as respectable until the late 1930s, and then it might be pilloried as 'suburban'.

11 Storm Jameson, 'Novels and novelists' and 'Apology for my life', in *Civil Journey* (Cassell, London, 1939), p. 83 and p. 19.

12 F. R. Leavis, *Mass Civilisation and Minority Culture* (Minority Press, Cambridge, 1930), p. 10. For Leavis the 'industrialisation' of literature is at once a 'levelling down' in class terms and a hybridisation: a kind of anarchy which de-centres all systems of discrimination. This is 'the plight of culture': 'The landmarks have shifted, multiplied and crowded upon one another, the distinctions and dividing lines have blurred away, the boundaries are gone and the arts and literatures of different countries and periods have flowed together' (p. 19). Fears about modernity as a cultural miscegenation – the threat to 'the Anglo-Saxon race' – surface in the singling out of jazz ('negro' music) by many critics. Storm Jameson, for example, maintains that bestsellers left audiences 'where they found them, confused by the noise of saxophones' (*Civil Journey*, p. 82).

13 'The Tosh Horse', in *The Strange Necessity* (Virago, London, 1987), p. 321.

14 ibid., p. 323.

15 Jameson, *Civil Journey*, pp. 18; 82; 84.

16 'Women and fiction' first appeared in *The Forum*, March 1929 and then in *Granite and Rainbow* (Hogarth Press, London, 1958); reprinted in Michèle Barrett (ed.), *Virginia Woolf: Women and Writing* (Women's Press, London, 1979), p. 51.

17 See Steedman, 'Women's biography and autobiography: forms of history, histories of forms' in Carr, *From My Guy to Sci-Fi*.

18 Even *Eve*, a high-society magazine for women, declared after the war that 'there has been a slump in sentimentalism' and 'misty-eyed emotionality' was dead: Cecil, *Heroines in Love*, p. 151. Of course romance came back, but differently.

19 Beauman, *A Very Great Profession*, p. 183.

20 See, for example, George Orwell's assumptions in 'Bookshop memories' (November 1936), in *The Collected Essays, Journalism and Letters of George Orwell*, vol. 1 (Penguin, Harmondsworth, 1970), p. 275.

21 G. C. Ramsey, *Agatha Christie: Mistress of Mystery* (Collins, London, 1968), p. 52.

22 The same divisions between 'high' and 'low' operate within the genre too: P. D. James, now published in large paperback format by Faber & Faber, appears more literary and more respectable than the other bestselling British 'queen of crime', Ruth Rendell. Their relation is rather like that which obtained between Sayers and Christie.

NICOLA HUMBLE

The Feminine Middlebrow Novel, 1920s to 1950s: Class, Domesticity, and Bohemianism

Any attempt to define the middlebrow novel in this period must inevitably run up against the monolith of modernism. In one sense middlebrow fiction is the 'other' of the modernist or avant-garde novel, the bugbear continually reviled by highbrow critics and literary experimenters as corrupting public taste and devaluing the status of the novel. Yet the feminine middlebrow also provides the brimming bowl into which recent revisers of the modernist canon have dipped for new plums: Rose Macaulay, Antonia White, and Elizabeth Bowen are among the once squarely middlebrow writers who have recently been co-opted into a newly femininized modernist history. For this revisionist project, modernism has traditionally been defined too narrowly because it has been unconsciously gendered masculine, and women writers excluded on the basis that their concerns with the domestic and the personal are inherently trivial. So Suzanne Clark's *Sentimental Modernism* (1991) argues that feminized discourses of emotion have been falsely excluded from the modernist project; Gillian Hanscombe and Virginia L. Smyers propose the term 'para-modernism' to extend the modernist literary phenomenon to a wide range of contemporary women writers, and Bonnie Kime Scott, editor of *The Gender of Modernism* (1990) goes as far as to suggest that 'the experimental, audience challenging, language-focused writing that used to be regarded as modernism' could be redefined as 'a gendered subcategory – "early male modernism", or "masculinist modernism"' of a much broader modernism that would allow the works of women their rightful place.[22] All these critics seek to elevate previously comparatively unregarded women novelists to the high status of modernists on the basis of experimental, symbolist, or anti-traditionalist elements in their work. While these attempts to reposition women writers within a 'serious' literary category are worthy ones, they are also problematic. 'Modernism' is a label that was applied retrospectively to the experimental writing of the early twentieth century, and would, of course, have meant little to writers at the time. We can renegotiate its definition endlessly, but it brings us no closer to seeing the literary map of the time as contemporaries would have seen it. Indeed, I would argue that the critical insistence, since the 1950s, on seeing the literature of this period solely in terms of modernism has significantly distorted our understanding. Rather than hack about at the definition of modernism in order to squeeze the women writers of the first half of the century into its confines, it seems to me more productive to employ the less slippery concepts of the highbrow or the avant-garde, which had specific, though continually contested, meanings for contemporaries. Equally, rather than extend the definition of the high-status highbrow to cover as much women's writing of the period as possible, I think it crucial to retain the sense of cultural boundaries that dominated contemporary thinking about literature; it is only by exploring the heavily patrolled border between intellectual, experimental fiction and the commercial middlebrow that we will find the places where the distinctions between these categories begin to break down, and interesting things escape.

'Middlebrow' and 'highbrow' are far from impermeable categories, and many texts shifted their status from one to the other, or were uneasily trapped in the no-man's land in-between. The curious dialogue-laden novels of Ivy Compton-Burnett are a good example of the latter: from the time of their first publication they possessed a profoundly indeterminate status – abstruse, effortful, and formally innovative, but so obsessed with class and domesticity as to attract an instant reader-cult that undermined their claims to high seriousness. Verbally complex works, yet produced to an unchanging formula, and cranked out on a virtually biennial basis for five decades, Compton-Burnett's novels challenge the distinction between high and middlebrow fiction. Virginia Woolf took her seriously as a highbrow rival, recording in her diary in 1937 the sleepless nights produced by the contrast of the favourable reviews received by Compton-Burnett's *Daughters and Sons* and those for her own *The Years*, yet the Hogarth Press had turned down the manuscript of Compton-Burnett's second novel in 1929, with Leonard Woolf declaring that 'She can't even write'.[23] Profoundly original, but wedded to the culture of the pre-war period, Compton-Burnett's novels offered highbrow difficulty without the modernist ideological commitment to the future, and the middlebrow pleasures of a self-indulgent snobbery and the anatomizing of family life without any concessions to the notion of reading as relaxation. Other hybrid writers of the period include Enid Bagnold, whose 1935 *National Velvet* achieved best-seller status despite what Claud Cockburn has aptly described as its 'high surrealism', and Elizabeth Bowen, who combines caustic gossip about class and domesticity with a stylized, mannered exploration of profoundly separate subjectivities that has much in common with Virginia Woolf's similar project.[24]

The conventional construction of modernism has, of course, long celebrated Woolf as its lone female exemplar. While it would be foolish to challenge her status as a profoundly original formal innovator, I would suggest that the gap between Woolf and her female contemporaries looked by no means as yawning in her lifetime as it has since appeared. Woolf herself repeatedly compared her work with that of other women novelists (such as Rose Macaulay and Rosamund Lehmann), evaluating their success and status against her own, and admitting jealousy at their talent in at least one case (that of Katherine Mansfield).[25] In at least some of her formulations on the nature and purpose of writing, she sees her own literary project as both specifically female, and shared by other women writers. In her essay 'Women and Fiction' of 1929, for example, she argues that contemporary women's fiction is 'far more genuine and far more interesting to-day than it was a hundred or even fifty years ago', because a lifting of some aspects of gender oppression has allowed women writers to extend their range from their own suffering to the lives of women in general.[26] The challenge, as she sees it, for the contemporary female novelist, is to represent the quotidian realities – both physical and psychological – of women's lives:

> Here again there are difficulties to be overcome, for, if one may generalise, not only do women submit less readily to observation than men, but their lives are far less tested and examined by the ordinary processes of life. Often nothing tangible remains of a woman's day. The food that has been cooked is eaten; the children that have been nursed have gone out into the world. Where does the accent fall? What is the salient point for the novelist to seize upon? It is difficult to say. Her life has an anonymous character which is baffling and puzzling in the extreme. For the first time, this dark country is beginning to be explored in fiction. (p. 82)

These challenges of representation, she claims, are repeatedly being met by recent women's fiction, which she praises for its honesty and courage, and its ability to speak in a specifically feminine voice but without bitterness: 'these qualities are much commoner than they were, and they give even to second- and third-rate work the value of truth and the interest of sincerity' (p. 82). On her own account, then, it is possible to read Woolf's fiction as part of a continuum with that of other women writers of the period, similarly searching for new means of representing women's changing historical circumstances. Looked at in such terms, Woolf's work shares significant concerns with that of her contemporaries: the hypersensitivity to the minutiae of class distinctions, and the meticulous tabulating of the pleasures and disappointments of the domestic day that we find in a novel like *To the Lighthouse*, for instance, are both, as I will argue extensively elsewhere, central features of the aesthetic of the feminine middlebrow.

As such overlaps and hybridity suggests, the middlebrow cannot ultimately be distinguished from the avant-garde highbrow on a formal basis: some highly popular works were formally experimental; some extremely abstruse novels had a cultish mode of production; and the queen of high modernism shared many of the themes and concerns of the average middlebrow women's writer. In fact, both the middlebrow and the highbrow need finally to be understood not as formal or generic categories, but as cultural constructs.

Just as much was invested in the assigning of particular texts to certain intellectual categories, so a great deal of cultural capital was at stake in the identification of particular classes of readers. The highbrow was a largely self-proclaimed creature, a member of the intellectual class comprised of writers, critics, academics, and literary publishers. The highbrow reader, as is seen in the pronouncements of Queenie Leavis, and other self-appointed guardians of the intellectual torch such as T. S. Eliot, conceived of himself as occupying a besieged fortress, resisting the onslaughts of an increasingly consumerist mass culture. Reading, for the highbrow, was properly effortful intellectual work, and he despised the development of a thriving market in escapist and entertaining reading matter. As guardians of literature, the highbrows set themselves against the rapidly expanding lowbrow threat posed by radio, the cinema, pulp fiction, and cheap magazines. These clearly promised to marginalize the purely literary element in the culture of the nation – but so too did the incursions of the middlebrow onto the hallowed ground of literary taste and value. While the highbrow reader was self-identified, the middlebrow reader – like middlebrow texts – was less likely to embrace the label wholeheartedly. He was nevertheless identified, and eagerly pursued, by writers and publishers and by the burgeoning numbers of book clubs and lending libraries. The middlebrow, as a cultural phenomenon, is characterized precisely by its commodification – its endless flexibility in the face of the changing demands of the market. It is this feature that its highbrow critics most condemned – but it is also the reason that they, as we have seen in the case of Queenie Leavis, consistently underestimated it. Immediately responsive to shifts in public tastes, almost paranoically aware of the latest trends – both popular and intellectual – the middlebrow was able to continually reinvent itself, incorporating highbrow experimentation, language, and attitudes almost as soon as they were formulated, and combining them with a mass accessibility and pleasurable appeal. As Janice Radway, author of one of the very few critical analyses of the book club phenomenon, has remarked, the middlebrow commodified 'not only particular books, but the whole concept of Culture itself'.[27] High culture, with all its associations of class and status, was available to buy in the form of the average middlebrow novel, which promised its readers instant and easy access to the very intellectual counters the highbrow so jealously guarded.

(2001)

Notes

22 Suzanne Clark, *Sentimental Modernism: Women Writers and the Revolution of the Word* (Bloomington: Indiana University Press, 1991); Gillian Hanscombe and Virginia L. Smyers, *Writing for Their Lives: The Modernist Women 1910–1940* (London: Women's Press, 1987); Bonnie Kime Scott (ed.), *The Gender of Modernism* (Bloomington: Indiana University Press, 1990), 4.
23 Richard Kennedy, *A Boy at the Hogarth Press* (Harmondsworth: Penguin, 1972), 82.

24 Cockburn, *Bestseller*, 181.
25 See e.g. *The Diary of Virginia Woolf*, ii: *1920–24*, ed. Anne Olivier Bell (London: The Hogarth Press, 1978), 57, 93, 138, 227, 314–15.
26 'Women and Fiction', *The Forum*, March 1929; republished in *Granite and Rainbow* (London: The Hogarth Press, 1958), 80–1.
27 Janice Radway, *A Feeling for Books: The Book-of-the-Month Club, Literary Taste and Middle-Class Desire* (Chapel Hill: University of North Carolina Press, 1997), 249.

SHARI BENSTOCK

'Afterword: The New Woman's Fiction'
Chick Lit: The New Woman's Fiction

Without question, chick lit calls attention to questions of authorship, audience, and subject matter. But in an era when anxieties about women's right to write have largely disappeared, authors ask new questions, taking different approaches to the dilemmas facing women in contemporary culture.

Chick-lit authors approach such dilemmas with humor. Their heroines bear little resemblance, for instance, to the "new woman" of a century before. The self-sufficient, independent women in Ellen Glasgow's "vein of iron" novels share little in common with the fallible, sometimes bumbling protagonists of chick lit. In *Barren Ground* (1925), for instance, a woman struggles to become a successful farmer. In Willa Cather's *The Song of the Lark* (1915), the heroine bravely forgoes marriage, opting for a career instead. The high seriousness and simmering anger characteristic of earlier feminist fiction has given way to comedy. Part of the undeniable appeal of chick-lit fiction lies in its suggestion to readers that we can be ourselves even when we're beside ourselves.

Chick lit's use of the diary form, journals, letters, and e-mail links it to the epistolary tradition and to the novel that emerged out of private modes of writing commonly associated with women. It also links contemporary chick lit to the novel of psychological development that emerged in the early twentieth century. Women such as Virginia Woolf and Dorothy Richardson moved away from the social considerations of the novel of manners to explore the internal mental and emotional life of a central female protagonist. Richardson's *Pilgrimage* (1918) presented a woman's development between the ages of seventeen and forty – the same period that is the focus of much chick lit – employing stream of consciousness to replicate her character's thoughts and feelings with uncommon detail and nuance. In *Mrs Dalloway* (1925) and *To the Lighthouse* (1927), Woolf did the same to capture the doubts, hopes, and reminiscences of women after World War I. Jean Rhys's *Good Morning Midnight* (1939) and Djuna Barnes's *Nightwood* (1936) powerfully represented the psychological torment of depression and psychosis. Well before them, in the closing pages of *The House of Mirth* (1907), Edith Wharton had used impressionistic interior monologue to capture Lily Bart's final moments. Although the somber tone of these novels divorces them from the lighter touch of chick lit, they share an interest in experimenting with modern means of communication. Just as the then cutting-edge technologies of the telephone, radio, telegraph, and cinema shaped modernist style, e-mail and instant messaging function in chick lit to capture the rapid, clipped pace of contemporary life and conversation.

The first-person, confessional mode of chick lit further enhances readers' identification. It also allies the genre with the equally popular contemporary genres of memoir and autobiography. The connection is not to the women of the 1950s and 1960s, such as Sylvia Plath and Anne Sexton, who railed against the restrictions of domestic life and the psychological damage it caused – loneliness, depression, and domestic violence – but to contemporary writers who look back not in anger or with self-pity but with humor stripped of sentimentality. Mary Karr, in *The Liar's Club* (1995), for example, treats traumatic events in her volatile childhood, such as fire, sexual assault, and her mother's mental illness, with an engaging mixture of horror and ironic distance. Her mother's depression is described as her "Empress Days," her parents' hangovers as "the Smirnoff flu." With wit, not sentimentality, chick-lit heroines recount their bafflement at their parents' behavior and expose their own flaws and failures.

(2006)

SUSAN SELLERS

Myth and Fairy Tale in Contemporary Women's Fiction

Derrida's notion of opening up the weave of writing to enable other meanings to come to the fore is a potentially empowering one for feminism, yet it leaves the question of what will happen to this tactic when confronted with the particular requirements of the genre unanswered. If the feminine writer adheres to Cixous's admonition that there can be no ordered beginnings and endings, no definitive characters, or events that follow a predetermined course, then isn't what she is writing the very antithesis of myth? If we adopt Kristeva's richly suggestive stance, how can our corporeal drives find expression in a mode of narration from which the personal has been successively erased? The difficulties confronting the feminist rewriter appear immense. Must we conclude, then, with Camille Paglia, that the feminist project of rewriting myth is both pointless and absurd?[114]

If Diane Purkiss is right, and altering internal patterns or attempting to express silenced or marginal voices leaves the central discourse inviolate, does it follow that feminists must begin again, from a place outside myth? Yet if we do this, we not only vacate the arena to allow myth's power to continue unimpeded, we also deprive ourselves of its undeniable force. I am also more optimistic than Irigaray or Purkiss about the potential impact of rewriting a myth. As Elisabeth Bronfen argues in a different context, the disruption caused leaves traces, so that the regained order contains a shift and is no longer the homogeneous realm from which difference is eradicated.[115] The work of feminist critic and myth-maker Mary Daly presents an example here. In a series of influential books, Daly works to dismantle the stranglehold of patriarchal myth and to create woman-focused words, images and tales.[116] For Daly, this metaphorical shape-shifting and gynocentric spinning opens up previously barred meanings and areas of experience, which have the capacity to unlock corresponding 'metamorphospheres' in us.[117] It is impossible, having once read Daly's etymological tracings and new glosses on words such as 'virgin', 'spinster' and 'hag', or laughed at her pun on 'phallosophy' and hilarious definition of patriarchy as 'Yahweh & Son: mythic paradigm for any corporation of cockocracy, for any all-male family business', to view their sources in the same light.[118] The problem, then, is not to avoid myth, but to find ways of rewriting it which do not return us to the negative prescriptions of the *logos*.

I see a first response to this dilemma in Derrida's insistence that the text will always slip away from us: just as the logocentric enterprise is never intact, so our own rewritings will always exceed and disrupt our intentions. We can actively encourage this process by leaving the web of the text open: as Derrida reminds us, 'to weave is first to make holes'.[119] Yet if we make too many holes we are in danger of writing something other than myth. Perhaps the answer lies in rethinking the conjunction between the old and the new – or the live and the dead, to borrow philosopher Paul Ricoeur's resonant phrase.[120] This would involve keeping and benefiting from those elements which are still potent for us, while discarding or revitalising those which are dead, deadly, or simply no longer appropriate. It would enable us to envisage rewritings not only as pleasurable reversals or ingenious tinkerings but as new embroideries, adding fresh images and colours to radically alter the picture. Feminist rewriting could thus include ironic mimicry and clever twists as well as a whole gamut of tactics that would open the myth from the inside as well as out, leaving in place enough of the known format to provide evocative points of reflection for its reader, but also encompassing different possibilities and other points of view. Marina Warner's rewriting of the tale of Susannah and the elders offers an illustration here, employing our knowledge of the original to complicate our relation to it through its invitation to identify with but also spy on Susannah. Warner reworks the existing template to prompt us to question our own roles as accomplices and voyeurs.[121]

My answer then is to try for the difficult and perhaps impossible balancing act. To follow the figure of Little Red Riding Hood and stick to enough of the path so as not to get lost completely, while taking in whatever flowers or strangers we encounter on the way. Critic Rosemary Jackson suggests that the fantastic nature of the genre can contribute to this: since it is free from many of the conventions that restrict our thinking it opens up spaces where unity and order are normally imposed.[122] She argues that its generic make-up disrupts the drive towards the institution of a single, reductive 'truth', introducing contradiction and polysemy. Jackson sees the movement of metamorphosis that is a persistent feature of myth as metonymic rather than metaphoric, since one object does not stand for another but rather slides into it, blurring the divisions and any concomitant hierarchy; she cites the psychoanalytic critic Jacques Lacan's contention that metonymy offers a means of eluding the repressive strictures of the social order to argue for its subversive power.[123] The honed quality of mythic symbolism also seems to me to provide rich potential since it encourages multiple interpretations, as the various configurations of the maze in Carol Shields' novel *Larry's Party* illustrates.[124] Some of Hélène Cixous's own feminine writings are notoriously difficult to read as they glide from word-play through dense allusion to disruption of all the 'rules' including those of grammar, punctuation and page layout, to the point where rebellion dissipates into chaos.[125] It is my contention that the rewriting of myth can circumvent some of these dangers, since the known forms operate as compass points around which we can weave new and different stories. Employing the existing weft and warp in this way replicates the psychoanalytic notion of holding, in which boundaries encourage the individual to progress. The double momentum of security and innovation similarly mirrors Kristeva's strategies for dissident writing, since it provides a context within which we can rend and renew our relation to the established order: prompting us to reject what unfairly binds us while reaffirming our allegiance to what is productive. As Kristeva points out, we must adopt the social-symbolic code in order to function, and our revolts will be fruitless unless they occur within it in ways that can be understood. Feminist rewriting can thus be thought of in two categories: as an act of demolition, exposing and detonating the stories that have hampered women, and as a task of construction – of bringing into being enabling alternatives.

(2001)

Notes

114 Camille Paglia, *Sexual Personae: Art and Decadence from Nefertiti to Emily Dickinson* (New Haven, Conn.: Yale University Press, 1990); for Paglia, mythology's identification of woman with nature is correct so that rewriting is both unnecessary and pointless since this truth will always re-emerge.

115   Bronfen, *Over Her Dead Body*, p. xii.
116   See Daly, *Gyn/Ecology*; *Pure Lust: Elemental Feminist Philosophy* (Boston: Beacon Press, 1984); and *Websters' First New Intergalactic Wickedary of the English Language* (1987; London: The Women's Press, 1988).
117   Daly, *Pure Lust*, p. 408.
118   These are all taken from Daly's *Wickedary*.
119   Kamuf (ed.), *A Derrida Reader*, p. 168.
120   Maria J. Valdès (ed.), *A Ricoeur Reader: Reflection and Imagination* (University of Toronto Press, 1991), p. 9.
121   Marina Warner, 'Now You See Me', *The Mermaids in the Basement* (1993; London: Vintage, 1994), pp. 121–36.
122   Jackson, *Fantasy: The Literature of Subversion*.
123   Ibid., p. 41; Jackson does, however, maintain that the happy endings of fairy tale have a counter-effect since they work to re-cover desire (p. 4). It is significant in this context that Ovid chose the title *Metamorphoses* for his collection of mythic tales.
124   Carol Shields, *Larry's Party* (London: Fourth Estate, 1997).
125   See, for example, Cixous's *Neutre* (Paris: Grasset, 1972), an extract of which is translated into English in Susan Sellers (ed.), *The Hélène Cixous Reader* (London: Routledge, 1994), pp. 3–16.

4

Towards Definitions of Feminist Writing

INTRODUCTION

Defining Feminist Writing

How would a reader recognize an example of feminist imaginative writing or feminist literary criticism? Are there certain definable characteristics that mark 'x' as a feminist text and 'y' as a non-feminist? Leaving aside for a moment all the problems around the word 'tradition' that we considered in Chapter 1, can we say that a tradition of women's writing is a tradition of *feminist* writing? Or, if this seems too all-embracing a definition, can we at least establish that the writing of declared feminists must be feminist? In short, is authorial intention everything? Alternatively, does the feminism lie in interpretation; could feminists agree on a definitive list of books that are more open than others to a feminist reading? Perhaps the nature of the readership is the key. Are the women-centred novels that Rosalind Coward mentions, in response to an earlier article by Rebecca O'Rourke, to be categorized as 'feminist' because lots of feminists read them? Or can the problem ultimately resolve itself as one of content? Does the placing of women's experience, ideas, visions, achievements at the centre of a piece of writing, or, as in Michèle Barrett's example, an art exhibition, make that work feminist?

The extracts from Coward and Barrett prove that these problems are not open to easy solutions. Both agree that we cannot take 'women's writing' to be a synonym for 'feminist writing'. Coward, for example, points out how similar women-centred novels are to conventional forms of popular and highly commercial fiction, so it does not follow that a fictional focus on women's experience is inevitably progressive. Barrett comments on Coward: 'Feminism, she argues, is an alignment of political interests and not a shared

Feminist Literary Theory: A Reader, Third Edition By Mary Eagleton   © 2011 Mary Eagleton

female experience; hence a tradition of women's art is of no particular importance.' While Barrett agrees that an emphasis on female experience does not *necessarily* make the work feminist, she is uneasy about Coward's rejection of the category: 'Whatever the problems of basing feminism on the experience shared by women, far greater problems arise in attempting completely to divorce feminism (as a political project) from women's experience.'

Furthermore, a closer examination of authorial intention raises more problems than solutions. Books conceived with the most laudable political motives can prove, on reading, to be lame and unconvincing. Conversely, books from authors with no particular sympathy for feminism are widely read by feminists and prove a rich vein for feminist criticism; much of Doris Lessing's work would illustrate this point. Readers too are unreliable guides. Coward makes clear that women-centred novels do not become feminist simply because feminists read them. On the other hand, Barrett believes that it was precisely the audience's 'reading' of Judy Chicago's art work, *The Dinner Party*, that made the event, rather than the specific work, feminist. As Barrett later writes: 'In this sense, although I disputed the claims of *The Dinner Party* to be an *intrinsically* feminist work I would not dispute that it is a feminist event. But this is because its meaning has been constructed, collectively, as such.'[1] Lillian Faderman's piece shows how all the same questions are present when one thinks of other forms of potentially feminist cultural production. As Barrett is questioning, 'When is women's art feminist art?' so Faderman is asking, 'What is lesbian literature?' She thinks about authorial intention and the changing position of the woman author, the historical construction of lesbianism, the nature of the subject-matter and the importance, or not, of a lesbian narrative or lesbian sexuality. And, underpinning all these thoughts are, again, those problem categories of 'identity' and 'experience'.

Another set of questions arises when considering feminist literary criticism. What makes it distinctive from other forms of criticism?[2] How should it relate to non-feminist criticism or to the practice of imaginative writing? Should feminist critics have a common political position and critical method? Are there critical methods which assist feminist politics and others which would hinder? The two extracts considered here, separated by over twenty years and radically different political and theoretical contexts, could be read as polar opposites in their attitudes to these issues. Cheri Register's response, to establish a 'prescriptive' feminist criticism, springs from a political agenda. Equally wary of any masculinist dominance in culture and of 'ivory tower academism', Register wants a literary criticism which is, above all, useful and 'can serve the cause of liberation'. But what she proposes is a highly dogmatic form of criticism, couched in authoritarian language – we keep being told what we should do, what is correct, or what is impermissible – and she offers a reductive analysis of the relationship between writing and politics. 'To earn feminist approval, literature must perform one or more of the following functions' illustrates the approach. Once again, a focus on female identity and experience is to the fore. Indeed, a whole series of terms – 'experience', 'truth', 'authentic', 'identity', 'realistic' – operate as either connecting or interchangeable buzzwords in the debate. The author must be 'authentic', telling the entire and unvarnished truth about her experiences and perceptions; the text should express a 'representative' female experience which we, the readers, can accept as an 'authentic reflection' of our lives; and each individual woman should be struggling to find her own 'true' identity, for which task strong, independent female characters may provide inspiring role-models. The intimation is that, hitherto, we have been presented with 'false' realities, 'false' images, 'unrepresentative' models, and that these, like dead skins, should be shed to find the 'true' reality and the 'authentic' selves at the core of our beings.

Elizabeth Weed's musing on the relationship between feminism and queer theory has nothing prescriptive about it.[3] Though she does attest to a connection with political movements, her focus is on subtleties of meaning – for example, the difference between 'meet', 'meeting' and 'and' or the various permutations within feminism/feminist theory/queer politics/queer theory. While the sex/gender debates of Weed's and Naomi Schor's collection may 'evoke an earlier feminist period' – that is, the time of Register's writing – the theoretical perspectives, tone and language are very different. And yet, in the qualifications and hesitancies of Register's extract concerning the relationship between 'life' and 'art', we glimpse a sub-text which is not that far from Weed's; it is rather that in Weed's extract the problems are more consciously recognized and more theoretically formulated.

Debates and Dialogues

The continuing work in feminist literary theory has been to move away from the prescriptive and to encourage debates both within feminism and with other critical discourses. In this section, we can get some indication of the criss-cross of argument that has taken place. First, how have Annette Kolodny, Elaine Showalter and Toril Moi approached the issue of critical openness? Kolodny's cry is not for prescription or definitions but for 'playful pluralism'. Concerned about both reductive readings and the wholesale rejection of non-feminist criticism, Kolodny suggests that feminist criticism should be viewed as *one* reading among many, taking part in an 'ongoing dialogue of competing potential possibilities'. This pluralism will not lead to chaos, she argues, but will prevent critics from privileging their work, and it will not simply reproduce the bourgeois appeal to pluralism because this version will stress, rather than deny, the workings of ideology. Showalter, however, writing in a period of rapid proliferation in critical theory, is concerned about what she sees as feminism's alarming attachment to the 'male theoretician' and women's intellectual and emotional investment, which constitutes an 'angry or loving fixation on male literature'.[4] Instead, she proposes 'gynocriticism', which will 'construct a female framework for the analysis of women's literature' and 'develop new models based on the study of female experience' – that word, 'experience', again. Moi's response to Kolodny is to worry whether she is not 'throwing the baby out with the bathwater'. If we accept an endless plurality of readings, we might, in so doing, endorse 'the most "masculinist" of criticism'. For instance, would Kolodny look upon the English language textbook which I had at school and which explained rhythm as 'the pulsating sounds that incite natives to kill' as simply an aspect of the plurality of interpretation? Moi is not looking for a prescriptive criticism, but she does see the need for a more analytical and evaluative approach than the one Kolodny suggests, and the same objection is made against Showalter's work. The critical suspicion that Showalter shows to the male-authored text should be directed equally to the female-authored text, suggests Moi. A too-ready sympathy for and identification with the female-authored text and a reluctance to see the text as 'sign' might do no service for feminism.

Reading Alice Jardine in conjunction with Showalter, and Rachel Bowlby alongside Jardine and Moi, produces further exchanges of ideas. In opposition to Showalter's 'gynocriticism', Jardine has coined the word 'gynesis'. Gynesis is but one manifestation from a series of critical practices – linguistic, postmodernist, psychoanalytic – that has rendered increasingly impossible the act of definition. As meanings have become unstable and diverse, any definition becomes not only elusive but untenable if one sees definition as linked to control. Gynocriticism will happily speak of female experience, culture and history – terms which gynesis finds questionable. The concepts which prescriptive criticism employs as self-evidently meaningful would be, for Jardine, the prompting for endless, deconstructive debates. Gynocriticism is concerned with women as real, historical persons, assigned by patriarchy to a female subculture, a place of both exclusion and autonomy. Gynesis does not see women's space as an empirically proven place within culture (the harem, for example), or within history (the female tradition, for instance); rather it discovers the 'feminine' or 'woman' as a gap, an absence, a 'nonknowledge' that has escaped the 'master narratives'. Yet both positions would agree that whoever, whatever this 'woman' is, she has the power to trouble and destabilise the dominant order. At the same time, as I summarise the material in terms of these antitheses, I am thinking of Bowlby's warning about 'simple, homologous oppositions'. Using Moi's *Sexual/ Textual Politics* and Jardine's *Gynesis: Configurations of Woman and Modernity*, Bowlby illustrates how even authors who are highly conscious of both theory and politics can have theoretical and political blind-spots. Moi and Jardine, Bowlby believes, construct their own texts in the very binary hierarchies they deprecate: French and American criticism emerge as separately defined modes, the French evidently superior to the American.

As rapidly as we deconstruct our premises, we reconstruct more. There never is a point where all is laid bare, luminously transparent to both author and reader.[5]

Two further propositions and responses can function as final examples of related ongoing debates – Nancy Fraser, Linda J. Nicholson and Robyn Wiegman on feminism's relation to postmodernism and bell hooks and Madhu Dubey on postmodernism's deployment of the concept of marginality. Fraser and Nicholson have, if not prescriptions, then suggestions as to how feminism might make use of postmodernism by maintaining a sense of the macro, choosing particular kinds of theorizing, espousing a comparativist stance and complicating our understanding of 'woman'. Postmodern feminism would be a 'tapestry composed of threads of many different hues'. Is this the same as 'playful pluralism' or, as Wiegman wonders, another form of mastery? Wiegman is full of cautions about feminism and postmodernism and their relation to knowledge. In particular, the catalogue of exclusions – gender, race, class – however conscientiously constructed, limits 'the potential excessibility of difference' both conceptually and politically. It is the conjunction of postmodernism, race and location that is the focus for hooks and Dubey. hooks looks to the margins as a 'site of radical possibility'. Drawing on her own experience of marginality as inequality, she re-conceives the margins as chosen and a place of counter-language and resistance. This careful positioning of herself in the margins is distinct from the colonizing occupation of the margins that she sees in other radicals, including some feminists. Despite hooks' claim that she is not romanticizing the margins, Dubey interprets her views as, precisely, 'the romance of the residual'. Rather than seeing black culture as postmodernism's mystified 'Other', 'the last vestige of authenticity', Dubey believes that black culture should be understood as part of postmodernism and its uneven development. As Dubey notes, the moves in hooks's essay from/to/within the margins are rhetorical and epistemological. Politically and materially, it is uncertain how the place of oppression becomes the place of resistance.

Reflections and Resistance

These dialogues illustrate the self-reflexive impetus in feminism which was particularly heightened around the period of the millennium as critics reviewed the scope and trajectory of feminist literary thought. It was a moment of taking stock, of evaluating what had been achieved and what still needed to be done.[6] Susan Stanford Friedman, remembering the principled but, often, acrimonious debates between a singular, universal *feminism* and multiple, pluralized *feminisms*, introduces 'a new singularization of feminism that assumes difference without reifying or fetishizing it'. In this extract, Friedman describes a 'locational feminism' which eschews universalism, on the one hand, and binarism, on the other, in an attempt to construct a politics sensitive to the specifics of time, place, difference and change. Friedman's deft and flexible strategy is a way of recognizing difference while not being inhibited by it. As Friedman asks us to rethink difference, so Isobel Armstrong returns us to 'the masters'. She offers a taxonomy of feminism or, as she calls it, 'a morphological sketch' that deliberately cuts across racial, national and disciplinary boundaries to suggest unexpected connections.[7] Her retrospective look divides the field into Expressive, Phallic and Ludic feminisms. The extract included here focuses on 'Phallic feminism', not to be confused with the 'phallic criticism' that Mary Ellmann describes in *Thinking About Women* (1968), so as to characterize those wings of feminism responsive to the work of Marx and Freud and, subsequently, Lacan. Armstrong indicates the potential and the pitfalls in feminism's negotiations with the master narratives and the danger that gender issues can get lost in 'the myth of power'.

For other critics, the millennium marked a reassessment of their own earlier work. In the extracts from Judith Butler and Toril Moi, two of the major names of feminist thought return to the books that first made their reputations to look at them again with older but fresh eyes. In the extract from *Undoing Gender*, Butler ruminates on continuing debates on sexual difference, the relation to heterosexism, the operation of sexual difference as a symbolic order, the possibilities of social change and the responses to her own work in these areas – all of which have relevance to feminist literary theory. Rereading *Sexual/Textual Politics*, Moi notices the occasional 'failure of voice' or 'example of theoretical alienation', but chiefly points to her renegotiation with poststucturalism.[8] Though still adhering to many earlier beliefs and processes of thought, she questions the views she held on binary oppositions, essentialism and subjectivity, and regrets some of her rhetorical strategies. Underlying her reflections is the figure of Simone de Beauvoir as the model of an intellectual woman. What unites both extracts is a common willingness to self-critique, to doubt the definitive and to keep asking questions.[9]

As the final three extracts illustrate, sometimes the best strategy is resistance – not to define, not to theorize, not to comment. Julia Kristeva tells us that 'woman can never be defined'. She dismisses the notion of 'being a woman' as 'absurd and obscurantist'. As with Jardine discussing gynesis, 'woman' is not tied to an identity, and feminist practice is characterized by 'negativity' in the sense that it is 'at odds with what already exists'. But Kristeva qualifies her claim with the word 'almost'. Here, she recognizes the political struggles in which women, identified *as women*, are necessarily still involved. Does feminism operate within the parameters of the hegemonic or does it hold a transformative potential? Kristeva talks of this issue in terms of uniting negativity with the 'ethical penchant in the women's struggle'. Barbara Christian's resistance is against theory itself. 'The race for theory' suggests the political import of theory as a controlling and defining mechanism, its priority over imaginative writing and the hectic pursuit of status as a theoretician. But Christian is also concerned with her 'race of theory', how black people may theorize in different ways and through imaginative forms. Christian does not actually name the particular critical theories to which she objects, though it seems that the scientism of structuralism is one target, but she does position herself as anti-humanist, anti-prescriptive, in favour of theory that is tied to practice and is she aware of how theory has become a commodity, a form of capital, which can determine whether or not one gets a job. Catherine Belsey is equally conscious of this final point. In *Desire: Love Stories in Western Culture* (Blackwell 1994), Belsey had included, as she says here, 'a tribute' to Toni Morrison, explaining why she would not be writing about Morrison's work, even though she valued it highly and it would clearly relate to the subject-matter of her study. Her argument was based not on a lack of knowledge or experience but on political issues of expropriation and career advancement. In this extract from an interview in 2000, Belsey, perceptively questioned by Marysa Demoor and Jürgen Pieters, has to explain and defend her position. For this critic, at this moment, in this situation, the most productive strategy is not only not to define but not to speak at all.[10]

Notes

1 Michèle Barrett, 'Feminism and the Definition of Cultural Politics', in Rosalind Brunt and Caroline Rowan (eds.), *Feminism, Culture and Politics* (London: Lawrence & Wishart, 1982) p. 57.

2 'What is feminist literary criticism?' is precisely the question Toril Moi addresses in her essay 'Feminist Literary Criticism', in Ann Jefferson and David Robey (eds.), *Modern Literary Theory: A Comparative Introduction* (London: Batsford, 1987).

3 For a further study on this relation, see: Diane Richardson, Janice McLaughlin and Mark E. Casey (eds.), *Intersections between Feminism and Queer Theory* (Basingstoke: Palgrave Macmillan, 2006).

4 For further comment by Showalter, see: 'Feminist Criticism in the Wilderness', in Showalter, *The New Feminist Criticism: Essays on Women, Literature and Theory* (London: Virago, 1986) and 'Critical Cross-Dressing; Male Feminists and the Woman of the Year' in Alice Jardine and Paul Smith (eds.), *Men in Feminism* (New York and London: Methuen, 1987).

5 One could trace these conversations further. Showalter responds to 'gynesis' in 'Women's Time, Women's Space: Writing the History of Feminist Criticism', in Shari Benstock (ed.), *Feminist Issues in Literary Scholarship* (Bloomington and Indianapolis: Indiana University Press, 1987). Toril Moi comments on Jardine in 'Feminism and Postmodernism: Recent Feminist Criticism in the United States', in Terry Lovell (ed.), *British Feminist Thought: A Reader* (Oxford: Blackwell, 1990).

6   In addition to the work discussed here, see: Robyn Wiegman 'Feminism's
    Apocalyptic Futures', *New Literary History*, vol. 31, no. 4 (2000), pp. 805–25;
    Wendy Brown 'Resisting Left Melancholy', *boundary 2* 26 (Fall, 1999), pp.
    19–27; Susan Gubar, 'What Ails Feminist Criticism?', *Critical Inquiry*, vol. 24,
    no. 4 (Summer, 1998), pp. 878–902, and the response and counter-response in
    the later issue: Robyn Wiegman, 'Critical Response: What Ails Feminist
    Criticism? A Second Opinion', *Critical Inquiry*, vol. 25, no. 2 (Winter, 1999),
    pp. 362–79, and Susan Gubar, 'Critical Response: Notations *in Medias Res*',
    Critical Inquiry, vol. 25, no. 2 (Winter, 1999), pp. 380–96. Gubar's original
    essay became part of her *Critical Condition: Feminism at the Turn of the
    Century* (New York: Columbia University Press, 2000) and Wiegman returns in
    a revised form to her debate with Gubar in 'Difference and Disciplinarity'
    (pp. 135–56) in Emory Elliott, Louis Freitas Caton and Jeffrey Rhyne (eds.),
    Aesthetics in a Multicultural Age (Oxford: Oxford University Press, 2002). See
    also Susan Stanford Friedman ' "Beyond" Gynocriticism and Gynesis: The
    Geographics of Identity and the Future of Feminist Criticism', *Tulsa Studies in
    Women's Literature*, vol. 15, no. 1 (Spring 1996), pp. 13–40. Of course, many
    journals had millennium special issues. The title of *Feminist Review* no. 61
    (Spring 1999) well captures the reflection on loss and gain at that juncture:
    'Snakes and Ladders: Reviewing Feminisms at Century's End'.
7   Armstrong, p. 208.
8   Some sense of the negative impact that *Sexual/Textual Politics* had at the time
    is evident in the discussion between Jane Gallop, Marianne Hirsch and Nancy
    K. Miller, 'Criticizing Feminist Criticism', in Marianne Hirsch and Evelyn Fox
    Keller (eds.), *Conflicts in Feminism* (New York: Routledge, 1990).
9   For the influence of Beauvoir on Moi, see: *Simone de Beauvoir: The Making of
    an Intellectual Woman* (Oxford: Blackwell, 1994) and for a further example of
    the dialogues I have been describing, see Moi's comments on Butler in *What is
    a Woman? And Other Essays* (Oxford: Oxford University Press, 1999).
10 For an earlier example of a critic carefully positioning herself and the kind of
    work she feels able to do, see: Nicole Ward Jouve, *White Woman Speaks with
    Forked Tongue: Criticism as Autobiography* (London: Routledge, 1991).

Rosalind Coward

' "This Novel Changes Lives": Are Women's Novels Feminist
Novels? A Response to Rebecca O'Rourke's Article
"Summer Reading" '
Feminist Review

Women-centred Writing

It is just not possible to say that women-centred writings have any necessary
relationship to feminism. Women-centred novels are by no means a new
phenomenon. The Mills and Boon romantic novels are written by, read by,
marketed for and are all about women. Yet nothing could be further from
the aims of feminism than these fantasies based on the sexual, racial and
class submission which so frequently characterise these novels. The plots and
elements of these novels are frequently so predictable that cynics have suggested that Mills and Boon's treasured authors might well be computers. Yet
the extraordinary rigidity of the formula of the novels, where the heroine
invariably finds material success through sexual submission and marriage,
does not prevent these publishers having a larger sales than Pan and Penguin.
The average print run for each novel is 115,000. While Mills and Boon may
have a highly individual market, their formulae are not so radically different
from romance fiction in general. Such immensely popular writers as Mary
Stewart and Georgette Heyer invariably have the experience of the heroine
at the centre, and concentrate on the vagaries of her emotions as the principal substance of the novel. In the cinema, the equivalent of the romantic
novel is melodrama, and melodrama is often promoted as 'women's pictures', suggesting that they are directed towards women as well as being
about women. Indeed it would not be stretching credibility too far to suggest
that the consciousness of the individual heroine has been a principal narrative device of the English novel in the last century, a fact which may well have
contributed to the relative presence of women writers in this field.

While this all shows how misguided it would be to mark a book of interest
to feminism because of the centrality it attributes to women's experiences, it
could be argued that what we loosely call feminist novels are qualitatively
different. But to make such a claim it would be necessary to specify in what
way 'women-centred' writing, allying itself with feminist politics, did mark
itself out as different. Some of the so-called feminist novels like *The Women's
Room* and *A Piece of the Night* do make explicit their allegiance to the
women's liberation movement. However, many of the others in roughly the
same genre do not. *Fear of Flying, Kinflicks* and *Loose Change* all fall into

this category. Yet the encounter with the milieu and aspirations of feminism often forms a central element in the narrative of these novels. And, the practice of consciousness raising – the reconstruction of personal histories within a group of women – sometimes forms the structure of the novel. Then there is a further category. Here we find novels like Kate Millett's *Sita* whose feminist commitment is guaranteed not so much by the content of the book as by the other theoretical and political writings of the author. And finally there is a whole host of novels which are adopted as honorary 'feminist novels', taking in such different writers as Doris Lessing, Fay Weldon and Alison Lurie. Their writings deal not so much with the milieu of contemporary feminism as with charting the experience of women's oppression.

Now, there is a certain convention within all these novels which does clearly mark them off from the romance genre for example. One striking feature is the frequency with which we meet with the quasi-autobiographical structure. *The Women's Room, Fear of Flying, Kinflicks, Sita* all foreground the writer, struggling to turn her experience into literature, even if this figure loiters in the background in god-like omnipotence as in *The Women's Room*. Moreover the 'voice' of the central protagonist, if not presenting itself directly as the author's voice, frequently offers itself as 'representative' of women in general, firstly claiming sexual experience as a vital terrain of all women's experience, sometimes also making generalities as to the oppressive nature of that experience. The distinctiveness of the genre has attracted attention; a Sunday Times colour supplement heading shows one response to the self-consciously 'representative' nature of these novels:

> Liberating the Libido. Getting sex straight was an essential first step along the noisy road to liberation; writing about it could be the next leap forward. Books by women surveying sex, and novels by women whose heroines savour sex are selling like hotdogs in America beating men into second place and turning the authoresses into millionairesses at the drop of a hard sell dust jacket.

I have raised this here in order to show that we do have a recognizable group of novels whose roots are, in a variety of ways, in the women's liberation movement but that their relation to feminism is not the necessary outcome of taking women's experience as central. But other questions arise in relation to this statement, questions as to whether the 'representativeness' which these novels claim is simply a reflection of 'feminist consciousness', or a propaganda device towards such a consciousness, or whether we have to be more cautious in analysing their structure and effects.

The Commercial Success of the Novels that Change Lives

Rebecca seems to imply that the widespread success of these novels can be attributed to a widespread diffusion of 'feminist consciousness'. In fact the disparity between the print runs of these novels and political texts gives rise to the exactly opposite suspicion in more cynical minds. Perhaps the kind of writing involved in *Kinflicks* or *The Women's Room* corresponds more closely to the structures of popular fiction rather than satisfying the incipient feminism of the population. The fact is that the space occupied by these novels is not so radically different from the conventional structures which make up the 'novelistic'. In other words that space of themes, modes of writing, hierarchies of appropriate statements which constitute these 'feminist novels' is not so utterly unlike those of popular fiction in general. We can isolate several aspects of this correspondence.

A dominant element in contemporary fiction has been that of the 'confessional' novel – the structuring of the novel, and the significant events of the narrative, around the voice of a principal protagonist describing her/his life. Novels like J. D. Salinger's *Catcher in the Rye* or *Lucky Jim* by Kingsley Amis bear an exceptionally strong resemblance to feminist works such as Alice Monroe's *Lives of Girls and Women* in this respect. But the similarity does not end here. For this structure has increasingly been characterized by the absolute centrality given to the experience of adolescence and young adulthood. In particular the experiences of this period have come to be almost synonymous with sexual experience. In drawing attention to the reception of feminist writers by the bourgeois press, I have already hinted how this preoccupation with the confession of sexual experience is one of the most characteristic features of contemporary feminist writings. Like the confessional novel in general, the novels by feminists also present the experience of sexuality as the significant experience of the novel. Whereas in romantic fiction (and indeed quite often in 'the classics') it was the events leading to marriage, or events disrupting love, which occupied the position of significant events, increasingly sexual experience is becoming sufficient.

Certain points can be made about the confessional form of these novels and their preoccupation with sexuality. An obvious point is that speaking about sexuality, and a preoccupation with sexuality, is not in and of itself progressive. Feminists have been involved for too long now in the analysis of images and ideologies to be conned into thinking that accounts of sexuality are progressive just because they take women's sexuality as their central concern. Criticism of pornography, which frequently highlights the sexual experiences of women, is just one example of representations of sexuality which feminists have actually contested.

It has been suggested that the centrality which the confession of sexuality has assumed and which is now an integral part of our culture does not in fact represent a radical break with the past. Michel Foucault (1978) for example has suggested that it represents a continuation of certain practices of dealing with sexuality which have been part of western culture for several centuries. He argues that sexuality has never been 'repressed' as such but has been the object of a variety of discourses for several centuries. In the past these discourses were frequently directed towards a control or negation of certain sexual practices, as with the medical and educational discourses of the Victorian period: they nevertheless had sexuality as their object. In Catholic countries, he suggests that the practice of the church confessional was taken over into scientific and social discourses, where once again sexuality became an object to be interrogated, spoken about, controlled. Again and again however, whatever the explicit aim of the discourses, sexuality was taken to be the element which revealed the 'true' and 'essential' nature of people. Foucault sees within this concern with sexuality the workings of power; the identity of the subject is found through discourses which multiply areas of pleasure and attention only to control, classify, subject. To deny a sudden rupture in the history of sexuality – from repression to liberation – does not mean that we have to go along with Foucault in suggesting that there have not been radical changes in the representations of sexuality themselves. For women, discourses on sexuality have changed importantly. The equation of female sexuality with the illicit and disgusting is no longer a dominant representation, and the possibilities of sexual enjoyment no longer focussed on motherhood, are changes for which feminism has fought.

Nevertheless these ideas are useful in this context. They indicate how the centrality which sexuality has assumed in the novel, either coyly in romantic preoccupations or explicitly in the confession of sexual experiences, has definite correspondences with other social practices. Within the novel, the 'confession' has appeared, structured by traditions, specific to the novel. In particular it has been influenced by the importance of narrative, which organizes a series of events or experiences as significant and progressing towards a meaningful conclusion. This space of time, or narrative, is one in which the central character or characters undergo an experience or series of experiences which radically affect their lives or transform their attitudes. The effect of this structure is to create a distinct ideology of knowledge and indeed life – that experience brings knowledge and possibly wisdom. But where women have been, and are, the central focus of the novel, a variation occurs. That variation is that the only space where knowledge or understanding for women is produced is across sexual experience – love, marriage, divorce or just sex. In romance for example, the significant space is that of encounter, love, (possibly) a hindrance and marriage; understanding is finding the proper mate. It is rare to find a novel such as Jane Austen's *Emma* where the sentimental lesson is combined with an intellectual lesson, that of discretion. An examination of novelistic practices – customs of the single central character, 'realistic' writing, the delineation of time as progressive and significant – would require a lengthy article but it is sufficient to bring them forward here to indicate that women centred novels are *not* the product of a feminist audience. Nor can we say that the structures of the realist novel are neutral and that they can just be filled with a feminist content. Indeed, it could be argued that the emergence of this particular form of 'women's writing' with its emphasis on sexual experience as the source of significant experience, might have the effect of confirming women as bearers of sentiment, experience and romance (albeit disillusioned).

It is quite clear that there are compelling similarities between 'novels that change lives' and contemporary fictional conventions, which should warn us against any simple designation of these novels as feminist. This does not mean that we cannot say anything about the emergence of this group of novels in their specificity, nor does it mean that there is nothing progressive about these novels. First of all, it is clear that female sexuality (as distinct from just female emotions) is becoming more and more an object to be interrogated, in a variety of social practices – film, sociological, psychological and 'sexological' studies. The novel's own history – its confessional form, and its highlighting of sexual events as significant time – make it particularly responsive to this preoccupation. And this preoccupation undoubtedly at a certain level represents a response to a problem: what is female sexual pleasure? Thus, though feminist writing may well be compromised by its uncritical use of the conventional forms of the novel, it is also an important presence in a popular form of fiction.

But it would also be limited to suggest that all the novels which we loosely designate feminist never escape beyond defining women entirely by their sexuality. Occasionally some go beyond the limits of the conventional novelistic forms and preoccupations. Doris Lessing and Fay Weldon, for example, both occasionally disrupt the conventions of the central narrative voice or character, and their writings suddenly become a myriad of historical, social and sexual concerns which do not 'belong' to an individual subjectivity. Where sexuality is treated as political this is occasionally the outcome and is one of the most interesting aspects of novels like these.

It is by paying attention to practices of writing, conventions of genre and their relation to other forms of writing, that we can differentiate between novels and assess their political effects. And it is only in conjunction with an analysis of the conventions internal to the text that we can understand marketing strategies.

MICHÈLE BARRETT

'Feminism and the Definition of Cultural Politics' *Feminism, Culture and Politics*

II. When is Women's Art Feminist Art?
This leads to a second problem. This is the question asked by Rosalind Coward in her article 'Are Women's Novels Feminist Novels?'.[1] Although Coward's piece is directed towards one particular review article on feminist fiction, her argument is in fact a generalized critique of a major (if not the

main) tendency in feminist literary criticism. She argues that feminists have emphasized the unity and continuity of women's creative work and have tended to confuse feminist art with, simply, women's art. Coward rejects this conflation of the two, and she suggests that the current popularity of 'women's fiction' is not necessarily feminist at all. Feminism, she argues, is an alignment of political interests and not a shared female experience; hence a tradition of women's art is of no particular importance.

This goes right to the nub of a number of controversial questions about feminism and culture. Is the recovery of women's artistic work of the past an integral part of our developing feminist project, or merely a sentimental resuscitation of marginalia better left in the obscurity to which establishment criticism has consigned it? What do we gain by elevating traditional crafts such as embroidery and knitting to the status of art objects and hanging them in galleries? What is the meaning of an art exhibition where the objects displayed are kitchen utensils or the careful record of a child's upbringing? How should we react to art that claims to be based on a 'female language' or on an artistic rendering of the female body and genitalia? In what sense might these various imaginative comments on women's experience be seen as 'feminist' art? Is a work of art feminist because the artist says it is, or the collective who produced it announce their feminist principles of work?

These questions were crystallized for me in a thought-provoking way by Judy Chicago's exhibition *The Dinner Party*, and although this has not yet been shown in Britain I want to use it to illustrate some points. The leaflet accompanying the show states that '... the goal of *The Dinner Party* is to ensure that women's achievements become a permanent part of our culture', and the scale of the exhibition matches this monumental aspiration.

The central conception is a triangular dining-table, along the sides of which are placed symbolic representations of thirty-nine women: pre-Christian goddesses; historical figures such as Sappho and Boadaceia; women like the suffragist Susan B. Anthony and the artist Georgia O'Keefe. (This dining-table echoes the 'last supper' so significant to our male-dominated Christian culture.) Each of the figures at the table has a place setting of a runner, cutlery, goblet and plate, whose different designs evoke her particular character. From these thirty-nine women the names of 999 less resoundingly famous, but still reasonably well-known, women radiate in inscriptions on the 'heritage floor'. Surrounding this central focus of the exhibition are banners designed for the entrance, documentation of the five year's work by Judy Chicago and her team of helpers, an exhibition of china-painting, and a display of congratulatory telegrams from feminist artists all over the world.

The size of the exhibition – completely devoted to women's achievements – is, literally, spectacular. When I saw it an entire floor of the San Francisco Museum of Modern Art had been given over to it. The dining-table itself totals nearly 150 feet in length, each woman's place setting using about three and a half feet of space. The combination of this impressive scale and the lavish, beautiful, solid, ceramics and embroidery made the experience of being there an obviously moving one for many women. Never before, it seemed, had women taken over the cultural arena in such a flamboyant and confident way. The atmosphere, too, was wonderful – bringing back all the most positive and sisterly dimensions of a large women's liberation conference since there were so many feminists there.

The experience of being there was for me a striking one and I warmed immediately to the project. It conveyed a real sense of women's achievements and perhaps we too frequently refuse to take pride in them. The feeling of straightforward gender-congratulation was a new and welcome one. Yet in other respects the exhibition was extremely disturbing.

First, it was clear from the documentation that Judy Chicago had not only conceived the project but had directed the work of her many assistants with a positively dictatorial zeal. The principles of collective work vaunted here were not so much the ones I might recognize as feminist but an attempt to recreate the 'school' or studio of an 'Artistic Genius' like Michelangelo. Although hundreds of people gave much time and work to the project it is Judy Chicago personally who has, apparently not unwillingly, made an international reputation from it.

Second, we have to question whether it is necessarily progress to retrieve embroidery and china-painting from the inglorious role of women's drudgery (or at best 'craft') and re-allocate them to the realm of 'high art'. This is undoubtedly the aim of the show, and it one that is fraught with problems. What has happened to previous radical artists who attempted to challenge prevailing definitions of the 'appropriate' contents of art galleries? This is not a reactionary question, for the answer is that by and large their iconoclasm has been effectively dampened by a versatile establishment and so their challenge to the institution has been converted into artistic novelty. To sail into the establishment without seeing this as a problem is to beg the question of what 'art' is and how it differs from other forms of work. It is not enough simply to get what women do recognized as 'art'.

Third, I found the uncritical exercise of ranking 'great women' rather disturbing. There is something rather crude in deeming (to take some British examples of the figures used) the composer Ethel Smythe and the writer Virginia Woolf as worthy of individual places at the dining-table, while Jane Austen and Dorothy Wordsworth merit only an inscription on the floor. The heroines of feminism are here graded, ranked according to a set of criteria that are highly subjective. (On what grounds was it decided that Eleanor of Acquitaine made a greater contribution to feminism than the Virgin Mary? Is there not something bizarre in ranking Emily Dickinson with the Primordial Goddess?) The list of names in the catalogue is studded with epithets like 'pioneer', 'prizewinning', 'cultural leader' and 'eminent intellectual' – all of them terms of evaluation which we have developed a critical stance towards. The search for heroines and role models, for the great women of history, is one which raises a number of difficulties.

Finally, there are the problems surrounding how these women are represented in the exhibition. It is, perhaps, unsurprising and even appropriate that mythological goddesses are symbolized through renderings of clitoral and vaginal imagery. We have little to know them by. But for other women, of whose lives and beliefs we know far more (since they are historical rather than mythological figures), the inevitable vaginal imagery is less appropriate. Less appropriate! I was in fact horrified to see a 'Virginia Woolf' whose image to me represented a reading of her life and work which contradicted all she had ever stood for. There she sits: a genital sculpture in deep relief (about four inches high) resting on a runner of pale lemon gauze with the odd blue wave embroidered on it. Gone is Woolf's theory of androgyny and love of gender ambiguity; gone the polemical public voice; gone the complex symbolic abstractions of her writing. I found this exclusive emphasis on genitalia, and the sentimentality of the trappings, a complete betrayal – as was the 'Emily Dickinson' whose vagina is trimmed with a white lace effect over the palest pink. Very few of our celebrated sisters manage to escape this dreadful posthumous fate. Ethel Smythe appears here as a rather fine grand piano on a background of grey pin-stripe, but this, one fears, is attributable to Chicago's perceptions of her as a dyke. It is in fact typical of Chicago's somewhat biologistic approach to feminism that various of her protagonists are credited for creating a 'female form' of art or literature in itself a controversial achievement since the possible existence of 'female' forms of art has yet to be established. The notion that some forms of art are intrinsically female (or male) is a dubious one.

All these reservations about *The Dinner Party* have a bearing on the problem of what can be said to be feminist art. This particular case is of interest in that Chicago's claims for the exhibition – that it serves her project of securing artistic recognition for women's achievements – crystallize one specific approach to feminist cultural politics. Her argument that women's art is systematically excluded from the artistic establishment is demonstrated by the fact that after an immensely popular American tour the show went into storage rather than on to Europe.

But problems still remain in (i) the difficulty of arriving at a consensus among feminists as to what constitutes 'feminist' art and (ii) the fact that the use of women's lives, histories and experience does not necessarily ensure the coherent, feminist, reading of Chicago's work that the artist appears to desire. In this sense the case of *The Dinner Party* does seem to me to illustrate the truth of Rosalind Coward's warning that women's art is not necessarily feminist art. Feminist art is not the same as any art which emphasizes women's experience.

We cannot, however, completely separate feminist art from women's experience and hence I would not go so far as Rosalind Coward when she writes:

> Feminism can never be the product of the identity of women's experiences and interests – there is no such unity. Feminism must always be the alignment of women in a political movement with particular political aims and objectives. It is a grouping unified by its *political interests*, not by its common experiences.[2]

Whatever the problems of basing feminism on the experience shared by women, far greater problems arise in attempting completely to divorce feminism (as a political project) from women's experience. This leads to the position that women's shared experience of oppression plays no significant part in the construction of a feminist cultural politics, which in turn must lead to the conclusion that feminist art could equally well be developed by (for instance) a man. Although an emphasis on women's experience, or the fact of female authorship, or indeed a concern with the female body, is not enough to make a work of art feminist I do not see how feminism can ever take women to be a dispensable category. So although I agree than an emphasis on women is not a sufficient condition to make cultural production feminist it must at least be a *necessary* condition. Put another way, feminist art could be seen as a category *within* a tradition of women's art but I fail to see how it could be generated outside it. It may be that in general women's art is only indirectly useful or inspiring to feminism, but it is not possible to conceive of a feminist art that could be detached from a shared experience of oppression.

(1982)

Notes

1   Rosalind Coward, ' "This Novel Changes Lives": Are Women's Novels Feminist Novels? A Response to Rebecca O'Rourke's Article "Summer Reading"', *Feminist Review*, 5 (1980). See previous extract.
2   Coward, ' "This Novel Changes Lives" ', p. 63.

LILLIAN FADERMAN

'What is Lesbian Literature? Forming a Historical Canon' *Profession of Desire: Lesbian and Gay Studies in Literature*

But must such works compose the extent of pre-1990s lesbian literature? What is lesbian literature? It has often been considered to be literature that deals with problems of coming out and coping with a homophobic society and with sexuality between women, as did *The Well of Loneliness*, the proto-typical lesbian novel. But if lesbian literature is limited to that subject mat-ter, it cannot go back much more than a hundred years, except for isolated instances, since "the lesbian" was seldom a recognized entity earlier. And if such literature must be written by a woman to be considered lesbian, its his-tory is even shorter since women of earlier eras seldom felt comfortable dealing with the subject of sexuality.

But perhaps literature need not confront the matter of same-sex sexuality head on to be "lesbian." Can we identify a lesbian sensibility in literature that may not be concerned specifically with lesbian sexuality and attendant matters? For example, if a work (especially one written before Hall broke the ice in 1928) criticizes heterosexual institutions, focuses on women apart from their erotic connection with men, and presents romantic friendships between women (which fall short of genital sexuality), is it lesbian? Willa Cather's *My Ántonia*, for instance, fulfills all those criteria and also presents a "male" narrator who is almost certainly a woman in masquerade. If a work evinces a fascination with androgyny and concerns itself with feminist protest, does it have a lesbian sensibility? Virginia Woolf's *Orlando* presents a character who keeps changing from male to female and back to male to illustrate the difficulties of women's plight. Is the argument for divining a lesbian sensibility in those works more persuasive when we know that both Cather and Woolf were lesbian?

Conversely, if an author is ostensibly nonlesbian, can we nevertheless consider her work lesbian if it concerns sexual love between women? Alice Walker's *The Color Purple*, set in black rural Georgia of the 1930s, suggests (realistically) that its characters are not aware of any lesbian "lifestyle" in America or even of the concept of "the lesbian." It leaves untouched such lesbian issues as coming out or battling homophobia. But it takes as its emo-tional center the nurturing, loving, and specifically sexual relationship between Celie and Shug. For Celie, the relationship remains erotically charged to the end of the novel and represents the only satisfactory sexual experience of her life. Do the absence of the word *lesbian*, the oblivion to the existence of a lesbian subculture, and the author's putative heterosexual-ity mandate that we cannot consider such a work lesbian literature? According to Bonnie Zimmerman's working definition, contemporary les-bian fiction (1969–89) must be written by self-declared lesbians because "the nature of lesbian fiction makes it impossible to separate the text from the imagination that engenders it" (15). But it is not easy to think of a text more critical of heterosexual institutions and more positive about the regen-erative effects of erotic love between women than *The Color Purple* or to conceive of how a "real lesbian imagination" could have engendered a more lesbian text.

Zimmerman also suggests that in lesbian literature of the 1970s and 1980s the central character must be "one who understands herself to be a lesbian" (15). While Zimmerman's definition is entirely appropriate to the political lesbian-feminist novels on which her study focuses, a different definition may be required for earlier novels, those written at a time when such consciousness was hard to come by and even harder to articulate in print, such as Louisa May Alcott's *Work* and Florence Converse's *Diana Victrix*. Such a definition would also cover novels that challenge the reader to struggle along with the main character to understand an inchoate lesbian development, for which the character may never have a descriptive term. In Carson McCullers's *A Member of the Wedding*, an adolescent girl crops her hair, takes a boy's name, fantasizes an androgynous existence where she can change her sex at will, assaults a young man who tries to kiss her, and by the end of the novel, enters into a satisfying relationship with another adolescent girl with whom she makes detailed plans to spend the rest of her life. Although Frankie is incapable of identifying herself as a lesbian, McCullers (herself a homosexual) presents what is almost a cliché in sexology: the adolescent history of "the lesbian." Writing in the years after World War II, under the constraint of self-censorship and possibly a not unrealistic fear of external censorship, McCullers did not dare permit even her third person narrator to state Frankie's lesbianism. But is it impossible to see the novel as lesbian because neither Frankie nor the narrator articulates what should be clear to the reader?

According to Zimmerman, the lesbian novel "places love between women, including sexual passion, at the center of its story" (15). While novels that follow that formula are clearly lesbian, must we eliminate from any "canon" (i.e., works we write about as lesbian scholars and recommend to students in our gay and lesbian literature classes, always with the distinct understanding that canons are mutable) a novel such as Jeanette Winterson's *Oranges Are Not the Only Fruit*, in which the center of the story is concerned with a girl's struggle in the context of a religious fundamentalist upbringing, and loving another woman erotically is shown to be only one of several ways in which she effects a break with her upbringing? Is it a contradiction in terms for a lesbian novel to focus on problems of, for example, frustrated ambition, on the trauma of aging, and on mortality, as they affect a character who just *happens* to be lesbian?

Can a work be seen as lesbian when it presents little or no awareness of erotic possibilities between women nor even a complaint about gender limitations? Barbara Smith, in "Toward a Black Feminist Criticism," argues that Toni Morrison's *Sula* is a lesbian novel not because Nel and Sula are lesbians but, rather, because the novel is critical of heterosexual institutions. Smith's analysis expands the definition of lesbian literature, but is it excessively liberal? Could we consider Sylvia Plath's "Daddy" a lesbian text because it provides a critique of heterosexual institutions (despite the homophobia of Plath herself)? And, if we reduce the point to its potential absurdity, since *The Well of Loneliness* privileges heterosexuality (a woman gives up her beloved, Mary, to a man because she believes that Mary will have an easier, happier life as his wife), must we see it as a heterosexual novel, despite its crucial role in the development of openly lesbian literature?

For some critics, a major difficulty in trying to formulate a canon of lesbian literature has been in deciding whether a work can be considered lesbian without doing violence to the writer's intention. But we must transcend the literality of insisting that lesbian literature, even works written before the 1970s, be by a self-declared lesbian (not many writers before the 1970s were making such declarations), be about a character "who understands herself to be a lesbian" (a certain sophistication is necessary for that understanding, and interesting characters often lack such insight), and include lesbian "sexual passion at the center of its story" (censorship laws in the past and self-censorship often mandated that the depiction of same-sex erotic love not be explicit). Perhaps a work might be considered lesbian, even if it lacks any of the criteria Zimmerman stipulates for the lesbian novel of the 1970s and 1980s, if it can be shown that lesbian subject matter is somehow encoded in it. Such encoding might be blatant to the contemporary reader, as it is in Gertrude Stein's 1923 piece "Miss Furr and Miss Skeene," which Stein published in *Vanity Fair* for predominantly heterosexual readers who undoubtedly thought that her constant reiteration of the word *gay* was nothing more than an instance of her wacky repetitive style or an ironic commentary on the sad life of "spinsters." Or the encoding might be more subtle, as in Nella Larsen's *Passing*, in which race and its attendant problems are possibly used as metaphors for the social and personal problems connected with lesbianism in the 1920s.

(1995)

CHERI REGISTER

'American Feminist Literary Criticism:
A Bibliographical Introduction'
Feminist Literary Criticism

Can feminists establish themselves as objective literary critics, given their political orientation?

The opponents of Phallic Criticism doubt whether any form of criticism can be truly objective; methods that appear to be non-ideological are actually supporting the status quo.[57] Nancy Hoffman thinks it not only impossible, but even undesirable, to create a feminist criticism that is totally objective. Her classroom method integrates objective distance and emotional involvement.[58] Feminist critics recognize that theirs is a specialized, highly political type of analysis, only one of many to which literature might be subjected. There are, however, varying opinions about feminist criticism's place in the spectrum that ranges between ivory tower academism and political activism. Lillian Robinson speaks from the political end:

> Some people are trying to make an honest woman out of the feminist critic, to claim that every "worthwhile" department should stock one. I am not terribly interested in whether feminism becomes a respectable part of academic criticism; I am very much concerned that feminist critics become a useful part of the women's movement.[59]

Because of its origin in the women's liberation movement, feminist criticism values literature that is of some use to the movement. Prescriptive Criticism, then, is best defined in terms of the ways in which literature can serve the cause of liberation. To earn feminist approval, literature must perform one or more of the following functions: (1) serve as a forum for women; (2) help to achieve cultural androgyny; (3) provide role-methods; (4) promote sisterhood; and (5) augment consciousness-raising. I would like to discuss these functions one by one.

In order to be useful as a *forum*, literature must allow forthright and honest self-expression, writing which is not constrained by pre-existing standards that may be alien to female culture. Virginia Woolf's first directive to female writers was: 'Above all, you must illumine your own soul with its profundities and its shallows, and its vanities and its generosities, and say what your beauty means to you or your plainness.' She regretted that the female author of the nineteenth century wrote with 'a mind which was slightly pulled from the straight, and made to alter its clear vision in deference to external authority.'[60] Ellen Morgan renews Woolf's advice: 'Feminist criticism should, I believe, encourage an art true to women's experience and not filtered through a male perspective or constricted to fit male standards.'[61] On the other hand, authors should not feel obligated to offer an exact representation of their own lives, but rather 'the fictional myths *growing out of their lives* and told by themselves for themselves.'[62] The arts must help people understand what female experience is, 'what it's like, what you think, how it operates. What it feels like to be us.'[63] Before literature can begin to perform the other functions, however, it must express female experience authentically, in all its variety. The emphasis on variety is apparent in the course syllabi in the *Female Studies* series. The works selected represent various ages, classes, and races of women. Tillie Olsen's 'Women: A List Out of Which to Read,' which appears in cumulative fashion in the *Women's Studies*

Newsletter (Old Westbury, New York: The Feminist Press), is an example of a growing tendency on the part of feminist critics and teachers to seek out materials that will compass the totality of the female life experience.

Once literature begins to serve as a forum, illuminating female experience, it can assist in humanizing and equilibrating the culture's value system, which has historically served predominantly male interests. That is, it can help to bring about *cultural androgyny*. Carolyn Heilbrun has reintroduced Woolf's 'androgyny' into the vocabulary of literary criticism in her book *Toward a Recognition of Androgyny* (New York: Alfred A. Knopf, 1973).[64] Other feminist critics agree that a 'female impulse' in literature is necessary for the achievement of cultural androgyny. Firestone expresses it succinctly: The 'development of "female" art … is progressive: an exploration of strictly female reality is a necessary step to correct the warp in a sexually biased culture. It is only after we have integrated the dark side of the moon into our world view that we can begin to talk seriously of universal culture.'[65] Of course, a pluralistic society like the one that exists in the United States must also draw on the experiences of its ethnic and regional groups if it is to be truly balanced.

Feminists often emphasize that they are not simply seeking more room for women in the present social order. They want a new social order founded on 'humanistic' values, some of which are traditionally 'female' and not respected in contemporary society. Those traditionally 'male' values that feminists believe harmful to the common good – excessive competition, for example – would be de-emphasized. Therefore, a female literary personage with 'masculine' characteristics does not necessarily meet with feminist approval. Ellen Harold, writing about Emma Peel, the heroine of 'The Avengers,' a British television series shown in the United States, comments: 'What is truly sad is that, though she is equal to a man and superior to most men, the measure of her competence is a strictly *macho* one – her capacity for violence. As an attempt at an emancipated woman she leaves something to be desired, for both men and women need new standards against which to measure themselves.'[66]

A literary work should provide *role-models*, instill a positive sense of feminine identity by portraying women who are 'self-actualizing, whose identities are not dependent on men.'[67] This function is particularly crucial in children's literature. In *Dick and Jane as Victims*, Women on Words and Images find fault with elementary school readers for reserving active mastery skills for boys – that is, creativity, ingenuity, adventurousness, curiosity, perseverance, bravery, autonomy – and describing girls as passive, docile, dependent, incompetent, and self-effacing. Adult women who are re-examining their lives may also depend on literature to introduce new possibilities and to help them evaluate the alternatives open to them. 'We cannot live in a certain way, we cannot see ourselves as the people we wish to be, until we perceive the wished-for life and self in our imaginations.'[68] To compensate for the death of satisfactory fictional role-models, feminist teachers are enlarging the definition of literature to include biography, autobiography, and memoirs. The syllabus for the Women's Biography Course offered at California State University in Sonoma illustrates the urgency of the search for role-models.[69]

It is important to note here that although female readers need literary models to emulate, characters should not be idealized beyond plausibility. The demand for authenticity supercedes all other requirements. Mary Anne Ferguson assigns works like Tillie Olsen's *Tell Me a Riddle* and Willa Cather's *My Antonia* to help her students 'realize that liberation involves hard choices; that it begins and ends with the self; that self-knowledge depends upon contact with the real world.'[70]

Literature should show women involved in activities that are not traditionally 'feminine', to speed the dissolution of rigid sex roles. It is not enough, however, to simply place a female character in a new occupation, with no corresponding change in her personality and behavior. Marion Meade describes the effects of the women's liberation movement on television heroines: although a few series feature female doctors or lawyers or television producers, the women's behavior and their relationships with men follow the familiar stereotyped pattern. They are caricatures, not realistic women, she says.[71]

The feminist movement in America is seeking to create a feeling of *sisterhood*, a new sense of community among women, in order to overcome group self-hatred, the animosity that many women feel for others of their sex as a result of isolation, competition for male attention, and belief in female inferiority. Virginia Woolf noticed the dearth of gratifying woman-to-woman relationships in literature:

> "Chloe liked Olivia," I read. And then it struck me how immense a change was there. Chloe liked Olivia perhaps for the first time in literature. Cleopatra did not like Octavia. And how completely *Antony and Cleopatra* would have been altered had she done so! ... All these relationships between women, I thought, rapidly recalling the splendid gallery of fictitious women, are too simple. So much has been left out, unattempted.[72]

In addition to testing new female–female (and female–male) relationships, a literary work can serve the cause of sisterhood by recounting experiences that the reader can identify as her own, experiences that are, perhaps, shared by many women. She will feel a common bond with the author and other readers who have similar reactions to the book. This is vital for adolescent readers, says Susan Koppelman Cornillon:

> We are all aware of the agony of adolescence in our culture, the evasive fumblings as we attempt to communicate about our fears and our needs and our anxieties without actually ever mentioning to anyone what they really are: the creation of elaborate private symbologies that enable us to grieve about our pimples, our sexual fantasies, our masturbation, the strange changes

happening to our bodies. But boys outgrow this secretiveness soon – because there is a vast wealth of literature for them to stumble on, both great and popular, classical and contemporary, pious and lewd, that assures them that, indeed, they are normal. Or even better, their suffering is portrayed as a prerequisite for maturity, if not a prelude to greatness.[73]

Literature might also enable a reader to emphasize with women whose subjective accounts of female reality differ from her own.

> Loving someone is wanting to know them. Insofar as we are able to learn and know of each other, we can acknowledge, and even in part assimilate into our own imaginative life, the thousand differences that have always been used as wedges to drive us apart. So that the experience of all women everywhere becomes, in a sense, our communal property, a heritage we bestow upon each other, the knowledge of what it has meant to be female, a woman in this man's world.[74]

In order to augment *consciousness-raising*, literature should provide realistic insights into female personality development, self-perception, interpersonal relationships, and other 'private' or 'internal' consequences of sexism. The reader can then note recurring problems and generalize from them with the aid of factual information about the status of women from other sources.[75] Feminist critics are far more concerned with exposing these private effects than with raising concrete issues, such as job discrimination and lack of child care facilities. In this age of mass communications, public forums, and official investigative committees, fiction is no longer the most effective means of arousing concern about measurable social problems. That is not to say that concrete political issues have no place in feminist-approved literature. But their presence must be consistent with the demands for authenticity and subjectivity prerequisite to an effective integration of the personal and the political. In disparaging didactic feminist poetry, Erica Jong noted, 'We all claim to believe that political oppression and personal feelings are related, and yet a great deal of the self-consciously polemical poetry that has come out of the Women's Movement reads like a generalized rant and it lacks any sort of psychological grounding. The poet has not really looked into herself and told it true. She has been content to echo simplistic slogans.'[76] Likewise, a fictional account of job discrimination that covers only the material consequences will not suffice. If the protagonist is, indeed, fully characterized, we will also see the private or psychic effects of discrimination. Ellen Morgan values a subtle rendering of both types of problems in which 'neo-feminist consciousness informs the novel as light informs a painting, rather than appearing as subject matter.'[77]

There is a precedent for this sort of personalized polemic in black literature. James Baldwin's novels are not single-issue tracts, but rather in-depth studies of individual examples of black humanity. Ralph Ellison's *Invisible Man* was successful not because it exposed conditions that were completely foreign to whites in America, but because it appealed to common, multiracial feelings of insignificance and alienation, showing how much more intense they are when institutionalized. Perhaps the difference between this and the muckraking and Socialist literatures of the early twentieth century is due to the fact that the victims have become the authors.[78]

Factual information about discrimination should be carefully integrated into a story with a larger focus, so that its presence seems natural. Joyce Nower warns, however, against condemning the author who merely translates position papers into fiction: 'A woman artist who writes a lousy story on a woman active in the Movement, or involved in getting an abortion, should be accorded the respect of critical appraisal: a lousy writer but important in that she is trying to use new materials.'[79] Ellen Morgan concurs: 'The capacity to teach and to delight which some of this work has would suggest that critical standards which deny literary legitimacy and value to [propagandistic] writing may be inadequate tools for [its] evaluation.'[80]

No feminist critic insists that a fictional work include political analysis.[81] The author need only describe the problems and offer some solutions, if the character herself can find them. The remaining tasks involved in consciousness-raising are left to the reader: to compare the problems encountered by female literary characters with her own, to explain similarities in terms of causes, and to decide on appropriate political action. Literature can thus augment the face-to-face consciousness-raising that is fundamental to the American women's liberation movement.

There is a potential conflict between the consciousness-raising function and the role-model function. A work that offers a thorough literary description of women's oppression may also feature a 'heroine' who is thoroughly oppressed and therefore unlikely to be emulated by female readers. Erica Jong, for one, is dissatisfied with 'all those so-called feminist novels in which women are depicted as helpless victims.'[82] The ideal feminist fictional work is one that fulfills all five functions in equilibrium. Rather than being driven to mental breakdown or suicide or immobility, the heroines of new feminist fiction will somehow manage to resist destruction, perhaps with the support and confidence of other women. Their outlook and behavior will presage a new social order that integrates the best aspects of 'female culture' with selected 'male' values.

(1975)

Notes

57 Lillian Robinson and Lise Vogel, 'Modernism and History,' *Images of Women in Fiction*, ed. Koppelman Cornillon, pp. 278–305; and Fraya Katz Stoker. 'The Other Criticism: Feminism vs. Formalism,' ibid., pp. 313–25.

58 Hoffman, 'A Class of Our Own,' pp. 14–27.

59   Robinson, 'Dwelling in Decencies,' p. 889.
60   Woolf, *A Room of One's Own*, pp. 93, 77.
61   Ellen Morgan to author, February 13, 1972.
62   Russ, 'What Can a Heroine Do?' p. 19.
63   Millett, 'Notes on the Making of *Three Lives*,' p. 2.
64   See also Carolyn Heilbrun, 'The Masculine Wilderness of the American Novel,' *Saturday Review*, January 29, 1972, pp. 41–4.
65   Firestone, *Dialectic of Sex*, p. 167.
66   Harold, 'A Look at Some Old Favorites,' pp. 44–5.
67   Martin, 'The Feminine Mystique in American Fiction,' p. 33.
68   Michele Murray, 'Introduction' to *A House of Good Proportion. Images of Women in Literature*, ed. Murray (New York: Simon and Schuster, 1973), p. 19.
69   *Female Studies VII*, ed. Rosenfelt, pp. 82–5.
70   Quoted in Showalter, 'Introduction: Teaching about Women, 1971,' p. x.
71   Marion Meade, 'On the Trail of the Liberated TV Heroine,' *Aphra* 2 (Spring 1971): 30–4.
72   Woolf, *A Room of One's Own*, p. 86.
73   Susan Koppelman Cornillon, 'The Fiction of Fiction,' *Images of Women in Fiction*, ed. Koppelman Cornillon, p. 115.
74   Millett, 'Introduction' to 'Prostitution: A Quartet,' p. 23. See also Hoffman, 'A Class of Our Own.'
75   See Morgan's critique of Alix Kates Schulman, *Memoirs of an Ex-Prom Queen* (New York: Alfred A. Knopf, 1972) in 'Humanbecoming,' pp. 197–204.
76   Erica Jong, 'Visionary Anger' (a review of Adrienne Rich, *Diving Into the Wreck*) *Ms*, July 1973, p. 31.
77   Morgan, 'Humanbecoming,' p. 197.
78   For a discussion of this earlier literature see Walter B. Rideout, *The Radical Novel in the United States, 1900–1954: Some Interrelations of Literature and Society* (Cambridge: Harvard University Press, 1956).
79   Joyce Nower to author, March 7, 1972.
80   Morgan, 'Humanbecoming,' p. 187.
81   With the possible exception of Kate Millett. In *Sexual Politics*, p. 139, she criticizes Virginia Woolf for not explaining the causes of Rhoda's suicidal misery in *The Waves*, but in 'Notes on the Making of *Three Lives*,' written two years later, she says that she would now rather *express* female experience than analyze it.
82   Jong, 'Visionary Anger,' p. 34.

ELIZABETH WEED

'Introduction'
Feminism Meets Queer Theory

When feminism meets queer theory, no introductions seem necessary. Both academic feminism and queer theory are connected, however directly or indirectly, to political movements outside the academy, in some cases to overlapping movements. Both are interdisciplinary modes of inquiry; both constitute themselves in critical relation to a set of hegemonic social and cultural formations. Indeed, the two are connected not only by commonalities but by affiliations. Queer theory, like lesbian and gay studies, has acknowledged its intellectual debts to feminist theory and women's studies, just as feminist theory has recognized the influence of queer theory. For many in the academy, feminism and queer theory are most easily understood as two branches of the same family tree of knowledge and politics, just as in most bookstores they are most easily found on shelves located side by side or back to back.

Since all this seems true enough, why entitle the volume "feminism *meets* queer theory"? If the purpose of the collection is to present some of the points of convergence and divergence between the two fields, why not give it the title of "the meeting of feminism and queer theory," or simply "feminism and queer theory"? Why a title that connotes a staging of strangeness or unpredictability?

The problem with the "and," of course, is that it too quickly renders its terms commensurable. To say that feminism and queer theory share commonalities and affiliations is not to say they are easily commensurable. In fact, they are clearly presented here as something of an unmatched pair: the unmodified "feminism" of the title would seem to be more properly paired with something like "queer politics" ("feminist politics meets queer politics"), just as "queer theory" would seem to be better matched with its counterpart, "feminist theory" ("feminist theory meets queer theory"). And yet, the solution is not to find a more proper couple, for if "feminism" and "queer theory" are an awkward pair, "feminist theory" and "queer theory" are no less so. Not only do the two bodies of theory have quite different historical formations, but because of these differences, the (various and complicated) relationships among feminist politics, women's studies, and feminist theory have no simple correspondence to the (various and complicated) relationships among queer politics, gay and lesbian studies, and queer theory.[1] Given the difficulty of finding a matched pair, the skewed coupling of the title remains unabashedly awry, suggesting, perhaps, a meeting that is not as straightforward as many academicians and bookstores might think.[2]

Still, why frame the collection of essays as a strange and even surprising meeting? The answer lies not so much in what queer theory represents, but in queer theory's representation of feminism – a representation that in the eyes of some feminist theorists renders feminism strangely unrecognizable. No matter how reluctant queer theory has been to pin itself down as a coherent set of theorizations,[3] it has been consistent about one aspect of its project: considerations of sex and sexuality cannot be contained by the category of gender. This is not, in itself, a controversial proposition. The problem, as Judith Butler shows in her argument "Against Proper Objects," is that in this formulation gender becomes the property of feminist inquiry while the proper study of sex and sexuality is located elsewhere.[4] This one move, the separation of gender from sex and sexuality, is by no means the only topic of conversation between feminism and queer theory–the essays in this volume address a number of other questions – but it is this move above all that makes the meeting of feminism and queer theory a strange one.

By rendering feminism unrecognizable – not to say illegible – to many feminist theorists, queer theory provokes a rethinking of earlier arguments that had seemed, if not resolved, at least displaced. That is, in engaging with queer theory, a number of the feminist theorists here are involved less in putting queer theory in its place – a place where many of the contributors also situate themselves – than in taking a close look at the odd sort of feminism queer theory presents them with. This means that one of the effects of the encounter is that "feminism" ineluctably, if unexpectedly, revisits itself. Running through the essays are debates about the sex/gender split, about whether gender or sexual difference is preferable as a category of analysis, about Freudian-Lacanian versus Foucauldian modes of theorizing. These debates evoke an earlier feminist period, in some cases a much earlier one. But like all "revisits," this one entails no simple reanimation of the past, no respectful return to former truths. The introduction of old arguments into the theoretical and political investments of the present serves, rather, to disturb the ground of both the old debates and the new, and this disturbance can only be enriching.

(1997)

Notes

1   For example, none of the undecidability of the term "women's studies" (see Gallop 13–21) is present in "gay and lesbian studies"; by the same token, none of the provocation of "queer theory" can be found in "feminist theory." Queer politics enact a split with gay and lesbian politics that overlaps but does not duplicate splits between "mainstream" feminist politics and lesbian politics or between feminist sexual liberationists and feminists against pornography. And so on.

2   One might ask why not call it a "queer" meeting, since the term "queer" sees itself as effecting essentially productive displacements or defamiliarizations. The question here would be through what route this particular encounter becomes productive.

3   As Lauren Berlant and Michael Warner say, queer theory has a very short history and "cannot be assimilated to a single discourse, let alone a propositional program.... Queer commentary takes on various shapes, risks, ambitions, and ambivalences in various contexts.... The danger of the label *queer theory* is that it makes its queer and nonqueer audiences forget these differences and imagine a context (theory) in which *queer* has a stable referential content and pragmatic force" (343–4).

4 Butler's argument engages with the introduction to *The Lesbian and Gay Studies Reader*, but it applies as well to queer theory. The latter breaks in some ways with lesbian and gay studies, but not with regard to the gender/sex-sexuality split.

ANNETTE KOLODNY

'Dancing through the Minefield: Some Observations on the Theory, Practice, and Politics of a Feminist Literary Criticism' *Feminist Studies*

What distinguishes our work from those similarly oriented 'social consciousness' critiques, it is said, is its lack of systematic coherence. Pitted against, for example, psychoanalytic or Marxist readings, which owe a decisive share of their persuasiveness to their apparent internal consistency as a system, the aggregate of feminist literary criticism appears woefully deficient in system, and painfully lacking in program. It is, in fact, from all quarters, the most telling defect alleged against us, the most explosive threat in the minefield. And my own earlier observation that, as of 1976, feminist literary criticism appeared 'more like a set of interchangeable strategies than any coherent school or shared goal orientation,' has been taken by some as an indictment, by others as a statement of impatience. Neither was intended. I felt then, as I do now, that this would 'prove both its strength *and* its weakness,'[48] in the sense that the apparent disarray would leave us vulnerable to the kind of objection I've just alluded to; while the fact of our diversity would finally place us securely where, all along, we should have been: camped out, on the far side of the minefield, with the other pluralists and pluralisms.

In our heart of hearts, of course, most critics are really structuralists (whether or not they accept the label) because what we are seeking are patterns (or structures) that can order and explain the otherwise inchoate; thus, we invent, or believe we discover, relational patternings in the texts we read which promise transcendence from difficulty and perplexity to clarity and coherence. But, as I've tried to argue in these pages, to the imputed 'truth' or 'accuracy' of these findings, the feminist must oppose the painfully obvious truism that what is attended to in a literary work, and hence what is reported about it, is often determined not so much by the work itself as by the critical technique or aesthetic criteria through which it is filtered or, rather, read and decoded. All the feminist is asserting, then, is her own equivalent right to liberate new (and perhaps different) significances from these same texts; and, at the same time, her right to choose which features of a text she takes as relevant because she is, after all, asking new and different questions of it. In the process, she claims neither definitiveness nor structural completeness for her different readings and reading systems, but only their usefulness in recognizing the particular achievements of woman-as-author and their applicability in conscientiously decoding woman-as-sign.

That these alternate foci of critical attentiveness will render alternate readings or interpretations of the same text – even among feminists – should be no cause for alarm. Such developments illustrate only the pluralist contention that, 'in approaching a text of any complexity ... the reader must choose to emphasize certain aspects which seem to him crucial' and that, 'in fact, the variety of readings which we have for many works is a function of the selection of crucial aspects made by a variety of readers.' Robert Scholes, from whom I've been quoting, goes so far as to assert that 'there is no single "right" reading for any complex literary work,' and, following the Russian formalist school, he observes that 'we do not speak of readings that are simply true or false, but of readings that are more or less rich, strategies that are more or less appropriate.'[49] Because those who share the term 'feminist' nonetheless practice a diversity of critical strategies, leading, in some cases, to quite different readings, we must acknowledge among ourselves that sister critics, 'having chosen to tell a different story, may in their interpretation identify different aspects of the meanings conveyed by the same passage.'[50]

Adopting a 'pluralist' label does not mean, however, that we cease to disagree; it means only that we entertain the possibility that different readings, even of the same text, may be differently useful, even illuminating, within different contexts of inquiry. It means, in effect, that we enter a dialectical process of examining, testing, even trying out the contexts – be they prior critical assumptions or explicitly stated ideological stances (or some combination of the two) – that led to the disparate readings. Not all will be equally acceptable to every one of us, of course, and even those prior assumptions or ideologies that are acceptable may call for further refinement and/or clarification. But, at the very least, because we will have grappled with the assumptions that led to it, we will be better able to articulate *why* we find a particular reading or interpretation adequate or inadequate. This kind of dialectical process, moreover, not only makes us more fully aware of what criticism is, and how it functions; it also gives us access to its future possibilities, making us conscious, as R. P. Blackmur put it, 'of what we have done,' 'of what can be done next, or done again,'[51] or, I would add, of what can be done differently. To put it still another way: just because we will no longer tolerate the specifically sexist omissions and oversights of earlier critical schools and methods does not mean that, in their stead, we must establish our own 'party line.'

In my view, our purpose is not and should not be the formulation of any single reading method or potentially procrustean set of critical procedures nor, even less, the generation of prescriptive categories for some dreamed of nonsexist literary canon.[52] Instead, as I see it, our task is to initiate nothing less than a playful pluralism, responsive to the possibilities of multiple critical schools and methods, but captive of none, recognizing that the many tools needed for our analysis will necessarily be largely inherited and only partly of our own making. Only by employing a plurality of methods will we protect ourselves from the temptation of so oversimplifying any text – and especially those particularly offensive to us – that we render ourselves unresponsive to what Scholes has called 'its various systems of meaning and their interaction.'[53] Any text we deem worthy of our critical attention is usually, after all, a locus of many and varied kinds of (personal, thematic, stylistic, structural, rhetorical, etc.) relationships. So, whether we tend to treat a text as a *mimesis*, in which words are taken to be recreating or representing viable worlds; or whether we prefer to treat a text as a kind of equation of communication, in which decipherable messages are passed from writers to readers; and whether we locate meaning as inherent in the text, the act of reading, or in some collaboration between reader and text – whatever our predilection, let us not generate from it a straitjacket that limits the scope of possible analysis. Rather, let us generate an ongoing dialogue of competing potential possibilities – among feminists and, as well, between feminist and nonfeminist critics.

The difficulty of what I describe does not escape me. The very idea of pluralism seems to threaten a kind of chaos for the future of literary inquiry while, at the same time, it seems to deny the hope of establishing some basic conceptual model which can organize all data – the hope which always begins any analytical exercise. My effort here, however, has been to demonstrate the essential delusions that inform such objections: If literary inquiry has historically escaped chaos by establishing canons, then it has only substituted one mode of arbitrary action for another – and, in this case, at the expense of half the population. And if feminists openly acknowledge ourselves as pluralists, then we do not give up the search for patterns of opposition and connection – probably the basis of thinking itself; what we give up is simply the arrogance of claiming that our work is either exhaustive or definitive. (It is, after all, the identical arrogance we are asking our nonfeminist colleagues to abandon.) If this kind of pluralism appears to threaten both the present coherence of and the inherited aesthetic criteria for a canon of 'greats,' then, as I have earlier argued, it is precisely that threat which, alone, can free us from the prejudices, the strictures, and the blind spots of the past. In feminist hands, I would add, it is less a threat than a promise.

(1980)

Notes

48 Annette Kolodny. 'Literary Criticism,' Review Essay in *Signs* 2, no. 2 (Winter 1976): 420.

49 Scholes, *Structuralism in Literature*, pp. 144–45. These comments appear within his explication of Tzvetan Todorov's theory of reading.

50   I borrow this concise phrasing of pluralistic modesty from M. H. Abrams's 'The Deconstructive Angel,' *Critical Inquiry* 3, no. 3 (Spring 1977): 427. Indications of the pluralism that was to mark feminist inquiry were to be found in the diversity of essays collected by Susan Koppelman Cornillon for her early and ground breaking anthology, *Images of Women in Fiction: Feminist Perspectives* (Bowling Green, Ohio: Bowling Green University Popular Press, 1972).

51   R. P. Blackmur, 'A Burden for Critics,' *The Hudson Review* 1 (1948): 171. Blackmur, of course, was referring to the way in which criticism makes us unconscious of how art functions; I use his wording here because I am arguing that that same awareness must also be focused on the critical act itself. 'Consciousness,' he avers, 'is the way we feel the critic's burden.'

52   I have earlier elaborated my objection to prescriptive categories for literature in 'The Feminist as Literary Critic,' Critical Response in *Critical Inquiry* 2, no. 4 (Summer 1976): 827–8.

53   Scholes, *Structuralism in Literature*, pp. 151–2.

Elaine Showalter

'Towards a Feminist Poetics'
Women Writing and Writing About Women

The Feminist Critique: Hardy

Let us take briefly as an example of the way a feminist critique might proceed, Thomas Hardy's *The Mayor of Casterbridge*, which begins with the famous scene of the drunken Michael Henchard selling his wife and infant daughter for five guineas at a country fair. In his study of Hardy, Irving Howe has praised the brilliance and power of this opening scene:

> To shake loose from one's wife; to discard that drooping rag of a woman, with her mute complaints and maddening passivity; to escape not by a slinking abandonment but through the public sale of her body to a stranger, as horses are sold at a fair; and thus to wrest, through sheer amoral wilfulness, a second chance out of life – it is with this stroke, so insidiously attractive to male fantasy, that *The Mayor of Casterbridge* begins.[8]

It is obvious that a woman, unless she has been indoctrinated into being very deeply identified indeed with male culture, will have a different experience of this scene. I quote Howe first to indicate how the fantasies of the male critic distort the text; for Hardy tells us very little about the relationship of Michael and Susan Henchard, and what we see in the early scenes does not suggest that she is drooping, complaining or passive. Her role, however, is a passive one; severely constrained by her womanhood, and further burdened by her child, there is no way that *she* can wrest a second chance out of life. She cannot master events, but only accommodate herself to them.

What Howe, like other male critics of Hardy, conveniently overlooks about the novel is that Henchard sells not only his wife but his child, a child who can only be female. Patriarchal societies do not readily sell their sons, but their daughters are all for sale sooner or later. Hardy wished to make the sale of the daughter emphatic and central; in early drafts of the novel Henchard has two daughters and sells only one, but Hardy revised to make it clearer that Henchard is symbolically selling his entire share in the world of women. Having severed his bonds with this female community of love and loyalty, Henchard has chosen to live in the male community, to define his human relationships by the male code of paternity, money and legal contract. His tragedy lies in realising the inadequacy of this system, and in his inability to repossess the loving bonds he comes desperately to need.

The emotional centre of *The Mayor of Casterbridge* is neither Henchard's relationship to his wife, nor his superficial romance with Lucetta Templeman, but his slow appreciation of the strength and dignity of his wife's daughter, Elizabeth-Jane. Like the other women in the book, she is governed by her own heart – man-made laws are not important to her until she is taught by Henchard himself to value legality, paternity, external definitions, and thus in the end to reject him. A self-proclaimed 'women-hater', a man who has felt at best a 'supercilious pity' for womankind, Henchard is humbled and 'unmanned' by the collapse of his own virile façade, the loss of his mayor's chain, his master's authority, his father's rights. But in Henchard's alleged weakness and 'womanishness', breaking through in moments of tenderness, Hardy is really showing us the man at his best. Thus Hardy's female characters in *The Mayor of Casterbridge*, as in his other novels, are somewhat idealised and melancholy projections of a repressed male self.

As we see in this analysis, one of the problems of the feminist critique is that it is male-oriented. If we study stereotypes of women, the sexism of male critics, and the limited roles women play in literary history, we are not learning what women have felt and experienced, but only what men have thought women should be. In some fields of specialisation, this may require a long apprenticeship to the male theoretician, whether he be Althusser, Barthes, Macherey or Lacan; and then an application of the theory of signs or myths or the unconscious to male texts or films. The temporal and intellectual investment one makes in such a process increases resistance to questioning it, and to seeing its historical and ideological boundaries. The critique also has a tendency to naturalise women's victimisation, by making it the inevitable and obsessive topic of discussion. One sees, moreover, in works like Elizabeth Hardwick's *Seduction and Betrayal*, the bittersweet moral distinctions the critic makes between women merely betrayed by men, like Hetty in *Adam Bede*, and the heroines who make careers out of betrayal, like Hester Prynne in *The Scarlet Letter*. This comes dangerously close to a celebration of the opportunities of victimisation, the seduction *of* betrayal.[9]

Gynocritics and Female Culture
In contrast to this angry or loving fixation on male literature, the programme of gynocritics is to construct a female framework for the analysis of women's literature, to develop new models based on the study of female experience, rather than to adapt male models and theories. Gynocritics begins at the point when we free ourselves from the linear absolutes of male literary history, stop trying to fit women between the lines of the male tradition, and focus instead on the newly visible world of female culture. This is comparable to the ethnographer's effort to render the experience of the 'muted' female half of a society, which is described in Shirley Ardener's collection, *Perceiving Women*.[10] Gynocritics is related to feminist research in history, anthropology, psychology and sociology, all of which have developed hypotheses of a female subculture including not only the ascribed status, and the internalised constructs of femininity, but also the occupations, interactions and consciousness of women. Anthropologists study the female subculture in the relationships between women, as mothers, daughters, sisters and friends; in sexuality, reproduction and ideas about the body; and in rites of initiation and passage, purification ceremonies, myths and taboos. Michelle Rosaldo writes in *Woman, Culture, and Society*,

> the very symbolic and social conceptions that appear to set women apart and to circumscribe their activities may be used by women as a basis for female solidarity and worth. When men live apart from women, they in fact cannot control them, and unwittingly they may provide them with the symbols and social resources on which to build a society of their own.[11]

Thus in some women's literature, feminine values penetrate and undermine the masculine systems which contain them; and women have imaginatively engaged the myths of the Amazons, and the fantasies of a separate female society, in genres from Victorian poetry to contemporary science fiction.

In the past two years, pioneering work by four young American feminist scholars has given us some new ways to interpret the culture of nineteenth-century American women, and the literature which was its primary expressive form. Carroll Smith-Rosenberg's essay 'The Female World of Love and Ritual' examines several archives of letters between women, and outlines the homosocial emotional world of the nineteenth century. Nancy Cott's *The Bonds of Womanhood: Woman's Sphere in New England 1780–1835* explores the paradox of a cultural bondage, a legacy of pain and submission, which none the less generates a sisterly solidarity, a bond of shared experience, loyalty and compassion. Ann Douglas's ambitious book, *The Feminization of American Culture*, boldly locates the genesis of American mass culture in the sentimental literature of women and clergymen, two allied and 'disestablished' post-industrial groups. These three are social historians; but Nina Auerbach's *Communities of Women: An Idea in Fiction* seeks the bonds of womanhood in women's literature, ranging from the matriarchal households of Louisa May Alcott and Mrs Gaskell to the women's schools and colleges of Dorothy Sayers, Sylvia Plath and Muriel Spark. Historical and literary studies like these, based on English women, are badly needed; and the manuscript and archival sources for them are both abundant and untouched.[12]

(1979)

Notes

8 Irving Howe, *Thomas Hardy* (London, 1968), p. 84. For a more detailed discussion of this problem, see my essay 'The Unmanning of the Mayor of Casterbridge' in Dale Kramer (ed.), *Critical Approaches to Hardy* (London, 1979).
9 Elizabeth Hardwick, *Seduction and Betrayal* (New York, 1974).
10 Shirley Ardener (ed.), *Perceiving Women* (London, 1975).
11 'Women, Culture, and Society: A Theoretical Overview' in Louise Lamphere and Michelle Rosaldo (eds.), *Women, Culture and Society* (Stanford, 1974), p. 39.
12 Carroll Smith-Rosenberg. 'The Female World of Love and Ritual: Relations Between Women in Nineteenth-Century America', *Signs: Journal of Women in Culture and Society*, vol. 1 (Autumn 1975), pp. 1–30; Nancy Cott, *The Bonds of Womanhood* (New Haven, 1977); Ann Douglas, *The Feminization of American Culture* (New York, 1977); Nina Auerbach, *Communities of Women* (Cambridge, Mass., 1978).

TORIL MOI

Sexual/Textual Politics: Feminist Literary Theory

Arguing that feminist criticism is a fundamentally 'suspicious' approach to literature, Kolodny sees the principal task of the feminist critic as that of examining the validity of our aesthetic judgments: 'What ends do those judgments serve, the feminist asks; and what conceptions of the world or ideological stances do they (even if unwittingly) help to perpetuate?' (15).[1] This is surely one of her most valuable insights.

The problem arises when she proceeds from this to a wholesale recommendation of *pluralism* as the appropriate feminist stance. Feminist criticism lacks systematic coherence, she argues, and this fact ('the fact of our diversity'), should 'place us securely where, all along, we should have been: camped out, on the far side of the minefield, with the other pluralists and pluralisms' (17). Feminists cannot and indeed should not provide that 'internal consistency as a system' that Kolodny ascribes to psychoanalysis and Marxism. In her discourse, these two theoretical formations come to figure

as monolithically oppressive blocks towering over the diversified, anti-
authoritarian feminist field. But it is not only untrue that Marxism and
psychoanalysis offer such a unified theoretical field; it is also surely doubtful
that feminist criticism is *that* diversified.[2] Kolodny acknowledges that feminist politics is the basis for feminist criticism; so that though we may argue
over what constitutes proper feminist politics and theory, that debate nevertheless takes place within a feminist political framework, much like debates
within contemporary Marxism. Without common political ground, there
can simply be no recognizable *feminist* criticism. In this context, Kolodny's
'pluralist' approach risks throwing the baby out with the bathwater:

> Adopting a "pluralist" label does not mean, however, that we cease to disa-
> gree; it means only that we entertain the possibility that different readings,
> even of the same text, may be differently useful, even illuminating, within dif-
> ferent contexts of inquiry.
>
> (18)

But if we wax pluralistic enough to acknowledge the feminist position as
just one among many 'useful' approaches, we also implicitly grant the most
'masculinist' of criticism the right of existence: it just *might* be 'useful' in a
very different context from ours.

Kolodny's intervention in the theoretical debate pays too little attention
to the role of politics in critical theory. When she states, correctly, that 'If
feminist criticism calls anything into question, it must be that dog-eared
myth of intellectual neutrality' (21), she still seems not to recognize that
even critical theory carries with it its own political implications. Feminist
criticism cannot just

> initiate nothing less than a playful pluralism, responsive to the possibilities of
> multiple critical schools and methods, but captive of none, recognizing that
> the many tools needed for our analysis will necessarily be largely inherited and
> only partly of our own making.
>
> (19)

Feminists must surely also conduct a political and theoretical evaluation of
the various methods and tools on offer, to make sure that they don't back-
fire on us.

[...]

In the first article, Showalter distinguishes between two forms of feminist
criticism. The first type is concerned with woman as reader, which Showalter
labels 'feminist critique'. The second type deals with woman as writer, and
Showalter calls this 'gynocritics'. 'Feminist critique' deals with works by

male authors, and Showalter tells us that this form of criticism is a 'historically grounded inquiry which probes the ideological assumptions of literary
phenomena' (25).³ This sort of 'suspicious' approach to the literary text
seems however to be largely absent from Showalter's second category, since
among the primary concerns of 'gynocritics' we find 'the history, themes,
genres and structures of literature by women' as well as the 'psychodynamics of female creativity' and 'studies of particular writers and works' (25).
There is no indication here that the feminist critic concerned with women as
writers should bring other than sympathetic, identity seeking approaches to
bear on works written by women. The 'hermeneutics of suspicion', which
assumes that the text is not, or not only, what it pretends to be, and therefore searches for underlying contradictions and conflicts as well as absences
and silences in the text, seems to be reserved for texts written by men. The
feminist critic, in other words, must realize that the woman-produced text
will occupy a totally different status from the 'male' text.

Showalter writes:

> One of the problems of the feminist critique is that it is male-oriented. If we
> study stereotypes of women, the sexism of male critics, and the limited roles
> women play in literary history, we are not learning what women have felt and
> experienced, but only what men have thought women should be.
>
> (27)

The implication is not only that the feminist critic should turn to 'gynocritics', the study of women's writings, precisely in order to learn 'what women
have felt and experienced', but also that this experience is directly available
in the texts written by women. The text, in other words, has disappeared, or
become the transparent medium through which 'experience' can be seized.
This view of texts as transmitting authentic 'human' experience is, as we
have seen, a traditional emphasis of Western patriarchal humanism. In
Showalter's case, this humanist position is also tinged by a good portion of
empiricism. She rejects theory as a male invention that apparently can only
be used on men's texts (27–8). 'Gynocritics' frees itself from pandering to
male values and seeks to 'focus ... on the newly visible world of female culture' (28). This search for the 'muted' female culture can best be carried out
by applying anthropological theories to the female author and her work:
'Gynocritics is related to feminist research in history, anthropology, psychology and sociology, all of which have developed hypotheses of a female subculture' (28). The feminist critic, in other words, should attend to historical,
anthropological, psychological and sociological aspects of the 'female' text;
in short, it would seem, to everything but the text as a signifying process.
The only influences Showalter appears to recognize as constitutive of the
text are of an empirical, extra-literary sort. This attitude, coupled with her

fear of 'male' theory and general appeal to 'human' experience, has the unfortunate effect of drawing her perilously close to the male critical hierarchy whose patriarchal values she opposes.

(1985)

Notes

1   All citations in this part of the extract are from Annette Kolodny, 'Dancing through the Minefield: Some Observations on the Theory, Practice and Politics of a Feminist Literary Criticism', *Feminist Studies*, vol. 6, no. 1 (Spring 1980).
2   Lukács, Brecht, Stalin, Trotsky, Benjamin, Gramsci and Althusser are all considered Marxists, and psychoanalysis comprises names as divergent as Freud, Adler, Jung, Reich, Horney, Fromm, Klein and Lacan.
3   All citations in this part of the extract are from Elaine Showalter, 'Towards a Feminist Poetics', in Mary Jacobas (ed.), *Women Writing and Writing about Women* (London: Croom Helm, 1979).

ALICE A. JARDINE

Gynesis: Configurations of Woman and Modernity

Gynesis

These new ways have not surfaced in a void. Over the past century, those master (European) narratives history, philosophy, religion which have determined our sense of legitimacy in the West have undergone a series of crises in legitimation. It is widely recognized that legitimacy is part of that judicial domain which, historically, has determined the right to govern, the succession of kings, the link between father and son, the necessary paternal fiction, the ability to decide who is the father – in patriarchal culture. The crises experienced by the major Western narratives have not, therefore, been gender-neutral. They are crises in the narratives invented by men.

Going back to analyze those narratives and their crises has meant going back to the Greek philosophies in which they are grounded and, most particularly, to the originary relationships posited between the *techné* and *physis*, *time* and *space*, and all the dualistic oppositions that determine our ways of thinking. And rethinking those oppositions has meant, among other things, putting their "obligatory connotations" into discursive circulation, making those connotations explicit in order, one would hope, to put them into question. For example, the *techné* and time have connoted the male; *physis* and space the female. To think new relationships between the *techné* and *physis*, time and space, and so on, within an atmosphere of crisis, has required backing away from all that has defined and immobilized the possibilities of their relationships in the history of Western philosophy, requestioning the major topics of that philosophy: Man, the Subject, Truth, History, Meaning. At the forefront of this rethinking has been a rejection by and within those narratives of what seem to have been the strongest pillars of their history: Anthropomorphism, Humanism, and Truth. And again, it is in France that, in my opinion, this rethinking has taken its strongest conceptual leaps, as "philosophy," "history," and "literature" have attempted to account for the crisis-in-narrative that is modernity.

In general, this has brought about, within the master narratives in the West, a vast self-exploration, a questioning and turning back upon their own discourse, in an attempt to create a new *space* or *spacing within themselves* for survivals (of different kinds). In France, such rethinking has involved, above all, a reincorporation and reconceptualization of that which has been the master narratives' own "nonknowledge," what has eluded them, what has engulfed them. This other-than-themselves is almost always a "space" of some kind (over which the narrative has lost control), and this space has been coded as *feminine*, as *woman*. It is upon this process that I am insisting in this study: the transformation of woman and the feminine into verbs at the interior of those narratives that are today experiencing a crisis in legitimation.

To designate that process, I have suggested what I hope will be a believable neologism: *gynesis* – the putting into discourse of "woman" as that *process* diagnosed in France as intrinsic to the condition of modernity; indeed, the valorization of the feminine, woman, and her obligatory, that is, historical connotations, as somehow intrinsic to new and necessary modes of thinking, writing, speaking. The object produced by this process is neither a person nor a thing, but a horizon, that toward which the process is tending: a *gynema*. This *gynema* is a reading effect, a woman-in-effect that is never stable and has no identity. Its appearance in a written text is perhaps noticed only by the feminist reader – either when it becomes insistently "feminine" or when women (as defined metaphysically, historically) seem magically to reappear within the discourse. This tear in the fabric produces in the (feminist) reader a state of uncertainty and sometimes of distrust – especially when the faltering narrative in which it is embedded has been articulated by a man from within a nonetheless still-existent discipline. When it appears in women theorists' discourse, it would seem to be less troubling. The still existent slippages in signification among feminine, woman, women, and what I am calling *gynesis* and *gynema* are dismissed (at least in the United States and increasingly by male feminist critics) as irrelevant *because* it is a woman speaking.

I have tried to introduce here briefly some of the reasons why feminists may not want to qualify, too rapidly, major texts of modernity in the West, especially in France, as necessarily feminist or antifeminist, most particularly when they are texts signed by women. I hope I have begun to convey, as well, how important I think it is for feminist theoreticians in France, England, the United States, and (especially) elsewhere to rethink the history, impact, place for, and possible future directions of contemporary interpretive modes with regard to feminist theory. For if, as I have only begun to suggest, modernity represents a perhaps unavoidable and, in any case, new kind of discursivity on, about, as woman, a valorization and speaking of woman, and if contemporary feminists are going to take modernity and its theorists seriously, then feminist theory must address some new and complex questions – questions that form the matrix of the pages to follow.

Are gynesis and feminism in contradiction, or do they overlap and interact with each other, perhaps even render each other inevitable, in some way? In what sense do certain of the texts of gynesis reintroduce very familiar representations of women in spite of themselves? To what extent is the process designated as feminine by those texts absolutely dependent on those representations? When we posit that process as one incarnated by *women*, are we not falling back into the anthropomorphic (or gynomorphic?) images thinkers of modernity have been trying to disintegrate?

On the other hand, in what ways do some of the major texts in question exceed those familiar representations of women? How do women theorists' texts of gynesis differ from those of male theorists; or French texts of gynesis from American ones? If the gynesis seemingly intrinsic to modernity is but the product of male fantasy, does that necessarily mean it offers no radical tools for women? How might these texts offer new ways of connecting the most radical insights of feminism to the larger questions facing the West as it moves toward a new century?

Most important, if modernity and feminism are not to become mutually exclusive and, at the same time, if feminism is not to compromise the quality of its attention to female stereotyping of whatever kind, what could be new strategies for asking new kinds of questions?

(1985)

RACHEL BOWLBY

'Flight Reservations: The Anglo-American/French
Divide in Feminist Criticism'
*Still Crazy After All These Years: Women, Writing
and Psychoanalysis*

Toril Moi's *Sexual/Textual Politics* does not belong autobiographically to the transatlantic mode, since the author is a Norwegian who was working at the time of writing in Britain.[8] But it is organised around the same type of contrast between American and French modes of feminist literary criticism, through long sections dealing with each. The book is a model of lucid exposition and argument, and it rapidly and deservedly established itself as an indispensable text for both students and teachers of literary theory.

Running through Moi's readings of different critical texts is a double criterion of political efficacy and distance from conventional liberal humanism, and it is in theoretical terms identified as French that American critics are found wanting: they tend to be confined to traditional conceptions of literature as the immediate transcription of experience, and of the transcription of female experience as the mark of genuine women's literature. Such an approach, as she argues, cannot accommodate a theory of representation. It takes 'man' and 'woman' as naturally given rather than symbolic categories, and in viewing language as a transparent medium, it reduces and refuses the complexity of the literary text. And so the book's title indicates its departure in a 'textual' direction away from what must now be seen as the too literalising argument of Kate Millett's diatribe against male authors in *Sexual Politics*: necessary as a first bash in 1969, but lacking in the analytically more complex tools that feminist criticism has subsequently acquired.[9]

As the proportion of interrogative sentences would suggest on its own, Alice Jardine's *Gynesis: Configurations of Woman and Modernity* is a less expository text than Toril Moi's. Jardine sets out to question both the apparent ease with which Franco-American feminist differences are articulated, and the facility with which the term 'feminist' is transported between the two countries, given its different connotations in each one. The book's neologistic title invokes what Jardine perceives as a constantly recurring focus of postmodernist enquiry in fiction and philosophy. 'Gynesis' would be:

> The putting into discourse of 'woman' as that *process* diagnosed in France as intrinsic to the condition of modernity; indeed, the valorization of the feminine, woman, and her obligatory, that is, historical connotations, as somehow intrinsic to new and necessary models of thinking, writing, speaking.[10]

Or again:

> *Gynesis*: a new kind of writing on the woman's body, a map of new spaces yet to be explored, with 'woman' supplying the only directions, the only images, upon which Postmodern Man feels he can rely.[11]

'Gynesis' in this sense of an exploration of textual spaces 'gendered feminine' is located or 'diagnosed' in male writers ranging from Derrida, Lacan and Deleuze to Lyotard, Baudrillard, Goux and Sollers, all of whose theoretical or fictional undoings of 'the paternal metaphor' under-pinning western discourse turn out to revolve around and explore the question of femininity.

Like Toril Moi, Alice Jardine is interested in modernist or postmodernist writing, and she links its emergence to the 'crisis in legitimation' more or less evident in western society since the beginning of the twentieth century. The loss of phallogocentric guarantees is precisely the moment at which the feminine becomes an open question: not a straightforward alternative to masculinity, or a known identity, but a virtual point towards or around which new kinds of question will cluster.

Gynesis has little to say about the issue of women's adequate representa-tion in literature: this would be the falsely universalising, realistic criterion rejected also by Moi. But Jardine's text does frequently refer to the problem-atic relation between this fluid 'gynesis' located in modern writing and a female personage variously invoked as 'the feminine reader' or 'the woman reader', to whom are attributed sceptical, common-sense responses to the theoretical propositions of 'gynesis'. In effect, it is as if this 'feminist reader' is none other than the pragmatic American whose simple formulations have to be corrected and complicated by French sophistication, just as in the ear-lier quotation Jardine declared that her 'questions themselves' were American, but their 'structure' was French.[12] Despite the alleged interac-tions and mutual transformations, 'gynesis' and 'feminism' remain as dis-tinct and opposed in Jardine's text as the French or American modes to which they are related.

The final chapter compares French and American postmodernist fiction by men, as represented in particular texts by Philippe Sollers, Thomas Pynchon and John Hawkes. While both the French writer and the Americans are concerned with the questions of interpretation, textuality and feminin-ity, the differences, for Jardine, are crucial. Concluding the analysis of the American writers, she states:

> This is a thematization of gynesis very different from the conceptual, textual, constitutive process of gynesis inherent to modernity as diagnosed in France. The 'woman-in-effect' in American male fiction, throughout its thematization of gynesis, is as far from the most radical tenets of modernity as it is close to the conceptual foundations of, among other things, (Anglo-)American femi-nist thought itself.[13]

The polarisation here between 'thematization' and 'gynesis' as 'process' reproduces what it accuses in the text, and comes precariously close to the type of static binary opposition – such as 'form versus content' – from which postmodernist and feminist thought, in the different and connected ways which Jardine's book so well describes, is said to have moved on.

Even in Jardine's own account, the opposition sometimes looks forced or arbitrary. The following paragraph says why the French fictional mode is better:

> The 'she' haunting much of the most important contemporary writing by men in France is at times angelic, at times monstrous. But 'she' is always seen, above all, as that which must be explored through an erotic merging at the interior of language, through a radical dismemberment of the textual body, a female body. *Woman*, as identity, may eventually reappear within the boundaries of that exploration, but never for long, usually separated from it, and always with duplicity.[14]

The 'she' as angel/monster, as ghostlike ('haunting') as dismembered body, and as duplicitous sounds uncannily familiar from somewhere. Without more specification of the difference, this could equally be read as the usual list of accusation levelled against a misogynist text, and thus as proof not of Sollers' difference, but of the fact that he remains locked in the conventional masculine fantasies of femininity which are attributed to the American writers.

It would seem, then, that however strong the assertion to the contrary, there is a tendency for the differences between American and French critical modes to be fixed into simple, homologous oppositions between stasis and process, theme and text, pragmatism and theory, realism and (post)modernism. This effect is reinforced by the representation of American feminist aims as outmoded or displaced by the passing of the universalising, egalitarian politics identified with pre-twentieth-century ideals. The universalising logic according to which women claim their rights as political subjects equal to men must now, apparently, be seen as part of a bygone stage of feminist debate; but it is also assumed to be the position from which Jardine's 'feminist reader' would put her questions to the French theoretical texts that come her way.

(1988)

Notes

8 Toril Moi, *Sexual/Textual Politics: Feminist Literary Theory* (London: Methuen, 'New Accents', 1985).
9 Ibid., pp. 24–31.
10 Jardine, op. cit., p. 25
11 Ibid., p. 52.
12 Ibid., p. 18.
13 Ibid., p. 257.
14 Ibid., p. 246.

NANCY FRASER AND LINDA J. NICHOLSON

'Social Criticism Without Philosophy: An Encounter
Between Feminism and Postmodernism'
Feminism/Postmodernism

Toward a Postmodern Feminism

How can we combine a postmodernist incredulity toward metanarratives with the social-critical power of feminism? How can we conceive a version of criticism without philosophy which is robust enough to handle the tough job of analyzing sexism in all its endless variety and monotonous similarity?

A first step is to recognize, *contra* Lyotard, that postmodern critique need forswear neither large historical narratives nor analyses of societal macrostructures. This point is important for feminists, since sexism has a long history and is deeply and pervasively embedded in contemporary societies. Thus, postmodern feminists need not abandon the large theoretical tools needed to address large political problems. There is nothing self-contradictory in the idea of a postmodern theory.

However, if postmodern-feminist critique must remain theoretical, not just any kind of theory will do. Rather, theory here would be explicitly historical, attuned to the cultural specificity of different societies and periods and to that of different groups within societies and periods. Thus, the categories of postmodern-feminist theory would be inflected by temporality, with historically specific institutional categories like the modern, restricted, male-headed, nuclear family taking precedence over ahistorical, functionalist categories like reproduction and mothering. Where categories of the latter sort were not eschewed altogether, they would be genealogized, that is, framed by a historical narrative and rendered temporally and culturally specific.

Moreover, postmodern-feminist theory would be nonuniversalist. When its focus became cross-cultural or transepochal, its mode of attention would be comparativist rather than universalizing, attuned to changes and contrasts instead of to covering laws. Finally, postmodern-feminist theory would dispense with the idea of a subject of history. It would replace unitary notions of woman and feminine gender identity with plural and complexly constructed conceptions of social identity, treating gender as one relevant strand among others, attending also to class, race, ethnicity, age, and sexual orientation.

In general, postmodern-feminist theory would be pragmatic and fallibilistic. It would tailor its methods and categories to the specific task at hand, using multiple categories when appropriate and forswearing the metaphysical comfort of a single feminist method or feminist epistemology. In short, this theory would look more like a tapestry composed of threads of many different hues than one woven in a single color.

The most important advantage of this sort of theory would be its usefulness for contemporary feminist political practice. Such practice is increasingly a matter of alliances rather than one of unity around a universally shared interest or identity. It recognizes that the diversity of women's needs and experiences means that no single solution, on issues like child care, social security, and housing, can be adequate for all. Thus, the underlying premise of this practice is that, while some women share some common interests and face some common enemies, such commonalities are by no means universal; rather, they are interlaced with differences, even with conflicts. This, then, is a practice made up of a patchwork of overlapping alliances, not one circumscribable by an essential definition. One might best speak of it in the plural as the practice of feminisms. In a sense, this practice is in advance of much contemporary feminist theory. It is already implicitly postmodern. It would find its most appropriate and useful theoretical expression in a postmodern-feminist form of critical inquiry. Such inquiry would be the theoretical counterpart of a broader, richer, more complex, and multilayered feminist solidarity, the sort of solidarity which is essential for overcoming the oppression of women in its "endless variety and monotonous similarity."

(1990)

ROBYN WIEGMAN

'Mapping the Lesbian Postmodern'
The Lesbian Postmodern

For a number of feminists who have approached the question of the postmodern, it is this circumvention of historical metanarrativity that defers any kind of positive embrace of the postmodern, especially as Lyotard's challenge to overarching narratives of history has been directed toward both Enlightenment and Marxian accounts of social being. Linda J. Nicholson and Nancy Fraser, for instance, worry that Lyotard's posting of modernist history moves political practice (as well as its legitimation and theorization) to the level of the local, thereby disabling "critique of broad-based relations of dominance and subordination along lines like gender, race, and class" ("Social Criticism Without Philosophy," 23). In response, they call for a postmodern feminism that eschews the foundationalism of

Western philosophies while attending "to large political problems" (34), a feminism that is "pragmatic and fallibilistic … using multiple categories when appropriate and forswearing the metaphysical comfort of a single feminist method or feminist epistemology. In short, this theory would look more like a tapestry composed of threads of many different hues than one woven in a single color" (35). This image of a tapestry is an arresting choice for the figuration of a postmodern feminism, not simply because of its unabashed pluralism but also because it emerges after the authors assure us that "there is nothing self-contradictory in the idea of a postmodern theory" (34). But wouldn't there be something politically useful for feminism in interpreting postmodernism as the nascent state of modernity, as precisely the embodiment and encodement of contradiction – as, in fact, the refusal to jettison contradiction in favor of modernity's quest for totality and coherence, for a singular and romantic tapestry, unified regardless of its many colored threads?

In this regard, one can imagine a feminism not only immensely aware of its self-contradiction, but committed to explorations of the contradictions of "self" through which the modern social subject is called into being. I am not suggesting here that feminism can marshal the postmodern by simply claiming – instead of repressing – contradiction even though much contemporary theory, feminist and non-feminist alike, often reduces the postmodern to a facile embrace of contradiction, multiplicity, and flux. As Diane Elam discusses and as Judith Roof notes in this volume, the knowledge of contradiction, inserted in the place of modernity's knowing subject of history, simply reverses the terms by which Enlightenment thought functions. Now we know that we can't possibly know, and in this we master the category of knowledge, overcoming its indeterminacy and instability. To move from the perceived coherence of the rational subject to one formed in contradiction and conflict does not in itself mark the postmodern. Nor can we rely on the fact of our awareness or reminism's deeply contradictory relation to modernity and patriarchy as the precondition for political transformation, as if the intellectual grasp we attain leads to liberation. This, too, is modernity claiming us. As such, one can only agree with Nancy Hartsock's assessment in her essay, "Foucault on Power" that, "for those of us who want to understand the world systematically in order to change it, postmodern theories at their best give little guidance" (159). But to counter her negative inflection, I'd have to add that the failure of postmodern theories to guide us to systematicity and the illusion of knowledge as liberating power is, indeed, quite rightly so – the very point at which modernity undoes itself by revealing its excess, the postmodern.

Hartsock's lament, echoed in a more nuanced way by Fraser and Nicholson, is a lament for the lost or (as she seems to feel) stolen map, for the teleological narrative of liberation, that epistemological relationship to the world that guarantees transcendence. But the postmodern doesn't provide the crystal ball that can lead us to the utopic "home" in the eye of the storm. It refuses, in fact, the impulse to forecast, forcing us instead to exist in the contradictions of a present that can never be entirely full to us either. For me, this is not nihilism or despair, not the end (or the beginning) of feminism. Nothing that dramatic or epochal. But it is something quite radically different from feminism's role as inquisitor and equalizer of modernity's gender biases. To reference feminism's role in modernity does not mean, however, that we must rush to discard such a role altogether (as though we could), recasting ourselves in the clothes of a postmodern new; such a move merely ups modernity's own ante by pretending that the postmodern succeeds the modern, that it has the teleological ability to birth itself anew. The postmodern doesn't transcend the modern; it rereads the modern, not from beyond, but from within.

Given this, what do we make of the often-leveled feminist criticism that the postmodern renders the contemporary significance of coordinates of gender, race, and class indeterminable at the level of broad-scale social organization and institutionalization? If, as we have seen with Huyssen, modernism's lack can be serviced by "women and minorities," what happens to categories of difference under the rubric of post/modernity once the forward thrust of Enlightenment narrativity has been challenged for its illusory epistemology and revealed as quite exceedingly Eurocentric and male? What I find most interesting when Fraser and Nicholson, to continue that example, cite the postmodern as making impossible a "critique of broad-based relations of dominance and subordination along lines like gender, race, and class" (23) is the way they tacitly assume that the categories of gender, race, and class are *fully adequate* to the task of defining and critiquing relations of domination. I would want to counter this assumption, especially in the context of contemporary feminist theory, whose energy has been turning increasingly to the elisions, exclusions, and amputations that the categorical litany of differences unwittingly produces.[10] For even as the multiplication of categories beyond the singularity of gender has made possible a rethinking of the complexities of women's varied social positioning, their conceptualization as discrete categories works precisely by cordoning off and hence limiting the potential excessibility of difference.

To play the game of categories, then, as Fraser and Nicholson seem to insist we must, is to wager the political for a conceptual framework that apprehends differences–their multiple, oversaturated, and contradictory formation – as parallel universes, separate and ultimately total in their knowability. While much recent feminist work, including my own,[11] tries to rethink the relationship between categories, to trace their contaminations and overdeterminations, it is not at all certain that the deep disparities between genders, races, and classes can be understood and/or ameliorated only within the conceptual field of gender, race, and class. After all, to speak of race is not to speak of or against racism, and we could well say the same of gender and sexism, sexuality and heterosexism, and class and classism. It might be the case, in fact, that the circulation of these categories in critical discourses functions quite often to short-circuit the interrogation of differences as well as the possibilities of the political itself. To lament the map, to dream the tapestry: these overtures to the political seal the fate of a future that has already been.

(1994)

Notes

10   I am thinking here in particular of the work of Hortense Spillers with its implicit insistence that categories don't simply overlap but so thoroughly saturate one another that gender (to take her prime example) rarely refers to the same constellation. Differences in racial positioning must therefore be understood to produce quite different (feminine) genders. See also Berlant in "National Brands/ National Body," who takes Spillers' point and develops it in a discussion of commodity culture.

11   My forthcoming study, *Economies of Visibility: Race and Gender in US Culture*, evinces my own grappling with categories of difference, focusing in particular on the way the discourse of sexual difference has been used to repeatedly reframe white racial supremacies. For those who may mistake my criticisms here as a dismissal of categories altogether, I can only reassert my central concern: we are investing too heavily in analyses based on "gender, race, and class (and/or sexuality)" as *the only means* – the only valid political territory – for thinking differences in order to eliminate hierarchies.

BELL HOOKS

Yearning: Race, Gender, and Cultural Politics

For me this space of radical openness is a margin – a profound edge. Locating oneself there is difficult yet necessary. It is not a "safe" place. One is always at risk. One needs a community of resistance.

In the preface to *Feminist Theory: From Margin to Center*, I expressed these thoughts on marginality:

> To be in the margin is to be part of the whole but outside the main body. As black Americans living in a small Kentucky town, the railroad tracks were a daily

reminder of our marginality. Across those tracks were paved streets, stores we could not enter, restaurants we could not eat in, and people we could not look directly in the face. Across those tracks was a world we could work in as maids, as janitors, as prostitutes, as long as it was in a service capacity. We could enter that world but we could not live there. We had always to return to the margin, to cross the tracks to shacks and abandoned houses on the edge of town.

There were laws to ensure our return. Not to return was to risk being punished. Living as we did – on the edge – we developed a particular way of seeing reality. We looked both from the outside in and from the inside out. We focused our attention on the center as well as on the margin. We understood both. This mode of seeing reminded us of the existence of a whole universe, a main body made up of both margin and center. Our survival depended on an ongoing public awareness of the separation between margin and center and an ongoing private acknowledgement that we were a necessary, vital part of that whole.

This sense of wholeness, impressed upon our consciousness by the structure of our daily lives, provided us with an oppositional world-view – a mode of seeing unknown to most of our oppressors, that sustained us, aided us in our struggle to transcend poverty and despair, strengthened our sense of self and our solidarity.

Though incomplete, these statements identify marginality as much more than a site of deprivation; in fact I was saying just the opposite, that it is also the site of radical possibility, a space of resistance. It was this marginality that I was naming as a central location for the production of a counter-hegemonic discourse that is not just found in words but in habits of being and the way one lives. As such, I was not speaking of a marginality one wishes to lose – to give up or surrender as part of moving into the center – but rather of a site one stays in, clings to even, because it nourishes one's capacity to resist. It offers to one the possibility of radical perspective from which to see and create, to imagine alternatives, new worlds.

This is not a mythic notion of marginality. It comes from lived experience. Yet I want to talk about what it means to struggle to maintain that marginality even as one works, produces, lives, if you will, at the center. I no longer live in that segregated world across the tracks. Central to life in that world was the ongoing awareness of the necessity of opposition. When Bob Marley sings, "We refuse to be what you want us to be, we are what we are, and that's the way it's going to be," that space of refusal, where one can say no to the colonizer, no to the downpressor, is located in the margins. And one can only say no, speak the voice of resistance, because there exists a counter-language. While it may resemble the colonizer's tongue, it has undergone a transformation, it has been irrevocably changed. When I left that concrete space in the margins, I kept alive in my heart ways of knowing reality which affirm continually not only the primacy of resistance but the necessity of a resistance that is sustained by remembrance of the past, which includes rec-ollections of broken tongues giving us ways to speak that decolonize our minds, our very beings. Once mama said to me as I was about to go again to the predominantly white university, "You can take what the white people have to offer, but you do not have to love them." Now understanding her cultural codes, I know that she was not saying to me not to love people of other races. She was speaking about colonization and the reality of what it means to be taught in a culture of domination by those who dominate. She was insisting on my power to be able to separate useful knowledge that I might get from the dominating group from participation in ways of know-ing that would lead to estrangement, alienation, and worse – assimilation and co-optation. She was saying that it is not necessary to give yourself over to them to learn. Not having been in those institutions, she knew that I might be faced again and again with situations where I would be "tried," made to feel as though a central requirement of my being accepted would mean par-ticipation in this system of exchange to ensure my success, my "making it." She was reminding me of the necessity of opposition and simultaneously encouraging me not to lose that radical perspective shaped and formed by marginality.

Understanding marginality as position and place of resistance is crucial for oppressed, exploited, colonized people. If we only view the margin as sign marking the despair, a deep nihilism penetrates in a destructive way the very ground of our being. It is there in that space of collective despair that one's creativity, one's imagination is at risk, there that one's mind is fully colonized, there that the freedom one longs for as lost. Truly the mind that resists colonization struggles for freedom one longs for as lost. Truly the mind that resists colonization struggles for freedom of expression. The struggle may not even begin with the colonizer; it may begin within one's segregated, colonized community and family. So I want to note that I am not trying to romantically re-inscribe the notion of that space of marginality where the oppressed live apart from their oppressors as "pure." I want to say that these margins have been both sites of repression and sites of resist-ance. And since we are well able to name the nature of that repression we know better the margin as site of deprivation. We are more silent when it comes to speaking of the margin as site of resistance. We are more often silenced when it comes to speaking of the margin as site of resistance.

Silenced. During my graduate years I heard myself speaking often in the voice of resistance. I cannot say that my speech was welcomed. I cannot say that my speech was heard in such a way that it altered relations between colonizer and colonized. Yet what I have noticed is that those scholars, most especially those who name themselves radical critical thinkers, feminist thinkers, now fully participate in the construction of a discourse about the "Other." I was made "Other" there in that space with them. In that space in the margins, that lived-in segregated world of my past and present. They did not meet me there in that space. They met me at the center. They greeted me as colonizers. I am waiting to learn from them the path of their resistance, of how it came to be that they were able to surrender the power to act as colonizers. I am waiting for them to bear witness, to give testimony. They say that the discourse on marginality, on difference has moved beyond a discussion of "us and them." They do not speak of how this movement has taken place. This is a response from the radical space of my marginality. It is a space of resistance. It is a space I choose.

I am waiting for them to stop talking about the "Other," to stop even describing how important it is to be able to speak about difference. It is not just important what we speak about, but how and why we speak. Often this speech about the "Other" is also a mask, an oppressive talk hiding gaps, absences, that space where our words would be if we were speaking, if there were silence, if we were there. This "we" is that "us" in the margins, that "we" who inhabit marginal space that is not a site of domination but a place of resistance. Enter that space. Often this speech about the "Other" annihilates, erases: "No need to hear your voice when I can talk about you better than you can speak about yourself. No need to hear your voice. Only tell me about your pain. I want to know your story. And then I will tell it back to you in a new way. Tell it back to you in such a way that it has become mine, my own. Re-writing you, I write myself anew. I am still author, authority. I am still the colonizer, the speaking subject, and you are now at the center of my talk." Stop. We greet you as liberators. This "we" is that "us" in the margins, that "we" who inhabit marginal space that is not a site of domination but a place of resistance. Enter that space. This is an intervention. I am writing to you. I am speaking from a place in the margins where I am different, where I see things differently. I am talking about what I see.

(1991)

Madhu Dubey

Signs and Cities: Black Literary Postmodernism

African-Americans can be cast in this double role – as both the worst victims and the redemptive agents of the postmodern condition – because material oppression often automatically translates into political opposition in postmodern cultural studies. Some striking examples, discussed in the following pages, are bell hooks's strategy of "choosing the margins," the "third worldism" espoused by Fredric Jameson, or Edward Soja's notion of "Thirdspace." In these and other instances, possibilities of critical resistance are situated in residual zones that somehow elude the dominant logic of postmodernism. This romance of the residual that beguiles so much postmodern thinking about race forms one of my principal targets of critique in *Signs and Cities*. To perceive African-American culture in residual terms is to exempt it from the contingencies of the postmodern condition. Locating black culture in pockets of sheer alterity within or outside contemporary social conditions, we inevitably primitivize this culture. Although primitivism can support sharp critiques of modernity, it can also all too easily slide over into fetishism of racial "others." Converting a structural position of relative powerlessness into a desirable ontological condition, we mine sites of material deprivation for their cultural capital. As cultural value increases in inverse proportion to political and economic power, aesthetic appreciation comes to compensate for and thereby mystify the realities of material suffering.

Not surprisingly, given the racialized logic of the residual, black culture in the postmodern era is persistently identified with oral and performance modes associated with the voice or the body and is often explicitly opposed to linguistic expression. For example, Cornel West contends that the "ur-text" of black culture is "neither a word nor a book" but instead the "guttural cry" or the "wrenching moan."[21] In one of the most widely read anthologies on postmodern culture, Andrew Ross's collection of essays, *Universal Abandon: The Politics of Postmodernism*, Anders Stephanson poses such questions as "Music is *the* black means of cultural expression, is it not?" or "The black community is more contestational than average America, is it not?"[22] – questions that are profoundly insulting, especially because they appear in the only piece treating black culture in a volume that otherwise applies the most discriminating forms of analysis to differences in postmodern culture.

It is not too difficult for cultural critics on the left to abjure the demonizing of African-American culture that lends force to accounts of postmodern crisis, such as, for example, in "underclass" or canon revision debates. But evidently it is much harder to resist romanticizing black culture as the last vestige of authenticity left in postmodern times, at once radically other and viscerally knowable. The obvious appeal of this approach is that it allows us to bypass the difficulties of mediation that are entailed in our intellectual work as cultural critics, to lay claim to political truths that are immediately apprehensible because they are said to inhere in the voice or the body, and thereby to certify that our theories have been honed on "the ragged edges of the Real."[23]

Cultural politics in the postmodern era might be better served by trying to grasp the racialized logic of uneven development that systematically links residual and dominant categories rather than through mystical evocations of the numinous reality, bodily presence, or sublime orality of

African-American culture. By this logic, we would view black culture as an integral part of the postmodern condition, without for a second losing sight of its historical specificity. The structural interdependence between various spheres that is essential to the concept of uneven development would have serious implications for cultural studies, making it harder for us to remand black culture to a zone of opaque otherness, a pure elsewhere to contemporary social conditions.

Once black culture is admitted to be as subject to social and technological mediation as any other culture in the postmodern era, its political salience could not hinge on a primal connection to bodily experience or material reality. An emphasis on mediation would move black culture out of a prelapsarian into a historical sphere, but, as is obvious from current academic accounts of hip-hop music, this alone would not neutralize the powerful lure of racial primitivism. Organicism can be an effect of technological fetishism, just as dire claims about the irreality of contemporary life breed desires for absolute epistemological guarantees.

[...]

An instance of this romance of the residual from African-American cultural studies is bell hooks's "Choosing the Margins as a Space of Radical Openness," an essay that has been widely taken up by advocates of postmodernism. The margin, or the space occupied by African-Americans, operates at two levels throughout hooks's essay. First, the margin is identified with certain sites of material oppression – the racially segregated areas to which African-Americans were confined in the rural South, and urban ghettoes, where African-Americans are susceptible to "every postmodern mode of dying" imaginable.[17] In the course of the essay, this "site of deprivation" is rhetorically converted into "a space of resistance" (149), which hooks does not link to a particular kind of social order. Hooks traces her journey from the margin, a physical place of oppression, to the center, here equivalent to mainstream U.S. society. But in this process, hooks chooses to continue inhabiting the margin, which must then refer to an epistemological standpoint rather than an actual place. Acknowledging the double inscription of the term *margin* in her essay, hooks asserts that "spaces can be real and imagined" (152). But what remains uncertain is the passage from one kind of space to the other: how exactly are the material sites of racial oppression transformed into spaces of resistance? The only clue hooks offers is that spaces "can be interrupted, appropriated, and transformed through artistic and literary practice" (152), suggesting that critical resistance is primarily conducted in the field of culture.

(2003)

Notes

21 Cornel West, "Black Strivings in a Twilight Civilization," in Cornel West and Henry Louis Gates Jr., *The Future of the Race* (New York: Vintage, 1996), 81.
22 Stephanson, "Interview with Cornel West," 276, 280.
23 Ibid., 277.

[...]

17 bell hooks, "Choosing the Margins as a Space of Radical Openness," in *Yearning: Race, Gender, and Cultural Politics* (Boston: South End Press, 1990), 148; hereafter cited parenthetically.

SUSAN STANFORD FRIEDMAN

*Mappings: Feminism and the Cultural
Geographies of Encounter*

In its advocacy of dialogic negotiation, *Mappings* polemically suggests that the time has come to reverse the past pluralization of feminisms based on difference, not to return to a false notion of a universal feminism that obliterates difference but rather to reinvent a singular feminism that incorporates myriad and often conflicting cultural and political formations in a global context. The move from *feminism* to *feminisms*, heralded in the United States by the publication in 1980 of Elaine Marks and Isabelle de Courtivron's classic anthology, *New French Feminisms*, insisted upon the acknowledgment of different feminist theories and movements both between and within national boundaries.[2] The plural form of the noun *feminism* forced a recognition of difference as a way of refusing the hegemony of one kind of feminism over another. Emerging out of the volatile and deep divisions within national and international kinds of feminism by the late 1970s, the politics of pluralization forcibly interrupted the tendency of some (especially white, heterosexual, western feminists) to attempt to speak for all, as if patriarchy were a monolithic cultural formation, as if women were the same everywhere, as if the female subject of feminism were homogeneous. This pluralization has contributed profoundly to the expansion and diversification of feminism; it has been vitally necessary, I strongly believe, for the development of a multicultural, international, and transnational feminism. Its very success, however, has spawned the need for a new singularization of feminism that assumes difference without reifying or fetishizing it. The borders between sites of feminism surely exist, but just as surely they are and must be transgressed. They are not fixed in stone, but shift with changing cultural formations, conditions, and alliances. Upon this fluidity, the survival and spread of feminism depends.

The feminism in the singular that I advocate assumes a locational epistemology based not upon static or abstract definition but rather upon the assumption of changing historical and geographical specificities that produce different feminist theories, agendas, and political practices.[3] A locational approach to feminism incorporates diverse formations because its positional analysis requires a kind of geopolitical literacy built out of a recognition of how different times and places produce different and changing gender systems as these intersect with other different and changing societal stratifications and movements for social justice. Locational feminism thus encourages the study of difference in all its manifestations without being limited to it, without establishing impermeable borders that inhibit the production and visibility of ongoing intercultural exchange and hybridity.

Locational feminism also acknowledges the travels and travails of feminism as it migrates across multiple borders, adapting itself to new conditions. Borrowing from Edward Said's account of "traveling theory," we need to acknowledge that feminism seldom arises in purely indigenous forms, but, like culture itself, develops syncretistically out of a transcultural interaction with others. Feminism's migrancy is "never unimpeded," to echo Said. "It necessarily involves processes of representation and institutionalization different from those at the point of origin. This complicates any account of the transplantation, transference, circulation, and commerce of theories and ideas" ("Traveling" 226). Locational feminism pays attention to the specificities of time and place, but unlike fundamentalist identity politics, it is not parochially limited to a single feminist formation and takes as its founding principle the multiplicity of heterogeneous feminist movements and the conditions that produce them. *Mappings* is itself a case in point for what it means to break out of a specifically American localism, for the influence of work (whether feminist or not) produced on or by people whose heritage is rooted in other parts of the world is pervasive – particularly South and Southeast Asia, the Caribbean, Africa, and Latin America.

Locational feminism requires a geopolitical literacy that acknowledges the interlocking dimension of global cultures, the way in which the local is always informed by the global and the global by the local. This is in part what Inderpal Grewal and Caren Kaplan advocate in their definition of a "transnational feminism" (*Scattered Hegemonies* 1–36) and what Gayatri Chakravorty Spivak calls for in her concept of "transnational literacy" (*Outside* 255–84). *Mappings* assumes that feminism needs to be understood in a global context, both historicized and geopoliticized to take into account its different formations and their interrelationships everywhere. As such, *Mappings* resists certain overly reductionist metanarratives of globalization. One such narrative is the notion that women suffer the same gender oppression in all societies, an approach to internationalizing feminism that bases affiliation solely on gender victimization, thus muting women's agency, ignoring cultural contextualizations, and suppressing understanding of gender's interaction with other constituents of identity. The commitment to universal human rights for women (which I share) should not be founded on a script of a uniform gender oppression that decontextualizes the condition of women in various locations.

Another such inadequate metanarrative bases its globalization on binaries of First World/Third World or the West/the Rest, telling the story of a unidirectional hegemony in which white/western people (always already) dominate people of color/nonwestern people. Whether it tells the history of the world through the lens of western modernity (colonialism) or western postmodernity (late-capitalist global markets), this narrative remains mired in the eurocentrism and ethnocentrism it deplores. It obscures how conquest and colonialism have been and still are worldwide phenomena, generated not only in the West but also in many other powerful societies. It ignores the rise of dominant cultures and civilizations in Asia, Africa, South America, the Caribbean, and Pacific Asia at various points in history, including the current ascendency of Asia in a phenomenon sometimes termed "the Asianization of the world" (Edward Friedman, "Rise of China"). It renders largely invisible the existence of stratification in nearly all (if not all) societies, inequities that highly complicate their interactions with western nations. Moreover, it does not take into account the historical agency of all individuals and groups, the role of intercultural exchange and symbiosis in all cultural formations, and the heterogeneity of both "the West" and "the Rest."

In resisting simplistically universalist and binarist narratives, *Mappings* undertakes a difficult negotiation between insistence on multidirectional flows of power in global context and continued vigilance about specifically western forms of domination. Given my own location in the United States (with its particular history and configuration of racism) and positionality as a white woman, I have found particularly challenging the need to acknowledge the material effects of racial privilege at the same time that I argue for broadening the American dialogue about race beyond its dominant templates of white/black, white/people of color, oppressor/oppressed. I remain convinced that a broadly comparative, global/locational feminism can change our analysis of "home" as well as "elsewhere," helping to break repetitive logjams of thought by casting the conditions of home in a new light and by illuminating the structures interlocking home and elsewhere.

The global contextualization that I advocate for feminism in *Mappings* is consistent with Spivak's various critiques of First World/Third World binaries as the route to internationalizing feminism. "I think we should also look at the West as differentiated," she says in an interview. "I'm not really that moved by arguments for homogenisation on both sides" (*Post-Colonial Critic* 39). She insists that "transnational feminism is neither revolutionary tourism, nor mere celebration of testimony" (*Teaching Machine* 39). She worries that if we take "the astonishing construction of a multicultural and multiracial identity for the United States" as the "founding principle for a study of globality, then we are off base" (279).[4] Instead, she suggests, "the point is to negotiate between the national, the global, and the historical as well as the contemporary diasporic. We must both anthropologize the West, and study the various cultural systems of Africa, Asia, Asia-Pacific, and the Americas as if peopled by historical agents" (278). A geopolitical, locational feminism travels globally in its thinking, avoiding the imposition of one set of cultural conditions on another, assuming the production of local agencies and conceptualization, and remaining attentive to the way these differences are continually in the process of modification through interactions within a global system of diverse, multidirectional exchanges.

(1998)

Notes

2 See also the widely used first and second editions of Robyn Warhol and Diane Price Herndl's *Feminisms*.

3 I resist in particular the conventional practice of identifying different feminisms according to such categories as reformist feminism, radical feminism, socialist feminism, Third World feminism, Black feminism, lesbian feminism, etc. The theory and political practice of feminists who are associated with such categories are frequently so overlapping or contradictory as to render the categories largely useless or misleading for analytic purposes. I find it useful to work with a definition of feminism based on two shared principles: (1) the oppression of women and (2) commitment to social change. The analysis of the origins and nature of oppression differs widely; so does the theory on the nature of and strategies for change. For discussions of the politics of location as a basis for feminist theory, see especially Rich, "Notes"; Caren Kaplan, *Questions* 143–87; Probyn; Mani; Grewal and Kaplan 1–36; Chandra Mohanty, "Feminist Encounters"; Smith and Katz; Clifford, "Notes"; and Dhareshwar.

4 Elsewhere Spivak expresses concern about the tendency to use race relations in the United States as a template for understanding race/ethnicity in global terms. "Don't forget the Third World at large," she says for example, "where you won't be able to dissolve everything into Black against White, as there is also Black against Black, Brown against Brown, and so on" (*Post-Colonial Critic* 65). In my view, the reduction of race relations in the United States to "Black against White" is also seriously misleading. For feminist discussions of multiculturalism in global context, see also Gunew and Yeatman; Grewal and Kaplan.

ISOBEL ARMSTRONG

The Radical Aesthetic

Phallic feminism has been, until recently, the dominant form of feminist theory. Until the early 1990s it seemed set fair to produce the central, generative debates in feminist thought. It always co-existed with Expressive and Ludic feminism, but it seemed to open new fields of knowledge in a way that made it the theoretical wing of the women's movement. This form of feminism is Phallic because its poetics derive from the two master discourses of the twentieth century, the new knowledges evolving from the work of Marx and Freud, and subsequently of Lacan. Phallic feminism works with the traditions of these forms of thought, questioning, reconfiguring and remaking them for a new gender theory. Feminist thinkers who are mutually hostile to each other intellectually can still belong to the category of Phallic critique. It is not that the two traditions are reconciled in Phallic feminism (though they sometimes are), but that they form the theoretical and ideological ground which structures the philosophical projects of women who *accept* the debates around Marx and Freud as the starting point of their own thought. Swinging between the different determinisms of both Marxism and Freudianism and the different understandings of cultural construction available through the theory of ideology and psychoanalysis, and bringing the insights of semiotics to these discourses as heuristic tools, these thinkers often elaborate an analysis which has called out such deeply imagined thought that this work has the force of poetry. This thought is so new that it shimmers with the strangeness and beauty of a poem, partly because it is aware that it is dealing with the stuff of the profound cultural myths of the twentieth century – which is not to say that myths do not call out belief. If the founding determinant of Marxist feminism is the anguish of class, the anguish of the Oedipal sacrifice is at the centre of psychoanalytical feminism. These take on an explanatory, causal force, however much they are re-read, re-visioned, re-described, understood as experience mediated through language and representation. The economic structure of women's oppression, the 'without' which organizes sexual difference, women's psychic lives and their entry into the symbolic order – these are the inexhaustible lyric themes of Phallic thought. And I call them lyric because the very nature of identity is at stake in this theory, how the 'I' is formed at the deepest psychic and social levels of being.

Julia Kristeva, of whom I have already spoken, Juliet Mitchell and Jacqueline Rose have been the formative critics of the psychoanalytical tradition. Juliet Mitchell extended her classic early work in *Psychoanalysis and Feminism* (1974), sharing with Jacqueline Rose the introduction to a collection of Lacan essays. These became the central text in a new phase of Phallic feminism, shifting, through Lacan, the emphasis of Freudian analysis from biologism to language and representation, from a literalized reading of feminine sexuality in terms of penis envy to the *structural* role of lack in the gender binary. 'Woman does not exist': the placing of woman in the space of lack, a fantasized other, the site of masculine self-elaboration, signifying the phallus through being its lack – these new conceptualizations promised an understanding of the genesis of gender formation and an explanation of the eternally unsymmetrical power relations constituted by sexual difference. It was undoubtedly the rigorous theorizing of a systematic symbolic order, which deterministically organized gender relations, that attracted feminist thinkers to the Lacanian model, and still does. Mastery's secret is not only revealed but given a logic. To anyone puzzled by the acceptance of a seemingly negative understanding of feminine sexuality, the Phallic critic replies, as Mitchell did, that Freudian/Lacanian thought does not offer a recommendation for a patriarchal society but an analysis of one.

And this is an intensely creative genre of feminism still. *Between Feminism and Psychoanalysis*, a collection of essays edited by Teresa Brennan in 1989, brought a new debate about the possibilities of remaining inside or outside Lacanian feminism into circulation.[5] Mary Jacobus's first essay in the intricate and subtle *First Things* (1995), 'Freud's mnemonic: screen memories and feminist nostalgia', declares her intention to shift attention from the symbolic order to the function of the Imaginary in culture and psychoanalysis. In a delicate argument with Freud and two major figures, Adrienne Rich and Jane Gallop, she suggests that the Oedipal moment retrospectively creates the pre-Oedipal and acts as a screen memory for an originary feminine 'fall' into sexuality. Yet the myth of an unmediated primal relation to the mother's body, explored so poignantly by Rich, is, she thinks, untenable. Instead she turns to Jane Gallop's re-theorizing of phallic loss as nostalgia to consider the powerful cultural imperative which associates nostalgia and women. Regret for loss repeats itself backwards from self to the irreparable loss of the phallic mother, to which the subject can never return for compensation: nostalgia is not so much a longing for completion but the alienation of the subject in an amnesia which attempts to forget phallic absence.

Phallic critique incorporates materialist thinking. This is in eclipse, though it shows signs of reviving, because the breakup of communism has led to a premature assumption that the materialist project is irrelevant, though the analysis of Marxist feminism and its philosophical project is actually of more importance than ever. Gayatri Chakravorty Spivak, exponent of an intricately theorized materialist deconstructive feminism, brings to bear the textual insights afforded by semiotics in a way which distinguishes her from other writers (such as Michèle Barrett in England or Christine Delphy in France).[6] She has sharply criticized her psychoanalytical Phallic contemporary, Julia Kristeva (though she isn't averse to psychoanalysis), for an idealist and self-serving reading of the 'Third World' women of China, and for a retreat to the maternal body and motherhood as a principle of feminine existence. I single Spivak out because in her work a materialist analysis of the economics of gender and race comes together with a critique of the 'epistemic violence' of imperialism in a post-structuralist world. *In Other Worlds* (1987) gathers some of the most impressive of her work. She is an agonistic critic, proceeding by the deconstructive mode of putting into question. She strenuously attempts to rethink basic concepts (such as the labour theory of value), which she thinks have been written out of contemporary discourse, by recalling both economic and textual theories of value. Her demonstration that the dematerializing and abstraction of labour and use value in the post-modern economic discourse of global capitalism is dependent upon the exploitation of 'Third World' women is complex and intricate, but she makes the brute reality of exploitation obvious (p. 167). Refusing either to sentimentalize use value or to commit herself to the textualization of labour or money, she treads a path through these extremes: 'Within this narrative replay of my argument in the previous pages it may be pointed out that, whereas Lehman Brothers, thanks to computers, "earned $2 million, for... 15 minutes of work", the entire economic text would not be what it is if it could not write itself as a palimpsest upon another text where a woman in Sri Lanka has to work 2,287 minutes to buy a T-shirt. The "post-modern" and "pre-modern era" are inscribed together' (p. 171). Her virtuosity demonstrates the continuing possibilities of Phallic Marxism. The journal *Feminist Economics* and the work of Regenia Gagnier (*Idylls of the marketplace*, 1987), who is interested in developing a post-modern feminist economics, are indications of the vitality of these traditions.

Are there problems associated with Phallic feminism's acceptance of the grand narratives of Marxism and psychoanalysis? The necessitarian, deterministic aspect of these theories dictates an analysis of certain inevitable structures of power – the symbolic order, the interpellated subject who is organized through the economic pressures of material conditions – and works with a myth of power. It is a short step from analysis to acceptance, from describing what is to accepting what must be – the *structural* necessity of forms of power – organizing discussion around, and presupposing, the very models that are critiqued. Thus Kristeva can insist upon the harsh necessity of feminine entry into the symbolic order with Greek fatalism, and Spivak can allow her discourse to be so ordered by a Marxist paradigm of colonial oppression that she asks a rhetorical question, 'Can the subaltern speak?, expecting the answer, "No". Generally speaking what Phallic feminism has done is to "post-modernize" these modern knowledges, opening out their determinisms and the fixity of power relations and oppression implied in their epistemologies by giving both psychoanalysis and materialism a semiotic turn. A limited agency opens up when fractures in the determining order, whether psychic or social/material, precipitate epistemic crisis, a crisis of language in which the sign and what it represents are in disjunction, allowing the subject a space in which to apprehend contradictions exposed by the mismatch of sign and experience. But agency *is* limited and may only consist in the release from ideological blindness. Oddly, in both psychoanalytical and Marxist paradigms of Phallic feminism, the political has a tendency to fall away, to get lost or immobilized, inhibited by the totalizing of political power itself. And gender issues themselves can disappear, can be absorbed by the myth of power.

(2000)

Notes

5   See Juliet Mitchell, *Psychoanalysis and Feminism*, particularly parts 3 and 4, 'Towards another symbolic', pp. 87–185.
6   Some of Gayatri Chakravorty Spivak's major work is collected in *In Other Worlds: Essays in Cultural Politics*. Her essay 'Scattered speculations on the question of value' and the work on subaltern issues in section 3 of this collection are particularly impressive. Her argument is extended in the essay, 'Can the subaltern speak? Marxism and the interpretation of culture'. Michèle Barrett's *Women's Oppression Today: Problems in Marxist Feminist Analysis* shows a hostility to psychoanalysis which was more characteristic of Marxist feminism of the 1980s than of feminism today.

TORIL MOI

What is a Woman? And Other Essays

Rereading *Sexual/Textual Politics* for the purpose of writing this preface was an interesting experience. I sound younger, and more inexperienced, theoretically and humanly. But I am glad to report that I recognize the voice. Although it is a voice that fails me from time to time, there is a freshness to it, a willingness to say exactly what I think, which carries a feeling of freedom.

The failure of voice is noticeable in a sentence such as this one, about the problems with the idea of the 'humanist self' (much quoted, I am afraid): 'As Luce Irigaray or Hélène Cixous would argue, this integrated self is in fact a phallic self, constructed on the model of the self-contained powerful phallus' (8). I don't think I can have believed this when I wrote it. I don't understand why every integral whole must be phallic, which is what I am saying here. It doesn't help that I say I have it from Irigaray and Cixous. This in fact makes it worse, since my subsequent chapters on them show that I am by no means pleased by their understanding of what a woman is. Beauvoir would call such failures of voice moments of inauthenticity. Today I would say I fail to stake myself in such claims, which is to say that I fail to take my own writing seriously enough.

In the same way, the very last paragraph of the book, the final reference to Derrida's utopian vision in 'Choreographies', is a reasonably good example of theoretical alienation. I remember very well putting the paragraph there as an afterthought. What I wanted to do, was to give a man the last word of my book, in order to unsettle the 'woman-centred' feminists who thought that feminist theory would have to dismiss 'male theory' entirely. I certainly succeeded in annoying those who believe that there is such a thing as 'male theory'. But in order to score an easy rhetorical point, I unfortunately forgot that I actually did not think of myself as a deconstructionist at all, so that the choice of *that* man was not exactly very thoughtful. I have to take responsibility for the resulting misunderstandings.

But *Sexual/Textual Politics* is also full of sentences that I *did* believe in, and still do. In the chapter on Irigaray, I write that we should 'aim for a society in which we have ceased to categorize logic, conceptualization and rationality as "masculine", not for one from which these virtues have been expelled altogether as "unfeminine" ' (160). A very Beauvoirean point. I see that I – rightly or wrongly – attribute the equally Beauvoirean thought that femininity is a patriarchal construct to Kristeva (see 166), and give this as my reason for liking her work better than that of Irigaray and Cixous. Today, I think I have developed these ideas in deeper and more thoughtful ways, but they are still fundamental to my way of being a feminist. I also like my tendency to argue through concrete examples, as for instance in the discussion of under what circumstances Irigaray's 'mimicry' might be a useful, neutral, or reactionary strategy for feminists (see 141–3).

The crucial difference, however, concerns poststructuralism. *Sexual/Textual Politics* is marked by poststructuralism. My new work is an attempt to work my way out from under poststructuralism (particularly in Chapter 1), and to see what happens when one goes elsewhere (particularly in Chapter 2). Anyone interested in the question of how my thought on questions such as essentialism, femininity, subjectivity, and so on has developed since the early 1980s, can probably easily work it out for herself. My sense is that my views on these matters, which owe a lot to various forms of poststructuralism, have developed and deepened, but not undergone any radical change. In Chapter 4 in this volume (another very recent essay) I give a brief overview of the motivations for my continuous interest in the subject as a subject of praxis – as the subject of acts, including speech acts. This interest is what constantly sends me back to thinkers such as Freud, Lacan, Kristeva, Bourdieu, Sartre, and Beauvoir, and from there to Wittgenstein, Austin, and Cavell. From this list it appears that my most genuine investment in poststructuralist thought always came through psychoanalysis, and only rarely through Derrida or Foucault. Subjectivity (and agency) has always been at the heart of my interests. This contrasts with my attitude to the concept of identity. As far as I can see, everything I have written is marked by a radical disinterest in the concept of identity. I neither posit nor deconstruct it, I simply do not use the term. Only now do I fully realize that this fundamental fact is the most Beauvoirean aspect of my thought.

Finally, however, there is the question of what I now think of as the metaphysical presuppositions of poststructuralism. Rereading it, I was astonished to see to what extent I avoid engaging with such metaphysics in *Sexual/Textual Politics*. On the whole, the book turns poststructuralist thought into a workable set of tools for feminist critique, no more and no less. The major reason for this is, of course, the fact that it was written by a socialist feminist who was already thinking a lot about Simone de Beauvoir. These fundamental commitments made me read French theory quite differently from feminists (not least in the US) who did not share these political and theoretical commitments. The fact that the whole book is structured as a series of readings of different theoretical texts, from Kate Millett and Mary Ellmann to Hélène Cixous and Julia Kristeva, also saves me from metaphysical mischief. When I make points that still hold up in my eyes, it is usually because they are presented as concrete analyses of a given text, and not at all as general metaphysical commitments.

My lack of interest in the foundational claims of deconstruction is surely the reason why most deconstructionists, particularly in the United States, thought the book banal and quite insufficiently Derridean. As late as in 1995 one deconstructive critic found it worth her while to point out that I grossly misunderstand Cixous because I persist in thinking of women as 'social beings' (Kamuf 75), and also, apparently, believe that 'theory's political responsibility begins and ends in a present "reality"' (Kamuf 74). Peggy Kamuf's thoughtful essay on Cixous, from which these quotes are taken, in fact raises all sorts of important issues – about what reading and writing as a feminist might mean, what we take words such as 'woman', 'style', 'reality', and 'social beings' to mean, and so on – issues that I would wish to engage with in a more serious fashion.[3] But sure: I do think it makes sense to say that women are social beings. And I certainly think that our political responsibility is to reality, which I take to mean the ordinary world we all inhabit. What I do not think, however, is that there is any need to speak of 'reality'.

My new essays are deeply concerned with the ordinary and the everyday. I now see poststructuralism as a form of thought that is too eager to lose itself in metaphysics (see Chapters 1 and 2 for this kind of claim). In short, the two new essays collected in Part I show why I would now challenge the mindset that produces the need to place scare quotes around words such as 'reality' or 'social beings'. They also show how hard the task of justifying this feeling intellectually actually is. As Wittgenstein teaches us, the task of freeing ourselves from the intellectual pictures that hold us captive is not only immensely hard, it is never done, for we are always going to find ourselves held by new metaphysical mirages, fall for new temptations to forsake the ordinary.

In *Sexual/Textual Politics* I find many traces of the metaphysics I now want to escape. I appear to believe that there is something intrinsically wrong with being part of a binary opposition (on what evidence? I ask myself today), I am quite insufficiently nuanced about when essentialism is a bad thing and when it doesn't matter, and I spend too much time using words like 'signifier' when 'word' would have been quite adequate. I also fail to explain properly why it is so terrible to see the subject as a non-contradictory master of its own world. Clearly, there are many situations in which it doesn't matter in the least what one thinks a self or a subject is. This didn't occur to me in 1984. In short, I sometimes write as if it is self-evident that some theoretical idea or other is intrinsically bad for feminist politics. Today I would call that theoreticism.

(1999)

Note

3   In Chapter 2 I do discuss style, and Chapter 1 is full of considerations of what the word 'woman' might mean. But 'reality' will have to be left for another day.

JUDITH BUTLER

Undoing Gender

In the first instance, at work in my exposition of this transition from sexual difference to gender trouble, or indeed, from sexual difference to queer theory (which is not the same, since "gender trouble" is but a moment of queer theory), there is a slippage between sexual difference as a category that conditions the emergence into language and culture, and gender as a sociological concept, figured as a norm. Sexual difference is not the same as the categories of women and men. Women and men exist, we might say, as social norms, and they are, according to the perspective of sexual difference, ways in which sexual difference has assumed content. Many Lacanians, for instance, argued with me that sexual difference has only a formal character, that nothing follows about the social roles or meanings that gender might have from the concept of sexual difference itself. Indeed, some of them evacuate sexual difference of every possible semantic meaning, allying it with the structural possibility for semantics, but having no proper or necessary semantic content. Indeed, they even argue that the possibility of critique emerges when one comes to understand how sexual difference has not only become concretized in certain cultural and social instances, but how it has become reduced to its instance, since this constitutes a fundamental mistake, a way of foreclosing the fundamental openness of the distinction itself.

So this is one way of answering me, and it comes from the formalist Lacanians: Joan Copjec and Charles Shepherdson, but also Slavoj Žižek. But there is a stronger feminist argument that implicitly or explicitly takes issue with the trajectory I have laid out. It is articulated most buoyantly, most persuasively, perhaps by Rosi Braidotti whose most recent work I consider as part of the chapter, "The End of Sexual Difference?" in this book.[2] I think the argument goes something like this: we must maintain the framework of sexual difference because it brings to the fore the continuing cultural and political reality of patriarchal domination, because it reminds us that whatever permutations of gender take place, they do not fully challenge the framework within which they take place, for that framework persists at a symbolic level that is more difficult to intervene upon. Critics such as Carol Anne Tyler argued, for instance, that it will always be different for a woman to enter into transgressive gender norms than it will be for a man, and that *Gender Trouble* does not distinguish strongly enough between these very different positions of power within society.

Others suggest that the problem has to do with psychoanalysis, and with the place and meaning of oedipalization. The child enters desire through triangulation, and whether or not there is a heterosexual pair who are functioning as the parents, the child will still locate a paternal and maternal point of departure. This heterosexual dyad will have symbolic significance for the child and become the structure through which desire is given form.

In a sense, there are important alternatives to be thought together here. I am not suggesting that they can or should be reconciled. It may be that they stand in a necessary tension to one another, and that this necessary tension now structures the field of feminist and queer theory, producing their inevitable tension and necessitating the contentious dialogue between them. It is important to distinguish among theorists of sexual difference who argue on biological grounds that the distinction between the sexes is necessary (Barbara Duden, the German feminist, tends to do this[3]), and those who argue that sexual difference is a fundamental nexus through which language and culture emerge (the structuralists and the non-gender-troubled post-structuralists do this). But then there is a further distinction. There are those who only find the structuralist paradigm useful because it charts the continuing power differential between men and women in language and society and gives us a way of understanding how deeply it functions in establishing the symbolic order in which we live. Among the latter, I think, there is a difference still between those who consider that symbolic order inevitable, and so ratify patriarchy as an inevitable structure of culture, and those who think that sexual difference is inevitable and fundamental, but that its form as patriarchal is contestable. Rosi Braidotti belongs to the latter. One can see why I have had such useful conversations with her.

The problem arises when we try to understand whether sexual difference is necessarily heterosexist. Is it? Again, it depends on which version you accept. If you claim that oedipalization presupposes heterosexual parenting or a heterosexual symbolic that exceeds whatever parenting arrangement – if there is one at work – then the matter is pretty much closed. If you think that oedipalization produces heterosexual desire, and that sexual difference is a function of oedipalization, then it seems that the matter is closed again. And there are those, such as Juliet Mitchell, who are presently troubled by this issue, even though she is the one who, in *Psycho-analysis and Feminism*, declared the patriarchal symbolic order not to be a changeable set of rules but to be "primordial law" (370).

I take the point that the sociological concepts of gender, understood as women and men, cannot be reducible to sexual difference. But I worry still, actively, about understanding sexual difference as operating as a symbolic order. What does it mean for such an order to be symbolic rather than social?[4] And what happens to the task of feminist theory to think social transformation if we accept that sexual difference is orchestrated and constrained at a symbolic level? If it is symbolic, is it changeable? I ask Lacanians this question, and they usually tell me that changes in the symbolic take a long, long time. I wonder how long I will have to wait. Or they show me a few passages in what is called the Rome Discourse, and I wonder if these passages are the ones to which we are supposed to cling for hope that things might eventually change. Moreover, I'm compelled to ask, is it really true that sexual difference at the symbolic level is without semantic content? Can it ever be? And what if we have indeed done nothing more than abstracted the social meaning of sexual difference and exalted it as a symbolic and, hence, presocial structure? Is that a way of making sure that sexual difference is beyond social contestation?

One might wonder after all of this why I want to contest sexual difference at all, but the abiding assumption of my earlier gender theory was that gender is complexly produced through identificatory and performative practices, and that gender is not as clear or as univocal as we are sometimes led to believe. My effort was to combat forms of essentialism which claimed that gender is a truth that is somehow there, interior to the body, as a core or as an internal essence, something that we cannot deny, something which, natural or not, is treated as given. The theory of sexual difference makes none of the claims that natural essentialism does. At least one version of sexual difference argued that it was the "difference" in every identity that precludes the possibility of a unified category of identity. There were, in this regard, at least two different kinds of challenges that *Gender Trouble* needed to meet, and I see now that I needed to separate the issues and hope that I have begun to do that in my subsequent work. Nevertheless, I still worry that the frameworks we commit ourselves to because they describe patriarchal domination well and may well recommit us to seeing that very domination as inevitable or as primary, more primary in fact than other operations of differential power. Is the symbolic eligible for social intervention? Does sexual difference really remain other to its instituted form, the dominant one being heterosexuality itself?

What was it I imagined? And how has the question of social transformation and politics changed in the interim?

(2004)

Notes

2   See also my interview with Rosi Braidotti, "Feminism By Any Other Name."
3   See Barbara Duden, *The Woman Beneath the Skin*.
4   I consider this issue at greater length in *Antigone's Claim: Kinship Between Life and Death*.

BARBARA CHRISTIAN

'The Race for Theory'
Gender and Theory: Dialogues on Feminist Criticism

I have seized this occasion to break the silence among those of us, critics, as we are now called, who have been intimidated, devalued by what I call the race for theory. I have become convinced that there has been a take-over in the literary world by Western philosophers from the old literary elite, the neutral humanists. Philosophers have been able to effect such a take-over because so much of the literature of the West has become pallid, laden with despair, self-indulgent, and disconnected. The New Philosophers, eager to understand a world that is today fast escaping their political control, have redefined literature so that the distinctions implied by that term, that is, the distinctions between everything written and those things written to evoke feeling as well as to express thought, have been blurred. They have changed literary critical language to suit their own purposes as philosophers, and they have re-invented the meaning of theory.

My first response to this realization was to ignore it. Perhaps, in spite of the egocentrism of this trend, some good might come of it. I had, I felt, more pressing and interesting things to do, such as reading and studying the history and literature of black women, a history that had been totally ignored, a contemporary literature bursting with originality, passion, insight, and beauty. But unfortunately it is difficult to ignore this new take-over, theory has become a commodity because that helps determine whether we are hired or promoted in academic institutions – worse, whether we are heard at all. Due to this new orientation, works (a word which evokes labor) have become texts. Critics are no longer concerned with literature, but with other critics' texts, for the critic yearning for attention has displaced the writer and has conceived of himself as the center. Interestingly in the first part of this century, at least in England and America, the critic was usually also a writer of poetry, plays, or novels. But today, as a new generation of professionals develops, he or she is increasingly an academic. Activities such as teaching or writing one's response to specific works of literature have, among this group, become subordinated to one primary thrust, that moment when one creates a theory, thus fixing a constellation of ideas for a time at least, a fixing which no doubt will be replaced in another month or so by somebody else's competing theory as the race accelerates. Perhaps because those who have effected the takeover have the power (although they deny it) first of all to be published, and thereby to determine the ideas which are deemed valuable, some of our most daring and potentially radical critics (and by *our* I mean black, women, Third World) have been influenced, even co-opted, into speaking a language and defining their discussion in terms alien to and opposed to our needs and orientation. At least so far, the creative writers I study have resisted this language.[1]

For people of color have always theorized – but in forms quite different from the Western form of abstract logic. And I am inclined to say that our theorizing (and I intentionally use the verb rather than the noun) is often in narrative forms, in the stories we create, in riddles and proverbs, in the play with language, since dynamic rather than fixed ideas seem more to our liking. How else have we managed to survive with such spiritedness the assault on our bodies, social institutions, countries, our very humanity? And women, at least the women I grew up around, continuously speculated about the nature of life through pithy language that unmasked the power relations of their world. It is this language, and the grace and pleasure with which they played with it, that I find celebrated, refined, critiqued in the works of writers like Toni Morrison and Alice Walker. My folk, in other words, have always been a race of theory – though more in the form of the hieroglyph, a written figure which is both sensual and abstract, both beautiful and communicative. In my own work I try to illuminate and explain these hieroglyphs, which is, I think, an activity quite different from the creating of the hieroglyphs themselves. As the Buddhists would say, the finger pointing at the moon is not the moon.

In this discussion, however, I am more concerned with the issue raised by my first use of the term, *the race for theory*, in relation to its academic hegemony, and possibly of its inappropriateness to the energetic emerging literatures in the world today. The pervasiveness of this academic hegemony is an issue continually spoken about – but usually in hidden groups, lest we, who are disturbed by it, appear ignorant to the reigning academic elite. Among the folk who speak in muted tones are people of color, feminists, radical critics, creative writers, who have struggled for much longer than a decade to make their voices, their various voices, heard, and for whom literature is not an occasion for discourse among critics but is necessary nourishment for their people and one way by which they come to understand their lives better. Clichéd though this may be, it bears, I think, repeating here.

The race for theory, with its linguistic jargon, its emphasis on quoting its prophets, its tendency towards 'Biblical' exegesis, its refusal even to mention specific works of creative writers, far less contemporary ones, its preoccupations with mechanical analyses of language, graphs, algebraic equations, its gross generalizations about culture, has silenced many of us to the extent that some of us feel we can no longer discuss our own literature, while others have developed intense writing blocks and are puzzled by the incomprehensibility of the language set adrift in literary circles. There have been, in the last year, any number of occasions on which I had to convince literary critics who have pioneered entire new areas of critical inquiry that they did have something to say. Some of us are continually harassed to invent wholesale theories regardless of the complexity of the literature we study. I, for one, am tired of being asked to produce a black feminist literary theory as if I were a mechanical man. For I believe such theory is prescriptive – it ought to have some relationship to practice. Since I can count on one hand the number of people attempting to be black feminist literary critics in the world today, I consider it presumptuous of me to invent a theory of how we *ought* to read. Instead, I think we need to read the works of our writers in our various ways and remain open to the intricacies of the intersection of language, class, race, and gender in the literature. And it would help if we share our process, that is, our practice, as much as possible since, finally, our work *is* a collective endeavor.

The insidious quality of this race for theory is symbolized for me by a term like 'Minority Discourse'[2] – a label that is borrowed from the reigning theory of the day but which is untrue to the literatures being produced by our writers, for many of our literatures (certainly Afro-American literature) are central, not minor. I have used the passive voice in my last sentence construction, contrary to the rules of Black English, which like all languages has a particular value system, since I have not placed responsibility on any particular person or group. But that is precisely because this new ideology has become so prevalent among us that it behaves like so many of the other ideologies with which we have had to contend. It appears to have neither head nor center. At the least though, we can say that the terms 'minority' and 'discourse' are located firmly in a Western dualistic or 'binary' frame which sees the rest of the world as minor, and tries to convince the rest of the world that it *is* major, usually through force and then through language, even as it claims many of the ideas that we, its 'historical' other, have known and spoken about for so long. For many of us have never conceived of ourselves only as somebody's *other*.

Let me not give the impression that by objecting to the race for theory I ally myself with or agree with the neutral humanists who see literature as pure expression and will not admit to the obvious control of its production, value, and distribution by those who have power, who deny, in other words, that literature is, of necessity, political. I am studying an entire body of literature that has been denigrated for centuries by such terms as *political*. For an entire century Afro-American writers, from Charles Chestnutt in the nineteenth century through Richard Wright in the 1930s, Imamu Baraka in the 1960s, Alice Walker in the 1970s, have protested the literary hierarchy of dominance which declares when literature is literature, when literature is great, depending on what it thinks is to its advantage. The Black Arts Movement of the 1960s, out of which Black Studies, the Feminist Literary Movement of the 1970s, and Women's Studies grew, articulated precisely those issues, which came *not* from the declarations of the New Western Philosophers but from these groups' reflections on their own lives. That Western scholars have long believed their ideas to be universal has been strongly opposed by many such groups. Some of my colleagues do not see black critical writers of previous decades as eloquent enough. Clearly they have not read Wright's 'A blueprint for Negro Writing', Ellison's *Shadow and Act*, Chesnutt's resignation from being a writer, or Alice Walker's 'In search of Zora Neale Hurston'.[3] There are two reasons for this general ignorance of what our writer-critics have said. One is that black writing has been generally ignored in the USA. Since we, as Toni Morrison has put it, are seen as a discredited people, it is no surprise, then, that our creations are also discredited. But this is also due to the fact that until recently, dominant critics in the Western world have also been creative writers who have had access to the upper-middle-class institutions of education and, until recently, our writers have decidedly been excluded from these institutions and in fact have often been opposed to them. Because of the academic world's general ignorance about the literature of black people, and of women, whose work too has been discredited, it is not surprising that so many of our critics think that the position arguing that literature is political begins with these New Philosophers. Unfortunately, many of our young critics do not investigate the reasons *why* that statement – literature is political – is now acceptable when before it was not; nor do we look to our own antecedents for the sophisticated arguments upon which we can build in order to change the tendency of any established Western idea to become hegemonic.

Notes

This essay is reprinted (with changes) with permission from Barbara Christian and first appeared in *Cultural Critique* 6 (Spring 1987): 51–63.

1 For another view of the debate this 'privileged' approach to Afro-American texts has engendered, see Joyce A. Joyce, ' "Who the Cap Fit:" unconsciousness and unconscionableness in the criticism of Houston A. Baker, Jr, and Henry Louis Gates, Jr', *New Literary History* 18 (1987): 371–84. I had not read Joyce's essay before I wrote my own. Clearly there are differences between Joyce's view and my own.

2 This paper was originally written for a conference at the University of California at Berkeley entitled 'Minority Discourse', and held on 29–31 May 1986.

3 See Ellison 1964; Farnsworth 1969; Gayle 1971; Jones, L. 1966; Neal 1971: pp. 357–74; Walker 1975; Wright 1937.

JULIA KRISTEVA

'Woman Can Never Be Defined'
New French Feminisms

Julia Kristeva: The belief that "one is a woman" is almost as absurd and obscurantist as the belief that "one is a man." I say "almost" because there are still many goals which women can achieve: freedom of abortion and contraception, day-care centers for children, equality on the job, etc. Therefore, we must use "we are women" as an advertisement or slogan for our demands. On a deeper level, however, a woman cannot "be"; it is something which does not even belong in the order of *being*. It follows that a feminist practice can only be negative, at odds with what already exists so that we may say "that's not it" and "that's still not it." In "woman" I see something that cannot be represented, something that is not said, something above and beyond nomenclatures and ideologies. There are certain "men" who are familiar with this phenomenon; it is what some modern texts never stop signifying: testing the limits of language and sociality – the law and its transgression, mastery and (sexual) pleasure – without reserving one for males and the other for females, on the condition that it is never mentioned. From this point of view, it seems that certain feminist demands revive a kind of naive romanticism, a belief in identity (the reverse of phallocratism), if we compare them to the experience of both poles of sexual difference as is found in the economy of Joycian or Artaudian prose or in modern music – Cage, Stockhausen.[3] I pay close attention to the particular aspect of the work of the avant-garde which dissolves identity, even sexual identities; and in my theoretical formulations I try to go against metaphysical theories that censure what I just labeled "a woman" – this is what, I think, makes my research that of a woman. Perhaps I should add something here, and it's not contradictory to what I just said. Because of the decisive role that women play in the reproduction of the species, and because of the privileged relationship between father and daughter, a woman takes social constraints even more seriously, has fewer tendencies toward anarchism, and is more mindful of ethics. This may explain why our negativity is not Nietzschean anger. If my work aims at broadcasting to the public precisely what this society censures in the avant-garde practice, then, I think, my work obeys ethical exigencies of this type. The whole problem is to know whether this ethical penchant in the woman's struggle will remain separated from negativity; in which case the ethical penchant will degenerate into conformity, and negativity will degenerate into esoteric perversion. The problem is on the agenda of the women's movement. But without the movement, no work of any woman would ever really be possible.

(1974)

Note

3   James Joyce, Antonin Artaud, John Cage, Karlheinz Stockhausen: writers and musicians included in the avant-garde canon. – Tr.

MARYSA DEMOOR AND JÜRGEN PIETERS

'Discursive Desire: Catherine Belsey's Feminism'
Feminist Review

Demoor and Pieters: Moving away from desire and love to sexual politics, to Toni Morrison and colonization of African American literature. Does not the fact that you refuse to deal with her work 'out of some kind of respect' stem from a misplaced fear of being criticized by African American feminist criticism? Does not such a deliberate silence about African American women writers lead to a marginalizaton of their work? Does such an attitude not continue the idea of unbridgeable polarities like black and white, just like the exclusion of male feminist critics would make feminist criticism an extreme, essentialist and undemocratic movement with men and women standing at opposite never to be reconciled extremes?

Belsey: I was very worried about the number of British PhDs being written on Toni Morrison and I felt agonized about the idea that white women might be putting Toni Morrison to work to advance their careers. When you look at it like that, it's politically disturbing. So I decided that I would not write about Toni Morrison, but I would in my declaration that I was not going to write about her just mention that I thought that she was the most brilliant novelist alive today. So in *Desire* I include a tribute to Toni Morrison. I think my feeling is this: first of all Toni Morrison doesn't need me. She is probably the greatest woman living novelist, and she has won a Nobel Prize. Second, she doesn't need me to interpret her, because the people most qualified to interpret her are the people who have access to the vocabulary that she uses, the heirs of that post-slavery culture. The people who themselves have lived the exploitation of African Americans are the ones best qualified to speak about it. What's more, they are the ones who are entitled to advance their careers. How many African American women have been employed in universities? And it seemed to me, since they have a privileged access to Toni Morrison's work, because they know the cultural context, they are the ones who should be becoming professors by writing about her, because for all those years they haven't had equal access to academic careers. It is for me to keep quiet and listen to them.

Demoor and Pieters: It is paradoxical that you say you don't have the vocabulary or cultural background to understand Toni Morrison yet you say she's the best novelist.

Belsey: It's not so much that I don't think I can understand her, it's that I'm not sure that by writing about her, I can serve any useful purpose, or add to what others have said. Of course, there are some things that I don't understand because inscribed in almost all those novels is a heritage of slavery.

Demoor and Pieters: That's not what makes it a good novel of course.

Belsey: Well, yes and no.

Demoor and Pieters: There are bad novels about slavery as well.

Belsey: What I mean is that there are nuances that I don't pick up. There must be nuances I miss because this is not a culture that I inhabit; it is geographically a long way away. British race relations are of a different kind and so

I don't have access that way either. But I think it is more that I feel that for me to advance my career writing about Toni Morrison is somehow improper.

Demoor and Pieters: What is it that you like so much about her novels?

Belsey: This is a difficult vocabulary for me, because I don't do literary value judgements, I haven't in twenty-five years. This is a private feeling; I don't speak as a professional here; I speak as a reader who is enraptured by her style, by the way that she can make you feel as if you speak an African American language by the end of those novels, as if you understand something you could not possibly have lived. And, simply as a novelist of desire, she writes in a way that I can recognize about the seductiveness of desire itself.

Demoor and Pieters: But then, if we follow your reasoning, men shouldn't be writing about women or women authors, an American heterosexual woman should not be writing about Jeanette Winterson because she's British and a lesbian or about a Victorian gay man, where there's a distance in time, gender and sexual nature.

Belsey: No, it isn't primarily the distance; it's the politics.

Demoor and Pieters: But there is a political tension between men and women, between heterosexuals and homosexuals?

Belsey: Yes, there is. I was annoyed when men started writing books about feminism. Let me try to explain it in terms of feminism, where it might make sense. When in the 1980s men in English departments began writing books about feminism, explaining what feminism was about, speaking for feminism, giving expositions of feminism, I became extremely irritated. This was a field that women had invented, and since women were at that time seriously under-represented in English departments, it seemed to me that women were the ones entitled to get published, to advance their careers by producing books of feminist criticism. It was a kind of colonization that was going on. Men, I felt, could write about everything else; they had the whole of the rest of the syllabus, the canon and beyond, to write about. I feel the same about Toni Morrison: the issue is primarily political. There are African American women who deserve jobs and don't have them, or deserve advancement and don't have it. Things are changing now and changing fast and I'm glad. But I think those women should be the ones who publish subtle, sophisticated, nuanced readings of Toni Morrison and get chairs on the basis of it, not me. Why me? I can write about everything else. I can write about Aphra Behn, for example. She's dead: no one has a special claim to Aphra Behn. I'd rather that women wrote about her, but I think feminism is now sufficiently established for that not to be so much the issue. Every English department in Britain in the last five years has been desperately looking for feminists to appoint. The endangered minority among my PhD students are now white heterosexual males. Nobody wants them. I've had cases where male PhD students who had done everything, published books, got their PhDs, could not get jobs, while women, feminists who hadn't even finished their PhDs walk into the first job they apply for. It's a political moment.

It is just that there are people who are more entitled to write about Toni Morrison than I am. Now, I will tell you something that in a way conflicts with this: Jane Moore and I have just brought out a second edition of *The Feminist Reader* that includes an essay by Morrison. But the reason for that is not for us to advance our careers, I hope, but to put her extremely brilliant analysis of literary racism on the syllabus. *The Feminist Reader* is a textbook, and we want this essay to be discussed in classes all over the English-speaking world.

Demoor and Pieters: But imagine Toni Morrison has not got the career she's got now and that you're the best qualified white woman academic to write about her, what would you do then?

Belsey: It's very hard to say, it's hypothetical. What I can say is that I have taught Toni Morrison and Alice Walker in a situation where there was nobody in my department better qualified to do it. Since for a long time I was the only woman, if they were going to be part of the curriculum, I had to teach them. Until we have solved the problem of race relations, until we have an equal world, until we have a world in which the white West is not exploiting the Third World and black races, until there is no longer any racial exploitation, these problems will remain problems.

(2000)

5

Writing, Reading
and Difference

INTRODUCTION

Writing Female or Feminine

Ellen Moers, looking at the use of bird metaphors in women's writing, concludes that there is something distinctive in the way women writers have used certain images. The tendency in Moers's argument is to see a link between particular metaphors and the social and historical position of women writers and women characters: so, given what we know of the restricted lifestyle of middle-class women in the nineteenth century, the caged bird metaphor in *Jane Eyre* is appropriate – almost predictable. But what is confusing in Moers's writing is the interchangeable use she makes of the terms 'feminine' and 'female' and, though it generally appears that she is talking about culture rather than biology, there are occasions when her use of 'female' instead of 'feminine' suggests that she is attributing to women some innate propensity to certain images or forms of language. This confusion of terminology poses a particular problem in understanding writing in French, since the adjective *féminin(e)* does not translate easily into English. Hence, problems of translation have become embroiled in arguments about the possible essentialism of certain French writers.[1]

Moers's method of textual analysis, searching for distinctive imagery, tones or stylistic devices, became a common one in Anglo-American criticism and, as we have seen in earlier chapters, important in uncovering a female tradition, in exploring the interconnections between women writers, and in establishing the methodology which Elaine Showalter termed 'gynocriticism'. But it was always an uncertain activity – and in several ways: no one wants to make extravagant claims about a uniformity in women's writing; the differences between women writers always seem to outnumber the similarities; moreover, there is no way of knowing whether any common factors are due to the writers' sex, their shared class or racial background, the demands of the literary form they employ, or any one of a dozen or more other factors. As Annette Kolodny warned as early as 1975, the thesis can operate as a self-fulfilling prophecy. If the explicit aim is to find stylistic similarities in women's writing, it is not surprising if, in that mass of material, some similarities are actually discovered.[2]

Mary Ellmann offers a different approach. She does not write of 'male' and 'female' but of 'masculine' and 'feminine' modes of writing, characterizing the 'masculine' in terms of an authority apparently absent in the so-called 'feminine'. Crucially, she presents this masculine voice as not necessarily the prerogative of the male writer; nor is the feminine voice possible only for women. Thus, in Simone de Beauvoir she discovers an adherence to the tone of authority which disappoints her, but in Norman Mailer, that most macho of writers, a delightful exhilarating abuse of it.[3] It is in writing which expresses the 'disruption of authority' or the 'disruption of the rational' that Ellmann finds the characteristics of 'what were previously considered feminine habits of thought'; there is an advantage, therefore, in the woman writer allying herself with 'a literature at odds with authority'. Rashness, daring, mockery, 'sudden alternations of the reckless and the sly, the wildly voluble and the laconic' are the stylistic qualities that can undercut the 'established masculine mode', and are, of course, precisely the qualities which Ellmann's own writing embodies.

In several ways Ellmann's remarks foreshadow, with striking prescience, subsequent developments in critical theory, particularly in poststructuralist and psychoanalytic thinking. For critics of these persuasions, the important issue, in Mary Jacobus's felicitous expression, is 'not the sexuality of the text but the textuality of sex' – in other words, not whether a text is authored by a man or a woman and the difference that might make, but how masculinity and femininity are produced in texts. Peggy Kamuf and Jacobus fear that in looking for the difference of women's writing, presumably with the laudable aim of illustrating its quality and uniqueness, one gets caught up in a form of biological determinism. Thus the 'distinctiveness' of women's writing becomes, merely and obviously, that it is writing produced by women. In addition, the emphasis on the author's name and sexual identity plays, with alarming ease, into the hands of the dominant order and its concepts of identity and meaning: 'the father's name and the index of sexual identity' (Kamuf); 'the woman author as origin and her life as the primary locus of meaning' (Jacobus). What starts as a radical move to focus on the specificity of women can be undermined and incorporated.

Though describing certain common themes and styles in women's writing, Julia Kristeva is cautious about any contention 'that a specifically female writing exists'. This is partly because, as indicated above, any similarities in women's (or men's) writing could be produced by a wide variety of factors and partly because, like Kamuf and Jacobus, Kristeva does not subscribe to the notion of a fixed sexual identity; on the contrary, she views sexual identity as 'constantly remade and reborn through the impetus provided by a play of signs'. Where she does suggests differences (for example, that in women's writing the emotion exceeds the expression or that women's writing shows less interest in composition), she makes clear that these are differences of degree – 'more often than in texts by men' – rather than absolute differences, and that they are the product of a complicated interplay between unconscious forces and linguistic signs; they are not the product of biological difference. Just as interesting to Kristeva is that which the woman writer does not say, cannot say, 'the speech of non-being', and this interest finds an echo in Jacobus's preoccupation with 'the gaps, the absences, the unsayable or unrepresentable of discourse'. This 'unspoken' is characterized as 'the feminine', but this is not 'the feminine' of subordination or docility or frivolity. Rather it is a gap in phallocentric culture for Jacobus; 'a "space" of some kind (over which the narrative has lost control)' for Alice Jardine (Chapter 4); for others, a potential at the margins. In short, the feminine has radical force.[4]

But Nancy Miller causes us to pause in this argument. Situating her remarks in the context of poststructuralist debates on writing and sexual difference and, particularly, Roland Barthes's highly influential concept of 'the death of the Author', Miller revives the question of authorial identity. While she fully recognizes the importance of Barthes's work for feminism and the role he has played within the US academy, while she is intrigued by Barthes's repeated killing off and resurrection of the author, it is still vital, believes Miller, to ask what all this means for the *woman* author. Taking into account the specifics of the 'historical, political, and figurative body of the woman writer' can lead to different conclusions and possibilities. There is a dangerous universalizing of '*the* author' or '*the* reader' in Barthes's position.

Difference and Reading

If the sex of the author cannot guarantee anything about the writing, what about the sex of the reader? Do men and women read differently? As we saw in the previous chapter, even if we feel sure about the sexual identity of the author or reader, the politics of the writing or reading are still in doubt: female reading does not mean feminist reading. Equally, if reading 'as a woman' is a position rather than an identity, does the reader's sex have any significance at all? Judith Fetterley's extract belongs to that period when American feminist criticism was preoccupied with the canon, finding women's place within it and, in Fetterley's case, considering the canon's deleterious effect on the woman reader. As Jonathan Culler indicates, Fetterley's objection is not to negative images of women, but 'to the way in which the dramatic structure of these stories induces women to participate in a vision of woman as the obstacle to freedom'. In Fetterley's view, the woman reader of the male-authored text is coerced into a position of 'immasculation' since the narrative strategies require that. Her necessary defence is to become 'a resisting reader'. Culler indicates what he terms 'two moments' in feminist criticism. In the first, women's experience has validated their reading; in the second, as we see in Fetterley's extract, the problem is precisely that women have not, could not, read 'as women'.[5]

Robert Scholes replies to Culler through an interchange with Jacques Derrida and he compares Derrida's claim to write 'from a feminine place' with Culler's argument about 'reading as a woman'. Scholes's worry about any dismissal of women's experience as a validating factor is a political concern. The rejection could be a way of diminishing women's authority to speak/read 'as members of a class who share that experience' or an opportunity for men to usurp that speaking/reading position (notice that Scholes sees Derrida's comments as a put-down). Scholes's conclusion is that women abandon at their peril concepts of experience and authority, though the deployment of such terms needs now to be more theoretically aware than in the gynocritical model. Throughout this debate, then, weaves an argument about the sex-identified reader (male or female), the possibility of reading out of that identity ('as a man' or 'as a woman'), the concept of 'experience' and the relation to gendered power differentials.[6]

In the extracts from Gayatri Chakravorty Spivak and Kate Flint, we see further incarnations of what Showalter (quoted in Culler) calls 'the *hypothesis* of the female reader'. The particular reader Spivak has in mind is 'a feminist reader or teacher in the USA' trying to make sense of a culturally different text.[7] Spivak's focus is Frédérique Marglin's *Wives of the God-king* (1985) which, she suggests, a reader of R. K. Narayan's novel *The Guide* (1980) might well use as a way of finding out more about temple dancers. Through her trenchant critique of Marglin, Spivak shows how becoming even an adequate reader of Narayan's novel would demand an understanding of cultural, linguistic, gender and class differences as well as knowledge about a particular dance form and debates about reading as both political and aesthetic practices. The basic answer to 'how to read' is knowledgeably, carefully, critically and self-consciously. This is daunting for 'our inquisitive feminist literary critic' and not always helped by another hypothetical reader, 'the Indian colleague or friend who is the US feminist's "native informant"' and who has her own reading problems to solve. For Flint, in her study of the figure of the woman reader in the Victorian and Edwardian periods, the problem is that her hypothetical reader has already, by the end of the eighteenth century, been constructed as vulnerable.[8] Morally, intellectually and emotionally, the woman reader is at risk, particularly from novels, and needs careful direction. Flint's detailed study historicizes the woman reader and explores both the deep cultural attachment – in medical and religious discourses, advice manuals, school texts, the periodical press, etc. – to this particular hypothesis of the woman reader and the ideological purposes to which this figure might be put.

Empirical studies of readerships have been concerned with the reader as neither a position nor a hypothesis, but as a real, embodied person and they offer another way of discovering what men and women actually read and whether those choices differ. Jan S. Fergus's demographic analysis of reader-ships in eighteenth-century England is based on the records of booksellers in five Midland towns between 1744 and 1807. Fergus discusses the problems of collecting the data – for example, the nature of the accounts kept by different booksellers, how women of all classes, servants and labourers are under-represented in comparison to tradesmen, professionals and gentle-man, the invisibility of the married woman – and yet can conclude that reading in the second half of the eighteenth century was not clearly gender-divided and that the female readership for fiction was not particularly large. Fergus's statistical enquiry leads to a conclusion similar to Flint's. The association of women with fiction may stem more from the anxieties of moralists and conduct book writers about the solitary and affective activity of women's fiction reading, and it occludes the significant role played by men as buyers, borrowers and readers of fiction. Two hundred years later, the survey by Jenny Hartley and Sarah Turvey of 284 reading groups in the UK indicates how differences in reading are still more complicated than one might at first assume.[9] These respondents show an awareness of difference, often as an obstacle to be overcome or accommodated, but those differences are to them matters of degree rather than significant.

Difference and 'French Feminism'
The rejection of difference as a binary opposition – male *versus* female; masculine *versus* feminine – has been most associated with what has been called 'French feminism'. According to binary thinking, the male and the masculine constitutes the norm, the positive and the superior; the female and the feminine is the aberration, the negative, the inferior. As Luce Irigaray suggests, 'the feminine finds itself defined as lack, deficiency, or as imitation and negative image of the subject'. In extolling the female, the woman writer does not break the pattern of patriarchal binary thought whereby the female is defined in relation to the male, but continues to operate 'within the terms of the existing system'. Difference as binary opposition is largely acceptable to the dominant order. Indeed, there is a long tradition of reactionary argu-ment which enthusiastically discusses the 'natural' differences between men and women. For example, with respect to language, girls are often seen as more verbal and fluent than boys, but then, also, women's language is labelled as bitchy or gossip, marked by the inconsequential. The implicit rider to this definition is that 'male' language is authoritative, rational and

appropriate to serious public platforms, and that, if women wish to improve their position, they must become adept in the use of this language. But this is not to say that the appeal to sexual difference is always reactionary in nature. The writers and critics we are considering here are well aware of how meaning can be differently constituted and take on new levels of significance. Thus, Jacobus can at once warn against the incipient biologism of the category 'women's writing' and, at the same time, recognize it as 'strategically and politically important', and Irigaray can advise that 'one must assume the feminine role deliberately'. In this context, the feminine is not a natural predisposition for women but the conscious utilization of a deconstructive method of mimicry. Irigaray stresses that this is a perilous undertaking: 'to try to recover the place of her [woman's] exploitation by discourse, without allowing herself to be simply reduced to it'.

For Hélène Cixous and Irigaray, the creative lies not in difference as opposition but in difference as multiplicity and heterogeneity. As Cixous says, 'you can't talk about *a* female sexuality, uniform, homogenous, classifiable into codes' ('Medusa'). Similarly, Irigaray, in prioritizing touch over sight, emphasizes the fluid oscillation and permeation of self-touching against the 'centrism' of phallic order. Cixous focuses on movement, abundance and openness. There is an expansive, jubilant creativity when she speaks of 'infinite richness' or the 'inexhaustible' or 'luminous torrents'. Far from the feminine being defined in relation to the masculine, it is, in Cixous's terms, that which escapes being 'theorized, enclosed, coded'. Both draw connections between the feminine practice of language and what Irigaray terms the 'disruptive excess' of female desire. On speaking, Cixous comments: 'Speak of her pleasure and, God knows, she has something to say about that, so that she gets to unblock a sexuality that's just as much feminine as masculine ...' ('Castration'). On writing, she exhorts: 'Write! Writing is for you, you are for you; your body is yours, take it' ('Medusa'). The variety and exuberance of writing links with the orgasmic overflowing of female pleasure, 'jouissance'. Because female desire, what women want, is so repressed or so misrepresented in a phallocentric society, its expression becomes a vital location for deconstructing that control.

These ideas on difference have been extremely productive, but their characterization as 'French feminism' or *l'écriture féminine* has equally been problematic. The concepts themselves, the importing of these ideas into, particularly, the US academy, and what their institutionalization signified for feminism have all needed close scrutiny. As we see in the extract from Domna Stanton, there was, in the early 1980s, a judicious attempt to weigh the impact of this transatlantic relationship, to evaluate, as Stanton indicates, the connection and the 'dis-connection' between the two approaches.[10] The theoretical complexity and the intensely impassioned, in the French examples, 'dis-connects' from the dominant empirical and materialist traditions of American and British thought with its interest in how women's writing is mediated, institutionalized, situated. But Stanton also resists any easy oppositions by pointing to the important insights of *l'écriture féminine* and to Anglo-American feminism's necessary dependency on its own long line of male theoretical masters. As we have already seen in Rachel Bowlby's remarks (Chapter 4), the construction of French and Anglo-American feminisms as two monolithic and oppositional blocks has never been either true or helpful and is, ironically, completely at odds with the notion of difference as plenitude.

Of the four names most frequently mentioned as 'French feminists' – Irigaray, Cixous, Kristeva and Monique Wittig – only one (Wittig) was actually born in France; each has a complex relationship to feminism and to each other's work; and, collectively, they represent only a small proportion of the diversity of feminisms taking place in France since circa 1968.[11] How did these few names come to represent 'French feminism'?[12] Claire Goldberg Moses's blunt assertion is that 'French feminism' is a 'made-in-America' product. Here she traces the main locations (conferences, journals, edited collections and surveys), the process by which the categories 'French intellectuals' or 'French writers' were reconceived as 'French feminists' and the role played by key members of French departments in US universities. As with the approach of Paul Lauter and Clare Hemmings (Chapter 1), the attention to detail becomes richly illustrative of larger questions.

In trying to show the major strands in contemporary feminist literary theory, I have, of course, compounded the problem that Moses discusses; the names and publications that I refer to in this collection are precisely the ones she rightly sees as over-determined. Understandably, this has irked even those who have most profited from the attention. So we see in the final extract, where Cixous is in discussion with Mireille Calle-Gruber, how strongly both have felt the constraint of Cixous's Anglo-American reputation with its focus on just a few texts from what has been a prolific output, and its insistence on Cixous as a theorist rather than a writer of 'poetry and philosophical reflexion'. Cixous understands those repeatedly-quoted texts as something deliberately produced, in a particular form, to meet a particular need. They are 'more visible than others', perhaps more directed, but they run the risk of appropriation. She certainly does not see them as having the emblematic status they are so often given.

Notes

1   For comment on this problem, see: Toril Moi, *Sexual/Textual Politics: Feminist Literary Theory* (London: Methuen, 1985), p. 97; Nicole Ward Jouve, *White Woman Speaks with Forked Tongue: Criticism as Autobiography* (London:

Routledge, 1991), p. 84; Judith Still, 'A Feminine Economy: Some Preliminary Thoughts', in Helen Wilcox et al. (eds.), *The Body and the Text: Hélène Cixous, Reading and Teaching* (Hemel Hempstead: Harvester Wheatsheaf, 1990).

2   Annette Kolodny, 'Some Notes on Defining a "Feminist Literary Criticism"', in *Critical Inquiry*, vol. 2, no. 1 (autumn 1975).

3   One remembers that Mailer was, along with D. H. Lawrence and Henry Miller, one of the three male writers most castigated by Kate Millett in *Sexual Politics* (London: Sphere, 1971).

4   Other influential discussions on writing and sexual difference would include: Elizabeth Abel (ed.), *Writing and Sexual Difference* (Chicago: Chicago University Press, 1982); Hester Eisenstein and Alice Jardine (eds.), *The Future of Difference* (Boston, MA: G. K. Hall, 1980); Nancy K. Miller (ed.), *The Poetics of Gender* (New York: Columbia University Press, 1986).

5   Note that the comments from Shoshana Felman to which Culler refers are to be found in Chapter 1.

6   On matters of gender and reading, see: Tania Modleski, 'Feminism and the Power of Interpretation: Some Critical Readings', in Teresa de Lauretis (ed.), *Feminist Studies/Critical Studies* (London: Macmillan, 1988); Elizabeth A. Flynn and Patrocinio P. Schweickart (eds.), *Gender and Reading: Essays on Readers, Texts, and Contexts* (Baltimore: Johns Hopkins University Press, 1986); Diana Fuss, 'Reading Like a Feminist', *Essentially Speaking: Feminism, Nature and Difference* (New York: Routledge, 1989); Sara Mills (ed.), *Gendering the Reader* (Hemel Hempstead: Harvester Wheatsheaf, 1994); Lynne Pearce, *Feminism and the Politics of Reading* (London: Arnold, 1997).

7   For further studies on reading a culturally different text, see: Elizabeth Abel, 'Black Writing, White Reading: Race and the Politics of Feminist Interpretation', *Critical Inquiry*, vol. 19, no. 3 (1983), pp. 470–98, later included with other relevant essays in Elizabeth Abel, Barbara Christian and Helene Moglen (eds.), *Female Subjects in Black and White: Race, Psychoanalysis, Feminism* (Berkeley, CA:, University of California Press, 1997). The interview with Catherine Belsey in Chapter 4 is also relevant here.

8   For further studies of the figure of the woman reader in earlier periods, see: Jacqueline Pearson, *Women's Reading in Britain 1750–1835: A Dangerous Recreation* (Cambridge: Cambridge University Press, 1999); Catherine J. Golden, *Images of the Woman Reader in Victorian British and American Fiction* (Gainesville, FL: University Press of Florida, 2003); Janet Badia and Jennifer Phegley (eds.), *Reading Women: Literary Figures and Cultural Icons from the Victorian Age to the Present* (Toronto: Toronto University Press, 2005); Joe Bray, *The Female Reader in the English Novel: From Burney to Austen* (London: Routledge, 2009).

9   For further work on reading groups and book clubs, see: Elizabeth Long, *Book Clubs: Women and the Uses of Reading in Everyday Life* (Chicago: University of Chicago Press, 2003) and Janice Radway, *Reading the Romance: Women, Patriarchy, and Popular Culture* (Chapel Hill: University of North Carolina Press, 1991). An extract from Radway's later work on book clubs is included in Chapter 6. Equally interesting are TV book clubs, particularly that of Oprah Winfrey. See the relevant chapter in Long; Mary J. Lamb, The 'Talking Life' of

Books: Women Readers in Oprah's Book Club, in Badia and Phegley, op. cit.; John Young, 'Toni Morrison, Oprah Winfrey and Postmodern Popular Audiences' *African-American Review*, vol. 35, no. 2 (Summer 2001), pp. 180–205; Cecilia Konchar Farr, *Reading Oprah: How Oprah's Book Club Changed the Way America Reads* (New York: State University of New York Press, 2005).

10   See also Ann Rosalind Jones, 'Writing the Body: Towards an Understanding of "L'Ecriture Féminine" ', *Feminist Studies*, vol. 7, no. 2 (Summer 1981) for a related exploration of this issue.

11   As indicative guides to these writers, see the following. On Irigaray: Rosi Braidotti, 'Radical Philosophies of Sexual Difference: Luce Irigaray', in *The Polity Reader in Gender Studies* (Cambridge: Polity Press, 1994) and the work of Margaret Whitford: 'Rereading Irigaray', in Teresa Brennan (ed.), *Between Feminism and Psychoanalysis* (London: Routledge, 1989); *The Irigaray Reader* (Oxford: Blackwell, 1991); *Luce Irigaray: Philosopher in the Feminine* (London: Routledge, 1991). On Cixous: Abigail Bray, *Hélène Cixous: Writing and Sexual Difference* (Basingstoke: Palgrave Macmillan, 2004) and the work of Susan Sellers: *The Hélène Cixous Reader* (London: Routledge, 1994); *Hélène Cixous: Authorship, Autobiography and Love* (Cambridge: Polity Press, 1996) and with Ian Blyth, *Hélène Cixous: Live Theory* (London: Continuum, 2004). On Kristeva: Toril Moi (ed.), *The Kristeva Reader* (Oxford: Blackwell, 1986); John Lechte, *Julia Kristeva* (London: Routledge, 1990); Kelly Oliver, *Reading Kristeva: Unraveling the Double-bind* (Bloomington: Indiana University Press, 1993). On Wittig: Namascar Shaktini (ed.), *On Monique Wittig: Theoretical, Political, and Literary Essays* (Urbana: University of Illinois Press, 2005); Robyn Wiegman, 'Un-remembering Monique Wittig', *GLQ: A Journal of Lesbian and Gay Studies*, vol. 13, no. 4 (2007), pp. 505–18.

12   For further responses to this question, see: Christine Delphy, 'The Invention of French Feminism: An Essential Move', *Yale French Studies*, 87 (1995), pp. 190–221; Oliver, op. cit.; Nancy Fraser and Sandra Lee Bartky (eds.), *Revaluing French Feminism: Critical Essays on Difference, Agency, and Culture* (Bloomington: Indiana University Press, 1992); and Bowlby, op. cit.

ELLEN MOERS

Literary Women

Is the bird merely a species of the littleness metaphor? Or are birds chosen because they are tortured, as little girls are tortured, by boys like John Reed, who 'twisted the necks of the pigeons, killed the little peachicks....'? Or because bird-victims can be ministered to by girl-victims – as in the scene where Jane, a prisoner in the nursery, tugs at the window sash to put out a few crumbs from her meager breakfast for the benefit of 'a little hungry robin, which came and chirruped on the twigs of the leafless cherry-tree nailed against the wall near the casement' – a metaphor which draws as much on the crucifixion as on country winters. Or is it because birds are beautiful and exotic creatures, symbols of half-promised, half-forbidden sensual delights, like the bird of paradise painted 'nestling in a wreath of convolvuli and rosebuds' on the china teaplate which Jane begs to take in her hands and examine closely, but is 'deemed unworthy of such a privilege'?

Because birds are soft and round and sensuous, because they palpitate and flutter when held in the hands, and especially because they sing, birds are universal emblems of love.

> My heart is like a singing bird
> Whose nest is in a watered shoot:

proclaims Christina Rossetti in her best-known poem, because 'the birthday of my life/Is come, my love is come to me.' Indeed, without birds, those patterns of animal monogamy, the Jane Eyre/Rochester love affair could not advance from romantic beginning to marital consummation. They meet on an icy moonlit road: Rochester, fierce and virile on a black horse, but lamed; and Jane – ' "Childish and slender creature! It seemed as if a linnet had hopped to my foot and proposed to bear me on its tiny wing." ' She peers at him through wide, inquisitive eyes 'like an eager bird'; she struggles in his arms 'like a wild frantic bird'; and when at last they are united, Rochester in his maimed blindness is like 'a royal eagle, chained to a perch, ... forced to entreat a sparrow to become its purveyor.'

[...]

Of all creatures, birds alone can fly all the way to heaven – yet they are caged. Birds alone can sing more beautifully than human voices – yet they are unheeded, or silenced. It is only when we hear the woman as well as the poet in Christina Rossetti that we sense the full force of her metaphor in 'A Royal Princess':

>Me, poor dove that must not coo –
>eagle that must not soar.

It is only when we explore the agonizing splits in the meaning to a girl of the bird itself – freedom against sexual fulfillment, love that also means murder by the hunter – that we can respond fully to 'A White Heron,' the poignant tale by Sarah Orne Jewett.

Whenever a girl stands at a window, as Jane Eyre does, and looks toward the winding white road that vanishes over the horizon, she yearns for the wings of liberty: 'for liberty I gasped; for liberty I uttered a prayer; it seemed scattered on the wind then faintly blowing.' Boys too gasp for liberty, but boys do not receive, they only send such valentines to young ladies as Mary Russell Mitford describes in *Our Village* as a sample of the newest in London taste: 'a raised group of roses and heartsease, executed on a kind of paper cut-work, which, on being lifted up, turned into a cage enclosing a dove – tender emblem!'

From Mary Wollstonecraft's *Maria* – to Brontë's *Jane Eyre* – to Anne Frank's *Diary of a Young Girl* – I find that the caged bird makes a metaphor that truly deserves the adjective female. And I am not at all surprised by George Eliot's and Virginia Woolf's delight in Mrs Browning's version of the caged bird metaphor in *Aurora Leigh*. The heroine's spinster aunt, that pattern of English propriety, had lived, Aurora says,

>A sort of cage-bird life, born in a cage,
>Accounting that to leap from perch to perch
>Was act and joy enough for any bird.
>Dear heaven, how silly are the things that live
>In thickets, and eat berries!
>   I alas,
>A wild bird scarcely fledged, was brought to her cage,
>And she was there to meet me. Very kind.
>Bring the clean water, give out the fresh seed.

So in *Jane Eyre*, when Rochester proposes an illicit sexual union, Jane fights to get free of the man she loves, but will not have on the wrong terms. ' "Jane, be still," ' he says, ' "don't struggle so, like a wild, frantic bird...." ' Her reply is touched with Brontë pomposity, but there is also Brontë wit in her use of a metaphor hallowed with female associations: ' "I am no bird; and no net ensnares me; I am a free human being with an independent will, which I now exert to leave you." ' In Brontë's work, both aspirations – to female freedom and moral freedom – are served by the bird metaphor, free flying.

(1978)

MARY ELLMANN

Thinking about Women

(1)

A generalization is in order at this point. Perhaps a third of future humanity will at some time during the course of their lives need an organ transplant. Terminal patients, victims of fatal accidents, condemned criminals who might be persuaded to will their healthy organs to society, and suicides, who number 22,000 a year in the United States, all die anyway. It will be a tragic waste if their organs are not made available to patients whose lives could be prolonged. With certain obvious qualifications, obtaining these organs involves questions of legal and social machinery rather than basic morality. We have not yet run quite full tilt into the moral dilemma.[1]

(2)

I know nothing of the circumstances surrounding Herbert Blau's resignation from the Lincoln Center Repertory Company, but it is a melancholy decision for which we all bear some measure of responsibility. Blau's tenure with the company was far from distinguished; it is hard to think of a single play produced by him at the Vivian Beaumont that stimulated any real excitement, expectation, or sense of adventure. But given the quality of the man himself and of his past work, we must surely look to other causes than artistic inadequacy for some clue to his failure.[2]

(3)

Whether the 'newer kind of shorter fiction' – be it a stylized snapshot as in Robbe-Grillet's 'The Secret Room' or a 'near-novel' as in Flannery O'Connor's 'Wise Blood' – marks a genuine departure is a moot point. The stories gathered by Mr Marcus may represent a rear-guard action, an after-life of the novel and the long tales of Conrad or Henry James. It is too early to tell. My own hunch is that the future of imaginative form lies elsewhere, in works part philosophic, part poetic, part autobiographical. It is, I think, the writings of Blake, of Nietzsche, of such solitary masters as Elias Canetti and Ernst Bloch, that contain the seeds of the next major literary genre. If the act of fiction is to reassert its claims on the adult mind, it will have to embody more knowledge, more intensity of thought and an awareness of language more in tune with that of Wittgenstein and Lévi-Strauss. What is, just now, more old-fashioned than a novel?[3]

The first statement sets off with an exemplary firmness, which opens the door for a bold prediction in turn. This prediction hurries past its own *perhaps* to appal the reader: must *a third* of all his descendants undergo this surgery? But to frighten is a subordinate effect of authority. Its chief effect is rather one of confidence, reason, adjustment and efficacy. These appear in the third sentence and come to an incomparable climax in the words *all die anyway*. How calmly the dead are found dead here! But no, there is regret – men may hang themselves anyway, but to bury their kidneys with them is a 'tragic waste.' In fact, the statement alienates the reader from the (defensible) goal of organ transplantation: why go to such lengths to keep bodies alive in a society habituated to accident, crime, capital punishment and despair?

But this is admittedly an extreme instance of the idiom. The topic, surgery, is in itself extreme. Only an exceptional self-confidence and aggressive purpose enable the surgeon to invade the body, which has for civilized laymen (except in moments of rage or hatred) a profound sanctity. One has to think of surgery as a virtuous barbarity, and expect barbaric terms to intrude upon explanations of its legitimate point of view. The second and third statements are more representative, however, in that they apply themselves to matters of no practical or physical urgency, and yet advance themselves along the same rhetorical route of authority as does the first statement. What unites the second and third is again the sensation of firmness, directness, confidence. They seem to me fair examples of critical prose now in this country, of an established masculine mode of speaking competently on esthetic issues. Particularly in the second passage, the decision with which even dull phrases are delivered makes them work. This decision dwindles somewhat in the third (where the *moot point* and the *hunch* are drains upon it), but here too the certainty with which even a predictable point is made establishes the effect of validity. 'What is, just now, more old-fashioned than a novel?' For a moment, while he bears the weight of this question, the reader is subdued, and cannot at once remember that in fact nothing is, just now, more old-fashioned than the question itself.

[…]

Unexpectedly, as though one found that some frivolous expenditure was practical after all, in this new idiom women writers move about with an ease they could not feel before. Again, I am not speaking of those who relentlessly prolong our evening with Elizabeth Barrett Browning (they will *not* get up and say, 'Enough of this lucrative distress. Call me a cab.'). Instead, I hope to define the way in which it is now possible for women to write well. Quite simply, having not had physical or intellectual authority before, they have no reason to resist a literature at odds with authority. There are, of course, those who prefer instead to wear hand-me-downs, to borrow now the certitude of the nineteenth century. One might say that the defect of Simone de Beauvoir is the authority of her prose: the absence of hesitation in hesitant times amounts to a presence, a tangible deficiency, a sense of obtuseness.

In better work by women now, while sentiment is avoided as stigmatic (as the inimical mark of their sex in others' minds), authority too is skirted – again, as in Mailer and Svevo, by deliberate rashness or by ironic constraint. The tenor of Mary McCarthy's remarks on *Macbeth* is rather different from that of E. E. Stoll's:

> He is a general and has just won a battle; he enters the scene making a remark about the weather. "So fair and foul a day I have not seen." On this flat note Macbeth's character tone is set. "Terrible weather we're having." "The sun can't seem to make up its mind." "Is it hot/cold/wet enough for you?" A commonplace man who talks in commonplaces, a golfer, one might guess, on the Scottish fairways, Macbeth is the only Shakespeare hero who corresponds to a bourgeois type: a murderous Babbitt, let us say.
>
> Macbeth has absolutely no feeling for others except envy, a common middle-class trait. He *envies* the murdered Duncan his rest, which is a strange way of looking at your victim.[4]

At once a comical and a suicidal wit: the intention of wit exceeds that of justice or plausibility. What is said is said more naturally and more quickly than what Stoll says, and the opinion of Macbeth is engaging. But wrong. One doesn't for a minute *accept* Macbeth as the general, the golfer, the Eisenhower. And the Babbitt reference is quite dead, like a hemline of the late thirties. The point of view is feminine, in the pejorative sense, not only in its wifely depreciation of Macbeth (Lady Macbeth's 'good sense' is later preferred to Macbeth's 'simple panic'), but also in its social narrowness. In its determination to make Macbeth middle-class, the criticism is middle-class itself. It is hard to imagine a more philistine conception of envy than that 'common middle-class trait.' But it is the rashness of the judgment which redeems it, its daring, its mocking diminution of a subject which God knows had taken on an institutionalized grandeur.[5] The rashness links Mary McCarthy, for all their disagreements, with Norman Mailer; the diminution with Svevo, and with now.

(1968)

Notes

1   Roy L. Walford, MD, 'A Matter of Life and Death,' *Atlantic*, August 1967, p. 70.
2   Robert Brustein, 'Saturn Eats His Children,' *New Republic*, January 28, 1967, p. 34.
3   George Steiner, 'The Search for New Genres,' *Book Week*, December 11, 1966, p. 16.

4   Mary McCarthy, 'General Macbeth,' *Harper's*, June 1962, pp. 35 and 37.
5   It is perhaps necessary to distinguish between varieties of rashness. The rashness
    of Mary McCarthy, which ousts conventional attitudes, is not the rashness, say,
    of Rebecca West: 'We were not alone. The house was packed with little girls,
    aged from twelve to sixteen, in the care of two or three nuns. They were, like any
    gathering of their kind in any part of the world, more comfortable to look at than
    an English girls' school. They were apparently waiting quite calmly to grow up.
    They expected it, and so did the people looking after them. There was no panic
    on anybody's part. There were none of the unhappy results which follow the
    English attempt to make all children look insipid and docile, and show no signs
    whatsoever that they will ever develop into adults. There were no little girls with
    poked chins and straight hair, aggressively proud of being plain, nor were there
    pretty girls making a desperate precocious proclamation of their femininity. But,
    of course, in a country where there is very little homosexuality, it is easy for girls
    to grow up into womanhood.' (*Black Lamb and Grey Falcon*, Vol. I, p. 163.)
        The final generalization is the clue: a person is obviously rash to allow herself
    to say anything so simple-silly. But the rashness is placid and auntlike. In the end,
    it reiterates an old point of view rather than risking a new one.

PEGGY KAMUF

'Writing Like a Woman'
Women and Language in Literature and Society

The opening chapter of Patricia Meyer Spacks's *The Female Imagination* is
on theorists (Simone de Beauvoir, Mary Ellmann, and Kate Millett), and it
concludes in this fashion: "So what is a woman to do, setting out to write
about women? She can imitate men in her writing, or strive for an imperson-
ality beyond sex, but finally she must write as a woman: what other way is
there?"[3] Spacks's study puts together readings of a list of literary works by
women in order to determine how, in her phrase, one "writes as a woman."
However, by limiting the field to works whose authors are women, the critic
finally gets caught in the kind of biological determinism, which, in other
contexts, is recognized as a primary instance of antifeminist sexism. Consider,
for example, this passage from the prologue:

Surely the mind has a sex, minds *learn* their sex – and it is no derogation of
the female variety to say so. At any rate, for readily discernible historical
reasons women have characteristically concerned themselves with matters
more or less peripheral to male concerns, or at least slightly skewed from
them. The differences between traditional female preoccupations and roles
and male ones make a difference in female writing. Even if a woman wishes
to demonstrate her essential identity with male interests and ideas, the
necessity of making the demonstration, contradicting the stereotype, allies

her initially with her sisters. And the complex nature of the sisterhood emerges in the books it has produced.[4]

Spacks's concept of female writing is one which must expand to include the works of a woman (de Beauvoir is her primary example) "who wishes to demonstrate her essential identity with male interests and ideas." Although the author sets out with a statement of faith in a psychological or cultural differentiation which can be characterized sexually ("Surely the mind has a sex ..."), she abandons this intuition without a second thought when she must account for a woman who, by her own reckoning, has a "male" mind. By adopting the biological distinction of male/female to define a cultural phenomenon, the critic demonstrates the impossibility of limiting that definition to what it "is" for, as it turns out, it "is" also what it "is not." By "female writing," we discover, Spacks quite banally understands works signed by biologically determined females of the species.

If the inaugural gesture of this feminist criticism is the reduction of the literary work to its signature and to the tautological assumption that a feminine "identity" is one which signs itself with a feminine name, then it will be able to produce only tautological statements of dubious value: women's writing is writing signed by women. Western culture has, of course, traditionally reserved a separate category for the intellectual or cultural productions of women, intimating their special status as exceptions within those realms where to "think male thoughts" is not to be distinguished from thinking in universals. Coming out of that tradition, we are also formed in the cult of the individual and the temptation which results to explain to ourselves artistic and intellectual productions as expressions, simple and direct, of individual experience. However, if these are principles establishing the grounds of a practice of feminist criticism, then that practice must be prepared to all itself with the fundamental assumptions of patriarchy which relies on the same principles.

If, on the other hand, by "feminist" one understands a way of reading texts that points to the masks of truth with which phallocentrism hides its fictions, then one place to begin such a reading is by looking behind the mask of the proper name, the sign that secures our patriarchal heritage: the father's name and the index of sexual identity.

(1980)

Notes

3 Patricia Meyer Spacks, *The Female Imagination* (New York: Knopf, 1975), p. 35.
4 Ibid., p. 7.

MARY JACOBUS

Reading Woman: Essays in Feminist Criticism

And yet the question "Is there a woman in the text?" remains a central one – perhaps *the* central one – for feminist critics, and it is impossible to answer it without theory of some kind. The respective answers given by Anglo-American and French criticism are defined, in part at least, by the inherent paradox of "theory." In America the flight toward empiricism takes the form of an insistence on "woman's experience" as the ground of difference in writing. "Women's writing," "the woman reader," "female culture" occupy an almost unchallenged position of authority in feminist critical discourse of this kind. The assumption is of an unbroken continuity between "life" and "text" – a mimetic relation whereby women's writing, reading, or culture, instead of being produced, reflect a knowable reality.[27] Just as one can identify a woman biologically (the unstated argument would run), so one can with a little extra labor identify a woman's text, a woman reader, the essence of female culture. Of course the category of "women's writing" remains as strategically and politically important in classroom, curriculum, or interpretive community as the specificity of women's oppression is to the women's movement. And yet to leave the question there, with an easy recourse to the female signature or to female being, is either to beg it or to biologize it. To insist, for instance, that *Frankenstein* reflects Mary Shelley's experience of the trauma of parturition and postpartum depression may tell us about women's lives, but it reduces the text itself to a monstrous symptom. Equally, to see it as the product of "bibliogenesis" – a feminist rereading of *Paradise Lost* that, in exposing its misogynist politics, makes the monster's fall an image of woman's fall into the hell of sexuality – rewrites the novel in the image not of books but of female experience.[28] Feminist interpretations such as these have no option but to posit the woman author as origin and her life as the primary locus of meaning.

By contrast, the French insistence on *écriture feminine* – on woman as a writing-effect instead of an origin – asserts not the sexuality of the text but the textuality of sex. Gender difference, produced, not innate, becomes a matter of the structuring of a genderless libido in and through patriarchal discourse. Language itself would at once repress multiplicity and heterogeneity – true difference – by the tyranny of hierarchical oppositions (man/woman) and simultaneously work to overthrow that tyranny by interrogating the limits of meaning. The "feminine," in this scheme, is to be located in the gaps, the absences, the unsayable or unrepresentable of discourse and representation.[29] The feminine text becomes the elusive, phantasmal inhabitant of phallocentric discourse, as Gradiva *rediviva* haunts Freud's

Delusions and Dreams, or, for the skeptical Girard, the narcissistic woman exercises her illusory power over the theory of narcissism. And yet, in its claim that women must write the body, that only the eruption of female jouissance can revolutionize discourse and challenge the Law of the Father, *écriture féminine* seems – however metaphorically – to be reaching not so much for essentialism (as it is often accused of doing) as for the conditions of representability. The theoretical abstraction of a "marked" writing that can't be observed at the level of the sentence but only glimpsed as an alternative libidinal economy almost invariably gives rise to gender-specific images of voice, touch, anatomy; to biologistic images of milk or jouissance. How else, after all, could the not-yet-written forms of *écriture féminine* represent themselves to our understanding? Not essentialism but representationalism is the French equivalent of Anglo-American empiricism – an alternative response to the indeterminacy and impenetrability of theory. If the woman in the text is "there," she is also "not there" – certainly not its object, not necessarily even its author. That may be why the heroine of feminist critical theory is not the silenced Irma, victim of Freudian theory, but the hysterical Dora whose body is her text and whose refusal to be the object of Freudian discourse makes her the subject of her own. Perhaps the question that feminist critics should ask themselves is not "Is there a woman in this text?" but rather: "*Is there a text in this woman?*"

(1986)

Notes

27 See Jonathan Culler's discussion of the concept of "the woman reader" in *On Deconstruction*, pp. 44–64.

28 See the respective readings of Frankenstein by Ellen Moers. "Female Gothic," in Levine and Knoepflmacher, *The Endurance of Frankenstein*, pp. 77–87, and by Gilbert and Gubar, "Horror's Twin: Mary Shelley's Monstrous Eve," *The Madwoman in the Attic*, pp. 213–47.

29 See, for instance, Hélène Cixous, "The Laugh of the Medusa," in Marks and de Courtivron, *New French Feminisms*, pp. 245–64, and "Castration or Decapitation," Annette Kuhn, trans., *Signs* (Autumn 1981), 7(1): 41–55; Luce Irigaray, "When Our Lips Speak Together," and "The Power of Discourse and the Subordination of the Feminine," in *This Sex Which Is Not One*. Catherine Porter, trans. (Ithaca: Cornell University Press, 1985), pp. 205–18, 68–85. For a recent critique of *écriture féminine*, see also Ann Rosalind Jones, "Writing the Body: Toward an Understanding of *L'Écriture Féminine*," *Feminist Studies* (Summer 1981), 7(2): 247–63, reprinted in Elaine Showalter, ed., *The New Feminist Criticism: Essays on Women, Literature, and Theory* (New York: Pantheon Books, 1985), pp. 361–77.

JULIA KRISTEVA

'Talking about Polylogue'
French Feminist Thought: A Reader

Julia Kristeva: If we confine ourselves to the *radical* nature of what is today called 'writing', that is, if we submit meaning and the speaking subject in language to a radical examination and then reconstitute them in a more polyvalent than fragile manner, there is nothing in either past or recent publications by women that permits us to claim that a specifically female writing exists. If it is true that the unconscious ignores negation and time, and is woven instead from displacement and condensation (hinted at by the metaphors of 'language' or 'matheme'), I should say that writing ignores sex or gender and displaces its difference in the discreet workings of language and signification (which are necessarily ideological and historical). Knots of desire are created as a result. This is one way, among others, of reacting to the radical split that constitutes the speaking subject. This eternally premature baby, prematurely separated from the world of the mother and the world of things, remedies the situation by using an invincible weapon: linguistic symbolization. Such a method deals with this fundamental change characterizing the speaking subject not by positing the existence of an *other* (another person or sex, which would give us psychological humanism) or an *Other* (the absolute signifier, God) but by constructing a network where drives, signifiers and meanings join together and split asunder in a dynamic and enigmatic process. As a result, a strange body comes into being, one that is neither man nor woman, young nor old. It made Freud dream of sublimation, and the Christians of angels, and it continues to put to modern rationality the embarrassing question of an identity that is sexual (among other things), and which is constantly remade and reborn through the impetus provided by a play of signs. The hasty attempt to contain the radical nature of this experience within a sexual identity is perhaps sometimes a means of modernizing or simply marketing an evasion of its most trenchant features.

On the other hand, in books written by women, we can eventually discern certain stylistic and thematic elements, on the basis of which we can then try to isolate a relationship to writing that is peculiar to women. But in speaking of these characteristics, for the moment I find it difficult to say if they are produced by something specific to women, by socio-cultural marginality, or more simply by one particular structure (for example hysteria) promoted by present market conditions from among the whole range of potential female qualities.

As regards the themes to be found in texts by women, they invite us to see, touch and smell a body made of organs, whether they are exhibited with satisfaction or horror. It is as if the effects giving rise to inter-subjective relations and social projects (ruled over by the phallus which is nowadays so disparaged) were here reduced to the level of secretions and intestines, carefully disguised by the culture of the past but now on open display. Moreover, these female writings, even at their most optimistic, seem underpinned by a lack of belief in any project, goal or meaning. It is as if no single Other could sustain their abrasive dissatisfaction, but that, paradoxically, without entertaining any illusions they call upon a host of others to fill this vacuum. This gives writings by women a content that is always psychological and often dissenting, disillusioned or apocalyptic – something all too easily interpreted as being political criticism. The epistolary genre or memoirs, as well as their offshoots, lend themselves best to this tendency. Finally, a great number of texts by women seem to be concerned at the moment with reformulating love. The Western conception of love (Christian or courtly love patronized by the combined figures of Christ and the Virgin Mary) today fails to satisfy the needs and desires of a woman's body. Feminism is the result of a crisis in religion which has shown up at its nodal point: namely its conception of love. We are not surprised, then, to read of women who proclaim another sort of love, whether for another woman or for children. This brings us into the obscure realm of primary narcissism or the archaic relationship which a woman has with her mother (an area over which Christianity has publicly drawn a veil or which it has carefully dismissed).[4]

As for the style of women's writings, I am struck by two permanent features. First, every time I read a text by a woman, I am left with the impression that the notion of the signifier as a network of distinctive marks is insufficient. It is insufficient because each of these marks is charged not only with a discriminating value which is the bearer of signification, but also with a drive or an emotional force which does not signify as such but which remains latent in the phonic invocation or in the gesture of writing. It is as if this emotional charge so overwhelmed the signifier as to impregnate it with emotion and so abolish its neutral status; but, being unaware of its own existence, it did not cross the threshold of signification or find a sign with which to designate itself. This holds as much for more modest writings as for those called risqué, where the expression (more often that in texts by men) falls short of the emotional charge which gives rise to it. Poetic language has always shared similar features, but female writings probably introduce into the day-to-day style of a particular age this abolition of the neutrality of the signifier that operates in close conjunction with a delusive and deluded signified. On the other hand, and perhaps as a consequence of this, women's writings exhibit a striking lack of interest (some would say lack of ability) in the art of composition. They fail to orchestrate signifiers as one might with musical staves. When a woman tries her hand at the architectonics of the word perfected by Mallarmé or Joyce, it generally leads to one of two things: either the art of composition gets bogged down in an artificially imposed structure that smacks of word-play or crossword puzzles, a sort of candid and consequently self-invalidating pataphysics; or else – and this is the solution which seems to me the more interesting – silence, and the unspoken, riddled with repetition, weave an evanescent canvas. This is where Blanchot saw the 'poverty of language' revealed and where some women articulate, through their sparing use of words and their elliptical syntax, a lacuna that is congenital to our monological culture: the speech of non-being ...

(1977)
Translated by Seán Hand

Note

4   I return to this in detail in my article, 'Héréthique de l'amour', *Tel Quel*, 74 (Winter 1977, pp. 30–49) (reprinted as 'Stabat Mater' in *Histories d'amour* (Paris: Denoël, 1983), tr. by Léon S. Roudiez as 'Stabat Mater' in *The Kristeva Reader*, ed. Toril Moi (Oxford: Blackwell, 1986, pp. 160–86)).

NANCY K. MILLER

Subject to Change: Reading Feminist Writing

So why remember Barthes, if this model of reading and writing by definition excludes the question of an identity crucial to feminist critical theory? Well, for one thing because Barthes's interest in the semiotics of literary and cultural activity – its pleasures, dangers, zones, and codes of reference – intersects thematically with a feminist emphasis on the need to situate, socially and symbolically, the practices of reading and writing. Like the feminist critic, Barthes maneuvers in the spaces of the tricky relations that bridge the personal and the political, the personal and the critical, the interpersonal and the institutional (his seminar, for example). Barthes translates seductively from within French thought the more arduous writings of Derrida, Lacan, Kristeva, for or into literature; and in the same gesture represents metonymically outside the Parisian scene (or in North American literature departments) most of the concepts that animate feminist (and other) literary critics not hostile to Theory's stories: currently, the post-structuralist epistemologies of the subject and the text, the linguistic construction of sexual identity.

In the preface to *Sade, Fourier, Loyola* (1971) Barthes returns to the problem of authorship: "For if," he writes, "through a twisted dialectic, the Text, destroyer of all subjects, contains a subject to love – *un sujet à aimer* – that subject is dispersed, somewhat like the ashes we strew into the wind after death" (8). And he continues poignantly in the same sentence, "were I a writer, and dead [*si j'étais écrivain, et mort*] how I would love it if my life, through the pains of some friendly and detached biographer, were to reduce itself to a few details, a few preferences, a few inflections, let us say: to 'biographemes'" (9). What interests me here, more than yet another nomination, another code, is Barthes's acknowledgment of the persistence of the subject as the presence in the text of perhaps not some*one* to love in person, but the mark of the need to be loved, the persistence of a peculiarly human(ist?) desire for connection. It is as though thinking of a writer's life – a "life" of Sade, a "life" of Fourier appended to a reading of their writing – generated a thinking of self: for Barthes then imagines himself "a writer."[3] But we have just seen the writer is already dead, his ashes scattered to the winds; and the self fatally dispersed. Thus no sooner is the subject restored metaphorically to a body through love, than he is dispersed figuratively through death. If one is to find the subject, he will not be in one place, but modernly multiple and atopic.

Will *she*?

The postmodernist decision that the Author is Dead and the subject along with him does not, I will argue, necessarily hold for women, and prematurely forecloses the question of agency for them. Because women have not had the same historical relation of identity to origin, institution, production that men have had, they have not, I think, (collectively) felt burdened by *too much* Self, Ego, Cogito, etc. Because the female subject has juridically been excluded from the polis, hence decentered, "disoriginated," deinstitutionalized, etc., her relation to integrity and textuality, desire and authority, displays structurally important differences from that universal position.

In Breaking the Chain, *Naomi Schor takes up Barthes's analysis in* S/Z *of the cultural discourse on "femininity," which he locates for the sake of argument in a passage from Balzac's* Sarrasine. *Curiously, this is also the passage that serves as the opening citation of "The Death of the Author": "This was woman herself...." (etc.) Following Schor's lead, it is interesting to puzzle the connections that for Barthes join* écriture *and "woman" in a definition of textuality that refuses a coherent subjectivity.*

In "Mapping the Postmodern" Andreas Huyssen asks: "Isn't the 'death of the subject/author' position tied by mere reversal to the very ideology that invariably glorifies the artist as genius, whether for marketing purposes or out of conviction and habit? ... [D]oesn't poststructuralism, where it simply denies the subject altogether, jettison the chance of challenging the ideology of the subject (as male, white, and middle-class) by developing alternative and different notions of subjectivity? (44).

In "Women Who Write Are Women," Elaine Showalter, arguing against Cynthia Ozick's belief (subsequently rearticulated by Gail Godwin in the same publication) that "writing transcends sexual identity, that it takes

*place outside of the social order," pointedly observes that in the gender
asymmetry of dominant culture "the female witness, sensitive or not, is still
not accepted as first-person universal" (33).*

It seems to me, therefore, that when the so-called crisis of the subject is
staged, as it generally is, within a textual model, that performance must then
be recomplicated by the historical, political, and figurative body of the
woman writer. (That is, of course, if we accept as a working metaphor the
location of women's subjectivity in female authorship.) Because the discourse of the universal historically has failed to include the testimony of its
others, it seems imperative to question the new doxa of subjectivity at this
juncture of its formation.

(1988)

Note

3   At the Cerisy colloquium of which he was the "prétexte," this phrase drew a
certain amount of attention. In his comments on the meaning of the phrase Barthes
situated his own relation to the historical context of writing *Sade/Fourier/Loyola*:
"It was the heyday of modernity and the text; we talked about the death of the
author (I talked about it myself). We didn't use the word writer [*écrivain*]: writers
were slightly ridiculous people like Gide, Claudel, Valéry, Malraux" (413–14).

JUDITH FETTERLEY

The Resisting Reader

Though one of the most persistent of literary stereotypes is the castrating
bitch, the cultural reality is not the emasculation of men by women but the
immasculation of women by men. As readers and teachers and scholars,
women are taught to think as men, to identify with a male point of view,
and to accept as normal and legitimate a male system of values, one of
whose central principles is misogyny.

One of the earliest statements of the phenomenon of immasculation, serving indeed as a position paper, is Elaine Showalter's "Women and the
Literary Curriculum." In the opening part of her article, Showalter imaginatively recreates the literary curriculum the average young woman entering
college confronts:

> In her freshman year she would probably study literature and composition,
> and the texts in her course would be selected for their timeliness, or their
> relevance, or their power to involve the reader, rather than for their absolute
> standing in the literary canon. Thus she might be assigned any one of the

texts which have recently been advertised for Freshman English: an anthology of essays, perhaps such as *The Responsible Man,* "for the student who wants literature relevant to the world in which he lives," or *Conditions of Men,* or *Man in Crisis: Perspectives on The Individual and His World,* or again, *Representative Men: Cult Heroes of Our Time,* in which thirty-three men represent such categories of heroism as the writer, the poet, the dramatist, the artist, and the guru, and the only two women included are the Actress Elizabeth Taylor and The Existential Heroine Jacqueline Onassis.... By the end of her freshman year, a woman student would have learned something about intellectual neutrality; she would be learning, in fact, how to think like a man.[8]

Showalter's analysis of the process of immasculation raises a central question: "What are the effects of this long apprenticeship in negative capability on the self-image and the self-confidence of women students?" And the answer is self-hatred and self-doubt: "Women are estranged from their own experience and unable to perceive its shape and authenticity.... they are expected to identify as readers with a masculine experience and perspective, which is presented as the human one.... Since they have no faith in the validity of their own perceptions and experiences, rarely seeing them confirmed in literature, or accepted in criticism, can we wonder that women students are so often timid, cautious, and insecure when we exhort them to 'think for themselves'?"[9]

The experience of immasculation is also the focus of Lee Edwards' article, "Women, Energy, and *Middlemarch.*" Summarizing her experience, Edwards concludes:

Thus, like most women, I have gone through my entire education – as both student and teacher – as a schizophrenic, and I do not use this term lightly, for madness is the bizarre but logical conclusion of our education. Imagining myself male, I attempted to create myself male. Although I knew the case was otherwise, it seemed I could do nothing to make this other critically real.

Edwards extends her analysis by linking this condition to the effects of the stereotypical presentation of women in literature:

I said simply, and for the most part silently that, since neither those women nor any women whose acquaintances I had made in fiction had much to do with the life I led or wanted to lead, I was not female. Alien from the women I saw most frequently imagined, I mentally arranged them in rows labelled respectively insipid heroines, sexy survivors, and demonic destroyers. As organizer I stood somewhere else, alone perhaps, but hopefully above them.[10]

Intellectually male, sexually female, one is in effect no one, nowhere, immasculated.

Clearly, then, the first act of the feminist critic must be to become a resisting rather than an assenting reader and, by this refusal to assent, to begin the process of exorcizing the male mind that has been implanted in us. The consequence of this exorcism is the capacity for what Adrienne Rich describes as re-vision – "the act of looking back, of seeing with fresh eyes, of entering an old text from a new critical direction." And the consequence, in turn, of this re-vision is that books will no longer be read as they have been read and thus will lose their power to bind us unknowingly to their designs. While women obviously cannot rewrite literary works so that they become ours by virtue of reflecting our reality, we can accurately name the reality they do reflect and so change literary criticism from a closed conversation to an active dialogue.

In making available to women this power of naming reality, feminist criticism is revolutionary. The significance of such power is evident if one considers the strength of the taboos against it:

> I permit no woman to teach ... she is to keep silent.
>
> *St Paul*

> By Talmudic law a man could divorce a wife whose voice could be heard next door. From there to Shakespeare: "Her voice was ever soft/Gentle, and low-an excellent thing in woman." And to Yeats: "The women that I picked spoke sweet and low/And yet gave tongue." And to Samuel Beckett, guessing at the last torture, The Worst: "a woman's voice perhaps, I hadn't thought of that, they might engage a soprano."
>
> *Mary Ellmann*[11]

> The experience of the class in which I voiced my discontent still haunts my nightmares. Until my face froze and my brain congealed, I was called prude and, worse yet, insensitive, since I willfully misread the play in the interest of proving a point false both to the work and in itself.
>
> *Lee Edwards*[12]

The experience Edwards describes of attempting to communicate her reading of the character of Shakespeare's Cleopatra is a common memory for most of us who have become feminist critics. Many of us never spoke; those of us who did speak were usually quickly silenced. The need to keep certain things from being thought and said reveals to us their importance. Feminist criticism represents the discovery/recovery of a voice, a unique and uniquely powerful voice capable of canceling out those other voices, so movingly described in Sylvia Plath's *The Bell Jar*, which spoke about us and to us and at us but never for us.

(1978)

Notes

8   *College English* 32 (1971), 855.
9   Ibid., 856–57.
10 *Massachusetts Review* 13 (1972), 226, 227.
11 *Thinking About Women* (New York: Harcourt Brace Jovanovich, 1968), pp. 149–50.
12 Edwards, p. 230.

JONATHAN CULLER

'Reading as a Woman'
On Deconstruction: Theory and Criticism after Structuralism

As Heilbrun suggests, reading as a woman is not necessarily what occurs when a woman reads: women can read, and have read, as men. Feminist readings are not produced by recording what happens in the mental life of a female reader as she encounters the words of *The Mayor of Casterbridge*, though they do rely heavily on the notion of the experience of the woman reader. Shoshana Felman asks, "Is it enough to be a woman in order to speak as a woman? Is 'speaking as a woman' determined by some biological condition or by a strategic, theoretical position, by anatomy or by culture?" ("Women and Madness: The Critical Phallacy," p. 3). The same question applies to "reading as a woman."

To ask a woman to read as a woman is in fact a double or divided request. It appeals to the condition of being a woman as if it were a given and simultaneously urges that this condition be created or achieved. Reading as a woman is not simply, as Felman's disjunctions might seem to imply, a theoretical position, for it appeals to a sexual identity defined as essential and privileges experiences associated with that identity. Even the most sophisticated theorists make this appeal – to a condition or experience deemed more basic than the theoretical position it is used to justify. "As a female reader, I am haunted rather by another question," writes Gayatri Spivak, adducing her sex as the ground for a question ("Finding Feminist Readings," p. 82). Even the most radical French theorists, who would deny any positive or distinctive identity to woman and see *le féminin* as any force that disrupts the symbolic structures of Western thought, always have moments, in developing a theoretical position, when they speak as women, when they rely on the fact that they *are* women. Feminist critics are fond of quoting Virginia Woolf's remark that women's "inheritance," what they are given, is "the difference of view, the difference of standard"; but the question then becomes, what is the difference? It is never given as such but must be produced. Difference is produced by differing. Despite the decisive and necessary appeal to the authority of women's experience and of a female reader's experience, feminist criticism is in fact concerned, as Elaine Showalter astutely puts it, "with the way in which the *hypothesis* of a female reader changes our apprehension of a given text, awakening us to the significance of its sexual codes" ("Towards a Feminist Poetics," p. 25, my italics).[7]

Showalter's notion of the *hypothesis* of a female reader marks the double or divided structure of "experience" in reader-oriented criticism. Much male response criticism conceals this structure – in which experience is posited as a given yet deferred as something to be achieved – by asserting that readers simply do in fact have a certain experience. This structure emerges explicitly in a good deal of feminist criticism which takes up the problem that women do not always read or have not always read as women: they have been alienated from an experience appropriate to their condition as women.[8] With the shift to the hypothesis of a female reader, we move to a second moment or level of feminist criticism's dealings with the reader. In the first moment, criticism appeals to experience as a given that can ground or justify a reading. At the second level the problem is precisely that women have not been reading as women. "What is crucial here," writes Kolodny, "is that reading is a *learned* activity which, like many other learned interpretive strategies in our society, is inevitably sex-coded and gender-inflected" ("Reply to Commentaries," p. 588). Women "are expected to identify," writes Showalter, "with a masculine experience and perspective, which is presented as the human one" ("Women and the Literary Curriculum," p. 856). They have been constituted as subjects by discourses that have not identified or promoted the possibility of reading "as a woman." In its second moment, feminist criticism undertakes, through the postulate of a woman reader, to bring about a new experience of reading and to make readers – men and women – question the literary and political assumptions on which their reading has been based.

In feminist criticism of the first sort, women readers identify with the concerns of women characters; in the second case, the problem is precisely that women are led to identify with male characters, against their own interests as women. Judith Fetterley, in a book on the woman reader and American fiction, argues that "the major works of American fiction constitute a series of designs upon the female reader." Most of this literature "insists on its universality at the same time that it defines that universality in specifically male terms" (*The Resisting Reader*, p. xii). One of the founding works of American literature, for instance, is "The Legend of Sleepy Hollow." The figure of Rip Van Winkle, writes Leslie Fiedler, 'presides over the birth of the American imagination; and it is fitting that our first successful homegrown legend should memorialize, however playfully, the flight of the dreamer from the shrew' (*Love and Death in the American Novel*, p. xx). It is fitting because, ever since then, novels seen as archetypally American – investigating or articulating a distinctively American experience – have rung the changes on this basic schema, in which the protagonist struggles against constricting, civilizing, oppressive forces embodied by woman. The typical protagonist, continues Fiedler, the protagonist seen as embodying the universal American dream, has been "a man on the run, harried into the forest and out to sea, down the river or into combat – anywhere to avoid 'civilization,' which is to say, the confrontation of a man and a woman which leads to the fall to sex, marriage, and responsibility."

Confronting such plots, the woman reader, like other readers, is powerfully impelled by the structure of the novel to identify with a hero who makes woman the enemy. In "The Legend of Sleepy Hollow," where Dame Van Winkle represents everything one might wish to escape and Rip the success of a fantasy, Fetterley argues that "what is essentially a simple act of identification when the reader of the story is male becomes a tangle of contradictions when the reader is female" (*The Resisting Reader*, p. 9). "In such fictions the female reader is co-opted into participation in an experience from which she is explicitly excluded; she is asked to identify with a selfhood that defines itself in opposition to her; she is required to identify against herself" (p. xii).

One should emphasize that Fetterley is not objecting to unflattering literary representations of women but to the way in which the dramatic structure of these stories induces women to participate in a vision of woman as the obstacle to freedom. Catherine in *A Farewell to Arms* is an appealing character, but her role is clear: her death prevents Frederic Henry from coming to feel the burdens she fears she imposes, while consolidating his investment in an idyllic love and in his vision of himself as a "victim of cosmic antagonism" (p. xvi). "If we weep at the end of the book," Fetterley concludes, "it is not for Catherine but for Frederic Henry. All our tears are ultimately for men, because in the world of *A Farewell to Arms* male life is what counts. And the message to women reading this classic love story and experiencing its image of the female ideal is clear and simple: the only good woman is a dead one, and even then there are questions" (p. 71). Whether or not the message is quite this simple, it is certainly true that the reader must adopt the perspective of Frederic Henry to enjoy the pathos of the ending.

Fetterley's account of the predicament of the woman reader – seduced and betrayed by devious male texts – is an attempt to change reading: "Feminist criticism is a political act whose aim is not simply to interpret the world but to change it by changing the consciousness of those who read and their relation to what they read" (p. viii). The first act of a feminist critic is "to become a resisting rather than an assenting reader and, by this refusal to assent, to begin the process of exorcizing the male mind that has been implanted in us" (p. xxii).

(1982)

Notes

7   Feminists criticism is, of course, concerned with other issues as well, particularly the distinctiveness of women's writing and the achievements of women writers. The problems of reading as a woman and of writing as a woman are in many respects similar, but concentration on the latter leads feminist criticism into areas that do not concern me here, such as the establishment of a criticism focused on women writers that parallels criticism focused on male writers. Gynocriticism, says, Showalter, who has been one of the principal advocates of this activity, is concerned "with woman as the producer of textual meaning, with the history, themes, genres, and structures of literature by women. Its subjects include the psychodynamics of female creativity; linguistics and the problem of a female language; the trajectory of the individual or collective female literary career; literary history; and, of course, studies of particular writers and works" ("Towards a Feminist Poetics," p. 25). For work of this kind, see Sandra Gilbert and Susan Gubar, *The Madwoman in the Attic*, and the collection edited by Sally McConnell-Ginet, Ruth Borker, and Nelly Furman, *Women and Language in Literature and Society* (New York: Praeger, 1980).

8   The analogy with social class is instructive: progressive political writing appeals to the proletariat's experience of oppression, but usually the problem for a political movement is precisely that the members of a class do not have the experience their situation would warrant. The most insidious oppression alienates a group from its own interests as a group and encourages it to identify with the interests of the oppressors, so that political struggles must first awaken a group to its interests and its "experience."

ROBERT SCHOLES

'Reading Like a Man'
Men in Feminism

Derrida is troubled by the same problems, which he addresses in a light and impromptu manner at the end of the conference from which I quoted him earlier. Here are three short passages from his final remarks:

> In other words if we consider for example what is called a writing man – for example me, to the extent that I'm supposed to be a man – then writing on woman should be less writing on woman than writing from or on the basis of (*depuis*) what comes to me from a feminine place.

Following Culler, we can rewrite this as a comment on reading:

> If we consider for example what is called a reading man – for example me, to the extent that I'm supposed to be a man – then reading as a woman should be less reading as a woman than reading from or on the basis of what comes to me from a feminine place.

Yes, possibly, but where is this "feminine place" and on what basis does a man have access to it? In deconstructive terms it is the trace of femininity that inevitably is inscribed in something defined as *not* feminine. But to reason in this way is to give the trace a positive status as a place or locus of the feminine. The "feminine place" here is perhaps not strictly deconstructive but Jungian. Still, one must wonder exactly what does come from this feminine place and how it might be recognized or authenticated as feminine. Derrida's awareness of the problem is suggested by his immediate restatement of it in terms of – of all things – voice.

> ... I too have learned from the *écoute* of women, from listening to the degree I can to a certain feminine voice.

Of special interest here is the qualification – "to the degree I can." What is it, we must ask, that sets limits to Derrida's ability to hear "a certain feminine voice"? Why does he need to suggest that he hears this voice less well than he hears other (presumably masculine) voices? What can it be other than his own membership in the class of males, with all that implies in the way of experience? At some level the concept of *experience*, which was earlier dismissed and replaced by the more docile and vulnerable concept of *essence*, is returning to trouble this text also.

Quite properly Derrida wants to complicate the question of gender, to deconstruct it,

> Because it's not such a simple thing when we say that whoever bears a masculine proper name, is anatomically male, etc., is a man. This feminine voice can pass through trajectories that are extremely multiple ... In other words, on the other side, and even in the most feminist women, the masculine voice is not silent. (p. 32).

After these words the text indicates "LAUGHTER." This laughter I read as symptomatic. Feminism and feminists have, however gently and gracefully, been put in their place – again. Whenever women speak up, it is the phallogocentric male voice speaking through them. And when they read actively and aggressively as members of the class, woman, are they then reading through male eyes as well? Or are they finally reading as women conscious of their own experience as members of a class who share that experience?

To put the problem another way, is there any difference between reading *as* a woman and reading *like* a woman? Can Mary actually read *as* a woman because she *is* a woman, or can she only read *like* a woman because no individual can ever be a woman? To put the question still another way, can John read *as* a woman or only *like* a woman? If neither John nor Mary can really read *as* a woman, and either one can read *like* a woman, then what's the difference between John and Mary? My own feeling is that until no one notices or cares about the difference we had better not pretend it isn't there. Above all, I think no man should seek in any way to diminish the authority which the experience of women gives them in speaking about that experience, and I believe that women should be very wary of critical systems that deny or diminish that authority.

Experience, of course, sets limits even as it confers authority. If some irreducible minimum of space or time separates us from our own experience, it is also true that this separation is never complete. We are subjects constructed by our experience and truly carry traces of that experience in our minds and on our bodies. Those of us who are male cannot deny this either. With the best will in the world we shall never read as women and perhaps not even like women. For me, born when I was born and living where I have lived, the very best I can do is to be conscious of the ground upon which I stand: to read not as but like a man.

(1987)

Gayatri Chakravorty Spivak

'How to Read a "Culturally Different" Book'
Colonial Discourse/Postcolonial Theory

Although (or perhaps precisely because) the dancer is not central to the novel, a feminist reader or teacher in the USA might wish to know a little more about the temple dancer in order to grasp the representation of Rosie/Nalini.

The source book most readily available to her is Frédérique Marglin's *Wives of the god-king* (1985).[12] Although for most metropolitan teachers of Commonwealth literature, the terrain of *The guide* exists as 'India', the reader might have specified it to herself as southern India from internal and external signals.[13] The state where Marglin did her field-work is not Narayan's south, but Orissa, where the south-east meets the northeast. How does the Orissan *devadāsi* (or *dei*), imprisoned in her own temple-community of women in a gender-hierarchy that mixes 'tradition' and 'modernity' in its unique blend, communicate with her counterpart in the south, in Mysore or Bangalore? Certainly not in their mother-tongue. In fact, it is unrealistic to think that there *can* be actual situations of communication between them. These are subaltern women, unorganised pre-capitalist labour, and it is not yet possible to think of them as *Indian* collectivities of resistance, although the Indian constitution appropriately thinks of them collectively as victims and thus offers a redress that has never been fully implemented in the individual states. Indeed, current feminist activism around this issue, dependent upon the direction and organisation of the women's movement in various regions, is much more forceful and visible in the states of Maharashtra, Karnataka and Tamil Nadu (roughly Narayan's area) than in Orissa, Marglin's field of work. The language barriers that allow the Indo-Anglian writer precisely to represent one of them as our implausible Rosie keeps her locked in isolated communities. The patriarchal system that informs *The guide* so that Raju can finally occupy the temple as saint makes the temple her prison.

(There are a very few rags-to-riches stories of the daughters of temple dancers becoming great *artistes*, but Narayan's focus on Rosie is too slight for us to feel that this is the point of her representation. To emphasise that point, Rosie's entry into secondary and post-secondary education would have had to be dramatised.)

Is literature obliged to be historically or politically correct? Because it is not, this sort of literary criticism is a category mistake, derided as 'politically correct'. But it should be considered that literature is not obliged to be formally excellent to entertain, either. Critical evaluation is dismissed as 'pedantic' by the real consumers of popular culture. Here again is class-negotiation. This way of reading, pointing at its cultural-political provenance, can be useful in the specific situation where the heterogeneous agency of the colonised in post-coloniality cannot be imagined, although the details of colonial history are known professionally.

As the feminist reader moves into *Wives of the god-king*, she notices a peculiar blandness in the reporting of the *devadāsī*'s prostitution. This curious apologetic finessing of judgement, invariably called cultural relativism, has become an unavoidable mark of the field-investigator who has become sensitive to the risks of neocolonial knowledge, but will compromise with it. This is perhaps exacerbated by the investigator who learns the social practice as artistic performance (in this case *Odissi* dance), now the property of the middle and upper middle classes.[14]

The transmogrification of female dance from male-dependent prostitution to emancipated performance helps the indigenous colonial elite to engage in a species of 'historical (hysterical) retrospection' which produces a golden age (Baudrillard 1983b, p. 16). Raju in *The guide* enters the hallucination without any particular historical thickening.

Dr Marglin's traffic with a great many Indian men, acknowledged in her book, is coded as exchange with a student of the *devadāsī*-system or a student of *Odissi*, eager cultural self-representation in response to altogether laudable white interest in our heritage; rather different from the traffic between men and women described in her chilling prose. It would be impossible to suspect from this account that feminists have internationally battled and are today battling (not the least in India) against this view of the role of the woman in reproduction:

The chastity of the wives of the temple brahmins is crucial not because it is they who transmit the characteristics of the caste and the *kula* to their children, but to ensure that only the produce of that species of seed that has been sown in it is the one that will be reaped and not the produce of some other species of seed. A woman, like a field, must be well guarded, for one wants to reap what one has sown and not what another has sown, since the produce of a field belongs to its owner. Such an idea was expressed long ago by Manu.... This theory by the ancient law-giver certainly corresponds well to what is the case today in Puri.... Women are like the earth, and the earth is one, although it is owned by many different types of men ... the woman palace servant (*dei*) told me that her mother answered her query [about menstruation rituals] ... in the following way: ... 'God has taken shelter' (in you).... 'You have married and you'll do the work of the god...'. The 'work of god' and 'the shelter of the god' she said referred to the fact that from that time on she would start her rituals in the palace and would become the concubine of the king. (1985, pp. 67, 73)

Wives of the god-king is a thoroughly vetted and rather well known book. It is hard to imagine that it was published in 1985! The author takes at face value the invocation of the golden age by Orientalist and bourgeois alike. The usual anti-Muslim explanation of the decay of Indian (read Hindu Aryan) culture under the Muslim rule, and hence the deterioration of the *devadāsis* into prostitutes, draws this from the author:

This view is representative of many if not most English-educated Indians today. The historical research necessary to confirm or refute the above statement was beyond my abilities, even if the records were available, which is highly doubtful. My training has prepared me to do ethnography, which happily the particular historical circumstances of Puri made possible. (p. 11)

'Ancient sources' are so regularly proclaimed that our inquisitive feminist literary critic will probably be daunted away; especially since there are repetitions of post-colonial piety and the claim that if Dr Marglin had been born a hundred years ago, her views would have coincided with those of Annie Besant, the noted Theosophist. Would the feminist investigator check this claim by consulting Mrs Besant's biography? Amrit Srinivasan has given a fine analysis of the relationship between the Theosophist interest in saving the dance rather than the dancer and the establishment of western-style residential schools for dance, like *Kalākshetra* (lit. the artistic field) in Madras by the indigenous elite.[15]

There seems nothing to link the women in Marglin with the world of *The guide* except to imagine that the daughters of one of these hapless women had been able to enter the educational system with nothing but her mother's good wishes as her resource.

And if the Indian colleague or friend who is the US feminist's 'native informant' happens to be a not untypical woman from the emancipated bourgeoisie, the work of her own uneven emancipation will have been undertaken by the slow acculturation of imperialism that is, in its neo-colonial displacement, the topic of our discussion. If this imaginary inform-ant happens to be a careful student of the dance form, she has learned the entire social ritual *as* ritual reverently museumised in an otherwise 'modern' existence. She might see the dance as directly expressive of female resistance in its very choreography. The result of this innocent ethnic validation is Cultural Studies as alibi.

Vigilance, then, about class as we read the novel and look for background. Impatient non-major students of required English courses often mutter, Can we not just read for pleasure? Their teachers were taught to offer a consola-tion from US New Criticism, Knowing the rules of the game does not detract from pleasure. But reading in the style of Cultural Studies, looking into the class provenance of form and information, may not enhance pleasure. The most it can do is to give a clue to the roadblocks to a too-quick enthusiasm for the other, in the aftermath of colonialism, even as it attempts to offer untrained resistance to the arrogance of the discipline.

(1994)

Notes

12 This book has been criticised by Indian scholars, but the politics of that criti-cism is itself a text for interpretation.

13 Narayan would like this not to be so (1989b, p. 32), and the Malgudi novels might have some unspecified regional specificity. *The guide* does not carry spe-cific regional signals.

14 Making dancing acceptable as a fully-fledged career, inserting *Odissi* into the classical repertoire, has its own 'feminist' histories, in quite a different space from subalternity. My conversations with Sanjukta Panigrahi, an *Odissi* dancer of my own generation and class, brought this home to me yet once again. This history must not be allowed to take first place. And the role of the quiet proto-feminist mothers of this generation who, working with immense innovativeness behind the scenes, made their daughters' career-freedom possible must not be obliterated in the accounts of the daughters' struggles.

15 See Srinivasan (1988). One wonders how seriously one should examine Marglin's claim of solidarity with Mrs Besant. Annie Besant (1847–1933) was a brilliant woman of extraordinary enthusiasms and unremitting activism: for Christianity, atheist secularism, socialism and Theosophy/India. It is well-known that her aim for India was 'Self-Government within the Empire' (in Kumar 1981, p. 139). Indeed, her Thesophist millenarianism 'was to bring about a universal, theocratic state under whose firm, wise rule men could not

but behave as brothers' (Taylor 1992, p. 277). As Taylor comments further, her 'historical account of India's spiritual past [was] heavily biased towards Hinduism.... Indians as well as Europeans blamed her for inciting race hatred and caste hatred.... "A democratic socialism controlled by majority votes, guided by numbers, can never succeed," she wrote as early as 1908; "a truly aristocratic socialism, controlled by duty, guided by wisdom is the next step upward in civilisation"' (pp. 311, 327, 313). Her attitude towards Indian women was consonant with her conviction that 'knowledge of British ways and political methods [would lead] to India's strengthening' (Kumar 1981, p. 102), and with her 'approval [of] a proletariat in the condition of a child, ready to be governed, ready to admit the superiority of its elders' (Taylor 1992, p. 313). I recommend a browse through a document like Besant's *Wake up, India* (1913) for a sense of her attitude to Indian women's education. It is no underestimation of her commitment, but a recognition of her historical inscription, to acknowledge that 'Victorian and Edwardian feminists collaborated in the ideological work of empire, reproducing the moral discourse of imperialism and embedding feminist ideology within it' (Burton 1990, p. 295). If Marglin's throwaway claim had been serious, her own invocation of a century's difference between herself and Besant would have led to considerations of the relationship between imperialism and neocolonialism, liberal humanism and cultural relativism. Who decolonises? And how?

KATE FLINT

The Woman Reader, 1837–1914

However, the volume of commentary on women's reading increased dramatically during the eighteenth century and the early years of the nineteenth. It can be found within general studies of literature, especially those examining the rapid growth of novel production; within the growing number of advice manuals aimed specifically at young girls and their mothers, and within fiction itself.[14] As in the earlier period, the anxieties expressed fall into easily identifiable categories. In particular, one encounters the familiar fear that young women will be corrupted by what they read, and, becoming preoccupied with the importance of romance, will seek perpetually for excitement; and the criticism that reading fiction, especially when carried to excess, wastes time which may more valuably be employed elsewhere. In the later years of the eighteenth century a new apprehension appears: that reading may teach politically seditious attitudes, especially, but not exclusively, challenging the role of the family and the position of woman in relation to authority. Mrs Mowbray, for example, in the conservative novelist Amelia Opie's *Adeline Mowbray* (1804), reads Locke's *The Conduct of the Understanding* as a child and then oversteps her filial place by recommending it to her parents as a text which will teach them how to 'think'. Her daughter, Adeline, finds that the reading to which she has been introduced by her mother encourages her to believe that marriage is something consecrated merely by mutual 'honour', without the need for civil ceremony. Inevitably, this leads to disaster.

In the final pages of her *Vindication of the Rights of Women*, Mary Wollstonecraft criticizes sentimental fiction for encouraging 'a romantic twist of the mind', a false view of human nature, and for teaching women to articulate 'the language of passion in affected tones', placing more reliance on their sensations than on their reason. The best way to correct a fondness for novels, she believes, 'is to ridicule them'.[15] This, of course, had already been done during the eighteenth century, and an examination of this ridicule is as revelatory of the growing variety of stereotypes, anxieties, and prescriptions concerning women and reading as is the range of more conspicuously serious material which is to be found in the rapidly growing advice literature and periodical reviews of the time.[16] Taken together, all these genres demonstrate the mid-eighteenth-century consolidation of the grounds on which Victorian attitudes to women's reading were to be based.

Charlotte Lennox anticipated Wollstonecraft's request for ridicule in *The Female Quixote* (1752), satirizing the influence of the heroic romance tradition, and concluding with the moralizing dialogue of the doctor on the dreadful effects such reading may have: 'The immediate tendency of these books ... is to give new fire to the passions of revenge and love: two passions which, even without such powerful auxiliaries, it is one of the severest labours of reason and piety to suppress.'[17] The theme of the mental stultification and blunted judgement which is induced by reading fiction was a recurrent one in the second half of the century. It was not necessarily central to a narrative, but used as a pointer to the interpretation of character. In Eliza Hamilton's *Letters of a Hindoo Rajah* (1796), for example, we find not only the deplorable example of the niece of the Dewan who had become addicted to novels, which 'by giving constant fuel to the vivid flame of youthful imagination, created such an insatiable craving for novelty, as rendered every other sort of reading, tasteless and insipid', but the fate of another susceptible novel-reader, Julia, who:

> has, it seems, suffered much from the unexpected metamorphosis of a charming swain; who, soon after he had introduced himself to her acquaintance, as a hero of exalted sentiment and tender sensibility, was unfortunately recognized by certain sagacious men, from a place called Bow-street, to be one of the tribe of Swindlers...[18]

A specific target is offered, famously, when the Radcliffean Gothic is mocked in *Northanger Abbey* and Henry Tilney, as part of his debunking, shows up to Catherine 'the liberty which her imagination had dared to take'.[19] If Austen is double-edged in her mockery here (for Catherine has plenty of justification for being apprehensive of her actual, rather than her imaginary, situation, given the undramatic but humanly damaging bigotry and selfishness that it contains), she returns with another twist in *Sanditon*. Here, she shows that it would be misguided to presume that only women might be affected adversely by what they read. The fanciful plot of seduction which Sir Edward develops, Austen indicates, was partly attributable to particular aspects of his indolent lifestyle:

> The truth was that Sir Edw: whom circumstances had confined very much to one spot had read more sentimental Novels than agreed with him. His fancy had been early caught by all the impassioned, & most exceptionable parts of Richardsons; & such Authors as have since appeared to tread in Richardson's steps, so far as Man's determined pursuit of Woman in defiance of every opposition of feeling & convenience is concerned, had since occupied the greater part of his literary hours, & formed his Character.[20]

The trope of satirizing human (and usually women's) gullibility when it comes to confusing the fictional world with the real is, of course, dependent for its didacticism on a further fiction: that the worlds which Arabella, Catherine, and others inhabit are, in their turn, 'real'. They are presented by the novel with a serious aim in view, such as warning the heroine/reader of the folly of eloping, or of not distinguishing carefully enough between love and passion.

(1993)

Notes

14 See Theodor Wolpers (ed.), *Gelebte Literatur in der Literatur: Studien zu Erscheinungsformen und Geschichte eines literarischen Motivs*, Abhandlungen der Akademie der Wissenschaft in Göttingen, Philologisch-Historische Klasse, Folge 3, Nr.152 (Göttingen, 1986).

15 Mary Wollstonecraft, *Vindication of the Rights of Women* (1792; repr. Harmondsworth, 1975), 305–9.

16 For full discussions on attitudes to reading, esp. women and reading, in the eighteenth century, see Peter de Bolla, *The Discourse of the Sublime: History, Aesthetics and the Subject* (Oxford, 1989), ch. 10; W. F. Gallaway, Jr., 'The Conservative Attitude Toward Fiction, 1770–1830', *PMLA* 55 (1940), 1041–59; Winfield H. Rogers, 'The Reaction against Melodramatic Sentimentality in the English Novel, 1796–1830', *PMLA* 49 (1934), 98–122; Kathryn Shevelow, *Women and Print Culture: The Construction of Femininity in the Early*

Periodical (1989); John Tinnon Taylor, *Early Opposition to the English Novel: The Popular Reaction from 1760 to 1830* (New York, 1943); Ioan Williams (ed.), *Novel and Romance 1700–1800: A Documentary Record* (1970). Eighteenth-century advice literature, and its relation to the education of girls, is discussed by Mitzi Myers, ' "A Taste for Truth and Reading": Early Advice to Mothers on Books for Girls', *Children's Literature Association Quarterly*, 12 (1987), 118–24.

17 Charlotte Lennox, *The Female Quixote* (1752; repr. Pandora: Mothers of the Novel, 1986), 420.

18 Eliza Hamilton, *Translation of the Letters of a Hindoo Rajah*, 2 vols. (1796), ii. 38, 337.

19 Jane Austen, *Northanger Abbey* (1818); repr. *The Works of Jane Austen*, ed. R. W. Chapman, vol. V., (1969), 199.

20 *Sanditon* (written 1817); *Works*, vi. (1972), 404.

JAN FERGUS

Provincial Readers in Eighteenth-Century England

Certainly, the Clay and Stevens records indicate that, overwhelmingly, men paid to buy and borrow fiction. Table 1.1.1 indicates that altogether, women bought 47 novels from the Clays and borrowed 67; adult men bought 184 and borrowed 153. The Stevens results are even more lopsided and undoubtedly underrepresent women's reading: women bought 17 novels and borrowed 12, men bought 231, borrowed 84. Schoolboys' recorded interest in novels far outstripped recorded women's, with a total of 105 purchases and 197 withdrawals. Table 1.1.2 tabulates customers and demonstrates that, even if we look at numbers of customers instead of numbers of purchases or borrowings, men still outnumber women (though less remarkably). Clay customers for novels include 7 all-male book clubs, 62 women, 127 adult men, and 110 schoolboys. Among adults, 41 women and 49 men borrowed novels, the closest that women come to matching men's consumption of fiction within the records. Stevens's customers for novels amount to ninety-three men and fifteen women altogether, plus three book clubs and the twenty-four women and fifty-seven men who were charged for reading in the circulating library, often at four shillings for three months. Thus, 77 provincial women bought and borrowed novels from the Clays and Stevens, compared to 220 adult men, or just under 26 per cent. Although women accounted, then, for a quarter of the adult customer base for fiction in these Midland areas, they accumulated just 13 per cent of the total transactions for novels (143 of 1,097).

Even at best provincial women never actually reach parity with men as customers for novels, but they come closest as borrowers. In the Stevens records, women make up about 30 per cent of subscribers to the circulating library for periods of a month or so to a year (twenty-four of eighty-one), a much better showing than they make as buyers: no withdrawals are indicated, however, just subscription costs. In the Clay records, again, women most nearly equal men as borrowers of fiction. Their visibility here probably arises because the Clays meticulously noted borrowing, often indicating volume by volume who had what for how long. The Clays' most ambitious circulating library, at Warwick, was the only one to attract more women than men as customers: twenty in nineteen months, out of more than three hundred credit customers, compared to seventeen male borrowers. If the Clay records for adults at Daventry, Rugby, and Lutterworth are added to those of Warwick, women closely follow men overall as patrons of the library (Table 1.1.1). Nonetheless, even borrowing novels – the cheapest way to obtain fiction, at 3*d.* a volume in Daventry, Rugby, and Lutterworth, as well as later in Cirencester, 2*d.* in Warwick, and the best way to leave a record in day books – does not reveal a predominantly female audience for fiction in the Midlands.

Although women did not dominate the provincial market for novels, those that did buy or borrow fiction did so in greater proportions than men. That is, a woman entering the Clay or Stevens shops was more likely than a man to take away a novel, even though she seems much less likely to have entered the shop at all. Figures in Table 1.1.2 make clear that while 20.5 per cent of the Clays' female customers for print consumed novels (62 of 302), just 7.3 per cent of adult men did so (127 of 1,750). Similarly, 22 per cent of Stevens's female customers for printed matter can be shown to have bought or borrowed novels (15 of 69) compared with 18 per cent of his male clientele (93 of 519). Women who patronized the Clays' shops in Daventry, Rugby, and Lutterworth were just as likely as men to subscribe to a magazine but were nearly three times as likely to withdraw or purchase a novel – though subscribing was much more common to both sexes than was consuming novels.

I have been implying here and elsewhere that buying and borrowing entail reading, but no such easy equation is possible, as we all know. Furthermore, the question of novels' circulation among buyers and borrowers is complex. Many people could read a purchased book, and considerable evidence exists in letters and elsewhere indicating that in the eighteenth century books of all kinds were read aloud and lent about among friends.[9] These could include borrowed books, though it is likely that such lending would occur within a small compass, probably within the borrower's household. Such books may have been read aloud to the whole family when time permitted, although to do so without declaring multiple readings (as discussed later in this chapter) was not strictly fair. In the small communities that Stevens and the Clays served, however, customers may have been rather scrupulous, like the

Table 1.1. Novels bought and borrowed; customers for all novels and for novels by women

1.1.1 Total numbers of novels bought and borrowed (novels written by women in parentheses):

Novels	Women	Men	Total
Clay records*, adults:			
Bought	47 (13)	184 (26)	231 (39)
Borrowed	67 (18)	153 (41)	220 (59)
Stevens records, adults:			
Bought	17 (4)	231 (54)	248 (58)
Borrowed	12 (7)	84 (38)	96 (45)
schoolboys:	Daventry	Rugby	Total
Bought	30 (6)	75 (14)	105 (20)
Borrowed	84 (9)	113 (33)	197 (42)
Novels obtained, all customers:			
	Women	Men and Boys	Total
Bought	64 (17)	520 (100)	584 (117)
Borrowed	79 (25)	434 (121)	513 (146)
Totals	143 (42)	954 (221)	1097 (263)

1.1.2. Total numbers of individual customers who buy and borrow novels:

	Clay				Stevens		All		
	women	men	Schoolboys		women	men	women	men*	
Customers			Daventry	Rugby					TOTAL
Buy novels	27	87	18	40	8	75	35	220	255
Borrow novels	41	49	24	51	9	37	50	161	211
Buy and borrow	6	9	10	13	2	19	8	51	59
Total customers for novels	62	127	32	78	15†	93†	77	330	407
Total Customers for print	302	1,750	79	611	69	519	371	2,959	3,330

*Clay sales and customers for Daventry, Rugby, Lutterworth, and Warwick included; book clubs' purchases appear under those for men and include 54 for Clay customers, 49 Stevens; but clubs are not counted among numbers of male customers. Warwick adult customers for publications come to 145 men and 45 women; no book clubs or schoolboys. Warwick customers for novels = 20 female borrowers, 2 female buyers (both also borrowed); 17 male borrowers, 3 male buyers, none who did both.

† In addition, 24 women and 57 men patronized Stevens' circulating library; withdrawals unknown.

Rudings who paid separately for borrowing *The Generous Inconstant* in October 1771. And certain neighbours shared borrowed books but paid separately for them: Mr Hindes of Priors Hardwick and Peter La Roque, the clergyman there, borrowed two volumes of Laurence Sterne's *Tristram Shandy* from John Clay shortly after they were published – and later did the same with Smollett's *Humphry Clinker*.

(2006)

Note

9   Patricia Howell Michaelson has compellingly analysed accounts of oral reading of novels in the eighteenth century in *Speaking Volumes: Women, Reading, and Speech in the Age of Austen* (Stanford: Stanford University Press, 2002).

JENNY HARTLEY

Reading Groups
A Survey Conducted in Association with Sarah Turvey

We asked groups if they read more books by men or by women, and if the sex of the author was an important factor. A small band of all-female groups has chosen to read only female authors, and a gay group we heard from picks books by men with a gay interest – though they admit to wearying recently of 'yet another depressing novel about AIDS'. Many all-women groups think that the gender of the author influences their choice, sometimes away from male authors:

–   *We avoid books for men by men.*
–   *More by women. We are aware of this and are actively looking for male authors with appeal – it's hard.*
–   *Mostly women – it is an issue apparently – we prefer women and make ourselves read men.*

Do men and women read differently? We compared male and female groups by gender of author, and found that more women read books by men than men read books by women. But not a great deal more: 53 per cent of the books all-female groups read are by men, whereas 36 per cent of the books male groups read are by women, i.e. about a third of the books men read are by women, and women read about half and half. This was a more even spread than we expected, especially given the conclusions drawn from a survey carried out in March 2000 for the Orange Prize for Fiction by Book Marketing Ltd. This research analysed the reactions of 200 respondents to the cover designs and titles of twenty books (not their contents), and claimed that 'women fail to seduce male readers': 'While 40 per cent of women surveyed said they would read books they believed appealed mainly to men, only 25 per cent of men said they would consider a book they felt was for women.' But do these figures, which are not dissimilar from ours, prove that 'Men are far more biased towards books written by men than women are to books written by women'? A bit more biased perhaps – but research on judging a book by its cover may be of more use to cover designers than anyone else. Interestingly, the overwhelming majority of groups in our survey agree either that the sex is not important, or that they like to strike a balance.

- *Equal – not that it's not important; make a conscious effort.*
- *Sex not important except appreciating our male member may not wish to read books aimed at women and which tend to be by women.*
- *Sex not important – ideas are.*

Men are generally thought to read less fiction than women, and the all-male groups in our survey – we only had a small number in this category – do pick slightly more non-fiction, biography in particular. Though not uncritically: Michael Heseltine in Michael Crick's version was succinctly dismissed by one group as 'a boring opportunist'. Another all-male group mentions going for 'lots of Roth'. And while women are choosing male authors, they aren't always enjoying them. Some of the lads get the thumbs down:

- Fever Pitch – *what a moaner, oh for heaven's sake grow up we all said – except for one male and one young girl.*
- High Fidelity – *over-hyped, and one-joke book which no one liked.*
- *Martin Amis's* Money – *vulgar and distasteful.*
- *Kingsley Amis – curmudgeonly.*

Mixed groups notice gender divisions:

- Snow Falling on Cedars *was generally preferred by the men in the group.*
- *We have two male members: this stops us making too many sweeping generalizations about men. In reading* Larry's Party *where there is a male protagonist it was very useful to have two male viewpoints. One man was the same age as Larry and so identified with the eras he lived through. As a woman I felt surely men are more insightful than Larry and was prepared to criticize Carol Shields for this portrayal until one of the male group members said he thought men were generally less insightful! An enlightening but depressing moment.*

(2001)

LUCE IRIGARAY

'The Powers of Discourse and the
Subordination of the Feminine'
This Sex Which Is Not One

But as we have already seen, even with the help of linguistics, psychoanalysis cannot solve the problem of the articulation of the female sex in discourse. Even though Freud's theory, through an effect of dress-rehearsal – at least as far as the relation between the sexes is concerned – shows clearly the function of the feminine in that scene. *What remains to be done, then, is to work at 'destroying' the discursive mechanism.* Which is not a simple undertaking.... For how can we introduce ourselves into such a tightly-woven systematicity?

There is, in an initial phase, perhaps only one 'path', the one historically assigned to the feminine: that of *mimicry*. One must assume the feminine role deliberately. Which means already to convert a form of subordination into an affirmation, and thus to begin to thwart it. Whereas a direct feminine challenge to this condition means demanding to speak as a (masculine), 'subject', that is, it means to postulate a relation to the intelligible that would maintain sexual indifference.

To play with mimesis is thus, for a woman, to try to recover the place of her exploitation by discourse, without allowing herself to be simply reduced to it. It means to resubmit herself – inasmuch as she is on the side of the 'perceptible', of 'matter' – to 'ideas', in particular to ideas about herself, that are elaborated in/by a masculine logic, but so as to make 'visible', by an effect of playful repetition, what was supposed to remain invisible: the cover-up of a possible operation of the feminine in language. It also means 'to unveil' the fact that, if women are such good mimics, it is because they are not simply resorbed in this function. *They also remain elsewhere*: another case of the persistence of 'matter', but also of 'sexual pleasure'.

Elsewhere of 'matter': if women can play with mimesis, it is because they are capable of bringing new nourishment to its operation. Because they have always nourished this operation? Is not the 'first' stake in mimesis that of re-producing (from) nature? Of giving it form in order to appropriate it for oneself? As guardians of 'nature', are not women the ones who maintain, thus who make possible, the resource of mimesis of men? For the logos?

It is here, of course, that the hypothesis of a reversal – within the phallic order – is always possible. Re-semblance cannot do without red blood. Mother-matter-nature must go on forever nourishing speculation. But this re-source is also rejected as the waste product of reflection, cast outside as what resists it: as madness. Besides the ambivalence that the nourishing phallic mother attracts to herself, this function leaves woman's sexual pleasure aside.

That *'elsewhere'* *of female pleasure* might rather be sought first in the place where it sustains ek-stasy in the transcendental. The place where it serves as security for a narcissism extrapolated into the 'God' of men. It can play this role only at the price of its ultimate withdrawal from prospection, of its 'virginity' unsuited for the representation of self. Feminine pleasure has to remain inarticulate in language, in its own language, if it is not to threaten the underpinnings of logical operations. And so what is most strictly forbidden to women today is that they should attempt to express their own pleasure.

That 'elsewhere' of feminine pleasure can be found only at the price of *crossing back through the mirror that subtends all speculation.* For this pleasure is not simply situated in a process of reflection or mimesis, nor on one side of this process or the other: neither on the near side, the empirical realm that is opaque to all language, nor on the far side, the self-sufficient infinite of the God of men. Instead, it refers all these categories and ruptures back to the necessities of the self-representation of phallic desire in discourse. A playful crossing, and an unsettling one, which would allow woman to rediscover the place of her 'self-affection'. Of her 'god', we might say. A god to which one can obviously not have recourse – unless its *duality* is granted – without leading the feminine right back into the phallocratic economy.

Does this retraversal of discourse in order to rediscover a 'feminine'
place suppose a certain work on/of language?
It is surely not a matter of interpreting the operation of discourse while remaining within the same type of utterance as the one that guarantees discursive coherence. This is moreover the danger of every statement, every discussion, *about Speculum.* And, more generally speaking, of every discussion *about* the question of woman. For to speak *of* or *about* woman may always boil down to, or be understood as, a recuperation of the feminine within a logic that maintains it in repression, censorship, nonrecognition.

In other words, the issue is not one of elaborating a new theory of which woman would be the *subject* or the *object*, but of jamming the theoretical machinery itself, of suspending its pretension to the production of a truth and of a meaning that are excessively univocal. Which presupposes that women do not aspire simply to be men's equals in knowledge. That they do not claim to be rivalling men in constructing a logic of the feminine that would still take onto-theologic as its model, but that they are rather attempting to wrest this question away from the economy of the logos. They should not put it, then, in the form 'What is woman?' but rather, repeating/interpreting the way in which, within discourse, the feminine finds itself defined as lack, deficiency, or as imitation and negative image of the subject, they should signify that with respect to this logic a *disruptive excess* is possible on the feminine side.

An excess that exceeds common sense only on condition that the feminine not renounce its 'style'. Which, of course, is not a style at all, according to the traditional way of looking at things.

This 'style', or 'writing', of women tends to put the torch to fetish words, proper terms, well-constructed forms. This 'style' does not privilege sight; instead, it takes each figure back to its source, which is among other things *tactile*. It comes back in touch with itself in that origin without ever constituting in it, constituting itself in it, as some sort of unity. *Simultaneity* is its 'proper' aspect – a proper(ty) that is never fixed in the possible identity-to-self of some form or other. It is always *fluid*, without neglecting the characteristics of fluids that are difficult to idealize: those rubbings between two infinitely near neighbours that create a dynamics. Its 'style' resists and explodes every firmly established form, figure, idea or concept. Which does not mean that it lacks style, as we might be led to believe by a discursivity that cannot conceive of it. But its 'style' cannot be upheld as a thesis, cannot be the object of a position.

And even the motifs of 'self-touching', of 'proximity', isolated as such or reduced to utterances, could effectively pass for an attempt to appropriate the feminine to discourse. We would still have to ascertain whether 'touching oneself', that (self-) touching, the desire for the proximate rather than for (the) proper(ty), and so on, might not imply a mode of exchange irreducible to any *centring*, any *centrism*, given the way the 'self-touching' of female 'self-affection' comes into play as a rebounding from one to the other without any possibility of interruption, and given that, in this interplay, proximity confounds any adequation, any appropriation.

But of course if these were only 'motifs' without any work on and/or with language, the discursive economy could remain intact. How, then, are we to try to redefine this language work that would leave space for the feminine? Let us say that every dichotomizing – and at the same time redoubling – break, including the one between enunciation and statement (*énoncé*), has to be disrupted. Nothing is ever to be *posited* that is not also reversed and caught up again in the *supplementarity of this reversal*. To put it another way: there would no longer be either a right side or a wrong side of discourse, or even of texts, but each passing from one to the other would make audible and comprehensible even what resists the recto-verso structure that shores up common sense. If this is to be practised for every meaning posited – for every word, *énoncé*, sentence, but also of course for every phoneme, every letter – we need to proceed in such a way that linear reading is no longer possible: that is, the retroactive impact of the end of each word, *énoncé*, or sentence upon its beginning must be taken into consideration in order to undo the power of its teleological effect, including its deferred action. That would hold good also for the opposition between structures of horizontality and verticality that are at work in language.

What allows us to proceed in this way is that we interpret, at each 'moment', the *specular make-up* of discourse, that is, the self-reflecting (stratifiable) organization of the subject in that discourse. An organization that maintains, among other things, the break between what is perceptible and what is intelligible, and thus maintains the submission, subordination, and exploitation of the 'feminine'.

This language work would thus attempt to thwart any manipulation of discourse that would also leave discourse intact. Not, necessarily, in the *énoncé*, but in its *autological presuppositions*. Its function would thus be to *cast phallocentrism, phallocratism*, loose from its moorings in order to return the masculine to its own language, leaving open the possibility of a different language. Which means that the masculine would no longer be 'everything'. That it could no longer, all by itself, define, circumvene, circumscribe, the properties of any thing and everything. That the right to define every value – including the abusive privilege of appropriation – would no longer belong to it.

(1977)
Translated by Catherine Porter (with Carolyn Burke)

HÉLÈNE CIXOUS

'The Laugh of the Medusa'
New French Feminisms

I shall speak about women's writing: about *what it will do*. Woman must write her self: must write about women and bring women to writing, from which they have been driven away as violently as from their bodies – for the same reasons, by the same law, with the same fatal goal. Woman must put herself into the text – as into the world and into history – by her own movement.

The future must no longer be determined by the past. I do not deny that the effects of the past are still with us. But I refuse to strengthen them by repeating them, to confer upon them an irremovability the equivalent of destiny, to confuse the biological and the cultural. Anticipation is imperative.

Since these reflections are taking shape in an area just on the point of being discovered, they necessarily bear the mark of our time – a time during which the new breaks away from the old, and, more precisely, the (feminine) new from the old (*la nouvelle de l'ancien*). Thus, as there are no grounds for establishing a discourse, but rather an arid millennial ground to break, what I say has at least two sides and two aims: to break up, to destroy; and to foresee the unforeseeable, to project.

I write this as a woman, toward women. When I say 'woman,' I'm speaking of woman in her inevitable struggle against conventional man; and of a universal woman subject who must bring women to their senses and to their meaning in history. But first it must be said that in spite of the enormity of the repression that has kept them in the 'dark' – that dark which people have been trying to make them accept as their attribute – there is, at this time, no general woman, no one typical woman. What they have *in common* I will say. But what strikes me is the infinite richness of their individual constitutions: you can't talk about *a* female sexuality, uniform, homogeneous, classifiable into codes – any more than you can talk about one unconscious resembling another. Women's imaginary is inexhaustible, like music, painting, writing: their stream of phantasms is incredible.

I have been amazed more than once by a description a woman gave me of a world all her own which she had been secretly haunting since early childhood. A world of searching, the elaboration of a knowledge, on the basis of a systematic experimentation with the bodily functions, a passionate and precise interrogation of her erotogeneity. This practice, extraordinarily rich and inventive, in particular as concerns masturbation, is prolonged or accompanied by a production of forms, a veritable aesthetic activity, each stage of rapture inscribing a resonant vision, a composition, something beautiful. Beauty will no longer be forbidden.

I wished that that woman would write and proclaim this unique empire so that other women, other unacknowledged sovereigns, might exclaim: I, too, overflow; my desires have invented new desires, my body knows unheard-of songs. Time and again I, too, have felt so full of luminous torrents that I could burst – burst with forms much more beautiful than those which are put up in frames and sold for a stinking fortune. And I, too, said nothing, showed nothing; I didn't open my mouth, I didn't repaint my half of the world. I was ashamed. I was afraid, and I swallowed my shame and my fear. I said to myself: You are mad! What's the meaning of these waves, these floods, these outbursts? Where is the ebullient, infinite woman who, immersed as she was in her naiveté, kept in the dark about herself, led into self-disdain by the great arm of parental-conjugal phallocentrism, hasn't been ashamed of her strength? Who, surprised and horrified by the fantastic tumult of her drives (for she was made to believe that a well-adjusted normal woman has a ... divine composure), hasn't accused herself of being a monster? Who, feeling a funny desire stirring inside her (to sing, to write, to dare to speak, in short, to bring out something new), hasn't thought she was sick? Well, her shameful sickness is that she resists death, that she makes trouble.

And why don't you write? Write! Writing is for you, you are for you; your body is yours, take it. I know why you haven't written. (And why I didn't write before the age of twenty-seven.) Because writing is at once too high, too great for you, it's reserved for the great – that is for 'great men'; and it's 'silly.' Besides, you've written a little, but in secret. And it wasn't good, because it was in secret, and because you punished yourself for writing, because you didn't go all the way, or because you wrote, irresistibly, as when we would masturbate in secret, not to go further, but to attenuate the tension a bit, just enough to take the edge off. And then as soon as we come, we go and make ourselves feel guilty – so as to be forgiven; or to forget, to bury it until the next time.

Write, let no one hold you back, let nothing stop you: not man; not the imbecilic capitalist machinery, in which publishing houses are the crafty, obsequious relayers of imperatives handed down by an economy that works against us and off our backs; and not *yourself*. Smug-faced readers, managing editors, and big bosses don't like the true texts of women – female-sexed texts. That kind scares them.

I write woman: woman must write woman. And man, man. So only an oblique consideration will be found here of man; it's up to him to say where his masculinity and femininity are at: this will concern us once men have opened their eyes and seen themselves clearly.[1]

Now women return from afar, from always: from 'without,' from the heath where witches are kept alive; from below, from beyond 'culture'; from their childhood which men have been trying desperately to make them forget, condemning it to 'eternal rest.' The little girls and their 'ill-mannered' bodies immured, well-preserved, intact unto themselves, in the mirror. Frigidified. But are they ever seething underneath! What an effort it takes – there's no end to it – for the sex cops to bar their threatening return. Such a display of forces on both sides that the struggle has for centuries been immobilized in the trembling equilibrium of a deadlock.

(1976)
Translated by Keith Cohen and Paula Cohen

Note

1   Men still have everything to say about their sexuality, and everything to write. For what they have said so far, for the most part, stems from the opposition activity/passivity from the power relation between a fantasized obligatory virility meant to invade, to colonize, and the consequential phantasm of woman as a 'dark continent' to penetrate and to 'pacify.' (We know what 'pacify' means in terms of scotomizing the other and misrecognizing the self.) Conquering her, they've made haste to depart from her borders, to get out of sight, out of body. The way man has of getting out of himself and into her whom he takes not for the other but for his own, deprives him, he knows, of his own bodily territory. One can understand how man, confusing himself with his penis and rushing in for the attack, might feel resentment and fear of being 'taken' by the woman, of being lost in her, absorbed or alone.

HÉLÈNE CIXOUS

'Castration or Decapitation?'
Signs: Journal of Women in Culture and Society

But first she would have to *speak*, start speaking, stop saying that she has nothing to say! Stop learning in school that women are created to listen, to believe, to make no discoveries. Dare to speak her piece about giving, the possibility of a giving that doesn't take away, but *gives*. Speak of her pleasure and, God knows, she has something to say about that, so that she gets to unblock a sexuality that's just as much feminine as masculine, "de-phallocentralize" the body, relieve man of his phallus, return him to an erogenous field and a libido that isn't stupidly organized round that monument, but appears shifting, diffused, taking on all the others of oneself. Very difficult: first we have to get rid of the systems of censorship that bear down on every attempt to speak in the feminine. We have to get rid of and also explain what all knowledge brings with it as its burden of power: to show in what ways, culturally, knowledge is the accomplice of power: that whoever stands in the place of knowledge is always getting a dividend of power: show that all thinking until now has been ruled by this dividend, this surplus value of power that comes back to him who knows. Take the philosophers, take their position of mastery, and you'll see that there is not a soul who dares to make an advance in thought, into the as-yet-unthought, without shuddering at the idea that he is under the surveillance of the ancestors, the grandfathers, the tyrants of the concept, without thinking that there behind your back is always the famous Name-of-the-Father, who knows whether or not you're writing whatever it is you have to write without any spelling mistakes.

Now, I think that what women will have to do and what they will do, right from the moment they venture to speak what they have to say, will of necessity bring about a shift in metalanguage. And I think we're completely crushed, expecially in places like universities, by the highly repressive operations of metalanguage, the operations, that is, of the commentary on the commentary, the code, the operation that sees to it that the moment women open their mouths – women more often than men – they are immediately asked in whose name and from what theoretical standpoint they are speaking, who is their master and where they are coming from: they have, in short, to salute ... and show their identity papers. There's work to be done against *class*, against categorization, against classification – classes. "Doing classes" in France means doing military service. There's work to be done against military service, against all schools, against the pervasive masculine urge to judge, diagnose, digest, name ... not so much in the sense of the loving precision of poetic naming as in that of the repressive censorship of philosophical nomination/conceptualization.

Women who write have for the most part until now considered themselves to be writing not as women but as writers. Such women may declare
that sexual difference means nothing, that there's no attributable difference
between masculine and feminine writing.... What does it mean to "take no
position"? When someone says "I'm not political" we all know what that
means! It's just another way of saying: "My politics are someone else's!"
And it's exactly the case with writing! Most women are like this: they do
someone else's – man's – writing, and in their innocence sustain it and give
it voice, and end up producing writing that's in effect masculine. Great care
must be taken in working on feminine writing not to get trapped by names:
to be signed with a woman's name doesn't necessarily make a piece of writing feminine. It could quite well be masculine writing, and conversely, the
fact that a piece of writing is signed with a man's name does not in itself
exclude femininity. It's rare, but you can sometimes find femininity in writings signed by men: it does happen.

Which texts appear to be woman-texts and are recognized as such
today, what can this mean, how might they be read?[4] In my opinion, the
writing being done now that I see emerging around me won't only be of
the kinds that exist in print today, though they will always be with us, but
will be something else as well. In particular we ought to be prepared for
what I call the "affirmation of the difference," not a kind of wake about
the corpse of the mummified woman, nor a fantasy of woman's decapitation, but something different: a step forward, an adventure, an exploration of woman's powers: of her power, her potency, her ever-dreaded
strength, of the regions of femininity. Things are starting to be written,
things that will constitute a feminine Imaginary, the site, that is, of identifications of an ego no longer given over to an image defined by the
masculine ("like the woman I love, I mean a dead woman"), but rather
inventing forms for women on the march, or as I prefer to fantasize, "in
flight," so that instead of lying down, women will go forward by leaps in
search of themselves.

There is work to be done on female sexual pleasure and on the production
of an unconscious that would no longer be the classic unconscious. The
unconscious is always cultural and when it talks it tells you your old stories,
it tells you the old stories you've heard before because it consists of the
repressed of culture. But it's also always shaped by the forceful return of a
libido that doesn't give up that easily, and also by what is strange, what is
outside culture, by a language which is a savage tongue that can make itself
understood quite well. This is why, I think, *political* and not just literary
work is started as soon as writing gets done by women that goes beyond the
bounds of censorship, reading, the gaze, the masculine command, in that
cheeky risk taking women can get into when they set out into the unknown
to look for themselves.

This is how I would define a feminine textual body: as a *female libidinal economy*, a regime, energies, a system of spending not necessarily carved out by culture. A feminine textual body is recognized by the fact that it is always endless, without ending: there's no closure, it doesn't stop, and it's this that very often makes the feminine text difficult to read. For we've learned to read books that basically pose the word "end." But this one doesn't finish, a feminine text goes on and on and at a certain moment the volume comes to an end but the writing continues and for the reader this means being thrust into the void. These are texts that work on the beginning but not on the origin. The origin is a masculine myth: I always want to know where I come from. The question "Where do children come from?" is basically a masculine, much more than a feminine, question. The quest for origins, illustrated by Oedipus, doesn't haunt a feminine unconscious. Rather it's the beginning, or beginnings, the manner of beginning, not promptly with the phallus in order to close with the phallus, but starting on all sides at once, that makes a feminine writing. A feminine text starts on all sides at once, starts twenty times, thirty times, over.

(1981)
Translated by Annette Kuhn

Note

4   There follows in the original a passage in which several categories of women's writing existing at the time (1975) are listed and discussed. These include: " 'the little girl's story,' where the little girl is getting even for a bad childhood," "texts of a return to a woman's own body," and texts which were a critical success, "ones about madwomen, deranged, sick women." The passage is omitted here, at the author's request, on the grounds that such a categorization is outdated, and that the situation with regard to women's writing is very much different now than it was five or six years ago (translator's note).

Domna C. Stanton

'Language and Revolution:
The Franco–American Dis-connection'
The Future of Difference

No less disturbing is the facile rejection of *écriture féminine* as too intellectual and elitist to be feminist. Admittedly, our understanding of Cixous, Kristeva, Irigaray, and others requires knowledge of philosophy, linguistics, and psychoanalytic theory. Even more, one must be willing to decipher dense texts replete with plays on words and devoid of normal syntactical constructions. Through their very mode of writing, however, these texts are striving to practice what they preach by subverting the syntax, the semantics, and even the Cartesian logic of the Logos. As Kristeva has written, '... playful language ergo disrupted law, violated, pluralized, maintained solely to allow a poly-valent, poly-logic game which leads to a conflagration of the essence of the Law....'[35] We American feminists tend to consider such wordplay virtuosic and exhibitionistic. We ignore the paradoxical disjunction between *what* we say and *how* we say it, and thus we continue to speak *about* subverting the patriarchal order in pellucid rationalistic discourse. Indeed, the charge of intellectualism and elitism directed at *écriture féminine* is connected to a serious lack of awareness about the nature of our own critical practice that verges on bad faith. Viewed within their specific contexts, Anglo-American feminist empiricism is certainly not any less intellectual than *écriture féminine*. The opposite could in fact be argued: for *écriture féminine* not only combines theory with a subjectivism that confounds the protocols of scholarly discourse, it also strives to break the phallologic boundaries between critical analysis, essay, fiction, and poetry. Moreover, those who maintain that *écriture féminine* is not feminist because it appropriates concepts from such 'seminal' thinkers as Saussure, Freud, Lacan, and Derrida choose to forget that it was not feminists but Anglo-American patriarchs who founded, and trained us in, the biographical, thematic, stylistic, sociohistorical, or Marxist literary criticism that we unquestioningly practice. Instead of blinding ourselves to the academic origins and present boundaries of our critical discourse, we should acknowledge that, when compared to the work of other women in our society, feminist scholarship is fundamentally both intellectual and privileged. That admission, however, should not be the cause for futile self-flagellation. Nor should it compound the existing, nefarious tendency to assign intellectuality, the capacity for abstraction and speculation, and the use of rigorous modes of analysis to the male, and intuitiveness, sensibility, and emotionality to the female – a type of thinking which validates traditional stereotypes, reinforces the tyranny of the binary, and thus strengthens the phallologocentric order. Rather, we should celebrate our own and all women's heterogeneous contributions to the demolition of the old and the building of a new order of thought and being.

This is not to suggest, however, that the presuppositions and goals of *écriture féminine* should be espoused without serious examination. American and French women should interrogate the premise that the global subversion of the Logos can be achieved through language, and we should question the proposition that there *can* exist a locus outside of the symbolic order from which woman might speak her difference. In *Les Guérillères* (1969), for example, Monique Wittig endorsed the notion that there is no reality outside the symbolic.[36] But whereas in that epic work she argued 'that in the first place the vocabulary of every language is to be examined, modified, turned upside down, that every word must be screened,'[37] in her recent paper 'The Straight Mind,' Wittig insists that emphasis on language has made French women writers lose sight of material reality[38] – a view which many American feminists might echo. We should also point out that French theorizing on the subversion of the Logos has tended to replace, and not merely to supplement, the kind of political activism which Americans consider crucial to their self-definition as feminists. Last, and as some recent French texts seem to confirm, a dis-connection with the *real* can lead to a regressive mystification of the 'feminine' and may yield nothing more than a new 'lingo,' a code doomed to repetition and extinction.[39]

(1980)

Notes

35   Kristeva, 'Un Nouveau type d'intellectuel: Le Dissident,' *Tel Quel* 74 ['Recherches féminines'] (Winter 1977): 5. '... Language enjouée donc loi bouleversée, violée, pluralisée, maintenue uniquement pour permettre un jeu polyvalent, poly-logique, qui conduit à l'embrasement de l'être de la loi....'
36   Monique Wittig, *Les Guérillères* (New York: Avon Books, 1973), trans. David Le Lay, p. 134.
37   Ibid.
38   See 'The Straight Mind,' *Questions féministes* 7 (December 1979); and *Feminist Issues* 1, 1 (Summer 1980).
39   In my view, this danger is immanent in the recurring identification of the female in *écriture féminine* with madness, antireason, primitive darkness, mystery, self-diffusion, and self-irridation, traits which represents a revalorization of tradi-tional 'feminine' stereotypes. I discuss this problem briefly in 'Parole et écriture: Women's Studies, USA,' *Tel Quel* 71–3 (Autumn 1977): 126. Françoise Colin, an editor of *Les Cahiers du GRIF*, has noted the danger signals of a new female 'lingo' and stressed the need for multiplicity and heterogeneity in 'polyglo(u) ssons' in *Les Cahiers du GRIF* 12 ['Parlez-vous francaise?: femmes et langages I'] (June 1976): 3–9.

CLAIRE GOLDBERG MOSES

'Made in America: "French Feminism" in Academia'
Feminist Studies

In my determination to trace the construction of a "made-in-America French feminism," I turned first to the earliest presentations of French writings translated and published in US feminist works. These appeared in *Signs*, which published English-language translations of Julia Kristeva and Hélène

Cixous in 1975 and 1976 and the first English-language analyses of the French movement in 1978. In 1980, *The Future of Difference*, edited by Hester Eisenstein and Alice Jardine, published papers from a Barnard College conference that included discussions by Jane Gallop, Carolyn Burke, and Domna Stanton, among others, of theories at work in Kristeva, Cixous, and Irigaray. In the same year Elaine Marks and Isabelle de Courtivron's *New French Feminisms: An Anthology* also appeared. In 1981, a cluster of articles "presenting and dissecting" French feminism was published in *Feminist Studies* and a "Special Section on French Feminist Theory" appeared in *Signs*. Toril Moi's *Sexual/Textual Politics: Feminist Literary Theory*, which opposed "French" to "Anglo-American" feminist thought and featured Cixous, Irigaray, and Kristeva, was published in England in 1985. Together these works were the foundational texts for the American- and also British-construction of the category "French feminism."

This construction was a process rather than a single event. Its first stage was the introduction to American audiences of Kristeva, Cixous, and Irigaray as French writers, although not yet as "French feminists." Consider the inaugural issue of *Signs*, which included a translated excerpt from Kristeva's *Des Chinoises* (On the Women of China). The accompanying editorial described Kristeva as "among the most provocative and respected contemporary French intellectuals"; nothing was said to connect her to feminism, and *Signs* did not then provide the biographical information about its authors that might have identified Kristeva's political affiliations. Nor did the editorial speak of the significance of *Des Chinoises* to French feminism. Readers unfamiliar with French writers – surely the vast majority of *Signs'* readers in 1975 – probably read the article for the light it might shed on Chinese women, not on France.

Readers introduced to Cixous in the pages of *Signs* would not have learned much that would place her in relation to a social and political movement. The editorial for the summer 1976 issue, which included Cixous's "Laugh of the Medusa" – a manifesto for what came to be called "écriture feminine" – described Cixous only as a "French writer, scholar, and initiator of a doctorate in women's studies at the University of Paris." A brief description of the essay, which had appeared in French the previous year, states only that it "calls for women to write a new female text." The editorial continues: "Her essay, which denies the legitimacy of 'phallic' intellectual schemes, exemplifies by its own texture the deregulation of past scholarship."

The slippage from "French writers" to "French feminists" seems to have begun with the essays by Carolyn Burke and Elaine Marks published in summer 1978 in *Signs*. Although both articles were still about French "writers," both also discussed the Movement de Libération des Femmes (MLF). Especially in view of the absence of any other analyses of French feminism in English-language periodicals, readers would reasonably conclude from this juxtaposition of writers and the MLF that French feminist activists were all novelists, philosophers, or critics. Marks's article, a review essay on women and literature in France, most prominently discussed Kristeva, Cixous, and Irigaray, although Marks also signaled the importance of Monique Wittig and listed several other writers – Simone de Beauvoir, Nathalie Sarraute, Marguerite Duras, Marguerite Yourcenar, as well as the more junior Catherine Clement, Claudine Hermann, Chantal Chawaf, Annie Leclerc, and Christiane Rochefort. Carolyn Burke's "Report from Paris: Women's Writing and the Women's Movement" purported to cover more than the literary scene but in fact also discussed only women writers. Burke explicitly conflated writers and the women's movement: after two introductory paragraphs on the birth of the women's liberation movement in the aftermath of May 1968, she describes a feminist practice that "brings into question, and into play, the transformational powers of language." The personalities Burke singled out for attention were Cixous, Kristeva, and Irigaray; the only movement group examined was Psychanalyse et politique. She noted Cixous's association with Psych et po and especially with its publishing house and bookstores. Although Burke hinted at criticism of Psych et po on the part of some other feminists, these other feminists were not identified.

It is important to keep in mind that both Burke and Marks are French-language literature specialists who traveled frequently to France in that context and who had a sensitive ear tuned to the political implications of writing and literary criticism. Then-associate editor at *Signs*, Domna Stanton is also a French-language literature specialist and most likely played the important role of obtaining, if not originating, these translations and analyses for *Signs*. Still, with only *Signs*, among feminist publications, publishing any French women at all, most US readers would have lacked the knowledge to recognize the omission of other forms of politically significant practice. In hindsight, it is the conflating of writers and critics with the women's movement that is most striking, although I am not certain I noticed it at the time. True, only Burke's "Report from Paris" even claimed to be covering something larger than academic, discipline-specific concerns – something we would take for a feminist movement. And the *Signs* editorials always identified Cixous, Kristeva, and Irigaray as French "writers" or "intellectuals," never as feminists. But I doubt that I was alone in reading into these articles an analysis of French "feminism." I assumed that Cixous was a feminist simply because she, like me, identified with a "women's liberation movement." Marks, in her review essay, informed us that Cixous and Psych et po had problematized the words "feminist" and "feminism"; but then again, in *The Second Sex*, Simone de Beauvoir, accepting the position of early-twentieth-century Marxists, had also dissociated herself from "feminism," assuming it to be class-biased and narrow in its interest.[27]

I think it not surprising, therefore, that in the United States the trio of already celebrated theorists – Cixous, Kristeva, and Irigaray – became identified with French feminism despite the protestations of at least Cixous and Kristeva that they were not feminists. By the end of the 1970s, the section of the Barnard College conference on "Difference" that was devoted to these particular women could be entitled "Contemporary Feminist Thought in France." This formulation in the Barnard conference papers, published as *The Future of Difference* in 1980, was reinforced by the publication in that same year of Elaine Marks and Isabelle de Courtivron's *New French Feminisms: An Anthology*, the volume I believe most significant of all for constructing "our" French feminism.[28]

(1998)

Notes

27 In "Debating the Present/Writing the Past: 'Feminism' in French History and Historiography," *Radical History Review*, no. 52 (winter 1992): 86, I have written that Beauvoir dissociated herself from feminism, because, in the late 1940s, she associated herself with a view of feminism's history that had been constructed prior to the First World War by socialist women. In 1907, in Stuttgart, the first international conference of socialist women had passed a resolution that "socialist women must not ally themselves with the feminists of the bourgeoisie, but lead the battle side by side with the socialist parties." From that time, socialist women began to refer to the "bourgeois feminist" movement, and they always did so disparagingly.
28 Hester Eisenstein and Alice Jardine, eds., *The Future of Difference* (Boston: G. K. Hall, 1980); and *New French Feminisms*.

HÉLÈNE CIXOUS AND MIREILLE CALLE-GRUBER

Hélène Cixous Rootprints: Memory and Life Writing

M.C-G.: By 'theory' you are referring in particular here to a north-American situation of which echoes are returning presently to Europe, and which, under the name of 'feminist theory', has excluded your books of fiction, limiting itself to a few essays or articles: 'The Laugh of the Medusa', 'Sorties', your participation in *The Newly Born Woman*. To carry out this amputation is unjust to your work which is plural; overflowing; which incessantly questions what it draws. The risk, with writing that is attentive to subtleties, is that laziness, deafness, or surprise should lead people to hear only one voice, to stop at a single aspect. That the reading should reduce and reify because this is easier.

One must wonder how this happens. What happens – or does not happen – when one does so little justice to a body of work. Admittedly, there is misunderstanding about the term 'theory': the writing you practise is more like a form of philosophical reflection that you lead through poetry. But the misunderstanding comes also from the fact that, in the very course of the work of fiction, you pursue an effort of lucidity: in the very place of writing's blindness – of which you are conscious. A kind of work that involves turning back on the sentence, that recycles, that reflects and flexes the flux of writing. Certain people misunderstand; consider it to be a theoretical treatment whereas it is a poetic treatment: incessant fictional practice. It's in the same linguistic dough, from the same pen, that poetry and philosophical reflexion weave a text. Which does not close itself in conceptualization, even locally. Hearing you speak of the concept which fixes, I thought of Derrida's sentence on the cover of *Circumfession*: 'As soon as it is poached by writing, the concept is done (for).'[2] It is clearly more than a simple pun. To the letter: at the speed of lightning, your text tries to say the 'raw', blood, tears, the body which is a 'state of meat'. (I am thinking of the self-portrait as a flayed animal in *First Days of the Year* which refers to Rembrandt; and *Déluge*: 'She remains alone with her terrible meat' p. 93.)

H.C.: I planted those essays *deliberately*, at a very dated, entirely historical moment, to mark off a field; so that we would not lose sight of it entirely – to have done something deliberately: that already tells you what it is! 'The Laugh of the Medusa' and other texts of this type were a conscious, peda-gogic, didactic effort on my part to class, to organize certain reflections, to emphasize a minimum of sense. Of common sense.

M.C-G.: You say 'dated, historical moment', that is to say, is it not, a politi-cal moment? *The Newly Born Woman* is a precisely circumstantial text that served as argumentational evidence at a moment in the struggle.

H.C.: I was inspired to write those texts by the urgency of a moment in the general discourse concerning 'sexual difference'. Which appeared to me to be confused and to be producing repression and loss of life and of sense. I would never have thought, when I began writing, that one day I would find myself making strategic and even military gestures: constructing a camp with lines of defence! It's a gesture which is foreign to me. I did do it. Because of ideological aggressions, all marked by intolerance – that were not addressed to me personally – all of a sudden I saw myself having an obliga-tion to become engaged to defend a certain number of positions. To do this, I left my own ground.

I do not regret it. To 'defend' is sometimes a necessity. But it is an ambiguous gesture: whoever defends him- or herself forbids [*qui se défend défend*], i.e. interdicts. And I do not like the regions where people lay down the law. In addition, this secondary gesture screens the principal act.

[...]

M.C-G.: I am always surprised that there is so little space, in the woman's movement, for the right to literary creativity. I am surprised also that people generally name Cixous–Irigaray–Kristeva together, amalgamating works between which I see mostly differences. Particularly: literary difference. Irigaray and Kristeva are theoreticians, they do not produce writer's works. However, it is the writer that I touch on in you. Where I touch down. One must recall that your field of action, indeed your combat, takes place in poetic writing, language, fiction.

H.C.: This happens because the texts of mine that are put into circulation are often texts that can easily be circulated and appropriated. They were made for this, by the way. The others are not read.

M.C-G.: Those other texts do not require the same threshold of readability. Nor the same kind of work.

H.C.: Exactly, but the situation then produces errors in evaluation: because to have an upright position, analogous to that of a theoretician, is not my intention.

M.C-G.: Are we in the process of saying that it is more difficult for a woman to be taken as a writer than as a theoretician?

H.C.: I must give several responses: it is easier for a woman to be accepted as a theoretician, that is to say, as less woman. And then, one cannot generalize your statement without caution because: as a woman, to be accepted as a writer ... well ... it depends a lot on the women ...

M.C-G.: ... it depends on the writer ...

H.C.: Of course, it depends on what she offers to the reader. In any case it's determined by the degree to which it can be appropriated. If you give a text that can be appropriated, you are acceptable. When the text runs far ahead of the reader and ahead of the author, or when the text simply runs, and requires the reader to run, and when the reader wishes to remain sitting, then the text is less well received.

M.C-G.: It does not all come from the fact of being a female or male writer, but from the way reading is most often considered in terms of appropriation.

H.C.: Unfortunately. While the reading that makes us happy is on the contrary reading that transports, with which we go off on a voyage, not knowing where. However, in my theoretical texts I use a 'form' of writing; but from time to time I resume. This is what happens in theoretical texts: there are moments when you sit down. And it is these moments, where you can sit down, where you can take, the moments of stopping, that make these texts more visible than others, those which dash off continually without stopping.

(1997)
Translated by Eric Prenowitz, London: Routledge

Note

2   *Dès qui'il est saisi par l'écriture, le concept est cuit*, playing on the bivalence of *saisir* (to grasp/to sear) and *cuire* (to finish off/to cook).

6

Locating the Subject

INTRODUCTION

What Is the Subject?

The reference to 'the subject' in this title can be understood in at least four ways. Firstly, it suggests the human subject and our concepts of what it means to be called, or to name oneself, 'a woman' or 'a man'. Linked with this is the notion of a *collective* subject, 'women'. Feminists, as we all know, speak frequently about women as a group, some even use the term 'class', with common needs and purposes. These categories have been much debated in recent years and the theorists mentioned in the first three extracts give some indication of the range of subject disciplines (here is a second meaning of the term 'subject') which have been preoccupied with this topic: for instance, psychoanalysis (Freud and Lacan); linguistics (Saussure and Beneviste); philosophy (Derrida); politics and ideology (Althusser). Feminism necessarily interrelates with these disciplines in trying to explore its specific focus on woman/women. The third meaning of 'subject' to consider here is subject as a discourse. We can think of feminism itself as a subject, a subject of inquiry, and consider what the implications are of this preoccupation with the human subject for the political and intellectual practice of feminism. As we have already begun to see, debates about the mutability of the subject, the relation between collectivity and difference, the gap between a postmodernist and an historical/materialist view of woman are important issues for politics and subjectivity but, equally, for reading and writing.

Julia Kristeva's and Jacqueline Rose's extracts can be read, to an extent, as defences of psychoanalysis and testimonies to its usefulness for feminism. Kristeva comments on the instability of language, meaning and subjectivity,

Feminist Literary Theory: A Reader, Third Edition By Mary Eagleton   © 2011 Mary Eagleton

and coins the phrase 'subject in process' to convey the sense of the subject as incomplete, always becoming, never stable. Similarly, Rose mentions the 'failure' of identity. This 'failure' is not to be interpreted as the inadequacy of certain individuals to achieve full subjecthood but rather 'the resistance to identity at the very heart of psychic life', and thus a 'failure' common to us all. Rose sees in this interpretation the possibility of a link between feminism and psychoanalysis; both locations recognize 'as more than a fact of individual pathology that most women do not painlessly slip into their roles as women if indeed they do at all'. Kristeva and Rose appreciate that there are psychological and political arguments to bring to this figure of the fragmented, unrealized/unrealizable female subject. To function, the individual needs to attain 'a certain type of stability' (Kristeva). This stability is an illusion, frequently challenged, but a vital illusion to maintain our everyday living. Moreover, to encourage political change, women may need a different sense of subjecthood, one which sees women as capable and purposeful. Feminism has to negotiate a passage between psychoanalysis and politics, and, in Rose's view, the idea of the subject as at odds with social norms offers a useful point of disjunction for any radical politics. It is an inconsistency in the social fabric which feminism can exploit.

The implication of Rose's reference to Louis Althusser is made clearer in Catherine Belsey's extract. Again using insights from psychoanalysis and linguistics, Belsey explores the construction of the individual through and in language. In Belsey's opinion, I am not an autonomous fully-formed individual who decides, periodically, to use language as a tool to express my views about the world. On the contrary, 'the subject is constructed in language and discourse': language makes me rather more than I make language. For Althusser the individual takes up the subject-positions which language and cultural norms permit her to adopt. Althusser uses the term 'interpellation' to describe the process by which ideology 'calls' or 'hails' the individual to her subject-position. Belsey, in quoting Althusser, reveals yet a fourth meaning of the term 'subject': the subject is 'also a *subjected being* who submits to the authority of the social formation'. Kristeva too explores this sense of accountability on the part of the subject – indeed, both use a legal metaphor – when she writes that 'our identities are constantly called into question, brought to trial, over-ruled'. Neither Althusser nor Kristeva would present the subject as merely a powerless victim of controlling forces. However, Althusser is interested in how ideology works and how individuals, *apparently* freely, adopt positions which in many respects are not in their interests. Thus, as Rose indicates, Lacan's psychoanalytical theories were open to a political reinterpretation by Althusser and both perspectives offer possibilities for feminists interested in the creation of, specifically, the female psyche and the interpellation of the female subject.[1]

Unsurprisingly, the form of writing that has been most explicitly interested in these questions is autobiography. The various renamings of the term are themselves indicative of the interrogation of the subject within the genre:

'autobiographics', 'biomythography', 'autogynography'.[2] Shoshana Felman's argument is that women, historically positioned as the Other, do not, as yet, have an autobiography. As Felman suggests, for women, a life 'is not entirely in their conscious possession'. Thus, Felman is suspicious about the equation between the autobiographical and the personal or confessional that has been a strong focus in feminism, not least when the personal meets with the professional in the form of the feminist literary critic. Her reference to 'getting personal' alludes to Nancy Miller's book of that name.[3] Felman doubts, both in her substantive argument and in her long footnotes, that there is any direct access to the story of women. Rather, women's autobiography is 'missing'.[4] It has to be struggled for through 'the bond of reading', by women reading themselves into a culture that has not recognized their difference or their trauma.[5] Janice A. Radway also turns to reading. She understands how her desiring and professional subjectivity was interpellated amidst selective reading, educational institutions and the socioeconomic world of the middlebrow. As Judith Fetterley indicates in Chapter 5, for this generation of women being educated meant an inculcation into a world of male achievement; it meant being taught to want a 'professional power', that of a specific gender, class and national identity.

Debates Between

Feminism's interest in the subject has taken it into debates with poststructuralism and postmodernism as much as into psychoanalysis, and always an imperative is to consider the political potential of any alliances.[6] In this section, we focus particularly on debates concerning agency and, as we have touched on earlier, debates on essentialism. Underpinning many of these discussions is the influential work of Judith Butler and her radical questioning of the binary oppositions that she sees as operating within feminism: I/self: Other; sex: gender; agency: construction; heterosexual: homosexual. Butler always resists any concept of a stable subject outside of culture. In her view, what our culture understands by feminine behaviour is not the product of a particular, settled identity; instead, our understanding of a female identity is produced, within signification, through the repeated performance of words and actions which we code as 'feminine'. Butler interprets the dispersal of identity as a liberating opportunity for the construction of new subjectivities and new political configurations, and conversely, she construes feminism's allegiance to identity politics as restrictive and limiting. The subtitle of her best-known study, *Gender Trouble: Feminism and the Subversion of Identity*, indicates her interest in the 'subversive' and in using the strategies of performance, parody and pastiche to undermine the status of 'the real' and 'the natural'.[7] In Butler's terms, the active agent of feminism is not lost but produced in the actions, and thus there is space for change, for the rules to be challenged or rewritten.

Seyla Benhabib's extract constitutes part of her ongoing disputation on postmodernism and the constitution of the subject, a debate she has undertaken in significant measure in disagreement with Butler.[8] She situates this essay within 'the new constellation formed by the coming together of global integration and apparent cultural fragmentation'.[9] Reviewing debates on subjectivity over the last twenty years, including those she has had with Butler, Benhabib proposes a 'narrative' model of subjectivity rather than the 'performativity' model associated with Butler. She makes use of Charles Taylor's metaphor of 'webs of interlocution' and suggests how this new constellation might encourage a re-evaluation of universalism and a role for the feminist theorist as critical intellectual and a cultural broker of new collective identities. Benhabib does not doubt that this is a challenge. The new universalism and the new sense of a collective identity must recognize difference and recognize, in a globalized word, the difference between a sense of security and belonging and a protectionist retreat from others.

Just as problematic as agency has been the debate on 'essence' and the role of essentialism in feminist thinking and politics. Linda Alcoff explores two strands in feminism – cultural feminism and poststructuralist feminism. She presents cultural feminists as concerned with the difference and uniqueness of women, the importance of feminine values, the need to valorize these qualities not dismiss them – in short, a female essence, perhaps biologically based, perhaps culturally produced. As we note from the start of Alcoff's extract, poststructuralist feminism sees 'woman' as a construct, a fiction with no essential characteristics. Briefly surveying some of the views of Derrida, Foucault and Kristeva, Alcoff discusses two attractions for feminism in poststructuralist thought: firstly, the emphasis on difference allows women to think beyond the prescriptiveness of normative gender identity; secondly, Alcoff finds a potential in poststructuralism's questioning of the construction of the subject.[10]

As ever there are also problems. By now we can appreciate that Alcoff's interrogation of the 'undecidability' of both text and 'woman' is a recurrent anxiety in feminist debates on the subject, though her stress on the political goals which, of necessity, require the invocation of 'woman' cannot be mentioned too often: 'How can we demand legal abortions, adequate child care, or wages based on compatible worth without invoking the concept "woman"?' A further reservation concerns the possible alliance between poststructuralism and liberal humanism around concepts of the subject. Could poststructuralism's deconstruction of gender, race and class at some level coincide with humanism's view of a *common* humanity? In a poststructuralist argument these terms would be in inverted commas to indicate their contingency; in a humanist argument they could be seen as false distinctions imposed upon our essential, universal subjectivity – a very different universal subjectivity from that proposed by Benhabib. Though theoretically at odds, Alcoff fears that in practice both positions could efface the importance to women of gender identity: one presents the identity as fictive; the other as peripheral.

The extracts from Teresa de Lauretis and Diana Fuss offer two interesting responses on this issue of essence, de Lauretis's directly concerned with

Alcoff's argument, both concerned with deconstructing the familiar opposition of essence against construct. De Lauretis questions Alcoff's formulation of the issues. Why construct the problem as a binary opposition ('Cultural Feminism versus Post-structuralism' is Alcoff's title), especially as within the essay there is evidence that feminist positions are more numerous and that the oppositional way of presenting the case has been superseded? Both de Lauretis and Fuss challenge this binary approach. De Lauretis warns against hierarchical relationships – essentialism as naïve, a constructionist view as theoretically aware. With an equally deconstructive move, Fuss turns the theoretical spotlight away from essentialism to check the validity of the constructionist claims. Firstly, Fuss queries whether the specificity of constructionist identities avoids essence or merely multiplies essentialist definitions. Secondly, she collapses the division between essence and construct and, intriguingly, suggests that the very concept of essentialism could 'operate as a deconstructionist strategy', embodying 'some strategic or interventionary value'. Thirdly, she reminds the constructionists that essence is also a sign: paradoxically, essence is without an essence. To dismiss essence as always reactionary is a notably undeconstructive response, an inability to recognize the play of signification. As Benhabib revives universalism, so Fuss recoups essentialism as a term to operate *within* deconstructionist debates.[11]

New and Diverse Subjectivities

Though feminists might deconstruct existing female subjectivities, they still construct others, more complex and diverse, and sometimes mythic figures that offer possibilities for new formulations. The examples to consider here are the cyborg (Donna Haraway), the *mestiza* and the migratory subject (Gloria Anzaldúa and Carol Boyce Davies), the lesbian and the queer subject (Monique Wittig and Eve Kosofsky Sedgwick). Several factors are held in common: the idea of shifting, reformulated identities; the critique of dualistic thinking – the product of 'the straight mind' (Wittig) and in need of 'massive uprooting' (Anzaldúa); the political importance of language – 'we work also at the level of language/manifesto, of language/action' (Wittig) and 'releasing the play of writing is deadly serious' (Haraway); and the turn to the autobiographical. Haraway, Anzaldúa and Boyce Davies make use of the concept of 'borders' and crossings. In one sense these are literal, physical borders, specifically the US/Mexico border for Anzaldúa, more generally for Haraway and Boyce Davies the many borders crossed by the migratory subject. But they are also metaphorical and conceptual borders. As Boyce Davies shows, the subject 'black' has no specific or defined meaning. The term has to be understood 'relationally, provisionally and based on location or position' and the possibilities proliferate when one is thinking of the black *female* subject. Similarly, in trying to understand the term 'African-American', meanings are multiple on both sides of the hyphen.

The repositioning of identities is evident if we consider also Wittig's and Sedgwick's extracts alongside Adrienne Rich's from Chapter 1. In its wide definition of 'lesbian', Rich's 'lesbian continuum' suggests that all women of a feminist or quasi-feminist consciousness are lesbian. Wittig's conclusion is quite the opposite. She wants to 'break off the heterosexual contract', to be free of the man/woman couple. She decries the 'heterosexual myths' circulating in psychoanalysis, the social sciences and anthropology with their aim 'to systematically heterosexualize that personal dimension...'. Thus, the radical logic of Wittig's argument is that the categories 'man' and 'woman' must disappear and the striking conclusion is not that all women are to some degree lesbians but that 'lesbians are not women', since to be a woman is to be caught in a heterosexual definition, 'woman' rather than 'man'. With Sedgwick too the security of subject-positions slips away. She responds to critiques of her position as 'a woman and a feminist writing (in part) about male homosexuality' by a 'queering' of identities and allegiances. There are uncertainties in identifying '*across* definitional lines', but as Sedgwick finds in her teaching, there are also uncertainties *within* largely homogeneous groups. The problematic prepositions – as, with, against – indicate both the values and limitations of various subject-positions.[12]

The new female subject is mobile and flexible, traversing all manner of psychological, linguistic and conceptual barriers. Along the way, she embraces contradiction, ambiguity, irony and revels in her illegitimacy. A difference in use of language lies in Anzaldúa's attachment to organicist metaphors – seas, corn, roots of trees – to embody regeneration and a new, more inclusive sense of wholeness. Against this, Haraway expresses an openness to the technological and a greater suspicion than Anzaldúa concerning myths of origin and fulfilment: 'The cyborg does not dream of community on the model of the organic family, this time without the Oedipal project. The cyborg would not recognize the Garden of Eden; it is not made of mud and cannot dream of returning to dust.'[13] Compare these words with Anzaldúa's conclusion: 'She becomes a *nahual,* able to transform herself into a tree, a coyote, into another person. She transforms the small "I" into the total Self.' There are mixed responses to the utopian aspects of these subjectivities. On the one hand, the utopian impulse constitutes an attempt to act/think beyond the dominant order. There is an invigorating animation in this mode. On the other hand, it is partly the utopianism that leads Kate Soper to a fundamental questioning of Haraway's cyborg. Despite Haraway's denials, Soper finds in her work a 'romantic-redemptive' thinking. Soper insists on a more politically situated and mediated view of the body and sexuality, even the necessary preservation of '[s]ome dualism and hierarchies'. As with Boyce Davies, there is a concern not to lose sight of the continuing legacies of exploitative histories and the material conditions that bind.

Notes

1　A useful introduction to various positions on subjectivity is Chris Weedon, 'Subjects' in Mary Eagleton (ed.), *A Concise Companion to Feminist Theory* (Oxford: Blackwell, 2003).

2　Leigh Gilmore, *Autobiographics: A Feminist Theory of Women's Self-Representation* (Ithaca, NY: Cornell University Press, 1994); Audre Lorde, *Zami: A New Spelling of My Name* (Trumansburg, NY: Crossing, 1983); Domna C. Stanton, 'Autogynography: Is the Subject Different?' in Donna C. Stanton (ed.), *The Female Autograph: Theory and Practice of Autobiography from the Tenth to the Twentieth Century* (Chicago: University of Chicago Press, 1984). The best collection of essays on autobiography, with a high level of representation about feminism, is Trev Lynn Broughton (ed.), *Autobiography: Critical Concepts in Literary and Cultural Studies* (Vols. I–IV) (London: Routledge, 2007).

3　Nancy K. Miller, *Getting Personal: Feminist Occasions and Other Autobiographical Acts* (New York: Routledge, 1991). See also Jane Tompkins, 'Me and My Shadow', *New Literary History*, vol. 19, no. 1 (1987), pp. 169–78. For responses to these essays and personal criticism generally, see Linda Anderson, 'Autobiography and Personal Criticism', in Gill Plain and Susan Sellers (eds.), *A History of Feminist Literary Criticism* (Cambridge: Cambridge University Press, 2007) and Toril Moi, *What is a Woman?: and Other Essays* (Oxford: Oxford University Press, 1999). Note how, in the 'Afterword' to Janet Badia and Jennifer Phegley (eds.), *Reading Woman: Literary Figures and Cultural Icons from the Victorian Age to the Present* (Toronto: University of Toronto Press, 2005), Kate Flint provides the personal history of childhood reading that her publisher had advised her not to include in *The Woman Reader*.

4　For a related argument, see Mary Evans, *Missing Persons: The Impossibility of Autobiography* (London: Routledge 1999) and Nicola King, *Memory: Narrative, Identity: Remembering the Self* (Edinburgh: Edinburgh University Press, 2000) on the part played by narrative and memory in the construction of the subject.

5　For a helpful explanation of Felman's position, its difference from 'personal criticism' and its relation to work on trauma and testimony, see the last chapter of Linda Anderson's *Autobiography* (London: Routledge, 2001).

6　As indicative examples, see Patricia Waugh, *Feminine Fictions: Revisiting the Postmodern* (London: Routledge, 1989); Kate Soper, 'Feminism, Humanism and Postmodernism', *Radical Philosophy*, no. 55 (Summer 1990); Joan W. Scott, 'Deconstructing Equality-Versus-Difference; or, the Uses of Poststructuralist Theory for Feminism', *Feminist Studies*, vol. 14, no. 1 (Spring 1988), pp. 33–50; Chris Weedon, *Feminist Practice and Poststructuralist Theory* (2nd edition) (Oxford: Blackwell, 1996); Kathi Weeks, *Constituting Feminist Subjects* (Ithaca, NY: Cornell University Press, 1998); Susan Lurie, *Unsettled Subjects: Restoring Feminist Politics to Poststructuralist Critique* (Durham, NC: Duke University Press, 1997).

7　Judith Butler, *Gender Trouble: Feminism and the Subversion of Identity* (New York and London: Routledge, 1990).

8 For a convenient, single-volume location for this dialogue alongside two other important voices in the debate, see Seyla Benhabib, Judith Butler, Drucilla Cornell and Nancy Fraser, *Feminist Contentions: A Philosophical Exchange* (New York: Routledge, 1995). On debates between Benhabib and Fraser, see Margot Canaday, 'Promising Alliances: The Critical Feminist Theory of Nancy Fraser and Seyla Benhabib', *Feminist Review*, no. 74 (2003), pp. 50–69.

9 Benhabib, p. 336.

10 Kristeva's argument might be more conditional than Alcoff credits. See the extract in Chapter 4 from 'Woman Can Never Be Defined', to which Alcoff refers here. Note how Kristeva qualifies the 'absurdity' of 'being a woman'.

11 In her footnote, Fuss sites Toril Moi's *Sexual/ Textual Politics* as an example of an anti-essentialist critique. Note how Moi in her later work (see the extract in Chapter 4) comes to the same conclusion as Fuss.

12 For responses on lesbian and queer identities and, specifically, Sedgwick's work, see Terry Castle, *The Apparitional Lesbian: Female Homosexuality and Modern Culture* (New York: Columbia University Press, 1993) and Judith Butler, *Bodies that Matter: On the Discursive Limits of 'Sex'* (New York: Routledge, 1993). For a very useful summary of positions in queer studies, see Noreen Giffney, 'Denormatizing Queer Theory: More than (simply) Lesbian and Gay Studies', *Feminist Theory*, vol. 5, no. 1 (2004), pp. 73–8.

13 For Haraway's essay accompanied by a series of responses, see Elizabeth Weed (ed.), *Coming to Terms: Feminism, Theory, Politics* (London: Routledge, 1989). See also Chela Sandoval, 'New Sciences: Cyborg Feminism and the Methodology of the Oppressed', in David Bell and Barbara M. Kennedy (eds.), The *Cybercultures Reader* (London: Routledge, 2000); on the elision of race in the figure of the cyborg and relevant essays on literary texts and representation, see Jenny Wolmark (ed.), *Cybersexualities: A Reader on Feminist Theory, Cyborgs and Cyberspace* (Edinburgh: Edinburgh University Press, 1999).

Julia Kristeva

'A Question of Subjectivity: An Interview'
Women's Review

Susan Sellers: As a professor of linguistics, and with publications on subjects ranging from philosophy to literary criticism, what led you also to train as a psychoanalyst?

Julia Kristeva: I don't believe one commits oneself to psychoanalysis without certain secret motivations ... difficulties living, a suffering which is unable to express itself. I talked to my psychoanalyst about this aspect of things and so today can speak about these motives for my work.

I wanted to examine the states at the limits of language; the moments where language breaks up in psychosis for example, or the moments where language doesn't yet exist such as during a child's apprenticeship to language. It seemed to me to be impossible to content oneself with a description which held itself to be objective and neutral in these two cases, because already the selection of examples presupposes a particular type of contact with the people who talk to you.

Also the interpretation of people's speech presupposes that you apply yourself to the meaning of what they say. I saw that there was no neutral objectivity possible in descriptions of language at its limits and that we are constantly in what psychoanalysis calls a 'transfer'. It seemed to me dishonest to apply this transfer without having myself undergone the experience of psychoanalysis.

Susan Sellers: An important part of your psychoanalytic research has been the process by which the individual acquires language. What does this 'process' entail?

Julia Kristeva: I used the term 'process' whilst I was working on the texts of Antonin Artaud. Artaud is an extremely disturbing writer in modern French literature, partly because he underwent a dramatic experience of madness and partly because he thought carefully about the music in language. Anyone who reads Artaud's texts will realize that all identities are unstable: the identity of linguistic signs, the identity of meaning and, as a result, the identity of the speaker. And in order to take account of this de-stabilization of meaning and of the subject I thought the term 'subject in process' would be appropriate. 'Process' in the sense of process but also in the sense of a legal proceeding where the subject is committed to trial, because our identities in life are constantly called into question, brought to trial, over-ruled.

I wanted to examine the language which manifests these states of instability because in ordinary communication – which is organized, civilized – we repress these states of incandescence. Creativity as well as suffering comprises these moments of instability, where language, or the signs of language, or subjectivity itself are put into 'process'. And one can extrapolate this notion and use it not just for the texts of Artaud but for every 'proceeding' in which we move outside the norms.

Susan Sellers: Writing about this process, one of the distinctions you have drawn in order to chart the development from non-differentiated infant to speaking subject is the distinction between 'the semiotic' and 'the symbolic'. Can you explain this distinction?

Julia Kristeva: In order to research this state of instability – the fact that meaning is not simply a structure or process, or that the subject is not simply a unity but is constantly called into question – I proposed to take into account two modalities or conditions of meaning which I called 'the semiotic' and 'the symbolic'. What I call 'the semiotic' takes us back to the pre-linguistic states of childhood where the child babbles the sounds s/he hears, or where s/he articulates rhythms, alliterations, or stresses, trying to imitate her/his surroundings. In this state the child doesn't yet possess the necessary linguistic signs and thus there is no meaning in the strict sense of the term. It is only after the mirror phase or the experience of castration in the Oedipus complex that the individual becomes subjectively capable of taking on the signs of language, of articulation as it has been prescribed – and I call that 'the symbolic'.

Susan Sellers: What actually happens during the mirror phase and the Oedipus complex?

Julia Kristeva: Identification takes place. What I call 'the semiotic' is a state of disintegration in which patterns appear but which do not have any stable identity: they are blurred and fluctuating. The processes which are at work here are those which Freud calls 'primary': processes of transfer. We have an example of this if we refer once again to the melodies and babblings of infants which are a sound image of their bodily instability. Babies and children's bodies are made up of erotogenic zones which are extremely excitable, or, on the contrary, indifferent, in a state of constant change, of excitation, or extinction, without there being any fixed identity.

A 'fixed identity': it's perhaps a fiction, an illusion – who amongst us has a 'fixed' identity? It's a phantasm; we do nevertheless arrive at a certain type of stability. There are several steps which lead to this stability and one step which has been accentuated by the French psychoanalyst Jacques Lacan is the specular identification which he calls 'the mirror phase'. In this phase one recognizes one's image in a mirror as one's self-image. It is a first identification of the chaotic, fragmented body, and is both violent and jubilatory. The identification comes about under the domination of the maternal image, which is the one nearest to the child and which allows the child both to remain close and to distance itself.

I see a face. A first differentiation takes place, and thus a first self-identity. This identity is still unstable because sometimes I take myself to be me, sometimes I confuse myself with my mother. This narcissistic instability, this doubt persists and makes me ask 'who am I?', 'is it me or is it the other?' The confusion with the maternal image as first other remains.

In order for us to be able to get out of this confusion, the classical pattern of development leads us to a confrontation inside the Oedipal triangle between our desire for the mother and the process of loss which is the result of paternal authority. In the ideal case, this finishes by stabilising the subject, rendering her/him capable both of pronouncing sentences which conform to the rules, to the law, and of telling her/his own story – of giving her/his account.

These are symbolic acquisitions that are pre-conditioned by a certain psychic experience which is the stabilization of the self in relation to the other.

(1986)

JACQUELINE ROSE

'Femininity and Its Discontents'
Feminist Review

Psychoanalysis has often been accused of 'functionalism'. It is accepted as a theory of how women are psychically 'induced' into femininity by a patriarchal culture, but is then accused of perpetuating that process, either through a practice assumed to be *prescriptive* about women's role (this is what women *should* do), or because the very effectiveness of the account as a *description* (this is what is demanded of women, what they are *expected* to do) leaves no possibility of change.

It is this aspect of Juliet Mitchell's pioneering book *Psychoanalysis and Feminism* which seems to have been taken up most strongly by feminists who have attempted to follow through the political implications of psychoanalysis as a critique of patriarchy.[1]

Thus Gayle Rubin, following Mitchell, uses psychoanalysis for a general critique of a patriarchal culture which is predicated on the exchange of women by men.[2] Nancy Chodorow shifts from Freud to later object relations theory to explain how women's childcaring role is perpetuated through the earliest relationship between a mother and her child, which leads in her case to a demand for a fundamental change in how childcare is organized

between women and men in our culture.³ Although there are obvious differences between these two readings of psychoanalysis, they nonetheless share
an emphasis on the social exchange of women, or the distribution of roles
for women, across cultures: 'Women's mothering is one of the few universal
and enduring elements of the sexual division of labour'.⁴

The force of psychoanalysis is therefore (as Janet Sayers points out)⁵
precisely that it gives an account of patriarchal culture as a trans-historical
and cross-cultural force. It therefore conforms to the feminist demand for a
theory which can explain women's subordination across specific cultures
and different historical moments. Summing this up crudely, we could say
that psychoanalysis adds sexuality to Marxism, where sexuality is felt to be
lacking, and extends beyond Marxism where the attention to specific
historical instances, changes in modes of production etc., is felt to leave
something unexplained.

But all this happens at a cost, and that cost is the concept of the unconscious.
What distinguishes psychoanalysis from sociological accounts of gender
(hence for me the fundamental impasse of Nancy Chodorow's work) is that
whereas for the latter, the internalization of norms is assumed roughly to
work, the basic premise and indeed starting-point of psychoanalysis is that
it does not. The unconscious constantly reveals the 'failure' of identity.
Because there is no continuity of psychic life, so there is no stability of sexual
identity, no position for women (or for men) which is ever simply achieved.
Nor does psychoanalysis see such 'failure' as a special-case inability or an
individual deviancy from the norm. 'Failure' is not a moment to be regretted
in a process of adaptation, or development into normality, which ideally
takes its course (some of the earliest critics of Freud, such as Ernest Jones,
did, however, give an account of development in just these terms). Instead
'failure' is something endlessly repeated and relived moment by moment
throughout our individual histories. It appears not only in the symptom, but
also in dreams, in slips of the tongue and in forms of sexual pleasure which
are pushed to the sidelines of the norm. Feminism's affinity with psychoanalysis rests above all, I would argue, with this recognition that there is a
resistance to identity at the very heart of psychic life. Viewed in this way,
psychoanalysis is no longer best understood as an account of how women
are fitted into place (even this, note, is the charitable reading of Freud).
Instead psychoanalysis becomes one of the few places in our culture where
it is recognized as more than a fact of individual pathology that most women
do not painlessly slip into their roles as women, if indeed they do at all.
Freud himself recognized this increasingly in his work. In the articles which
run from 1924 to 1931,⁶ he moves from that famous, or rather infamous,
description of the little girl struck with her 'inferiority' or 'injury' in the face
of the anatomy of the little boy and wisely accepting her fate ('injury' as the
fact of being feminine), to an account which quite explicitly describes the

process of becoming 'feminine' as an 'injury' or 'catastrophe' for the complexity of her earlier psychic and sexual life ('injury' as its *price*).

Elizabeth Wilson and Janet Sayers are, therefore, in a sense correct to criticize psychoanalysis when it is taken as a general theory of patriarchy or of gender identity, that is, as a theory which explains how women wholly internalize the very mode of being which is feminism's specific target of attack; but they have missed out half the (psychoanalytic) story. In fact the argument seems to be circular. Psychoanalysis is drawn in the direction of a general theory of culture or a sociological account of gender because these seem to lay greater emphasis on the pressures of the 'outside' world, but it is this very pulling away from the psychoanalytic stress on the 'internal' complexity and difficulty of psychic life which produces the functionalism which is then critized.

The argument about whether Freud is being 'prescriptive' or 'descriptive' about women (with its associated stress on the motives and morals of Freud himself) is fated to the extent that it is locked into this model. Many of us will be familiar with Freud's famous pronouncement that a woman who does not succeed in transforming activity to passivity, clitoris to vagina, mother for father, will fall ill. Yet psychoanalysis testifies to the fact that psychic illness or distress is in no sense the prerogative of women who 'fail' in this task. One of my students recently made the obvious but important point that we would be foolish to deduce from the external trappings of normality or conformity in a woman that all is in fact well. And Freud himself always stressed the psychic cost of the civilizing process for all (we can presumably include women in that 'all' even if at times he did not seem to do so).

All these aspects of Freud's work are subject to varying interpretation by analysts themselves. The first criticism of Freud's 'phallocentrism' came from inside psychoanalysis, from analysts such as Melanie Klein, Ernest Jones and Karen Horney who felt, contrary to Freud, that 'femininity' was a quality with its own impetus, subject to checks and internal conflict, but tending ultimately to fulfilment. For Jones, the little girl was 'typically receptive and acquisitive' from the outset; for Horney, there was from the beginning a 'wholly womanly' attachment to the father.[7] For these analysts, this development might come to grief, but for the most part a gradual strengthening of the child's ego and her increasing adaptation to reality, should guarantee its course. Aspects of the little girl's psychic life which were resistant to this process (the famous 'active' or 'masculine' drives) were defensive. The importance of concepts such as the 'phallic phase' in Freud's description of infantile sexuality is not, therefore, that such concepts can be taken as the point of insertion of patriarchy (assimilation to the norm). Rather their importance lies in the way that they indicate, through their very artificiality, that something was being *forced*, and in the concept of psychic life with which they were accompanied. In Freud's work they went hand in hand with an increasing awareness of the difficulty, not to say impossibility of the path to normality for the girl, and an increasing stress on the fundamental divisions, or splitting, of psychic life. It was those who challenged these concepts in the 1920s and 1930s who introduced the more normative stress on a sequence of development, and coherent ego, back into the account.

I think we go wrong again, therefore, if we conduct the debate about whether Freud's account was developmental or not entirely in terms of his own writing. Certainly the idea of development is present at moments in his work. But it was not present *enough* for many of his contemporaries, who took up the issue and reinstated the idea of development precisely in relation to the sexual progress of the girl (her passage into womanhood).

'Psychoanalysis' is not, therefore, a single entity. Institutional divisions within psychoanalysis have turned on the very questions about the phallo-centrism of analysts, the meaning of femininity, the sequence of psychic development and its norms, which have been the concern of feminists. The accusations came from analysts themselves. In the earlier delates, however, the reproach against Freud produced an account of femininity which was more, rather than less, normative than his own.

The politics of Lacanian psychoanalysis begin here. From the 1930s, Lacan saw his intervention as a return to the concepts of psychic division, splitting of the ego, and an endless (he called it 'insistent') pressure of the unconscious against any individual's pretension to a smooth and coherent psychic and sexual identity. Lacan's specific target was 'ego-psychology' in America, and what he saw as the dilution of psychoanalysis into a tool of social adaptation and control (hence the central emphasis on the concepts of the ego and identification which are often overlooked in discussions of his ideas). For Lacan, psychoanalysis does not offer an account of a developing ego which is 'not *necessarily* coherent',[8] but of an ego which is 'necessarily *not* coherent', that is, which is always and persistently divided against itself.

Lacan could therefore be picked up by a Marxist like Althusser not because he offered a theory of adaptation to reality or of the individual's insertion into culture (Althusser added a note to the English translation of his paper on Lacan criticizing it for having implied such a reading),[9] but because the force of the unconscious in Lacan's interpretation of Freud was felt to undermine the mystifications of a bourgeois culture proclaiming its identity, and that of its subjects, to the world. The political use of Lacan's theory therefore stemmed from its assault on what English Marxists would call bourgeois 'individualism'. What the theory offered was a divided subject out of 'synch' with bourgeois myth. Feminists could legitimately object that the notion of psychic fragmentation was of little immediate political advantage to women struggling for the first time to find a voice, and trying to bring together the dissociated components of their life into a political programme. But this is a very different criticism of the political implications of psychoanalysis than the one which accuses it of forcing women into bland conformity with their expected role.

(1983)

Notes

First published in *Feminist Review*, 14 (Summer 1983), pp. 5–21, this essay was originally requested by the editors of *Feminist Review* to counter the largely negative representation of psychoanalysis which had appeared in the journal, and as a specific response to Elizabeth Wilson's 'Psychoanalysis: psychic law and order', *Feminist Review*, 8 (Summer 1981). (See also Janet Sayers, 'Psychoanalysis and personal politics: a response to Elizabeth Wilson', *Feminist Review*, 10 (1982).) As I was writing the piece, however, it soon became clear that Elizabeth Wilson's article and the question of *Feminist Review*'s own relationship to psychoanalysis could not be understood independently of what has been – outside the work of Juliet Mitchell for feminism – a fairly consistent repudiation of Freud within the British Left. In this context, the feminist debate over Freud becomes part of a larger question about the importance of subjectivity to our understanding of political and social life. That this was in fact the issue became even clearer when Elizabeth Wilson and Angie Weir published an article 'The British women's movement' in *New Left Review*, 148 (November–December 1984), which dismissed the whole area of subjectivity and psychoanalysis from feminist politics together with any work by feminists (historians and writers on contemporary politics) who, while defining themselves as socialist feminists, nonetheless query the traditional terms of an exclusively class-based analysis of power.

1   Juliet Mitchell, *Psychoanalysis and Feminism* (Allen Lane, London, 1974).
2   See Gayle Rubin, 'The traffic in women'; and for a critique of the use of Lévi-Strauss on which this reading is based, Elizabeth Cowie, 'Woman as sign', *m/f*, 1978, pp. 49–63.
3   Nancy Chodorow, *The Reproduction of Mothering* (University of California Press, Berkeley, 1978).
4   Ibid., p. 3.
5   Janet Sayers, 'A response to Elizabeth Wilson', *Feminist Review*, 10 (1981), pp. 91–5.
6   Sigmund Freud, 'The dissolution of the Oedipus complex' (1924); 'Some psychical consequences of the anatomical distinction between the sexes' (1925); 'Female sexuality' (1931), *Standard Edition of Complete Psychological Works* (Hogarth, London, 1955–74), vol. 19.
7   Ernest Jones, 'The phallic phase', *International Journal of Psycho-Analysis*, 14 (1933), p. 265; Karen Horney, 'On the genesis of the castration complex in women' (1924), in *Feminine Psychology* (London, 1967), p. 53.
8   Elizabeth Wilson, 'Reopening the case – feminism and psychoanalysis', opening seminar presentation in discussion with Jacqueline Rose, London 1982. This was the first of a series of seminars on the subject of feminism and psychoanalysis

which ran into 1983; see articles by Parveen Adams, Nancy Wood and Claire Buck, *m/f*, 8 (1983).
9   Louis Althusser, 'Freud and Lacan', see publisher's note in *Lenin and Philosophy and Other Essays* (London, 1971), pp. 189–90.

CATHERINE BELSEY

Critical Practice

The destination of all ideology is the subject (the individual in society) and it is the role of ideology to *construct people as subjects*:

> I say: the category of the subject is constitutive of all ideology, but at the same time and immediately I add that *the category of the subject is only constitutive of all ideology in so far as all ideology has the function (which defines it) of 'constituting' concrete individuals as subjects*. (ibid, [*Louis Althusser, Lenin and Philosophy*, London, Longman, 1971] p. 160)

Within the existing ideology it appears 'obvious' that people are autonomous individuals, possessed of subjectivity or consciousness which is the source of their beliefs and actions. That people are unique, distinguishable, irreplaceable identities is 'the elementary ideological effect' (*ibid*, p. 161).

The obviousness of subjectivity has been challenged by the linguistic theory which has developed on the basis of the work of Saussure. As Emile Benveniste argues, it is language which provides the possibility of subjectivity because it is language which enables the speaker to posit himself or herself as 'I', as the subject of a sentence. It is through language that people constitute themselves as subjects. Consciousness of self is possible only through contrast, differentiation: 'I' cannot be conceived without the conception 'non-I', 'you', and dialogue, the fundamental condition of language,[11] implies a reversible polarity between 'I' and 'you'. 'Language is possible only because each speaker sets himself up as a *subject* by referring to himself as *I* in his discourse' (Benveniste [*Problems in General Linguistics*, Miami University Press] 1971, p. 225). But if language is a system of differences with no positive terms, 'I' designates only the subject of a specific utterance. 'And so it is literally true that the basis of subjectivity is in the exercise of language. If one really thinks about it, one will see that there is no other objective testimony to the identity of the subject except that which he himself thus gives about himself' (*ibid*, p. 226).

Within ideology, of course, it seems 'obvious' that the individual speaker is the origin of the meaning of his or her utterance. Post-Saussurean linguistics, however, implies a more complex relationship between the individual and meaning, since it is language itself which, by differentiating between concepts, offers the possibility of meaning. In reality, it is only by adopting the position of the subject within language that the individual is able to produce meaning. As Jacques Derrida puts it,

> what was it that Saussure in particular reminded us of? That 'language [which consists only of differences] is not a function of the speaking subject'. This implies that the subject (self-identical or even conscious of self-identity, self-conscious) is inscribed in the language, that he is a 'function' of the language. He becomes a *speaking* subject only by conforming his speech … to the system of linguistic prescriptions taken as the system of differences … (Derrida [*Speech and Phenomena*, Northwestern University Press] 1973, pp. 145–6)

Derrida goes on to raise the question whether, even if we accept that it is only the signifying system which makes possible the speaking subject, the signifying subject, we cannot nonetheless conceive of a non-speaking, non-signifying subjectivity, 'a silent and intuitive consciousness' (*ibid*, p. 146). The problem here, he concludes, is to define consciousness-in-itself as distinct from consciousness of something, and ultimately as distinct from consciousness of self. If consciousness is finally consciousness of self, this in turn implies that consciousness depends on differentiation, and specifically on Benveniste's differentiation between 'I' and 'you', a process made possible by language.

The implications of this concept of the primacy of language over subjectivity have been developed by Jacques Lacan's reading of Freud.[12] Lacan's theory of the subject as constructed in language confirms the *decentring* of the individual consciousness so that it can no longer be seen as the origin of meaning, knowledge and action. Instead, Lacan proposes that the infant is initially an 'hommelette' – 'a little man and also like a broken egg spreading without hindrance in all directions' (Coward and Ellis [*Language and Materialism*, London, Routledge and Kegan Paul] 1977, p. 101). The child has no sense of identity, no way of conceiving of itself as a unity, distinct from what is 'other', exterior to it. During the 'mirror-phase' of its development, however, it 'recognizes' itself in the mirror as a unit distinct from the outside world. This 'recognition' is an identification with an 'imaginary' (because imaged) unitary and autonomous self. But it is only with its entry into language that the child becomes a full subject. If it is to participate in the society into which it is born, to be able to act deliberately within the social formation, the child must enter into the symbolic order, the set of signifying systems of culture of which the supreme example is language. The child who refuses to learn the language is 'sick', unable to become a full member of the family and of society.

In order to speak the child is compelled to differentiate; to speak of itself it has to distinguish 'I' from 'you'. In order to formulate its needs the child learns to identify with the first person singular pronoun, and this identification constitutes the basis of subjectivity. Subsequently it learns to recognize itself in a series of subject-positions ('he' or 'she', 'boy' or 'girl', and so on) which are the positions from which discourse is intelligible to itself and others. 'Identity', subjectivity, is thus a matrix of subject-positions, which may be inconsistent or even in contradiction with one another.

Subjectivity, then, is linguistically and discursively constructed and displaced across the range of discourses in which the concrete individual participates. It follows from Saussure's theory of language as a system of differences that the world is intelligible only through discourse: there is no unmediated experience, no access to the raw reality of self and others. Thus,

> As well as being a system of signs related among themselves, language incarnates meaning in the form of the series of positions it offers for the subject from which to grasp itself and its relations with the real. (Nowell-Smith ['A Note on History/Discourse', *Edinburgh 76 Magazine* no. 1] 1976, p. 26)

The subject is constructed in language and in discourse and, since the symbolic order in its discursive use is closely related to ideology, in ideology. It is in this sense that ideology has the effect, as Althusser argues, of constituting individuals as subjects, and it is also in this sense that their subjectivity appears 'obvious'. Ideology suppresses the role of language in the construction of the subject. As a result, people 'recognize' (misrecognize) themselves in the ways in which ideology 'interpellates' them, or in other words, addresses them as subjects, calls them by their names and in turn 'recognizes' their autonomy.[13] As a result, they 'work by themselves' (Althusser 1971, p. 169), they 'willingly' adopt the subject-positions necessary to their participation in the social formation. In capitalism they 'freely' exchange their labour-power for wages, and they 'voluntarily' purchase the commodities produced. And it is here that we see the full force of Althusser's use of the term 'subject', originally borrowed, as he says, from law. The subject is not only a grammatical subject, 'a centre of initiatives, author of and responsible for its actions', but also a *subjected being* who submits to the authority of the social formation represented in ideology as the Absolute Subject (God, the king, the boss, Man, conscience):

> the individual *is interpellated as a (free) subject in order that he shall submit freely to the commandments of the Subject, i.e. in order that he shall (freely) accept his subjection. (ibid, p. 169)*

(1980)

Notes

11   The signals emitted to each other by bees preclude the possibility of dialogue and are therefore not to be confused with language (Benveniste, pp. 49–54; Lacan 1977a, pp. 84–5).

12   Work by and on Lacan is becoming increasingly available in English (see Notes on Further Reading, 1.3).

13   I have stressed the role of interpellation in the constitution of subjectivity, although Althusser himself also lays considerable emphasis on the metaphor of imaginary recognition in the mirror-structure of ideology (1971, pp. 167–8). This concept, derived from Lacan's analysis of the mirror-phase, is open to criticism. The notion of recognition by the subject of itself and of the Absolute Subject implies a subject prior to ideology which does the recognizing – 'Something must recognize that which it is to be' (Hirst 1976, p. 404). As Hirst goes on to argue, Althusser's position compels him to argue that the child is 'always-already' a subject, awaited as a subject even before its birth, in the certainty that it will bear its Father's Name (Althusser 1971, pp. 164–5). But children do not possess subjectivity at birth; they are not ' "knowing" subjects independent of their formation and training as social beings' (Hirst 1976, p. 406). Subjectivity, I have suggested, is to be understood above all as a linguistic construct, and the recognition (misrecognition) performed by the subject is most usefully understood as its identification with the *I* of language and then with the I AM of the Absolute Subject to which it accepts its subjection (Althusser 1971, p. 169). The set of subject-positions which make action possible are products of discourse, and it is the network of discourses which is the site of ideology in its specificity.

Shoshana Felman

What Does a Woman Want? Reading and Sexual Difference

Feminism, I will thus suggest, is indeed for women, among other things, reading literature and theory with their own life – a life, however, that is not entirely in their conscious possession. If, as Adrienne Rich acutely points out, rereading or "re-vision – the act of looking back, of seeing with fresh eyes, of entering an old text from a new critical direction – is for women more than a chapter in cultural history: it is an act of survival," it is because survival is, profoundly, a form of autobiography.

Reading autobiographically is, however, an activity and a performance far more complex than the mere project – and the mere stylistic trend – of "getting personal."[16] Because as educated women we are all unwittingly possessed by "the male mind that has been implanted in us," because though women we can quite easily and surreptitiously read literature as men, we can just as easily "get personal" with a borrowed voice – and might not even know *from whom* we borrow that voice. "Getting personal" does not guarantee that the story we narrate is wholly ours or that it is narrated in our own voice. In spite of the contemporary literary fashion of feminine confessions and of the recent critical fashion of "feminist confessions," I will suggest that *none of us, as women, has as yet, precisely, an autobiography.* Trained to see ourselves as objects and to be positioned as the Other, estranged to ourselves, we have a story that by definition cannot be self-present to us, a story that, in other words, is not a story, but *must become* a story.[17] And it cannot *become* a story except through the *bond of reading,* that is, through the *story of the Other* (the story read by other women, the story of other women, the story of women told by others), insofar as this story of the Other, as *our own* autobiography, *has as yet precisely to be owned.* I will suggest that it cannot be owned by our attempting a direct access to ourselves as women ("getting personal") or by our pretending to leave culture or to step outside the text (by becoming a "resisting reader"). Rather, I will here propose that we might be able to engender, or to access, our story only indirectly – by conjugating literature, theory, and autobiography together through the act of reading and by reading, thus, into the texts of culture, at once our sexual difference and our autobiography as missing.

I should hasten to explain that by adopting the generic "we" in what I have just written ("I will suggest that none of us, as women, has as yet, precisely, an autobiography"), I am not proposing to speak in the name of women: the "we" is a rhetorical structure of address, not a claim for epistemological authority. I am speaking not *for* women, but *to* women. My utterance is meant as a *speech act,* not as a constative *representation;* it is a cognitive suggestion, an intuition, but its rhetorical force is primarily performative. The contemporary female autobiographical self-consciousness is a crucially important, innovative theoretical and critical resource, and I do not mean to underestimate or undercut its strategic value. But I do propose here to *unsettle* the very notion of autobiography, precisely insofar as we have *settled* into it (I feel) a little too impatiently and self-complacently, as though we could be sure that we already have – in culture or in life – "a room of our own."

As what follows will make clear, this book is, among other things, the account of how I made the discovery – and the experience – of my own autobiography as missing, and why this *missing* of my own autobiography appears to me today to be characteristic of the female condition. I am mainly speaking for myself. And yet I venture to propose this insight as a metaphor for the dilemmas and the problematic of autobiography for women, since the observations of my personal experience cannot invalidate it with respect to any woman I know, and since I have gained this self-understanding, once again, once indirectly, by listening to other women speak about themselves, by looking closely at the stories (which narrated, ultimately, the absence of a story or, what amounts to the same thing, the presence of too many stories) of a number of close female friends.

(1993)

Notes

16   See Nancy Miller, *Getting Personal* (New York: Routledge, 1991) for a subtly nuanced feminist position that identifies, however, the autobiographical with the personal and the confessional. Miller points to the contemporary "outbreak of self-writing," which "(although it is not practiced uniquely by feminists or women) can be seen to develop out of feminist theory's original emphasis on the analysis of the personal: ... the current proliferation in literary studies of autobiographical or personal criticism," and comments:

> The spectacle of a significant number of critics getting personal in their writing, while not, to be sure, on the order of a paradigm shift, is at least the sign of a turning point in the history of critical practices.... In the face of the visible extremes of racism or misogyny, or the equally violent silences of theoretical discourses from which all traces of embodiment have been carefully abstracted, the autobiographical project might seem a frivolous response. How can I propose a reflection about an ethics in criticism ... from these individualistic grounds? But the risk of a limited personalism, I think, is a risk worth taking. ("Preface," *Feminist Confessions*, ix–x, xiv)

This equation between the autobiographical and the "confessional" is commonly encountered in current feminist criticism and perception. See, for instance, the excellent introduction of the editors to the section, "Autobiography," in the anthology entitled *Feminisms:* "When the writer's presence seems to tear through the fabric of the academic text – revealing glimmers of the lived experience that forms the context for scholarly writing – "confessional" moments occur in otherwise conventional prose.... The confessional mode can also govern an entire essay.... In this new form of academic writing, autobiography merges with scholarship, and a personal voice begins – if only tentatively – to take shape in expository prose" (Robyn R. Warhol and Diane Price Herndl, eds., *Feminisms: An Anthology of Literary Theory and Criticism* [New Brunswick, NJ: Rutgers University Press, 1991], 1033).

For a different perspective, which insists on analyzing, on the contrary, the radical gap and consequent differentiation between "the autobiographical" and the illusions of the personal, see (in the same anthology) Shari Benstock's study of Virginia Woolf ("Authorizing Autobiography") and its critique of what might be called the mystique of traditional autobiography ("definitions of autobiography that stress self-disclosure and narrative account"), insofar as this tradition gravitates around the delusion of a coherent (or "organic") self. In contrast to this mystique, says Benstock, the modern feminine autobiographical project (as embodied by Virginia Woolf) stresses language as "a principle of separation and division" through which the "self" is at the same time constructed and decentered: " 'Writing the self' is therefore a process of simultaneous sealing and splitting that can *only trace fissures of discontinuity*. This process may take place through 'the individual's special, peculiar psychic configuration,' but it is never an act of 'consciousness' pure and simple" (ibid., 1054, emphasis mine).

17   My point here is different from the one developed by Carolyn Heilbrun in her moving and effective essay, *Writing a Woman's Life* (New York: Ballantine Books, 1988). Heilburn argues that women have been hindered in their quest for accomplishment because "power and control" have always been "declared unwomanly." As a result, "women have been deprived of the narratives, or the texts, plots, or examples, by which they might assume power over–take control of–their own lives" (17). "Power is the ability to take one's place in whatever discourse is essential to action and the right to have one's part matter" (18). Thus, women suffer from the fact that they have "no models on which to form their lives" (25). Heilbrun's enterprise is to provide new models in narrating the life stories of exceptional women and in attempting to "face systematically" the "choices and pain of the women who did not make a man the center of their lives" (31), women who wrote themselves a "life beyond convention" (96) and thereby contributed to "transform female destiny" (120) and to create, specifically, "new stories" (122), having "moved beyond the categories our available narratives have provided for women" (131).

My argument is that *our own autobiography is not available to us*, not simply because we have no models and because, inhabiting male plots, we are enjoined not to transgress convention and to leave the realm of accomplishment to men (to live around a male center) but because we cannot simply *substitute ourselves as center* without regard to the *decentering* effects of language and of the unconscious, without acute awareness of the fact that our own relation to a linguistic frame of reference is never self-transparent. We can neither simply "write" our stories nor decide to write "new" stories, because we *do not know* our stories, and because the decision to "rewrite" them is not simply external to the language that unwittingly writes us. My emphasis is on the unavailability for women, not simply of "power" but of knowledge, and self-knowledge; on the unavailability, that is, not only of new models but of new linguistic *structures of address*.

The question of a model is one of origins, of sources. The question of address is one of goals, of destinations. Life as a complex relation to the Other (to society, to history) poses not merely the question, "What model do I imitate?" "What structure of otherness do I identify myself with?" but also, "What structure of otherness do I address myself to (in my speeches and my actions)?"

This is why the key, in my perspective, is in *learning how to read* (rhetorical, psychoanalytical, political, ethical) *structures of address* and in attempting, through the reading, to transform or "rewrite" these structures not merely from the vantage point of *one* language (in whose ethnocentric, pseudotransparent medium we will simply substitute one center for another, in shifting from male-centered plots to female-centered stories) but from the *cross-cultural* perspective of the difference and the interaction between different languages and cultures.

For a study of autobiography that insists, precisely, on a multicultural, multiracial, multilinguistic perspective, and yet that tries to analyze how women writers from different races and different languages, those specifically "who must survive (and write) in the interval between different cultures and languages," nonetheless share not just conflicts and dilemmas but common concerns, strategies, and ways of coping, see Françoise Lionnet, *Autobiographical Voices: Race, Gender, Self-Portraiture* (Ithaca: Cornell University Press, 1989).

JANICE A. RADWAY

A Feeling for Books: The Book-of-the-Month Club,
Literary Taste, and Middle-Class Desire

Most of the books I read that year, as I turned fifteen, similarly celebrated the achievements of heroic men. Together with *Marjorie Morningstar*; *Gods, Graves, and Scholars*; and *To Kill a Mockingbird*, they tutored me about the value of a public world rendered significant by "serious" problems and "momentous" events. If they argued that this world had to be humanized and enlivened by the actions of individuals with extraordinary warmth and compassion, they nonetheless suggested that its compass could only be taken by people with broad knowledge and special training. What these books taught me to want, then, was a professional's power, a power lodged in books, honed in institutions of higher learning, and wielded in the name of greater knowledge.

The knowledge I wanted knew few limits. *Kon-Tiki* suggested that intellectual work might eventually take me to a place like the South Pacific, put me on a raft with a few other intrepid souls, and set me to proving a theory passionately held. *The Ugly American* suggested that I might actually understand why talk of dominoes and this strange-sounding country, Vietnam, with its even stranger-sounding cities, such as Dien Bien Phu and Hue, had suddenly begun to occupy so much time on the news programs I watched religiously. If the book was profoundly nationalist in its assumption that the United States was destined to bring its superior democracy to lesser states misguidedly enamored of communism, it also suggested that a commitment to the truth, to greater knowledge, might push one to criticize one's country constructively in the interest of greater global responsibility. Indeed the book's authors counseled me that "to the extent that our foreign policy is humane and reasonable, it will be successful. To the extent that it is imperialistic and grandiose, it will fail" (267). These sentiments provided fertile ground later for my participation in my generation's antiwar movement. But they also further reinforced my emergent professionalist aspirations with the exhortation, "We do not need the horde of 1,500,000 Americans – mostly amateurs – who are now working for the US overseas. What we need is a small force of well-trained, well-chosen, hard-working and dedicated professionals.... They must speak the language of the land of their assignment, and they must be more expert in its problems than are the natives" (284). I wanted to be such a person.

The books selected by the Book-of-the-Month Club and sent by Mr Shymansky suggested that knowledge was so powerful, in fact, that it might even enable me to understand the inexplicable events that had shaped my parents' adult lives and the history of the twentieth century, that is, the events of World War II. I cannot recall a moment when I first learned about the war or the figure of Adolf Hitler. These events were part of the everyday texture of my childhood because my father's wartime picture albums documenting his years in the Air Force were always ready to hand. Every time I pulled them down from the front closet to admire the uniformed crew of his B-24 or to puzzle over the aerial photos of bombs dropping on German cities, my mother or father would haltingly try to explain why the war was fought, who Adolf Hitler was, and what he had done. But those events always still felt just beyond comprehension, unexplained, and inexplicable. Perhaps that is why I was willing to attempt a book whose narrative fragmentation I found very difficult – *The Wall*, by John Hersey. Maybe that is why I plowed through William Shirer's 1,250 pages of *The Rise and Fall of the Third Reich*. Rereading Shirer's daunting narrative now, I cannot imagine that I actually read the whole thing then. But I certainly wanted to, and even more, I know I wanted to say that I had. I suspect, in fact, that my desire to make sense of these most incomprehensible events of a generally baffling century was widely shared and the very thing that made Shirer's the most popular book ever sent out by the Book-of-the-Month Club. Even if the book was not fully read in every case, it promised those who ordered it, held it in their hands, paged through it, and perhaps made their way through only the first few chapters that a singular, dedicated man, armed with a relentless desire to know and an endless willingness to read papers, documents, letters, and books, could actually comprehend the incomprehensible.

When Dr Waugh finally sliced through my cast with a tiny, buzzing saw in October 1964, liberating me at last from the house and that bedroom, I returned to school. Freed of my plaster armor, I felt terribly fragile at first and very small. I worried about girlish things – whether I could return to the cheerleading squad or what I would look like in a dress again. Mr Shymansky's books already seemed an incidental part of a distant past, books that had provided only a stay against boredom, easy enough to forget, and certainly not worth mentioning to anyone. Their effects remained, though, steeling me for a future almost the way the bone grafts now straightening my spine enabled me to walk fully upright for the first time in two years. Although I was not aware of it, their powerful evocation of the riches to be found in the world of knowledge and expertise enabled me to dismiss those cheerful, cartoonish diagrams I found in my SAT booklet only a year later. Those diagrams claimed that girls with a certain SAT score would complete fewer years of higher education and make less money than boys with exactly the same score. I was determined that this would not happen to me. I wanted to be as familiar with a professional world as Atticus was and as authoritative as he seemed to be. I was determined not to take up my place on that porch Scout saw looming in her own future, nor did I want any part of the house in Mamaroneck next to Marjorie's. Books, reading, and the worlds they revealed were the hope Mr Shymansky and the Book-of-the-Month Club gave me, the hope that I might breach the pink cotton walls of the feminine penitentiary.

For me Mr Shymansky's middlebrow books accomplished many things. They staved off loneliness and peopled an imagination starved by enforced isolation. At the same time they preserved desire by delineating objects I might aim for at the very moment when I felt crushed by the necessity to contain every familiar want I had ever known, the desire to hang out with my friends, to ride downtown, to make the cheerleading squad, to go to a dance. Less immediately, perhaps, they surveyed, mapped, and made sense of an adult world. They described that world as one where the irreducible individual was a given, where knowledge was revered, and where expertise was to be sought after with intensity and a sense of purpose. They provided materials for self-fashioning as a result, and models to emulate. In the end they fostered my entry into middle-class selfhood and pointed me in direction of the professional middle class.

There were terrible costs, though, among them the repudiation of my gender demanded by the still-masculine image of professionalism. Indeed, I took my place in college classrooms where we read only a handful of books by women. As an undergraduate, the only female writers I read were the Brontës, Jane Austen, Emily Dickinson, and Edith Wharton. No Margaret Fuller, no Kate Chopin, no Gertrude Stein, no Djuna Barnes, no Virginia Woolf, and not even George Eliot. The women we read about – Carrie Meeber, Lady Brett Ashley, Hester Prynne, Caddie Compson, and Temple Drake – all seemed to meet an awful fate. Similarly, the way of reading we were taught required our subordination to an all-powerful text, whose flinty, virile power was always highlighted by its rejection of a feminine sentimentalism. It did not occur to me to ask what was wrong with sentiment. I was too intent on the goal of acquiring the particular form of technical expertise I found so compelling, expertise about literature and high culture. I wanted the authority that seemed to follow from knowing books and understanding how to read them. I wanted to command all that New York had once signified.

(1997)

Seyla Benhabib

'Sexual Difference and Collective Identities: The New Global Constellation'
Signs: Journal of Women in Culture and Society

During historical periods such as ours, in which economic-technological and political changes effect a restructuring of millions of lives, the search for certainty grows. The more fluid the environment becomes, the more unpredictable and opaque it grows and the more we retreat into the walls of our certainties, into the markers of the familiar. Hence globalization is accompanied by demands for isolationism, for protectionism, for raising even higher and making even sturdier the walls that divide us and them.

Theories of fragmentary and dispersed subjectivity, which were so fashionable at the height of postmodernism, ignored these demands for stability and understanding. The dispersal of the subject – yes, indeed, the "death" of the subject – was thought to be a good thing. Yet the search for coherence in an increasingly fragmentary material and cultural world and the attempt to generate meaning out of the complexities of life stories are not wrong, or unjust, or meaningless. The challenge in the new constellation is the following: Can there be coherent accounts of individual and collective identity that do not fall into xenophobia, intolerance, paranoia, and aggression toward others? Can the search for coherence be made compatible with the maintenance of fluid ego boundaries? Can the attempt to generate meaning be accompanied by an appreciation of the meaningless, the absurd, and the limits of discursivity? And finally, can we establish justice and solidarity at home without turning in on ourselves, without closing our borders to the needs and cries of others? What will democratic collective identities look like in the century of globalization?

One consequence of the new constellation for issues of sexual difference and collective identity is a renewed respect for the universal. The feminist movement in the 1980s lived through a "hermenuetics of suspicion." Every claim to generalization was suspected of hiding a claim to power on the part of a specific group; every attempt to speak in the name of "women" was countered by myriad differences of race, class, culture, and sexual orientation that were said to divide women. The category "woman" itself became suspect; feminist theorizing about woman or the female of the species was dubbed the hegemonic discourse of white, middle-class, professional, heterosexual women. We are still reeling from the many divisions and splinterings, the amoeba-like splittings, of the women's movements.

I sense, however, a new awareness afoot – a recognition of interdependence among women of different classes, cultures, and sexual orientations;[14] more significantly, I detect a renewed respect for the moral and political legacy of universalism out of which the women's movements first grew in the eighteenth and nineteenth centuries. Consider the remarkable "Universalism" issue of the journal *differences*. In "French Feminism Is a Universalism," Naomi Schor writes,

> And yet just as some women have resisted the critique of universalism, so, too, universalism has clung to life. This refusal simply to fade away gracefully is indicated by the recent return of the universal among some of the feminists and postmodernist theorists who at other times and in other situations wholeheartedly

embraced the critique of universalism. I count myself among them.... If Auschwitz dealt the Enlightenment ideal of universalism – a notion rejected by fascism–a death blow, what may pass for the repetition of Auschwitz, the ongoing ethnic cleansing in Bosnia-Herzegovina, has if not revived universalism then called into question the celebration of particularisms, at least in their regressive ethnic form. (1995, 28)

A further consequence of the new constellation is a reconceptualization of the position of the feminist theorist as a critical intellectual. In *Situating the Self* I used the metaphor of the exile to explicate the possibility of social and cultural criticism, which, while being situated and context-bound, nonetheless aspired to transcend its own parish walls. I argued that "the social critic who is in exile does not adopt the 'view from nowhere' but the 'view from outside the walls of the city,' wherever those walls and those boundaries might be. It may indeed be no coincidence that from Hypatia to Diotima to Olympe de Gouges and to Rosa Luxemburg, the vocation of the feminist thinker and critic has led her to leave home and the city walls" (Benhabib 1992b, 228). The metaphor of exile to describe the vocation of the feminist critic has received a spirited objection from Rosi Braidotti in her provocative *Nomadic Subjects*. Braidotti agrees with me that we must empower women's political agency without falling "back on a substantialist vision of the subject," but she objects to my emphasis on exile:

> The central figuration for postmodern subjectivity is not that of a marginalized exile but rather that of an active nomadism. The critical intellectual camping at the city gates is not seeking readmission but rather taking a rest before crossing the next stretch of desert. Critical thinking is not a diaspora of the elected few but a massive abandonment of the logocentric "polis," the alleged "center" of the empire, on the part of critical and resisting thinking beings. Whereas for Benhabib the normativity of the phallogocentric regime is negotiable and reparable, for me it is beyond repair. Nomadism is therefore also a gesture of nonconfidence in the capacity of the "polis" to undo the power foundations on which it rests. (1994, 32)

This is an eloquent characterization of some fundamental differences. However, Braidotti has an unrealistic conception of identity. For her, matters of identity seem infinitely deconstructable figurations. She defines nomadic consciousness as "not taking any kind of identity as permanent. The nomad is only passing through; s/he makes those necessarily situated connections that can help her/him to survive, but s/he never takes on fully the limits of one, national fixed identity. The nomad has no passport – or has too many of them" (1994, 33).

Yet there is an enormous difference between having no passport and having too many. The refugee, the illegal immigrant, the asylum seeker who has no passport also has no protection from the collective and organized power of her or his fellow human beings. She or he is at the mercy of border patrols, emigration officials, international relief organizations (see Benhabib 1998). She has lost, in Hannah Arendt's famous words, "the right to have rights" – that is, the right to be recognized as a moral and political equal in a human community (1951, 290; see also Benhabib 1996b). In a century in which statelessness and the condition of being a refugee have become global phenomena, this is not a matter to be taken lightly. To have too many passports is usually the privilege of the few. Nation-states are still loath to recognize the status of dual citizenship; it is only rare circumstances of family, work, and political history that place one in this situation. I would agree with Braidotti that the complexity of our cultural, ethnic, racial, linguistic identities and heritages are not reflected in our passports, in our identities as nationals of this or that state. However, we must have the right to become members of a polity, and the rules of entry into a polity must be fair and in accordance with human dignity. To achieve this, we must indeed renegotiate the normativity of the "logocentric polis." The feminist theorist at the present is one of the brokers in this complex renegotiation of sexual difference and new collective identities.

(1999)

Note

14   The work of María Lugones on *mestizaje* (1994) and Gloria Anzaldúa (1987, 1990) and Norma Alarcón (1990) on cultural interstitiality deal with parallel themes. I would like to thank my student Edwina Barvosa (1998) for drawing my attention to Chicana women's writing and multiplex identities.

Linda Alcoff

'Cultural Feminism versus Post-Structuralism: The Identity Crisis in Feminist Theory'
Signs: Journal of Women in Culture and Society

The attraction of the post-structuralist critique of subjectivity for feminists is two-fold. First, it seems to hold out the promise of an increased freedom for women, the "free play" of a plurality of differences unhampered by any predetermined gender identity as formulated by either patriarchy or cultural feminism. Second, it moves decisively beyond cultural feminism and liberal feminism in further theorizing what they leave untouched: the construction of subjectivity. We can learn a great deal here about the mechanisms of sexist oppression and the construction of specific gender categories by relating these to social discourse and by conceiving of the subject as a cultural product. Certainly, too, this analysis can help us understand right-wing women, the reproduction of ideology, and the mechanisms that block social progress. However, adopting nominalism creates significant problems for feminism. How can we seriously adopt Kristeva's plan for only negative struggle? As the Left should by now have learned, you cannot mobilize a movement that is only and always against: you must have a positive alternative, a vision of a better future that can motivate people to sacrifice their time and energy toward its realization. Moreover, a feminist adoption of nominalism will be confronted with the same problem theories of ideology have, that is, Why is a right-wing woman's consciousness constructed via social discourse but a feminist's consciousness not? Post-structuralist critiques of subjectivity pertain to the construction of all subjects or they pertain to none. And here is precisely the dilemma for feminists: How can we ground a feminist politics that deconstructs the female subject? Nominalism threatens to wipe out feminism itself.

Some feminists who wish to use post-structuralism are well aware of this danger. Biddy Martin, for example, points out that "we cannot afford to refuse to take a political stance 'which pins us to our sex' for the sake of an abstract theoretical correctness.... There is the danger that Foucault's challenges to traditional categories, if taken to a 'logical' conclusion ... could make the question of women's oppression obsolete."[32] Based on her articulation of the problem with Foucault we are left hopeful that Martin will provide a solution that transcends nominalism. Unfortunately, in her reading of Lou Andreas-Salome, Martin valorizes undecidability, ambiguity, and elusiveness and intimates that by maintaining the undecidability of identity the life of Andreas-Salome provides a text from which feminists can usefully learn.[33]

However, the notion that all texts are undecidable cannot be useful for feminists. In support of his contention that the meaning of texts is ultimately undecidable, Derrida offers us in *Spurs* three conflicting but equally warranted interpretations of how Nietzsche's texts construct and position the female. In one of these interpretations Derrida argues we can find purportedly feminist propositions.[34] Thus, Derrida seeks to demonstrate that even the seemingly incontrovertible interpretation of Nietzsche's works as misogynist can be challenged by an equally convincing argument that they are not. But how can this be helpful to feminists, who need to have their accusations of misogyny validated rather than rendered "undecidable"? The point is not that Derrida himself is antifeminist, nor that there is nothing at all in Derrida's work that can be useful for feminists. But the thesis of undecidability as it is applied in the case of Nietzsche sounds too much like yet another version of the antifeminist argument that our perception of sexism is based on a skewed, limited perspective and that what we take to be misogyny is in reality helpful rather than hurtful to the cause of women. The declaration of undecidability must inevitably return us to Kristeva's position, that we can give only negative answers to the question, What is a woman? If the category "woman" is fundamentally undecidable, then we can offer no positive conception of it that is immune to deconstruction, and we are left with a feminism that can be only deconstructive and, thus, nominalist once again.[35]

A nominalist position on subjectivity has the deleterious effect of degendering our analysis, of in effect making gender invisible once again. Foucault's ontology includes only bodies and pleasures, and he is notorious for not including gender as a category of analysis. If gender is simply a social construct, the need and even the possibility of a feminist politics becomes immediately problematic. What can we demand in the name of women if "women" do not exist and demands in their name simply reinforce the myth that they do? How can we speak out against sexism as detrimental to the interests of women if the category is a fiction? How can we demand legal abortions, adequate child care, or wages based on comparable worth without invoking a concept of "woman"?

Post-structuralism undercuts our ability to oppose the dominant trend (and, one might argue, the dominant danger) in mainstream Western intellectual thought, that is, the insistence on a universal, neutral, perspectiveless epistemology, metaphysics, and ethics. Despite rumblings from the Continent, Anglo-American thought is still wedded to the idea(l) of a universalizable, apolitical methodology and set of transhistorical basic truths unfettered by associations with particular genders, races, classes, or cultures. The rejection of subjectivity, unintentionally but nevertheless, colludes with this "generic human" thesis of classical liberal thought, that particularities of individuals are irrelevant and improper influences on knowledge. By designating individual particularities such as subjective experience as a social construct, post-structuralism's negation of the authority of the subject coincides nicely with the classical liberal's view that human particularities are irrelevant. (For the liberal, race, class, and gender are ultimately irrelevant to questions of justice and truth because "underneath we are all the same." For the post-structuralist, race, class, and gender are constructs and, therefore, incapable of decisively validating conceptions of justice and truth because underneath there lies no natural core to build on or liberate or maximize. Hence, once again, underneath we are all the same.) It is, in fact, a desire to topple this commitment to the possibility of a worldview – purported in fact as the best of all possible worldviews – grounded in a generic human, that motivates much of the cultural feminist glorification of femininity as a valid specificity legitimately grounding feminist theory.[36]

(1988)

Notes

32   Martin, 16–17.
33   Ibid., esp. 21, 24, and 28.
34   See Derrida, *Spurs*, esp. 57 and 97.
35   Martin's most recent work departs from this in a positive direction. In an essay coauthored with Chandra Talpade Mohanty, Martin points out "the political limitations of an insistence on 'indeterminacy' which implicitly, when not explicitly, denies the critic's own situatedness in the social, and in effect refuses to acknowledge the critic's own institutional home." Martin and Mohanty seek to develop a more positive, though still problematized, conception of the subject as having a "multiple and shifting" perspective. In this, their work becomes a significant contribution toward the development of an alternative conception of subjectivity, a conception not unlike the one that I will discuss in the rest of this essay ("Feminist Politics: What's Home Got to Do with It?" in Lauretis, ed. [n. 18 above], 191–212, esp. 194).
36   A wonderful exchange on this between persuasive and articulate representatives of both sides was printed in *Diacritics* (Peggy Kamuf, "Replacing Feminist Criticism," *Diacritics* 12 [1982]: 42–7; and Nancy Miller, "The Text's Heroine: A Feminist Critic and Her Fictions," *Diacritics* 12 [1982]: 48–53).

Teresa de Lauretis

'Upping the Anti (Sic) in Feminist Theory'
Conflicts in Feminism

The title of Alcoff's essay, "Cultural Feminism versus Post-structuralism: The Identity Crisis in Feminist Theory," bespeaks some of the same problems: a manner of thinking by mutually oppositional categories, an agonistic frame of argumentation, and a focus on division, a "crisis in feminist theory" that may be read not only as a crisis *over* identity, a metacritical doubt and a dispute among feminists as to the notion of identity, but also as a crisis *of* identity, of self-definition, implying a theoretical impasse for feminism as a whole. The essay, however, is more discerning, goes much further than its title suggests, and even contradicts it in the end, as the notion of identity, far from fixing the point of an impasse, becomes an active shifter in the feminist discourse of woman.[5]

Taking as its starting point "the concept of woman," or rather, its redefinition in feminist theory ("the dilemma facing feminist theorists today is that our very self-definition is grounded in a concept that we must deconstruct and de-essentialize in all of its aspects"), Alcoff finds two major categories of responses to the dilemma, or what I would call the paradox of woman (p. 406). Cultural feminists, she claims, "have not challenged the defining of woman but only that definition given by men" (p. 407), and have replaced it with what they believe a more accurate description and appraisal, "the concept of the essential female" (p. 408). On the other hand, the poststructuralist response has been to reject the possibility of defining woman altogether and to replace "the politics of gender or sexual difference … with a plurality of difference where gender loses its position of significance" (p. 407). A third category is suggested, but only indirectly, in Alcoff's unwillingness to include among cultural feminists certain writers of color such as Moraga and Lorde in spite of their emphasis on cultural identity, for in her view "their work has consistently rejected essentialist conceptions of gender" (p. 412). Why an emphasis on racial, ethnic, and/or sexual identity need not be seen as essentialist is discussed more fully later in the essay with regard to identity politics and in conjunction with a third trend in feminist theory which Alcoff sees as a new course for feminism, "a theory of the gendered subject that does not slide into essentialism" (p. 422).

Whereas the narrative structure underlying Weedon's account of feminist theories is that of a contest where one actor successively engages and defeats or conquers several rivals, Alcoff's develops as a dialectics. Both the culturalist and the poststructuralist positions display internal contradictions: for example, not all cultural feminists "give explicitly essentialist formulations of what it means to be a woman" (p. 411), and their emphasis on the affirmation of women's strength and positive cultural roles and attributes has done much to counter images of woman as victim or of woman as male when in a business suit; but insofar as it reinforces the essentialist explanations of those attributes that are part and parcel of the traditional notion of womanhood, cultural feminism may, and for some women does, foster another form of sexist oppression. Conversely, if the poststructuralist critique of the unified, authentic subject of humanism is more than compatible with the feminist project to "deconstruct and de-essentialize" woman (as Alcoff puts it, in clearly poststructuralist terms), its absolute rejection of gender and its negation of biological determinism in favor of a cultural-discursive determinism result, as concerns women, in a form of nominalism. If "woman" is a fiction, a locus of pure difference and resistance to logocentric power, and if there are no women as such, then the very issue of women's oppression would appear to be obsolete and feminism itself would have no reason to exist (which, it may be noted, is a corollary of poststructuralism and the stated position of those who call themselves "post-feminists"). "What can we demand in the name of women," Alcoff asks, "if 'women' do not exist and demands in their name simply reinforce the myth that they do?" (p. 420).

The way out – let me say, the sublation – of the contradictions in which are caught these two mainstream feminist views lies in "a theory of the subject that avoids both essentialism and nominalism" (p. 421), and Alcoff points to it in the work of a few theorists, "a few brave souls," whom she rejoins in developing her notion of "woman as positionality": "woman is a position from which a feminist politics can emerge rather than a set of attributes that are 'objectively identifiable'" (pp. 134–435). In becoming feminist, for instance, women take up a position, a point of perspective, from which to interpret or (re)construct values and meanings. That position is also a politically assumed identity, and one relative to their sociohistorical location, whereas essentialist definitions would have woman's identity or attributes independent of her external situation; however, the positions available to women in any sociohistorical location are neither arbitrary nor undecidable. Thus, Alcoff concludes,

> If we combine the concept of identity politics with a conception of the subject as positionality, we can conceive of the subject as nonessentialized and emergent from a historical experience and yet retain our political ability to take gender as an important point of departure. Thus we can say at one and the same time that gender is not natural, biological, universal, ahistorical, or essential and yet still claim that gender is relevant because we are taking gender as a position from which to act politically. (p. 433)

I am, of course, in agreement with her emphases on issues and arguments that have been central in my work, such as the necessity to theorize experience in relation to practices, the understanding of gendered subjectivity as "an emergent property of a historicized experience" (p. 431), and the notion that identity is an active construction and a discursively mediated political interpretation of one's history. What I must ask, and less as a criticism of Alcoff's essay than for the purposes of my argument here, is: why is it still necessary to set up two opposing categories, cultural feminism and poststructuralism, or essentialism and anti-essentialism, thesis and antithesis, when one has already achieved the vantage point of a theoretical position that overtakes them or sublates them?

Doesn't the insistence on the "essentialism" of cultural feminists reproduce and keep in the foreground an image of "dominant" feminism that is at least reductive, at best tautological or superseded, and at worst not in our interests? Doesn't it feed the pernicious opposition of low versus high theory, a low-grade type of critical thinking (feminism) that is contrasted with the high-test theoretical grade of a poststructuralism from which some feminists would have been smart enough to learn? As one feminist theorist who's been concurrently involved with feminism, women's studies, psychoanalytic theory, structuralism, and film theory from the beginning of my critical activity, I know that learning to be a feminist has grounded, or embodied, all of my learning and so en-gendered thinking and knowing itself. That engendered thinking and that embodied, situated knowledge (in Donna Haraway's phrase)[6] are the stuff of feminist theory, whether by "feminist theory" is meant one of a growing number of feminist critical discourses – on culture, science, subjectivity, writing, visual representation, social institutions, etc. – or, more particularly, the critical elaboration of feminist thought itself and the ongoing (re)definition of its specific difference. In either case, feminist theory is not of a lower grade than that which some call "male theory," but different in kind; and it is its essential difference, the essence of that triangle, that concerns me here as a theorist of feminism.

Why then, I ask again, continue to constrain it in the terms of essentialism and anti-essentialism even as they no longer serve (but did they ever?) to formulate our questions? For example, in her discussion of cultural feminism, Alcoff accepts another critic's characterization despite some doubt that the latter "makes it appear too homogeneous and ... the charge of essentialism is on shaky ground" (p. 411). Then she adds:

> In the absence of a clearly stated position on the ultimate source of gender difference, Echols *infers* from their emphasis on building a feminist free-space and woman-centered culture that cultural feminists hold some version of essentialism. I share Echols's *suspicion*. Certainly, *it is difficult to render the views of Rich and Daly into a coherent whole without supplying a missing premise* that there is an innate female essence. (p. 412; emphasis added)

But why do it at all? What is the purpose, or the gain, of supplying a missing premise (innate female essence) in order to construct a coherent image of feminism which thus becomes available to charges (essentialism) based on the very premise that had to be supplied? What motivates such a project, the suspicion, and the inferences?

(1990)

Notes

5 Since Alcoff refers extensively to my own work, this essay is in a sense a dialogue with her and with myself – that dialogue in feminist critical writing which often works as a variation of consciousness raising or better, its transformation into a significant form of feminist cultural practice, and one not always reducible to "academic" activity.
6 Donna Haraway, "Situated Knowledges: The Science Question in Feminism and the Privilege of Partial Perspective," *Feminist Studies* 14, no. 3 (Fall 1988): 575–99.

Diana Fuss

Essentially Speaking: Feminism, Nature and Difference

Despite the uncertainty and confusion surrounding the sign "essence," more than one influential theorist has advocated that perhaps we cannot do without recourse to irreducibilities. One thinks of Stephen Heath's by now famous suggestion, "the risk of essence may have to be taken" ("Difference" [*Screen* vol. 19, no. 3] 1978, 99). It is poststructuralist feminists who seem most intrigued by this call to risk essence. Alice Jardine, for example, finds Stephen Heath's proclamation (later echoed by Gayatri Spivak) to be "one of the most thought-provoking statements of recent date" ("Men in Feminism: Odor di Uomo Or Compagnons de Route?" in Jardine and Smith, [*Men in Feminism*, London, Methuen] 1987, 58). But not all post-structuralist feminists are as comfortable with the prospect of re-opening theory's Pandora's box of essentialism. Peggy Kamuf warns that calls to risk essentialism may in the end be no more than veiled defenses against the unsettling operations of deconstruction:

> How is one supposed to understand essence as a *risk* to be run when it is by definition the non-accidental and therefore hardly the apt term to represent danger or risk? Only over against and in impatient reaction to the decon-struction of the subject can "essence" be made to sound excitingly dangerous and the phrase "the risk of essence" can seem to offer such an appealing invitation.... "Go for it," the phrase incites. "If you fall into 'essence,' you can always say it was an accident." ("Femmeninism," in Jardine and Smith 1987, 96)

In Kamuf's mind, risking essence is really no risk at all; it is merely a clever way of preserving the metaphysical safety net should we lose our balance walking the perilous tightrope of deconstruction.

But the call to risk essence is not merely an "impatient reaction" to decon-struction (though it might indeed be this in certain specific instances); it can also operate as a deconstructionist strategy. "Is not strategy itself the real risk?" Derrida asks in his seminar on feminism ("Women in the Beehive," in Jardine and Smith 1987, 192). To the deconstructionist, strategy of any kind is a risk because its effects, its outcome, are always unpredictable and unde-cidable. Depending on the historical moment and the cultural context, a strategy can be "radically revolutionary or deconstructive" or it can be "dangerously reactive" (193). What is risky is giving up the security – and the fantasy – of occupying a single subject-position and instead occupying two places at once. In a word, "we have to negotiate" (202). For an example of this particular notion of "risk" we can turn to Derrida's own attempts to dare to speak as woman. For a male subject to speak as woman can be radi-cally de-essentializing; the transgression suggests that "woman" is a social space which any sexed subject can fill. But because Derrida never specifies *which* woman he speaks as (a French bourgeois woman, an Anglo-American lesbian, and so on), the strategy to speak as woman is simultaneously re-essentializing. The risk lies in the difficult negotiation between these apparently contradictory effects.

It must be pointed out here that the constructionist strategy of specifying more precisely these sub-categories of "woman" does not necessarily preclude essentialism. "French bourgeois woman" or "Anglo-American lesbian," while crucially emphasizing in their very specificity that "woman" is by no means a monolithic category, nonetheless reinscribe an essentialist logic at the very level of historicism. Historicism is not always an effective counter to essentialism if it succeeds only in fragmenting the subject into multiple identities, each with its own self-contained, self-referential essence. The constructionist impulse to specify, rather than definitively counteracting essentialism, often simply redeploys it through the very strategy of historicization, rerouting and dispersing it through a number of micropolitical units or sub-categorical classifications, each presupposing its own unique interior composition or metaphysical core.

There is an important distinction to be made, I would submit, between "deploying" or "activating" essentialism and "falling into" or "lapsing into" essentialism. "Falling into" or "lapsing into" implies that essentialism is inherently reactionary – inevitably and inescapably a problem or a mistake.[14] "Deploying" or "activating," on the other hand, implies that essentialism may have some strategic or interventionary value. What I am suggesting is that the political investments of the sign "essence" are predicated on the subject's complex positioning in a particular social field, and that the appraisal of this investment depends not on any interior values intrinsic to the sign itself but rather on the shifting and determinative discursive relations which produced it. As subsequent chapters will more forcefully suggest, the radicality or conservatism of essentialism depends, to a significant degree, on *who* is utilizing it, *how* it is deployed, and *where* its effects are concentrated.

It is important not to forget that essence is a sign, and as such historically contingent and constantly subject to change and to redefinition. Historically, we have never been very confident of the definition of essence, nor have we been very certain that the definition of essence is to *be* the definitional. Even the essence/accident distinction, the inaugural moment of Western metaphysics, is by no means a stable or secure binarism. The entire history of metaphysics can be read as an interminable pursuit of the essence of essence, motivated by the anxiety that essence may well be accidental, changing and unknowable. Essentialism is not, and has rarely been, monolithically coded. Certainly it is difficult to identify a single philosopher whose work does not attempt to account for the question of essentialism in some way; the repeated attempts by these philosophers to fix or to define essence suggest that essence is a slippery and elusive category, and that the sign itself does not remain stationary or uniform.

The deconstruction of essentialism, rather than putting essence to rest, simply raises the discussion to a more sophisticated level, leaps the analysis up to another higher register, above all, keeps the sign of essence in play, even if (indeed *because*) it is continually held under erasure. Constructionists, then, need to be wary of too quickly crying "essentialism." Perhaps the most dangerous problem for anti-essentialists is to see the category of essence as "always already" knowable, as immediately apparent and naturally transparent. Similarly, we need to beware of the tendency to "naturalize" the category of the natural, to see this category, too, as obvious and immediately perceptible *as such*. Essentialism may be at once more intractable and more irrecuperable than we thought; it may be essential to our thinking while at the same time there is nothing "quintessential" about it. To insist that essentialism is always and everywhere reactionary is, for the constructionist, to buy into essentialism in the very act of making the charge; *it is to act as if essentialism has an essence.*

(1989)

Note

14 Toril Moi's *Sexual/Textual Politics* provides a particularly good example of how this locution can be used to dismiss entire schools of feminist thought – in Moi's case, to discredit "Anglo-American" feminism. Moi's sweeping criticism of writers as diverse as Elaine Showalter, Myra Jehlen, Annette Kolodny, Sandra Gilbert, and Susan Gubar consists mainly in mapping out in detail the points in which their analyses "slip into" essentialism and therefore "reinscribe patriarchal humanism." Such an ostensibly anti-essentialist critique can only be built on the grounds of the twin assumptions that essentialism is, in essence, "patriarchal" and that "patriarchal humanism" has an essence which is inherently, inevitably reactionary.

DONNA HARAWAY

'A Manifesto for Cyborgs: Science, Technology, and Socialist Feminism in the 1980s'
Socialist Review

The cyborg is a creature in a post-gender world; it has no truck with bisexuality, pre-Oedipal symbiosis, unalienated labor, or other seductions to organic wholeness through a final appropriation of all the powers of the parts into a higher unity. In a sense, the cyborg has no origin story in the Western sense; a "final" irony since the cyborg is also the awful apocalyptic *telos* of the "West's" escalating dominations of abstract individuation, an ultimate self untied at last from all dependency, a man in space. An origin story in the "Western," humanist sense depends on the myth of original unity, fullness, bliss and terror, represented by the phallic mother from whom all humans must separate, the task of individual development and of history, the twin potent myths inscribed most powerfully for us in psychoanalysis and Marxism. Hilary Klein has argued that both Marxism and psychoanalysis, in their concepts of labor and of individuation and gender formation, depend on the plot of original unity out of which difference must be produced and enlisted in a drama of escalating domination of woman/nature. The cyborg skips the step of original unity, of identification with nature in the Western sense. This is its illegitimate promise that might lead to subversion of its teleology as star wars.

The cyborg is resolutely committed to partiality, irony, intimacy, and perversity. It is oppositional, utopian, and completely without innocence. No longer structured by the polarity of public and private, the cyborg defines a technological polis based partly on a revolution of social relations in the *oikos*, the household. Nature and culture are reworked; the one can no longer be the resource for appropriation or incorporation by the other. The relationships for forming wholes from parts, including those of polarity and hierarchical domination, are at issue in the cyborg world. Unlike the hopes of Frankenstein's monster, the cyborg does not expect its father to save it through a restoration of the garden; i.e., through the fabrication of a heterosexual mate, through its completion in a finished whole, a city and cosmos. The cyborg does not dream of community on the model of the organic family, this time without the Oedipal project. The cyborg would not recognize the Garden of Eden; it is not made of mud and cannot dream of returning to dust. Perhaps that is why I want to see if cyborgs can subvert the apocalypse of returning to nuclear dust in the manic compulsion to name the Enemy. Cyborgs are not reverent; they do not re-member the cosmos. They are wary of holism, but needy for connection – they seem to have a natural feel for united front politics, but without the vanguard party. The main trouble with cyborgs, of course, is that they are the illegitimate offspring of militarism and patriarchal capitalism, not to mention state socialism. But illegitimate offspring are often exceedingly unfaithful to their origins. Their fathers, after all, are inessential.

[...]

I want to conclude with a myth about identity and boundaries which might inform late twentieth-century political imaginations. I am indebted in this story to writers like Joanna Russ, Samuel Delany, John Varley, James Tiptree, Jr, Octavia Butler, Monique Wittig, and Vonda McIntyre.[29] These are our storytellers exploring what it means to be embodied in high-tech worlds. They are theorists for cyborgs. Exploring conceptions of bodily boundaries and social order, the anthropologist Mary Douglas should be credited with helping us to consciousness about how fundamental body imagery is to world view, and so to political language.[30] French feminists like Luce Irigaray and Monique Wittig, for all their differences, know how to write the body; how to weave eroticism, cosmology, and politics from imagery of embodiment, and especially for Wittig, from imagery of fragmentation and reconstitution of bodies.[31]

American radical feminists like Susan Griffin, Audre Lorde, and Adrienne Rich have profoundly affected our political imaginations – and perhaps restricted too much what we allow as a friendly body and political language.[32] They insist on the organic, opposing it to the technological. But their symbolic systems and the related positions of ecofeminism and feminist paganism, replete with organicisms, can only be understood in Sandoval's terms as oppositional ideologies fitting the late twentieth century. They would simply bewilder anyone not preoccupied with the machines and consciousness of late capitalism. In that sense they are part of the cyborg world. But there are also great riches for feminists in explicitly embracing the possibilities inherent in the breakdown of clean distinctions between organism and machine and similar distinctions structuring the Western self. It is the simultaneity of breakdowns that cracks the matrices of domination and opens geometric possibilities. What might be learned from personal and political "technological" pollution? I will look briefly at two overlapping groups of texts for their insight into the construction of a potentially helpful cyborg myth: constructions of women of color and monstrous selves in feminist science fiction.

Earlier I suggested that "women of color" might be understood as a cyborg identity, a potent subjectivity synthesized from fusions of outsider identities and in the complex political-historical layerings of her (Audre Lorde) "biomythography," *Zami*.[33] There are material and cultural grids mapping this potential. Audre Lorde captures the tone in the title of her *Sister Outsider*. In my political myth, Sister Outsider is the offshore woman, whom US workers, female and feminized, are supposed to regard as the enemy preventing their solidarity, threatening their security. Onshore, inside the boundary of the United States, Sister Outsider is a potential amidst the races and ethnic identities of women manipulated for division, competition, and exploitation in the same industries. "Women of color" are the preferred labor force for the science-based industries, the real women for whom the world-wide sexual market, labor market, and politics of reproduction kaleidoscope into daily life. Young Korean women hired in the sex industry and in electronics assembly are recruited from high schools, educated for the integrated circuit. Literacy, especially in English, distinguishes the "cheap" female labor so attractive to the multinationals.

Contrary to orientalist stereotypes of the "oral primitive," literacy is a special mark of women of color, acquired by US black women as well as men through a history of risking death to learn and to teach reading and writing. Writing has a special significance for all colonized groups. Writing has been crucial to the Western myth of the distinction of oral and written cultures, primitive and civilized mentalities, and more recently to the erosion of that distinction in "post-modernist" theories attacking the phallogocentrism of the West, with its worship of the monotheistic, phallic, authoritative, and singular work, the unique and perfect name.[34] Contests for the meanings of writing are a major form of contemporary political struggle. Releasing the play of writing is deadly serious. The poetry and stories of US women of color are repeatedly about writing, about access to the power to signify; but this time that power must be neither phallic nor innocent. Cyborg writing must not be about the Fall, the imagination of a once-upon-a-time wholeness before language, before writing, before Man. Cyborg writing is about the power to survive, not on the basis of original innocence, but on the basis of seizing the tools to mark the world that marked them as other.

The tools are often stories, retold stories, versions that reverse and displace the hierarchical dualisms of naturalized identities. In retelling origin stories, cyborg authors subvert the central myths of origin of Western culture. We have all been colonized by those origin myths, with their longing for fulfillment in apocalypse. The phallogocentric origin stories most crucial for feminist cyborgs are built into the literal technologies – technologies that write the world, biotechnology and microelectronics – that have recently textualized our bodies as code problems on the grid of C^3I. Feminist cyborg stories have the task of recoding communication and intelligence to subvert command and control.

Figuratively and literally, language politics pervade the struggles of women of color; and stories about language have a special power in the rich contemporary writing by US women of color. For example, retellings of the story of the indigenous woman Malinche, mother of the mestizo "bastard" race of the new world, master of languages, and mistress of Cortés, carry special meaning for Chicana constructions of identity. Cherríe Moraga in *Loving in the War Years* explores the themes of identity when one never possessed the original language, never told the original story, never resided in the harmony of legitimate heterosexuality in the garden of culture, and so cannot base identity on a myth or a fall from innocence and right to natural names, mother's or father's.[35] Moraga's writing, her superb literacy, is presented in her poetry as the same kind of violation as Malinche's mastery of the conquerer's language – a violation, an illegitimate production, that allows survival. Moraga's language is not "whole"; it is self-consciously spliced, a chimera of English and Spanish, both conquerer's languages. But it is this chimeric monster, without claim to an original language before violation, that crafts the erotic, competent, potent identities of women of color. Sister Outsider hints at the possibility of world survival not because of her innocence, but because of her ability to live on the boundaries, to write without the founding myth of original wholeness, with its inescapable apocalypse of final return to a deathly oneness that Man has imagined to be the innocent and all-powerful Mother, freed at the End from another spiral of appropriation by her son. Writing marks Moraga's body, affirms it as the body of a woman of color, against the possibility of passing into the unmarked category of the Anglo father or into the orientalist myth of "original illiteracy" of a mother that never was. Malinche was mother here, not Eve before eating the forbidden fruit. Writing affirms Sister Outsider, not the Woman-before-the-Fall-into-Writing needed by the phallogocentric Family of Man.

(1985)

Notes

29 Katie King, "The Pleasure of Repetition and the Limits of Identification in Feminist Science Fiction: Reimaginations of the Body after the Cyborg," California American Studies Association, Pomona, 1984. An abbreviated list of feminist science fiction underlying themes of this essay: Octavia Butler, *Wild Seed, Mind of My Mind, Kindred, Survivor*, and *Dawn*; Suzy McKee Charnas, *Motherliness*; Samuel Delany, *Tales of Neveryon*; Anne McCaffrey, *The Ship Who Sang*, and *Dinosaur Planet*; Vonda McIntyre, *Superluminal* and *Dreamsnake*; Joanna Russ, *Adventures of Alyx, The Female Man*; James Tiptree, Jr, *Star Songs of an Old Primate*, and *Up the Walls of the World*; John Varley, *Titan, Wizard*, and *Demon*.

30 Mary Douglas, *Purity and Danger* (London: Routledge & Kegan Paul, 1966) and *Natural Symbols* (London: Cresset Press, 1970).

31 French feminisms contribute to cyborg heteroglossia. Carolyn Burke, "Irigaray through the Looking Glass," *Feminist Studies*, vol. 7, no. 2 (Summer 1981): 288–306; Luce Irigaray, *Ce sexe qui n'en est pas un* (Paris: Minuit, 1977); Luce Irigaray, *Et l'une ne bouge pas sans l'autre* (Paris: Minuit, 1979); Elaine Marks and Isabelle de Courtivron, eds., *New French Feminisms* (Amherst: University of Massachusetts Press, 1981); *Signs*, vol. 7, no. I (Autumn, 1981), special issue on French feminism; Monique Wittig, *The Lesbian Body*, trans. David Le Vay (New York: Avon, 1975; *Le corps lesbien*, 1973). See especially *Feminist Issues: A Journal of Feminist Social and Political Theory* (1980 ff.); and Claire Duchen, *Feminism in France: From May '68 to Mitterrand* (London: Routledge & Kegan Paul, 1986).

32 But all these poets are very complex, not least in treatment of themes of lying and erotic, decentered collective and personal identities. Susan Griffin, *Women and Nature: The Roaring Inside Her* (New York: Harper & Row, 1978); Audre Lorde, *Sister Outsider* (New York: Crossing Press, 1984); Adrienne Rich, *The Dream of a Common Language* (New York: Norton, 1978).

33 Audre Lorde, *Zami, a New Spelling of my Name* (New York: Crossing Press, 1982); Katie King, "Audre Lorde: Layering History/Constructing Poetry," in "Canons without Innocence," PhD dissertation, UCSC, 1987.

34   Jacques Derrida, *Of Grammatology*, trans. and Introd. Gayatri Chakravorty
     Spivak (Baltimore: Johns Hopkins University Press, 1976), esp. part II, "Nature,
     Culture, Writing"; Claude Lévi-Strauss, *Tristes Tropiques*, trans. John Russell
     (New York, Atheneum, 1961), esp. "The Writing Lesson"; Henry Louis Gates,
     Jr, "Writing 'Race' and the Difference It Makes," in " 'Race,' Writing and
     Difference," special issue of *Critical Inquiry*, ed. Gates, vol. 12, no. 1 (Autumn
     1985): 1–20; Douglas Kahn and Diane Neumaier, eds., *Cultures in Contention*
     (Seattle: Real Comet Press, 1985); Walter Ong, *Orality and Literacy: The
     Technologizing of the Word* (New York: Methuen, 1982); Cheris Kramarae and
     Paula Treichler, *A Feminist Dictionary* (Boston: Pandora, 1985).

35   Cherrie Moraga, *Loving in the War Years* (Boston: South End Press, 1983). The
     sharp relation of women of color to writing as theme and politics can be
     approached through: "The Black Woman and the Diaspora: Hidden Connections
     and Extended Acknowledgements," An International Literacy Conference,
     Michigan State University, October 1985; Mari Evans, ed., *Black Women Writers:
     A Critical Evaluation* (Garden City, NY: Doubleday/Anchor, 1984); Barbara
     Christian, *Black Feminist Criticism* (New York: Pergamon, 1985); Dexter Fisher,
     ed., *The Third Woman: Minority Women Writers of the United States* (Boston:
     Houghton Mifflin, 1980); several issues of *Frontiers*, esp. vol. 5 (1980), "Chicanas
     en el Ambiente Nacional" and vol. 7 (1983), "Feminisms in the Non-Western
     World"; Maxine Hong Kingston, *China Men* (New York: Knopf, 1977); Gerda
     Lerner, ed., *Black Women in White America: A Documentary History* (New York:
     Vintage, 1973); Paula Giddings, *When and Where I Enter: The Impact of Black
     Women on Race and Sex in America* (Toronto: Bantam, 1985); Cherrie Moraga
     and Gloria Anzaldúa, eds., *This Bridge Called My Back: Writings by Radical
     Women of Color* (Watertown, Mass.: Persephone, 1981); Robin Morgan, ed.,
     Sisterhood Is Global (Garden City, NY: Anchor/Doubleday, 1984). The writing of
     white women has had similar meanings: Sandra M. Gilbert and Susan Gubar, *The
     Madwoman in the Attic* (New Haven: Yale University Press, 1979); Joanna Russ,
     How to Suppress Women's Writing (Austin: University of Texas Press, 1983).

Gloria Anzaldúa

Borderlands/La Frontera: The New Mestiza

These numerous possibilities leave *la mestiza* floundering in uncharted seas.
In perceiving conflicting information and points of view, she is subjected to
a swamping of her psychological borders. She has discovered that she can't
hold concepts or ideas in rigid boundaries. The borders and walls that are
supposed to keep the undesirable ideas out are entrenched habits and
patterns of behavior; these habits and patterns are the enemy within. Rigidity
means death. Only by remaining flexible is she able to stretch the psyche
horizontally and vertically. *La mestiza* constantly has to shift out of habitual
formations; from convergent thinking, analytical reasoning that tends to use

rationality to move toward a single goal (a Western mode), to divergent thinking,[4] characterized by movement away from set patterns and goals and toward a more whole perspective, one that includes rather than excludes.

The new *mestiza* copes by developing a tolerance for contradictions, a tolerance for ambiguity. She learns to be an Indian in Mexican culture, to be Mexican from an Anglo point of view. She learns to juggle cultures. She has a plural personality, she operates in a pluralistic mode – nothing is thrust out, the good the bad and the ugly, nothing rejected, nothing abandoned. Not only does she sustain contradictions, she turns the ambivalence into something else.

She can be jarred out of ambivalence by an intense, and often painful, emotional event which inverts or resolves the ambivalence. I'm not sure exactly how. The work takes place underground – subconsciously. It is work that the soul performs. That focal point or fulcrum, that juncture where the mestiza stands, is where phenomena tend to collide. It is where the possibility of uniting all that is separate occurs. This assembly is not one where severed or separated pieces merely come together. Nor is it a balancing of opposing powers. In attempting to work out a synthesis, the self has added a third element which is greater than the sum of its severed parts. That third element is a new consciousness – a mestiza consciousness – and though it is a source of intense pain, its energy comes from continual creative motion that keeps breaking down the unitary aspect of each new paradigm.

En unas pocas centurias, the future will belong to the mestiza. Because the future depends on the breaking down of paradigms, it depends on the straddling of two or more cultures. By creating a new mythos – that is, a change in the way we perceive reality, the way we see ourselves, and the ways we behave – *la mestiza* creates a new consciousness.

The work of *mestiza* consciousness is to break down the subject – object duality that keeps her a prisoner and to show in the flesh and through the images in her work how duality is transcended. The answer to the problem between the white race and the colored, between males and females, lies in healing the split that originates in the very foundation of our lives, our culture, our languages, our thoughts. A massive uprooting of dualistic thinking in the individual and collective consciousness is the beginning of a long struggle, but one that could, in our best hopes, bring us to the end of rape, of violence, of war.

La encrucijada/The Crossroads

> A chicken is being sacrificed
> at a crossroads, a simple mound of earth
> a mud shrine for *Eshu*,
> *Yoruba* god of indeterminacy,

> who blesses her choice of path.
> She begins her journey.

Su cuerpo es una bocacalle. La mestiza has gone from being the sacrificial goat to becoming the officiating priestess at the crossroads.

As a mestiza I have no country, my homeland cast me out; yet all countries are mine because I am every woman's sister or potential lover. (As a lesbian I have no race, my own people disclaim me; but I am all races because there is the queer of me in all races.) I am cultureless because, as a feminist, I challenge the collective cultural/religious male-derived beliefs of Indo-Hispanics and Anglos; yet I am cultured because I am participating in the creation of yet another culture, a new story to explain the world and our participation in it, a new value system with images and symbols that connect us to each other and to the planet. *Soy un amasamiento*, I am an act of kneading, of uniting and joining that not only has produced both a creature of darkness and a creature of light, but also a creature that questions the definitions of light and dark and gives them new meanings.

We are the people who leap in the dark, we are the people on the knees of the gods. In our very flesh, (r)evolution works out the clash of cultures. It makes us crazy constantly, but if the center holds, we've made some kind of evolutionary step forward. *Nuestra alma el trabajo*, the opus, the great alchemical work; spiritual *mestizaje*, a "morphogenesis,"[5] an inevitable unfolding. We have become the quickening serpent movement.

Indigenous like corn, like corn, the *mestiza* is a product of crossbreeding, designed for preservation under a variety of conditions. Like an ear of corn – a female seed-bearing organ – the *mestiza* is tenacious, tightly wrapped in the husks of her culture. Like kernels she clings to the cob; with thick stalks and strong brace roots, she holds tight to the earth – she will survive the crossroads.

Lavando y remojando el maiz en agua de cal, despojando el pellejo. Moliendo, mixteando, amasando, haciendo tortillas de masa.[6] She steeps the corn in lime, it swells, softens. With stone roller on *metate*, she grinds the corn, then grinds again. She kneads and moulds the dough, pats the round balls into *tortillas*.

> We are the porous rock in the stone *metate*
> squatting on the ground.
> We are the rolling pin, *el maiz y agua*,
> *la masa harina. Somos el amasijo.*
> *Somos lo molido en el metate.*
> We are the *comal* sizzling hot,
> the hot *tortilla*, the hungry mouth.
> We are the coarse rock.
> We are the grinding motion,

the mixed potion, *somos el molcajete*.
We are the pestle, the *comino*, *ajo*, *pimienta*,
We are the *chile colorado*,
the green shoot that cracks the rock.
We will abide.

(1987)

Notes

4 In part, I derive my definitions for "convergent" and "divergent" thinking from Rothenberg, 12–13.
5 To borrow chemist Ilya Prigogine's theory of "dissipative structures." Prigogine discovered that substances interact not in predictable ways as it was taught in science, but in different and fluctuating ways to produce new and more complex structures, a kind of birth he called "morphogenesis," which created unpredictable innovations. Harold Gilliam, "Searching for a New World View," *This World* (January, 1981), 23.
6 *Tortillas de masa harina*: corn tortillas are of two types, the smooth uniform ones made in a tortilla press and usually bought at a tortilla factory or supermarket, and *gorditas*, made by mixing *masa* with lard or shortening or butter (my mother sometimes puts in bits of bacon or *chicharrones*).

CAROLE BOYCE DAVIES

Black Women, Writing and Identity: Migrations of the Subject

For these reasons, I want to activate the term "Black"[19] relationally, provisionally and based on location or position. The term "Black," oppositional, resisting, necessarily emerges as whiteness seeks to depoliticize and normalize itself. Still "Black" is only provisionally used as we continue to interrogate its meaning and in the ongoing search to find the language to articulate ourselves.

In locating identity within the context of assailment, interrogation and belatedness, Homi Bhabha cites Fanon's "The Fact of Blackness"[20] in which Blackness activates itself as a response to these three. Blackness, marginalized, overdetermined and made stereotypic stands in for the human figure which is located and disrupted. But what of Black femaleness or Black womanness? For it is the additional identity of femaleness which interferes with seamless Black identity and is therefore either ignored, erased or "spoken for." One still finds some women trying to say that they want to speak only as an African or as a "Black," and not as a woman,[21] as if it were possible to divest oneself of one's gender and stand as neutered within the context of palpable and visible historical, gendered and racialized identities. Black men have often claimed the space of speaking only in terms of their race with the assumption that their gender remains unmarked. But their manhood is often frontally identified in these assertions.

It is at this point "when we enter"[22] that one gets the convergence (at least of race and gender) and hence the challenging of specific identities. If following Judith Butler,[23] the category of woman is one of performance of gender, then the category Black woman, or woman of color, exists as multiple performances of gender and race and sexuality based on the particular cultural, historical, geopolitical, class communities in which Black women exist. Those complicating locations of these multiple and variable subject positions are what I propose to explore in this study.

A similar interrogation of the term African-American explodes its often synonymous identification with "United Staters" of African descent ("Black Americans"). It is also significant that in the United States, the term "Black" does not include other "Third World" peoples (Asians, Arabs, Latino/as) as it does in the United Kingdom. For in the United States, the historical convergence between "race" and "nationality" has kept separate, for the most part, all the possibilities of organizing around related agendas and has operated in terms of polarizations of various races. It has also either sublimated racial differences or reified them in essential ways. Interrogating "African-American" as a defining terminology first mandates moving beyond the limited definition of what is "American."[24] In this way, "African-American" could correctly refer to the African peoples of the Americas: North America, the Caribbean and South America. Yet, since the term "American" has become synonymous with United States imperialistic identity, would the "other Americas" being colonized (both internally and externally) by the United States of America want to claim such a monolithic identification? Perhaps not, especially since the term "America" is also identified with European "discovery" and the destruction of native communities and nations. But perhaps yes, for tactical self-assertive reasons as Canadians or South Americans and Caribbeans sometimes do. Nancy Morejon would suggest that the term "America" is insufficient to discuss the entire spectrum of socio-historical interactions. She therefore uses the interesting formulation, for example, of "Amerindia" which embraces the continent extending from north to south geographically and which captures the extent to which the First People (Amerindians) made possible the emergence of Afro-America.[25]

The other half of the claimed "African-American" identity, "African," is a term based on another misnaming and an attempt to create a monolithic construction out of a diverse continent of peoples, cultures, nations and experiences. "Africa" becomes important as a defining term only in opposition to what is European or what is American. African historians indicate, for example, that the term "African" (derived from the terms Afri, Afriqui or Afrigi) was originally the name of a small Tunisian ethnic group which then began to be applied to a larger geographical area ranging from what is now eastern Morocco to Libya. For the Romans, "Africa *proconsularis*" was an administrative, territorial category.[26] Unpacking the archeology and genealogy of the term "Africa" is an important exercise in our understanding of how the politics of conquest and domination are so fundamentally linked to naming. The origin of the term "Africa" for colonialist, administrative reasons and its subsequent application to an entire continent (again for administrative, colonialist reasons), has implications for how African peoples (particularly in the diaspora) begin to activate monolithic categories of heritage and identity, as, for example, "Afrocentricity." The political basis of identity formation is a central issue in all of these interrogations. For, again, in the diaspora, under Pan-Africanist ideologies, the reconstruction of "Africa" as homeland occurred, also for management of reality. As resistance to European domination, monolithic constructions of Africa posed an alternative identity and did duty against the European deployment of its reality and its attempt to redefine the identities of large numbers of people taken from their native homelands.

(1994)

Notes

19 See, for example, F. James Davis, *Who is Black? One Nation's Definition*, Philadelphia, Pennsylvania State University Press, 1991; and essays in Ronald Takaki, ed., *From Different Shores. Perspectives on Race and Ethnicity in America*, London, Oxford University Press, 1987; and essays in Henry Louis Gates, Jr., ed., *"Race," Writing, and Difference*, Chicago, Ill. and London, University of Chicago Press, 1985; and Jack D. Forbes, *Africans and Native Americans. The Language of Race and the Evolution of Red-Black Peoples*, Urbana and Chicago, Ill., University of Illinois Press, 1993, which discusses the various classifications, for discussion of some of the complexity of the history of racial identifications.

20 Editor of *Nation and Narration*, London and New York, Routledge, 1990, citing Frantz Fanon, "The Fact of Blackness," from his *Black Skin, White Masks* at symposium on "Identity in Question," CUNY Graduate Center, New York, November 16, 1991.

21 As did Lauretta Ngcobo at the African Writers in Exile Conference, London, March 29, 1991.

22 See Paula Giddings, *When and Where I Enter. The Impact of Black Women on Race and Sex in America*, New York, Bantam, 1984.

23 *Gender Trouble. Feminism and the Subversion of Identity*, New York and London, Routledge, 1990.

24 I have found Michael Hanchard's work on this, especially his "Identity, Meaning and the African-American," *Social Text*, 24, 1990, pp. 31–42 and "Racial Consciousness and Afro-Diasporic Experiences. Antonio Gramsci Reconsidered,"

Socialism and Democracy, 3, Fall, 1991, pp. 83–106, and my several discussions with him in Brazil and in the US helpful and supportive examinations of my thoughts on this issue.

25   Her presentation, "The Invisible Afro-America," in which she discussed this was given at SUNY Binghamton University on April 1, 1993.

26   From a conversation with Prof. Akbar Muhammad, African historian, SUNY Binghamton, November 20, 1991. See also Christopher Miller's *Blank Darkness. Africanist Discourse in French*, Chicago, Ill., University of Chicago Press, 1985, pp. 6–14, and his "Theories of Africans. The Question of Literary Anthropology," in Gates Jr., *"Race," Writing and Difference*, pp. 281–300, which discusses a variety of African philosophical and literary positions on the meaning of "African" and concludes by asking that critics "reconsider the applicability of all our critical terms [and] looking to traditional African cultures for terms they might offer" (p. 300). See also V.Y. Mudimbe's *The Invention of Africa*, Bloomington and Indiannapolis, Indiana University Press, 1988, and London, James Currey, 1988.

Monique Wittig

'The Straight Mind'
Feminist Issues

Yes, straight society is based on the necessity of the different/other at every level. It cannot work economically, symbolically, linguistically, or politically without this concept. This necessity of the different/other is an ontological one for the whole conglomerate of sciences and disciplines that I call the straight mind. But what is the different/other if not the dominated? For heterosexual society is the society which not only oppresses lesbians and gay men, it oppresses many different/others, it oppresses all women and many categories of men, all those who are in the position of the dominated. To constitute a difference and to control it is an "act of power, since it is essentially a normative act. Everybody tries to show the other as different. But not everybody succeeds in doing so. One has to be socially dominant to succeed in it."[7]

For example, the concept of difference between the sexes ontologically constitutes women into different/others. Men are not different, whites are not different, nor are the masters. But the blacks, as well as the slaves, are. This ontological characteristic of the difference between the sexes affects all the concepts which are part of the same conglomerate. But for us there is no such thing as being-woman or being-man. "Man" and "woman" are political concepts of opposition, and the copula which dialectically unites them is, at the same time, the one which abolishes them.[8] It is the class struggle between women and men which will abolish men and women.[9] The concept of difference has nothing ontological about it. It is only the way that the masters interpret a historical situation of domination. The function of difference is to mask at every level the conflicts of interest, including ideological ones.

In other words, for us, this means there cannot any longer be women and men, and that as classes and categories of thought or language they have to disappear, politically, economically, ideologically. If we, as lesbians and gay men, continue to speak of ourselves and to conceive of ourselves as women and as men, we are instrumental in maintaining heterosexuality. I am sure that an economic and political transformation will not dedramatize these categories of language. Can we redeem *slave?* Can we redeem *nigger, negress?* How is *woman* different? Will we continue to write *white, master, man?* The transformation of economic relationships will not suffice. We must produce a political transformation of the key concepts, that is of the concepts which are strategic for us. For there is another order of materiality, that of language, and language is worked upon from within by these strategic concepts. It is at the same time tightly connected to the political field, where everything that concerns language, science and thought refers to the person as subjectivity and to her/his relationship to society. And we cannot leave this within the power of the straight mind or the thought of domination.

If among all the productions of the straight mind I especially challenge the models of the Structural Unconscious, it is because: at the moment in history when the domination of social groups can no longer appear as a logical necessity to the dominated, because they revolt, because they question the differences, Lévi-Strauss, Lacan, and their epigones call upon necessities which escape the control of consciousness and therefore the responsibility of individuals.

They call upon unconscious processes, for example, which require the exchange of women as a necessary condition for every society. According to them, that is what the unconscious tells us with authority, and the symbolic order, without which there is no meaning, no language, no society, depends on it. But what does women being exchanged mean if not that they are dominated? No wonder then that there is only one Unconscious, and that it is heterosexual. It is an Unconscious which looks too consciously after the interests of the masters[10] in whom it lives for them to be dispossessed of their concepts so easily. Besides, domination is denied; there is no slavery of women, there is difference. To which I will answer with this statement made by a Rumanian peasant at a public meeting in 1848: "Why do the gentlemen say it was not slavery, for we know it to have been slavery, this sorrow that we have sorrowed." Yes, we know it, and this science of oppression cannot be taken away from us.

It is from this science that we must track down the "what-goes-without-saying" heterosexual, and (I paraphrase the early Roland Barthes) we must not bear "seeing Nature and History confused at every turn."[11] We must make it brutally apparent that psychoanalysis after Freud and particularly Lacan have rigidly turned their concepts into myths – Difference, Desire, the

Name-of-the-father, etc. They have even "over-mythified" the myths, an operation that was necessary for them in order to systematically heterosexualize that personal dimension which suddenly emerged through the dominated individuals into the historical field, particularly through women, who started their struggle almost two centuries ago. And it has been done systematically, in a concert of interdisciplinarity, never more harmonious than since the heterosexual myths started to circulate with ease from one formal system to another, like sure values that can be invested in anthropology as well as in psychoanalysis and in all the social sciences.

This ensemble of heterosexual myths is a system of signs which uses figures of speech, and thus it can be politically studied from within the science of our oppression; "for-we-know-it-to-have-been-slavery" is the dynamic which introduces the diachronism of history into the fixed discourse of eternal essences. This undertaking should somehow be a political semiology, although with "this sorrow that we have sorrowed" we work also at the level of language/manifesto, of language/action, that which transforms, that which makes history.

In the meantime, in the systems that seemed so eternal and universal that laws could be extracted from them, laws that could be stuffed into computers, and in any case for the moment stuffed into the unconscious machinery, in these systems, thanks to our action and our language, shifts are happening. Such a model, as for example, the exchange of women, reengulfs history in so violent and brutal a way that the whole system, which was believed to be formal, topples over into another dimension of knowledge. This dimension of history belongs to us, since somehow we have been designated, and since, as Lévi-Strauss said, we talk, let us say that we break off the heterosexual contract.

So, this is what lesbians say everywhere in this country and in some others, if not with theories at least through their social practice, whose repercussions upon straight culture and society are still unenvisionable. An anthropologist might say that we have to wait for fifty years. Yes, if one wants to universalize the functioning of these societies and make their invariants appear. Meanwhile the straight concepts are undermined. What is woman? Panic, general alarm for an active defense. Frankly, it is a problem that the lesbians do not have because of a change of perspective, and it would be incorrect to say that lesbians associate, make love, live with women, for "woman" has meaning only in heterosexual systems of thought and heterosexual economic systems. Lesbians are not women.

(1980)

Notes

7   Claude Faugeron and Philippe Robert, *La Justice et son public et les représentations sociales du système pénal* (Paris: Masson, 1978).

8   See, for her definition of "social sex," Nicole-Claude Mathieu, "Notes pour une définition sociologique des catégories de sexe," *Epistémologie Sociologique* 11 (1971). Translated as *Ignored by Some, Denied by Others: The Social Sex Category in Sociology* (pamphlet), Explorations in Feminism 2 (London: Women's Research and Resources Centre Publications, 1977), pp. 16–37.

9   In the same way that in every other class struggle the categories of opposition are "reconciled" by the struggle whose goal is to make them disappear.

10   Are the millions of dollars a year made by the psychoanalysts symbolic?

11   Roland Barthes, *Mythologies* (New York: Hill and Wang, 1972), p. 11.

Eve Kosofsky Sedgwick

Epistemology of the Closet

In the Introduction to *Between Men* I felt constrained to offer a brief account of how I saw the political/theoretical positioning of "a woman and a feminist writing (in part) about male homosexuality";[44] my account was, essentially, that this was an under-theorized conjunction and it was about time someone put her mind to it. Issues of male homosexuality are, obviously, even more integral to the present volume, and the intervening years have taught me more about how important, not to say mandatory, such an accounting must be – as well as how almost prohibitively difficult. I don't speak here of the question of anyone's "right" to think or write about the subjects on which they feel they have a contribution to make: to the degree that rights can be measured at all, I suppose this one can be measured best by what contribution the work does make, and to whom. Beyond the difficulty of wielding a language of rights, however, I find that abstractive formulations like that phrase in the Introduction to *Between Men* always seem to entail a hidden underpinning of the categorical imperative, one that may dangerously obscure the way political commitments and identifications actually work. Realistically, what brings me to this work can hardly be that I am *a* woman, or *a* feminist, but that I am this particular one. The grounds on which a book like this one might be persuasive or compelling to you, in turn, are unlikely to be its appeal to some *bienpensant*, evenly valenced lambency of your disinterested attention. Realistically, it takes deeply rooted, durable, and often somewhat opaque energies to write a book; it can take them, indeed, to read it. It takes them, as well, to make any political commitment that can be worth anything to anyone.

What, then, would make a good answer to implicit questions about someone's strong group-identification across politically charged boundaries, whether of gender, of class, of race, of sexuality, of nation? It could never be a version of "But everyone *should* be able to make this identification." Perhaps everyone should, but everyone does not, and almost no one makes more than a small number of very narrowly channeled ones. (A currently plausible academic ideology, for instance, is that everyone in a position of class privilege *should* group-identify across lines of class; but who hasn't noticed that of the very few US scholars under 50 who have been capable of doing so productively, and over the long haul, most also "happen to have been" red diaper babies?) If the ethical prescription is explanatory at all – and I have doubts about that – it is anything but a full explanation. It often seems to me, to the contrary, that what these implicit questions really ask for is narrative, and of a directly personal sort. When I have experimented with offering such narrative, in relation to this ongoing project, it has been with several aims in mind.[45] I wanted to disarm the categorical imperative that seems to do so much to promote cant and mystification about motives in the world of politically correct academia. I wanted to try opening channels of visibility – toward the speaker, in this case – that might countervail somewhat against the terrible one-directionality of the culture's spectacularizing of gay men, to which it seems almost impossible, in any powerful gay-related project, not also to contribute. I meant, in a sense, to give hostages, though the possible thud of them on the tarmac of some future conflict is not something I can contemplate. I also wanted to offer (though on my own terms) whatever tools I could with which a reader who needed to might begin unknotting certain overdetermined impactions that inevitably structure these arguments. Finally, I have come up with such narrative because I desired and needed to, because its construction has greatly interested me, and what I learned from it has often surprised me.

A note appended to one of these accounts suggested an additional reason: "Part of the motivation behind my work on it," I wrote there, "has been a fantasy that readers or hearers would be variously – in anger, identification, pleasure, envy, 'permission,' exclusion – stimulated to write accounts 'like' this one (whatever that means) of their own, and share those."[46] My impression, indeed, is that some readers of that essay have done so. An implication of that wishful note was that it is not only identifications *across* definitional lines that can evoke or support or even require complex and particular narrative explanation; rather, the same is equally true of any person's identification with her or his "own" gender, class, race, sexuality, nation. I think, for instance, of a graduate class I taught a few years ago in gay and lesbian literature. Half the students in the class were men, half women. Throughout the semester all the women, including me, intensely uncomfortable with the dynamics of the class and hyperconscious of the problems of articulating lesbian with gay male perspectives, attributed our discomfort to some obliquity in the classroom relations between ourselves and the men. But by the end of the semester it seemed clear that we were in the grip of some much more intimate dissonance. It seemed that it was among the group of women, all feminists, largely homogeneous in visible respects, that some nerve of individually internal difference had been set painfully, contagiously atremble. Through a process that began, but *only* began, with the perception of some differences among our mostly inexplicit, often somewhat uncrystallized sexual self-definitions, it appeared that each woman in the class possessed (or might, rather, feel we were possessed by) an ability to make one or more of the other women radically and excruciatingly doubt the authority of her own self-definition as a woman; as a feminist; and as the positional subject of a particular sexuality.

I think it probable that most people, especially those involved with any form of politics that touches on issues of identity – race, for instance, as well as sexuality and gender – have observed or been part of many such circuits of intimate denegation, as well as many circuits of its opposite. The political or pedagogical utility or destructiveness of those dissonant dynamics is scarcely a given, though perhaps it must always be aversive to experience them. Such dynamics – the denegating ones along with the consolidating ones – are not epiphenomenal to identity politics, but constitute it. After all, to identify *as* must always include multiple processes of identification *with*. It also involves identification *as against*; but even did it not, the relations implicit in *identifying with* are, as psychoanalysis suggests, in themselves quite sufficiently fraught with intensities of incorporation, diminishment, inflation, threat, loss, reparation, and disavowal. For a politics like feminism, furthermore, effective moral authority has seemed to depend on its capacity for conscientious and nonperfunctory enfoldment of women alienated from one another in virtually every other relation of life. Given this, there are strong political motives for obscuring any possibility of differentiating between one's identification *as* (a woman) and one's identification *with* (women very differently situated – for bourgeois feminists, this means radically less privileged ones). At least for relatively privileged feminists of my generation, it has been an article of faith, and a deeply educative one, that to conceive of oneself as a woman at all must mean trying to conceive oneself, over and over, as if incarnated in ever more palpably vulnerable situations and embodiments. The costs of this pressure toward mystification – the constant reconflation, as one monolithic act, of *identification with/as* – are, I believe, high for feminism, though its rewards have also been considerable. (Its political efficacy in actually broadening the bases of feminism is still, it seems to me, very much a matter of debate.) *Identification with/as* has a distinctive resonance for women in the oppressively tidy dovetailing between old ideologies of women's traditional "selflessness" and a new one of feminist commitment that seems to begin with a self but is legitimated only by willfully obscuring most of its boundaries.

(1991)

Notes

44. *Between Men*, p. 19.
45. The longest such narrative appears as "A Poem Is Being Written," *Representations*, no. 17 (Winter 1987): 110–43. More fragmentary or oblique ones occur in "Tide and Trust," *Critical Inquiry* 15, no. 4 (Summer 1989): 745–57; in Chapter 4 of the present book; and in "Privilege of Unknowing."
46. "A Poem Is Being Written," p. 137.

Kate Soper

'Of OncoMice and FemaleMen: Donna Haraway on Cyborg Ontology'
Women: A Cultural Review

Leaving aside these ontological and epistemological unclarities, however, let us turn to what is perhaps the more relevant and interesting normative aspects of her argument. Why is it that we are asked to view the cyborg as having socialist-feminist Utopian potential? Why should we advocate cyborg existence rather than insist that any compelling Utopian vision must respect the specificity of the human being?

One part of Haraway's response echoes the naturalism of the deep ecologists who emphasize our affinities with other animals. 'Nothing', she argues, 'convincingly settles the separation of human and animal'; 'many feminists affirm the pleasure of connection of human and other living beings'; 'movements for animal rights are not irrational denials of human uniqueness, but clearsighted recognition of this connectedness'.[10] Yet whatever one thinks of these claims (and I personally believe they require far more qualification and sceptical appraisal than Haraway anywhere accords them – a neglect which is all the stranger given her clear understanding of the risks of sociobiological reductionism),[11] it is difficult to see how this part of her argument avoids the romantic-redemptive framework of thinking about nature which she professes to want to avoid. The standard move of the animal liberationists is to *oppose* the body to the machine, the organic and suffering flesh to the indifference and alienation of bio-technology and agribusiness. Where, then, does this leave a cyborg politics? And how can this approval for the natural connectedness of all animal species be reconciled with the anti-naturalism of her (wildly indiscriminate) attack on the 'racism' of those who appeal to the idea of a 'natural' species in their objections to genetic engineering?[12]

The other part of her answer gestures to the Utopian potentials of cybernetics, although there is rather little here in the way of exemplification. Haraway wants a 'cyberfeminism' rather than recourse to 'nature' because she thinks that a nature-invoking politics is inevitably pulled into essentialist positions on female being, feminist projections of 'woman' as innocent, maternal and victimized, and so on. Only by refusing to root a feminist politics in bodily integrity, she argues, can one do justice to the 'partial, fluid, sometimes aspect of sex and sexual embodiment', and thereby avoid the heterosexual and maternal 'norms';[13] and it is in this spirit that she applauds the FemaleMen, cyborg monsters, mutants and experiments in 'technological pollution' of the personal and political that 'people' cyberpunk writings and feminist science fiction.[14] But this seems based on a quite unjustified assumption that there is no alternative between a total (and often wholly fantastic) flight from 'nature' and the acceptance of patriarchal constructions of the female body and sexuality. In reality, is it only in the appeal to the bodily integrity, anguish and suffering of the oppressed subject that one can ultimately ground the demand for release from distorting or confining identities, or call for improved cultural understandings of what it is to be cast as subordinate. Nor does this argument anywhere properly ground its implication that heterosexuality is the restraining, repressive and merely contingent convention from which all other forms of sexuality must offer liberation. Heterosexuality, one may argue, is no more mere 'norm' than is homosexuality mere 'counter-norm'. Both dispositions will always be experienced in particular cultural contexts and mediated through the specific representations, familial institutions, forms of tolerance or intolerance associated with those contexts. But these mediations are not the desires, passions, lusts, obsessions and compulsions which they mediate; and it is these sexual, emotional energies which generate and empower the challenges to conventional forms of intolerance or institutional norms, and not some bloodless objection to convention as such. It is difficult to know what sense to make of the appeal to the 'fluid and partial' nature of female sexuality if we are not to construe it as an assertion of the need to release a flow of natural desires from the dams of cultural constraints. This appeal *is itself* an appeal to respect bodily integrity.

If to argue along these lines is, as Jill Marsden, a sympathetic but to my mind somewhat naive, commentator on Haraway puts it, to be guilty of dualistic thinking–of 'locating the notion of the cyborg within a precritical understanding of the machine', of demonstrating 'a humanist prejudice against the idea of machinic nature'[15]–then so be it. Some dualism and hierarchies have to be preserved as a condition of observing the 'responsibility' in the construction of boundaries which Haraway herself calls for even as she also advocates pleasure in their confusion. The refusal to blur the machine-body boundary is, for example, of critical conceptual importance to the condemnation of torture. So, too, is the refusal to blur the human-animal divide out of respect for the distinctive pleasures and pains of human love and sexuality. It is Haraway's ultimate awareness of this which renders her work so equivocal and inconsistent in its political message. In this sense

Marsden is quite right to complain about the confusion in Haraway's demand for responsibility:

> If we do not choose to be cyborgs, *can* we choose responsibilities for machines? Are 'we' still in control? This is a variant of the problem that hampers Haraway's endeavour to inject 'progressive' politics into a systemic conception of power.... In fear of losing the possibility of acting politically she re-anthropomorphises control ... In insisting on 'political accountability' and ethical obligation, Haraway struggles to rescue 'A Cyborg Manifesto' from the charge of technological determinism, but in so doing weakens the case for understanding technological revolution and biological evolution as symbiotic.[16]

While, for Marsden, all this represents a capitulation to the slave morality which cyberfeminism otherwise 'so refreshingly ignores', a refusal to face the full trauma of dismantling the biological order, and a cowardly reversion to humanist values,[17] it figures for me as reluctant and confused testimony to Haraway's understanding of the self-defeating quality of cybernetic anti-humanism.

(1999)

Notes

10   Ibid., pp. 151–2.
11   There is no space here to pursue these issues, but see my anti-naturalist or humanist argument in *What is Nature? Culture, Politics and the Non-Human*, Oxford: Blackwell, 1995, esp. chs. 2 and 5.
12   Cf. *Modest Witness*, pp. 60–2.
13   *Simians, Cyborgs and Women*, p. 180.
14   Ibid., pp. 173–81.
15   Jill Marsden, 'Virtual Sexes and Feminist Futures: The Philosophy of "Cyberfeminism"', *Radical Philosophy* 78, July–August 1996, 8–9, 13.
16   Ibid., p. 14.
17   Ibid., pp. 14–15.

7

Writing 'Glocal'

INTRODUCTION

Definitions, Positions and Parameters

Ever since Virginia Woolf asked for 'a room of one's own', it has been clear
that space is an essential factor in women's literary production and, in recent
years, feminism's intense involvement with postcolonial theory has enhanced
its awareness of space alongside a continuing interest in temporality. There
is a space of settled places, locations, homes and nations, but also a space of
diasporic, transnational and nomadic movements, of border-crossings and
the liminal, of the *unheimliche*. Our understanding of what the spatial
means for feminist literary theory operates within globalized economies,
including the publishing industry, migratory shifts of people, new national-
isms and heightened ethnic identities. Writing, then, is inevitably 'glocal',
both global and local.

The first three extracts are examples of attempts to define terms but not
in any easy, resolved sense. Every term suggests connotations, contexts,
relations and parameters.[1] Sangeeta Ray describes the subject-matter of her
book as an examination of 'the rival and shifting representations of the
Indian woman in British imperial and Indian colonial and postcolonial
writings after 1857'.[2] In this extract, introducing her chapter on Anita
Desai's *Clear Light of Day* and Bapsi Sidhwa's *Cracking India*, we see how
this apparent clarity and simplicity of purpose is, of necessity, complicated
by a wealth of other factors: terminology, the instability and yet relation
between categories – in Ray's case 'nationality' and 'gender' – historical
moment and geographical/cultural placings, authorial location, reception
and readerships, and the potential and limitations of critical fields. Similarly,

Feminist Literary Theory: A Reader, Third Edition By Mary Eagleton   © 2011 Mary Eagleton

Avtar Brah's study is a wide-ranging exploration of the diasporic experience in the contemporary period, bringing to bear social, cultural, political and economic interpretations of difference, space, 'race' and gender. She coins the phrase 'diaspora space' to describe that position, important to the feminist literary critic, where geography, cultural production, the individual subject and theory could be mutually productive.

However, as Ray, Brah and Reina Lewis all indicate, the theoretical is itself a diverse space and the critic has to be alert to strategies and effects. Ray is highly conscious of the 'packaging' of categories such as 'third world', 'postcolonial' and 'Asian American', and the need for the teacher – and, one could add, any reader – 'to be vigilant against the creation of facile and seamless links'. Brah's approach is, at once, critical and deconstructive, and relational, looking for the changing connections between different social and cultural formations; we need, she suggests, 'a kind of *theoretical creolisation*'. Lewis's theoretical awareness is equally flexible. In exploring harem literature produced by women authors in the early decades of the twentieth century, she questions the scope and tenets of 'masculinist histories of Orientalism', feminist postcolonial theory and Turkish historical studies.[3] Looking at the specific position of these Ottoman women, in terms of gender, ethnicity and class, reveals their agency and questions our theoretical simplicities.

First World/Third World/Speaking/Reading

The term 'third world' has been among the most debated in feminist, postcolonial and development studies, though its origins lay in economics.[4] Despite its strategic value in naming and focusing on an oppressed group, the term has been critiqued for its homogenizing of difference and for defining people always in relation to colonialism and imperialism; rather than redressing inequalities, the 'third world' continues to find itself in a position of inferiority with respect to the 'first world'. For feminist literary scholars, the recurring questions underpinning this relationship are: who is speaking and how is she speaking; to whom is she speaking and on behalf of whom is she speaking; how does she read me; how do I read her?

Gayatri Chakravorty Spivak's work has long been preoccupied with these questions. The extract included here is constructed around two problematic scenes. In the first, she attempts to understand the conjunction of a young woman from Sudan, a Saudi Arabian university, structural functionalism and clitoridectomy; in the second, she remembers a conversation which, as a child, she overheard between two washerwomen on her grandfather's estate. Both scenes lead Spivak to the most profound philosophical and political questions: 'not merely who am I? but who is the other woman? How am I naming her? How does she name me?' Such questioning relates directly to issues of knowledge production, to what happens in universities, to how feminists might construct a literary tradition or feminist literary theory. The intractable problem is how – or whether – academic 'first world' feminists and illiterate Indian women can speak together with understanding, without patronage or exploitation – 'what can I do *for* them?' – with a full recognition of both community and diversity.[5]

Chandra Talpade Mohanty is acutely aware of all these dilemmas. Her first footnote debates the description 'third world' and her opening page points to the danger of seeing both Western and 'third world' women in monolithic terms: to set up any categories, to make any generalized comment is to start a discussion. Mohanty's emphasis is on a structural relationship which is also a power relationship, and which positions the subordinated group as 'Other'. Thus, the Western woman, feminist or not, is the normative female subject; the 'third world' woman is the difference, the deviation and unrepresented. Furthermore, as Trinh T. Minh-ha indicates, the problem lies not only between categories but within categories: 'the generic "woman", like its counterpart, the generic "man", tends to efface difference within itself'. Mohanty's interest is in the textual strategies employed by Western feminists which reinscribe and legitimate this power imbalance. Despite protestations of global sisterhood, despite its position as a critical discourse within its own culture, feminism may be limiting and demarking 'third world' women in ways that reproduce colonialist attitudes. Trinh reinforces this point in her reference to the Western feminist preoccupation with footbinding, genital mutilation and *suttee*. She would not see any of these as unproblematic practices beyond discussion. The question is *how* to discuss them without constructing the 'third world' woman as ignorant, without agency and needing to be rescued.

Trinh indicates additional ways in which the 'first world' academic feminist retains a superior position in relation to the 'third world'. The 'third world' woman becomes a subject of 'special' (for which read 'marginal') interest. Trinh quotes Kristeva's title, 'woman can never be defined' (see Chapter 4), and illustrates with a range of examples the discursive play that surrounds the 'third world' woman. Not only is the term 'third world' constantly reformulated as geopolitical changes take place, but the glib distinction between 'first world' and 'third world' cannot be easily maintained: 'The Master is bound to recognize that His Culture is not as homogeneous, as monolithic as He believed it to be.' As in Mohanty's work, the complexity and power politics of these subject positions are central to Trinh's argument.

The extracts from Sara Suleri and Rey Chow reveal how ongoing are these debates. Mohanty and Trinh frame their comments with careful reservations, but Sara Suleri believes there are still problems with the deployment of these categories. She sees in Mohanty an attachment to binarism and an untenable 'claim to authenticity', and in Trinh, an unfulfilled theoretical project that relies too much on 'the naked category of lived experience'. These are consequences both of the very real difficulty in bringing together feminist and postcolonial theories and of the danger of romanticizing and sentimentalizing the marginal. (We might remember Madhu Dubey's similar concern with the significance of the margin in Chapter 4.) Chow, discussing what she describes as the 'lures of diaspora', returns us to where Spivak began, on the position of the 'third world' woman intellectual. Like Suleri, Chow is cautious of 'authenticity' and the duplicitous 'charms' of the position from which she is expected to speak, but still feels it is important to name 'Chinese woman intellectuals'.[6] To do so is not to elevate them but to 'place on them the burden of a kind of critical awareness' with regard to their location within Western universities, their distance from the 'native land' and their own part in the production of a particular 'third world'.

Textual Strategies
Self-evidently, fiction has given wonderful expression to our changing sense of multiculturalism, transnationalism and a globalized world, but of equal interest to critics has been the history of travel writing, a genre of cultural movement, exploration and encounter – not only with the Other but, often, in a reappraisal of the self.[7] It is for this reason that travel writing often shades into autobiography, and descriptions of action and movement are interspersed with reflection and stasis.[8] Feminist literary critics have been especially preoccupied with women as travellers, sometimes as part of conquests, and the textual strategies they have employed in their accounts. Here one can see colonial and imperial discursive power at play, not only in administrative functions, in the home as much as elsewhere, but in legitimizing power, conceptualizing the process of colonial expansion to oneself and to varied audiences, and as a symbolic violence where language might act alongside or as a substitute for legal sanctions and physical violence.

Mary Louise Pratt looks at two nineteenth-century women travel writers in South America, Flora Tristan and Maria Graham, and suggests that their narrative strategies differ significantly from those of the 'capitalist vanguard'. Though they enjoy the same privileges as the men, the narrative structure of their writing, its focus, their use of a language 'that is explanatory but non-technical', places them at odds with the male accounts, while their rejection of the sentimental positions them at odds with the norms of middle-class femininity. What is to be known and investigated is, for women, the self as much as the environment or the locale. The diverse positionings of these women travel writers is clear also in Laura E. Franey's study. Amidst the various forms of imperial violence is the 'verbal violence' of women travel writers and, as these women recount, the somatic effects produced on the African body. Franey concentrates on three accounts – Amelia Edwards's *A Thousand Miles up the Nile* (1877), Cornelia Speedy's *My Wanderings in the Soudan* (1884) and Mary Kingsley's *Travels in West Africa* (1897). She describes the common attribution in the Victorian period of linguistic competence to white women and Africans of both sexes. This is, at best, a 'soft' power, at worst a confirmation that neither group had any access to real power. Franey notes how these women travellers make use of this verbal power to establish their own legitimacy – indeed, superiority – and to identify with the colonial cause; their language becomes a verbal weapon.

We have already seen in Chapter 2 how the production and marketing of women's writing is an aspect of the interrogative movements between centre and peripheries, and how there is now a 'writing back' to the centre by those who do not support the metropolis. Yet, as Amal Amireh and Lisa Suhair Majaj here demonstrate, those movements may still be determined 'by the balance in power relations governing First World–Third World interactions'.[9] In reading globally, issues of translation, selection, literary form, marketing and reviewing, academic agendas in criticism and teaching all determine what is read and, to some extent, how it is read.[10] Amireh and Majaj point to the danger of 'third world' women's texts being 'transformed by the reception context, their meanings reproduced and reshaped to fit local agendas'. As Chow has also made clear, there is both a self-interest and a politics in the actions of apparently disinterested agents. And if literary production is a problem, so is literary criticism. Benita Parry reviews the work of various feminist critics involved in, as her chapter title indicates, 'reading the signs of empire in metropolitan fiction'. What Parry deplores is what she sees as the over-casual links between the literary and the sociopolitical. Through the use of analogy or metaphors or tropes, an equivalence is presumed between gender politics and the politics of race or empire, or between the domestic and the colonial. Such connections can become 'cognitive blind spots rather than cognitive insights'; they hide difference and hide, as Franey also makes clear, the collusion of women writers in the colonial or imperial project.

Places, Spaces and Locations

Adrienne Rich's influential essay, 'Notes toward a Politics of Location', is predicated on a deep understanding of the human subject as situated in a specific body, time, place and context, with consequences for one's relations, actions and responsibilities.[11] At this point in her essay, Rich is considering the privilege of whiteness and how her own awareness of that privilege was enhanced by certain events – attending to the words and actions of black people in the USA, reading the poetry of Cuban women, going to a conference in Nicaragua, watching the news on TV. Unless one attends to the specifics of location, feminists could get caught in a deadly 'either/or', frighteningly similar to the rhetoric of Cold War politics. But Caren Kaplan believes that Rich is caught in her own 'either/or'.[12] Rich has an established history of working with 'women of colour' in the USA, but, Kaplan suggests, it is not 'home' but 'away' – her trip to a conference in Nicaragua in the early 1980s – that prompts her rethinking about the hegemony of the North American white woman. In Kaplan's view, Rich moves from one binary view – the relative positions of 'women of colour' and white women in the USA – to another – the relative positions of North American women and South America women – and this risks losing sight of the complexity of the position of 'women of colour' in the USA. One could add that it also risks losing sight of the complexity of the location of South American women. This is not to discount Rich's essay; rather it is to continue to explore the politics of location as 'a strenuously contested and dynamically stressed term'.

Kaplan shows how our understanding of place or location is so often dependent on a relation – 'home' or 'away', here rather than there, national or immigrant. One of the attractions of Anzaldúa's *mestiza*, as we saw in Chapter 6, is that she avoids placement on one side or the other of the border. In the extracts that follow, we consider three different locations – the land to be explored and conquered, the home and the nation. In each case, space is gendered and 'woman' takes on a symbolic and iconographic meaning. Anne McClintock discusses the role of discourse in European imperial conquest and woman's place in what she calls 'a porno-tropics for the European imagination', where both the search for land and the search for knowledge are gendered, eroticized and productive of violence. Feminizing the land allows the male conqueror 'naturally' to reassert authority in the threatening spaces of the threshold and the unknown. Susan Strehle's study of fiction by women from six different locations is based on the premise that reading the local or the national effectively demands an understanding of the global and the transnational. In doing this, Strehle, unlike Parry, sees a role for homologies and correspondences. Specifically, Strehle explores, semantically, discursively and through responses of nostalgia, the relation between 'home' and 'homeland'.[13] She considers the roles women have played as writers, guardians of and prisoners in the home, and as symbolic embodiments of the home and homeland. Elleke Boehmer describes how in nationalist and independence struggles, the subject is coded as male.[14] For women there is a gap between a symbolic femininity, what Boehmer calls 'iconic recognition', and a material experience of continuing subordination. The link between nationalism, masculinity and writing establishes a 'ring of identity' from which women are excluded. Boehmer mentions the response of women writers in exploring matriarchal myths but is more interested in experimental, resistant forms of writing which can constitute a textual disruption. Women writers, suggests Boehmer, may search for a 'narrative territory' where they can claim their own identity and question the nationalist narrative that has excluded them.

Rosi Braidotti's concluding extract is a salutary reminder of the problems and potential of women's writing and feminist theory in a globalized world. Braidotti distinguishes 'the nomad' from 'the migrant'. She equates the nomad with the 'woman of ideas' and applauds the circulation of ideas; their nomadic nature is the best security for their survival. The migrant, in Braidotti's view, is not circulating but going from one place to another, often in abject circumstances. As we have seen elsewhere in this chapter, there is an urgent project to find a relation between 'the nomadic intellectual and the migrant women'.

Notes

1 For further helpful examples of the exploration of terms, see Sneja Gunew, *Haunted Nations: The Colonial Dimensions of Multiculturalisms* (London: Routledge, 2004); Anne McClintock, 'The Angel of Progress: Pitfalls of the Term "Post-colonialism"', *Social Text* (Spring 1992), pp. 1–15; Ania Loomba, *Colonialism/Postcolonialism* (London: Routledge, 1998); Leela Gandhi, *Postcolonial Theory: A Critical Introduction* (St Leonards, NSW: Allen & Unwin, 1998); *Contemporary Women's Writing*, vol. 3, no. 1 (June 2009), a special issue on diaspora edited by Emma Parker.

2 Ray, p. 9.

3 Equally interesting is Lewis's other work on Orientalism. See *Gendering Orientalism: Race, Femininity and Representation* (London: Routledge, 1996) and her comments on women as the producers of Orientalist images, not simply the product of the Orientalist gaze.

4 As debates have developed, practices in writing 'third world' have varied in terms of using, or not using, inverted commas and initial capital letters. Except where quoting, I am keeping to the practice of 'third world'.

5 Spivak returns to these questions in her work on subaltern studies. See, for example, relevant essays in *In Other Worlds: Essays in Cultural Politics* (New York and London: Methuen, 1987) and 'Can the Subaltern Speak?', in Cary Nelson and Lawrence Grossberg (eds.), *Marxism and the Interpretation of Culture* (Basingstoke: Macmillan, 1988), pp. 271–313. See also Spivak's reflections on 'French feminism', in 'French Feminism Revisited', *Outside in the Teaching Machine* (London: Routledge, 1993).

6 For related work, see: Julia Kristeva's much critiqued study, *About Chinese Women* (trans. Anita Barrows) (London: Marion Boyars, 1977); Jinhua Emma Teng, 'The Construction of the "Traditional Chinese Woman" in the Western Academy: A Critical Review', *Signs: Journal of Women in Culture and Society*, vol. 22, no. 1 (Autumn 1996), pp. 115–51; Rey Chow (ed.), *Modern Chinese Literary and Cultural Studies in the Age of Theory* (Durham, NC: Duke University Press, 2000).

7 In addition to work discussed here, see: Sara Mills, *Discourses of Difference: Women's Travel Writing and Colonialism* (London: Routledge, 1991); Alison Blunt, *Travel, Gender and Imperialism* (New York: Guilford Press, 1994); Cheryl McEwan, *Gender, Geography and Empire: Victorian Women Travellers in East Africa* (Aldershot: Ashgate, 2000); Sidonie Smith, *Moving Lives: Twentieth-Century Women's Travel Writing* (University of Minnesota Press: Minneapolis, 2001).

8 For instance, Brah uses an autobiographical mode in her Introduction. See also the fusion of autobiography and location in the *testimonios* of Latin American women, discussed in Doris Somner, ' "Not Just a Personal Story": Women's *Testimonios* and the Plural Self', in Bella Brodski and Celeste Schenck (eds.), *Life/Lines: Theorizing Women's Autobiography* (Ithaca, NY: Cornell University Press, 1988) and Gillian Whitlock, *The Intimate Empire: Reading Women's Autobiography* (London and New York: Cassell, 2000), which examines the relation between colonial culture and autobiography.

9 For discussion of the concept of 'writing back', see Bill Ashcroft, Gareth Griffiths and Helen Tiffin (eds.), *The Empire Writes Back: Theory and Practice in Postcolonial Literatures*, 2nd edition (London: Routledge, 2002).

10 Note how other commentators, such as Spivak and Madhu Dubey, have pointed out the appeal to the West of the realist text, interpreted as history or ethnography, rather than experimental writing. The author becomes, in Spivak's term, the 'native informant'. See Spivak, 'Questions of Multiculturalism', in Sarah Harasym (ed.), *The Postcolonial Critic: Interventions, Interviews, Dialogues* (New York: Routledge, 1990) and Dubey, *Black Women Novelists and the Nationalist Aesthetic* (Bloomington: Indiana University Press, 1994). One could equally say that, post-Rushdie, the ideal text for Western marketing is polyvocal and carnivalesque.

11 For a similar strategy, see June Jordan, *Moving Towards Home: Political Essays* (London: Virago, 1989) and Elly Bulkin, Minnie Bruce Pratt and Barbara Smith, *Yours in Struggle: Three Feminist Perspectives on Anti-Semitism and Racism* (Ithaca, NY: Firebrand, 1984).

12 See other work by Kaplan on the politics of location in 'Deterritorializations: The Rewriting of Home and Exile in Western Feminist Discourse', *Cultural Critique*, no. 6 (Spring 1987), pp. 187–98 and 'The Politics of Location as Transnational Feminist Practice', in Inderpal Grewal and Kaplan (eds.), *Scattered Hegemonies: Postmodernity and Transnational Feminist Practice* (Minneapolis: University of Minneapolis Press, 1994).

13 For further studies of 'home', see: Inderpal Grewal, *Home and Harem: Nation, Gender, Empire, and the Cultures of Travel* (Durham, NC: Duke University Press, 1996); Rosemary Marangoly George, *The Politics of Home: Postcolonial Relocations and Twentieth-Century Fiction* (Berkeley: University of Berkeley Press, 1996); Roberta Rubenstein, *Home Matters: Longing and Belonging, Nostalgia and Mourning in Women's Fiction* (Basingstoke: Palgrave Macmillan, 2001); Susan Stanford Friedman, 'Bodies on the Move: A Poetics of Home and Diaspora', *Tulsa Studies in Women's Literature*, vol. 23, no. 2 (Fall 2004), pp. 189–214.

14 For other work on gender and nationalism, see: Eavan Boland, *Object Lessons: The Life of the Woman and the Poet in Our Time* (London: Vintage, 1996); C. L. Innes, *Woman and Nation in Irish Literature and Society 1880–1935* (Brighton: Harvester, 1993); Neluka Silva, *The Gendered Nation: Contemporary Writings from South Asia* (Delhi: Sage, 2004).

SANGEETA RAY

*En-gendering India: Woman and Nation in Colonial
and Postcolonial Narratives*

Discussions of nationalism and gender in third world literature are further compounded when one shifts the location of certain writers loosely grouped under this category to other sites. The two writers I have chosen here could also be classified as writers of the South Asian diaspora and even as South Asian American writers. During the last ten years, Anita Desai has spent a large part of her time teaching at US universities, and her latest novel is set in Iowa. Interestingly, Desai began to gain recognition in the United States only after the publication of *Baumgartner's Bombay* in 1988, although she has been writing since the 1960s.[3] *Baumgartner's Bombay*, according to Desai, was successful in the United States "not because of its Indian material but because of its Jewish material. It's aroused a great deal of curiosity and interest among Jewish readers ... and people are interested in the element of the war, the Nazis and then the Holocaust" (Jussawalla and Dasenbrock 168–69). Bapsi Sidhwa, a Parsi from Pakistan, moved to the United States in 1983 and has lived in Charleston, Atlanta, Houston, Cambridge, and New York. She had published two novels, *The Bride* and *The Crow Eaters*, before she came to the States, but it was her novel *Cracking India* that introduced her to a North American audience. The novel had originally been published in Britain with the title *Ice-Candy Man*.

It is important to highlight a writer's multiple locations not just to complicate any easy categorization but also to allow for a more nuanced exploration of the praxis of cultural contact, "otherness," marginality, domination, and change. Postcolonial studies in the US academy has often been accused of being preoccupied with things South Asian/Indian. While there may be some truth in that, it is also the case that South Asians have only very recently been included in discussions about "Asians" in North America. As we read and teach postcolonial writers in the United States, we must pay increasing attention to ways in which we classify them to better unpackage categories such as third world, postcolonial, and Asian American and reveal the discursive, contingent nature of such descriptive labels. For example, if *Cracking India* is a particularly inflected postcolonial fictional account of the partition, *An American Brat* by the same novelist is a coming-of-age novel that depicts the trials and tribulations of a young Parsi immigrant woman in the United States. It shares a number of themes and tropes with other, more familiar Asian American novels.

A writer such as Sidhwa may herself state that "I don't know the Americans very well enough to write of *purely* American characters. I will use people from my part of the world in America – the expatriate, the immigrant experience if you like, how they interact here with the American" (Jussawalla and Dasenbrock 219; emphasis added). Alternatively, she may produce contradictory explanatory frameworks for an evaluation of her writings, as does Desai. In an interview Desai reveals that her recent work is more cross-cultural because after living in the United States, "a screen has come between me and India. I can't simply ignore this experience abroad – it's too over-whelming, it demands to be dealt with, somehow grappled with" (177). At the same time she implicitly refutes this characterization of her work when she asserts that she feels "extremely isolated ... removed to a society with which I have no *natural* link whatsoever" (179; emphasis added).

It therefore becomes all the more crucial for the postcolonial teacher in a US institution, often herself emblematic of some originary "otherness," to critique the very shoring up of a unique ahistorical American or Indian identity by those very writers who in their fiction set out to delineate the ways in which identities in general are subject to ongoing negotiation and reconstruction. It is incumbent on us consistently to foreground discursive positionings of both reader and writer, to initiate reading strategies that emphasize the ways in which terms such as "postcolonial," "Asian American," "South Asian," or "Indian" are part and parcel of differentially situated micro- and macronarratives that create the need for identitarian and territorializing nomenclatures even as we question those very needs and impulses. With respect to the gradually evolving connections between postcolonial and South Asian/Indian American identity formations in the United States, we need to be vigilant against the creation of facile and seamless links. Even as we demand inclusion of certain South Asian postcolonial texts in discussions of Asian American literature, we must scrutinize the complex and often contradictory socioeconomic and historical realities that constitute the various groups that make up Asian America in terms of patterns of immigration and issues of class, caste, religion, gender, and sexuality.

Although both novels I discuss can be grouped with texts that concern the themes of migration, travel, exile, and repudiation of one's originary community, they must be read in terms of their particular location within the formations of new nation-states in the wake of a specific history of colonization. Furthermore, both novels represent a vision of gendered agency that is intimately tied to a certain class and education which must be taken into account when one generalizes about the condition of the colonial and post-colonial South Asian woman. The depiction of a specific colonial and postcolonial society, upper class and Hindu in one novel and upper class and Parsi in another, might also help us understand the construction of a particular genealogy of South Asian immigration to the United States, a genealogy that privileges the second wave of professional, post-1965 immigrants. My readings of the two novels are situated within the debates about the status and nature of third world literature provided at length in the introduction, and I hope that the brief discussion of the multiply mediated locations of these two writers will extend my own analysis of their representations of gender, partition, and postindependent India.

(2000)

Note

3   Anita Desai belongs to the second generation of Indian authors writing in English, and after Rushdie she is probably the most recognized both in India and abroad. Her first novel, *Cry the Peacock*, was published in 1963. The first generation of authors writing in English began to work in the 1930s. They included Raja Rao, R. K. Narayan, Mulk Raj Ananad, and G. V. Desani. Anita Desai is a particularly interesting figure; with a Bengali father and a German mother, she grew up in Delhi, where she has lived for most of her life and which she still calls home.

AVTAR BRAH

Cartographies of Diaspora: Contesting Identities

The concepts of diaspora, borders, and multi-axial locationality together offer a conceptual grid for historicised analyses of contemporary trans/national movements of people, information, cultures, commodities and capital. The concept of diasporas presupposes the idea of borders. Correspondingly, the concept of border encapsulates the idea of diasporising processes. The two are closely intertwined with the notion of the politics of location or dislocation. The three concepts are immanent. I wish to propose the concept of *diaspora space* as the site of this immanence. Diaspora space is the intersectionality of diaspora, border, and dis/location as a point of confluence of economic, political, cultural, and psychic processes. It is where multiple subject positions are juxtaposed, contested, proclaimed or disavowed; where the permitted and the prohibited perpetually interrogate; and where the accepted and the transgressive imperceptibly mingle even while these syncretic forms may be disclaimed in the name of purity and tradition. Here, tradition is itself continually invented even as it may be hailed as originating from the mists of time. What is at stake is the infinite experientiality, the myriad processes of cultural fissure and fusion that underwrite contemporary forms of transcultural identities. These emergent identities may only be surreptitiously avowed. Indeed, they may even be disclaimed or suppressed in the face of constructed imperatives of 'purity'. But they are inscribed in the late twentieth-century forms of syncretism at the core of culture and subjectivity (Hall 1990; Coombes 1992).

The concept of diaspora space references the global condition of 'culture as a site of travel' (Clifford 1992) which seriously problematises the subject position of the 'native'. Diaspora space is the point at which boundaries of inclusion and exclusion, of belonging and otherness, of 'us' and 'them', are contested. My argument is that diaspora space as a conceptual category is 'inhabited', not only by those who have migrated and their descendants, but equally by those who are constructed and represented as indigenous. In other words, the concept of *diaspora space* (as opposed to that of diaspora) includes the entanglement, the intertwining of the genealogies of dispersion with those of 'staying put'. The diaspora space is the site where *the native is as much a diasporian as the diasporian is the native*. However, by this I do not mean to suggest an undifferentiated relativism. Rather, I see the conceptual category of diaspora space in articulation with the four modes of theorising of difference that I have proposed in Chapter Five, where 'difference' of social relation, experience, subjectivity and identity are relational categories situated within multi-axial fields of power relations. The similarities and differences across the different axes of differentiation – class, racism, gender, sexuality, and so on – articulate and disarticulate in the diaspora space, marking as well as being marked by the complex web of power.

In the diaspora space called 'England', for example, African-Caribbean, Irish, Asian, Jewish and other diasporas intersect among themselves as well as with the entity constructed as 'Englishness', thoroughly re-inscribing it in the process. Englishness has been formed in the crucible of the internal colonial encounter with Ireland, Scotland and Wales; imperial rivalries with other European countries; and imperial conquests abroad. In the post-war period this Englishness is continually reconstituted via a multitude of border crossings in and through other diasporic formations. These border crossings are territorial, political, economic, cultural and psychological. This Englishness is a new ensemble that both appropriates and is in turn appropriated by British-based African-Caribbean-ness, Asian-ness, Irishness and so on. Each of these formations has its own specificity, but it is an ever-changing specificity that adds to as well as imbues elements of the other. What I am proposing here is that border crossings do not occur only across the dominant/dominated dichotomy, but that, equally, there is traffic within cultural formations of the subordinated groups, and that these journeys are not *always* mediated through the dominant culture(s). In my schema such cultural ensembles as British Asian-ness, British Caribbean-ness, or British Cypriot-ness are cross-cutting rather than mutually exclusive configurations. The interesting question, then, is how these British identities take shape; how they are internally differentiated; how they interrelate with one another and with other British identities; and how they mutually reconfigure and decentre received notions of Englishness, Scottishness, Welshness, or Britishness. *My argument is that they are not 'minority' identities, nor are they at the periphery of something that sees itself as located at the centre, although they may be represented as such.* Rather, through processes of decentring, these new political and cultural formations continually challenge the minoritising and peripheralising impulses of the cultures of dominance. Indeed, it is in this sense that Catherine Hall (1992) makes the important claim that Englishness is just another ethnicity.

I have argued that feminist theorisation of the politics of location is of critical relevance to understanding border positionalities. This, however, is not to minimise the importance of other theoretical and political strands in illuminating diasporising border processes. Insights drawn from analyses of colonialism, imperialism, class, and gay and lesbian politics, for instance, are equally indispensable. Earlier, we noted the growing currency of the term 'border theory' to reference analytical perspectives that, *inter alia*, address some of these aspects. This term jostles with others, such as 'post-colonial theory' and 'diaspora theory'. Here, I am less concerned about the overlaps or differences between and across these conceptual terrains. The point I wish to stress is that these theoretical constructs are best understood as constituting *a point of confluence and intersectionality* where insights emerging from these fields inhere in the production of analytical frames capable of addressing multiple, intersecting, axes of differentiation. In other words, it is a space of/for theoretical crossovers that foreground processes of power inscribing these interrelationalities; a kind of *theoretical creolisation*. Such creolised envisioning is crucial, in my view, if we are to address fully the contradictions of modalities of enunciation, identities, positionalities and standpoints that are simultaneously 'inside' and 'outside'. It is necessary in order to decode the polymorphous compoundedness of social relations and subjectivity. The concept of diaspora space which I have attempted to elaborate here, and my analysis of 'difference' in a previous chapter, are firmly embedded in a theoretical creolisation of the type described above.

(1996)

REINA LEWIS

Rethinking Orientalism: Women, Travel and the Ottoman Harem

This book takes an interdisciplinary approach to evidence of Ottoman women's social and cultural agency to intervene on a number of fronts in discussions about the value and limits of Orientalism as a discourse and as a theoretical paradigm. Its focus on sources with a female point of origin brings a new element to existing challenges to masculinist histories of Orientalism. Introducing Ottoman sources also provides an example of 'indigenous' cultural agency that demonstrates the other side of the classic Orientalist paradigm. That these sources are by Ottoman women is particularly important because they speak of practices of resistance that are charged by differences of both ethnicity *and* gender. This is not to privilege their Orientalised status as a mark of 'purity' within imperial and gender inequalities, nor to understand gender as a homogeneous or stable category. Rather, the importance given to the different ethnic and class positions of these writers undercuts any singularity that might be accorded to the category of Oriental or Ottoman (or third world) woman, thus also interrupting some of the orthodoxies that have emerged in contemporary feminist postcolonial theory. To this is added a critical attention to the hybrid reformulations of Western cultural forms that emerge from the specific social, cultural and political historical situations from which these individuals speak. This is done in order to address the impact of these differently enunciated voices on their audiences in the West and the East, emphasising the complex overlapping addressees constructed by their writing.

But as well as their reading publics, they were also writing for each other. A central tenet of my argument is the importance of the dialogue between the Ottoman authors and Grace Ellison, through which some of their books came into being and their textual strategies can be evaluated. Presented also as emblematic of other such dialogues (see Lewis and Micklewright 2004), this serves to illustrate that the Orientalised Ottoman woman (presumed to be silenced rather than speaking) was in fact engaged in diverse forms of political and cultural activity. It also demonstrates that Ottoman women were connected textually and socially to a web of other women (and men) throughout and beyond the region, all of whom, constituting a series of segregated and unsegregated publics, recognised the importance of their writing activities. In restoring these sources to view this book characterises the segregated domains of Ottoman women as spaces of political agency and cultural production. It thereby contributes to the recasting of critical thinking about the institutional and symbolic significance of the harem – that most fertile space of the Orientalist imagination.

Despite the exponential growth of postcolonial studies and although Turkey and the Ottoman Empire feature large in representations associated with Orientalism, little attention has been paid to the case of Turkey, or to the Middle East more generally. Yet, Turkey and the late Ottoman Empire provide another paradigm for the analysis of (competing) colonial powers and the political and cultural effects of Euro-American imperial policy. This book, then, can also be understood as an intervention into postcolonial historiography and theory, using the Ottoman study as corrective to the narrowness of what postcolonial studies (often taking the South Asian experience as paradig-matic) regards as the colonial and the postcolonial. A transfer of attention to the postcolonialities of the Middle East would, as Deniz Kandiyoti urges, diversify this picture geographically and methodologically, by recognising 'not only the historical specificity of their colonial encounters but also the very different modalities and temporalities of their insertion into world capitalist markets' (Kandiyoti 2002: 282). She identifies three factors – global market relations, local social stratification and the differing roles of religion – as essen-tial for the construction of postcolonial analyses that can take into account 'struggles over resources, legitimacy and meaning' (Kandiyoti 2002: 294–5).[3] It is in this context, at the conjunction of two fields, that this book hopes to operate, introducing to postcolonial studies the specificities of the late Ottoman situation (which only briefly after the First World War involved direct European colonial rule) and bringing to the reading of Ottoman sources the critical perspectives of postcolonial and gender theory.

This is not to present these different fields of scholarly endeavour as either securely bounded or internally unified. So, for example, if Turkey has usually been outside the scope of postcolonial studies, Ottoman women have until very recently generally been outside the scope of Turkish historical studies. Paradoxically, one area where women's history does feature large is in Turkish republican historiography which has always given a heightened role to the celebration of the Anatolian woman liberated by the revolution. But it has had little to say about the struggle of women for those rights or the history of women's activism in the late Ottoman period (with the exception of the nationalist heroine Halide Edib). Indeed it is only recently that scholar-ship has turned to the study of the late Ottoman period. The reasons for this as Zehra Arat (1999c) and Elizabeth Frierson (1995) both argue, were politi-cal and linguistic. The politically motivated break from the Ottoman past, seen most dramatically in the adoption of the Latin script in 1928, 'kept the following generations completely detached from their past' (Arat 1999c: 10) and helped promulgate acceptance of republican historiography. The inabil-ity of generations raised after the establishment of the republic to read Ottoman records went hand-in-hand with what Frierson characterises as a 'sense of civilisational superiority to the Ottomans' which was so entrenched that 'foreignness in the case of Ottoman history, is not entirely a matter of national boundaries' (Frierson 1995: 57). Nationalist history, in depreciating all that was linked with the immediately pre-republican past, denied the agency of Ottoman women, picturing them as helpless slaves to sultanic and religious despotism (Frierson 1995: 57) from which the nationalists were held to have liberated the entire population. This volume is, among other things, directed as a contribution to the developing analysis of how Ottoman women were active in seeking their own liberation in their own terms.

(2004)

Note

3   For an excellent overview see also Cole and Kandiyoti (2002) and the special issue of *International Journal of Middle East Studies* (34:2, 2002) to which it is the introduction.

GAYATRI CHAKRAVORTY SPIVAK

'French Feminism in an International Frame'
Yale French Studies

A young Sudanese woman in the Faculty of Sociology at a Saudi Arabian University said to me, surprisingly: 'I have written a structural functionalist dissertation on female circumcision in the Sudan.' I was ready to forgive the sexist term 'female circumcision.' We have learned to say 'clitoridectomy' because others more acute than we have pointed out our mistake.

But Structural Functionalism? Where 'integration' is 'social control [which] defines and *enforces* ... a degree of *solidarity*'? Where 'interaction, seen from the side of the economy,' is defined as 'consist[ing] of the supply of income and wealth applied to purposes strengthening the persistence of cultural patterns?'[1] Structural functionalism takes a 'disinterested' stance on society as functioning structure. Its implicit interest is to applaud a system – in this case sexual – because it functions. A description such as the one below makes it difficult to credit that this young Sudanese woman had taken such an approach to clitoridectomy:

> In Egypt it is only the clitoris which is amputated, and usually not completely. But in the Sudan, the operation consists in the complete removal of all the external genital organs. They cut off the clitoris, the two major outer lips (*labia majora*) and the two minor inner lips (*labia minora*). Then the wound is repaired. The outer opening of the vagina is the only portion left intact, not however without having ensured that, during the process of repairing, some narrowing of the opening is carried out with a few extra stitches. The result is that on the marriage night it is necessary to widen the external opening by slitting one or both ends with a sharp scalpel or razor so that the male organ can be introduced.[2]

In my Sudanese colleague's research I found an allegory of my own ideological victimage:

The 'choice' of English Honors by an upper-class young woman in the Calcutta of the fifties was itself highly overdetermined. Becoming a professor of English in the US fitted in with the 'brain drain.' In due course, a commitment to feminism was the best of a collection of accessible scenarios.

The morphology of a feminist theoretical practice came clear through Jacques Derrida's critique of phallocentrism and Luce Irigaray's reading of Freud. (The stumbling 'choice' of French avant-garde criticism by an undistinguished Ivy League PhD working in the Midwest is itself not without ideology-critical interest.) Predictably, I began by identifying the 'female academic' and feminism as such. Gradually I found that there was indeed an area of feminist scholarship in the US that was called 'International Feminism:' the arena usually defined as feminism in England, France, West Germany, Italy, and that part of the Third World most easily accessible to American interests: Latin America. When one attempted to think of so-called Third World women in a broader scope, one found oneself caught, as my Sudanese colleague was caught and held by Structural Functionalism, in a web of information retrieval inspired at best by: 'what can I do *for* them?'

I sensed obscurely that this articulation was part of the problem. I rearticulated the question: What is the constituency of an international feminism? The following fragmentary and anecdotal pages approach the question. The complicity of a few French texts in that attempt could be part both of the problem – the 'West' out to 'know' the 'East' determining a 'westernized Easterner's' symptomatic attempt to 'know her own world'; or of something like a solution, – reversing and displacing (if only by juxtaposing 'some French texts' and a 'certain Calcutta') the ironclad opposition of West and East. As soon as I write this, it seems a hopelessly idealistic restatement of the problem. I am not in a position of choice in this dilemma.

To begin with, an obstinate childhood memory.

I am walking alone in my grandfather's estate on the Bihar–Bengal border one winter afternoon in 1949. Two ancient washerwomen are washing clothes in the river, beating the clothes on the stones. One accuses the other of poaching on her part of the river. I can still hear the cracked derisive voice of the one accused: 'You fool! Is this your river? The river belongs to the Company!' – the East India Company, from whom India passed to England by the Act for the Better Government of India (1858); England had transferred its charge to an Indian Governor-General in 1947. India would become an independent republic in 1950. For these withered women, the land as soil and water to be used rather than a map to be learned still belonged, as it did one hundred and nineteen years before that date, to the East India Company.

I was precocious enough to know that the remark was incorrect. It has taken me thirty-one years and the experience of confronting a nearly inarticulable question to apprehend that their facts were wrong but the fact was right. The Company does still own the land.

I should not consequently patronize and romanticize these women, nor yet entertain a nostalgia for being as they are. The academic feminist must learn to learn from them, to speak to them, to suspect that their access to the political and sexual scene is not merely to be *corrected* by our superior theory and enlightened compassion. Is our insistence upon the especial beauty of the old necessarily to be preferred to a careless acknowledgment of the mutability of sexuality? What of the fact that my distance from those two was, however, micrologically you defined class, class-determined and determining?

How, then, can one learn from and speak to the millions of illiterate rural and urban Indian women who live 'in the pores of' capitalism, inaccessible to the capitalist dynamics that allow us our shared channels of communication, the definition of common enemies? The pioneering books that bring First World feminists news from the Third World are written by privileged informants and can only be deciphered by a trained readership. The distance between 'the informant's world,' her 'own sense of the world she writes about,' and that of the non-specialist feminist is so great that, paradoxically, *pace* the subtleties of reader-response theories, here the distinctions might easily be missed.

This is not the tired nationalist claim that only a native can know the scene. The point that I am trying to make is that, in order to learn enough about Third World women and to develop a different readership, the immense heterogeneity of the field must be appreciated, and the First World feminist must learn to stop feeling privileged *as a woman*.

[...]

As soon as one steps out of the classroom, if indeed a 'teacher' ever fully can, the dangers rather than the benefits of academic feminism, French or otherwise, become more insistent. Institutional changes against sexism here or in France may mean nothing or, indirectly, further harm for women in the Third World.[44] This discontinuity ought to be recognized and worked at. Otherwise, the focus remains defined by the investigator as subject. To bring us back to my initial concerns, let me insist that here, the difference between 'French' and 'Anglo-American' feminism is superficial. However unfeasible and inefficient it may sound, I see no way to avoid insisting that there has to be a simultaneous other focus: not merely who am I? but who is the other woman? How am I naming her? How does she name me? Is this part of the problematic I discuss? Indeed, it is the absence of such unfeasible but crucial questions that makes the 'colonized woman' as 'subject' see the investigators as sweet and sympathetic creatures from another planet who are free to come and go; or, depending on her own socialization in the colonizing cultures, see 'feminism' as having a vanguardist class fix, the liberties it fights for as luxuries, finally identifiable with 'free sex' of one kind or another. Wrong, of course. My point has been that there is something equally wrong in our most sophisticated research, our most benevolent impulses.

(1981)

Notes

1   Bert F. Hoselitz, 'Development and the Theory of Social Systems,' in M. Stanley, ed., *Social Development* (New York: Basic Books, 1972), pp. 44, 45. I am grateful to Professor Michael Ryan for drawing my attention to this article.

2   Nawal El Saadawi, *The Hidden Face of Eve: Women in the Arab World* (London: Zed Press, 1980), p. 5.

[...]

44   To take the simplest possible American examples, even such innocent triumphs as the hiring of more tenured women or adding feminist sessions at a Convention might lead, since most US universities have dubious investments, and most Convention hotels use Third World female labor in a most oppressive way, to the increasing proletarianization of the women of the less developed countries.

Chandra Talpade Mohanty

'Under Western Eyes: Feminist Scholarship and Colonial Discourses'
Third World Women and the Politics of Feminism

Any discussion of the intellectual and political construction of "third world feminisms" must address itself to two simultaneous projects: the internal critique of hegemonic "Western" feminisms, and the formulation of autonomous, geographically, historically, and culturally grounded feminist concerns and strategies. The first project is one of deconstructing and dismantling; the second, one of building and constructing. While these projects appear to be contradictory, the one working negatively and the other positively, unless these two tasks are addressed simultaneously, "third world" feminisms run the risk of marginalization or ghettoization from both mainstream (right and left) and Western feminist discourses.

It is to the first project that I address myself. What I wish to analyze is specifically the production of the "third world woman" as a singular monolithic subject in some recent (Western) feminist texts. The definition of colonization I wish to invoke here is a predominantly *discursive* one, focusing on a certain mode of appropriation and codification of "scholarship" and "knowledge" about women in the third world by particular analytic categories employed in specific writings on the subject which take as their referent feminist interests as they have been articulated in the US and Western Europe. If one of the tasks of formulating and understanding the locus of "third world feminisms" is delineating the way in which it resists and *works against* what I am referring to as "Western feminist discourse," an analysis of the discursive construction of "third world women" in Western feminism is an important first step.

Clearly Western feminist discourse and political practice is neither singular nor homogeneous in its goals, interests, or analyses. However, it is possible to trace a coherence of *effects* resulting from the implicit assumption of "the West" (in all its complexities and contradictions) as the primary referent in theory and praxis. My reference to "Western feminism" is by no means intended to imply that it is a monolith. Rather, I am attempting to draw attention to the similar effects of various textual strategies used by writers which codify Others as non-Western and hence themselves as (implicitly) Western. It is in this sense that I use the term *Western feminist*. Similar arguments can be made in terms of middle-class urban African or Asian scholars producing scholarship on or about their rural or working-class sisters which assumes their own middle-class cultures as the norm, and codifies working-class histories and cultures as Other. Thus, while this essay focuses specifically on what I refer to as "Western feminist" discourse on women in the third world, the critiques I offer also pertain to third world scholars writing about their own cultures, which employ identical analytic strategies.

It ought to be of some political significance, at least, that the term *colonization* has come to denote a variety of phenomena in recent feminist and left writings in general. From its analytic value as a category of exploitative economic exchange in both traditional and contemporary Marxisms (cf. particularly contemporary theorists such as Baran [*The Political Economy of Growth*, New York, Monthly Review Press] 1962, Amin [*Imperialism and Unequal Development*, New York, Monthly Review Press] 1977, and Gunder-Frank [*Capitalism and Underdevelopment in Latin America*, New York, Monthly Review Press] 1967) to its use by feminist women of color in the US to describe the appropriation of their experiences and struggles by hegemonic white women's movements (cf. especially Moraga and Anzaldúa [*This Bridge Called my Back: Writings by Radical Women of Color*, New York, Kitchen Table Press] 1983, Smith [*Home Girls: A Black Feminist Anthology*, New York, Kitchen Table Press] 1983, Joseph and Lewis [*Common Differences: Conflicts in Black and White Feminist Perspectives*, Boston, Beacon Press] 1981, and Moraga [*Loving in the War Years*, Boston, South End Press] 1984), colonization has been used to characterize everything from the most evident economic and political hierarchies to the production of a particular cultural discourse about what is called the "third world."[1] However sophisticated or problematical its use as an explanatory construct, colonization almost invariably implies a relation of structural domination, and a suppression – often violent – of the heterogeneity of the subject(s) in question.

My concern about such writings derives from my own implication and investment in contemporary debates in feminist theory, and the urgent political necessity (especially in the age of Reagan/Bush) of forming strategic coalitions across class, race, and national boundaries. The analytic principles discussed below serve to distort Western feminist political practices, and limit the possibility of coalitions among (usually white) Western feminists and working-class feminists and feminists of color around the world. These limitations are evident in the construction of the (implicitly consensual) priority of issues around which apparently *all* women are expected to organize. The necessary and integral connection between feminist scholarship and feminist political practice and organizing determines the significance and status of Western feminist writings on women in the third world, for feminist scholarship, like most other kinds of scholarship, is not the mere production of knowledge about a certain subject. It is a directly political and discursive *practice* in that it is purposeful and ideological. It is best seen as a mode of intervention into particular hegemonic discourses (for example, traditional anthropology, sociology, literary criticism, etc.); it is a political praxis which counters and resists the totalizing imperative of age-old "legitimate" and "scientific" bodies of knowledge. Thus, feminist scholarly practices (whether reading, writing, critical, or textual) are inscribed in relations of power – relations which they counter, resist, or even perhaps implicitly support. There can, of course, be no apolitical scholarship.

The relationship between "Woman" – a cultural and ideological composite Other constructed through diverse representational discourses (scientific, literary, juridical, linguistic, cinematic, etc.) – and "women" – real, material subjects of their collective histories – is one of the central questions the practice of feminist scholarship seeks to address. This connection between women as historical subjects and the re-presentation of Woman produced by hegemonic discourses is not a relation of direct identity, or a relation of correspondence or simple implication.[2] It is an arbitrary relation set up by particular cultures. I would like to suggest that the feminist writings I analyze here discursively colonize the material and historical heterogeneities of the lives of women in the third world, thereby producing/re-presenting a composite, singular "third world woman" – an image which appears arbitrarily constructed, but nevertheless carries with it the authorizing signature of Western humanist discourse.[3]

I argue that assumptions of privilege and ethnocentric universality, on the one hand, and inadequate self-consciousness about the effect of Western scholarship on the "third world" in the context of a world system dominated by the West, on the other, characterize a sizable extent of Western feminist work on women in the third world. An analysis of "sexual difference" in the form of a cross-culturally singular, monolithic notion of patriarchy or male dominance leads to the construction of a similarly reductive and homogeneous notion of what I call the "third world difference" – that stable, ahistorical something that apparently oppresses most if not all the women in these countries. And it is in the production of this "third world difference" that Western feminisms appropriate and "colonize" the constitutive complexities which characterize the lives of women in these countries. It is in this process of discursive homogenization and systematization of the oppression of women in the third world that power is exercised in much of recent Western feminist discourse, and this power needs to be defined and named.

(1991)

Notes

This essay would not have been possible without S. P. Mohanty's challenging and careful reading. I would also like to thank Biddy Martin for our numerous discussions about feminist theory and politics. They both helped me think through some of the arguments herein.

1 Terms such as *third* and *first world* are very problematical both in suggesting oversimplified similarities between and among countries labeled thus, and in implicitly reinforcing existing economic, cultural, and ideological hierarchies which are conjured up in using such terminology. I use the term *"third world"* with full awareness of its problems, only because this is the terminology available to us at the moment. The use of quotation marks is meant to suggest a continuous questioning of the designation. Even when I do not use quotation marks, I mean to use the term critically.

2 I am indebted to Teresa de Lauretis for this particular formulation of the project of feminist theorizing. See especially her introduction in de Lauretis, *Alice Doesn't: Feminism, Semiotics, Cinema* (Bloomington: Indiana University Press, 1984); see also Sylvia Wynter, "The Politics of Domination," unpublished manuscript.

3 This argument is similar to Homi Bhabha's definition of colonial discourse as strategically creating a space for a subject people through the production of knowledges and the exercise of power. The full quote reads: "[colonial discourse is] an apparatus of power.... an apparatus that turns on the recognition and disavowal of racial/cultural/historical differences. Its predominant strategic function is the creation of a space for a subject people through the production of knowledges in terms of which surveillance is exercised and a complex form of pleasure/ unpleasure is incited. It (i.e. colonial discourse) seeks authorization for its strategies by the production of knowledges by coloniser and colonised which are stereotypical but antithetically evaluated" (1983, 23).

Trinh T. Minh-ha

Woman, Native, Other: Writing Postcoloniality and Feminism

Woman can never be defined. Bat, dog, chick, mutton, tart. Queen, madam, lady of pleasure. MISTRESS. *Belle-de-nuit*, woman of the streets, girl. Lady and whore are both bred to please. The old Woman image-repertoire says She is a Womb, a mere baby's pouch, or "nothing but sexuality." She is a passive substance, a parasite, an enigma whose mystery proves to be a snare and a delusion. She wallows in night, disorder, and immanence and is at the same time the "disturbing factor (between men)" and the key to the beyond. The further the repertoire unfolds its images, the more entangled it gets in its attempts at capturing Her. "Truth, Beauty, Poetry – she is All: once more all under the form of the Other. All except herself,"[27] Simone De Beauvoir wrote. Yet, even with or because of Her capacity to embody All, Woman is the lesser man, and among male athletes, to be called a woman is still resented as the worst of insults. "Wo-" appended to "man" in sexist contexts is not unlike "Third World," "Third," "minority," or "*color*" affixed to *woman* in pseudo-feminist contexts. Yearning for universality, the generic "woman," like its counterpart, the generic "man," tends to efface difference within itself. Not every female is "a real woman," one knows this through hearsay ... Just as "man" provides an example of how the part played by women has been ignored, undervalued, distorted, or omitted through the use of terminology presumed to be generic, "woman" more often than not reflects the subtle power of linguistic exclusion, for its set of referents rarely includes those relevant to Third World "female persons." "All the Women Are White, All the Blacks are Men, But Some of Us Are Brave" is the title given to an anthology edited by Gloria T. Hull, Patricia Bell Scott, and Barbara Smith. It is, indeed, somehow devious to think that WOMAN also encompasses the Chinese with bound feet, the genitally mutilated Africans, and the one thousand Indians who committed *suttee* for one royal male. Sister Cinderella's foot is also enviably tiny but never crooked! And, European witches were also burnt to purify the body of Christ, but they do not pretend to "self-immolation." "Third World," therefore, belongs to a category apart, a "special" one that is meant to be both complimentary and complementary, for First and Second went out of fashion, leaving a serious Lack behind to be filled.

Third World?

To survive, "Third World" must necessarily have negative *and* positive connotations: negative when viewed in a vertical ranking system – "underdeveloped" compared to over-industrialized, "underprivileged" within the already Second sex – and positive when understood sociopolitically as a subversive, "non-aligned" force. Whether "Third World" sounds negative or positive also depends on *who* uses it. Coming from you Westerners, the word can hardly mean the same as when it comes from Us members of the Third World. Quite predictably, you/we who condemn it most are both we who buy in and they who deny any participation in the bourgeois mentality of the West. For it was in the context of such mentality that "Third World" stood out as a new semantic finding to designate what was known as "the savages" before the Independences. Today, hegemony is much more subtle, much more pernicious than the form of blatant racism once exercised by the colonial West. I/i always find myself asking, in this one-dimensional society, where I/i should draw the line between tracking down the oppressive mechanisms of the system and aiding their spread. "Third World" commonly refers to those states in Africa, Asia and Latin America which called themselves "non-aligned," that is to say, affiliated with neither the Western (capitalist) nor the Eastern (communist) power blocs. Thus, if "Third World" is often rejected for its judged-to-be-derogative connotations, it is not so much because of the hierarchical, first-second-third order implied, as some invariably repeat, but because of the growing threat "Third World" consistently presents to the Western bloc the last few decades. The emergence of repressed voices into the worldwide political arena has already prompted her (Julia Kristeva) to ask: "How will the West greet the awakening of the 'third world' as the Chinese call it? Can we [Westerners] participate, actively and lucidly, in this awakening when the center of the planet is in the process of moving toward the East?"[28] Exploited, looked down upon, and lumped together in a convenient term that denies their individualities, a group of "poor" (nations), having once sided with neither of the dominating forces, has slowly learned to turn this denial to the best account. "The Third World to Third World peoples" thus becomes an empowering tool, and one which politically includes all non-whites in their solidarist struggle against all forms of Western dominance. And since "Third World" now refers to more than the geographically and economically determined nations of the "South" (versus "North"), since the term comprises such "developed" countries as Japan and those which have opted for socialist reconstruction of their system (China, Cuba, Ethiopia, Angola, Mozambique) as well as those which have favored a capitalist mode of development (Nigeria, India, Brazil), there no longer exists such a thing as a unified unaligned Third World bloc. Moreover, Third World has moved West (or North, depending on where the dividing line falls) and has expanded so as to include even the remote parts of the First World. What is at stake is not only the hegemony of Western cultures, but also their identities as unified cultures. Third World dwells on diversity; so does First World. This is our strength and our misery. The West is painfully made to realize the existence of a Third World in the First World, and vice versa. The Master is bound to recognize that His Culture is not as homogeneous, as monolithic as He believed it to be. He discovers, with much reluctance, He is just an other among others.

(1989)

Notes

27   Simone De Beauvoir, *The Second Sex* (1952, rpt New York: Bantam, 1970), p. 223.
28   Julia Kristeva, "Woman Can Never Be Defined," trans. Marilyn A. August, *New French Feminism*, ed. E. Marks and I. De Courtivon (Amherst: Univ. of Massachusetts Press, 1980), p. 139.

SARA SULERI

'Woman Skin Deep: Feminism and the Postcolonial Condition'
Critical Inquiry

In the context of contemporary feminist discourse, I would argue, the category of postcolonialism must be read both as a free-floating metaphor for cultural embattlement and as an almost obsolete signifier for the historicity of race. There is no available dichotomy that could neatly classify the ways in which such a redefinition of postcoloniality is necessarily a secret sharer in similar reconfigurations of feminism's most vocal articulation of marginality, or the obsessive attention it has recently paid to the racial body. Is the body in race subject or object, or is it more dangerously an objectification of a methodology that aims for radical subjectivity? Here, the binarism that informs Chandra Mohanty's paradigmatic essay, "Under Western Eyes: Feminist Scholarship and Colonial Discourses," deserves particular consideration. Where Mohanty engages in a particular critique of "Third World Woman" as a monolithic object in the texts of Western feminism, her argument is premised on the irreconcilability of gender as history and gender as culture. "What happens," queries Mohanty, "when [an]assumption of 'women as an oppressed group' is situated in the context of Western feminist writing about third world women?" What happens, apparently, begs her question. In contesting what she claims is a "colonialist move," Mohanty proceeds to argue that "Western feminists alone become the true 'subjects' of this counter-history. Third World women, on the other hand, never rise above the debilitating generality of their 'object' status."[4] A very literal ethic underlies such a dichotomy, one that demands attention to its very obviousness: how is this objectivism to be avoided? How will the ethnic voice of womanhood counteract the cultural articulation that Mohanty too easily dubs as the exegesis of Western feminism? The claim to authenticity – only a black can speak for a black; only a postcolonial subcontinental feminist can adequately represent the lived experience of that culture – points to the great difficulty posited by the "authenticity" of female racial voices in the great game that claims to be the first narrative of what the ethnically constructed woman is deemed to want.

This desire all too often takes its theoretical form in a will to subjectivity that claims a theoretical basis most clearly contravened by the process of its analysis. An example of this point is Trinh Minh-ha's treatise, *Woman, Native, Other,*[5] which seeks to posit an alternative to the anthropological twist that constitutes the archaism through which nativism has been apprehended. Subtitled *Writing Postcoloniality and Feminism*, Trinh's book is a paradigmatic meditation that can be essentialized into a simple but crucial question: how can feminist discourse represent the categories of "woman" and "race" at the same time? If the languages of feminism and ethnicity are to escape an abrasive mutual contestation, what novel idiom can freshly articulate their radical inseparability? Trinh's strategy is to relocate her gendering of ethnic realities on the inevitable territory of postfeminism, which underscores her desire to represent discourse formation as always taking place after the fact of discourse. It further confirms my belief that had I any veto power over prefixes, *post-* would be the first to go – but that is doubtless tangential to the issue at hand. In the context of Trinh's methodology, the shape of the book itself illuminates what may best be called the endemic ill that effects a certain temporal derangement between the work's originary questions and the narratives that they engender. *Woman, Native, Other* consists of four loosely related chapters, each of which opens with an abstraction and ends with an anecdote. While there is a self-pronounced difference between the preliminary thesis outlined in the chapter "Commitment from the Mirror-Writing Box" to the concluding claims in "Grandma's Story," such a discursive distance is not matched with any logical or theoretical consistency. Instead, a work that is impelled by an impassioned need to question the lines of demarcation between race and gender concludes by falling into a predictable biological fallacy in which sexuality is reduced to the literal structure of the racial body, and theoretical interventions within this trajectory become minimalized into the naked category of lived experience.

When feminism turns to lived experience as an alternative mode of radical subjectivity, it only rehearses the objectification of its proper subject. While lived experience can hardly be discounted as a critical resource for an apprehension of the gendering of race, neither should such data serve as the evacuating principle for both historical and theoretical contexts alike. "Radical subjectivity" too frequently translates into a low-grade romanticism that cannot recognize its discursive status as *pre-*rather than *post-*. In the concluding chapter of Trinh's text, for example, a section titled "Truth and Fact: Story and History" delineates the skewed idiom that marginal subjectivities produce. In attempting to proclaim an alternative to male-identified objectivism, Trinh-as-anthropologist can only produce an equally objectifying idiom of joy:

> Let me tell you a story. For all I have is a story. Story passed on from generation to generation, named Joy. Told for the joy it gives the storyteller and the listener. Joy inherent in the process of storytelling. Whoever understands it also understands that a story, as distressing as it can be in its joy, never takes anything away from anybody. [*WNO*, p. 119]

Given that I find myself in a more acerbic relation both to the question of the constitution of specific postcolonialisms and of a more metaphoric postcolonial feminism, such a jointly universalist and individualist "joy" is not a term that I would ordinarily welcome into my discursive lexicon. On one level, its manipulation of lived experience into a somewhat fallacious allegory for the reconstitution of gendered race bespeaks a transcendence – and an attendant evasion – of the crucial cultural issues at hand. On a more dangerous level, however, such an assumption serves as a mirror image of the analyses produced by the critics of political rectitude. For both parties, "life" remains the ultimate answer to "discourse." The subject of race, in other words, cannot cohabit with the detail of a feminist language.

Trinh's transcendent idiom, of course, emanates from her somewhat free-floating understanding of "postcoloniality": is it an abstraction into which all historical specificity may be subsumed, or is it a figure for a vaguely defined ontological marginality that is equally applicable to all "minority" discourses? In either case, both the categories of "woman" and "race" assume the status of metaphors, so that each rhetoric of oppression can serve equally as a mirrored allegory for the other. Here, *Woman, Native, Other* is paradigmatic of the methodological blurring that dictates much of the discourse on identity formation in the coloring of feminist discourse. To privilege the racial body in the absence of historical context is indeed to generate an idiom that tends to waver with impressionistic haste between the abstractions of postcoloniality and the anecdotal literalism of what it means to articulate an "identity" for a woman writer of color. Despite its proclaimed location within contemporary theoretical – not to mention post-theoretical – discourse, such an idiom poignantly illustrates the hidden and unnecessary desire to resuscitate the "self."

(1992)

Notes

4   Chandra Talpade Mohanty, "Under Western Eyes: Feminist Scholarship and Colonial Discourses," *Third World Women and the Politics of Feminism*, ed. Mohanty, Ann Russo, and Lourdes Torres (Bloomington, Ind., 1991), p. 71.
5   See Trinh T. Minh-ha, *Woman, Native, Other: Writing Postcoloniality and Feminism* (Bloomington, Ind., 1989); hereafter abbreviated *WNO*.

REY CHOW

Writing Diaspora: Tactics of Intervention in Contemporary Cultural Studies

In naming "Chinese women intellectuals," thus, my intention is not to establish them as a more authentic group of investigators whose claim to "women" in the Chinese field would exclude that of other investigators.

Naming here is, first and foremost, a way to avoid repeating the well-worn discursive paradigm of Orientalism, in which the peoples of the non-West are taken factographically as "objects" without consciousness while the historical privileges of speaking subjects – in particular the privilege of "having" consciousness – remain unarticulated.

Second, naming is also a way of *not giving in* to the charms of an alterity in which so many of the West's "others" are now called upon to speak. Naming is not so much an act of consolidating power as it is an act of making explicit the historical predicament of investigating "China" and "Chinese women," especially as it pertains to those who are ethnically Chinese and/ or sexually women.

Third, it follows that naming the investigators amid the current "multicultural" interest in "women" in non-Western fields is also a means of accentuating the otherwise *muted* fact of intellectual women's privilege as intellectuals and thus (particularly in the Chinese context) as members of the elite. While this privilege is, at this point, hardly acknowledged in the masculinist explorations of modernity, nationhood, and literature, because masculinist explorations are themselves preoccupied with their own minority and womanhood vis-à-vis the West, it is peremptory that women investigators, especially Chinese women investigators investigating the history of Chinese women's social subordination, handle the mode of their speech – which historically straddles the elite and the subaltern – with deliberate care. In naming them as such, therefore, my point is to place on them the burden of a kind of critical awareness that has yet to be articulated in their field. The weight of each of the terms under which they work – Chinese, women, intellectual – means that their alliances with other discursive groups, as well as their self-reflection on their own positions, must always be astute. Both practices, allying with others and reflecting on oneself, are by necessity more demanding than a blanket dismissal of names and identities as "essentialist."[27] Such a dismissal is often the result of an ahistorical espousal of "difference" and "femininity" as is found in some influential theories which, by equating the feminine with the negative and the unrepresentable, dismiss all processes of identification as positivistic. (A good case in point is the work of Julia Kristeva, which is popular with many feminist critics despite Kristeva's unwillingness to name "woman"[28] and to name herself "feminist.") The question on which to insist, however, is not "to name or not to name" but: What is to be gained or lost in naming what and whom, and by whom?

What I am arguing can also be stated in a different way: What are we doing talking about modern Chinese literature and Chinese women in the North American academy in the 1990s? As such activities of speaking and writing are tied less to the oppressed women in Chinese communities "back home" than to our own intellectual careers in the West, we need to unmask ourselves through a scrupulous declaration of self-interest. Such declaration does not clean our hands, but it prevents the continuance of a tendency, rather strong among "third world" intellectuals in diaspora as well as researchers of non-Western cultures in "first world" nations, to sentimentalize precisely those day-to-day realities from which they are distanced.

The diasporic postcolonial space is, as I already indicate, neither the space of the native intellectual protesting against the intrusive presence of foreign imperialists in the indigenous territory nor the space of the postcolonial critic working against the lasting effects of cultural domination in the home country (now an independent "nation") after the phase of territorial imperialism. In the case of China, it is necessary to remember that "Chinese" territory, with the exceptions of Taiwan from 1895 to 1945, Hong Kong from 1842 to 1997, and Macau (occupied by the Portuguese since the mid-sixteenth century) from 1887 to 1997, was never completely "colonized" over a long period by any one foreign power, even though the cultural effects of imperialism are as strong as in other formerly colonized countries in Asia, Africa, and Latin America. One could perhaps say that such cultural effects of foreign dominance are, in fact, *stronger*: they are most explicit, paradoxically, when one sees how the mainland Chinese can hold on to the illusion – born of modern Western imperialism but itself no less imperialistic – of a "native land," a *zuguo*, that was never entirely captured and that therefore remains glorious to this day.

The space of "third world" intellectuals in diaspora is a space that is removed from the "ground" of earlier struggles that were still tied to the "native land." Physical alienation, however, can mean precisely the intensification and aestheticization of the values of "minority" positions that had developed in the earlier struggles and that have now, in "third world" intellectuals' actual circumstances in the West, become defunct. The unselfreflexive sponsorship of "third world" culture, including "third world" women's culture, becomes a mask that conceals the hegemony of these intellectuals over those who are stuck at home.

For "third world" intellectuals, the lures of diaspora consist in this masked hegemony. As in the case of what I call masculinist positions in the China field, their resort to "minority discourse," including the discourse of class and gender struggles, veils their own fatherhood over the "ethnics" at home even while it continues to legitimize them as "ethnics" and "minorities" in the West. In their hands, minority discourse and class struggle, especially when they take the name of another nation, another culture, another sex, or another body, turn into signifiers whose major function is that of discursive exchange for the intellectuals' self-profit. Like "the people," "real people," "the populace," "the peasants," "the poor," "the homeless," and all such names, these signifiers *work* insofar as they gesture toward another place (the lack in discourse-construction) that is "authentic" but that cannot be admitted into the circuit of exchange.

What happens eventually is that this "third world" that is produced, circulated, and purchased by "third world" intellectuals in the cosmopolitan diasporic space will be exported "back home" in the form of values – intangible goods – in such a way as to obstruct the development of the native industry. To be sure, one can perhaps no longer even speak of a "native industry" as such in the multinational corporate postmodernity, but it remains for these intellectuals to face up to their truthful relation to those "objects of study" behind which they can easily hide – as voyeurs, as "fellow victims," and as self-appointed custodians.

Hence the necessity to read and write against the lures of diaspora: Any attempt to deal with "women" or the "oppressed classes" in the "third world" that does not at the same time come to terms with the historical conditions of its own articulation is bound to repeat the exploitativeness that used to and still characterizes most "exchanges" between "West" and "East." Such attempts will also be expediently assimilated within the plenitude of the hegemonic establishment, with all the rewards that that entails. No one can do without some such rewards. What one can do without is the illusion that, through privileged speech, one is helping to save the wretched of the earth.[29]

(1993)

Notes

27 The extensiveness of the philosophical, political, and feminist arguments about "essentialism" is such that I can merely point to it here. Two recent publications readers can consult are Diana Fuss, *Essentially Speaking* (New York: Routledge, 1989), and *differences* 1.2 (Summer 1989), a special issue on essentialism.

28 "In 'woman' I see something that cannot be represented, something that is not said, something above and beyond nomenclatures and ideologies." Kristeva, "Woman Can Never Be Defined," trans. Marilyn A. August, in Elaine Marks and Isabelle de Courtivron, eds., *New French Feminisms* (New York: Schocken Books, 1981), p. 137.

29 I want to acknowledge those who have contributed to the final version of this chapter. I have benefited from comments made by Wendy Larson and Lydia Liu at the conferences at Iowa and in New Orleans. Continual discussions with Kwai-cheung Lo, Tonglin Lu, and Ming-bao Yue about this chapter and other related issues give me the support of a strong critical community. Most of all, I am indebted to Yu-shih Chen for a forceful and enabling critique, which made me restate my concerns with a clarity that had been previously missing.

Mary Louise Pratt

Imperial Eyes: Travel Writing and Transculturation

In structuring their travel books, I have suggested, the capitalist vanguardists often relied on the goal-directed, linear emplotment of conquest narrative. Graham's and Tristan's accounts do not, though they might have. They are emplotted in a centripetal fashion around places of residence from which the protagonist sallies forth and to which she returns. Both women begin their accounts by taking up residence in an urban center (Graham in Valparaiso and Tristan in Arequipa). Though both do make lengthy inland journeys into the country or across it to other cities, it is this initial fixed positioning that organizes the narrative. Urban-based rather than rural, the women's accounts follow a different descriptive agenda as well. Social and political life are centers of personal engagement; each shows a strong ethnographic interest. In the accounts of the capitalist vanguard, interventionist goals often produce a reactive, judgemental energy. Though they share many of those goals, Graham and Tristan have little immediate stake in the outcomes of what goes on around them and write along more interpretive, analytical lines. They reject sentimentality and romanticism almost as vehemently as the capitalist vanguard did. For them identity in the contact zone resides in their sense of personal independence, property, and social authority, rather than in scientific erudition, survival, or adventurism. No less than the men, these women travelers occupy a world of servants and servitude where their class and race privilege is presupposed, and meals, baths, blankets, and lamps appear from nowhere.

"I took possession of my cottage at Valparaiso," begins Graham in her entry for May 9, 1822, "and feel an indescribable relief in being quiet and alone."[37] It is ten days since her arrival in Chile, a week since her husband's burial. For both Graham and Tristan, the indoor world is the seat of the self; both privilege their houses and above all their private rooms as refuges and sources of well-being. Graham describes her house in detail, including the views from the doors and windows: initially Chile will be seen from within. (One is reminded of Anna Maria Falconbridge looking out into the slave-yard from a parlor window.) It must be underscored, however, that the indoor, private world here does not mean family or domestic life, but in fact their absence: it is the site above all of solitude, the private place in which the lone subjectivity collects itself, creates itself in order to sally forth into the world. Tristan, lodged in the homes of her relatives, repeatedly depicts herself violating social convention by retiring to her room to collect herself. The rooms themselves become allegories of her subjective and relational states:

> This room, at least twenty-five feet long and twenty-five feet high, was lit by a single tiny window set high in the wall.... The sun never penetrated this

suite, which in its shape and atmosphere was not unlike an underground cave. A profound sadness pervaded my soul as I examined the place my family had allotted me.[38]

The predictable fact that domestic settings have a much more prominent presence in the women's travel accounts than in the men's (where one is hard pressed indeed to find even an interior description of a house) is a matter not just of differing spheres of interest or expertise, then, but of modes of constituting knowledge and subjectivity. If the men's job was to collect and possess everything else, these women travelers sought first and foremost to collect and possess themselves. Their territorial claim was to private space, in personal, room-sized empire. From these private seats of selfhood, Graham and Tristan depict themselves emerging to explore the world in circular expeditions that take them out into the public and new, then back to the familiar and enclosed. One version of this paradigm was of course the rounds of visiting so prominent in urban social life, for men and women. Both women moved in elite creole and expatriate circles. Graham takes her readers to visit the governor, to have tea with her landlady, to call on educated women like the poet Mercedes Marín del Solar. Tristan, less tolerant of Peruvian society, complains repeatedly of the tedium of continual visiting. Her interest was roused rather by local spectacles like Holy Week processions, a mystery play, carnival celebration, and, we shall see below, a civil war.

Equally pertinent to these books is the more specifically exploratory activity identified with urban middle-class women in the early nineteenth century. The political work of social reformers and charity workers included the practice of visiting prisons, orphanages, hospitals, convents, factories, slums, poorhouses, and other sites of social management and control. German critic Marie-Claire Hoock-Demarle uses the term *exploratrice sociale* ("social exploratress") to discuss the work of Flora Tristan and her German contemporary Bettina von Arnim.[39] In Peru Tristan takes a great interest in the life of Arequipa's numerous convents, and visits a military encampment, a flour mill, and a sugar plantation as well as

a hospital, a madhouse, and an orphanage, all three for the most part, very badly maintained.... The obligations of charity are thought to be satisfied if the children are given just enough to sustain their miserable existence; what is more, they receive no education or training, so any who survive become beggars.[40]

The label fits Maria Graham as well. Graham's social explorations in Chile include visits to a prison, an artisan village, ports, markets, and religious retreats for young girls: "There under the direction of an old priest, the young creatures who retire thus are kept praying night and day, with so little food and sleep that their bodies and minds alike become weakened."[41]

As such quotations recall, written or spoken critique is integral to social exploration as a political practice. Obviously this institutional critique differs from the taste-based denunciation of American living habits offered by the capitalist vanguard – though both are equally anchored in class values. Another branch of the civilizing mission, social reformism might be said to constitute a form of female imperial intervention in the contact zone. This is not to say, of course, that the critique of taste belonged exclusively to men. Flora Tristan indulges in it with gusto, and with more flair than many male writers. Arequipan cuisine she finds "detestable":

> The valley of Arequipa is very fertile, yet the vegetables are poor. The potatoes are not floury, the cabbages, lettuce, and peas are hard and tasteless. The meat is dry, and the poultry is as tough as if it had come out of the volcano.... The only things I really enjoyed in Arequipa were the cakes and other dainties made by the nuns.[42]

Hoock-Demarle's study of social exploratresses focuses in particular on the language women writers used to recount their explorations and frame their critiques. The terminology of "exploratresses" and "exploration" is introduced by Hoock-Demarle to distinguish the work of these "contesta-tory women" from officialist "research" and "researchers" (*enquêtes, enquêtrices*), whose authoritative discourse was statistical and technical description. Aiming at broad audiences, she argues, the social exploratresses avoided specialized statistical languages anchored in expertise, and instead called upon novelistic practice to express their findings, producing a "subtle fusion of the literary and the social carried out at the level of style." The rejection of statistical description had everything to do, of course, with the oppositional and often specifically anti-statist momentum of their work. Their adaptation of realist novelistic language, says Hoock-Demarle, enabled the social exploratresses to

> avoid the trap of bureaucratic technicity, the preserve of official masculine discourse, which they recognize has little impact on the masses. They also escape from the facile socio-sentimentality that is beginning, not without success, to exploit the genre of the pamphlet.[43]

Hoock-Demarle's stylistic observations are pertinent to both Tristan's and Graham's South American writings. Visiting the seaside resort of Chorrillos near Lima, for example, the ever inquisitive Tristan makes an excursion to a sugar refinery ("Up to then I had only seen sugar in the Botanical

Gardens in Paris"). She describes the place experientially in a language that is explanatory but non-technical:

> I was very interested in the four mills used to crush the canes; they are powered by a waterfall. The aqueduct which brings the water to the refinery is very fine and cost a great deal to build because of the difficulties of the terrain. I went over to the huge shed where the vats for boiling the sugar are housed, then we proceeded to the adjoining refinery where the sugar is separated from the molasses.[44]

Not surprisingly the visit provides an occasion for a verbal attack on slavery and plantation economics. Tristan presents the critique novelistically through a long dramatized dialogue with the plantation owner, in which she plays the heroine of the enlightenment. The tactics are those of the realist, not the sentimental novel, however.

(1992)

Notes

37   Maria Graham, *Journal of a Residence in Chile during the year 1822*, London, Longman et al., and John Murray, 1824, p. 115.

38   Tristan, op. cit., pp. 98–9. See also the description of her convent cell "like a Parisian boudoir," p. 194. This is the first English translation of Tristan's book. Like most, it has been substantially abridged from the 600-page original. The 1979 French edition by Maspero is cut by about one-fourth. The full edition I consulted was the 1946 Spanish translation by Emilia Romero, Lima, Editorial Antártica, 1946, republished in 1971 by Moncloa-Campodonico, also in Lima.

39   Marie-Claire Hoock-Demarle, "Le Langage littéraire des femmes enquêtrices," in Stéphane Michaud, ed., *Un fabuleux destin: Flora Tristan*, Dijon, Editions Universitaires, 1985. See also Magda Portal et al., *Flora Tristan: Una reserva de utopía*, Centro de la Mujer Peruana Flora Tristan, 1985; Dominique deSanti, *Flora Tristan, la femme révoltée*, Paris, Hachette, 1972; Jean Baelen, *La Vie de Flora Tristan: Socialism et féminisme au 19e siècle*, Paris, Seuil, 1972; Rosalba Campra, "La imagen de América en *Peregrinations d'une paria* de Flora Tristan: experiencia autobiográfica y tradición cultural," in *Amérique Latine/Europe*, special issue of *Palinure*, Paris, 1985–6, pp. 64–74.

40   Tristan, op. cit., p. 121.

41   Graham, op. cit., p. 271.

42   Tristan, op. cit., pp. 122–3. Graham, by contrast, finds "potatoes of the very first quality. Cabbages of every kind; lettuces inferior only to those of Lambeth ..." and so on (op. cit., p. 132).

43   Hoock-Demarle, op. cit., pp. 105–6.

44   Tristan, op. cit., p. 281.

Laura E. Franey

Victorian Travel Writing and Imperial Violence: *British Writing on Africa 1855–1902*

There are striking similarities between these discussions of women's verbal capabilities and travel writers' emphasis on the linguistic prowess of Africans, both male and female, thereby lending credence to the idea that in the Victorian period "the public stereotype of the African was [...] similar in many respects to the prevailing mythology about women."[6] Nearly all of the major mid-Victorian explorers who crisscrossed the continent in search of scientific information, converts to Christianity, new lands for British conquest, or personal fulfillment, commented on what they perceived – or at least what they wished to portray – as Africans' physical weakness and their concomitant expertise in the realm of language use. Frequently, they state that Africans employ violent and/ or eloquent language rather than physical weapons such as guns or fists when they engage in conflicts with one another. For instance, Stanley's *Through the Dark Continent* tells of a "bloodless," verbal – and, according to Stanley, "comic" – internecine war in the great lakes region of East Africa:

> From this position [the warriors] opened on the enemy volleys of tongue abuse, which lasted for hours; until at last both sides, fatigued with the wordy encounter and hoarse with the prolonged vituperative exercise, mutually consented to defer the battle until next day. [...] On the third day the wordy war was resumed, until both tribes, exhausted from the bloodless conflict, mutually agreed that they would postpone the war with spears to an indefinite period.
>
> (2:69)

An understanding of verbal prowess as an African technique to establish authority also figures prominently in the travel narratives of Richard Burton. In *The Lake Regions of Central Africa* (1861), Burton praises the ability of his African interpreter, Muinyi Wazira, to force some indigenous people to step back off the road and "gaze" in fright simply by "open[ing] upon them the invincible artillery of his tongue" (59). Likewise, John Mackenzie, a missionary in southern Africa, states in *Day-Dawn in Dark Places* (1883) that "while the Bechwanas [sic] sometimes fight with their spears, they decidedly prefer to do so with their tongues, and are indeed much better qualified for the latter warfare than for the former."[7]

This last statement, about Africans apparently being "better qualified" for linguistic warfare than for physical contests, gives us a clue as to the reasons why Victorian explorers (and Victorian men more generally) may have felt comfortable ascribing verbal power to Englishwomen and to Africans of both genders. Assertions about discursive capabilities seem not to have been intended or interpreted as indicators of those groups' political or cultural authority; rather, they seem intended as manifestations of those groups' alienation from authority because power continued to be thought of mainly in physical terms. In other words, within late-nineteenth-century culture white men could afford to grant women and Africans access to speech precisely because they did not conceive of such access as a significant method by which one might gain or maintain political, social and cultural hegemony.

Recognizing the significance of Victorian associations of women and Africans with verbal power leads to questions about how women travel writers situated themselves in relation both to different types of violence and to the development of European empires. As we saw in the first chapter of this study, women travelers sometimes wrote about physical violence in ways that supported the introduction of European sovereignty. Yet on the whole women's travel narratives do not feature a great amount of somatic harm. Instead, they first establish that women and Africans share a view of language as powerful and perhaps almost magical and then go on to foreground verbal conflicts between Africans and Europeans – and especially verbal conflicts between Africans and the women travelers themselves. In so doing, they demonstrate an awareness of cultural constructs of their shared verbal power with Africans, but they do not capitalize upon that shared quality to assert solidarity with Africans and thereby to challenge patriarchal and racial norms. Instead, the scenes of linguistic conflict they stage always conclude with the established hegemony of the European participant in the debate.

By defining discourse as a part of the "colonial contest" (a phrase utilized by Anne McClintock in *Imperial Leather* [1995]) that is equal to, if not more important than, physical struggle, women travelers stake out a path that allows them to contribute in their own way to European political hegemony in Africa. Even if women cannot participate in one-on-one disciplinary violence or large-scale military campaigns because they are physically smaller and weaker than men, these travelers seem to suggest, they are capable of using words as effective weapons. Emphasizing verbal prowess as the most effective way for Europeans to vanquish African resistance to racial hierarchy and imperial governance, the three women travelers whose narratives we shall study here – Amelia Edwards, Cornelia Speedy, and Mary Kingsley – essentially push Africans out of the linguistic space that women and Africans had previously been thought to share and thereby demonstrate a commitment to imperial structures.

(2003)

Notes

6 Catherine Barnes Stevenson, "Female Anger and African Politics: The Case of Two Victorian 'Lady Travellers,'" *Turn-of-the-Century Women* 2, no. 1 (1985): 14. On page 8, Stevenson cites a very striking passage from H. Rider Haggard's *Allan Quatermain* (1887) that illustrates the perceived similarity between women and Africans: "My dear young lady, what are those pretty things around your own neck? – they have a strong family resemblance, especially when you wear that very low dress, to the savage woman's beads. Your habit of turning round and round to the sound of horns and tom-toms, your fondness for pigments and powders, the way in which you love to subjugate yourself to the rich warrior who has captured you in marriage, and the quickness with which your taste in feathered headdresses varies – all these things suggest touches of kinship."

7 John Mackenzie, *Day-Dawn in Dark Places* (London: Cassell, 1883), 220–1. Like Mackenzie, David Livingstone observed about the Tswana that "Their disputes are usually conducted with great volubility and noisy swearing" (*Missionary Travels and Researches in South Africa*, New York: Harper, 1858, 503).

AMAL AMIREH AND LISA SUHAIR MAJAJ

'Introduction'
Going Global: The Transnational Reception of Third World Women Writers

This project is situated at a historical moment of increasing globalization. It is, by now, a critical commonplace to note the accelerated movement of capital, populations, and cultural artifacts across national borders. For the most part, this has been a movement from center to periphery, as material and cultural products from the First World flood the markets of the Third World. But, as many recent studies have shown, this flow is not unidirectional. Third World populations – workers, students, immigrants, and postcolonial intellectuals – constitute a significant portion of most First World metropolitan centers, creating a "Third World" *within* the First World. Whereas Hollywood productions often seem to hold a position of cultural dominance across the globe, other cultural artifacts do travel to the center from the peripheries: Brazilian *telenovelas*, Mexican soap operas, Indian cinema, "world music," and of course postcolonial literature such as the texts discussed in this collection (see, for instance, Featherstone, 65; Grewal and Kaplan, 13–17). As Ella Shohat and Robert Stam argue, "It is simplistic to imagine an active First World unilaterally forcing its products on a passive Third World …

[moreover] there are powerful reverse currents as a number of Third World countries (Mexico, Brazil, India, Egypt) dominate their own markets and even become cultural exporters" (Shohat and Stam, *Unthinking Eurocentrism*, 31).

However, this cultural flow from the peripheries to the center is still governed by the balance in power relations governing First World–Third World interactions. In general, as Barbara Harlow notes, the Third World "is seen to provide the raw materials for the 'First World's' critical apparatus that will transform that material into consumable commodities for its properly schooled readership" (190; see also Mitchell, 475). Moreover, as Mary E. John reminds us, "Just what arrives in other places is itself a product of the relations of power and marginality that structure the circulation of knowledge within nations" (69–70). Contexts of reception significantly influence not only how specific works are read, but also which texts are translated, marketed, reviewed, and taught, and which issues are prioritized. We need, therefore, to keep in view the "difficult negotiation between insistence on multidirectional flows of power in global context and continued vigilance about specifically western forms of domination" (Friedman, 6).

Moreover, as Edward Said has argued in his essay "Traveling Theory," a theory or idea that travels to different contexts gets partly or fully accommodated or incorporated and is "to some extent transformed by its new uses, its new position in a new time and place" (227). Said's argument can be extended to all cultural products, including Third World women's texts, which, in the process of moving across national/cultural boundaries, are transformed by the reception context, their meanings reproduced and reshaped to fit local agendas. The essays in this collection focus on these traveling texts within their old and new contexts. In tracing the production and transformation of textual meanings within shifting contexts of reception, these essays examine how the publishing, circulation, and teaching of texts in both First and Third Worlds reproduce, alter, or challenge the asymmetries of power among different groups of people; how Third World women are themselves constructed in the process of transnational mediation to meet First World expectations; and how the politics of inclusion and exclusion shape the formation of multicultural, feminist, and postcolonial canons. In so doing, the essays probe both the possibilities and the limitations of feminist and multiculturalist projects in a global age.

In order to even begin to examine the reception of Third World women writers and their texts, we must first acknowledge the material apparatuses that make possible this "migration" or cultural flow. Obviously, Third World women's texts do not "travel" by accident. Unless originally written in English, they must be translated and then published; they must be distributed; and they must be brought to the attention of readers through critical apparatuses such as reviewing and through institutional forums such as inclusion in university courses. Market forces play a significant role in such processes: decisions about translating, editing, publishing, distributing, and course adoption are all made with economic as well as literary factors in mind. Third World women's texts are thus commodified, as literary decisions come together with marketing strategies and assessments of audience appeal (ranging from interest in the "exotic" to feminist solidarity) to foreground certain texts and repackage or silence others.

For instance, which books are chosen for translation in the first place? Those that uphold assumptions about Third World women as victims of religion, patriarchy, tradition, and poverty, and that play upon the fascination with "difference"? Or those that challenge expectations of "Third World" experience, presenting women as active agents within their own cultures? The answer often depends on a publisher's assessment of marketability, which is itself based on predictions of a range of factors, including popular appeal, classroom utility, and the like. Thus, books deemed capable of crossing categories, such as novels whose "realism" makes them usable not only in literature classes but also in sociology, political science, or history classes, are often chosen for translation over books of poetry or *avant garde* fiction, which are typically viewed as commanding a narrower literary market. Similarly, the issues that come into play during the translation process itself – for instance, decisions to shorten or reshape a text – are addressed with a target audience and sales figures in mind.

The overall relationship between Third World women writers and their texts on the one hand and First World readers and mediators on the other hand is shaped by these market forces. The translators, editors, publishers, and critics who make Third World women's texts available and known in First World contexts function not simply as disinterested literary specialists, but also as what Mike Featherstone calls "design professionals," filling a role similar to that of the "cultural specialists and intermediaries working in the film, television, music, advertising, fashion, and consumer culture industries" (61). As "design professionals," these literary intermediaries not only determine the availability and physical appearance of a book, but also shape textual meanings. They thus participate in what André Lefevere, in his discussion of English patronage of African literature written in English, calls "patronage by stipulation." As Lefevere observes, "Patronage selects the themes that can be treated, emphasizes certain techniques and rejects others, according to the changing appreciation of elements of the poetics" (467).

(2000)

Benita Parry

Postcolonial Studies: A Materialist Critique

It is noticeable that the authors of such readings are predominantly women whose principal interest appears to be in gender domination within the metropolis. In discussing *Daniel Deronda* one such critic situates Gwendolen's social representativeness within 'a scheme of political *allegory*' which constitutes 'an urgently topical piece of social criticism' where the social drama of private life is symbolically and *actually* connected to Britain's involvement in the rise of a racist nationalism.[15] Of *The Moonstone* another has proposed that a novel in which the plots of courtship and colonialism are aligned comes to inscribe 'an *analogy* between sexual and imperial domination', the interpenetrated representations of empire and the domestic scene demonstrating 'how the hierarchies of gender and class that undergird British culture *replicate* the politics of colonialism'.[16] In related mode discussion of *Mansfield Park* has noted the affinities between patriarchal domination of women in the homeland and plantocratic power over slaves. For one commentator the novel is a 'eurocentric post-abolition narrative' which displays the degradations of both the colonial situation and domestic gender relationships by *reenacting* the conditions of an Antiguan estate in the social intercourse of an English country-house;[17] for another the slave trade offers a convenient *metaphor* for class and gender wrongs at home, the confluence of abolitionist and emergent feminist discourses providing the space for a 'critique of the moral blight underlying Mansfield's beauty' which extends to interrogating the ethical basis for Sir Thomas's authority overseas.[18]

Similar analyses are reiterated in discussion of *Jane Eyre*, the classic that has generated the greatest number of studies alert to its formerly disregarded or unnoticed colonial allusions and implications. For one critic 'Jane's struggle to overcome the class and gender restrictions placed on her is articulated though colonial tropes of bondage and liberation', and her progress is seen to follow 'the itinerary of colonialism from the abolition of slavery in the West Indies to the civilizing mission in India';[19] while another sees *Jane Eyre* as one of those key nineteenth-century novels which in presenting metropolitan feminist interests, deploys 'a vocabulary and imagery of oppressed oriental womanhood'.[20] Stretching the analogy, Susan Meyer – who remarks that colonialism features figuratively in all of Charlotte Brontë's novels – finds that *Jane Eyre* condenses the *historical alliance* between the ideology of male domination and the ideology of colonial domination, men's relationships with colonized people standing in for their relationships with white women, and racial otherness functioning to signify gender oppression.[21] Moreover, having observed the fiction's deployment of colonial tropes, Meyer goes on to infer that women novelists who were resistant to patriarchy were therefore *predisposed* to oppose colonialism (*Imperialism at Home*, p. 11). Not only does this argument imply that all oppressions are congruent, even equivalent, but it neglects evidence of the *conformity* with the ideology of empire displayed both by women writers and feminist movements in the late nineteenth century: as Sally Ledger points out, 'the middle-class feminists of the 1890s themselves had a considerable ideological investment in notions of empire'; and Laura Chrisman has shown that 'for many nineteenth-century white English women writers, it was precisely through collusion with, and not opposition to, hierarchical notions of ethnic and cultural difference, that feminist identity was articulated'.[22] Such willing participation in the dominant ethos points to fissures in the interrelationship between gender, class and imperial politics, rather than to their integration[23] – disjunctions also apparent in working-class complicity with the ideology of empire and participation in its practice.

The critic may be aware that 'the women novelists who use race as a metaphor are in some sense emptying out the vehicle "enslaved Jamaican blacks" ... of its full significance', or diverting 'our attention away from all the other things we might think about were we to think, say, of the peoples of India without the guidance and restraint of metaphor'.[24] All the same, the yoking of the terms is justified on the grounds that such tropological transference opens the door to the way the history of British colonialism finds its way into the fictions.[25] And this way, it seems, is by suturing gender subordination at home with the conditions of slavery and colonialism abroad. In 'Race and Gender: the Role of Analogy in Science', Nancy Stepan has argued that because interactive metaphors shape our perceptions and actions while neglecting or suppressing information that does not fit the similarity, 'they tend to lose their metaphoric nature and be taken literally'.[26] Indeed the commentaries I have mentioned actively collude with the work of interactive metaphors: for even though the expositions reveal that the colonial tropes used to dramatize metropolitan dominations are without coordinating connectives within the fictions, the critics undertake to rearticulate the *unsecured metaphoric* linkages between the juxtapositions of colonial and gender oppressions as if these constituted *conceptual knowledge* about both the systematic operation of sexism and imperialism, and the ideological coalescence of gender, race and class discourses as 'intertwined subsets' and 'mutually reinforcing categories'.

I suggest that those who seek to install parity between the egregious oppressions legitimated by a politics of empire and the subordination of middle-class Englishwomen by a male-dominated bourgeois society are committing a category error by linking two distinct social realities. As a consequence they occlude the historical, ideological, experiential and discursive specificity of slavery, colonial rule and British class society.

A caution against this careless conflation can be found in the ironic distinction made by Jane Fairfax in *Emma*: having assured the importunate Mrs Elton of her confidence in finding employment – 'There are places in town, offices, where inquiry would soon produce something – offices for the sale, not quite of human flesh, but of human intellect' – Jane Fairfax has then to reassure her obtuse interlocutor ('Oh! my dear! human flesh! You quite shock me; if you mean a fling at the slave trade …!') that she is referring not to the slave trade but 'the governess-trade … widely different, certainly, as to the guilt of those who carry it on; but as to the greater misery of the victims, I do not know where it lies' (*Emma*, 1816, Chapter 35).[27]

To enunciate the enactment of metropolitan gender relations in an abolitionist vocabulary does not ensure that this will emerge as 'anti-colonialist', as is evident in the rhetorical and narrative strategies of *Jane Eyre*, where a simultaneity of identification with and disassociation from the conditions of slavery, colonialism and domestic class relationships is revealed.[28] Neither do the analogies used by the fiction necessarily produce a coherent critique of a social order simultaneously sustaining patriarchal, colonial and class inequalities. Yet so certain are the critics of the fiction's concerted opposition to all oppressions, including the domestic class system, that they neglect to remark on the novels' silence about the long process of violent indigenous expropriation which had enabled the establishment of a Mansfield Park and a Thornfield Hall. Hence when observing the novels' critical view of Sir Thomas Bertram and Mr Rochester as patriarchal figures and beneficiaries of colonial estates, the commentators do not attend to the writings' stance on the legitimacy of these figures as hereditary English landowners. Not every large landowner was implicated in colonial ventures, but the fortunes of all were built on one or another process of dispossession and increased through one or another system of exploitation. Perhaps then tropological correlatives between the domestic and the colonial are a symptom of cognitive blind spots rather than cognitive insight about the exercise and effects of both class and imperial power.

(2004)

Notes

15   Katherine Bailey Lineham, 'Imperialism in *Daniel Deronda*', *Texas Studies in Literature and Language*, vol. 34, no. 3 (1992), pp. 325–46. Lineham's argument proceeds from citing Deirdre David's claim that Gwendolen Harleth's 'psychological imperialism' serves as 'a *metaphor* for her class and her culture', the domestic and sexual politics of her private life being linked 'to *actual* imperialist policies of colonization and exploitation', pp. 327–8.

16   Tamar Heller, *Dead Secrets: Wilkie Collins and the Female Gothic* (New Haven: Yale University Press, 1992), pp. 144–5.

17 Moira Ferguson, '*Mansfield Park*: Slavery, Colonialism and Gender', *Oxford Literary Review*, vol. 13, nos. 1–2 (1991), pp. 118–39.

18 Susan Fraiman, 'Jane Austen and Edward Said: Gender, Culture, and Imperialism, *Critical Inquiry*, vol. 21 (1995), pp. 805–21, 810.

19 Jenny Sharpe, *Allegories of Empire: the Figure of Woman in the Colonial Text* (Minneapolis: University of Minnesota Press, 1993), p. 28.

20 Suvendrini Perera, *Reaches of Empire* (New York: Columbia University Press, 1991), p. 81.

21 Susan Meyer, *Imperialism at Home: Race and Victorian Women's Fiction* (Ithaca: Cornell University Press, 1996), pp. 22–3.

22 'The New Woman and the Crisis of Victorianism', and 'Empire, "Race" and Feminism at the Fin de Siècle: the Work of George Egerton and Olive Schreiner', in *Cultural Politics at the Fin de Siècle*, ed. Sally Ledger and Scott McCracken (Cambridge: Cambridge University Press, 1995), pp. 32, 35–6, 45.

23 Equally troubling is the claim that white women inhabiting or travelling in colonized territories were inclined to be critical of their compatriots, and therefore produced more sympathetic accounts of native peoples. See Sara Mills, *Discourses of Difference: Women's Travel Writing and Colonialism* (London: Routledge, 1991) and Mary Louise Pratt, *Imperial Eyes: Travel Writing and Transculturation* (London: Routledge, 1992).

24 Meyer, *Imperialism at Home*, p. 22.

25 Meyer, *Imperialism at Home*, p. 23.

26 In *Anatomy of Race*, ed. David Theo Goldberg (Minneapolis: University of Minnesota Press, 1990), p. 52.

27 For the context of the conversation, and Bristol as a slave port and a favoured retirement place for West Indian merchants and slave traders, see Baum, *Mind-Forg'd Manacles*, p. 6.

28 Cora Kaplan, ' "A Heterogeneous Thing": Female Childhood and the Rise of Racial Thinking in Victorian Britain', in *Human All Too Human*, ed. Diana Fuss (London: Routledge, 1996), pp. 184–5. See also Carl Plasa, who suggests that, despite the text's scepticism towards its own rhetorical moves, the literality and historicity of slavery in *Jane Eyre* is obscured by the novel's use of the moral language of the abolitionists to dramatize domestic oppression; ' "Silent Revolt": Slavery and the Politics of Metaphor in *Jane Eyre*', in *The Discourse of Slavery: Aphra Behn to Toni Morrison*, ed. Carl Plasa and Betty J. Ring (London: Routledge, 1994).

ADRIENNE RICH

Blood, Bread, and Poetry: Selected Prose 1979–1985

To come to terms with the circumscribing nature of (our) whiteness.[9] Marginalized though we have been as women, as white and Western makers of theory, we also marginalize others because our lived experience is thoughtlessly white, because even our "women's cultures" are rooted in some Western tradition. Recognizing our location, having to name the ground we're coming from, the conditions we have taken for granted – there is a confusion between our claims to the white and Western eye and the woman-seeing eye,[10] fear of losing the centrality of the one even as we claim the other.

How does the white Western feminist define theory? Is it something made only by white women and only by women acknowledged as writers? How does the white Western feminist define "an idea"? How do we actively work to build a white Western feminist consciousness that is not simply centered on itself, that resists white circumscribing?

It was in the writings but also the actions and speeches and sermons of Black United States citizens that I began to experience the meaning of my whiteness as a point of location for which I needed to take responsibility. It was in reading poems by contemporary Cuban women that I began to experience the meaning of North America as a location which had also shaped my ways of seeing and my ideas of who and what was important, a location for which I was also responsible. I traveled then to Nicaragua, where, in a tiny impoverished country, in a four-year-old society dedicated to eradicating poverty, under the hills of the Nicaragua-Honduras border, I could physically feel the weight of the United States of North America, its military forces, its vast appropriations of money, its mass media, at my back; I could feel what it means, dissident or not, to be part of that raised boot of power, the cold shadow we cast everywhere to the south.

I come from a country stuck fast for forty years in the deep-freeze of history. Any United States citizen alive today has been saturated with Cold War rhetoric, the horrors of communism, the betrayals of socialism, the warning that any collective restructuring of society spells the end of personal freedom. And, yes, there have been horrors and betrayals deserving open opposition. But we are not invited to consider the butcheries of Stalinism, the terrors of the Russian counterrevolution alongside the butcheries of white supremacism and Manifest Destiny. We are not urged to help create a more human society here in response to the ones we are taught to hate and dread. Discourse itself is frozen at this level. Tonight as I turned a switch searching for "the news," that shinily animated silicone mask was on television again, telling the citizens of my country we are menaced by communism from El Salvador, that communism – Soviet variety, obviously – is on the move in Central America, that freedom is imperiled, that the suffering peasants of Latin America must be stopped, just as Hitler had to be stopped.

The discourse has never really changed; it is wearingly abstract. (Lillian Smith, white anti-racist writer and activist, spoke of the "deadly sameness" of abstraction.)[11] It allows no differences among places, times, cultures, conditions, movements. Words that should possess a depth and breadth of allusions – words like *socialism, communism, democracy, collectivism* – are stripped of their historical roots, the many faces of the struggles for social justice and independence reduced to an ambition to dominate the world.

Is there a connection between this state of mind – the Cold War mentality, the attribution of all our problems to an external enemy – and a form of feminism so focused on male evil and female victimization that it, too, allows for no differences among women, men, places, times, cultures, conditions, classes, movements? Living in the climate of an enormous either/or, we absorb some of it unless we actively take heed.

(1987)

Notes

9   Gloria I. Joseph, "The Incompatible Ménage à Trois: Marxism, Feminism and Racism," in *Women and Revolution,* ed. Lydia Sargent (Boston: South End Press, 1981).
10   See Marilyn Frye, *The Politics of Reality* (Trumansburg, NY: Crossing Press, 1983), p. 171.
11   Lillian Smith, "Autobiography as a Dialogue between King and Corpse," in *The Winner Names the Age,* ed. Michelle Cliff (New York: W. W. Norton, 1978), p. 189.

CAREN KAPLAN

Questions of Travel: Postmodern Discourses of Displacement

The key to Rich's politics of location, then, lies in her recognition that as marginal as white, Western women appear to be in relation to the real movers and shakers in this world – white men – there are others made marginal by white, Western women themselves. Rich desires "us" to take responsibility for these marginalizations, to acknowledge "our" part in this process in order to change these unequal dynamics: "The movement for change is a changing movement, changing itself, demasculinizing itself, de-Westernizing itself, becoming a critical mass that is saying in so many different voices, languages, gestures, actions: it must change; we ourselves can change it."[57] How does a feminist movement for social change "de-Westernize" itself? Rich proposes a politics of location in which white, North American feminists explore the meaning of "whiteness," "recognizing our location, having to name the ground we're coming from, the conditions we have taken for granted."[58]

Although Rich had been moving in the direction of such a deconstructive moment for some time, without the critiques of Audre Lorde, Barbara Smith, Michelle Cliff, and other US women of color with whom Rich worked throughout this period, her notion of a politics of location would not have been as fully formulated. "De-Westernizing," then, could be seen to begin at "home." Yet her fullest critique of her earlier "chauvinism" is written out not within the parameters of domestic conversations but in the aftermath of a trip abroad. In its first articulation as a term, therefore, a politics of location could be seen as a *suppression* of discussions of differences between white women and women of color *within* the geographic boundaries of the United States in favor of a new binary: US white women and the victims of US foreign policies. This floating boundary between "us" and "them" is set by Rich depending upon her travels, her feminist agendas, and her point of view. The subject of US women of color and their disparate and linked histories of diaspora and immigration along with contradictory and complex political positions vis-à-vis US nationalist identities and agendas have no place in this formulation.

Thus, despite her efforts to account for the politics of location, Rich remains locked into the conventional opposition of the global-local nexus as well as the binary construction of Western and non-Western. She deconstructs the equalizations of "global feminism" (the "common world of women" scenario) by homogenizing the location of "North American feminist." Yet in her earlier deconstructions of North American differences between women Rich had seemed to ignore or discount global distinctions. Such oscillations are predictable in binary constructions that depend upon generalized polar opposites. The root of the particular problem at work in Rich's essays on a politics of location can be traced to her attachment to the convention of travel as transformation. Unable to critique the inherently binary nature of Western travel paradigms, Rich completely rewrites her "home" in terms of "away." Yet over ten years of coalition work with women of color in the United States might account for many of the ideas found in the politics of location essays. The issue of accountability is not only between North and South American women, then, but among women at home in the United States as well.

Rich's deconstructive practice appears to have captured the imagination of a range of Euro-American critics who seek to bridge poststructuralist destabilizations of master narratives and materially based political concerns.[59] Sensitive to poststructuralist charges of essentialism toward any fixed positions, the theorists of location seek to negotiate between ahistorical mystifications of identity made in the name of political movements and antihistorical universalizations made in the name of philosophical purity. Thus Rich's essays on the politics of location have encouraged decentering moves as critics examine their positions vis-à-vis geopolitics. For example, Neil Smith and Cindi Katz point to what they term a crucial "double shift" in Rich's critical practice: "The brilliance of Rich's formulation is that it maintains the relationality of social identity without slipping into a formless relativism, and at the same time disarranges the received fixity of social *and* geographical location."[60] Rich, they argue, questions the "very process through which the base map of different locations" is drawn, linking social and geographical location in a dynamic relation. Parting ways with Euro-American "global" feminism's vision of a unitary world of women, Rich acknowledges the problematic power of mapping, naming, and establishing agendas.

This practice of a politics of location, however, conflates "Western" and "white," reinscribing the centrality of white women's position within Euro-American feminism. A further danger lies in the removal of the term from the context of debates about feminist accountability to celebrations of cultural relativism, expressing a transnational "fiesta" of differences that mystify and codify power relations. While some readings of Rich (such as Chandra Mohanty's 1987 essay on the politics of experience)[61] have integrated this specific formulation into feminist, anti-imperialist cultural criticism, the circulation of Rich's notion of a politics of location does not always emphasize her concerns about race and imperialism.[62] With such homogenizations in mind, Lata Mani, in "Multiple Mediations," argues for a revised politics of location that demonstrates that "the relation between experience and knowledge is now seen to be not one of correspondence but one fraught with history, contingency, and struggle."[63] In this practice, a politics of location operates as a strenuously contested and dynamically stressed term, signaling debate and transformative theorizing.

(1996)

Notes

57 Rich, *Blood, Bread, and Poetry*, 225.
58 Ibid., 219.
59 For a useful introduction to this project see Weedon, *Feminist Practice and Poststructuralist Theory*.
60 Smith and Katz, "Grounding Metaphor," 77.
61 Mohanty, "Feminist Encounters."
62 I have discussed some of the readings of Rich's term that produce more relativist or managed diversity approaches in my essay, "The Politics of Location as Transnational Feminist Practices," in Grewal and Kaplan, *Scattered Hegemonies*, 137–154.
63 Mani, "Multiple Mediations," 4.

ANNE McCLINTOCK

Imperial Leather: Race, Gender, and Sexuality
in the Colonial Context

The European porno-tropics had a long tradition. As early as the second century AD, Ptolemy wrote confidently of Africa that "the constellation of Scorpion, which pertains to the pudenda, dominates that continent."[1] Leo Africanus agreed that there was "no nation under heaven more prone to venerie" than "the Negros."[2] Francis Bacon's Hermit was visited by the Spirit of Fornication, who turned out to be a "little foule, ugly Aethiope."[3] John Ogilby, adapting the writings of Olfert Dapper, rather more tactfully informed his readers that west Africans were distinguished by "large propagators,"[4] while the planter Edward Long saw Africa as "the parent of everything that is monstrous in nature."[5] By the nineteenth century, popular lore had firmly established Africa as the quintessential zone of sexual aberration and anomaly – "the very picture," as W. D. Jordan put it, "of perverse negation."[6] The *Universal History* was citing a well-established and august tradition when it declared Africans to be "proud, lazy, treacherous, thievish, hot and addicted to all kinds of lusts."[7] It was as impossible, it insisted, "to be an *African* and not lascivious, as it is to be born in *Africa* and not be an African."[8]

Within this porno-tropic tradition, women figured as the epitome of sexual aberration and excess. Folklore saw them, even more than the men, as given to a lascivious venery so promiscuous as to border on the bestial. Sir Thomas Herbert observed of Africans "the resemblance they bear with Baboons, which I could observe kept frequent company with the Women."[9] Long saw a lesson closer to home in the African spectacle of female sexual excess, for he identified British working-class women as inhabiting more naturally than men the dangerous borders of racial and sexual transgression: "The lower class of women in *England*," he wrote ominously, "are remarkably fond of the blacks."[10] The traveler William Smith likewise warned his readers of the perils of traveling as a white man in Africa, for, on that disorderly continent, women "if they meet with a Man they immediately strip his lower Parts and throw themselves upon him."[11]

During the Renaissance, as the "fabulous geography" of ancient travel gave way to the "militant geography" of mercantile imperialism and the triangular trade, so the bold merchant ships of Portugal, Spain, Britain and France began to draw the world into a single skein of trade routes.[12] Mercantile imperialism began to be emboldened by dreams of dominating not only a boundless imperium of commerce but also a boundless imperium of knowledge. Francis Bacon (1561–1626) gave exemplary voice to the immodesty of intellectual Renaissance expansionism. "My only earthly wish," he wrote, "is ... to stretch the deplorably narrow limits of man's dominion over the universe to their promised bounds."[13] But Bacon's vision of a world-knowledge dominated by Europe was animated not only by an imperial geography of power but also by a gendered erotics of knowledge: "I come in very truth," he proclaimed, "leading to you Nature with all her children to bind her to your service and make her your slave."[14]

All too often, Enlightenment metaphysics presented knowledge as a relation of power between two gendered spaces, articulated by a journey and a technology of conversion: the male penetration and exposure of a veiled, female interior; and the aggressive conversion of its "secrets" into a visible, male science of the surface. Bacon deplored the fact that "while the regions of the material globe ... have been in our times laid widely open and revealed, the intellectual globe should remain shut up within the narrow limits of old discoveries."[15] Voyaging into the enigma of infinity, there to unlock "Nature's secrets," Faust likewise cried out:

> New roads lie open to me. I
> Shall pierce the veil that hides what we desire,
> Break through to realms of abstract energy.[16]

Knowledge of the unknown world was mapped as a metaphysics of gender violence – not as the expanded recognition of cultural difference – and was validated by the new Enlightenment logic of private property and possessive individualism. In these fantasies, the world is feminized and spatially spread for male exploration, then reassembled and deployed in the interests of massive imperial power. Thus, for Rene Descartes, the expansion of male knowledge amounted to a violent property arrangement that made men "masters and possessors of nature."[17] In the minds of these men, the imperial conquest of the globe found both its shaping figure and its political sanction in the prior subordination of women as a category of nature.

Women as the Boundary Markers of Empire
What is the meaning of this persistent gendering of the imperial unknown? As European men crossed the dangerous thresholds of their known worlds, they ritualistically feminized borders and boundaries. Female figures were planted like fetishes at the ambiguous points of contact, at the borders and orifices of the contest zone. Sailors bound wooden female figures to their ships' prows and baptized their ships – as exemplary threshold objects – with female names. Cartographers filled the blank seas of their maps with mermaids and sirens. Explorers called unknown lands "virgin" territory. Philosophers veiled "Truth" as female, then fantasized about drawing back

the veil. In myriad ways, women served as mediating and threshold figures by means of which men oriented themselves in space, as agents of power and agents of knowledge.

The following chapters explore, in part, the historically different but persistent ways in which women served as the boundary markers of imperialism, the ambiguous mediators of what appeared to be – at least superficially – the predominantly male agon of empire. The first point I want to make, however, is that the feminizing of terra incognita was, from the outset, a strategy of violent containment – belonging in the realm of both psychoanalysis and political economy. If, at first glance, the feminizing of the land appears to be no more than a familiar symptom of male megalomania, it also betrays acute paranoia and a profound, if not pathological, sense of male anxiety and boundary loss.

As Columbus' and Haggard's images suggest, the erotics of imperial conquest were also an erotics of engulfment. At one level, the representation of the land as female is a traumatic trope, occurring almost invariably, I suggest, in the aftermath of male boundary confusion, but as a historical, not archetypal, strategy of containment. As the visible trace of paranoia, feminizing the land is a compensatory gesture, disavowing male loss of boundary by reinscribing a ritual excess of boundary, accompanied, all too often, by an excess of military violence. The feminizing of the land represents a ritualistic moment in imperial discourse, as male intruders ward off fears of narcissistic disorder by reinscribing, as natural, an excess of gender hierarchy.

Mary Douglas points out that margins are dangerous.[18] Societies are most vulnerable at their edges, along the tattered fringes of the known world. Having sailed beyond the limits of their charted seas, explorers enter what Victor Turner calls a liminal condition.[19] For Turner, a liminal condition is ambiguous, eluding "the network of classifications that normally locate states and positions in cultural space."[20] There on the margins between known and unknown, the male conquistadors, explorers and sailors became creatures or transition and threshold. As such, they were dangerous, for, as Douglas writes: "Danger lies in transitional states....The person who must pass from one to another is himself in danger and emanates danger to others."[21] As figures of danger, the men of margins were "licensed to waylay, steal, rape. This behaviour is even enjoined on them. To behave anti-socially is the proper expression of their marginal condition."[22] At the same time, the dangers represented by liminal people are managed by rituals that separate the marginal ones from their old status, segregating them for a time and then publicly declaring their entry into their new status. Colonial discourse repeatedly rehearses this pattern – dangerous marginality, segregation, reintegration.

(1995)

Notes

1   Quoted in Peter Fryer, *Staying Power: The History of Black People in Britain* (London: Pluto Press, 1984), p. 139.

2   John Leo Africanus, *A Geographical Historie of Africa*, trans. John Pory (London: Georg. Bishop, 1600), p. 38.

3   Francis Bacon, *New Atlantis: A Worke Unfinished*, in Francis Bacon, *Sylva sylvarum or, a natural history in ten centuries* (London: William, 1670), p. 26.

4   John Ogilby, *Africa: Being an Accurate Description of the Regions of Aegypt, etc.* (London: Tho. Johnson, 1670), p. 451.

5   Edward Long, *The History of Jamaica*, (London: T. Lowndes, 1774), pp. 382–3.

6   Winthrop D. Jordan, *White Over Black: American Attitudes Toward the Negro, 1550–1812* (New York: W. W. Norton, 1977), p. 7.

7   *The Modern Part of the Universal History*, vol. V (T. Osborne etc., 1760), pp. 658–9.

8   *The Modern Part of the Universal History*, p. 659.

9   Sir Thomas Herbert, *Some years travel into divers parts of Africa, and Asia the Great* (London: R. Scot, 1677), p. 18.

10   Edward Long, *Candid Reflections* (London: T. Lowndes, 1772), p. 48.

11   William Smith, *A New Voyage to Guinea* (London: John Nourse, 1745), pp. 221–2.

12   The term "fabulous geography" is Michael Taussig's, in *Shamanism, Colonialism and the Wild Man: A Study in Terror and Healing* (Chicago: The University of Chicago Press, 1987), p. 15. Joseph Conrad first coined the term "militant geography" in his essay "Geography and Some Explorers," in *Last Essays* (London: J. M. Dent & Sons, 1926), p. 31. For a history of the demise of colonial slavery, see Robin Blackburn, *The Overthrow of Colonial Slavery; 1776–1848* (London: Verso, 1988).

13   Benjamin Farrington, *The Philosophy of Francis Bacon: An Essay on Its Development from 1603 to 1609 With New Translations of Fundamental Texts* (Chicago: Chicago University Press, 1964), p. 62. See Ludmilla Jordanova, *Sexual Visions: Images of Gender in Science and Medicine Between the Eighteenth and Twentieth Centuries* (New York: Harvester Wheat-sheaf, 1989). See also E. F. Keller, *Reflections on Gender and Science* (New Haven: Yale University Press, 1985), especially chs. 2 and 3; Susan Griffin, *Woman and Nature: The Roaring Inside Her* (New York: Harper & Row, 1978); and Genevieve Lloyd, *The Man of Reason: "Male" and "Female" in Western Philosophy* (Minneapolis: Minnesota University Press, 1984).

14   Farrington, ibid., p. 62. For the gendering of Bacon's vision of science, see Carolyn Merchant, *The Death of Nature: Women, Ecology and the Scientific Revolution* (San Francisco: Harper and Row, 1980), especially ch. 7.

15   Francis Bacon, *Novum Organum* in *The Works of Francis Bacon*, James Spedding, Robert Ellis, and Douglas Heath, eds. (London: Longmans, 1870), p. 82.

16   Goethe, *Faust*, Part 1, quoted in Jordanova, *Sexual Visions*, p. 93.

17   Rene Descartes, *Discourse on Method and the Meditations* (Harmondsworth: Penguin, 1968), p. 78.
18   Mary Douglas, *Purity and Danger* (London: Routledge & Kegan Paul, 1966), p. 63.
19   Victor Turner, *The Ritual Process: Structure and Anti-Structure* (Ithaca: Cornell University Press, 1969).
20   Turner, *The Ritual Process*, p. 95.
21   Douglas, *Purity and Danger*, p. 78.
22   Douglas, *Purity and Danger*, p. 79.

SUSAN STREHLE

Transnational Women's Fiction: Unsettling Home and Homeland

While later chapters will be concerned to speak and read locally, I want to begin by thinking globally about conjunctions between home and homeland and tracing some of their intersecting foundations and functions. As a first principle, both home and nation draw on and perpetuate a fundamentally patriarchal authority, hardly unique to these two institutions. By no accident, the discourse of home and nation points to this authority in allied ways, so that nations – "motherlands" and "fatherlands" – have "founding fathers" and patriarchal homes have "governors." The word "home" points outward – it derives from the Anglo-Saxon *ham* which, as John Hollander observes, "designates a village or town, an estate or possession"; Hollander also notes that "the modern Turkish *yurt* (= tent) contracts down from the wide reaches of the Old Turkic word for 'country' or 'fatherland' " (40). The verb "to domesticate" implies lording it over: it "is akin to dominate, which derives from *dominus*, lord of the *domum*, the home," writes McClintock (35). While home may be linked with women's influence and activity in Western culture, the terms identify a controlling patriarchal power that operates at home as it does in the nation. This power also functions, writes Ketu Katrak, in postcolonial societies inflected by racism: "The domestic, familial arena is the most legitimized space for male domination even when, or particularly when, the male faces racism outside the home" (238).

Both home and homeland are theoretical, virtual, or, in Benedict Anderson's terms, imagined communities, built on the appeal of "a deep, horizontal comradeship," even though patriarchal authority and political power make the real structure far more vertical and hierarchical (16). Home, like homeland, is an ideal that links "fraternity, power and time meaningfully together" in shared sacrifice and triumph (40). While houses, apartments, and other dwelling places are tangible, concrete spaces, "home," in the sense I am invoking, is fully as abstract and invisible, as loaded with emotional and ideological investment, as related to religious imagining and to the hope for immortality, as the concept of nation. Writing about patriotism, Anderson identifies the language of "political love" with "the vocabulary of kinship (motherland, *Vaterland, patria*) or that of home," both idioms denoting a natural tie, "something unchosen," a bond carrying "a halo of disinterestedness" (131). As communities offering innate, disinterested solidarity, home and homeland are able to summon the degree of unquestioning loyalty required for the sacrifice of life in their defense. Bonds of attachment to nation and home are reinvigorated by perceptions of threat or loss, as suggested by the resurgence of nationalism in the United States after September 11, 2001.

As implied by the importance of enforceable borders and lockable doors, home and homeland are imagined communities based on the exclusion or assimilation of the foreign. Those who can be admitted to the "fraternity" of "deep, horizontal comradeship" are included; they belong as kin, inside home and nation. Others must be kept outside – those who differ or whose race, caste, religion, gender, or sexuality renders them unfit to be assimilated to the homogeneous collective. Said invokes "the fundamentally static notion of *identity* that has been the core of cultural thought during the era of imperialism": the idea "that there is an 'us' and a 'them,' each quite settled, clear, unassailably self-evident" (1993: xxv). For Kaplan, excluding "them" defines both home and nation. She points out that "domestic" relies on an opposition to "foreign": "*Domestic* has a double meaning that links the space of the familial household to that of the nation, by imagining both in opposition to everything outside the geographic and conceptual border of the home" (2002: 25). Erecting borders and boundaries to enclose the exclusive space of home/ land enables the construction of a homogeneous "identity" (one single "us" or "fraternity"). From this perspective, discriminations of race, gender, class, caste, religion, and nationality are basic to home and homeland – put simply, home/land is constitutionally racist, sexist, and chauvinistic.

Another important link between home and homeland is their pledge of an ideal blend of security with personal freedom as the basis for a powerful sentimental appeal. In an essay published in *Subaltern Studies*, Qadri Ismail articulates the "bind between 'home' and 'nation'" as a promise of "absolute" security in communal identity:

> Such security is to be found, ideally at least, only at home: a space that provides not just physical security, but is also without claustrophobia and dysphoria. Metaphorically speaking, nationalism promises to take its nationals home, to end homelessness and homesickness, represents itself as the exclusive and ultimate cure for nostalgia.
>
> (218–19)

Yet these promises are impossible, Ismail argues. For one thing, nationalism constructs women as subordinate to men and thus "women cannot find home in nation"; for another, in keeping the promises, nationalism would have exhausted its obligations and rendered itself obsolete, so "nationalism cannot and does not keep its promises (to its nationals)" (218–19). In fact, Ismail concludes, the logic of nationalism "demands that it conserve, nurture and foster nostalgia, not rebut or terminate it" (281). Ismail's provocative analysis suggests a necessary functional gap between the promises made by nations and homes – a paradisiacal balance between perfect security and perfect freedom – and their imperfect delivery. The promise reminds people of what they feel they have lost, and thus it feeds a nostalgic investment in the home/land by the very impossibility of its achievement. The delivery is considerably worse, as we would expect, for those of unprivileged gender, race, caste, or religion. I would add to Ismail's claims the argument that women, commonly held to be the keepers of home, cannot find home in home either, nor can people whose ethnicity or poverty renders them "foreign" within their culture.

(2008)

Elleke Boehmer

Stories of Women: Gender and Narrative in the Postcolonial Nation

This then means that a woman seeking to claim a place or an identity in most fields of national activity faces multiple perils of self-contradiction. Literature as a medium of self-expression offers a representative case. Within African nationalism, for instance, especially that of the immediate pre- and post-independence periods, writing provided the middle classes with an important source of national myth-making and dreaming. For a writer to be a nationalist, was to be that much more a worthy writer, as well as that much more self-assertively male – in relation to which equation the figure of woman was habitually regarded as the vehicle or medium of male creativity, as for example in Wole Soyinka's work. The circle of mutually reinforcing identities shut – and still shuts – women out.

A woman might choose to crack this ring of identity by attempting to repossess matriarchal myths. For some women the reclaimed myth of an age-old, long-suffering 'Afrika' – Walker's Africa/Goddess/Mother presiding over the '500,000 years' of human history covered by *The Temple of My Familiar* – has continued to hold out much promise of communion and liberation. The South African dramatist Gcina Mhlope, for example, has expressed her loyalty to this mythical maternal entity, speaking of the 'Women of my country' as 'Mother Africa's loved daughters'.[21] Motherhood remains closely linked to the configuration of African, Caribbean and South Asian women's identities in many of the sociocultural contexts they inhabit.[22] Yet the problematic facing mother-oriented women is whether and how such apparently redemptive symbols might be separated from those which continue to shore up a system of gender-tagged national authority. After all, the idealisation and possible fetishisation of mother figures bears an uncanny resemblance to the monolithic aspects of male-centred nationalism, just as to the romanticisation of conquered land under colonialism. Subscribing to the unitary icon may therefore threaten to defeat women's objectives of affirming their own particular mode of being.

Given that men have to a large extent monopolised the field of nationalist identity and self-image, women have in many cases sought to evolve other strategies of selving – less unitary, more dispersed and multifarious, more alive to the contradictions involved in the process of self-making. The challenge is not only that the patriarchal roots and sources that inform nationalist images must be in some way confronted. It is also that it is necessary to explore forms of women's self-representation that would counterpoise the inherited symbolic languages of gender as well as the grand stories of the nation. In this, despite influential national traditions of male authorship, writing – experimental, exploratory, nuanced, ironic – holds out fruitful possibilities of redress. Fredric Jameson, speaking here as a Marxist, not as a 'Third World' critic, has referred to such redress as the 'restoration of an essentially dialogical ... horizon'.[23]

In the case of Africa, for instance, it is the case that, if literature in the past has constituted something of a nationalist and masculinist preserve, then, simply by writing, women directly confront and face down the male prerogative. In writing, as many postcolonial women critics have by now recognised, women express their own reality, unsettle male-focused (and other exclusionary) narratives, and so question received notions of national character and experience. But writing is more than this, too. To write is not only to speak for one's place in the world. It is also to *make* one's own place and narrative, to tell the story of oneself, to create an identity. It is in effect to deploy what in another context might be called a typical nationalist strategy. As Simon Gikandi once put it: 'To write is to claim a text of one's own; textuality is an instrument of territorial possession ... narrative is crucial to our discovery of selfhood'.[24]

This idea of self-creation through narrative intersects with the Kristevan concept of excess in writing. Julia Kristeva observes, à propos of Barthes's criticism, that writing is transformative, operating through the displacement of what is already signified, bringing forth the not-yet-imagined and the transgressive.[25] Indebted to Bakhtin, yet concentrating on women's expression in particular, Kristeva maintains that language – the symbolic order, syntactic completion – is threatened by the irruption of the heterogeneous, the disorderly, the semiotic, that which lies outside language though is finally only conceivable within it. Such irruption, which for Kristeva constitutes the

poetic, comes about, among other methods, through a process aptly demonstrated by Flora Nwapa, that is, 'transposition', the shift between literary
and linguistic media that creates possibilities for polysemy. Through writing,
through claiming a text – and a narrative territory – women sign into and at
the same time subvert a nationalist narrative that has excluded them as
negativity, as corporeal and unclean, or as impossibly idealised.

Possibilities for the disruption and/or transformation of a masculine
nationalist text can therefore be seen to operate in two main ways in women's
writing: the *textual* and the (broadly) *temporal/territorial*. The first occurs
through the medium of the text, in the substance of the writing, and involves
interrupting the language of official nationalist discourse and literature with
a women's vocality. Nationhood is so bound up in textuality, in 'definitive'
histories and official languages and mythologies, that to compose a substantially different kind of text, using vernacular, non-literary and phatic forms
that are part of people's everyday experience, is already to challenge normative discourses of nationhood – even where, as in Rushdie's *Midnight's
Children* (1981), that discourse announces itself as always-already multi-
voiced. Moreover, as this suggests, these different forms of composition
manifest, crucially, *within* the poetics of the text, as nuance, emphasis and
ironic juxtaposition – disruption is not expressed merely at the level of
externalised, 'protest' writing.

Yet, because national identity rests on received images of national history
and topography, the second method of transformation is as important. It
involves *changing the subjects* that have dominated the nationalist text – and
therefore questioning the centrality of the male-defined nation as *the* key
historical player in the post-independence period. Where women tell the
story of their own experience, they map their own geographical perspectives,
scry their own history and so, necessarily, contest official representations of
a nationalist reality. They implicitly – and in some cases explicitly – challenge
the nation's definition of itself through territorial claims, through the
reclamation of the past and the canonisation of heroes. At the same time they
also lever the icons of heroes and national mothers from their dominant
positions as mascots and symbols of the quintessential national experience.

(2005)

Notes

21   Gcina Mhlope, 'We are at war', in Susan Brown (ed.), *LIP from South African
     Women* (Johannesburg: Ravan, 1983), pp. 159–60.
22   See Juliana Makuchi Nfah-Abbenyi, *Gender in African Women's Writing*
     (Bloomington: Indiana University Press, 1997), p. 35; Filomena Steady (ed.),
     The Black Woman Cross-Culturally (Cambridge, MA: Schenkman, 1981),

p. 29. While the present study acknowledges the importance of motherhood and of mother figures to African and South Asian women, it also wishes to consider women writers' concerns with identities configured in contradistinction to the institution of motherhood.

23 Fredric Jameson, *The Political Unconscious: Narrative as a Socially Symbolic Act* (London: Methuen, 1981), p. 87.

24 Simon Gikandi made this point as early as 'The politics and poetics of national formation: recent African writing', *ACLALS Triennial Conference* paper, University of Kent, Canterbury, 24–31 August 1989, pp. 1–20, and has interestingly elaborated it in his work since, as, for example, in *Reading Chinua Achebe* (London: James Currey, 1991). See also Richard Kearney, *On Stories* (London: Routledge, 2002).

25 Julia Kristeva, *Desire in Language*, trans. Léon S. Roudiez (Oxford: Blackwell, 1987), in particular the essay, 'How does one speak to literature?', pp. 92–123.

Rosi Braidotti

Nomadic Subjects: Embodiment and Sexual Difference in Contemporary Feminist Theory

The image of female exile can be complemented by that of the nomad and of the migrant. I shall take the nomad as the prototype of the "woman of ideas":[14] in the history of women's struggle the international dimension is implicit from the start. Not only is feminism as such an international movement, like most other major social movements of this century but at the intellectual level also the very conceptual structure of women's studies is the result of intense international networking. As an example: the single most important feminist book of this century, *The Second Sex*, by Simone de Beauvoir, appeared in France in 1949, and although it raised a few eyebrows and many nasty comments, it did not trigger a revolution. We had to wait till the 1960s and the American second wave of the women's struggle for Beauvoir's book to become recognized as the earth-shaking analysis it is. It was not until Kate Millett, Ti-Grace Atkinson, and Shulamith Firestone dedicated their works to Beauvoir that *The Second Sex* produced what we would today call women's studies. A transatlantic connection was needed for a book published in 1949 in Paris to be greeted in Europe, via the United States, as a revolutionary work.[15] Had the Americans not done so, the book's subversive potential might have remained latent. This is only one of the many discontinuities one can find in the history of feminist ideas: internationalization is, for women, a way of preserving their fragile heritage.

This point is obviously not restricted to women's studies or to feminist thought. The history of ideas as a whole is made of such disconnection, of transatlantic loops and gaps; once again one may think here of the international dimension as a variation on the theme of the "archive," that is to say of stocking, preserving, and reproducing a symbolic capital. Internationalization can also be a resistance tactic; it can allow for certain ideas to survive despite the accidents of history; it can create continuity out of disruptions. The nomadic nature of ideas is their safest safeguard. For example, the fate of the central European Jews after the rise of Nazism: a whole wave of exiles from Germany and neighboring countries emptied the European intelligentsia of its most brilliant subjects. Most of these exported to the English-speaking world such notions as Marxism, psychoanalysis, phenomenology – not to speak of the hard or exact sciences, which simply made American culture the leader of the western world. The history of ideas is always a nomadic story; the physical displacement is just a way of preserving in time certain ideas, so that they do not get lost. Ideas are as mortal as human beings and as subjected as we are to the crazy twists and turns of history.

Next to this, the other image we want to evoke is that of the migrant. Contrary to the nomad, the migrant has a clear destination: it goes from one point in space to another for a very clear purpose. The question of migration is important in that it has concretely created in every European culture a series of foreign subcultures of which women tend to be the loyal guardians and perpetuators.

Migrant women constitute the bulk of what we would call the "domestic foreigners" in our postindustrial metropolis. These people who speak a language and embody cultural values so different from the dominant ones tend to be forgotten in all the debates about international perspectives. When will we accept that internationalization begins at home? How close are we, the "white" intellectual women, to the migrant women who have even fewer citizen rights than we have? How sensitive are we to the intellectual potential of the foreigners that we have right here, in our own backyard? We would ask those of my readers who plan to have an international career and become professional jet-setters: how much do you know about the foreignness of these people? For internationalization to become a serious practice, we must work through this paradox of proximity, indifference, and cultural differences between the nomadic intellectual and the migrant women.

Notes

14   Dale Spender, *Women of Ideas* (London/Boston/Melbourne: Ark Publications, 1982).

15   Many American feminists have commented on this trans-Atlantic connection, especially Alice Jardine and Domna Stanton; see Hester Eisenstein and Alice Jardine, *The Future of Difference* (Boston: G. K. Hall, 1980).

Bibliography of Extracts

The following list gives bibliographical information on all the extracts included in this *Reader*. To help in locating material, I have, on occasions, given details of later editions and other sources.

ALCOFF, Linda 'Cultural Feminism versus Post-structuralism: The Identity Crisis in Feminist Theory', *Signs: Journal of Women in Culture and Society*, vol. 13, no. 3 (1989). Widely anthologised, including Linda Nicholson (ed.), *The Second Wave* (New York and London: Routledge, 1996).

AMIREH Amal and MAJAJ Lisa Suhair Introduction to *Going Global: The Transnational Reception of Third World Women Writers* (New York and London: Garland Publishing, Inc., 2000).

ANZALDÚA, Gloria *Borderlands/La Frontera: The New Mestiza* (San Francisco: Aunt Lute, 1987). Twentieth anniversary and 3rd edition, 2007. The relevant chapter is included in Linda S. Kauffman (ed.), *American Feminist Thought at Century's End: A Reader* (Oxford: Basil Blackwell, 1993).

ARMSTRONG, Isobel 'Christina Rossetti: Diary of a Feminist Reading', in Sue Roe (ed.), *Women Reading Women's Writing* (Brighton: Harvester, 1987).

ARMSTRONG, Isobel *The Radical Aesthetic* (Oxford: Blackwell, 2000).

ARMSTRONG, Nancy *Desire and Domestic Fiction: A Political History of the Novel* (Oxford: Oxford University Press, 1987).

BARRETT, Michèle 'Feminism and the Definition of Cultural Politics', in Rosalind Brunt and Caroline Rowan (eds.), *Feminism, Culture and Politics* (London: Lawrence and Wishart, 1982).

BELSEY, Catherine *Critical Practice* (London: Methuen, 1980; 2nd edition 2002).

BENHABIB, Seyla 'Sexual Difference and Collective Identities: The New Global Constellation', *Signs: Journal of Women in Culture and Society*, vol. 24, no. 2 (1999).

BENSTOCK, Shari 'Afterword: The New Woman's Fiction', in Suzanne Ferriss and Mallory Young (eds.), *Chick Lit: The New Woman's Fiction* (New York: Routledge, 2006).

BLACK WOMAN TALK COLLECTIVE 'Black Woman Talk', *Feminist Review*, no. 17 (1984).

BOEHMER, Elleke *Stories of Women: Gender and Narrative in the Postcolonial Nation* (Manchester: Manchester University Press, 2005).

BOWLBY, Rachel 'Flight Reservations: The Anglo-American/French Divide in Feminist Criticism', in *Still Crazy After All These Years: Women, Writing and Psychoanalysis* (London and New York: Routledge, 1992). Reissued in the Routledge Revivals Series, 2010.

BOYCE DAVIES, Carole *Black Women, Writing, and Identity: Migrations of the Subject* (London and New York: Routledge, 1994).

BRAH, Avtar *Cartographies of Diaspora: Contesting Identities* (London and New York: Routledge, 1996).

BRAIDOTTI, Rosi *Nomadic Subjects: Embodiment and Sexual Difference in Contemporary Feminist Theory* (New York: Columbia University Press, 1994).

BRANT, Clare 'Varieties of Women's Writing', in Vivien Jones (ed.), *Women and Literature in Britain 1700–1800* (Cambridge: Cambridge University Press, 2000).

BUTLER, Judith *Undoing Gender* (New York and London: Routledge, 2004).

CHOW, Rey *Writing Diaspora: Tactics of Intervention in Contemporary Cultural Studies* (Bloomington and Indianapolis: Indiana University Press, 1993).

CHRISTIAN, Barbara 'The Race for Theory', in Linda Kauffman (ed.), *Gender and Theory: Dialogues on Feminist Criticism* (Oxford: Basil Blackwell, 1989). Also anthologised in Bill Ashcroft et al. (eds.), *The Post-Colonial Studies Reader* (London: Routledge, 1995). An earlier version can be found in *Cultural Critique* 6 (Spring 1987).

CIXOUS, Hélène 'Castration or Decapitation?', *Signs: Journal of Women in Culture and Society*, vol. 7, no. 1 (Autumn 1981). Also available in Robert Davis and Ronald Schleifer (eds.), *Contemporary Literary Criticism: Literature and Cultural Studies* (New York: Longman, 1989).

CIXOUS, Hélène 'The Laugh of the Medusa', in Elaine Marks and Isabel de Courtivron (eds.), *New French Feminisms: An Anthology* (Brighton: Harvester, 1981). Also available in *Signs: Journal of Women in Culture and Society*, vol. 1, no. 4 (Autumn 1976); Dennis Walder (ed.), *Literature in the Modern World* (Oxford: Oxford University Press and the Open University, 1990); Robyn R. Warhol and Diane Price Herndl (eds.), *Feminisms: An Anthology of Literary Theory and Criticism* (New Jersey: Rutgers University Press, 1991; 2nd edition 1997).

CIXOUS, Hélène et al. 'Conversations', in Susan Sellers (ed.), *Writing Differences: Readings from the Seminar of Hélène Cixous* (Milton Keynes: Open University Press, 1988).

CIXOUS, Hélène and Mireille Calle-Gruber *Hélène Cixous Rootprints: Memory and Life Writing* (London: Routledge, 1997).

COWARD, Rosalind *Female Desire: Women's Sexuality Today* (London: Paladin, 1984).

COWARD, Rosalind ' "This Novel Changes Lives": Are Women's Novels Feminist Novels? A Response to Rebecca O'Rourke's Article "Summer Reading" ', *Feminist Review*, no. 5 (1980). Anthologised in Elaine Showalter (ed.), *The New Feminist Criticism: Essays on Women, Literature and Theory* (London: Virago, 1986).

CULLER, Jonathan 'Reading as a Woman', *On Deconstruction: Theory and Criticism after Structuralism* (London: Routledge, 1982).

DE LAURETIS, Teresa 'Upping the Anti (sic) in Feminist Theory', in Marianne Hirsch and Evelyn Fox Keller (eds.), *Conflicts in Feminism* (London: Routledge, 1990). Also available in Simon During (ed.), *The Cultural Studies Reader* (London: Routledge, 1993; 2nd edition 1999).

DEMOOR, Marysa and PIETERS, Jürgen 'Discursive Desire: Catherine Belsey's Feminism', *Feminist Review*, no. 66 (Autumn 2000).

DUBEY, Madhu *Signs and Cities: Black Literary Postmodernism* (Chicago: University of Chicago Press, 2003).

duCILLE, Ann 'On Canons: Anxious History and the Rise of Black Feminist Literary Studies', in Ellen Rooney (ed.), *The Cambridge Companion to Feminist Literary Theory* (Cambridge: Cambridge University Press, 2006).

EAGLETON, Mary 'Mapping Contemporary Women's Fiction after Bourdieu', *Women: A Cultural Review*, vol. 19, no. 1 (Spring 2008).

ELLMANN, Mary *Thinking About Women* (London: Virago, 1979.) First published 1968.

EZELL, Margaret J. M. *Writing Women's Literary History* (Baltimore and London: Johns Hopkins University Press, 1993).

FADERMAN, Lillian 'What Is Lesbian Literature? Forming a Historical Canon', in George E. Haggerty and Bonnie Zimmerman (eds.), *Professions of Desire: Lesbian and Gay Studies in Literature* (New York: Modern Language Association of America, 1995).

FARWELL, Marilyn R. *Heterosexual Plots and Lesbian Narratives* (New York and London: New York University Press, 1996).

FELMAN, Shoshana 'Women and Madness: The Critical Phallacy', *Diacritics*, vol. 5, no. 4 (1975). Included in her collection *What Does a Woman Want? Reading and Sexual Difference* (Baltimore and London: Johns Hopkins University Press, 1993). Anthologised in Robyn R. Warhol and Diane Price Herndl (eds.), *Feminisms: An Anthology of Literary Theory and Criticism* (New Jersey: Rutgers University Press, 1991; 2nd edition 1997) and Catherine Belsey and Jane Moore (eds.), *The Feminist Reader: Essays in Gender and the Politics of Literary Criticism* (London: Macmillan, 1989; 2nd edition 1997).

FELSKI, Rita *Doing Time: Feminist Theory and Postmodernist Culture* (New York: New York University Press, 2000).

FERGUS, Jan *Provincial Readers in Eighteenth-Century England* (Oxford: Oxford University Press, 2006).

FETTERLEY, Judith *The Resisting Reader* (Bloomington: Indiana University Press, 1978).

FLINT, Kate *The Woman Reader, 1837–1914* (Oxford: Oxford University Press, 1993).

FORRESTER, Viviane 'What Women's Eyes See', in Elaine Marks and Isabel de Courtivron (eds.), *New French Feminisms: An Anthology* (Brighton: Harvester Press, 1981). First published 1976.

FRANEY, Laura *Victorian Travel Writing and Imperial Violence: British Writing on Africa 1855–1902* (Basingstoke: Palgrave Macmillan, 2003).

FRASER, Nancy and NICHOLSON, Linda J. 'Social Criticisms Without Philosophy: An Encounter between Feminism and Postmodernism', in Linda J. Nicholson (ed.), *Feminism/Postmodernism* (New York and London: Routledge, 1990).

FRIEDMAN, Susan Stanford *Mappings: Feminism and the Cultural Geographies of Encounter* (Princeton, NJ: Princeton University Press, 1998).

FUSS, Diana *Essentially Speaking: Feminism, Nature and Difference* (London: Routledge, 1989).

GILBERT, Sandra M. and GUBAR, Susan *The Madwoman in the Attic: The Woman Writer and the Nineteenth-Century Literary Imagination* (New Haven and London: Yale University Press, 1979; 2nd edition 2000).

HARAWAY, Donna 'A Manifesto for Cyborgs: Science, Technology, and Socialist Feminism in the 1980s', *Socialist Review*, vol. 15, no. 18 (1985). In varying forms included in Haraway's *Simians, Cyborgs, and Women: The Resurrection of Nature* (New York: Routledge, 1991); Elizabeth Weed (ed.), *Coming to Terms: Feminism, Theory, Politics* (London: Routledge, 1989); Linda J. Nicholson (ed.), *Feminism/Postmodernism* (London: Routledge, 1990); Simon During (ed.), *The Cultural Studies Reader* (London: Routledge, 1993; 2nd edition 1999).

HARTLEY, Jenny (with Sarah Turvey) *Reading Groups* (Oxford: Oxford University Press, 2001).

HEMMINGS, Clare 'Telling Feminist Stories', *Feminist Theory*, vol. 6, no. 2 (2005).

hooks, bell 'Choosing the Margin as a Space of Radical Openness' in *Yearning: Race, Gender and Cultural Politics* (London: Turnaround, 1991).

HUGGAN, Graham *The Postcolonial Exotic: Marketing the Margins* (London: Routledge, 2001).

HUMBLE, Nicola *The Feminine Middlebrow Novel, 1920s to 1950s: Class, Domesticity and Bohemianism* (Oxford: Oxford University Press, 2001).

IRIGARAY, Luce 'The Powers of Discourse and the Subordination of the Feminine', *This Sex Which Is Not One* (Ithaca, NY: Cornell University Press, 1985). First published in French in 1977. Essay included in Margaret Whitford (ed.), *The Irigaray Reader* (Oxford: Basil Blackwell, 1991).

JACKSON, Rosemary *Fantasy: The Literature of Subversion* (London: Methuen, 1981).

JACOBUS, Mary *Reading Woman: Essays in Feminist Criticism* (London: Methuen, 1986).

JARDINE, Alice *Gynesis: Configurations of Woman and Modernity* (Ithaca, NY: Cornell University Press, 1985).

KAMUF, Peggy 'Writing Like a Woman', in Sally McConnell-Ginet et al. (eds.), *Women and Language in Literature and Society* (New York: Praeger, 1980).

KAPLAN, Caren *Questions of Travel: Postmodern Discourses of Displacement* (Durham, NC: Duke University Press, 1996).

KAPLAN, Cora (ed.) Elizabeth Barrett Browning, *Aurora Leigh and Other Poems* (London: Women's Press, 1978).

KOLODNY, Annette 'Dancing Through the Minefield: Some Observations on the Theory, Practice, and Politics of a Feminist Literary Criticism', *Feminist Studies*, vol. 6, no. 1 (Spring 1980). Included in Elaine Showalter (ed.), *The New Feminist*

Criticism: Essays on Women, Literature and Theory (London: Virago, 1986); Robyn R. Warhol and Diane Price Herndl (eds.), *Feminisms: An Anthology of Literary Theory and Criticism* (New Jersey: Rutgers University Press, 1991; 2nd edition 1997).

KRISTEVA, Julia 'Woman Can Never Be Defined', in Elaine Marks and Isabel de Courtivron (eds.), *New French Feminisms: An Anthology* (Brighton: Harvester Press, 1981). First published as 'La Femme, ce n'est jamais ça' in *Tel Quel* (Autumn, 1974).

KRISTEVA, Julia 'A Question of Subjectivity: An Interview', *Women's Review*, no. 12 (Oct., 1986). Included in Philip Rice and Patricia Waugh (eds.), *Modern Literary Theory: A Reader* (London: Edward Arnold, 1989; 4th edition London: Bloomsbury Academic, 2001).

KRISTEVA, Julia 'Talking About *Polylogue*', in Toril Moi (ed.), *French Feminist Thought: A Reader* (Oxford: Basil Blackwell, 1987). First published as 'A Partir de *Polylogue*' in *Revue des Sciences Humaines*, vol. XLIV, no. 168 (Oct.–Dec. 1977).

LANSER, Susan S. 'Towards a Feminist Narratology', *Style*, vol. 20, no. 3 (Fall 1986).

LAUTER, Paul 'Race and Gender in the Shaping of the American Literary Canon: A Case Study from the Twenties', (first published 1983) in Judith Newton and Deborah Rosenfelt (eds.), *Feminist Criticism and Social Change: Sex, Class and Race in Literature and Culture* (New York and London: Methuen, 1985). Included in Lauter's own collection, *Canons and Contexts* (Oxford: Oxford University Press, 1991).

LEWIS, Reina *Rethinking Orientalism: Women, Travel and the Ottoman Harem* (London: I. B. Tauris, 2004).

LIGHT, Alison *Forever England: Femininity, Literature and Conservatism between the Wars* (London: Routledge, 1991).

LOVELL, Terry 'Writing Like a Woman: A Question of Politics', in Francis Barker et al. (eds.), *The Politics of Theory* (Colchester: University of Essex, 1983).

McCLINTOCK, Anne *Imperial Leather: Race, Gender, and Sexuality in the Colonial Context* (New York and London: Routledge, 1995).

McDOWELL, Paula *The Women of Grub Street: Press, Politics, and Gender in the Literary Marketplace 1678–1730* (Oxford: Clarendon Press, 1998).

McGRATH, Kathryn 'Pushed to the Margins: The Slow Death and Possible Rebirth of the Feminist Bookstore', *Feminist Collections*, vol. 25, no. 3 (Spring 2004).

MILLER, Nancy K. 'Parables and Politics: Feminist Criticism in 1986', *Paragraph*, vol. 8 (Oct. 1986).

MILLER, Nancy K. *Subject to Change: Reading Feminist Writing* (New York: Columbia University Press, 1988).

MITCHELL, Juliet 'Femininity, Narrative and Psychoanalysis', in *Women: The Longest Revolution* (London: Virago, 1984).

MOERS, Ellen *Literary Women* (London: Women's Press, 1978).

MOHANTY, Chandra Talpade 'Under Western Eyes: Feminist Scholarship and Colonial Discourses', in Ann Russo Mohanty and Lourdes Torres (eds.), *Third World Women and the Politics of Feminism* (Bloomington and Indianapolis: Indiana University Press, 1991). Also available in Meenakshi Gigi Durham and

Douglas M. Kellner (eds.), *Media and Cultural Studies: Key Works* (Oxford: Blackwell, 2006) and Mohanty's own collection, *Feminism without Borders: Decolonizing Theory and Practicing Solidarity* (Durham, NC: Duke University Press, 2004). Earlier versions are to be found in *Boundary 2*, vol. 12, no. 3/ vol. 13, no. 1 (Spring/Fall 1984) and *Feminist Review*, no. 30 (Autumn 1988).

MOI, Toril *Sexual/Textual Politics: Feminist Literary Theory* (London: Methuen, 1985; 2nd edition 2002).

MOI, Toril *What is a Woman? And other Essays* (Oxford: Oxford University Press, 1999).

MOSES, Claire Goldberg 'Made in America "French Feminism" in Academia', *Feminist Studies*, vol. 24, no. 2 (Summer 1998).

MURRAY, Simone *Mixed Media: Feminist Presses and Publishing Politics* (London: Pluto Press, 2004).

NGCOBO, Lauretta 'Editor's Introduction', *Let It Be Told: Essays by Black Women in Britain* (London: Virago, 1988).

OHMANN, Carol 'Emily Brontë in the Hands of Male Critics', *College English*, vol. 32, no. 8 (May 1971).

OLSEN, Tillie *Silences* (London: Virago, 1980) (first published 1978). A 25th anniversary edition with supplementary material was published by the Feminist Press, City University, New York in 2003.

PARRY, Benita *Postcolonial Studies: A Materialist Critique* (London and New York: Routledge, 2004).

PONNUSWAMI, Meenakshi 'Small Island People: Black British Women Playwrights', in Elaine Aston and Janelle Reinelt (eds.), *The Cambridge Companion to Modern British Women Playwrights* (Cambridge: Cambridge University Press, 2000).

PRATT, Mary Louise *Imperial Eyes: Travel Writing and Transculturation* (London and New York: Routledge, 1992).

RADWAY, Janice A. *A Feeling for Books: The Book-of-the-Month Club, Literary Taste, and Middle-Class Desire* (Chapel Hill and London: University of North Carolina Press, 1997).

RAY, Sangeeta *En-Gendering India: Woman and Nation in Colonial and Postcolonial Narratives* (Durham, NC: Duke University Press, 2000).

REGISTER, Cheri 'American Feminist Literary Criticism: A Bibliographical Introduction', in Josephine Donovan (ed.), *Feminist Literary Criticism: Explorations in Theory* (Kentucky: University Press of Kentucky, 1975).

RICH, Adrienne 'Compulsory Heterosexuality and Lesbian Existence', *Blood, Bread, and Poetry: Selected Prose 1979–1985* (London: Virago, 1987). Also available in Henry Abelove, Michèle Aina Barale and David M. Halperin (eds.), *The Lesbian and Gay Studies Reader* (New York: Routledge, 1993).

RICH, Adrienne 'Notes toward a Politics of Location', *Blood, Bread and Poetry: Selected Prose 1979–1985* (London: Virago, 1987). Included in Reina Lewis and Sara Mills (eds.), *Feminist Postcolonial Theory: A Reader* (London: Routledge, 2003).

ROSE, Jacqueline 'Femininity and Its Discontents', *Feminist Review*, no. 14 (1983). Revised in Rose's *Sexuality in the Field of Vision* (London: Verso, 1986). Included in Terry Lovell (ed.), *British Feminist Thought: A Reader* (Oxford: Basil Blackwell, 1990).

SCHELLENBERG, Betty A. *The Professionalization of Women Writers in Eighteenth-Century Britain* (Cambridge: Cambridge University Press, 2005).

SCHOLES, Robert 'Reading Like a Man' in Alice Jardine and Paul Smith (eds.), *Men in Feminism* (New York and London: Methuen, 1987).

SEDGWICK, Eve Kosofsky *Epistemology of the Closet* (London: Harvester Wheatsheaf, 1991).

SELLERS Susan, *Myth and Fairy Tale in Contemporary Women's Fiction* (Basingstoke: Palgrave, 2001).

SHOWALTER, Elaine *A Literature of Their Own: British Women Novelists from Brontë to Lessing* (London: Virago 1978; 2nd edition, 1999).

SHOWALTER, Elaine 'Toward a Feminist Poetics', in Mary Jacobus (ed.), *Women Writing and Writing about Women* (London: Croom Helm, 1979). Included in Showalter's edited volume, *The New Feminist Criticism: Essays on Women, Literature and Theory* (London: Virago, 1986); Rick Rylance (ed.), *Debating Texts: A Reader in 20th Century Literary Theory and Method* (Milton Keynes: Open University Press, 1987); Philip Rice and Patricia Waugh (eds.), *Modern Literary Theory: A Reader* (London: Edward Arnold, 1989; 4th edition London: Bloomsbury Academic, 2001).

SMITH, Barbara 'Toward a Black Feminist Criticism', *Conditions: Two*, vol. 1, no. 2 (Oct. 1977). Anthologised in Judith Newton and Deborah Rosenfelt (eds.), *Feminist Criticism and Social Change: Sex, Class and Race in Literature and Culture* (New York and London: Methuen, 1985) and Elaine Showalter (ed.), *The New Feminist Criticism: Essays on Women, Literature and Theory* (London: Virago, 1986).

SOPER, Kate 'Of OncoMice and Female Men: Donna Haraway on Cyborg Ontology', *Women: A Cultural Review*, vol. 10, no. 2 (1999).

SPENCER, Jane *The Rise of the Woman Novelist: From Aphra Behn to Jane Austen* (Oxford: Basil Blackwell, 1986).

SPENCER, Jane *Literary Relations: Kinship and the Canon 1660–1830* (Oxford: Oxford University Press, 2005).

SPIVAK, Gayatri Chakravorty 'French Feminism in an International Frame', *Yale French Studies*, no. 62 (1981). Included in Spivak's collection, *In Other Worlds: Essays in Cultural Politics* (New York and London: Methuen, 1987) and Mary Eagleton (ed.), *Feminist Literary Criticism* (London: Longman, 1991).

SPIVAK, Gayatri Chakravorty 'How to Read a "Culturally Different" Book', in Francis Barker, Peter Hulme and Margaret Iverson (eds.), *Colonial Discourse/Postcolonial Theory* (Manchester: Manchester University Press, 1994). Included in Donna Landry and Gerald McClean (eds.), *The Spivak Reader* (New York and London: Routledge, 1996).

SQUIRES, Claire *Marketing Literature: The Making of Contemporary Writing in Britain* (Basingstoke: Palgrave Macmillan, 2007).

STANTON, Domna C. 'Language and Revolution: The Franco-American Dis-Connection', in Hester Eisenstein and Alice Jardine (eds.), *The Future of Difference* (Boston: G. K. Hall, 1980).

STREHLE, Susan *Transnational Women's Fiction: Unsettling Home and Homeland* (Basingstoke: Palgrave Macmillan 2008).

SULERI, Sara 'Woman Skin Deep: Feminism and the Postcolonial Condition', *Cultural Critique*, no. 18 (Summer 1992). See also Kwame Anthony Appiah and Henry Louis Gates (Jr.) (eds.), *Identities* (Chicago: University of Chicago Press, 1995).

TRINH T. Minh-ha *Woman, Native, Other: Writing Postcoloniality and Feminism* (Bloomington and Indianapolis: Indiana University Press, 1989).

WARHOL, Robyn R. *Having a Good Cry: Effeminate Feelings and Pop-Culture Forms* (Columbus, Ohio: Ohio State University Press, 2003).

WEED, Elizabeth 'Introduction', in Weed and Naomi Schor (eds.), *Feminism Meets Queer Theory* (Bloomington and Indianapolis: Indiana University Press, 1997).

WEEDON, Chris *Feminist Practice and Poststructuralist Theory* (Oxford: Basil Blackwell, 1987; 2nd edition 1996).

WIEGMAN, Robyn 'Introduction: Mapping the Lesbian Postmodern', in Laura Doan (ed.), *The Lesbian Postmodern* (New York: Columbia University Press, 1994).

WILLIAMS, Linda R. 'Happy Families? Feminist Reproduction and Matrilineal Thought', in Isobel Armstrong (ed.), *New Feminist Discourses: Critical Essays on Theories and Texts* (London: Routledge, 1992).

WITTIG, Monique *The Straight Mind and Other Essays* (London: Harvester Wheatsheaf, 1992). The relevant essay was originally published as 'The Straight Mind', *Feminist Issues*, vol. 1, no. 1 (Summer 1980).

WOOLF, Virginia *A Room of One's Own* (1929). There are several editions of *A Room of One's Own*. Particularly useful are the combined volumes of *A Room of One's Own* and *Three Guineas*, ed. Michèle Barrett (Harmondsworth, Middlesex: Penguin, 1993) and the World's Classics combined volume, ed. Morag Shiach (Oxford: Oxford University Press, 1992).

WOOLF, Virginia 'Professions for Women', *The Death of the Moth* (1942). Included in several collections: Michèle Barrett (ed.), *Virginia Woolf: Women and Writing* (London: Women's Press 1975; 2nd edition 1992); Rachel Bowlby (ed.), *Virginia Woolf: The Crowded Dance of Modern Life* (Harmondsworth, Middlesex: Penguin, 1993); David Bradshaw (ed.), *Virginia Woolf: Selected Essays* (Oxford: Oxford University Press, 2008).

Index

Feminist Literary Theory: A Reader, Third Edition By Mary Eagleton © 2011 Mary Eagleton